# THE HISTORY OF
# THE FORMER HAN DYNASTY

# THE HISTORY OF
# THE FORMER HAN DYNASTY

BY
## PAN KU

*Translation, Volume Three*

IMPERIAL ANNALS XI AND XII
AND
THE MEMOIR OF WANG MANG

A Critical Translation with Annotations
by
## HOMER H. DUBS
Professor of Chinese, Oxford University

With the Collaboration of
P'AN LO-CHI

———

BALTIMORE
WAVERLY PRESS, INC.
1955

The preceding volumes of this translation were awarded the Stanislas Julien prize for 1947 by the Académie des Belles-Lettres et Inscriptions, Institut de France.

# FOREWORD

This First Part of Volume Three completes the translation of the Former Han "Imperial Annals". Part Two will continue the history of those times by presenting a translation of "The Memoir of Wang Mang". The period covered by the two parts is that when Wang Mang first became important and later dominated China. This imperial maternal relative began to affect the government some thirty years before he came to the throne, so that the reigns of the last two Former Han emperors belong to his period. A translation of their "Annals" would be seriously incomplete without the parallel and subsequent account of Wang Mang's life and reign. By including that chapter, the history of China is continued to the beginning of the Later Han period.

To the many persons who have given me assistance and advice in this work I here tender my heartiest thanks. In the notes I have tried to mention those to whom I am indebted, but many, who have contributed incidental suggestions, could not be named for lack of space.

More than to anyone else, I am indebted to Professor J. J. L. Duyvendak. He has patiently gone over the whole material and has given me the benefit of his profound knowledge. To him I owe many apt renderings and corrections. My Chinese collaborator, Mr. L. C. P'an, worked with me for two years and a summer while a student in the United States. I owe much to his patient industry and aid. Next to them I am indebted to Mr. Piet van der Loon, who, during the hard winter of 1944–45 in Holland and the subsequent year, worked over the chapter on Wang Mang together with an unrevised typescript of this translation and furnished me with a volume containing 360 remarks on as many passages. Dr. Duyvendak, at whose suggestion he engaged in this task, furthermore furnished me with his comments upon Mr. van der Loon's work. Many of these corrections constituted improvements that I have thankfully adopted. I have been fortunate in my friends and have tried to welcome criticisms, adverse ones even more than favorable ones, from whatever source they have come. As far as possible without unduly burdening the notes with names, I have indicated the sources of any substantial aid. For the rest, I can only express here my deep gratitude to all those who have helped me. The correct translation of a difficult Chinese text can only be achieved by the cooperation of many minds—here two heads are better than one and three are better than two.

To the Carnegie Corporation of New York and the American Council of Learned Societies I owe the financial assistance without which this work would have been impossible. Duke University, through its Research Council, has made grants for the purchase of needed books and for the clerical assistance. The Committee on Chinese Studies of the American Council of Learned Societies has aided substantially in the publication of this book. To the Library of Congress and to Dr. A. W. Hummel, Chief of its Division of Orientalia, I am indebted for the use of its facilities and for advice and encouragement. I have however not hesitated to exercise my own judgment upon all the suggestions offered me, so that I alone must bear the blame for any errors in this volume.

The Chinese text for chapters XCIX and XXIV was written out by Mr. John T. Find, Arlington, Virginia.

HOMER H. DUBS

*University College*
*Oxford, England*
April, 1948

# TABLE OF CONTENTS

# THE HISTORY OF THE FORMER HAN DYNASTY

## CHAPTER XI

## EMPEROR HSIAO-AI

## INTRODUCTION

### Summary of the period

The short reign of Emperor Ai (7-1 B.C.) constituted a temporary eclipse to the power of the Wang clan and Wang Mang. The Emperor himself, a sickly young man, attempted to imitate the "strong" government of Emperor Wu, but only succeeded in becoming a tool, first of his grandmother and then of his favorite's family. As a result of the Emperor's attempt to rule in person, the period is full of intrigues: concerning the maternal relatives of the Emperor, concerning a certain revelation, and concerning Tung Hsien$_{2a}$. Attention is centered in the court; external events continued to be uneventful. The influence of Han Confucianism, which reached its apogee in the reign of Wang Mang, continued to grow. This introduction will deal with the events and forces necessary to understand the background of this chapter, matters which are not explained in the chapter itself (for further details, cf. the Onomasticon and Glossary). It, like the other imperial annals, is rather a chronological summary than what occidentals would call a history.

### The intrigues of Emperor Ai's various maternal relatives

The reign of Emperor Ch'eng had fixed, as a dynastic practise, the Confucian principle of favoring imperial relatives (11: 4b). Relatives on the paternal side, who were potential rivals for the imperial throne, were given kingdoms or marquisates and were carefully watched. When Emperor Ai was continually ill, the Queen of King Yang of Tung-p'ing, Liu Yün$_{2a}$, an imperial fourth cousin, who was descended from Emperor Hsüan, was discovered to have made magical imprecations against the Emperor, with the purpose of bringing her husband to the imperial throne. She, her husband, and her uncle (who was an imperial physician) were executed and the informers were ennobled. Imperial paternal relatives, who might benefit from any harm done to the imperial person, were ordinarily kept away from the court and drastically repressed. The imperial power was thus left to the imperial maternal relatives.

Emperor Ai had however four sets of maternal relatives. The Wang clan's power rested upon the fact that the mother of Emperor Ch'eng,

1

now entitled the Grand Empress Dowager nee Wang, was still alive. She was the Emperor's adoptive grandmother and the head of the imperial clan. Due to her influence, Wang Mang had been put in charge of the government as Comander-in-chief just five months before Emperor Ch'eng had died. The Chao clan owed its influence to Emperor Ch'eng's second wife, the famous Chao Fei-yen. Emperor Ai had nominally been made the son of Emperor Ch'eng; this lady was consequently the Emperor's adoptive mother and was now made the Empress Dowager. Her relatives were given noble titles and positions. Emperor Ai had in addition his own maternal relatives. His grandmother, the former imperial Brilliant Companion, now the Queen Dowager nee Fu, had been Emperor Yüan's favorite, and her son, Liu K'ang$_{1a}$, had become the King of Ting-t'ao. His son, Liu Hsin$_5$, now Emperor Ai, had been born of a Concubine nee Ting, so that there was also a Ting clan. The Fu and Ting clans, because they were out of the court, worked together, opposing the Wang clan, which had entrenched itself in the court. Thus the situation was ripe for abundant jealousies and intrigues.

The Chao clan was quickly eliminated. Within half a year, an industrious Director of the Retainers dug up the facts about Emperor Ch'eng's imperial infanticides (cf. *HFHD*, II, 369–72), which were due to Chao Fei-yen's younger sister. This sister had previously committed suicide, but, when the facts became known, they occasioned such a revulsion that her male relatives were all dismissed from their positions and titles and were exiled. Because of Emperor Ai's debt to the Empress Dowager nee Chao, she was not touched and retained her title. Without any male relatives in the court, she was helpless.

Before his death, Emperor Ch'eng had endeavored to prevent any conflict between the various clans among the maternal relatives of his successor by separating Liu Hsin$_5$, the future Emperor Ai, from his own family and restricting him to intercourse with the imperial family. Emperor Ch'eng appointed Lin Ching$_{3b}$, another descendant of Emperor Hsüan, as the King of Ting-t'ao, to be the successor of Emperor Ai's father, so that the new Emperor would not have any further obligation to his natural father's clan. When Liu Hsin$_5$ came to the capital as the Imperial Heir-apparent, Emperor Ch'eng separated him from his actual grandmother and mother, establishing them in the Lodge for the Princes of Ting-t'ao, while Liu Hsin$_5$ went to the Heir-apparent's palace. (We may perhaps see Wang Mang's hand in these moves.) Emperor Ch'eng was not even going to allow them to see Liu Hsin$_5$, but the Empress Dowager nee Wang reminded her son that Liu Hsin$_5$ had been reared by his grandmother, so that the Queen Dowager should have the privileges given a nurse. She was accordingly allowed to visit her grandson once every ten days.

The Queen Dowager nee Fu was an indomitable and high-tempered woman, who would not easily yield up her opportunity for power and prestige. She was capable in intrigue and had previously almost succeeded in having her son, Liu K'ang$_{1a}$, made the Imperial Heir-apparent in place of Emperor Ch'eng. She had taken her grandson away from his mother and had raised him herself, teaching and directing him, thus acquiring an ascendancy over him. She had paid large bribes to the Wang and Chao clans, in order that her grandson should be preferred as Heir-apparent over his cousin. Now she was not willing to lose the opportunity of reaping her reward.

After Emperor Ch'eng's death, the future Emperor Ai found himself without anyone in the court upon whom he could rely. It was filled with the adherents of the Wang and Chao clans. Four days before he took the throne, his maternal uncle, Ting Ming, and his maternal great-uncle, Fu$_4$ Yen, were enfeoffed as marquises. These ceremonies were performed by the Queen Dowager nee Fu, who had no real authority to do so (97 B: 20a). Since however these appointments would have been made anyway, this illegality was not challenged, although there was some disapproval of the Fu clan's greediness. Probably the Queen Dowager felt these appointments were essential, in order that the new Emperor would not be left without aid in the court; for an Emperor, without any courtiers to recommend what he wanted done, would be helpless. The visits of his grandmother were still limited to once every ten days, and his mother was also allowed to make such visits. The two ladies were established in Kuei Palace, in another part of the city, two miles distant. This palace was however connected by a private elevated passageway with Wei-yang Palace (where the Emperor lived), so that it was possible to go from one to the other without making a formal royal progress. The Queen Dowager nee Fu accordingly went morning and evening by this elevated passageway to the Emperor, instructing and advising him. A steadfast refusal of his grandmother's wishes would have been unthinkable, for it would have violated the Confucian principle of filial piety, in which all noble children were trained. Thereafter the Ting and Fu clans needed only to discover and report the faults of those who stood in their way, in order to achieve control over the court.

As soon as Emperor Ai came to the throne, the Empress Dowager nee Wang tactfully ordered Wang Mang, who had previously controlled the government, to resign. He did so, but Emperor Ai could not permit his predecessor's chief minister to resign immediately, for such an act would have implied that the new ruler would not filially continue the policies of his predecessor.   So Wang Mang (who probably expected such a result and may have instigated the Empress Dowager's action) was continued in office.

Then strife arose concerning precedence between the Emperor's actual grandmother, the Queen Dowager nee Fu, and his nominal grandmother, the Grand Empress Dowager nee Wang.   An official memorialized that, according to classical principles, a mother should receive honor when her son becomes honorable, so that the Emperor's mother should receive an imperial title.   Shih$_1$ Tan and Wang Mang however opposed the proposal, and Emperor Ai did not want immediately to go contrary to the advice of his highest ministers, so let the matter drop.   Instead of that, Emperor Ch'eng's old officials, who had been put in power by the Wang clan, were dropped one by one, being accused of some crime or other.   When Wang Mang saw that he had incurred the enmity of the Queen Dowager nee Fu, he again asked to resign.   This time he was allowed to do so and was asked to remain at the court with high honors, but no official post.   Two years later he was sent away from the court to his estates.   The Grand Empress Dowager nee Wang, who was not herself aggressive or interested in politics, was not interfered with.   The titles of the Queen Dowager nee Fu and the Concubine nee Ting were raised.

Fu Hsi, a paternal cousin of the Queen Dowager and the ablest member of the Fu clan, succeeded Wang Mang as Commander-in-chief.   When he opposed female influence in the government and refused to raise the titles of the Emperor's mother and grandmother still further, he too was dismissed from his position and sent away from the court.   As one after another of the court officials were removed, the Emperor's mother and grandmother were given higher and higher titles, until there were four Empresses Dowager in the court: nee Wang, nee Chao, nee Fu, and nee Ting.   The latter died in 5 B.C.; two years later the Empress Dowager nee Fu was at last given the same title as her former rival, the Grand Empress Dowager nee Wang; both ladies had borne sons to Emperor Yüan.   The Grand Empress Dowager nee Fu had previously succeeded in legally murdering her other former rival for Emperor Yüan's favor, the Queen Dowager nee Feng of Chung-shan.   This active and ambitious Empress Dowager thus triumphed over those who held to a strict construction of proprieties (the Confucians who had tried to prevent her elevation), but she died a year later.   Meanwhile the clans of the Emperor's mother and grandmother had been highly honored: the Ting clan counted among its members two marquises, one Commander-in-chief, six generals, ministers, and officials ranking at two thousand piculs, and more than ten Palace Attendants and Division Heads. The Fu clan (including the Chang clan, that of the Empress Dowager nee Fu's half-brother) numbered among its members six marquises, two Commander-in-chiefs, six ministers or officials ranking at two thousand piculs, and more than ten Palace Attendants or Division Heads. These high officials of course distributed positions liberally to their henchmen and relatives. Thus a spoils system was put into full play in ancient China by the maternal relatives of the emperor.

## Emperor Ai's strong rule and his execution of Wang Chia$_{1a}$

In his government, Emperor Ai imitated Emperor Wu by not retaining any official in office for long, and by executing several of them. In this short period of six years, there were five Lieutenant Chancellors, seven Commanders-in-chief, and eleven Grandee Secretaries. Two Lieutenant Chancellors and one Grandee Secretary were executed. The most flagrant case was that of Wang Chia$_{1a}$ (not a member of Wang Mang's clan). He was an honest, self-respecting, and capable official, who opposed Emperor Ai's desire to advance and enrich his favorite, Tung Hsien$_{2a}$. When the treason of the Emperor's fourth cousin, Liu Yün$_{2a}$, was reported, Emperor Ai substituted the name of Tung Hsien$_{2a}$ for that of the person who had transmitted this information, thus obtaining an excuse for ennobling his favorite. Later the Emperor sent an order to the Lieutenant Chancellor and Grandee Secretary to make Tung Hsien$_{2a}$ a full marquis. These officials however knew the (unwritten) constitutional practise, that the Emperor can only act on the motion of his high ministers, and refused to make the necessary recommendations. The Emperor was thus blocked. But in a few months he issued an edict making this enfeoffment. Thus Emperor Ai, following the example of Emperor Wu, broke down this important provision in the Han constitution. When the Empress Dowager nee Fu died, Emperor Ai sent to these two highest ministers her testamentary edict, which ordered the granting of estates to her relatives and to Tung Hsien$_{2a}$. Wang Chia$_{1a}$ sealed and returned this edict to the Emperor, probably because he suspected that the name of Tung Hsien$_{2a}$ was a forgery, thus again blocking the Emperor. When the Commandant of Justice and others had investigated Liu Yün$_{2a}$, they concluded that this King was innocent, and ordered him tried again. Emperor Ai thought that they were trying to curry favor with the King, and dismissed them. A few months later there was a general amnesty, after which Wang Chia$_{1a}$ recommended the dismissed Commandant of Justice and his associates for official position. That was too much for Emperor Ai. He charged Wang Chia$_{1a}$ with having been unjust and with attempting to mislead the throne. The case was committed to the important courtiers. Some fifty, including K'ung Kuang, who then had high hopes of being again made Lieutenant Chancellor, supported the Emperor's charges; ten recommended mercy.

A century earlier, a high spirited noble would have taken poison rather than go to jail; but that chivalric age had passed. Wang Chia$_{1a}$ was a high-minded Confucian; his conscience was clear and he recognized that he had acted for the best interests of the state. He refused the poison his subordinates offered him and went to jail. Emperor Ai was angry that this stubborn minister should have thus again blocked his efforts to put him out of the way, and sent a committee of high officials to argue him down. But Wang Chia$_{1a}$ justified his actions and condemned Tung Hsien$_{2a}$ and his relatives as flatterers. The dismissed minister was starved in prison and died twenty days later. A prison sentence was then frequently merely a milder form of capital punishment than public execution. Martyrs for their moral convictions were not lacking among Han Confucians. After Emperor Ai's death, Wang Mang ordered Wang Chia$_{1a}$ listed as a faithful minister, restored his marquisate to his son, and gave him the posthumous name, Faithful (Marquis Chung).

## Supernatural revelations influence governmental policy

This reign witnessed the appearance of revelations or oracle books (*ch'an*) that affected government policy. These revelations were a natural development from the Confucian practise of interpreting visitations and portents as having a meaning for government policies. The theory of the five powers as determining history was first elaborated by Tsou Yen (iv cent. B.C.), and became popular in Confucian circles through its appearance in the "Great Plan," which became a chapter in the *Book of History*. This theory had as one of its consequences the doctrine that dynasties rise and fall in accordance with the dominating power. After the Han dynasty had been on the throne for a century and its virtual collapse during the last years of Emperor Wu's reign, people accordingly began to speculate what would be the next dynasty. In 78 B.C., Kuei Hung, who had studied Tung Chung-shu's interpretation of the *Kung-yang Commentary* and who was then a minor court official, interpreted a portent as indicating the end of the Han dynasty and the appearance of a new dynasty with the surname Kung-yang. He was executed for treason, but speculation continued. One belief was that $3 \times 70 = 210$ years was the period a dynasty endured, which era, counting from 206 B.C., would end in A.D. 4 (cf. 99 A: n. 34.5). In the reign of Emperor Ch'eng, a certain Kan Chung-k'o from the Ch'i commandery wrote a book in twelve chapters, which he said was a revelation from a spirit named the Essence of the Red Lord (Ch'ih-ching-tzu), by whose power Emperor Kao had killed the serpent blocking his path (*HS* 1 A: 7a) and had seated his dynasty on the throne. In this book, Kan Chung-k'o evidently reasoned, on a calendrical basis, that the Han dynasty, if it was to continue, must again receive a mandate from Heaven, and asserted that the Essence of the Red Lord had come down to teach the dynasty how to secure this mandate. Kan Chung-k'o was thus supporting the Han dynasty against interpretations like that of Kuei Hung. Kan Chung-k'o's book seems to have been the first of the "revelations." (Kuei Hung was later said to have written a book of revelations, which did not appear until the first century A.D., when a pretender surnamed Kung-sun appeared, so that this book was probably a forgery.) Liu Hsiang$_{4a}$ had been asked by Emperor Ch'eng to report on the correctness of this revelation. He had memorialized that this doctrine was not classical, and was an attempt to deceive the Emperor and to mislead the crowd. Kan Chung-k'o was imprisoned, tortured, and died; his disciples were dismissed from office.

When it was discovered that Emperor Ch'eng had killed his own infant sons, thus leaving himself without a natural heir, and when sundry portents occurred, people came increasingly to feel that the Han dynasty had actually decayed. This opinion was confirmed by the fact that Emperor Ai was continually ill, with some disease like arthritis, and also that he had no natural heir. He was told about Kan Chung-k'o's revelation. The matter was submitted to Liu Hsiang$_{4a}$'s son, Liu Hsin$_{1a}$, who again condemned the doctrine as unclassical. Other courtiers, however, supported this new teaching, and Emperor Ai summoned Kan Chung-k'o's chief disciples to several audiences. They told the Emperor that he should change the year-period and take a new title, whereby he would secure lengthened life and an heir, as well as freedom from his illness, etc. On July 13, 5 B.C., he followed their advice, taking new, long, and flowery names.

A month later, the bearers of the revelation, emboldened by their success, proposed further changes. They now said that the highest ministers should be dismissed, and those courtiers who had supported the revelation should be given the vacant positions. That was too much for the ministers. Emperor Ai's illness had not improved, so that the supporters of the revelation could not point to any verification of their promises. The Emperor was persuaded that the revelation was groundless; he rescinded his edict and committed Kan Chung-k'o's disciples to the officials; these disciples were sentenced for having deceived the Emperor, an inhuman crime, and were executed.  This incident marks the first important influence upon government policies by revelations, which were to play such a large part in the reign of Wang Mang and later times.

### The popular cult of the Mother Queen of the West

The popular excitement in the spring and summer of 3 B.C., connected with the worship of the Mother Queen of the West (Hsi-wang-mu), deserves careful notice.  Unfortunately we know little about it; all the relevant passages are to be found in the text and notes under this date.  The Mother Queen of the West figures in ancient Chinese legends and grave-sculptures before and after this date.  She was then supposed to be an immortal, dwelling in the far western K'un-lun Mountains, in a grotto inside a metal house in a stone city, and to have three green birds who brought her food to this desert place.  She had a human body, a leopard's tail, tiger's teeth, which latter were good for whistling, and brilliant white tangled hair, in which she wore a peculiar high jade hair-ornament.  She was probably now represented as offering to her devotees a means of escaping death from starvation and becoming as immortal as she was.

This incident seems to have been a soteriological religion promising immortality, in many respects similar to the Bacchic religion of ancient Greece.  The drought brought it popularity.  The present Shantung, where it started, is still susceptible to this sort of ecstatic, revivalistic religious agitation.  It did not affect the bureaucracy or court, hence is merely mentioned in the *History* as a curious incident, a portent requiring explanation.

### Tung Hsien$_{2a}$'s meteoric rise and fall

The rise of Tung Hsien$_{2a}$ shows how far a completely worthless person could go by imperial favor.  He was merely a handsome and pliable lad in the Heir-apparent's suite, who was made a Gentleman when Emperor Ai came to the throne, and became the Emperor's catamite.  He was promoted from one post to another, all the while continuing in personal attendance upon the Emperor.  In the course of ten months, he had accumulated a hundred million cash in grants and rewards.  When he did not leave the Palace on the regular days for vacation, the Emperor arranged that Tung Hsien$_{2a}$'s wife might enter the palace inner apartments, with the result that his wife and children lived there.  The Emperor took Tung Hsien$_{2a}$'s younger sister as a Brilliant Companion, giving her the rank next to the Empress.  Tung Hsien$_{2a}$, his wife, or his sister were continually in attendance upon the Emperor.  His father was made a minister and noble; his father-in-law and brother were given court positions;

a large and splendid residence was built for him just outside the palace portal and a splendid burial place was prepared beside the imperial tomb. Jewels and weapons were given him from the palace workshops, even better ones than those the Emperor secured. By an imperial forgery, he was given a marquisate and an estate. When Wang Chia$_{1a}$ opposed this proposed enfeoffment, he was removed and finally executed.

The Emperor's maternal uncle, Ting Ming, was Commander-in-chief, and he too disapproved of Tung Hsien$_{2a}$. Emperor Ai dismissed this minister and also retired Fu$_4$ Yen, the imperial great-uncle. Thus the Emperor's infatuation with a boy led him to break with both his own maternal clans. He was thus left without any loyal followers in the court except the Tung clan. The latter clan contained no one of ability. It seems not to have been interested in politics except to enrich itself. Tung Hsien$_{2a}$ was finally made Commander-in-chief, the controlling position in the ministry, although he was only in his twenty-second year. His younger brother was given Tung Hsien$_{2a}$'s former position and the whole Tung clan were made Palace Attendants, Division Chiefs, etc., receiving greater favors than had even been bestowed upon the Emperor's maternal clans. The Emperor seems even to have come to believe that the Han dynasty, because of the succession of the elements, must inevitably be soon succeeded by a different dynasty (cf. Ku Chieh-Kang, *Ku-shih-pien*, V, 465–77). Once, at a feast, the Emperor even calmly talked about resigning the throne to his favorite. Wang Hung, a cousin of Wang Mang, happened to be in attendance. He immediately remonstrated, telling the Emperor that the empire was no plaything, for it had been received from his ancestors and must be transmitted to his descendants, thus invoking the Confucian exaltation of filial piety. Emperor Ai was plainly displeased, at which circumstance the imperial attendants were frightened and Wang Hung left the room. Thus imperial infatuation was carried to the extreme.

When Emperor Ai died suddenly without an heir and without having appointed a successor, his mother and grandmother had previously died and his maternal relatives had been deprived of their positions, possibly because the Emperor continued to hope that Tung Hsien$_{2a}$ would inaugurate a new dynasty. But the latter was wholly incapable of doing so, even though he possessed the imperial seals of office. The imperial authority naturally reverted to the Grand Empress Dowager nee Wang, the senior of the two surviving Empress Dowagers. During his last years, after Emperor Ai had broken with his maternal clans, he had begun recalling the Confucians whom he had displaced from their positions when he took the throne. At this time Wang Mang had been praised by those who took the civil service examinations, so that he had been recalled to the capital and had been there during the last year of Emperor Ai's reign, without however being given a post.

On the day of the imperial death, the Grand Empress Dowager, who probably had previously been instructed what to do, immediately went to the emperor's palace and collected the imperial seals of state. Thereby she took to herself the imperial authority. She then asked Tung Hsien$_{2a}$ about the regulations for imperial mourning, which he, as the highest minister, would be required to conduct. The young man was distraught and in all likelihood completely ignorant of such matters, so could only beg her pardon. She remarked that Wang Mang had previously conducted the mourning for Emperor Ch'eng and sent a messenger galloping to summon him.

Wang Mang, like most of the other courtiers, could not endure Tung Hsien$_{2a}$. The latter was now impeached for negligence in caring for the Emperor and imprisoned in the palace. He had no influential friends outside of his own clan. Wang Mang then told the Grand Empress Dowager that public opinion disapproved of the favorite. The day after the emperor died, Wang Mang had her order Tung Hsien$_{2a}$ dismissed from his position and sent to his residence. The latter and his relatives were so frightened that, on the same day, both he and his wife committed suicide in order to save the rest of their clan. The two were buried that same night. The whole Tung clan were dismissed from their positions and exiled, and their wealth sold. It amounted to 4,300,000,000 cash. Tung Hsien$_{2a}$'s body was exhumed, stripped, and reburied meanly. Thus the imperial favorite received his reward.

## The influence of Confucianism

During this period, the influence of Confucianism continued unabated. The high officials continued to be Confucians. Learned men were recommended for the highest posts. There came indeed to be two parties in the imperial court: the Fu and Ting clans, who defended their positions and sought wealth and influence, and the Confucians (to whom Wang Mang belonged), who comprised the bulk of the bureaucracy and stood for a strict construction of court proprieties and for moral ideals. In spite of this division, Confucian influence continued to be strong, for the imperial maternal relatives owed their influence to the Confucian teaching of favoring one's relatives, hence, even when they dismissed the Confucians from high office, they continued to cultivate Confucianism and favor those Confucians who would accord with them. There was no thought, on the part of any important personage, of changing from Confucianism to any other philosophy.

K'ung Kuang, a lineal descendant of Confucius and one of the great scholars of the empire, was installed as Lieutenant Chancellor on the day Emperor Ch'eng died; he was dismissed in two years, because he opposed the raising of the Empress Dowager nee Fu's title. Three years later, he was recalled to court when she died, and was soon reappointed to his old post. He had meanwhile learned to be more pliable to the Emperor's wishes, lending his consent to the condemnation of Wang Chia$_{1a}$ and treating Tung Hsien$_{2a}$ deferentially. A very learned Confucian who was at the same time a lineal descendant of Confucius could not be neglected, for such a person would be an ornament to any Chinese court. The post of Commander-in-chief, which actually dominated the government, was, however, except for brief intervals, kept in the hands of imperial relatives or of the imperial favorite, Tung Hsien$_{2a}$. Through his concurrent position as Intendant of the Affairs of the Masters of Writing, the Commander-in-chief controlled the most important source of imperial information. Under Emperor Ai, this control was not as important as previously, for the Empress Dowager nee Fu and Tung Hsien$_{2a}$ both had direct access of the imperial person. Thus Confucian influence, while important, was partly checked by the imperial maternal relatives and favorite.

Confucian influence also showed itself in certain reforms. The practise of mourning for a parent to the third year was revived (cf. App. I). An attempt was made to restrict the amount of land and slaves one person could own (11: 2b, 3a). This edict was however tabled because the imperial maternal relatives and favorite found it inconvenient. At the same time certain imperial ateliers were abolished and a few other humanitarian laws were enacted (11: 3a, b). A new ruler was expected to show his devotion to Confucian principles in his government, and reforms such as these were enacted because Confucians urged them. The Wang clan, not to be outdone, distributed its private fields to the poor people (11: 4a); but this does not mean that they gave up the estates from which their income as marquises was derived—their estates were government, not private fields. Their generosity was probably limited to their lands near the capital, rents from which (at least part of which were paid in grain) would be more convenient for a court official than income from distant estates in the provinces. Wang Mang may have foreseen that he would eventually be exiled from the court; this generous gift aided greatly in inducing people to urge the recall of Wang Mang, four years later.

### A temporary rectification of high official titles, following classical models

The most interesting effect of Confucianism was the change of official titles—a phenomenon that became pronounced under Wang Mang. A cardinal Confucian principle was the imitation of ancient practises.

About 8 B.C., Ho Wu, who was then Grandee Secretary, memorialized that in ancient times, when life was simple, government business was divided among the three highest ministers (*San-kung*), whereas now, when there were not available officials who had as great ability as those of ancient times, the duties of the three ancient highest ministers were concentrated in the hands of the Lieutenant Chancellor. He suggested the appointment of the three highest ministers as in ancient times (83: 13b). Emperor Ch'eng asked Chang Yü$_{3a}$, a retired Lieutenant Chancellor and Confucian, about the matter; the latter agreed, whereupon the title of Grandee Secretary was changed to Grand Minister of Works, and he was given the same salary and rank as the Lieutenant Chancellor and Commander-in-chief. There probably was at the same time also a division of responsibility, so that some of the Lieutenant Chancellor's duties were given to the Grand Minister of Works.

But many who discussed the matter said that ancient and present times required different institutions and that the Han official titles, from that of the Emperor down to that of the Accessory Officials, were different from those of ancient times, so that a change in merely the titles and duties of the three highest officials would make no difference in the quality of the government (83: 14a). After the Confucian Ho Wu had been dismissed for lack of filial piety, and Chu Po, an adherent of the Fu clan, became Grand Minister of Works, he memorialized that dynasties do not need to imitate one another, that when Emperor Kao received the Mandate of Heaven to found the Han dynasty, he had established a Grandee Secretary as second in rank to the Lieutenant Chancellor and had given him the duty of correcting the laws and institutes, with the result that the empire had now been calm for two centuries. Hence the change of Grandee Secretary to Grand Minister of Works would not secure the blessing of Heaven. So he recommended that titles be changed back again (83: 14b). Emperor Ai accordingly made the change, and in 5 B.C. installed Chu Po as Grandee Secretary.

The Han dynasty had adopted the practise of the Ch'in dynasty in dividing the country into counties (*hsien*) and grouping these into commanderies (*chün*), each containing about a dozen prefectures or more, over which there was set a Commandery Administrator to act as satrap of the region, usually with the rank of two thousand piculs. In 106 B.C., Emperor Wu had grouped these commanderies into thirteen divisions or provinces (*chou*), and appointed to each province an Inspector of a Regional Division (*Pu-tz'u-shih*), with the rank of six hundred piculs, whose business it was to make the circuit of his commanderies and report any irregularities. Feudal kingdoms (which later became smaller than commanderies) were governed by a Chancellor (Hsiang), who was appointed by the imperial court, so that there had come to be little difference, outside of titles, between the government of commanderies and of kingdoms. Both were supervised by the same Inspectors.

In 8 B.C., Ho Wu memorialized that this Han practise was contrary to Confucian classical principles, according to which the superior should govern the inferior, not the reverse. So he had Emperor Ch'eng change the Inspectors to Provincial Shepherds (*Chou-mu*), a title taken from the *Book of History*, and rank them at fully two thousand piculs, so that their rank should be higher than that of Administrators.

Two years later (6 B.C.), Chu Po however pointed out that when Inspectors ranked lower than Administrators, the former had been stimulated to activity by the hope of being promoted to be one of the 103 Administrators or Chancellors, so that an efficient Inspector had had lively hopes of promotion. But when these officials became Shepherds and were given a high rank, they had available for promotion only the dozen ministerial positions at the imperial court. Consequently they lost their incentive to activity; the better ones merely guarded themselves for fear of committing a fault and sullying their record, while the wicked ones were unrestrained, since there was no one to watch them. Local administrations were consequently left without supervision and government degenerated. So Chu Po recommended the abolition of Shepherds and the restoration of the Inspectors. This change was made in 5 B.C. Thus the practical bureaucrat showed more wisdom than the Confucian. One of the reasons for the inefficiency of Wang Mang's provincial administration was undoubtedly that he reestablished Provincial Shepherds in order to accord with classical Confucian ideas.

When an eclipse of the sun happened on a New Year's day (Feb. 5, 2 B.C.), followed within a month by the death of the Empress Dowager nee Fu, Emperor Ai was deeply impressed, and in that very month summoned K'ung Kuang back to court, asking him to explain the portent. The latter said that government matters had not been right and should be reformed (81: 19a–20a). Since the Emperor's grandmother was no longer alive and the Emperor had broken with his maternal clans, while the Tung clan showed no disposition to interfere in government policies, Emperor Ai turned to the Confucians again, recalling those whom he had dismissed at the beginning of his reign. When, a year later, a second solar eclipse occurred, Emperor Ai interpreted it as a warning and, through Confucian influence, restored the arrangement under which government control was divided among the three ancient highest ministers. In the scholastic interest of uniformity, a new title was also given to the Lieutenant Chancellor, and these three officials were now entitled *Ta-szu-t'u* (Grand Minister Over the Masses), *Ta-szu-ma* (Commander-in-chief), and *Ta-szu-k'ung* (Grand Minister of Works). This arrangement did not last long, for Emperor Ai died within a month and in the next year Wang Mang changed these titles again. The change is however interesting as showing that the tendency to change titles and to adopt ancient phraseology and ancient governmental arrangements was inherent in Han Confucianism, and that Wang Mang merely took it from that powerful current of influence.

## Chapter XI

# THE ELEVENTH [IMPERIAL ANNALS]

### THE ANNALS OF [EMPEROR HSAIO]-AI

相中尉皆國二千石故盡從之上令誦詩通習能說他日問中山王獨

朝獨從傅上怪之以問定陶王對曰令諸侯王朝得從其國二千石傅

文辭法律元延四年入朝盡從傅相中尉時成帝少弟中山孝王亦來

孝哀皇帝元帝庶孫定陶恭王子也母曰丁姬年三歲嗣立爲王長好

漢書十一

哀紀第十一

Emperor Hsiao-ai was the grandson of Emperor Yüan by a concubine and the son of King Kung of Ting-t'ao, [Liu K'ang₁ₐ]. His mother was the Concubine [nee] Ting. When he was in his third year, he succeeded [his father] and was set up as King. When he grew up, he delighted in words and phrases and in the laws and statutes.[1.2]  *22 B.C.[1.1]*

In [the period] Yüan-yen, the fourth year, he came [to Ch'ang-an] to pay court, followed by all [his high officials], his Tutor, his Chancellor, and his Commandant of the Capital. At that time the youngest brother of Emperor Ch'eng, King Hsiao of Chungshan, [Liu Hsing], also came to pay court, followed [only] by his Tutor. The Emperor thought it strange, and asked [Liu Hsin₅, the future Emperor Ai], about it. The King of Ting-t'ao, [Liu Hsin₅] replied, "According to the [imperial] ordinances, when vassal kings come to pay court, they are permitted to be accompanied by the [officials ranking at] two thousand piculs in their kingdoms. The Tutor, Chancellor, and Commandant of the Capital are all [officials ranking at] two thousand piculs in a kingdom, hence I am accompanied by them all." The Emperor ordered him to recite from the *Book of Odes*, and he understood and was versed in it, and was able to explain it.  *9 B.C.*

On another day, [the Emperor] asked the King of Chung-shan, [Liu Hsing], in what law or ordinance

---

[1.1] Cf. *HS* 14: 23a.

[1.2] These phrases (the first one is repeated on 11: 8b) may well refer to the matters discussed by the school of circumstances and names or penological terminology; cf. 9: n. 1.2.

[it was ordered that he should be] accompanied only by his tutor, and he was unable to reply. [The Emperor] ordered him to recite from the *Book of History*, and he broke off [in the middle of his recitation]. Moreover, [at an imperial feast], when he had been granted food in the presence of [the Emperor], he was the last to finish eating; when he arose, his stockings came down, [for] their ties had become **1b\***
*1b†* loosened. Because of these [facts], Emperor Ch'eng considered that he was incapable, and esteemed the King of Ting-t'ao, [Liu Hsin₅], as capable, often exalting his abilities.

**1b‡** At this time the grandmother of the King, the Queen Dowager [of Ting-t'ao, nee] Fu, had come with the King to pay court, and privately sent presents to the Brilliant Companion [nee] Chao, whom the Emperor favored, and to the Emperor's maternal uncle, the General of Agile Cavalry and Marquis of Ch'ü-yang, Wang Ken. The Brilliant Companion [nee Chao] and [Wang] Ken saw that the Emperor had no sons, and also wished beforehand to attach themselves [to the coming ruler] by a plan for the distant future, so both in turn praised the King of Ting-t'ao and urged the Emperor to make him his successor. Emperor Ch'eng of his own volition also exalted [Liu Hsin₅'s] ability, and, after having put the bonnet of virility upon him, sent him 9 B.C. [back to his kingdom]. At that time he had [reached] his seventeenth year.

8 B.C. The next year, [the Emperor] sent the Bearer of Mar. 20[1.3] the Gilded Mace, Jen Hung, as Acting Grand Herald, with credentials, to summon the King of Ting-t'ao to [come and] be established as the Imperial Heir-apparent. [Liu Hsin₅ however] excused himself, saying, "Your servant has been favored in being

---

[1.3] *HS* 10: 14b; 80: 10a.

*Light upright numbers indicate the paging in the Ching-yu ed., reprinted in the Commercial Press' Po-na Series of the "Twenty-four Histories".

†Italic numbers indicate the paging in the Palace ed. or Wu-ying Tien ed., reprinted in the *Szu-pu Pei-yao*.

‡Bold-face numbers indicate the paging in the Wang Hsien-ch'ien's *Han-shu Pu-chu*, as in previous volumes.

十七矣明年使執金吾任宏守大鴻臚持節徵定陶王立為皇太子謝曰臣幸
長久計皆更稱定陶王勸帝以為嗣成帝亦自美其材為加元服而遣之時年
幸趙昭儀及帝舅票騎將軍曲陽侯王根昭儀及根見上亡子亦欲豫自結為
此以為不能而賢定陶王數稱其材時王祖母傅太后隨王來朝私賂遺上所
從傅在何法令不能對令誦書又廢及賜食於前後飽起下襪係解成帝由

後之誼語在外戚傳綏和二年三月成帝崩四月丙午太子卽
月餘立楚孝王孫景爲定陶王奉恭王祀所以獎厲太子專爲
留國邸旦夕奉問起居侯有聖嗣歸國守藩書奏天子報聞後
寬仁敬承祖宗奉順神祇宜蒙福祐子孫千億之報臣願且得
得繼父守藩爲諸侯王材質不足以假充太子之宮陛下聖德

permitted to succeed his father in charge of a tributary [kingdom] and to become a vassal king. My ability and nature is inadequate for use as the occupant of the Heir-apparent's palace. Your Majesty is sage and virtuous, generous and benevolent. [Your Majesty] has respectfully succeeded his ancestors and has upheld and been obedient in the care of the gods in heaven and earth. It is proper that your [Majesty] should receive happiness and blessing thru the reward of 'thousands and millions of descendants.'[1.4] Your servant is willing temporarily to be permitted to remain in the prince's lodge of his kingdom [at the imperial capital], morning and evening to present himself [to your Majesty] to ask [about your Majesty's] health, and to wait until there may be an imperial heir, [whereupon your servant] will return to his kingdom and [remain] in charge of his tributary [state]." When the memorial was presented, the Son of Heaven replied, "[We] have heard it."[1.5]  *2a*

More than a month later, [Emperor Ch'eng] established [Liu] Ching[3b], a grandson of King Hsiao of Ch'u, [Liu Ao], as King of Ting-t'ao, to uphold the sacrifices to King Kung [of Ting-t'ao, Liu K'ang], in order to encourage and incite the Heir-apparent to apply himself solely to the purpose of being [the Emperor's] successor. A discussion is in the "Memoir of the [Imperial] Relatives by Marriage."  Dec.[1.6]

In [the period] Sui-ho, the second year, the third month, Emperor Ch'eng died, and in the fourth month, on [the day] *ping-wu*, the Heir-apparent took

97B: 17a
*2a*
7 B.C.
II
2a[1.7]Apr. 17
May 7

[1.4] A quotation from the *Book of Odes*, III, II, v, 2 (Legge, p. 482).

[1.5] Implying tacit disapproval. Emperor Ch'eng planned to separate the future Emperor Ai from his own family and make him an Imperial Son. Emperor Ai's relatives refused to allow him to be separated from them.

[1.6] *HS* 10: 15b.

[1.7] *HS* 10: 16a.

the imperial throne and presented himself in the Temple of [Emperor] Kao. He honored the Empress Dowager [nee Wang] with the title, Grand August Empress Dowager, and the Empress [nee Chao] with the title, Empress Dowager. He [granted] a general amnesty to the empire, granted one quadriga of horses to each king's son of the imperial house who was enregistered,[2.2] to the officials and common people, noble ranks, to [each] hundred households, an ox and wine, and to the Thrice Venerable, the Filially Pious, the Fraternally Respectful, the [Diligent] Cultivators of the Fields, widowers, widows, orphans, and childless, silk.

May 17[2.1]

The Grand Empress Dowager [nee Wang] issued an imperial edict honoring King Kung of Ting-t'ao, [Liu K'ang], as Sovereign Kung [of Ting-t'ao]. In the fifth month, on [the day] ping-hsü, [the Emperor] established the Empress nee Fu [as Empress]. An imperial edict said, "[According to the principle of] the *Spring and Autumn*, [in the *Kung-yang Commentary*] that 'a mother becomes honorable because of her son,'[2.3] [We] honor the Queen Dowager [nee Fu] of Ting-t'ao with the title, Empress Dowager Kung, and the Concubine [nee] Ting [of Ting-t'ao with the title, Empress Kung, and establish for each an entourage, a Supervisor of the Household, and the

June 16

2b

貴尊定陶太后曰恭皇太后丁姬曰恭皇后各置左右
尊為恭皇五月丙戌立皇后傅氏詔曰春秋母以子
恭王為恭皇五月丙戌立皇后傅氏詔曰春秋母以子
牛酒三老孝弟力田鰥寡孤獨帛太皇太后詔尊定陶
大赦天下賜宗室王子有屬者馬各一駟吏民爵百戶
皇帝位謁高廟尊皇太后曰太皇太后皇后曰皇太后

[2.1] *HS* 97 B: 14a.

[2.2] Yen Shih-ku (581–645) explains, "*Yu-shu* 有屬 means that his relationship had not been extinguished, so that he was still [of the proper relationship] to wear mourning." In 9: 2b and 10: 2b Emperors Yüan and Ch'eng are each recorded as having at the beginning of their reigns made grants to the members of the imperial house who 有屬籍; Emperor Ai, in similarily making grants, would hardly have meant anything different from what they did. Then the phrase here is merely an abbreviation for the phrase used in the "Annals of Emperors Yüan" and "Ch'eng." Those who rebelled or were sentenced for crime and their descendants were dropped from the imperial house, cf. 6: 4b. The practise of considering relationship to have lapsed after a certain number of generations is recognized in 12: 3a; cf. n. 3.1. This phrase is also found in 8: 7a.

[2.3] A quotation from the *Kung-yang Commentary* (iii cent. B.C.) to the *Spring and Autumn*, 1: 7b, Dk. Yin, Yr. I.

父侯皇曰
事迫太鄭
食諡后聲
邑滿弟淫
如父侍而
長忠中亂
信封光聖
宮丁祿王
中周大所
宮明夫放
追爲趙其
尊陽欽罷
傅安爲樂
父侯新府
爲皇成曲
崇后侯陽
祖父六侯
侯晏月根
丁爲詔

詹父侯
事爲迫
食褒諡
邑德滿
如侯父
長封忠
信舅侯
宮丁舅
中周子
宮爲滿
追陽爲
尊侯平
博安周
父侯
爲舅
崇子
祖滿
侯爲
丁孔
   鄉
   侯

income of an estate, like [the occupants of] the
Ch'ang-hsin Palace and the Inner Palace.[2.4]  [We]
posthumously honor the father of [the Empress
Dowager nee] Fu as the Marquis [through Whom the
Emperor] Renders Homage to an Ancestor, and the
father of [the Empress nee] Ting as the Marquis in
Recompense to his Virtue."  The maternal uncle [of
the Emperor], Ting Ming, had been made the Mar-      May 3[2.5]
quis of Yang-an, his maternal uncle's son, [Ting]
Man, was made Marquis of Ping-chou, and [Ting]      June 19[2.5]
Man's father, [Ting] Chung, was posthumously
[granted] the posthumous name, Marquis Huai of
P'ing-chou.  The Empress [nee Fu's] father, [Fu4]
Yen, had become the Marquis of K'ung-hsiang, and    May 3[2.5]
the younger brother of the Empress Dowager [nee
Chao], the Palace Attendant and Imperial Household
Grandee Chao Ch'in_b, became the Marquis of         June 22[2.5]
Hsin-ch'eng.[2.5]

In the sixth month, an imperial edict said, " 'The   July
melodies of Cheng are licentious'[2.6] and bring disorder into music.  They were banished by the Sage-   2b
kings.[2.7]  Let the Bureau of Music be abolished."
For the Marquis of Ch'ü-yang, [Wang] Ken, who

[2.4] Ying Shao (ca. 140–206) explains, "The mother of Emperor Ch'eng, the Empress
Dowager [nee] Wang, lived in the Ch'ang-hsin Palace."  "The Ch'ang-hsin Palace" was
then an indirect way of referring to this Empress Dowager; the "Inner Palace" was
similarly an indirect reference to the Empress; cf. Glossary *sub* Inner Palace.  Li Ch'i
(fl. ca. 200) remarks, "The Concubine [nee] Fu was to be [treated] like [the occupant of]
the Ch'ang-hsin [Palace] and the Concubine nee Ting like [the occupant of] the Inner
Palace."

[2.5] According to 18: 24a, b and Shih1 Tan's memorial in 86: 16a, Ting Ming and
Fu Yen had been enfeoffed on May 3, four days before Emperor Ai came to the throne;
Ting Man and Chao Ch'in_b were enfeoffed on June 19 and 22, respectively (18: 24b, 22b).

[2.6] A quotation from a saying of Confucius in *Analects* XV, x, 6.  Cf. Legge's
"Concluding Note" to his translation of the *Book of Odes* I, vii, "The Odes of Cheng,"
p. 149.

[2.7] Another allusion to *Analects* XV, x, 6 where Confucius directs a disciple to "banish
the melodies of Cheng."   For this dismissal of 441 out of a total of 829 imperial musicians,
cf. 22: 34b–37a; Glossary *sub* Bureau of Music.

had previously as Commander-in-chief initiated the plan for [the dynasty's] gods of the soils and grains, [whereby Emperor Ai had been appointed Heir-apparent], there was added to his enfeoffment [the

**2b** income of] two thousand households, and for the Grand Coachman, the Marquis of An-yang, [Wang] Shun[4b], who had seconded and guided [the Emperor before he was appointed] and had been his former benefactor, there was added to his enfeoffment [the income of] five hundred households.  Moreover, for the Lieutenant Chancellor, K'ung Kuang, and the Grand Minister of Works, the Marquis of Fan-

**3a** hsiang, Ho Wu, there was added to each of their enfeoffments [the income of] a thousand households.[2.8]

An imperial edict said, "The King of Ho-chien, [Liu] Liang, has mourned for his Queen Dowager to the third year and so has become a sign-post to the imperial house.[2.9]  Let his enfeoffment be increased

前戶封鄉王
以太五侯良
大僕百何喪
司安戶武太
馬陽及益后
建侯丞封三
社舜相各年
稷輔孔千爲
策導光戶宗
益有大詔室
封舊司曰儀
二恩空河表
千益氾閒益

[2.8] The above paragraph is probably a quotation from the imperial edict making these awards, but, since Pan Ku does not precede it by writing, "An edict *also* said," he plainly did not mean it to be read as a quotation.

[2.9] Yen Shih-ku says, "*Yi$_1$-piao* 儀表 means that he should be a model in the rites and ceremonies (*yi$_1$*)."  But Wang Nien-sun (1744–1832) points out that *HS* 90: 21a, speaking of the "Tyrannical Officials," says "Those who were incorrupt were qualified to be *yi$_1$-piao*," as showing that Yen Shih-ku's interpretation is inadequate.  He continues, "In my opinion, a standing post which directs people was called a *yi$_1$* and was also called a *piao*.  The *Shuo-wen* [(ca. 100) 6A: 4b says], '*Yi$_2$* 樣 is a plank 榦 [laid horizontally as the casing in making an earthen wall.  It comes] from the 'wood' [radical] and *yi$_4$* 義 as the sound.'  The classics and the 'traditions' (ancient commentaries) interchange [*yi$_2$*] and *yi$_1$*.  Hence the *Erh-ya* [(before and during Han times) 2: 7a, says, '*Yi$_1$* is a plank.'  [Kao Yu (fl. 205–212), in] a note to the *Lü-shih Ch'un-ch'iu*, Bk. 25, ch. 6[p. 10a, says], 'A *piao* is a post.'  [Wilhelm, p. 446, translates *piao* as "Stange."]  Hence when [a person's] virtue and conduct were adequate to serve as a model for people, he was called a sign-post (*piao-yi*).  [The *Li-ki* (ca. i cent. B.C.)], Bk. XXX, 4 [Legge, II, 353; Couvreur, II, 516, says], 'The superior should be careful in what he likes and dislikes, for he is a sign-post (*piao*) to the common people,' and Cheng [Hsüan, (127–200)] comments, 'The common people follow their prince as a shadow follows a gnomen (*piao*).'  Hsün-tzu [ca. 320–235 B.C.] roll VIII, fascicle XII [p. 4a, says], 'The prince is the gnomen (*yi$_1$*).  When the gnomen (*yi$_1$*) is straight, then its shadow is straight.'

封萬戶又曰制節謹度以防奢淫為政所先百王
不足其議限列有司條奏諸王列侯得名田國中
民多畜奴婢田宅亡限與民爭利百姓失職重困
列侯在長安及公主名田縣道關內侯吏民名田

by ten thousand households."

It also said, " 'Frugality in expenditure and caution in action,'[2.10] in order to prevent extravagance and excess, are the first things in government and the unvarying way of all the [true] kings. [But] the vassal kings, the full marquises, the princesses, and the officials [ranking at] two thousand piculs, together with powerful and rich common people, keep [many] male and female slaves, cultivated fields and residences without limit. They compete with the common people in profitable [enterprises] so the people lose their occupations and suffer severely without enough [to live on]. Let regulations for the restriction [of these matters] be discussed."[2.11]

The high officials memorialized detailed [regula- **3a** tions as follows], "The vassal kings and full marquises are to be permitted to own private cultivated fields in their states; the privately owned cultivated fields in the prefectures or marches of full marquises who [live] in Ch'ang-an and of princesses and the privately owned cultivated fields of Marquises of the Imperial Domain, officials, and common people are

These [passages] prove that $yi_1$ was the same as *piao*. *Kuan-tzu* [iii cent. B.C.] roll 20, fascicle 64 [p. 8b, says], 'Rules and laws are the sign-posts ($yi_1$-*piao*) for the many common people; the rules of proper conduct and moral principles are the sign-posts ($yi_1$-*piao*) for honorable and humble [persons].' *Huai-nan-tzu* [d. 122 B.C.], ch. 9 [p. 1a, says], 'His words are embroideries and his actions are his sign-posts ($yi_1$-*piao*).' The *Tso-chuan* [(iv cent. B.C.), Dk.] Wen, Yr. VI [Legge, 242[9], Couvreur I, 471 says], 'They proclaimed the standard and model [for tribute], and led them by their examples (*piao*-$yi_1$).' Then whether it says $yi_1$-*piao* or *piao*-$yi_1$, the meaning is the same. [Yen] Shih-ku ... did not know that a $yi_1$-*piao* ... was a standing post, and also did not know that $yi_1$ was a word borrowed for $yi_2$." This phrase is also used in *SC* 130: 9. Cf. also *HFHD*, I, p. 244, n. 1.

For the implications of this edict upon the practise of mourning to the third year, cf. app. I.

[2.10] A phrase from the *Classic of Filial Piety* 2: 1a, ch. 3, I. Chen's trans., p. 18.

[2.11] The language of this edict is taken from Shih[1] Tan's memorial, quoted in 24A: 20a, b.

3a all not to be allowed to exceed thirty *ch'ing*.[3.1] The male and female slaves of the vassal kings [shall be limited to] two hundred persons; those of full mar-
3b quises and princesses, to a hundred persons; and those of Marquises of the Imperial Domain, officials, and the common people, to thirty persons. Those [slaves] in their sixtieth year and over or in their tenth year and under are not to be counted in this number. No merchants are to be allowed to own private cultivated land or become officials.[3.2] Those who violate [this order] shall be sentenced according to the Code. Those who [after three years] own private cultivated land or keep male or female slaves more than the [allowed] number, shall all have them

者以律論諸名田畜奴婢過品皆
在數中賈人皆不得名田爲吏犯
三十人列侯公主百人關內侯吏民
百人皆得過三十頃諸侯王奴婢
無皆得過三十頃諸侯王奴婢二

[3.1] Ju Shun (fl. dur. 189–265) explains, "To own private cultivated land (*ming-t'ien* 名田 [名 = 'to possess']) in their states [refers to land] within the states from which they received their income. In addition to collecting the land-tax and tax on products, [vassal kings and marquises] were also personally permitted to own three thousand *mou* of private cultivated land (*szu-t'ien* 私田). As to 'owning private cultivated land (*ming-t'ien*) in the prefectures and marches': [according to] the first section in [the dynastic] ordinances, those nobles who [lived] in their states and who owned private cultivated land (*ming-t'ien*) in other prefectures should be fined [the equivalent of] two taels of gold. [But] now some full marquises had not gone to their states; altho they received the income of the land-tax and tax on produce from their distant states, they were also themselves permitted to have cultivated land (*t'ien*) in other prefectures or marches. Princesses were similarily treated. [But these lands] were not permitted to exceed three thousand mou." For a discussion of these private lands, cf.; 陳伯瀛, 中國田制叢考, pub. by Commercial Press, ch. 3. Tung Chung-shu seems to have been the first to suggest limiting the size of private lands, cf. *HS* 24 A: 17a. Emperor Ai's edict was made as a result of Shih₁ Tan's suggestion (*HS* 24 A: 20a). Wang Hsien-ch'ien states that *ming-t'ien* is the same as *chan-tien* 占田, which latter phrase is used in *Han-chi* 28: 1b.

[3.2] The regulation that those enregistered in market-places and their sons and grandsons were not allowed to be officials dates back to the time of Emperor Kao or earlier. Cf. *HS* 24 B: 4a[11].

*HS* 24 A: 20b also quotes this edict adding, "The period [for final compliance with this edict] shall end with the third year." The passage continues, "[At this] time the price of cultivated fields, residences, and male and female slaves became low. The Ting and Fu [clans] were [however] employed [on important government] matters and Tung Hsien₂ₐ became great and honorable, all [of whom found this edict] inconvenient. [So the enforcement of this] edict was temporarily postponed to a latter [time]. Thereupon it was tabled and not put into effect."

輸除任子令及
之物皆止無作
繡難成害女紅
服官諸官織綺
沒入縣官齊三

confiscated and delivered over the imperial government."

[The production of] those articles in the Three Offices for Garments in the Ch'i [Commandery] and in various offices which weave figured silks and [make] embroidery, which are difficult to produce or are injurious to women's work,[3.3] were all stopped and [such goods] were not to be made or transported [to the capital]. The ordinance [concerning] the giving of office to a son[3.4] was done away with, together with

[3.3] For the Three Offices for Garments in the Ch'i Commandery, cf. Glossary, *sub voce* The reference to "women's work" is reminiscent of Emperor Ching's edict, where the term is explained. Cf. 5: 9a, *HFHD*, I, 328, & n. 9.4.

The text is ambiguous: Ju Shun interprets it: "Those which are being made and are already completed, and those which are not yet completed shall all be stopped and shall not again be made. All shall be transported to the depot nearest the Office." But Yen Shih-ku writes, "Ju [Shun's] explanation is mistaken. It merely means that those which are not yet completed shall not be made, and those which are already completed shall not be transported." Wang Hsien-ch'ien comments, "The two explanations of Ju [Shun] and Yen [Shih-ku] are [both] mistaken. Hu San-hsing [1230–1287, in a note to the *Tzu-chih T'ung-chien* 33: 7a] says, 'The Three Offices for Garments in Ch'i together with the various offices for weaving shall all not make articles difficult to complete in order to transport them [to the capital].'"

[3.4] Ying Shao comments, "[As to] the ordinance [concerning] the giving office to sons, the Comment in the *Han-[chiu]-yi* [by Wei Hung, (fl. dur. 25–57; this passage has dropped out of that book, much of which has been lost; it has been replaced in its "Appendix" of fragments, A: 3a), says], 'Officials [ranking at] two thousand piculs and above, who have attended to [government] affairs for three full years, are permitted to obtain the position of Gentleman for one of [their brothers or half-brothers] of the same father [or these persons' sons], or for a son.' [Such persons however] were not selected for their virtue, hence [the order] was done away with." (Yen Shih-ku, following a comment of Fu Ch'ien (125–195) to *HS* 36: 6a, interprets 任 as meaning the same as 保, "guarantee," but Chou Shou-ch'ang (1814–1884) replies that in view of the provision in the Han Code, quoted by Ying Shao, guarantors were not necessary.)

Tung Chung-shu (56: 13a) and Wang Chi₅ₐ (72: 7a) had protested against this practise. Its abolition constituted a strengthening of the examination system.

At various times in the Later Han period persons are stated to have been made Gentlemen of the court (*lang*) because of their close relationship to high officials (*HHS*, M. 31: 14a, 17b; M. 9: 10b–11a; M. 27: 4a, 6a; M. 35: 6a; M. 51: 13a, b). But in each case this appointment was probably a special act of imperial grace. In A.D. 121, one son, nephew, or younger brother of each one of the highest ministers, high ministers, colonels, and masters of writing was made a Gentleman or Member of the Heir-apparent's Suite. This act was also a special favor; it is listed along with grants of general amnesty to the common

the laws about slandering [the government][3.5] and
**3b** calumny. Palace Maids in the Lateral Courts [of
the Wei-yang Palace] who were in their thirtieth
year and under were sent out [of the harem] and
married off; government male and female slaves who
were in their fiftieth year and above were freed and
made commoners. The prohibition [was made] that
the commanderies and kingdoms should not be permitted to present famous wild animals [to the imperial court]. The salaries of officials [ranking at]
three hundred piculs[3.6] and under was increased.
Officials who were oppressive or tyrannical were investigated in order that from time to time they
might be dismissed. The high officials were not permitted to bring up former matters that had happened
previous to an amnesty.[3.7] When the fathers or
mothers of Erudits or their Disciples died, they were
**4a** given leave for mourning to the third year.[3.8]
**Autumn** In the autumn, [it was decided that] the Marquis
of Ch'ü-yang, Wang Ken, and the Marquis of Ch'eng-

誹之官奴婢五十以上免爲庶人年三十以下出嫁
謗詆欺法掖庭宮人年三十以
得獻名獸益吏三百石以下奉察吏殘賊無
酷虐者以時退有司無得舉赦前往事博
士弟子父母死予寧三年秋曲陽侯王

people and grants of cash or silk to the Honored Ladies at the imperial tombs, the royal
princesses, ministers, and lesser officials (*HHS*, An. 5: 15a). This grant establishes that
the abolition of 7 B.C. was maintained, except for special imperial favors. In A.D. 146
it was however enacted that the sons of officials ranking at 600 piculs and over could enter
the Imperial University and that the best ten of these sons should be made Gentlemen
of the court or Members of the Heir-apparent's Suite (*HHS*, An. 6: 17b). Thus the
practise of giving office to sons was partially and qualifiedly renewed.

[3.5] This law had seemingly been ineffectively abolished by Emperor Wen; cf. 4: 10b.

[3.6] The Official ed. (1739) carelessly reads 而 for 石.

[3.7] Shen Ch'in-han (1775–1832) remarks, "This edict was probably occasioned by the
[Director] of the Retainers, Chieh Kuang, memorializing the deeds of the [Brilliant Com-
panion] nee Chao." It was probably an attempt to protect the life of her sister, the
Empress Dowager nee Chao. Cf. *HFHD*, II, ch. X, Introduction, pp. 369–372; Glossary,
*sub* Brilliant Companion nee Chao.

[3.8] Yen Shih-ku explains, "*Ning* 寧 means to dwell at home and wear mourning
garments." The Official ed. has the word "previously (*ch'ien* 前)" at the beginning of
this sentence, before the words for "Erudits" (*po-shih*), with the note, "The Sung Ch'i
[ed., xi or xii cent.] says, '[In the phrase] *"Ch'ien po-shih,"* one text does not have the
word "ch'ien."'" This word was dropped in the Ching-yu ed. (1034–5). On this period
of mourning, cf. App. I.

根成都侯王況皆有罪根就國況
免爲庶人歸故郡詔曰朕承宗廟
之重戰戰競競懼失天心閒者日
月亡光五星失行郡國比比動地
酒者河南潁川郡水出流殺人民

tu, Wang K'uang₄ₐ, had both committed crimes; [Wang] Ken went to his estate; [Wang] K'uang₄ₐ  *3b* was dismissed [from his title] and became a commoner, returning to his native commandery.[3.9]

An imperial edict said, "Since We have succeeded to the heavy [responsibilities] of the [imperial] ancestral temples, [We] have been trembling and circumspect, fearing that [We] might depart from the will of Heaven. [But] recently the sun and moon have lost their brilliance, the five planets have lost their paths, and the commanderies and kingdoms have frequently [suffered from] movements of the Earth.[3.10] Recently in the Ho-nan and Ying-ch'uan Commanderies, streams have overflowed and have carried away and killed some of the common people,  **4a**

[3.9] *HS* 18: 19b and 98: 11a report that these two persons were sentenced because, before Emperor Ch'eng's tomb was completed, they had married imperial concubines and had held a feast at which there was singing and dancing, (cf. Glossary, *sub* Wang, Grand Empress Dowager nee). Hence abstinence from festivities was now required for far more than merely the thirty-six days after an emperor's death stipulated by Emperor Wen. Cf. 4: 20a.

Another curious event happened at this time. *HS* 27 Ca: 21b says, "In the second year of [the period] Sui-ho, the eighth month, on [the day] *keng-shen* [Huang gives no such day in the eighth month, but if the intercalary month, which he inserts after the seventh month, is changed to come after the eighth month, this date is Sept. 18, 7 B.C.], a man of the T'ung Hamlet in the Cheng [county], Wang Pao, clothed in carmine garments, with a small bonnet, and girt with a two-edged sword, entered thru the Northern Major's Gate and the Eastern Gate of the [Wei-yang Palace] Hall, went up into the Front Hall and entered the Extraordinary Room, loosened the ribbon of a curtain, knotted and girded himself with it, beckoned to the Chief in the offices in the Front Hall, Yeh, and others, saying, 'The Lord of Heaven ordered me to live here.' Yeh and the others arrested, bound, and examined him. [Wang] Pao had been a soldier of the [Chief] Grand Questioner to the Major [in Charge of Official Carriages], and was suffering from insanity, so that he himself did not know the circumstances under which he had entered the palace. He was sent to prison and died."

[3.10] The Official ed. inverts the order of 地動.

*HS* 27 Ca: 9a says, "In the ninth month, on [the day] *ping-ch'en* [Nov. 13], there was an earthquake. From the capital to the northern borders, in more than thirty commanderies and kingdoms, the inner and outer city walls were ruined. Altogether it killed 415 people."

ruining and demolishing[4.1] their cottages. [Owing to] Our lack of virtue, the common people have suffered punishment in [Our] place. We have been greatly dismayed and have already sent an Imperial Household Grandee to travel about, inspect, and report [the names] and registration [in which those who have suffered are located], granting for each dead person three thousand cash for a coffin. Let it be ordered that in the counties and towns which have been injured by flood, together with those other commanderies and kingdoms which have suffered four-tenths or more from a [calamitous] visitation, the common people whose property does not [amount to] fully 100,000 [cash] shall all not [be required] to pay this year's land-tax or poll-taxes."[4.2]

I
6 B.C.
Feb./Mar.

In [the period] Chien-p'ing, the first year, in the spring, the first month, an amnesty [was granted] to the empire. The Palace Attendant and Colonel of Cavalry, the Marquis of Hsin-ch'eng, Chao Ch'in_b, and the Marquis of Ch'eng-yang, Chao Hsin_1b, who had both committed crimes, were dismissed [from their titles], made commoners, and exiled to the Liao-hsi [Commandery].[4.3]

4b

The Grand Empress Dowager [nee Wang] issued an imperial edict that the cultivated fields which had not been [used for] tombs, belonging to the Wang clan who were imperial relatives by marriage, should all be distributed to the poor people.[4.4]

Mar./Apr.

In the second month, an imperial edict said, "Verily [We] have heard that the Sage-kings, in their government, considered the securing of capable

詔外家王氏田非冢塋皆以賦貧民二月詔曰蓋聞聖王之治以得賢爲首
侍中騎都尉新成侯趙欽成陽侯趙訢皆有罪免爲庶人徙遼西太皇太后
無出今年租賦建平元年春正月赦天下
棺錢人三千其令水所傷縣邑及他郡國災害什四以上民貲不滿十萬皆
壞敗廬舍朕之不德民反蒙辜朕甚懼焉已遣光祿大夫循行舉籍賜死者

----

[4.1] The Official ed. inverts the order of 壞敗.

[4.2] A hundred thousand cash [which was equivalent to ten catties of gold] was the value of a middle-class family's estate; Cf. 4: 21a.

[4.3] They were both brothers of the Brilliant Companion nee Chao, who had been responsible for imperial infanticide. Cf. *HFHD* II, 369–372; Glossary, *sub vocibus*.

[4.4] *HS* 27 Cb: 25a says, "In Chien-p'ing I, i, on [the day] *ting-wei* [Mar. 4], ten meteorites fell in the [Commandery] of Po-ti."

王太后媛弟宜鄉侯馮參有罪皆自殺
二千石中都官郎吏金錢帛各有差冬中山孝
各一人三月賜諸侯王公主列侯丞相將軍中
孝弟惇厚能直言通政事延于側陋可親民者
其與大司馬列將軍中二千石州牧守相舉

persons as the most important [of matters]. Let [the Lieutenant Chancellor, K'ung Kuang, the Grand Minister of Works, Shih₁ Tan], with the Commander-in-chief, [Fu Yen], the full Marquises, the generals, [officials ranking at] fully two thousand piculs, the Provincial Shepherds, the Administrators, and the Chancellors each recommend one person who is filially pious, fraternally respectful, true and honest, able to speak frankly, who understands government matters, and has arisen[4.5] from a mean condition, so is able to love the common people."

**4b** *4a* / Apr./May

In the third month, [the Emperor] granted to the vassal kings, the princesses, the full marquises, the Lieutenant Chancellor, [K'ung Kuang], the generals, [officials ranking at] fully two thousand piculs, [officials] in the imperial capital offices, the Gentlemen, and [minor] officials, gold, cash, and silk, to each proportionately.[4.6]

Winter

In the winter, the Queen Dowager, [Feng] Yüan, of King Hsiao of Chung-shan, [Liu Hsing], and her younger brother, the Marquis of Yi-hsiang, Feng Ts'an, who had [been charged with] having committed a crime, both killed themselves.[4.7]

---

[4.5] Yü Yüeh (1821–1906) declares that *yen* 延 is a copyist's error for an ancient form of 起. Without this emendation, as Wang Nien-sun remarks, the clause beginning with *yen* interrupts the sentence and must have been displaced. According to Yen Shih-ku's comment (A.D. 641), *yen* was already in his text.

Liu Pin (1022–1088) remarks that this edict must have been a command to the Lieutenant Chancellor and Grand Minister of Works as well as to the officials mentioned; their titles have hence been inserted into the translation.

[4.6] *HS* 27 Cb: 25a says, "In the ninth month, on [the day] *chia-ch'en* [Oct. 27], two meteorites fell in Yü [in the kingdom of Liang]."

[4.7] The Queen Dowager had been a rival of the Empress Dowager nee Fu for Emperor Yüan's favor, and was hated by her; her younger sister had now been falsely charged with plotting an attempt on the life of Emperor Ai. Cf. Glossary, *sub* Feng, Brilliant Companion nee.

Chou Shou-ch'ang glosses on 11: 4a, "The *Ku-chin-chu* [ca. 300, (we have been unable to find this passage there) says], 'In the first year of Emperor Ai, a fungus of immortality

II
5 B.C.
Apr./May

In the second year, in the spring, the third month, [the title of] Grand Minister of Works was abolished, and [the former title of] Grandee Secretary was restored.[4.8]

May/June

In the summer, the fourth month, an imperial edict said, "The institutes of the Han dynasty stress the favoring of [imperial] relatives in order to manifest the honoring of those who should be honored.

5a

In the title of Sovereign Kung of Ting-t'ao, [Liu K'ang], it is not proper that he should again be called 'of Ting-t'ao.' [We] honor the Empress Dowager Kung [nee Fu] with the title, the Emperor's

**5a**

Grand Empress Dowager; she is to be called [the occupant of] the Yung-hsin Palace.[5.1] The Empress Kung [nee Ting] is to be entitled the Emperor's Empress Dowager; she is to be called [the occupant of] the Chung-an Palace. There is to be established a Temple to Sovereign Kung in the [imperial] capital." An amnesty was granted to convicts in the empire.

[The Emperor] abolished the [office of] Provincial Shepherds and reestablished [their occupants as] Inspectors.

July 9

In the sixth month, on [the day] *keng-shen*, the Emperor's Empress Dowager nee Ting died. The

下徒罷州牧復刺史六月庚申帝太后丁氏崩上
皇后曰帝太后稱中安宮立恭皇廟于京師赦天
復稱定陶尊恭皇太后稱永信宮恭
漢家之制推親親以顯尊尊定陶恭皇之號不宜
二年春三月罷大司空復御史大夫夏四月詔曰

grew on a laurel magnolia tree of the rear slaughter-house.' Chung Chang-t'ung's [180–220] *Ch'ang-yen* [lost; fragments in the *Yü-han Shan-fang Chi-yi Shu;* this passage is in B: 5b, and is recovered from the *Yi-wen Lei-chü* (vii cent.) ch. 89, and from the *T'ai-p'ing Yü-lan* (978–983), 960: 4a] says, 'In the time of Emperor Ai of the Han [dynasty, (the *Yü-lan* says, "Emperor An")], there were prodigies which grew on an arbor-vitae tree of an eastern gallery (behind the Yen-yü stables) in the Ch'ang-lo Palace, and on a mimosa tree at the southern door of the Long Lane. Those who discussed them considered that they were fungi of immortality. The courtiers all congratulated [the Emperor] and received grants.' "

[4.8] Wang Hsien-ch'ien remarks that this change was the result of a request by Chu Po. The change in the title of Provincial Governors below was also due to his recommendation. Cf. Introduction, p. 13.

[5.1] Cf. 11: 2a & n. 2.4.

曰朕聞夫婦一體詩云穀則異室死則同穴昔季武子成寢杜氏　之殯在西階下請合葬而許之附葬之禮自周與焉郁郁乎文哉　吾從周孝子事亡如事存帝太后宜起陵恭皇之園遂葬定陶發　陳留濟陰近郡國五萬人穿復土待詔夏賀良等言赤精子之讖　漢家曆運中衰當再受命宜改元易號詔曰漢與二百載曆數開

Emperor declared, "We have heard that husband and wife are one flesh. The *Book of Odes* says,

　'When living, we occupy different apartments,

But when dead, we shall share the same grave.'[5.2] Anciently, 'When Viscount Wu, Chi-[sun Su], had completed his private apartments, and at the foot of his western steps there was' a corpse 'of the Tu clan, [the head of that clan] begged permission to bury [the wife of the deceased] together with [her husband],' and '[Chi-sun Su] permitted it.'[5.3] The rite of associating [husband and wife] in burial arose in the Chou [period].[5.4] 'How complete and elegant *4b* was its culture! I follow the Chou [practises].'[5.5] A filial son 'serves the dead as he served the living.'[5.6] It is proper that for the Emperor's Empress Dowager there should be raised a tumulus in the funerary park of King Kung." She was thereupon buried in [the kingdom of] Ting-t'ao. Fifty thousand persons from Ch'en-liu, Chi-yin, and neighboring commanderies and kingdoms were mobilized to dig and replace *5b* the earth.

The Expectant Appointee Hsia Ho-liang and others spoke of revelations from Ch'ih-ching-tzu, that the Han dynasty had come upon [a time of] decay in the midst of [the period of time allotted to it] by its destiny, so that it must again receive the Mandate [of Heaven; hence] it was proper that [the Emperor] should change the year-period and alter *July 13[5.7]* his title. The imperial edict said, "The Han [dynasty] arose two hundred years [ago], and many *5b* times in succession it has begun [new] year-periods.

[5.2] *Book of Odes*, I, VI, ix, 3 (Legge, I, 121).

[5.3] A quotation (with a variation in two words) from the *Li-ki*, II, ɪ, i, 3 (Legge, I, 121; Couvreur, I, 109–110).

[5.4] Cf. *Li-ki*, ibid.

[5.5] Quoted from a saying of Confucius in *Analects* III, xiv.

[5.6] Quoted from the *Doctrine of the Mean*, xix, 5 (Legge, p. 403; Couvreur, *Li Ki*, II, 447; Legge, *Li Ki*, II, 311).

[5.7] Cf. 99 A: 34b and 11: 6a. On this incident, cf. Introduction, pp. 6–8.

August Heaven has sent down its aid to [Us] who have no ability, so that the Han [dynasty's] estate should a second time be permitted to have the portents for receiving the Mandate [of Heaven]. Though We are not virtuous, who [are We that We] should dare not to listen [to the will of Heaven]?

"Now [that We are to receive] this great Mandate which is the foundation of [all] government, [We] must certainly give [everyone in] the empire [an opportunity to] renew himself. Let a general amnesty [be granted] to the empire. Let the second year of [the period] Chien-p'ing become the first year of [the period] T'ai-ch'u-yüan-chiang. [Let Our] title be the Sovereign Emperor of Great Peacefulness Who Makes Known the Sageness of the Liu

5a  [House].[5.8]  For the graduations on the clepsydra,

元命事天年
皇之之下號
天符元以曰
降朕命建陳
非之必平聖
材不與二劉
之德天年太
佑曷下爲平
漢敢自太皇
國不新初帝
再通其元漏
獲夫大將刻
受基赦元以
           元百

[5.8] This edict is given in greater fullness in 75:32b, which passage is much clearer.

The Official ed. has not "yüan-chiang," the last two words of the new year-period, and quotes the Sung Ch'i ed. as saying that some editor "did not understand that the name [of the year-period] included four words, so excised the two words 'yüan-chiang', which is an error. Later I obtained a T'ang text [before xi cent.] in which the words 'yüan-chiang' are really preserved." All four words of this name are found in *HS* 75: 32b and 99 A: 34b. Ch'i Shao-nan remarks that T'ai-ch'u was a year-period in Emperor Wu's reign, and would not be repeated in this reign. "[The Emperor] must have been misled by the sayings of these magicians who invented this name with four words to show that there was a renaissance. Altho [this name of a year-period] was not actually established, nevertheless the names [of year-periods] in later ages which contain four words began with this one." This name may possibly be translated, "The Primordial and Great Grand Beginning."

It is almost impossible to be sure about the meaning of a magical title such as that taken by the Emperor, viz., "Ch'en-sheng Liu T'ai-p'ing Huang-ti." Wang Mang took them as a prophecy of his usurpation; cf. 99 A: 34b. Li Fei (prob. iii cent.) says, "*Ch'en* is to lead. It means that he obtained spiritual leading. The sage is the Liu [house]." Ju Shun however says, "[The rulers of the state of] Ch'en, [the first word in the Emperor's title], were the descendants of Shun. Wang Mang was a descendant of [the rulers of] Ch'en. These were deceptive words which made plain that [Wang] Mang would usurp [the throne] and set himself up [as emperor]. However [Hsia Ho-liang and Emperor Ai] did not know that." Wei Chao (197–273/4) says, "It made known and published (*ch'en*) the virtue of the sage Liu [house]." Yen Shih-ku adds, "The two explanations of Ju [Shun] and Wei [Chao] are [both] correct," and Hu San-hsing remarks ironically

二西初自賀
十北陵安良
爲原勿八等
度上徙月建
七永郡詔言
月陵國曰改
以亭民時元
渭部使詔易
城爲得夏號

[let] 120 [graduations per day] be used as the measure of their size."[5.9]

6a

In the seventh month, on the plain northwest of   Aug.
Wei-ch'eng, in the Yung-ling Commune section [of   6a
the prefecture], there was made the Emperor's tomb,
[with the order], "Do not remove the common people
from the commanderies and kingdoms [to this place],
in order that [the people] may not be disturbed."

In the eighth month, an imperial edict said, "The   Sept.
Expectant[6.1] Appointee Hsia Ho-ling and others gave
advice that [We] should change the year-period,

"If Wei [Chao's] explanation is not far from the truth, then Ju [Shun's] explanation is
like magic. Since Yen [Shih-ku] considers that both explanations are correct, which one
shall we follow?"

[5.9] Yen Shih-ku remarks, "Previously in the clepsydra, for a day and night together
there were 100 graduations 亥. Now [the Emperor] increased them by twenty." Wang
Mang later established 120 graduations; cf. 99 A: 35a. Shen Ch'in-han remarks, "If a
hundred graduations are divided equally among twelve [double]-hours, one [double]-hour
has 8 graduations and 20 divisions 分. Now 120 graduations were used, so that one
[double]-hour had ten graduations. The *Wu-tai Hui-yao* [by Wang Po (922–982), 10:
13a, 14a, 13b, says], 'In the [Posterior] Chin [dynasty, in the period] T'ien-fu III, [ii
Mar., 938], the Director of the Imperial Observatory memorialized, ... "The various
*Classics on the Graduations of the Clepsydra* [(there were five books by this title listed
even as early as the *Sui History's* "Treatise on Arts and Literature") all consider that in
a day and night there are one hundred graduations, which are divided among twelve
[double]-hours, so that each [double]-hour has 8 graduations and a third.... Sixty
divisions make one graduation, so that one [double]-hour has 8 graduations and 20 divisions." ' The *Sui Dynastic History* [begun 622], 19: [26a ff, which gives a full account
of the apportionment of clepsydra graduations among the various hours and their changes,
says], 'In 507, Emperor Wu considered that if the hundred graduations [of the clepsydra]
in a day and night were divided equally among the twelve double-hours, a double-hour
would have 8 graduations and there still would be some excess divisions [of a graduation].
So he considered that a day and night should have 96 graduations, so that one double-
hour should have eight whole graduations.' [Other schemes were also tried, by which
some double-hours had more graduations that others.] In the present [Ch'ing] dynasty,
the imperial almanacs use the arrangement [of Emperor Wu]. Each [double]-hour has 8
equal graduations, and each graduation has 15 divisions, without any distinction between
long graduations and short graduations."

[6.1] Ch'ien Ta-chao (1744–1813) declares that 時 should be emended to 侍. The
Official ed. has the latter reading. It is also found in the version of this edict on *HS*
75: 32b.

alter [Our] title, and increase the [number of] graduations on the clepsydra, whereby [We] could [secure] permanent peace for the clan [ruling] the state. We mistakenly listened to the advice of [Hsia] Ho-liang and the others, hoping to obtain blessings for [all] within the [four] seas. [But] in the end there was no happy verification [of their promises]; they have all gone contrary to the Classics, turned their backs on ancient [practises], and are not in accordance with the needs of the times. The decree of the

July 13　sixth month and [the day] *chia-tzu*, except for the order of an amnesty, is all expunged. [Hsia] Ho-liang and the others have gone contrary to the [right] Way and misled the crowd; they are to be committed [the charge of] the high officials." They all suffered [death] for their crimes.

　　　　The Lieutenant Chancellor, [Chu] Po, the Grandee Secretary, [Chao] Hsüan₂ₐ, and the Marquis of K'ung-hsiang, [Fu₄] Yen, had committed crimes; [Chu] Po

Sept. 21[6.2]　killed himself, [Chao] Hsüan's death-[penalty] was reduced by three[6.3] degrees, and [Fu₄] Yen was sentenced to have one-fourth of the households [in his estate] cut off. A discussion is in the "Memoir of

83: 16a–17a　[Chu] Po."[6.4]

III　　　　In the third year, in the spring, the first month,

增益漏刻可以永安國家朕過聽賀良等言冀為海內獲福卒亡

嘉應皆違經背古不合時宜六月甲子制書非赦令也皆蠲除之

賀良等反道惑眾下有司皆伏辜丞相博御史大夫玄孔鄉侯晏

有罪博自殺減死二等論晏削戶四分之一語在博傳

三年春正月

---

[6.2] *HS* 19 B: 49a.

[6.3] The present text and the *Han-chi* 28: 7b read "two degrees"; but *HS* 83: 17a⁴ and the *Tzu-chih T'ung-chien* 34: 5b read "three degrees." Hu San-hsing explains, "[Whoever]" has his capital punishment reduced three degrees, becomes a convict servitor or concubine."

These three officials had conspired, at the instigation of the Emperor's Grand Empress Dowager nee Fu, to have her nephew, Fu Hsi, dismissed. The latter was the most capable member of the Fu clan, but had opposed elevating the title of the Emperor's Grand Empress Dowager. Cf. Glossary, *sub* Chu Po.

[6.4] *HS* 27 Ca: 18b says, "In Chien-p'ing II, in the [Commandery] of Ting-hsiang, a male horse bore a colt with three legs, which followed the herd in drinking and eating." *Ibid.* 19b says, "In [the period] Chien-p'ing, in the [Commandery] of Yü-chang, there was a boy who metamorphosed and became a girl, was married, became a man's wife, and gave birth to a child."

立廣德夷王弟廣漢爲廣平王癸卯帝太太后所居桂宮正殿火三月

己酉丞相當薨有星孛于河鼓夏六月立魯頃王子郚鄉侯閔爲王冬

十一月壬子復甘泉泰時汾陰后土祠罷南北郊東平王雲雲后謁安

成恭侯夫人放皆有罪雲自殺詔放棄市

四年春大旱關東

[the Emperor] made [Liu] Kuang-han[a], the younger brother of King Yi of Kuang-tê, [Liu Yün-k'o], the King of Kuang-p'ing.    4 B.C. Jan./Feb. **6b** *5b* 6b

On [the day] *kuei-mao*, there was a fire in the Main Hall of the Kuei Palace where the Emperor's Grand Empress Dowager [nee Fu] lived.[6.5]    Feb. 17

In the third month, on [the day] *chi-yu*, the Lieutenant Chancellor [P'ing] Tang died. A comet appeared in the [constellation] Ho-ku.[6.6]    Apr. 24

In the summer, the sixth month, [the Emperor] established the Marquis of Wu-hsiang, [Liu] Min[3a], the son of King Ch'ing of Lu, [Liu Feng1], as King [of Lu].    July/Aug.

In the winter, the eleventh month, on [the day] *jen-tzu*, [the Emperor] reestablished the Altar to the Supreme [One] at the Kan-ch'üan [Palace] and the Temple to Sovereign Earth at Fen-yin [as places for regular imperial sacrifices] and disestablished [the places in] the southern and northern suburbs [for the suburban sacrifices].[6.7]    Dec. 23

The King of Tung-p'ing, [Liu] Yün[2a], [Liu] Yün[2a]'s Queen, Yeh, and Fang, the Lady of Marquis Kung of An-ch'eng [Wang Ch'ung[2a]], had all committed crimes; [Liu] Yün[2a] killed himself; Yeh and Fang were publicly executed.[6.8]

In the fourth year, in the spring, [the first month],[6.9] there was a great drought. East of the [Han-ku] Pass the common people carried in pro-    IV 3 B.C. Feb./Mar.

[6.5] *HS* 27 A: 16a says it was in the Hall of Vast Peace in that palace.

[6.6] Williams lists this comet as no. 53.

[6.7] These places had been last reestablished by the Empress Dowager nee Wang in Apr., 7 B.C. Cf. 10: 16a.

[6.8] These women had tried by magical means to bring about the death of Emperor Ai, in order that Liu Yün[2a] might become Emperor. Cf. Glossary, *sub* Liu Yün[2a].

*HS* 27 Bb: 17b says, "In Chien-p'ing III, at P'ing-tu in the [Commandery] of Tung-lai there were produced seven large fish, 80 feet long and 11 feet high, all of whom died." They were probably whales.

[6.9] Wang Nien-sun remarks that *HS* 27 Ca: 22a, in recounting this matter, prefaces it with "In the first month"; the next event in 11: 6b is prefaced with "in the second

cession the wands of the Mother Queen of the West.
They passed thru commanderies and kingdoms and
went west thru the [Han-ku] Pass to the imperial
capital.  The common people [there] also collected
and sacrificed to the Mother Queen of the West.
Some by night took fire up on top of buildings, beat
drums, and cried out, exciting and frightening one
another.

**7a**
Mar./Apr.
In the second month, [the Emperor] enfeoffed a
younger cousin of the Emperor's Grand Empress
Dowager [nee Fu], the Palace Attendant, Fu Shang,
as Marquis of Ju-ch'ang, and the son of a younger
[half]-brother of the [Emperor's Grand] Empress
Dowager [nee Fu] by the same mother, the Palace
7a  Attendant Cheng Yeh, as Marquis of Yang-hsin.  In

民至火太后
傳京上太母
行師屋太同
西民擊后弟
王又鼓從子
母會號弟侍
籌聚呼侍中
經祠相中鄭
歷西驚傅業
郡王恐商為
國母二為陽
西或月汝信
入夜封昌侯
關持帝太三

month"; the *Han-chi* 29: 1a also prefaces its account with "in the first month"; hence
these words should be in this passage too.

This interesting soteriological religion is described in two other passages, which are
appended here: *HS* 27 Ca: 22a says, "In Chien-p'ing IV, the first month, the common
people were excited and ran, [each] holding a stalk of straw or of hemp, carrying them on
and passing them to one another, saying, 'I am transporting the wand of [the goddess's
edict].'  Those who passed along and met on the roads were as many as thousands.
Some let down their hair and walked barefoot.  Some at night broke door-bars and some
climbed over walls, entering [houses].  Some rode chariots or on horseback, galloping
fast, making [themselves] post-messengers to transmit and transport [the wands].  They
passed and traveled thru 26 commanderies or kingdoms and came to the imperial capital.

"That summer, in the imperial capital, the common people of the commanderies and
kingdoms met together in the wards, lanes, and foot-paths, making sacrifices and setting
out utensils for tablets [like dice to throw lots, probably for divination], singing and
dancing, sacrificing to the Mother Queen of the West.  They also transmitted a written
message which said, 'The Mother informs her people that those who wear this writing
will not die.  Let those who do not believe my words look below their door hinges, where
there will be white hairs.'  In the autumn it stopped."

*HS* 26: 59b adds, "In [Chien-p'ing], the fourth year, the first month, the second month,
and the third month [Feb.–May], the common people frightened each other, crying out
and running, transmitting wands [containing] the edict [of the goddess], and sacrificing
to the Mother Queen of the West.  They also said, 'People with eyes [placed] vertically
will come.'"

Tu Yeh interpreted this event as portending weakness in the government, because

元壽元年春正月辛丑朔日有蝕之詔曰朕獲保宗

慮者

八月恭皇園北門災冬詔將軍中二千石舉明兵法有大

六百石及天下男子爵六月尊帝太太后爲皇太太后至秋

皆以告東平王封列侯語在賢傳夏五月賜中二千石孫寵

月侍中駙馬都尉董賢光祿大夫息夫躬南陽太守

the third month, the Palace Attendant and Chief Commandant of Attendant Cavalry, Tung Hsien[2a], the Imperial Household Grandee, Hsi-fu Kung, and the [former] Grand Administrator of Nan-yang [Commandery], Sun Ch'ung, were all enfeoffed as full marquises because they had informed on the King of Tung-p'ing, [Liu Yün[2a]]. A discussion is in the "Memoir of [Tung] Hsien[2a]."    Apr./May

   93: 9a

In the summer, the fifth month, [the Emperor] granted noble titles to [officials ranking from] fully two thousand piculs to those of six hundred piculs, also to the males of the empire. In the sixth month, he honored the Emperor's Grand Empress Dowager [nee Fu, with the title,] August Grand Empress Dowager. In the autumn, the eighth month, there was a visitation [of fire] to the North Gate of the Funerary Park for Sovereign Kung, [Liu K'ang].    June/July    July/Aug.    6a    Sept./Oct.

In the winter, an imperial edict [ordered] the generals and [officials ranking at] fully two thousand piculs to recommend those who understood military affairs and who had great plans [for the empire's future].[7.1]    Winter

In [the period] Yüan-shou, the first year, in the spring, the first month, on [the day] hsin-ch'ou, the first day of the month, there was an eclipse of the sun.[7.2] The imperial edict said, "We have been permitted to protect the [imperial] ancestral temples,    I    2 B.C.    Feb. 5

of its domination by the evil Ting and Fu clans. Pan Ku says that the Grand Empress Dowager nee Wang and Wang Mang responded to this portent when he destroyed the Ting and Fu clans. Cf. 27 Ca: 22a, b.

Chavannes, *La Sculpture sur pierre en Chine*, pl. XXXVIII, in the third register of the gable; *Mission archeologique dans la Chine Septentrionale*, Plates, 88, vol. I, fig. 161, 162, also vol. I[1], fig. 1237, and p. 80 reproduce Han grave sculptures in which devotees offer branches to the Mother Queen of the West, which are these wands. Cf. also Introduction, p. 8; Glossary, *sub* Mother Queen of the West; "An Ancient Chinese Mystery Cult," *Harvard Theological Review*, 35, Oct., 1942, 221–240.

[7.1] This edict is quoted in greater detail in 45: 17a, b.

[7.2] Cf. Appendix II for eclipses. This eclipse brought about the downfall of Sun Ch'ung and Hsi-fu Kung (45: 17b, 18a) and served to bring K'ung Kuang and Wang

and, [altho We are] neither wise nor clever, [We have] toiled day and night, taking no leisure for repose. Nevertheless, the *Yin* and *Yang* have not been in accord, so that the great multitude do not have enough [to live on]. We have not yet perceived [where lies] the blame for this [state of affairs], and have frequently [ordered Our] ministers to be attentive [to their duties], expecting that [We] might have hopes [of improvement in the government. But] to the present, the high officials, in administering the laws, have not yet attained [Our] goal [of good government]. Some esteem oppressiveness and cruelty and utilize the power [of the government] to obtain fame, while gentle and good, magnanimous and forgiving [people] fall into destruc-

7b tion and extinction. For this reason murderous brigands have increased more and more, while harmony and concord have daily declined, the people are resentful, and have no place to repose themselves.

"Recently on the first day of the first month there was an eclipse of the sun. The blame for that [event] is not far [to seek]—it lies upon Ourself.

7b Let the ministers and grandees each do their utmost and make all efforts to lead the officials, taking care to appoint benevolent persons and to degrade and send far away injurious villains, with the purpose of securing tranquillity for the common people. They should make Our faults known and not be silent about anything. Let them, with the generals, the full marquises, and [officials ranking at] fully two thousand piculs, each recommend one person who is capable and good, sincere and upright, and able to speak frankly. A general amnesty [is granted to] the empire."

Mang back to the capital (81: 18b, 19a; 99 A: 3b). Pao Hsüan recommended that Tung Hsien₂ₐ also be sent away and that Ho Wu, Shih₁ Tan, P'eng Hsüan, and Fu Hsi be recalled (72: 24a).

廟不明不敏宿夜憂勞未皇寧息惟陰陽不調元元不贍未睹厥咎婁救公卿庶

幾有望至今有司執法未得其中或上暴虐假執獲名溫良寬柔陷於亡滅是故

殘賊彌長和睦日衰百姓愁怨靡所錯躬酒正月朔日有蝕之厥咎不遠在余一

人公卿大夫其各悉心勉帥百寮敦任仁人黜遠殘賊期於安民陳朕之過失無

有所譚其與將軍列侯中二千石舉賢良方正能直言者各一人大赦天下

丁巳皇太太后傅氏崩三月丞相嘉有罪下獄死秋九月

二年春正月匈奴單于烏孫大昆彌來朝二月歸國單于

不說語在匈奴傳夏四月壬辰晦日有蝕之五月正三公

官分職大司馬衛將軍董

On [the day] *ting-szu*, the August Grand Empress Dowager nee Fu died.　　Feb. 21

In the third month, the Lieutenant Chancellor [Wang] Chia[1a] who had committed a crime, was sent to prison, where he died.[7.3]　　Apr./May *6b*

In the autumn, the ninth month, the Commander-in-chief and General of Agile Cavalry, Ting Ming, was dismissed. The bronze tortoise and snake door-knocker heads on the gate to the Hall in the Temple of [Emperor] Hsiao-yüan cried out.　　Oct.

In the second year,[7.4] in the spring, the first month, the *Shan-yü* of the Huns and the Greater *K'un-mi* of the Wu-sun came to pay court. In the second month, they returned to their states. The *Shan-yü* was not pleased. A discussion is in the "Memoir of the Huns."[8.1]　　8a 1 B.C. Feb./Mar. Mar./Apr. 8a 94B: 14b, 15a

In the summer, the fourth month, on [the day] *jen-hsu*,[8.2] the last day of the month, there was an eclipse of the sun.　　June 20

In the fifth month, [the titles of] the three highest ministers were corrected and their duties divided: the Commander-in-chief and General of the Guard, Tung　　June/July

---

[7.3] Wang Chia[1a] was a capable and loyal official, who prevented Emperor Ai from promoting and enriching his catamite, Tung Hsien[2a]. After an amnesty, he recommended some officials whom the Emperor had previously dismissed, so he was accused of having misdirected the state and misled the Emperor, which was an inhuman crime. He was sent to prison, where he starved to death. In 4 A.D., Wang Mang had him listed as a faithful minister. This judicial murder was perhaps Emperor Ai's greatest crime.

[7.4] Chang Chao (1691–1745) remarks that the Academy ed. (1124) prefixes "Yüan-shou" to the words "second year," the use of which words is contrary to the practise of the history, hence they are an interpolation.

[8.1] *Tzu-chih T'ung-chien* 35: 11a (following *HS* 94 B: 14b) points out that the *Shan-yü* was not pleased because he had been lodged in the Grape Lodge of the Shang-lin Park in order that the planet Jupiter might repress and overcome the evil influences the *Shan-yü* had brought with him in coming from the north (*Yin*). Cf. de Groot, *Die Hunnen*, p. 261, n. 1.

[8.2] The text reads *jen-ch'en*, but calculation shows that *ch'en* is an error for *hsü*. Cf. App. II, ii.

Hsien$_{2a}$, became the Commander-in-chief; the Lieutenant Chancellor, K'ung Kuang, became the Grand Minister of the Masses; and the Grandee Secretary, P'eng Hsüan, became the Grand Minister of Works.[8.3] [The latter] was enfeoffed as Marquis of Ch'ang-p'ing. The duties of the Director of Uprightness and the Director of the Retainers were to be corrected, and a Minister of Brigands was to be created.

Before the matter was settled, in the sixth month, on [the day] *mou-wu*, the Emperor died in the Wei-yang Palace. In the autumn, the tenth[8.4] month, on [the day] *jen-yin*, he was buried in the Yi Tomb.

In eulogy we say: When [Emperor] Hsiao-ai was a tributary king and then entered the palace of the Heir-apparent, his vocabulary was large[8.5] and intelligent, [so that even when] he was young, he [had already] obtained a good renown. He observed the period of [Emperor] Hsiao-ch'eng, when 'blessings left the' imperial 'house'[8.6] and [the Emperor's] power was transferred to his maternal [relatives]. For this reason, when [Emperor Ai] attended court, he frequently executed his great officials, seeking to strengthen the might of the ruler and to imitate [Emperors] Wu and Hsüan. In his nature he did

*Margin notes (left):*
Aug. 15
**8b**
Nov. 27
*7a*
**8b**

*Chinese text (right column, read top to bottom, right to left):*

賢爲大司馬丞相孔光爲大司徒御史大夫彭宣爲大司
空封長平侯正司直司隸造司寇職事未定六月戊午帝
崩于未央宮秋九月壬寅葬義陵贊曰孝成哀自爲藩王及
充太子之宮文辭博敏幼有令開睹孝成世祿去王室權
柄外移是故臨朝娶誅大臣欲彊主威以則武宣雅性

---

[8.3] Hu San-hsing, in a note to the *Tzu-chih T'ing-chien* 35: 11a, explains, "The division of duties was that the Commander-in-chief took charge of military matters, the Grand Minister of the Masses took charge of matters concerning the people, and the Grand Minister of Works took charge of matters concerning the waters and the earth."

The Sung Ch'i ed. says that the Chiang-nan text (prob. x–xiii cent.) has 官 before the 職.

[8.4] The present text says "ninth month," but Huang lists no *jen-yin* day in that month. Fu Tsan, in a note, says that from the death to the burial was to the 105th day. Szu-ma Kuang, in his *Tzu-chih T'ung-chien K'ao-yi* 2, 9b notes that the 105th day after the death was in the tenth month, so emends "ninth" to "tenth." I have adopted that suggestion. *Han-chi* 29: 13b dates the burial in the ninth month, on the day *jen-ch'en*, which is also impossible, for Huang also puts that day in the tenth month.

[8.5] A phrase reminiscent of *SC* 47: 84 (= *Mh* V, 421), where the *Spring and Autumn* is said to be 約文辭而指博 "condensed in its language, but extensive in its allusiveness."

[8.6] A quotation from *Analects* XVI, iii.

不　覽　卽　年　不
好　卜　位　濡　永
聲　射　痿　劇　哀
色　武　痺　饗　哉
時　戲　末　國

not care for music or women. At times he watched boxing,[8.7] archery, and military sports. When he ascended the throne, he had arthritis,[8.8] and in his latter years [his arthritis] gradually became worse. He did not long enjoy the rule. How sad![8.9]

[8.7] *HS* 70: 5a says that Kan Yen-shou "was examined in boxing and made an Attendant at the Gate." Meng K'ang (ca. 180–260) and Su Lin (fl. 196–227) say that *pien* 卞 or 弁 is 手搏.

[8.8] Ju Shun comments, "The pronunciation of *wei* 痿 is that of the *fan-jui* 蹞 踤 cross-bow. The sickness in which one cannot cross his two feet is called *wei*." Yen Shih-ku says that *fan-jui* is the name of a cross-bow and means to press with both feet. Shen Ch'in-han adds, "In stretching this cross-bow one has to use the feet, hence it became the name of the cross-bow." These were probably the extremely stout crossbows used by "skilled soldiers."

[8.9] A pun; the word for "sad" is *ai*, the Emperor's posthumous name.

# APPENDIX I

## THE CUSTOM OF MOURNING TO THE THIRD YEAR

The custom of mourning for parents to the third year was urged by Confucius,[1] seemingly because it reinforced the virtue of filial piety.[2] It was vehemently attacked by Moh-tzu,[3] and defended by Mencius[4] and Hsün-tzu.[5] However, even in the state of Lu at the time of Mencius, it was still an uncommon practise. When he urged it upon the Duke of T'eng, after the death of Duke T'ing, the court advisors memorialized the Duke saying, "None of the former princes of Lu, which kingdom we honor, observed [this practise of mourning to the third year], neither have any of our own former princes observed it."[6] In its extreme form, when the son spent his time weeping and in partial fasting, cutting himself off from his usual pursuits, this custom could only have originated among aristocrats, for no one else had the leisure to devote two years and more to such a practise.

This custom of mourning to the third year seems to have remained a specifically Confucian practise. Emperor Wen, in his posthumous edict of 157 B.C., condemned it and limited mourning for an emperor to the thirty-sixth day after his burial.[7] That period was thereafter adopted by officials in mourning for their own parents.[8] Even the famous Confucian bibliophile, Liu Tê, King Hsien of Ho-chien (d. 130 B.C.), seems not to have followed the custom of mourning to the third year. We have the citation of his deeds by his Commandant of the Capital,[9] and it says nothing about his having mourned to the third year, even though he is said to have cultivated Confucian practises in his rites and robes. Thus the attack of Moh-tzu upon the Confucian mourning rites and Emperor Wen's condemnation of this practise seems to have led the Confucians themselves to dispense with this practise until their doctrine secured an

---

[1] *Analects* XVII, xxi.

[2] Dubs, *Hsüntze, the Moulder*, p. 148 ff.

[3] Y. P. Mei, *The Works of Motse*, ch. 25.

[4] *Mencius*, III, I, ii, 2 (Legge, p. 236).

[5] Dubs, *The Works of Hsüntze*, p. 239 ff.

[6] *Mencius*, III, I, ii, 3 (Legge, p. 237).

[7] *HS* 4: 20a; *HFHD* I, 270, n. 3.

[8] *HS* 84: 4b.

[9] *HS* 53: 2a, b.

unchallenged hold upon official China. It remained quite uncommon to the end of the first century B.C., for in 7 B.C. Emperor Ai considered this practise unusual and so meritorious that he rewarded King Hui of Ho-chien, Liu Liang, a descendant of King Hsien, by a complimentary edict and an increase by ten thousand households in the size of his king-dom, for having mourned to the third year for his mother, the Queen Dowager.[10] In the same year Erudits and their Disciples, who were the teachers in the Confucian Imperial University, were allowed to take leave to the third year to mourn for their parents.[11] The practise of mourning to the third year seems thus to have first been propagated widely during the latter part of the first century B.C.

The Han dynasty stressed filial piety in many ways. The *Classic of Filial Piety* was a textbook studied by all; the Han Emperors (except the first) were all given the word *"hsiao* 孝, filially pious" as the first part of their posthumous names. They made occasional grants to Filially Pious people and had persons recommended for the bureaucracy because of their filial piety. Emperor Ai considered a lack of filial conduct as sufficient grounds for dismissing even the highest official.[12] Hence it is quite natural, when Confucianism came to be well established and an attempt was made to fulfil all its requirements, that the practise of mourning to the third year should have been revived and adopted by those who were careful in their Confucianism and had the leisure to follow this custom.

Yet the practise was slow in spreading. It was not until Jan. 1, 117 A.D. that the Empress nee Teng, while ruling for Emperor An, "for the first time permitted high officials, [those ranking at] two thousand piculs, and Inspectors to perform the mourning to the third year,"[13] at the end of which time they were returned to their former posts. This provision was confirmed by later emperors. At the suggestion of Ch'en Chung,[14] on Dec. 25, 120, Emperor An "again decided that high officials [and those ranking at] two thousand piculs and over should wear mourning to the third year."[15] The actual period was twenty-five months.[16] In 154,

[10] *HS* 11: 2b.
[11] *HS* 11: 3b.
[12] Cf. Glossary, *sub* Ho Wu.
[13] *HHS*, An. 5: 12b.
[14] *HHS*, Mem. 36: 13b.
[15] *HHS*, An. 5: 16a.
[16] *HHS*, Mem. 36: 13a.

Emperor Huan "again permitted Inspectors [and officials ranking at] two thousand piculs to perform the mourning to the third year,"[17] and in Apr./May 159 he "again decided that Inspectors [and officials ranking at] two thousand piculs should perform the mourning to the third year."[18] Thus only at the end of the Later Han period was the mourning to the third year performed by the high officials as an example to the empire.

[17] *HHS*, An. 7: 6b.
[18] *Ibid.*, 8b.

# APPENDIX II

## ECLIPSES DURING THE REIGN OF EMPEROR AI

i. In Yüan-shou I, i (the first month), on the day *hsin-ch'ou*, the first day of the month, an eclipse of the sun is recorded (11: 7a). *HS* 27 Cb: 16a adds, "It was not total, [but] like a hook, and was 10 degrees in [the constellation] Ying-shih, in the same month and day as that in the seventh year of Emperor Hui."

Huang, *Concordance des chronologies néoméniques*, gives this date as Feb. 5, 2 B.C., for which day Oppolzer, *Canon der Finsternisse*, calculates his solar eclipse no. 2879. He charts the path of totality as passing along the Yangtze River. Calculation of this eclipse according to Neugebauer, *Astronomische Chronologie*, shows that at Ch'ang-an it reached a magnitude (totality = 1.00) of 0.85 at 7:45 a.m. local time, and that the path of totality passed through the present Lhassa, Southern Szechuan, southern Hunan and Foochow. The sun was in longitude 314° = 317° R.A. The first and principal star in Ying-shih, α, Pegasi was then in 319° R.A. It is interesting that a total eclipse was not reported when it went so far south.

In the 10 years between this and the preceding recorded eclipse, no solar eclipses were visible in China.

ii. *HS* 11: 8a states, in Yüan-shou II, "the summer, *fourth* month, on [the day] *jen-ch'en*, the last day of the month, there was an eclipse of the sun." *Han-chi* 29: 12b merely states, "In the summer, the *fourth* month, there was an eclipse of the sun." *HS* 27 Cb: 16a however states, "In [Yüan-shou] II, the *third* month, on [the day] *jen-ch'en*, the last day of the month, there was an eclipse of the sun." Huang gives no *jen-ch'en* day in the fourth month, but makes that day the last day of the third month, May 21, 1 B.C. He gives the last day of the fourth month as a *jen-hsü* day, June 20, 1 B.C., for which day Oppolzer calculates his solar eclipse no. 2882. He gives none for the other date. Calculation of this partial eclipse by Neugebauer's tables shows that it reached a magnitude of 0.06 at sunset, 5:08 p.m. local time at Ch'ang-an.

It is then evident that *jen-ch'en* 辰 is a mistaken reading for *jen-hsü* 戌 (a natural error), and that someone who knew that *jen-ch'en* could not have been the last day of the fourth month corrected the record in ch. 27. Astronomers must have been looking for this eclipse, else they would not have perceived it. In the 16 months between this and the preceding recorded eclipses, no solar eclipses were visible in China.

43

# THE HISTORY OF THE FORMER HAN DYNASTY

## CHAPTER XII

## EMPEROR HSIAO-P'ING

## INTRODUCTION

### Summary of the period

The reign of Emperor P'ing (1 B.C.–A.D. 6), is the period during which Wang Mang consolidated his control of the government in such a fashion that he could not later be removed. Emperor P'ing was only in his ninth year when he came to the throne and he died before he was capped (the ceremony marking the attainment of a youth's majority), so that during this whole period Wang Mang actually wielded the imperial authority. He eliminated the influence of any imperial relatives, except his own clan. He raised himself from one honor to another by the ingenious use of Confucian humility. He married his daughter to the Emperor, against the opposition of the Grand Empress Dowager. He secured the loyal cooperation of Confucians, especially the famous Liu Hsin[1a]. This period was thus one of conspicuous success on the part of Wang Mang. After Emperor P'ing had died, Wang Mang was charged with regicide, but that allegation may have been merely propaganda. These matters will be discussed seriatim.

### The nature of this "Annals"

This chapter, like the other "Imperial Annals," does not pretend to be what we would call a history of the period. It is actually an expanded chronological summary, useful for purposes of convenient reference. The actual history is to be found in the other parts of this large book, especially in the "Memoirs," and most of all in the "Memoir of Wang Mang," a translation of which is appended to this chapter. The part of that "Memoir" devoted to these six years is more than twice as long as are these "Imperial Annals." That "Memoir" should accordingly be read in connection with these "Imperial Annals."

### Wang Mang's orderly solution of a dynastic crisis

This reign began with a dynastic crisis, for at the death of Emperor Ai there was no heir to the throne. Emperor Wen had established the dynastic practice that the reigning Emperor designates one of his sons as his successor by making him Heir-apparent (4: 5b–6b). Emperor Ai

44

however had no sons and appointed no Heir-apparent. There were, moreover, no living descendants of his predecessor, Emperor Ch'eng. Fortunately such a crisis had occurred twice before in Han Times: at the death of the Empress Dowager nee Lü and at the death of Emperor Chao. Each time the high officials had deliberated over the matter and had selected the nearest suitable relative of the deceased monarch. Ho Kuang had legitimized his choices of emperors by enacting them in imperial edicts issued by the Empress Dowager. Wang Mang followed this precedent: he selected the grandson and only surviving descendant of Emperor Yüan, Liu Chi-tzu, a first cousin of Emperor Ai, and enthroned him. This boy was only in his ninth year, so could not rule in person; the Grand Empress Dowager nee Wang, his step-grandmother, who, as the "mother of the dynasty" and regent, had been ruling for the two months between the death and the enthronement, continued to attend court and decide matters. She entrusted the government to Wang Mang, her grand-nephew, who was now in his forty-fifth year.

## Wang Mang's revenge upon Emperor Ai's maternal relatives

Before the new Emperor was enthroned, Wang Mang began his revenge upon Emperor Ai's maternal relatives, who had previously turned Wang Mang out of power and out of the court. The Empress Dowagers nee Fu and nee Ting had both died; the only lady remaining of their clans was the Empress nee Fu of Emperor Ai. She had had no children, so Wang Mang had the Grand Empress Dowager issue an edict commanding the Empress to retire to another palace, because of the crimes of her elder cousin, the deceased Empress Dowager nee Fu. Some months later she was dismissed from her rank and made a commoner, whereupon she committed suicide. At the death of Emperor Ai, the Fu and Ting clans possessed no male relatives who could intercede with the ruler for them, hence these clans became helpless. Fu Yen, the brother of the Empress Dowager, was dismissed from his marquisate and exiled to Ho-p'u Commandery, in the southernmost peninsula of the present Kuangtung. The members of the Ting clan were sent back to their natal commanderies. The Grand Empress Dowager nee Fu and the Empress Dowager nee Ting were posthumously degraded in their titles and merely entitled the Mother (nee Fu) of King Kung of Ting-t'ao and the [Royal] Concubine nee Ting. In 5 A.D., Wang Mang argued the Grand Empress Dowager nee Wang into permitting him to have the tombs of these two ladies opened, their official seals taken away and destroyed, the body of the lady nee Fu transported from the capital to Ting-t'ao, and to have them both reburied in simple wooden coffins, like concubines (which had been their original rank). Their tumuli were levelled and thorns were planted at these places. Wang Mang did not forget an injury.

The Empress Dowager nee Chao was degraded and removed from the imperial palace at the same time as was the Empress nee Fu. This famous beauty, Chao Fei-yen, was the sister of the Favorite Beauty nee Chao, who had been responsible for Emperor Ch'eng's infanticides. She would have been punished for her sister's crimes when they were discovered at the beginning of Emperor Ai's reign, except for the fact that Emperor Ai was indebted to her. Wang Mang was not so indebted, and had her removed to the palace for dismissed empresses. She was later dismissed from her title, whereupon she too committed suicide.

## The dynastic principle that there should be only one imperial line of descent

Probably Wang Mang's motive in removing these ladies was not merely revenge, but also to eliminate the evil effect of imperial maternal relatives in the court. He was not willing to yield up his power to a new clan. The moral corruption, extravagance, and misuse of the government to enrich themselves on the part of the Wang and Chao clans in the reign of Emperor Ch'eng and of the Fu and Ting clans in the reign of Emperor Ai had convinced many intelligent persons that imperial maternal relatives were injurious to the state. When, at the death of Emperor Ai, the Grand Empress Dowager nee Wang asked the ministers to recommend someone to control the government, the General of the Van, Ho Wu, and the General of the Left, Kung-sun Lu, had both become convinced that the government should be in the hands of neither the imperial clan nor of any imperial maternal clan. They therefore independently recommended each other for the post of Commander-in-chief. But this policy was contrary to the Confucian moral principle that people generally (including the ruler) should favor their relatives, and the circumstance that these two ministers recommended each the other proved fatal. The other ministers all recommended Wang Mang, who was accordingly given the position. Wang Mang had Ho Wu and Kung-sun Lu accused of plotting to advance each other; they were dismissed and sent to their homes. Four years later Ho Wu was arrested in connection with the affair of Wang Yü, whereupon Ho Wu committed suicide.

Because of his unhappy experience with the Fu and Ting clans, Wang Mang did not even allow the new Emperor's mother, the Concubine nee Wei, nor her relatives to come to the imperial capital. The Wei clan had previously been connected with the imperial court: it had furnished

46

Emperors Hsüan and Yüan each with a Favorite Beauty, who bore each a child, as well as furnishing a concubine for Emperor Ch'eng's half-brother. This latter girl was the mother of Liu Chi-tzu, Emperor P'ing. Wang Mang evidently feared the power of such a clan, which knew well the customs in the imperial court and had old connections in the capital.

Instead of allowing this Wei clan to repeat the exploits of the Fu clan, Wang Mang had its members all kept in the kingdom of Chung-shan, where Liu Chi-tzu had been King. His intention was to establish the principle that there is only one imperial family, and that when, because of the failure of a natural heir, some scion from another branch of the imperial clan was elevated to the throne, this person should become exclusively a member of the imperial family, so that his own close relatives must not be considered close imperial relatives or treated as such. Thus the number of imperial maternal relatives, who might interfere in the government, was to be restricted (and the Wang clan continued in power without any rivals). Emperor Ch'eng had attempted to put this principle in force just before his death (possibly at the instigation of Wang Mang), but Emperor Ai, through the influence of his grandmother, had rejected and acted contrary to it.

Wang Mang appointed another scion of the imperial clan as King of Chung-shan to act as the son of Liu Chi-tzu's father, and sent to his mother, the Concubine nee Wei, a royal seal and cord, installing her as the Queen of King Hsiao of Chung-shan, with a whole county as her private estate, from which she received the income. Her uncle and younger brother were both made Marquises of the Imperial Domain, and her three younger sisters were given the title of Baronetess, with an estate of two thousand households. Her first cousin was made Queen to the new King of Chung-shan. But honor and wealth would not make up to her for her absent son. Unlike the Concubine nee Ting, who, without objecting, allowed her son, Emperor Ai, to be taken from her, the Queen nee Wei was said to be disconsolate, weeping day and night for her child, who had no near relative by him to guard or care for him.

Wang Yü, Wang Mang's eldest son, disapproved of his father's policy. He was afraid that there would come to be a feud between the Wei and Wang clans, which would be disastrous to the Wang clan when the new Emperor came of age. Wang Yü secretly communicated with the Wei clan, urging them to ask permission to come to the imperial court. Wang Yü's clique furthermore attempted to terrify Wang Mang into acceding to their request by playing upon his superstition with false portents (99 A: 16a, b). When the matter was discovered (A.D. 3), Wang Mang had his son executed, together with the Wei clan and hundreds of others. Only Liu Chi-tzu's mother was left alive, retaining her title and estate. When Wang Mang usurped the throne, she was dismissed from her title and made a commoner; a year or so later she died. Thus Wang Mang was left unchallenged in control of the imperial court.

### The nature of Wang Mang's position and power

During the reign of Emperor P'ing, Wang Mang was not the legal ruler of the state, but merely its most important minister. He was the Commander-in-chief and Intendant of Affairs of the Masters of Writing, who could be dismissed at will by the actual regent, the Grand Empress Dowager nee Wang. By this time, the Commander-in-chief concerned himself little with the army; this official had become the dominating minister in the civil government. He made appointments in the bureaucracy, cited officials for promotion or demotion, proposed governmental policies, and acted as chief consultant to the ruler. The other ministers had become for the most part virtual executive officers to the Commander-in-chief. The latter's authority over the other ministers was exercised by memorializing the throne that they be ordered to execute certain policies, and then advising the throne to consent to the proposal. Since the rejection of an important official's advice in an important matter meant that this official must resign or be dismissed, a great official was consequently often reluctant to offer advice, and, when asked to do so, often allowed less important members of the court to propose the policy he favored. At the same time, this custom made the throne very reluctant to refuse an important minister's advice, since the throne might find it difficult to discover another person who would be as suitable as the dismissed minister. Thus a minister could sometimes compel the throne to accept an unwelcome policy. On the other hand, under an aggressive ruler, ministers could frequently be dismissed and sometimes punished for offering suggestions that were unpleasant to the throne. Thus Wang Mang could wield the imperial power, even though he was not actually the regent.

The Grand Empress Dowager nee Wang had no taste for ruling; she was a quiet old lady, who upheld the best traditions of Chinese wifely virtue, being loyal to her husband and her relatives, complaisant to her husband's relatives, going her own quiet way without interfering with others. She had originally supported Wang Mang in 8 B.C. because her brother, Wang Ken, had recommended him as Commander-in-chief. But she was not altogether blind to his faults, and did not trust him completely. Since she was a woman, she was immured in her palace, and Wang Mang saw to it that only those favorable to him had access to her. Thus she was brought around to accede to his plans.

## How Wang Mang established himself securely and obtained a following

Wang Mang's gradual rise in power and popularity is so well recounted in his "Memoir" that it is unnecessary to repeat it here. It will be sufficient to point out the steps he took and the general principles upon which he operated, stressing nuances that may not be so clear to a casual reader and mentioning facts not found in these two chapters.

When Wang Mang was first put into power, he took care to surround himself with people whom he could influence. The pliant K'ung Kuang, a descendant of Confucius, had been Grand Minister Over the Masses and had recommended Wang Mang to the Grand Empress Dowager. Wang Mang treated him respectfully, retained him in office, and promoted his son-in-law, Chen Han, who later became one of Wang Mang's intimate followers. Wang Mang also attached Wang Shun$_{4b}$ to himself, because the latter was loved and trusted by the Grand Empress Dowager. This man was a son of the Grand Empress Dowager's first cousin who had been the Commander-in-chief, Wang Yin. Then Wang Mang proceeded to get rid of his possible opponents.

The person whose influence with the Grand Empress Dowager Wang Mang most feared was Wang Li$_{5a}$, who was own half-brother to her and her closest living relative. There was also her nephew, Wang Jen, a son of Wang T'an$_{2b}$, another half-brother of the Grand Empress Dowager. Wang Jen bore the same relationship to her that Wang Mang did. Both Wang Li$_{5a}$ and Wang Jen were courageous and plain-speaking; as close relatives they had access to her, so that Wang Mang needed to remove them in order to establish his own power securely. Wang Li$_{5a}$ was perhaps the worst reprobate in the Wang clan, so much so that he had been passed over when, in the reign of Emperor Ch'eng, the post of Commander-in-chief had been passed about among the brothers of the Grand Empress Dowager. Wang Mang prepared a petition to the Grand Empress Dowager, enumerating the crimes of Wang Li$_{5a}$ and Wang Jen, and had Chen Han take it to K'ung Kuang, with the request that he memorialize those matters in his own name. K'ung Kuang was timid and did not like to refuse, so did as he was told. Wang Mang liked to act by indirection; he would hint to his followers what he wanted done and allow them to propose these matters for action. Then he could

49

approve or disapprove as the circumstances dictated and yet not seem to have been taking the initiative.

When the petition regarding Wang Li$_{5a}$ and Wang Jen reached the Grand Empress Dowager, Wang Mang advised her to assent to it. When she did not want to part with her last independent sources of information, Wang Mang insisted, putting her in the position of either having to reject K'ung Kuang and himself or send away her brother and nephew. She yielded, and thus gave herself into the control of Wang Mang. Three years later, Wang Mang involved Wang Li$_{5a}$ and Wang Jen in the affair of Wang Yü, and compelled them both to commit suicide.

Thus Wang Mang, partly by persuasion and partly by a relentless use of the governmental power, eliminated any possible rivals. He filled the court with his own followers, eliminating all who would oppose him. Most of the bureaucracy willingly followed Wang Mang. He was the legal deputy of the imperial power; the custom of delegating the imperial power to the outstanding imperial maternal relative had regularly been practised for half a century, consequently it may be said to have become part of the (unwritten) constitution. The people had been trained to follow the imperial authority, so that any reforms, short of a rebellion, had to be authenticated by the emperor. Power and wealth lay in the giving of Wang Mang, hence few officials were willing to refuse his leadership. Only a very few of the more squeamish officials, in particular the Grand Minister of Works, P'eng Hsün, and his successor, Wang Ch'ung$_{2b}$, were willing to sacrifice their careers because of their dislike for the way Wang Mang was doing things. These two in succession asked to resign. They had not actually opposed Wang Mang and were respected by intelligent people, so he had to allow them to go. But he disliked their leaving and refused to bestow upon them the parting gifts customarily given at the resignation of an honored official. They could merely retire from the court to their homes and keep quiet about their opinions. Wang Mang distributed noble titles and positions liberally to his loyal followers and was praised on all sides.

## How Wang Mang secured unprecedented honors and popularity

No sooner had Wang Mang established his followers in the bureaucracy than he proceeded to seek for fame and popular support. The method he employed was an ingenious use of a Confucian principle: the virtue of yielding to others. He induced his followers to demand certain honors for him from the throne and then systematically refused those honors. The custom of first refusing great honors had long been used. Emperor

Kao refused the throne thrice when it was offered to him (*Mh* II, 380). Emperor Wen refused it five times (*HS* 4: 4a). Emperor Ai thought it best to refuse at first (11: 1b). Wang Mang excelled them all in humility by refusing, not at merely five times, but firmly and stubbornly.

Confucian tradition contained the statement that when the Duke of Chou, so honored by Confucius and his followers, was regent for the infant King Ch'eng, someone from the Yüeh-shang brought a white pheasant as tribute. Wang Mang, who in his youth had made a thorough study of Confucianism and its traditions, had the officials in the southern-most Chinese commandery reminded of this fact, and, at the first New Year's court of the new reign, some persons who called themselves Yüeh-shang accordingly appeared with an albino pheasant. No Chinese or member of the Office for Interpreting (*Yi-guan*) at the court could under-stand their language, so that it had to be translated by a succession of interpreters before it could be rendered into Chinese. To such distant regions had Wang Mang's virtue penetrated!

It made quite a stir at the court. The Confucians were pleased to recognize this obscure tradition, and the courtiers likened Wang Mang to Ho Kuang, who had so nobly conducted the dynasty through the minority of Emperors Chao and Hsüan, and to the Duke of Chou him-self. Thus was confirmed Mencius' statement (IV, B, i, 3) that at intervals of a thousand years, like sages appear. When the Grand Em-press Dowager hinted her suspicions, the courtiers had the opportunity of lauding Wang Mang to the skies, and proposed that Wang Mang should be given the title of Duke Giving Tranquillity to the Han Dynasty. At that time, the two highest existing noble titles were King and Marquis. The title of king was given only to sons of emperors and their heirs who succeeded them. Outside the Liu clan there were no kings. The Han dynasty had not previously enfeoffed any dukes, so that this title ele-vated Wang Mang above all the other nobles except the dozen-odd kings. When Wang Mang insistently refused this honor, keeping to his bed in order to avoid it, and the petitioners insisted that it should be granted to him, the Grand Empress Dowager was advised and forced to do as Wang Mang had planned: to grant high honors to Wang Mang's asso-ciates, K'ung Kuang, Wang Shun₄ᵦ, Chen Feng, and Chen Han, and then to grant still higher honors to Wang Mang, before he could be induced to rise and accept his title. He still however refused some of her grants, and advised her instead to bestow titles and grants upon members of the imperial clan and common people. Thus Wang Mang, by the simple device of obdurantly refusing honors, was enabled, without seeming to take the initiative, to secure important grants for his followers and also to avoid the jealousy of the imperial clan and people by having additional grants bestowed upon them. A more effective means to popularity could hardly have been found.

When this scheme had been so successful, Wang Mang sought for plenary power in the government. He again hinted his desires to his associates. At their suggestions, the Grand Empress Dowager, who did not want to be disturbed by the details of government, easily granted to Wang Mang full authority to decide all except the most important matters, such as enfeoffments to noble titles. She probably thought that this grant would make no practical difference in the government. Thus Wang Mang controlled the whole administration by right as well as in practise. He responded by having the Grand Empress Dowager make a great grant to the poor people and then lauding her extravagantly for it.

In order to make himself a close relative of the reigning emperor, thus securing his position in case the Grand Empress Dowager should die, Wang Mang next planned to marry his daughter to the boy Emperor. Again he proceeded by indirection. He first proposed that the Emperor be married, in order that the imperial line be continued. The Grand Empress Dowager agreed, and ordered the presentation of suitable girls. It was the custom that the mother of the Emperor should choose his wife. The Grand Empress Dowager, who was the young Emperor's legal mother, did not approve of her nephew too whole-heartedly; Wang Mang was afraid that she would pass over his own daughter, so called attention to this girl by publicly refusing to offer her under a plea of humility. The Grand Empress Dowager really opposed the match in her heart and seems to have thought it would be a good thing to check his growing power by putting another clan in power, for she issued an edict withdrawing all girls of the Wang clan from the competition.

But Wang Mang had become too popular. His daughter was of the right age; he outranked all other nobles in the empire, except those of the Liu clan, whose daughters could not be espoused because they bore the same surname as the Emperor; and he had acquired a great fame through his distribution of favors and grants to the people. It was then the custom that any one could come to the imperial palace and present petitions advising the ruler. Many families of those who hoped to enter the bureaucracy had moved to the capital commanderies, in order to study at the Imperial University or with the many Confucian masters who had congregated there, so that there was probably a larger proportion of literate persons in that region than elsewhere in the empire. These people hoped to attract the attention of the ministers and so attain office. Since Wang Mang controlled the giving of offices, and the proposal suited them, these people crowded to the portals of the Grand Empress Dowager at the rate of more than a thousand a day, offering petitions which protested that the daughter of Wang Mang was the most suitable person to be made the Empress. The ministers and grandees prostrated themselves in her courts, making similar requests. Wang Mang politely sent his personal attendants to turn them away, but the petitioners naturally paid no attention. Thus popular opinion, mobilized by Wang Mang's refusal, forced the Grand Empress Dowager to discontinue the competition among the girls and select Wang Mang's daughter. The other families were placated by selecting eleven of their girls as imperial concubines. It was an outstanding victory of intrigue, directed by a master mind, in which Wang Mang completely outmaneuvered his great-aunt.

There was a Confucian tradition that in Chou times, when the Son of Heaven took a wife from a noble whose state was small, the Son of Heaven augmented that noble's fief to be at least a hundred *li* square, i.e., nine million *mou* or over four hundred thousand acres. A sycophant marquis of the Liu clan accordingly memorialized that Wang Mang's fief should be augmented to that size, and the courtiers added that he should be given two hundred million cash as a betrothal present. He declined both presents, accepting only forty million cash, and distributing most of that among the new imperial concubines. Then the courtiers said that he had not received enough, so he was given a further sum, whereupon he distributed part of it among his own poor relatives. After the marriage had been celebrated, the ministers likened Wang Mang to Yi Yin and the Duke of Chou, the two greatest ministers in ancient history, and proposed that Wang Mang be given the same title as they had had, that his sons be ennobled, and he be given honors similar to those the Duke of Chou had received. Wang Mang again refused, the matter was again debated by the ministers, and petitions again poured in from the people. His two remaining sons were made marquises, his mother was made a Baronetess, he was given an official title higher than any other previous minister, and a special seal with the title, "Ruling Governor, Grand Tutor, and Commander-in-chief." The other ministers were ordered to address him in special humble terms. Ten chariots and a host of elite troops and attendants formed his train. Altogether some 487,572 persons signed petitions, urging that he be honored. (This number was likely taken from a memorial to the Grand Empress Dowager, summarizing these documents.) Thus Wang Mang, by a showy Confucian humility and generosity, captured the imaginations of the people. No one before his time and few since then have excited so much enthusiasm.

### How Wang Mang secured the loyalty of Liu Hsin[1a]

Among those whose loyalty he secured was the famous scholar, Liu Hsin[1a]. Even after Wang Mang usurped the throne and took away imperial and royal honors from the Liu clan, Liu Hsin still remained loyal, until just before Wang Mang's death, when the mounting resentment against Wang Mang, together with an astrological portent and a prophecy, led Liu Hsin finally to head an abortive rebellion (cf. 99 C: 22b–24a). The fact that an outstanding member of the imperial clan and a famous Confucian scholar should have become one of Wang Mang's most loyal supporters and highest officials is so remarkable that it is worth while studying the means by which Wang Mang secured this man's loyalty.

During the reign of Emperor Ch'eng (in 28–25 B.C.), Liu Hsin[1a] had been ordered to assist his father, Liu Hsiang[4a], in cataloging the imperial private library. Emissaries were sent about the country to collect ancient manuscripts, and people were encouraged to present their books to the imperial library. Thus there was gathered the magnificent imperial collection, whose catalog, extracted from that published by Liu Hsin, is to be found in *HS* ch. 30, the "Treatise on Arts and Literature."

In the course of this study, Liu Hsin came upon some books that had previously been neglected, particularly the *Tso-chuan* and some writings in ancient characters said to have been discovered about 150 B.C., when tearing down the wall of Confucius' house. These writings were said to have been presented to Emperor Wu about 100 B.C. by K'ung An-kuo. The ancient writings secured then or at other times included some 39 chapters of the lost *Book of Rites* (i.e., part of the present *Chou-li*), and 16 chapters of the *Book of History*. As a good Confucian, who esteemed everything that came from the ancient Chou period, Liu Hsin was deeply impressed, especially by the *Tso-chuan*. It was in the form of a commentary upon the *Spring and Autumn*, which latter was thought to have been compiled by Confucius. (The *Tso-chuan*, according to Maspero and Karlgren, actually dates from the end of the iv century B.C. It has been dated in Han times, but I see no adequate evidence for that dating. There are however doubtless minor interpolations datable in Han times, such as the data for the ancestry of Emperor Kao; cf. *HFHD* I, 148, n.1.) Tso Ch'iu-ming, its reputed author, is mentioned in the *Analects*; Liu Hsin[1a] argued, with a young man's enthusiasm, that Tso Ch'iu-ming had talked personally with Confucius, so that his commentary on the *Spring and Autumn* should be elevated to a place above those by Kung-yang and Ku-liang, which had previously been the only authorized commentaries, for the latter authors had not known Confucius in person, hence were not so likely to have transmitted his conceptions. Liu Hsin sought out those persons who knew the traditional explanation of the *Tso-chuan*, studied with them, and made new discoveries by comparing its text with that of the *Spring and Autumn*. His father, Liu Hsiang, was however an adherent of the orthodox Ku-liang Commentary, and remained unimpressed by Liu Hsin's arguments.

In his youth, Wang Mang had known Liu Hsin, as he had known every other person of any consequence in the capital. The two had been associated when they were Gentlemen at the Yellow Gate, and Wang Mang had been impressed by the scholar. When Emperor Ai came to the throne, Wang Mang recommended Liu Hsin to the new Emperor. He was given some honorary positions and asked to complete his father's work in the imperial private library. Liu Hsin now proposed to set up the books he esteemed as authoritative Confucian books for study in the Imperial University, i.e., as authoritative Classics: the *Tso-chuan*, the Mao text of the *Book of Odes* (the one now extant), the *Chou-li*, and the ancient text chapters from the *Book of History*. When this matter was presented to the Erudits, who were the professors in the Imperial University, they opposed the innovation, and did not even deign to discuss the matter. Liu Hsin felt the cut deeply, and sent a letter to the court, reproaching the Erudits bitterly. They resented his words, one eminent scholar even asking to resign. One of the three highest ministers, a Confucian scholar, was so enraged that Emperor Ai had to intervene in order to protect Liu Hsin. The latter left the court in order to save his life and spent the remainder of Emperor Ai's reign in disgrace as an administrator of distant commanderies.

When Wang Mang came to power after the death of Emperor Ai, he recalled Liu Hsin and gave him an honorary position at the capital. Wang Mang then granted what Liu Hsin had been fighting for—the establishment of the *Tso-chuan*, the Mao text of the *Odes*, the *Chou-li*, and the ancient text of the *Book of History* as authoritative subjects for study at the Imperial University and for the civil service examinations (88: 25b, 26a). Thus Liu Hsin became attached to Wang Mang through his Confucian loyalties. Wang Mang made him his Hsi-and-Ho, which was Wang Mang's title for the state treasurer, and had him build a *Ming-t'ang* and a *Pi-yung*, two Confucian ceremonial buildings. Thereupon he was made a marquis and was put in charge of divination, fixed the calendar, and wrote out his famous *San-t'ung* astronomical theory. He became an influential advisor of Wang Mang, recommending the Confucian precedents that guided Wang Mang's conduct. He fixed the new regulations for officials' marriages, burials, betrothments, etc. Thus Wang Mang really gave Liu Hsin the opportunity to do his life's work and rewarded him with high office and great honors. In addition, the Confucian doctrine of the five elements, which had become accepted in part through the efforts of Liu Hsin's father, plainly pointed to Wang Mang as the next emperor. It is hence not surprising that when Wang Mang usurped the throne, Liu Hsin should have continued to be loyal.

Most of the influential Confucians were likewise loyal to Wang Mang, because the latter had shown himself loyal to Confucian principles. He not only erected Confucian ceremonial buildings, he also enlarged the Imperial University, increasing the number of authorized classics and establishing five Erudits for each classic. Ten thousand houses were erected for its students, a thousand students and teachers were appointed, a market-place and government granary were established for this new town. Each year, a hundred of its best graduates were taken into the government service by competitive examination. In A.D. 4, Wang Mang also summoned to the capital all the teachers of the empire who had as many as eleven pupils, all those who could teach and explain ancient books on the classics, astronomy, divination, revelations, music, the calendar, military arts, and philology. Thus he gathered thousands of the most learned men in the empire, collected and supported them at the imperial palace, and made use of their learning. In the previous summer, he had ordered the establishment of public schools in commanderies, prefectures, districts, and even in villages; now he probably sent most of these teachers to the government schools. Thus he gathered thousands of the empire's scholars, collected and supported them at the imperial palace, and then gave them government positions. In this way he attached to himself practically the entire body of learned people in the empire. Wang Mang thus invented the method, used so effectively by the Ch'ing and other dynasties, of reconciling learned people to a new ruler or dynasty by giving them scholarly employment in government enterprises.

After Wang Mang took the throne, he continued to honor Liu Hsin, finally making him the State Master, one of the four greatest ministers, and ennobling him as a Duke. Liu Hsin recommended to Wang Mang, as models for government, various practises mentioned in the *Chou-li* and elsewhere in Confucian tradition, and Wang Mang adopted these Confucian precedents. Many of his famous economic reforms came about in this manner. Wang Mang married his son and heir to Liu Hsin's daughter. In these ways, Wang Mang bound Liu Hsin to him by the greatest honors and the closest possible ties. Only when these ties were broken by Wang Mang himself, did Liu Hsin think of rebelling. Liu Hsin was Wang Mang's guide and advisor in Confucian matters. Liu Hsin thus owed his fame, his opportunity, and his fortune to Wang Mang. Under the circumstances, he could hardly have been otherwise than loyal to such a benefactor.

## Did Wang Mang murder Emperor P'ing?

When Emperor P'ing died on Feb. 3, A.D. 6, he was still a minor. He was born in 9 B.C., so that he may have been fully fourteen years old. When, in Oct., A.D. 7, Chai Yi raised the standard of revolt against Wang Mang, the rebels sent messengers about the country alleging that Wang Mang had poisoned Emperor P'ing. This charge was almost universally believed in Later Han times, but we may well discount the prevalence of that belief, for a sequent Han dynasty would be likely to encourage it.

It is of course impossible to determine the truth of such a charge, for we have absolutely no direct evidence on this matter. Events inside the palace could hardly be known except through the testimony of its inmates, most of whom could not leave the place; Wang Mang controlled the palace and its inhabitants for a subsequent period long enough to have silenced any possible witnesses. The absence of any testimony does not thus afford any presumption in either direction.

There were reasons enough to have predisposed Wang Mang to such a murder. He was not above committing such a deed. To hush up his son's adultery, he had the commissioner who investigated the matter murdered and buried in the jail (99 C: 11a). He was not slow in demanding the lives of any who opposed him, even of the highest families; he even executed three of Liu Hsin[1a]'s children (99 C: n. 23.2), and did not hesitate to execute his own son together with hundreds of persons in connection with the plot of Wang Yü (99 A: 16b). Wang Mang showed an utter callousness concerning human affections; he kept Emperor P'ing's mother away from her son, even though she is said to have wept day and night.

Wang Mang furthermore had adequate motives for murdering Emperor P'ing. Wang Mang had prevented any of Emperor P'ing's maternal relatives from coming to the imperial capital, and, when the plot of

Wang Yü was discovered, he had executed all these relatives, except Emperor P'ing's mother. The young Emperor P'ing hence had a serious grievance against Wang Mang, and may well have expressed his feelings in his adolescent years. Wang Mang might have suspected he would be unable to control the Emperor, once the latter came of age, and that he might even be made to suffer on some trumped-up charge. The capping of the Emperor, which ceremony marked his coming of age, was moreover delayed until after his death. (That circumstance does not however indicate any delinquency on Wang Mang's part. The regular age for capping, according to Confucian principles, was the fifteenth year; in Han times, however, the age of capping varied: Emperor Chao was not capped until his eighteenth year, while Emperor Ho was capped in his thirteenth year.) Wang Mang loved power and may well have planned to continue his power by initiating another regency. There is a circumstantial account of the poisoning (12: n. 10.2), but it was not used by Pan Ku and is intrinsically questionable. (A dose of poison does not act only fourteen days after it was administered.) Thus there is some evidence tending to show that Wang Mang may have committed regicide.

There are however certain circumstances that lead us to doubt whether Wang Mang really did murder his lord. He probably realized the grave difficulties that would arise concerning the succession to the throne. Emperor P'ing was the last of Emperor Yüan's living descendants; a successor would have to be picked from among the descendants of Emperor Hsüan, who was Emperor Ch'eng's grandfather, so that the successor would be four or five generations removed from his imperial ancestor (Liu Ying was actually the fifth generation). There was also the danger that further pretended sons of Emperor Ch'eng would appear to claim the throne. Wang Mang's uncle, Wang Li$_{5a}$, had sponsored one such pretender. Wang Mang may well have furthermore anticipated opposition to an infant successor and a serious rebellion, such as that actually raised by Chai Yi. While the imperial clan had been rendered powerless by the separation of its members, giving them only quite small fiefs, and watching them carefully (long the imperial policy), other officials might nevertheless rebel. The empire had so long been faithful to the Liu clan that its loyalties could not be changed easily. These reasons of state would likely have deterred Wang Mang from attempting an assassination.

Confucian tradition, to which Wang Mang was bound, condemned regicide and exalted faithfulness on the part of ministers. Confucius' own model, who had come to be esteemed by all Confucians as an ideal and sage, was the Duke of Chou, who had loyally laid down his regency when his lord came of age. Wang Mang had frequently been compared to the Duke of Chou and doubtless aspired for the same high reputation as this ideal figure, who was exalted above kings and emperors. Ho Kuang, who had ruled during the reigns of Emperors Chao and Hsüan, was highly esteemed in recent times. Indeed, if Emperor P'ing had not died, Wang Mang would doubtless have come down in history as the greatest minister of Han times, a model for succeeding ages, a regent like the Duke of Chou, whose fame outshone that of emperors themselves. Thus the death of Emperor P'ing may well have seemed a terrible calamity to Wang Mang and he very likely considered that it deprived him of his opportunity for a great Confucian fame.

Wang Mang had attempted to bind Emperor P'ing to himself by secure ties. He married his daughter to the Emperor and in 5 A.D. cut the Tzu-wu Road for the purpose of magically bringing it about that Emperor P'ing should have a son by her. If she had had a son, Wang Mang, as the grandfather of the Heir-apparent and father-in-law of the Emperor, the minister who ruled during the Emperor's minority, would have been secure in his position and untouchable, even by an emperor. Public opinion would have defended against almost any charge a minister with such a high reputation and close relationship.

It is somewhat unlikely that Wang Mang actually planned to usurp the throne until some time after the death of Emperor P'ing. The knife-cash were not issued until June/July, A.D. 7; when Wang Mang actually came to the throne and changed the dynasty, he found these knife-cash an embarrassment, for the word "Liu," the surname of the Han dynasty, contains the words "metal" and "knife," so that Wang Mang had to do away with these knife-coins in order to prevent their magical influence from injuring him (24 B: 21b). While such a magical influence of knife-cash upon the dynastic name might possibly have been neglected in A.D. 7, yet a person so concerned with magical influences as Wang Mang would have been likely to have known their magical meaning, and would hardly have issued them if he had any definite plans for changing the dynasty. Pan Ku states that Wang Mang planned to take the throne only after Chai Yi's rebellion had quickly been crushed.

There is also the fact that Emperor P'ing had been a sickly child, who had been "continually ill" (98: 11b[11]), so that he was not at all strong, and could easily have been carried off by illness, just as was Emperor Ai. Wang Mang seems to have done everything that a loyal minister should have done to prevent this death. When, in the winter of A.D. 5/6,

Emperor P'ing was ill, Wang Mang made a vow to the Supreme One, in which he offered his own life for that of the Emperor. The vow was stored in a metal-bound coffer, just as the Duke of Chou had done in a similar case when King Ch'eng was ill. The coffer was not opened until A.D. 23 (99 A: 24b; C: 22b). Wang Mang was superstitious and relied much upon magic, so that he probably took this vow seriously. He furthermore did not kill the succeeding Emperor, the Young Prince, Liu Ying₁ₐ. This child grew up, and, after Wang Mang's death, actually ascended the throne for a time. Furthermore when Chai Yi rebelled in A.D. 7 and when the rebels finally entered Kuan-chung in A.D. 23, Wang Mang made a dramatic appeal to Heaven for aid, in the latter case, setting out, at the place for sacrifice to Heaven, his mandates by means of portents, and asking Heaven to strike him dead by a thunderbolt if he had done wrong (99 C: 25a). When a superstitious man acts thus, it is good evidence that his conscience is clear of any such heinous sins as regicide.

There is thus much evidence to show that Wang Mang was innocent of the charge that he had poisoned his lord, and that this charge was propaganda on the part of those who rose in rebellion against him. It is of course impossible to be certain, and the evidence is far from conclusive. In the end, one's judgment will depend upon one's estimate of Wang Mang's character. That character was evil enough: he was callous to suffering, impatient of any opposition and ready to execute any subordinates and even his own children and grandchildren who presumed to oppose him or even make awkward suggestions (cf. the execution of Wang Chien₄, 98: 14b). But he was a whole-hearted Confucian. Confucianism exalted loyalty and comdemned regicide as a heinous sin. My own opinion is that Wang Mang was too good a Confucian to have murdered Emperor P'ing.

## Chapter XII

# THE TWELFTH [IMPERIAL ANNALS]

### THE ANNALS OF [EMPEROR HSIAO]–P'ING

漢書十二　孝平皇帝元帝庶孫中山孝王子也母曰衛姬年　三歲嗣立為王元壽二年六月哀帝崩太皇太后　詔曰大司馬賢年少不合衆心其上印綬罷賢即　日自殺新都侯王莽為大司馬領尚書事秋七月

平紀第十二

Emperor Hsiao-p'ing was the grandson, by a concubine, of Emperor Yüan and the son of King Hsiao of Chung-shan, [Liu Hsing]. His mother was called the Concubine [nee] Wei. When [Emperor P'ing] was in his third[1.1] year, he succeeded [his father] and was established as King [of Chung-shan].

In [the period] Yüan-shou, the second year, the sixth month, Emperor Ai died. The Grand Empress Dowager [nee Wang issued] an imperial edict saying, "Since the Commander-in-chief, [Tung] Hsien$_{2a}$ is young and it does not accord with popular opinion [to have him control the government], let him deliver up his seal and cord and be dismissed [from his office]." The same day[1.3] [Tung] Hsien$_{2a}$ committed suicide. The Marquis of Hsin-tu$_c$, Wang Mang, was made Commander-in-chief and Intendant of the Affairs of the Masters of Writing.

In the autumn, the seventh month, [the Grand

II

1 B.C.

Aug. 15[1.2]

Aug. 16[1.3]

Aug. 17[1.3]

Aug./Sept.

---

[1.1] Ch'en Ching-yün (1670–1747) would emend "third" to "second" because *HS* 97 B: 21b reports that Emperor P'ing was born in 9 B.C. and was in his second year when his father died, and because *HS* 12: 1b says he was in his ninth year when he came to the throne. But *HS* 14: 23b records that his father first became King in 37 B.C. and reigned altogether to the thirtieth year; hence his father died in 8 B.C. Emperor P'ing succeeded his father in 7 B.C. (14: 23b) and became Emperor in 1 B.C., which was the ninth year of his life. So there is no reason to emend the text; Ch'en Ching-yün seems not to have understood that in Han times ages were counted by *elapsed full* years, not by elapsed *calendar* years as at present; so that a child born just before New Year's was *not* then considered after New Year's to be in his second (calendar) year, as at present. Cf. Glossary *sub* Hsiao-ai, Emperor.

[1.2] Cf. 11: 8a.

[1.3] The Sung Ch'i ed. (xi or xii cent.) notes that the T'ang text (before xi cent.) does not have the words 即日. The dates of Tung Hsien's dismissal and death and of Wang Mang's appointment are found in 19 B: 51a.

Empress Dowager nee Wang] sent the General of Chariots and Cavalry, Wang Shun₄ᵦ, and the Grand Herald, Tso Hsien, as messengers bearing credentials, to go and invite the King of Chung-shan, [Liu Chi-tzu], to come [to the capital and take the throne].

Sept. 15     On [the day] *hsin-mao*, the Empress Dowager nee Chao was degraded and made the Empress of [Emperor] Hsiao-ch'eng. She was made to retire and live in the Northern Palace. The Empress nee Fu of Emperor Ai was [also] made to retire and live in

**1b** Kuei Palace. The Marquis of K'ung-hsiang, Fu₄

**1b** Yen, the [former] Privy Treasurer, Tung Kung, and others were all dismissed from their offices and noble

*1b* titles and exiled to the Ho-p'u [Commandery].

Oct. 17     In the ninth month, on [the day] *hsin-yu*, the King of Chung-shan, [Liu Chi-tzu], ascended the imperial throne and was presented [to the imperial ancestors] in the Temple of [Emperor] Kao.[1.4] A general amnesty [was granted] to the empire. The Emperor was in his ninth year, so the Grand Empress Dowager [nee Wang] attended court. The Commander-in-chief, [Wang] Mang, controlled the government and "the officials attended to their several duties in obedience to"[1.5] [Wang] Mang.

An imperial edict said, "Verily an ordinance of amnesty is [an instrument] for the purpose of giving the empire [an opportunity of making] a new beginning. It is sincerely hoped that it may cause the people to correct their conduct, purify themselves, and preserve their lives. In the past,[1.6] the high officials have frequently brought up in their memorials matters previous to an amnesty, including them [with their present charges, in order to] increase [the severity of peoples'] greater or lesser crimes, [with

始誠欲令百姓改行絜己全其性命也性者有司多舉奏赦前事累增罪過
太后臨朝大司馬莽秉政百官總己以聽於莽詔曰夫赦令者將與天下更
官爵徙合浦九月辛酉中山王卽皇帝位謁高廟大赦天下帝年九歲太皇
成皇后退居北宮哀帝皇后傅氏退居桂宮孔鄉侯傅晏少府董恭等皆免
遣車騎將軍王舜大鴻臚左咸使持節迎中山王辛卯貶皇太后趙氏為孝

[1.4] Liu Pin (1022–1088) notes that this was the 64th day after Emperor Ai's death.
[1.5] A quotation from *Analects* XIV, xliii, 2.
[1.6] Ch'ien Ta-chao (1744–1813) says that the second 性 should be 往. The Official ed. (1739) has that emendation.

誅如詔書爲虧恩以不道論定著令布告天下使明知之
陷以小疵妨大材自今以來有司無得陳赦前事置奏上有不
亡之義諸有臧及內惡未發而薦舉者皆勿案驗令士屬精鄉進
辜事有名之士則以爲難保廢而弗舉甚謬於赦小過舉賢材
殊心自新之意也及選舉者其歷職

the result that] they have executed or ruined guiltless [people, which practise] is almost opposite to the intention of emphasizing fidelity and being careful about punishments [and to induce criminals] to purify their hearts and renew themselves. More- 2a
over, in their selections and recommendations [for appointment], if a gentleman has [already] held various offices, has been experienced in [government] affairs, and has acquired a reputation, then [the high officials] consider that [such a person] would be difficult to guarantee, hence, when [such a person has been] dismissed, he is not recommended [again, which practise] is quite contrary to the principle of 'pardon- ing small transgressions and recommending those who are capable and able.'[2.1]  [In the case of] who- ever has taken bribes or [has committed] hidden evils which have not yet become known, if he is recommended for a position, let all [such matters] not be investigated judicially, in order that [such] 2a
gentlemen may whet their innermost beings and en- deavor to improve themselves, and that small flaws may not hamper great talents.  From this time and henceforth, high officials shall not be permitted to present matters previous to an amnesty and put them in a memorial to the Emperor.  If anyone acts contrary to this written edict, he is acting against the [imperial] favor, [hence] it shall be judged as an inhuman [deed.  Let this order] be established and published as a [permanent] ordinance and be pub- lished and made known to the empire to cause it to 2a
be clearly known."[2.2]

[2.1] A saying of Confucius found in *Analects* XIII, ii, 1.  Emperor Ai had previously issued an order to this same effect: cf. 11: 3b.

[2.2] Very probably Wang Mang is thinking of Wang Chia[1a], who was done to death by Emperor Ai, because, after an amnesty, he had recommended some persons whom Em- peror Ai had previously dismissed on suspicion of crime (cf. Introduction to ch. XI, pp. 5–6; Glossary *sub* Wang Chia[1a]).  Ho Ch'uo (1661–1722) says, "By this [ordinance, Wang] Mang was ensnaring and attracting people who had been rejected, discarded, and despised, by giving them unhoped for extraordinary favors, in order that he might use

I
A.D. 1
Feb./Mar.

In [the period] Yüan-shih, the first year, in the spring, the first month, the head of the Yüeh-shang tribe, [whose speech had to be] repeatedly interpreted, presented tribute of one white pheasant and two black pheasants.[2.3] An imperial edict had the three highest ministers use them for sacrifice in the [imperial] ancestral temples.

Various courtiers [thereupon] memorialized, saying, "The merits and virtuous deeds of the Commander-in-chief, [Wang] Mang, are equal to those of the Duke of Chou. He should be granted the title, the Duke Giving Tranquillity to the Han [Dynasty]." His enfeoffment and those of the Grand

**2b**
**99A: 5a-6b.**

Master K'ung Kuang and others were all increased. A discussion is in the "Memoir of [Wang] Mang."

There was granted, on this special occasion, to the common people of the empire one step in noble rank and to the officials who [then] held positions [ranking at] two hundred piculs and over, the full salary of their rank, like the regular [occupant of that posi-

**2b**

tion].[2.4] [Liu] K'ai-ming, the Heir-apparent of the

級吏在位二百石以上一切滿秩如真立
孔光等皆益封語在莽傳賜天下民爵一
司馬莽功德比周公賜號安漢公及太師
黑雉二詔使三公以薦宗廟羣臣奏言大
元始元年春正月越裳氏重譯獻白雉一

them for his own purposes." In A.D. 210, (Cf. *San-kuo Chih*, 1: 28b), Ts'ao Ts'ao, in his famous "Order Requesting Worthy Persons to Come," similarly said, "If one must be an incorrupt person and then only be given position, how could [Duke] Huan of Ch'i have come in his epoch to be Lord Protector?" Ho Ch'uo, after quoting the above passage, remarks sarcastically, "Usurpers and rebels always seek for their own kind."

[2.3] The head of the Yüeh-shang tribe is mentioned in the *Bamboo Annals* (Legge, *Shoo-King*, Prolegomena, p. 146). The *T'ai-p'ing Yü-lan*, 917: 8b quotes the *Hsiao-ching Yüan-sheng Ch'i* (prob. Former Han period), fragments B: 23a, as saying, "In the time of King Ch'eng of the Chou [dynasty], the Yüeh-shang presented a white pheasant. They are 30,000 *li* distant from the capital. When a true king is unsurpassed in his sacrifices and moderate in his repasts and robes, then [these people] appear [with a white pheasant]." Cf. Introduction, p. 51; Glossary *sub* Yüeh-shang.

[2.4] The implications of this statement have been debated. Ju Shun (fl. dur. 198–265) says, "When the officials in the various offices are first given new positions, they are all tried as acting [occupants of their positions] for a year, and then made regular [occupants of their positions] with their full salary. When Emperor P'ing took the throne, he therefore granted to them to be regular [occupants of their positions]." Shen Ch'in-han (1775–1832) moreover points out that Ho Hsiu (129–182), in a note to the *Kung-yang Commentary*, 2: 5b *sub* Duke Yin, III, Autumn, says, "At that time, altho [a person] was a

故明子宣六
東爲成帝人
平王成都耳皆
王故爲孫爲
雲桃中信列
太鄉山等侯
子頃王三
開侯封十

former King of Tung-p'ing, [Liu] Yün$_{2a}$, was established as King [of Tung-p'ing. Liu] Ch'eng-tu, the son of the former Marquis Ch'ing of T'ao-hsiang, [Liu Hsüan$_{1d}$], was made King of Chung-shan [to succeed Emperor P'ing's father]. Thirty-six great-grandsons of Emperor Hsüan, [including Liu] Hsin$_{4g}$ and others, were all made full marquises.[2.5]

2b

hereditary grandee, because he had the heart of a filial son, he could not endure at once to take his father's position, hence he followed the ancient [practises] and was first tried [in that position] for a year, and then was given a [regular] mandate [as his father's successor] in his ancestral Temple." Shen Ch'in-han concludes, "The practise of the Han [dynasty], follows from this principle that when [an official] was first given a new position, he was tried as an acting [occupant of that position], and [after] a year he was made the regular [occupant of that position]."

But Yen Shih-ku (581–645) writes, "This explanation, [that of Ju Shun], is mistaken. At that time among the various offices there were those who were being tried as acting [occupants of those positions], consequently [the Emperor] specially granted an unusual act of favor and it was merely ordered that they should [be treated] the same as the regular [occupants of those positions]. It was not that all those officials who were given new positions must all be regarded as acting [occupants of those positions] on trial. Yi-ch'ieh一切 [means] 'temporarily,' not 'regularly'." Yi-ch'ieh is also found in 76: 15a, 16a, where Ju Shun glosses that yi-ch'ieh means "temporarily 權時也." Wang Ch'i-yüan (xix cent.) approves of Yen Shih-ku's interpretation that this was a temporary favor on this special occasion, and not a permanent enactment concerning future appointees.

Liu Pin however says, "I say that altho the officials' salaries were nominally [a certain number of piculs per year], they all were not [paid] the full [amount of] that number [of piculs]. When Emperor P'ing ascended the throne, favors were extended, hence he granted and ordered that [officials should be paid] the full salary of their rank, for example, that [an official ranking at] two thousand piculs should get double ten hundred [piculs]. Yen [Shih-ku] in a note to HS 19 [A: 1a, concerning] the differences of officials' salaries, speaks of these [circumstances]. His note reads, '[According to] the Han Code, the three highest ministers were nominally [ranked at] ten thousand piculs, [but] the salary of each [one] was 350 hu of grain per month. Those who nominally [ranked at] fully 2000 piculs [received] 180 hu per month. [Those ranked at] 2000 piculs [received] 120 hu, and [those ranked at] equivalent to 2000 piculs [received] 100 hu,' etc. According to the comment in the HHS, [Tr. 28: 14b, from which Yen Shi-ku has taken the above figures], those [whose nominal salaries] were fixed at 1000 piculs or less received a certain proportion of their nominal salary in a year. [But this payment] was added to in the time of [Emperor] Kuang-wu [ruled A.D. 25–57], and was not an old practise of the Former Han [dynasty]."

[2.5] HS 99 A: 19b notes this last appointment in Jan./Feb., A.D. 5. But HS 15 B: 38a, b, 40a–44a, 53a–55b lists 35 appointments on Apr. 10, A.D. 1, in addition to that of Liu Hsin$_4$ (ibid., 50a), so that ch. 99 is mistaken. All were great-grandsons of Emperor

3a　　The Grand Coachman, Wang Yün, and others, twenty-five persons [in all], when previously there had been a discussion about honoring the Queen Dowager [nee] Fu of Ting-t'ao with a [higher] imperial title, had held to classical principles, had not flattered her desires or followed erroneous [principles]; the General of the Right, Sun Chien, was the great official who was [Wang Mang's] military assistant;[3.1] the Grand Herald, [Tso] Hsien, had previously discussed [that matter] correctly, had not flattered [the Queen Dowager], later he had been sent, bearing credentials, to go and invite the King of Chung-shan, [Liu Chi-tzu], to come [to take the throne]; also the Superintendant of the Imperial House, Liu Pu-o, the Bearer of the Gilded Mace, Jen Ts'en[b], the General of the Gentlemen-of-the-Palace, K'ung Yung, the Prefect of the Masters of Writing, Yao Hsün, and the Grand Administrator of the P'ei Commandery, Shih Hsü—because all these [persons] had previously shared in initiating the plan [whereby Emperor P'ing came to the throne], had gone to the east to invite him to ascend the throne, had been perfectly adept, or had worked diligently and laboriously in performing their duties, they were granted the noble rank of Marquis of the Imperial Domain with the income of estates, to each proportionately. Noble ranks were granted to the officials in the prefectures and towns thru which the Emperor passed on his way to assume the throne, [ranking at] two thousand piculs and less, down to the Accessory

3a　Officials, to each proportionately.

　　It was also ordered that vassal kings, dukes, full marquises, and marquises of the imperial domain who had no sons but had grandsons, if [any of these nobles] had raised as sons the sons of their full or

太僕王惲等二十五人前議定陶傅太后尊號守經法不阿指從邪右將軍孫建

爪牙大臣大鴻臚咸前正議不阿後奉節使迎中山王及宗正劉不惡執金吾任

岑中郎將孔永尚書令姚恂沛郡太守石詡皆以前與建策東迎卽位奉事周密

勤勞賜爵關內侯食邑各有差賜帝徵卽位前所過縣邑吏二千石以下至佐史

爵各有差又令諸侯王公列侯關內侯亡子而有孫若子同產子者皆得以為嗣

---

Hsüan; 99 A: 19b states they were 曾孫, so that *jen-sun* 耳孫 must here mean "greatgrandson." The genealogy of Liu Hsin[4] in 15 B: 50a confirms this statement. Cf. *HFHD* I, 176, n. 3.

[3.1] On the phrase, "talons and teeth," cf. 99 A: n. 5.4.

公者石大償
列復以行其
侯其上三義
嗣屬年輔陵
子其老舉民
有為致籍家
罪吏仕吏不
耐舉者民妨
以廉參以殿
上佐分元中
先史故壽者
請補祿二勿
宗四以年發
室百一倉天
屬石與卒下
未天之時吏
盡下終橫舍
而吏其賦亡
以比身斂得
罪二遣者置
絕千諫

half-brothers, they should all be permitted to make [these nephews] their heirs; and that for heirs of dukes and full marquises who had committed crimes [requiring the punishment] of shaving the whiskers or above, [the officials] should beg [the Emperor's permission] before [such persons were punished]. There were restored to registration those [members of] the imperial house whose registration had not yet lapsed [because they had become too distantly related to the Emperor], but whose [registration] had been cut off because of crimes.[3.2] Those [members of the imperial house] who were officials were to be recommended [for promotion] as incorrupt persons; [those members of the imperial house] who were Accessory Officials were to be given vacancies [ranking at] four hundred piculs. For officials of the empire who [had   *3a* the rank of] equivalent to 2000 piculs or above and   **3b** were aged and retired, their former salary was to be divided in three and one [third] was to be given to them to the end of their life.

A Grandee-remonstrant was sent to inspect the three capital commanderies and report the [names and] registrations of the officials and common people who in the time of haste and confusion during the second year of [the period] Yüan-shou [had paid]   1 B.C. the extraordinary taxes and collections. They were to be repaid the value [of what they had paid]. The tombs of the common people at the Yi Tomb which did not interfere with the interior of the Hall [at the Yi Tomb] were not to be opened.[3.3] The officials and common people[3.4] of the empire were not to be

[3.2] Hu San-hsing (1280–1287) explains, "It means that those should have their registration restored who were related [so that in mourning] they uncovered an arm and wore the mourning head-dress or were more [closely related], who because of crime had been cut off the register [of the imperial house]." Cf. 11: n. 2.2.

[3.3] The Yi Tomb was that of Emperor Ai, the buildings attached to which were probably still being erected, since Emperor Ai had not made preparations for his own demise. Private tombs previously at that locality were not to be disturbed, unless they interfered with the Hall at that Tomb.

[3.4] The Official ed. has emended *shê* 舍 to *min* 民. It quotes the Sung Ch'i ed. as saying that the T'ang text (before xi cent.) does not have the word *li* 吏. The Ching-yu

3b permitted to lay up productive implements or articles.[3.5]

Mar./Apr. In the second month, there were established the Office of the Hsi-and-Ho, ranking at two thousand piculs, and the Clerk for the Provinces and the Master of the Houses, [both] ranking at six hundred piculs, to spread the [orthodox] teaching and culture, to prohibit irregular sacrifices, and to banish the songs of Cheng.[3.6]

Mar. 20 On [the day] yi-wei, in the funerary chamber at the Yi Tomb [of Emperor Hsiao-ai], the ghost's garments were in their casket, and on the [day] ping-
Mar. 21 shen at dawn the garments were outside of it on the
4a bed.[3.7] The Prefect of the Funerary Chamber reported it as an urgent grievous vicissitude, and a suovetaurilia was sacrificed. In the summer, the
June 10 fifth month, on [the day] ting-szu, the first day of the month, there was an eclipse of the sun.[4.1] A general amnesty [was granted] to the empire; the ministers, generals, and [officials ranking at] fully two thousand piculs were each to recommend one person who was honest and sincere and able to speak
3b frankly.

什六在牢軍
器百柳祠中
儲石中夏二
偫班丙五千
二教申月石
月化旦丁舉
置禁衣巳敦
羲淫在朔厚
和祀外日能
官放牀有直
秩鄭上蝕言
二聲寢之者
千乙令大各
石未以赦一
外義急天人
史陵變下
閭寢聞公
師神用卿
秩衣太將

ed. (1034) has li-min; the Chi-ku Ko ed. (1642) has li-shê. Chou Shou-ch'ang (1814–1884) points out that various texts have li-min, and that Yen Shih-ku (581–645) does not explain li-shê, so that his text must also have had li-min.

[3.5] Yen Shih-ku says, "According to the military law, five men make a pentad (group of five), and two groups of five make a decade, who therefore have their implements and articles in common. Hence [people] generally call productive implements shih-ch'i 什器 [i.e., implements belonging to a decade]. It was also like those who today are with the army or do forced service: ten persons constitute a 'fire' and share their provisions and arrangements." This term is also found in 12: 6a.

Chia Yi, in HS 48: 27a[7,8], uses chih 置 -ch'i with a similar meaning, "When people today lay up things (chih-ch'i), if they lay them up (chih) in a safe place, they are safe, [while] if they lay them up (chih) in dangerous places, they are in danger. The affections of the empire are in no way different from things (ch'i)—they are where the Son of Heaven places (chih) them."

[3.6] For irregular (or unlawful) sacrifices cf. HS 25 A: 4a; Li-ki 5: 11a (Couvreur I. 100; Legge, I, 116). "Songs of Cheng" denotes licentious music; cf. Analects XV, x, 6.

[3.7] For a similar incident, cf. 99 C: 8b.

[4.1] For eclipses, cf. App. I.

六月使少傅左將軍豐賜帝母中山孝王姬璽書拜為中山

孝王后賜帝舅衞寶寶弟玄爵關內侯賜帝女弟四人號皆

曰君食邑各二千戶封周公後公孫相如為襃魯侯孔子後

孔均為襃成侯奉其祀追諡孔子曰襃成宣尼公罷明光宮

及三輔馳道天下女徒已論歸家顧山錢月三百

In the sixth month, the Junior Tutor[4.2] and General of the Left, [Chen] Feng, was sent to grant to the Emperor's mother, the Concubine [nee Wei] of King Hsiao of Chung-shan, [Liu Hsing], a document sealed with the imperial seal, and to install her as the Queen of King Hsiao of Chung-shan. There were granted to the Emperor's maternal uncle, Wei Pao and to [Wei] Pao's younger brother, [Wei] Hsüan[a], the noble rank of Marquis of the Imperial Domain. There was granted, to all of the Emperor's three[4.3] sisters, the title of Baronetess, with the income of an estate of two thousand households for each.

July/Aug.

Kung-sun Hsiang-ju, a descendant of the Duke of Chou, was made the Marquis in Recompense to [the Duke of] Lu. A descendant of Confucius, K'ung Chün, was made Marquis in Recompense for Perfection, to uphold the sacrifices [to Confucius]. Confucius was posthumously given the posthumous name and title, Duke Hsüan-ni in Recompense for Perfection.[4.4]

4a

Ming-kuang Palace together with the imperial pathways in the three capital [commanderies] were abolished. The female convicts of the empire who had already been sentenced [were ordered] to return home [and pay][4.5] three hundred cash per month for

---

[4.2] The Sung Ch'i ed. says that *fu4* 傅 (Junior Tutor) is in some texts written as *fu3* 府 (Privy Treasurer). *HS* 19 B: 52a writes *fu3*; 97 B: 22a writes *fu4*. Chou Shou-ch'ang in a note to this passage, suggests that *fu4* should be amended to *fu3*; Wang Hsien-ch'ien (1842–1918), in a note to 19 B: 52a, suggests that *fu3* should be emended to *fu4*. *HS* 99 A: 6a records that Chen Feng was appointed Junior Tutor, one of the Four Coadjutors, so that *fu4* is certainly the correct reading.

[4.3] The text says "four," but 97 B: 22a, in recounting these sisters, says there were three and enumerates their names and titles. *HS* 99 A: 16a, in recounting the events at this time, does not mention these Baronetesses. Hence "four" should be emended to "three" (Chou Shou-ch'ang). *Han-chi* 30: 2a follows this passage in writing "four"; *Tzu-chih T'ung-chien* 35: 17b has emended it to "three."

[4.4] Ch'ien Ta-chao remarks that Hsüan-ni as a name for Confucius originated in this enactment.

[4.5] Wang Hsien-ch'ien says that the meaning requires the insertion of 出 before the word 顧. *Tzu-chih T'ung-chien* 35: 18a has this word.

On the term 'mountain hire,' Ju Shun says, "In the first section of the [dynastic]

**4b** 'mountain hire.' One chaste wife in a district was exempted [from taxes].

There were established one Assistant to the Privy Treasurer [in Charge of] the Seas and one Assistant [in charge of] Fruits,[4.6] and [also] thirteen Divisional Assistants to the Grand Minister of Agriculture, [each] one having for his district one province, [with the duty of] encouraging agriculture and sericulture.[4.7]

The Grand Empress Dowager [nee Wang] dispensed with ten prefectures of her private estate from which she received income and confided them to the Grand Minister of Agriculture, who was regularily to keep separate accounts of their land-tax and pay [this sum] out, using it to assist poor people.

復貞婦鄉一人置少府海丞果
丞各一人大司農部丞十三人
人部一州勸農桑太皇太后省
所食湯沐邑十縣屬大司農常
別計其租入以贍貧民

ordinances [it was ordained] that women who had committed crimes should work as convicts and to the sixth month should be employed [to work on] the mountains. That [the Emperor] had them 'return home' means that they ought to have been cutting trees on the mountains, [but] he permitted them to send [a substitute] and pay cash in hire for the value of their work. Hence it is called 'mountain hire.'" Ying Shao (ca. 140–206) says, "The ancient punishment of 'spiritual firewood' [cf. *HFHD*, I, p. 177, n. 1] was taking firewood from the mountains for the use of the [imperial] ancestral temples. Now [the ruler] caused female convicts to pay cash to hire [people to cut] firewood, hence it is called 'mountain hire'." Yen Shih-ku adds, "Ju [Shun's] explanation comes near [the truth]. It means that the female convicts whose sentences for crime have already been imposed shall all be set free, return to their homes, and not themselves do forced labor; instead he ordered that they should pay three hundred cash per month to hire people. He performed this [act of] grace in order to spread the virtue of the Grand Empress Dowager [nee Wang] and accord her beneficent government to women." Shen Ch'in-han adds, "Since in *HS* 66: [8b] rich Gentlemen who pay money [to gain holidays] are called 'mountain Gentlemen', [the name for] female convicts who pay money are likewise called 'mountain hire'. The meaning is similar [to that of the other name]." Cf. Glossary, *sub* Yang Yün.

[4.6] Yen Shih-ku explains that they were put in charge of the taxes upon sea [products] and upon fruits, respectively.

[4.7] Hu San-hsing explains, "Emperor Wu had Sang Hung-yang establish several tens of Divisional Assistants to the Grand Minister of Agriculture, who separately had for their districts [certain] commanderies and kingdoms, and had control of the Equalization and Transportation and the Salt and Iron [government monopolies]. Now thirteen persons were employed to have charge of the thirteen provinces, [respectively], as their districts."

秋二年春黄支國獻犀牛詔曰皇帝二名通于器物今更名　九月赦天下徒以中山苦陘縣爲中山孝王后湯沐邑

合於古制使太師光奉太牢告祠高廟夏四月立代孝王　玄孫之子如意爲廣宗王江都易王孫盱台侯宮爲廣川

王廣川惠王曾孫倫爲廣德王　之子如意爲廣宗王

In the autumn, the ninth month, an amnesty [was granted] to the convicts of the empire. *4a*  Oct./Nov.

The K'u-hsing prefecture in [the kingdom of] Chung-shan was made the private estate of the Queen [nee Wei] of King Hsiao of Chung-shan, [Liu *4b* Hsing].

In the second year, in the spring, the state of II Huang-chih offered a rhinoceros [in tribute].[4.8] A.D. 2

An imperial edict said, "The two [words in] the Spring personal name of the Emperor are connected with a utensil. Now [We] change [Our] personal name in conformity with the ancient regulations."[4.9] He sent the Grand Master, [K'ung] Kuang, to present a suovetaurilia and give information [of the change] in a sacrifice at the Temple of [Emperor] Kao.

In the summer, the fourth month, [Liu] Ju-yi[b], a May son of a great-great-grandson of King Hsiao of Tai, [Liu Ts'an], was made King of Kuang-tsung; [Liu] *5a* Kung[1a], a grandson of King Yi of Chiang-tu, [Liu Fei[1]], and [the son of] the Marquis of Hsü-yi, [Liu Meng-chih], was made King of Kuang-shih;[5.1] and [Liu] Lun, a great-grandson of King Hui of Kuang-ch'uan, [Liu Yüeh[5a]], was made King of Kuang-tê.

[4.8] Yen Shih-ku explains, "The rhinoceros has the shape of a water buffalo and a head like a pig, with four legs; it is like an elephant in its black color. It has one horn in front of its forehead, and on its nose has another small horn." For a translation of the passage in the *HS* describing trading voyages into the Indian Ocean and the location of this place, cf. Glossary *sub* Huang-chih. Also cf. C. W. Bishop, "Rhinoceros and Wild Ox in Ancient China," *China Journal XVII*, no. 6 (June 1933), p. 330. Wang Mang had sent a messanger with an order to the king of Huang-chih that he should present a live rhinoceros. Cf. *HS* 28 Bii: 68a, b; *Tzu-chih T'ung-chien* 35: 18b.

[4.9] Emperor P'ing's first personal name, Chi-tzu 箕子, means 'dustpan'; it is found in 14: 23b. His name was changed to K'an 衎, 'rejoice,' in conformity with the precedent set by Emperor Hsüan (cf. 8: 13b). This rare word would not be troublesome as a taboo. Hsün Yüeh (148–209), in a note to 12: 1a and Meng K'ang (ca. 180–260), here furnish the latter name.

[5.1] *HS* 14: 14b and 53: 7a both record that Liu Kung was the *son of* the Marquis of Hsü-yi; hence 子 should be in the text at this point.

The text names this kingdom as Kuang-ch'uan 川, 14: 14b names it Kuang-shih 世, and 53: 7a names it Kuang-ling 陵. *HS* 14: 20b lists other kings of Kuang-ling down

[Ho] Yang, a great-grandson of a paternal cousin of the former Commander-in-chief and Marquis of Po-lu, Ho Kuang; [Chang] Ch'ing-chi, a great-great-grandson of the Marquis of Hsüan-p'ing, Chang Ao; [Chou] Kung, a great-great-grandson of the Marquis of Chiang, Chou P'o; and [Fan] Chang, the son of a great-great-grandson of the Marquis of Wu-yang, Fan K'uai, were all enfeoffed as full marquises, so that [these] noble titles were revived. There were granted to Li Ming-yu, the great-great-grandson of the former Marquis of Ch'ü-chou, Li Shang, and to

5a [descendants of] other [former marquises], 113 per-
5b sons [in all],[5.2] the noble rank of Marquis of the Imperial Domain, with the income of estates, to each proportionately.

In the commanderies and kingdoms there was a great drought and [plague of] locusts;[5.3] in Ch'ing
4b Province it was especially severe, so that its common

侯食邑各有差郡國大旱蝗青州尤甚
酇商等後玄孫玄孫酇明友等百一十三人爵關內
樊噲玄孫之子章皆為列侯復爵賜故曲周侯
平侯張敖玄孫慶忌絳侯周勃玄孫共舞陽侯宣
封故大司馬博陸侯霍光從父昆弟曾孫陽宣侯

to the time of Wang Mang's usurpation, so that Kuang-ling is certainly a mistake. Kuang-ch'uan was the name of a kingdom whose name had been changed to Hsin-tu_a (q.v. in Glossary) and made a kingdom, the king of which at this time was Liu Ching_3b. Ch'ien Ta-hsin (1728–1804) remarks that a piece of Liu Ching_3b's territory would hardly have been taken away from him to make a new kingdom of Kuang-ch'uan, as must have been done if that name had been used. Shen Ch'in-han notes that *ch'uan* and *shih* might easily have been mistaken for each other, and says that several thousand households might have been taken from Hsin-tu_a to make the kingdom of Kuang-ch'uan. *Han-chi* 30: 2b has copied the reading Kuang-ch'uan; so has *Tzu-chih T'ung-chien* 35: 19a. But the *Comment to the Shui-ching* 23: 3b, sub the Ying-kou River, says, "The Kuo River also goes east and passes north of the city of Kuang-hsiang 廣鄉. Ch'üan Ch'eng [fl. dur. 135–220] glosses, 'In Hsiang-yi 襄邑 there is the Shê-ch'iu 蛇丘 Commune, which is the former Kuang-hsiang. It was changed to be Kuang-shih. Emperor Shun of the Later Han [dynasty] in 135 A.D. enfeoffed the Palace Attendant Chih T'ien [not mentioned in the *HHS*] as the marquis [of this place]. His marquisate was Kuang-hsiang.' " Then the reading in ch. 14, Kuang-shih, is probably correct, and the text should be emended accordingly. The error was probably caused by attraction to the following Kuang-ch'uan.

[5.2] *Han-chi* 30: 2b reads "130 persons"; *Tzu-chih T'ung-chien* 35: 19a says "117 persons," including the full marquises.

[5.3] *HS* 27: Bb: 20b says, "In Yüan-shih II, in the autumn, locusts were everywhere in the empire."

民流亡安漢公四輔三公卿大夫吏民爲百困之獻其田宅者二百三十

人以口賦貧民遣使者捕蝗民捕蝗詣吏以石斗受錢天下民貲不滿二萬

及被災之郡不滿十萬勿租稅民疾疫者舍空邸第爲置醫藥賜死者一家

六戸以上葬錢五千四戸以上三千二戸以上二千罷安定呼池苑以爲安

民縣起官寺市里慕徒貧民縣次給食至徒所賜田宅什器假與犁牛種食

people became vagrants. The Duke Who Gives Tranquillity to the Han [Dynasty, Wang Mang], the four Coadjutors [K'ung Kuang, Wang Mang, Wang Shun4b, and Chen Feng], the three highest ministers [Ma Kung, Wang Mang, and Chen Feng], the high ministers, grandees, officials, and common people, 230 persons [in all], presented their fields and residences in behalf of suffering and indigent people,[5.4] to be distributed among the poor people in accordance with their number. Messengers were sent to catch the locusts; the common people who caught locusts and brought them to the officials received cash in accordance with the [number of] piculs [of weight] or *tou* [of measure of the locusts]. The common people of the empire whose property was not as much as 20,000 [cash], together with those in the commanderies which suffered from the visitation, [whose property] was not as much as 100,000 [cash], were not to pay the land-tax or poll-taxes. The common people who [suffered from] the epidemic were lodged in the empty [commandery or princes'] lodges and residences, and physicians and medicines were provided for them. Grants were made for the dead: for six corpses or over in one family, five thousand cash for burial; for four corpses or over, three thousand [cash]; and for two corpses or over, two thousand [cash]. Hu-t'o Park in Anting [Commandery] was abolished and made Anming prefecture. Government offices and buildings, 6a market-places and hamlets were built [there], and poor people were solicited to remove [there]. In the counties where they lodged [as they were moving], they were given food, and when they reached 5b the places to which they were removed, they were granted fields, residences, productive instruments, and were made loans of oxen for plowing, and of seed

[5.4] Wang Hsien-ch'ien says that 姓 is omitted after 百; the Official ed. has this word. For the Coadjutors, cf. Glossary. For a parallel account, cf. 99 A: 7b.

and food.  Five hamlets were also built within the city of Ch'ang-an with two hundred residences, for the poor people to dwell in.[5.5]

Autumn     In the autumn, [each] commandery recommended one brave and warlike person possessing self-control, who was intelligent in military methods.  [They were ordered] to go to [the office of the Major in Charge of] Official Carriages [to await official appointment].

Nov. 23     In the ninth month, on [the day] *mou-shen*, the last day of the month, there was an eclipse of the sun.  An amnesty [was granted] to the criminals of the empire.   Internuncios and Division Heads of the Commander-in-chief, forty-four persons [in all], bearing credentials, were sent to inspect the border

5a     troops.  A Captain under the Bearer of the Gilded Mace, Ch'en Mou, was sent, [with the right] to use a bell and drum, who solicited three hundred brave and daring officials and gentlemen from Ju-nan and Nan-yang [Commanderies], who [in turn] remonstrated with and persuaded the robbers on the [Yangtze] River and lakes, Ch'eng Chung, and others, more than two hundred persons, all to come out voluntarily [and present themselves to the officials].  They were sent to the places where their

6b     homes were, and were held to do service.[6.1]  [Ch'eng] Chung was removed to Yün-yang and was granted public fields and a residence.

Winter     In the winter, [the officials ranking at] fully two thousand piculs were [ordered] yearly to recommend

6a     one person who had equitably judged law-cases.

III     In the third year, in the spring, there was an

---

[5.5] *HS* 27 Cb: 25a says, 'In Yüan-shih II, vi, (July), two meteorites fell in the Chü-lu [Commandery]."

[6.1] Yen Shih-Ku explains, "They went to their native counties and towns and performed [the payment of] the land taxes and conscript service."   Ho Chuo adds, *"Shou-shih* 收事 is like when at present they are enrolled in the militia of the hamlets as runners."

又起五里於長安城中宅二百區以居貧民秋舉勇武有節明兵法郡一人詣公車

九月戊申晦日有蝕之赦天下徒使謁者大司馬掾四十四人持節行邊兵遣執金

吾候陳茂假以鉦鼓募汝南南陽勇敢吏士三百人諭說江湖賊成重等二百餘人

皆自出送家在所收事重徙雲陽賜公田宅冬中二千石舉治獄平歲一人

生送終嫁娶奴婢田宅器械之品
立軺併馬夏安漢公奏車服制度吏民養
公卿大夫博士郎吏家屬皆以禮娶親迎
傅又詔光祿大夫劉歆等雜定婚禮四輔
詔有司為皇帝納采安漢公莽女語在莽
三年春

imperial edict [from the Grand Empress Dowager nee Wang] that the high officials should present the proposal [of marriage][6.2] on behalf of the Emperor to the daughter of the Duke Who Gives Tranquillity to the Han Dynasty, [Wang] Mang. A discussion is in the "Memoir of [Wang] Mang." There was also an imperial edict to the Imperial Household Grandee Liu Hsin[1a] and others that they should fix marriage rites for various [ranks], and that the four Coadjutors, the ministers, grandees, Erudits, Gentlemen, and officials, and [the members of] their households must all be married according to the rites: they must themselves go to fetch [their wives] standing in an small chariot with [a pair of] horses yoked abreast.[6.3]

In the summer, the Duke Who Gives Tranquillity to the Han Dynasty, [Wang Mang], memorialized the regulations for chariots and garments and the [various] classes [into which] officials and people [are divided with respect to] caring for their living [parents], accompanying [their dead] to the last [resting-place,[6.4] conducting] betrothals and marriages, and [possessing] male and female slaves, cultivated fields and residences, vessels and utensils.

A.D. 3
Spring

99 A: 8b-10a

Summer

5b

---

[6.2] A phrase from *Yi-li* 4: 1a (Steele I, 18) and *Li-ki* XLI, 1 (Legge, II, 428; Couvreur, II, 641). Cf. 99 A: n. 9.4.

[6.3] Fu Ch'ien (ca. 125–195) explains, "*Yao* 軺 (a small chariot) . . . is a small chariot in which one rides standing up. *Ping-ma*, 併馬 [means] yoked with two horses attached to the same yoke." Cf. also *HFHD* I, 107, n. 3 for the "small chariot." Yen Shih-ku remarks, "These regulations were [now] newly fixed."

The *Yi-li* (Steele, III, 8a) and *Li-chi*, ch. 40 (Legge, II, 429; Couvreur II, 624) direct that the groom shall to the bride's house to fetch her; the *Yi-li* (*ibid.*, 4: 6b) specifies a quadriga 乘; neither of these classics seem to mention the "small chariot."

*HS* 27 Bb: 7a says, "In Yüan-shih III, i [Feb./Mar.], Heaven rained plants of a sort like that in the period Yung-kuang [42 B.C.]." Cf. 9: n. 9.2. Cf. W. Eberhard, *Beiträge zur Kosmologischen Spekulation*", p. 27.

[6.4] An allusion to *Mencius* IV, ii, xiii (Legge, p. 322).

I do not find anywhere an explanation of these sumptuary regulations regarding slaves, fields, etc. It may have been a reenactment of Emperor Ai's law; cf. 11: 3a.

Official altars to the gods of the grains were estab-
**7a** lished,[6.5] together with offices for schools: in the
commanderies and kingdoms they were called seminaries (*hsüeh*), and in the counties, marches, [prin-
cesses'] estates, and marquises' states they were
called academies (*hsiao*).[7.1]　In academies and semi-

立 學 曰 邑 校
官 官 學 侯 校
稷 郡 縣 國 學
及 國 道 曰

[6.5] About 205 B.C., Emperor Kao "ordered the prefectures to make public altars to
the gods of the soils 公社" (*HS* 25 A: 18a).　*HS* 25 B: 22a, b says, "[Wang] Mang
said, . . . 'When the sage Han [dynasty] arose, rites and ceremonies were somewhat fixed,
so that there are already official altars to the gods of the soils, [but] there are not yet
any official altars to the gods of the grains.'　Thereupon behind the official altars to
the gods of the soils there were established official altars to the gods of the grains.　Yü
of the Hsia [dynasty] was made the coadjutor to receive the offerings together with the
official gods of the soils; Prince Millet was made the coadjutor to receive the offerings
with the official gods of the grains.　[At the] altars to the gods of the grains there were
planted paper mulberry trees."　(Reference from Ju Shun.)

Fu Tsan (fl. ca. 285) explains that passage as follows, "Emperor Kao did away with
the Ch'in [dynasty's] altars to the gods of the soils and grains and established the Han
[dynasty's] altars to the gods of the soils and grains [cf. *HS* 1 A: 30b], which the *Book
of Rites* [IX, i, 20 (Legge, I, 425; Couvreur, I, 586)] calls the Grand Altar to the Gods
of the Soils (*T'ai-shê*).　At this time there was also established the official altar to the
gods of the soils, Yü of the Hsia [dynasty] being made their coadjutor, which is called
[in the *Book of Rites* XX, 6 (Legge, II, 206; Couvreur, II, 265)] the royal altar to the
gods of the soils (*Wang-shê*).　Cf. the *Han [Dynasty's] Ordinances for Sacrifices* [lost].
But official altars to the gods of the grains had not yet been established.　At this [time]
they were first established.　At the Restoration [of the Han dynasty, Emperor] Kuang-wu
did not establish official altars to the gods of the grains, which [situation] has been inherited down to the present [time]."

There seem thus to have been two sets of altars to the gods of the soils and grains:
the Grand Altar, i.e. the altar of the dynasty, and the Royal Altar, i.e. the state altar.
Emperor Kao had established a dynastic altar to the gods of the soils and grains and a
state altar to the gods of the soils; Wang Mang now added a state altar to the grains,
which Emperor Kuang-wu did not reestablish.

Yen Shih-ku interprets the passage in ch. 12 to mean that the official altars to the gods
of the grains had previously been established at the rear of the altars to the gods of the
soils, and that now these altars were changed and set up at another place, not near the
altars to the gods of the soils.

[7.1] *Li-shih*, 5: 3a–4b (by Hung Kua, 1117–1184), quotes a stele to the Chief of the
P'iao-yang county, P'an Ch'ien, found in 1143 and dated Dec. 14, 181, in which P'an
Ch'ien is praised for having opened a school at this place.　In the title of this inscription,
the school is called a *hsiao-kuan* 校官.　Shen Ch'in-han says that this inscription proves
that county schools were called *hsiao*.

置經師一人鄉曰庠聚曰序序庠置孝經師一人陽
陵任橫等自稱將軍盜庫兵攻官寺出囚徒大司徒
掾督逐皆伏辜安漢公世子宇與帝外家衞氏有謀
宇下獄死誅衞氏
四年春正月郊祀高祖以配天宗祀孝文以配上帝

naries there was established one Master of the Classics. In districts they were called lycea (*hsiang*), and in the villages they were called palestrae (*hsü*). In lycea and palestrae there was established one Master of the *Classic of Filial Piety*.[7.2]     6b

At Yang-ling, Jen Heng with others styled himself a general, robbed arms from the arsenal, attacked the offices and buildings, and set free the imprisoned convicts. A Division Head of the Grand Minister over the Masses supervised the pursuit [of these rebels]. They all suffered for their crimes.

[Wang] Yü₃, the heir of the Duke Who Gives Tranquillity to the Han Dynasty, [Wang Mang], had plotted with the maternal relatives of the Emperor, the Wei clan. [Wang] Yü₃ was sent to prison and died; the Wei clan were executed.[7.3]

In the fourth year, in the spring, the first month,   IV
the suburban sacrifice (*chiao*) was performed to the   A.D. 4
Eminent Founder, [Emperor Kao], making him the   Feb./Mar.
coadjutor of Heaven, and the sacrifice to the greatest exemplar (*tsung*) was performed to [Emperor] Hsiao-wen, making him the coadjutor of the Lords on High.[7.4]

[7.2] These four names for schools were taken from *Mencius* III, I, iii, 10 (Legge, p. 242). Wen Tang Weng first established schools in Shu Commandery about 140 B.C. and was so successful in thus developing that region that Emperor Wu shortly afterwards ordered the commanderies and kingdoms to establish seminaries and academies. In 41 B.C., Emperor Yüan ordered the commanderies and kingdoms to establish Retainers for the Classics; cf. 9: n. 9.6.

Wei Chao (197–273/4) says, "[Places] smaller than districts (*hsiang* 鄉) are called *chü* 聚 (villages)." *HS* 24 A: 4b states that in hamlets 里 there were palestrae and in districts there were lycea. *Ibid.* 4a defines a hamlet as 25 families and a district as 2500 households.

[7.3] For the incident concerning Wang Yü, cf. 99 A: 16a, b; Introduction, pp. 47–48.

*T'ai-p'ing Yü-lan* (978–983) 717: 4b quotes the *Ku-chin Chu* (ca. 300; this passage is not found in that book today) as saying, "In Yüan-shih III, at the funerary park west of the Yen Tomb, [that of Emperor Ch'eng], the great mirrors in front of the door to the imperial throne inside the funerary chamber of the divinity all [had on them drops of] clear liquid, as if they had the appearance of having perspired."

[7.4] Cf. *HS* 25 B: 20a–21a and 99 A: 17a. Wang Mang was imitating the examples

[The title of] the Duke Honoring and Continuing [the Ancestral Sacrifices of] the Yin [dynasty, K'ung Ho-ch'i], was changed to be Duke of Sung and [the title of] the Duke Who Succeeds to the Greatness of the Chou [Dynasty, Chi Tang, was changed] to be Duke of Cheng.

An imperial edict said, "Verily when [the relations between] husband and wife are correct, then father and son love [each other] and human relationships are stable. Previously an imperial edict ordered the high officials to exempt chaste wives and [permit] female convicts to return home, [by which the Emperor] in truth wished to avoid depravity and to protect chastity and faithfulness. Moreover

6a upon very aged and very young persons,[7.5] punishments are not employed. [This is] what the sage-kings have instituted.

"Harsh and oppressive officials however frequently arrest and imprison the family and relatives of those who violate the law, their wives and daughters, their aged and weak, causing them to be resentful and injuring [the imperial] cultural influence. The people [have suffered] bitterness on this account. Let it be clearly ordered to all the officials that

7a women, unless they have themselves violated the law, and males in their eightieth year or above or in their seventh year or under, unless someone in their household has been sentenced for inhumanity or [unless] they have been ordered in an imperial edict by name to be arrested, in all other cases all [such persons]

男子年八十以上七歲以下家非坐不道詔所名捕它皆
屬婦女老弱搆怨傷化百姓苦之其明敕百僚婦女非身犯法者及
悼之人刑罰所不加聖王之所制也惟苛暴吏多拘繫犯法者親及
人倫定矣前詔有司復貞婦歸女徒誠欲以防邪辟全貞信及眊
改殷紹嘉公曰宋公周承休公曰鄭公詔曰蓋夫婦正則父子親

of the ancients as recounted in the *Classic of Filial Piety*, 5: 1b (Legge, ch. IX, p. 477), "Anciently the Duke of Chou made the suburban sacrifice (*chiao*) to Prince Millet, making him the coadjutor of Heaven, and made the sacrifice to the exemplar (*tsung*) to King Wen in the *Ming-t'ang*, making him the coadjutor of the Lord(s) on High."

[7.5] Yen Shih-ku says, "[Persons aged] eighty are called *mao* 眊. Those in their seventh year are called *tao* 悼. *Mao* is an appellation for the aged, referring to their dim sight; the *tao* are those persons who have not yet become men, and for whose death it is proper to sorrow and feel saddened (*tao*)." For the classical definition, cf. *Li-ki* I, I, i, 27 (Couvreur I, 9; Legge, I, 66).

無令天假卿
得二下節以
繫月遣分下
其丁太行至
當未僕天六
驗立王下百
者皇惲覽石
即后等觀宗
驗王八風室
問氏人俗有
定大置賜屬
著赦副九

shall not be permitted to be imprisoned,[7.6] and let **7b**
those who must be examined be immediately examined and questioned.[7.7] Let this be established
and published as a [permanent] ordinance."

In the second month, on [the day] *ting-wei*, the    Mar. 16
Empress nee Wang was established [as Empress]
and a general amnesty [was granted] to the empire.
The Grand Coachman, Wang Yün, and others,
eight persons [in all], were sent out. [For them]
were established Associates, to whom they lent their
credentials,[7.8] [which Associates were sent] to travel
about the empire separately, to examine and observe
[the people's] customs.[7.9] There were granted to
the nine high ministers and those [ranking] lower,
[down] to [those ranking at] six hundred piculs, and
to the [members of] the imperial house who were

---

[7.6] *Li-ki* I, I, i, 27 (Couvreur, I, 9; Legge, I, 66) contains the provision that persons
in their seventh year and under or in their eightieth year and over were not to undergo
(mutilating) punishments. In 195 B.C., Emperor Hui exempted the aged and very young
from the mutilating punishments (*HS* 2: 3a). In 141 B.C., those in their eightieth year
and over and in the eighth (or seventh) year and younger, together with suckling babes,
blind musicians, and dwarfs, were not to be shackled in prison. In 62 B.C., those over
80 were exempted from all punishments, except for heinous crimes. In 20 A.D. Emperor Ch'eng ordered that capital sentences for children in their seventh year or under
must be reported to the Commandant of Justice, and that they should be allowed to
ransom themselves (23: 19a, b). Now it was ordered that women and men under seven
or over eighty should not be imprisoned, except for heinous crimes. (References from
*Yü Yüeh*.) This enactment was modelled on the principle in the *Chou-li* 36: 2a (Biot,
II, 356) *sub* the *Szu-tz'u*, that the young and weak, the aged, and the stupid should be
pardoned. The Han laws thus gradually approached Confucian ideals.

[7.7] Yen Shih-ku explains, "They should go to the place where they live to question
them," but Chou Shou-ch'ang replies that Yen Shih-ku is probably explaining this
ordinance by that of Emperor Kuang-wu in 27 A.D. (*HHS*, An. 1 A: 22b, 23a), which
repeats this order, but uses *chiu* 就 instead of *chi* 即. These two words are different
and cannot be used to explain each other. *Han-chi* (by Hsün Yüeh, 148–209) 30: 4b,
writes *tsê* 則, which Wang Hsien-ch'ien states was anciently a synonym of *chi*.

[7.8] The principals "bore" credentials, which they "lent" to their associates (Hu San-
hsing). These credentials enabled them to wield, temporarily and for a specific purpose,
the imperial authority.

[7.9] For the report of these eight messengers, cf. 99 A: 23b; for their names, cf. 12:
n. 9.4.

enregistered, noble ranks, from [the rank] of Fifth Rank Grandee and above, to each proportionately. There were granted to the common people of the empire one step in noble rank, and to widowers, widows, orphans, childless, and aged, silk. In the

**Summer** summer, the Empress [nee Wang] was presented in the Temple of [Emperor] Kao. There was added to the Duke Who Gives Tranquillity to the Han Dynasty, [Wang Mang], the title of Ruling Governor, and there was granted to the Lady Dowager of the Duke, [the mother of Wang Mang], the title, the

**8a** Baronektess of Apparent Merits. The Duke's sons, [Wang] An[1a] and [Wang] Lin[1a] were both enfeoffed as full marquises.

The Duke Who Gives Tranquillity to the Han Dynasty, [Wang Mang], memorialized [the plans for] and set up the *Ming-t'ang* and the *Pi-yung*.[8.1]

**6b 7b** The Temple of [Emperor] Hsiao-hsüan was honored and made that of the Central Exemplar; the Temple of [Emperor] Hsiao-yüan became that of the Eminent Exemplar;[8.2] the Son of Heaven was to make offerings and sacrifices [at these temples] from generation to generation.

[8.3] Hsi-hai Commandery was established, and those in the empire who had violated the prohibitions were exiled to inhabit it.

The King of Liang, [Liu] Li[5a], who had committed crimes, killed himself.[8.4]

---

[8.1] Cf. *HS* 99 A: 18b.

[8.2] Wang Hsien-ch'ien remarks that Wang Mang honored Emperor Yüan in order to please the Grand Empress Dowager nee Wang, who was the wife of Emperor Yüan.

[8.3] The Official ed. has at this point the word for "in the winter." It quotes the Sung Ch'i ed. as saying that the new edition (unknown) drops the word for "winter." The Ching-yu ed. (1034) has that word; the Chi-ku Ko ed. (1642) has excised it. Chou Shou-ch'ang adds that since the word for "in the winter" is found below (12: 8b), that word should be dropped here.

For the incident of the Hsi-hai Commandery, cf. 99 A: 23b–24b.

[8.4] Liu Li[5a] had committed incest and many murders, but had avoided punishment; he was finally sentenced to dismissal and exile for having had communication with the

籍者爵自五大夫以上各有差賜天下民爵一級鰥寡孤

夫人號曰功顯君封公子安臨皆為列侯安漢公奏立明

堂辟雍尊孝宣廟為中宗孝元廟為高宗天子世世獻祭

置西海郡徙天下犯禁者處之梁王立有罪自殺

分京師置前煇光後丞烈二郡更公卿大夫八十一元

士官名位次及十二州名分界郡國所屬罷置改易天

下多事吏不能紀冬大風吹長安城東門屋瓦且盡

五年春正月祫祭明堂諸侯王二十八人列侯百二十

人

The imperial capital was divided and there were established the two commanderies of the Displayer of Splendor in the South and the Successor to the Magnificence in the North. The official titles and rankings of the ministers, grandees, and eighty-one First Officers were changed, together with the names, **8b** divisions, boundaries, and the commanderies and kingdoms which belonged [to each] of the twelve provinces. The abolitions, establishings, changes, and alterations in the empire made so much work that the officials could not record them.[8.5]

In the winter, a great gale blew off almost all of **Winter** the tiles from the buildings at the eastern gates of the city-wall of Ch'ang-an.

In the fifth year, in the spring, the first month, the **V** *hsia* ancestral sacrifice to all the ancestors together **A.D. 5** was performed in the *Ming-t'ang;*[8.6] twenty-eight **Jan./Feb.** vassal kings,[8.7] one hundred twenty full marquises

Wei clan, whereupon he was forced to commit suicide. His death may have occurred in the preceding year. Cf. Glossary, *sub voce.*

[8.5] The only change in official titles I have found recorded for this time is from Superintendent of the Imperial House to Elder of the Imperial House (19 B: 52b). Probably these other titles were later changed again, so that historians did not trouble to record such short-lived alterations.

[8.6] Ying Shao remarks, "According to the rites, [every] five years there should be two grand sacrifices, one *ti* 禘 [a common offering to all the ancestors in the fifth year] and one *hsia* 祫 [a similar offering in the third year]. At the *hsia* [sacrifice], those shrines which have been removed to the temple of the first ancestor, together with the tablets of those shrines which have not yet been removed, are all jointly given offerings in [the shrine of] the first ancestor." This remark is based on *Kung-yang Commentary* 13: 3b, 4a (Dk. Wen, II, viii). Cf. Maspero, *La Chine Antique*, pp. 249–250.

[8.7] Ch'ien Ta-hsin finds that only 22 vassal kings were reigning at this time: the King of Ch'eng-yang, Liu Li$_4$ (14: 6b), the King of Tzu-ch'uan, Liu Yung$_{3b}$ (14: 7b), the King of Ho-chien, Liu Shang$_{4b}$ (14: 13b), the King of Lu, Liu Min$_{3a}$ (14: 14b), the King of Chao, Liu Yin$_{6a}$ (14: 15a), the King of Ch'ang-sha, Liu Lu-jen (14: 16a), the King of Kuang-p'ing, Liu Kuang-han (14: 16b), the King of Chiao-tung, Liu Yin$_2$ (14: 18a), the King of Liu-an, Liu Yü$_{5a}$ (14: 18b), the King of Chen-ting, Liu Yang (14: 19a), the King of Szu-shui, Liu Ching$_5$ (14: 19b), the King of Kuang-yang, Liu Chia$_{1b}$ (14: 20a), the King of Kuang-ling, Liu Shou$_{3a}$ (14: 20b), the King of Kao-mi, Liu Shen (14: 21a), the King of Huai-yang, Liu Yin$_{4b}$ (14: 21b), the King of Tung-p'ing, Liu K'ai-ming (14:

and more than nine hundred scions of the imperial
house were summoned to assist in the sacrifices.
When the rites were ended, all [had a certain number

8a  of] households added [to their estates] or they were
granted noble ranks, and [they were granted] money
and silk or their official ranks were increased or they
were given vacancies as officials, to each proportionately.

An imperial edict [from the Grand Empress Dow-
ager] said, "Verily, [We] have heard that when the
[ancient] lords and kings governed the common
people by their virtue, their next [principle] was to
favor their relatives, in order that [their influence
might thereby] reach to others.[8.8] Anciently Yao
harmonized his nine [classes of] kindred[8.9] and Shun

7a  generously promoted [his kindred].[8.10] Because of
the Emperor's youth, We have temporarily been

9a  directing the government of the state. [We] have
reflected that the scions of the imperial house are all
descendants of the Grand Founder, Emperor Kao, or
of his brothers, [King] Ch'ing of Wu, [Liu Chung,
and King] Yüan of Ch'u, [Liu Chiao]; that, since
the beginning of the Han [dynasty] to the present,
[they have multiplied and have become] more than
a hundred thousand persons; and that altho they
are related to [such persons as] kings and marquises,
they have been unable mutually to control each
other, and so some have fallen into punishment for
crime. The cause [for this situation is that the im-
perial] teaching and instruction has not reached them.
Does not the *Memoir* say, 'When princes are generous

宗有舜孫及能莫
室差惇敍兄相能
子詔之吳頃相
九曰以楚或
百蓋皇元陷
餘聞帝之入
人帝幼後刑
徵王年漢罪
助以且元教
祭德統至訓
禮撫國今不
畢民政十至
皆其惟有之
益次宗餘咎
戶親室萬也
賜親子人傳
爵以皆雖不
及相太有云
金及祖王乎
帛也高侯君
增昔皇之子
秩堯帝屬篤
補睦子
吏九
各族

21b), the King of Chung-shan, Liu Ch'eng-tu (20: 22a), the King of Ch'u, Liu Yü[1a] (20:
22b), the King of Hsin-tu[a], Liu Ching[3b] (14: 22b), the King of Kuang-tsung, Liu Ju-yi[b]
(14: 13a), the King of Kuang-shih, Liu Kung[1a] (14: 14b), and the King of Kuang-tê, Liu
Lun (14: 18a). The King of Liang, Liu Yin[1b] (14: 12a), was not appointed until the
second or the intercalary month of this year, so is not included.

[8.8] Alluding to *Mencius* I, i, vii, 12 (Legge, p. 143).

[8.9] An allusion to *Book of History* I, i, 2 (Legge, p. 17; Couvreur, p. 2).

[8.10] An allusion to *ibid.* II, iii, 1 (Legge, p. 69; Couvreur, p. 44). Karlgren, BMFED,
20, 106f, gl. 1297, does not express the full force of "giving thin proper order to" a king's
kindred.

於　國　察　以　令
親　置　不　歲　漢
則　宗　從　正　與
民　師　教　月　文
興　以　令　賜　王
於　糾　有　宗　靈
仁　之　寃　師　臺
其　致　失　帛　周
為　教　職　各　公
宗　訓　者　十　作
室　焉　宗　匹　洛
自　二　師　義　同
太　千　得　和　符
上　石　因　劉　太
皇　選　郵　歆　僕
以　有　亭　等　王
來　德　書　四　惲
族　義　言　人　等
親　者　宗　使　八
各　以　伯　治　人
以　為　請　明
世　宗　以　堂
氏　師　聞　辟
郡　考　常　雍

to their relatives, then the common people are stirred to mutual kindnesses'?[9.1]

"For the imperial house [which has descended] from the Grand Emperor, the clan, each [member of which] has inherited his surname [of Liu], let Masters to the Imperial Clan be established in the commanderies and kingdoms in order to control them and bring [the imperial] teaching and instruction to them. Let [the officials who rank at] two thousand piculs select those who are virtuous and well-principled to be the Masters to the Imperial Clan. They should examine and investigate those who do not follow [the imperial] teaching and ordinances and those who have suffered injustice and lost their positions. Masters of the Imperial Clan are permitted to take advantage of the postal stations in writing letters to ask the Elder of the Imperial House to make requests [of Us] in order that [We] may hear of it. Regularily every year in the first month, the Masters of the Imperial Clan shall each be granted ten bolts of silk."[9.2]

The Hsi-and-Ho, Liu Hsin[1a], and others, four persons [in all],[9.3] who had been sent to prepare the *Ming-t'ang* and *Pi-yung*, had brought it about that the Han [dynasty] had happy presages similar to those of King Wen [when he built] his Spiritual Tower and to those of the Duke of Chou [when he built the city of] Lo; the Grand Coachman, Wang Yün, and others, eight persons [in all], who had been

8b

7b

9b

---

[9.1] *Analects* VIII, ii, 2 (Soothill, p. 383).

[9.2] Ho Ch'uo remarks, "At that time the vassal kings were all like ordinary common people, not worth being afraid of. Yet because [the imperial clan] was a multitude of more than a hundred thousand [persons, Wang Mang] thought that [the members of] the Liu [clan] might join together and start trouble. Hence he secretly appointed those of them who were closely leagued with the Wang clan and would injure the imperial house, in order secretly to restrain and repress the imperial clan, not to teach and instruct them." Such comments appear to be unsupported suspicions.

[9.3] These four were Liu Hsin[1a], P'ing Yen, K'uang Yung, and Sun Ch'ien, according to *HS* 18: 29a, b.

sent to investigate [the people's] customs, had propagated [the imperial] virtue and culture, so that all the kingdoms had become harmonious;[9.4] all [these twelve persons] were enfeoffed as full marquises.

June 29[9.5]

The [following sorts of persons] were summoned to the place where [the Emperor] was: those in the empire who comprehended and understood the lost classics, the ancient records, astrological phenomena, astronomical calculations, the musical tubes, philology, Shih [Chou's] *Fascicles*, the magical and technical arts, materia medica, together with those who taught the Five Classics, the *Analects*, the *Classic of Filial Piety*, and the *Erh-ya*. For these there were yoked small chariots with singly sealed

9a [passports][9.6] to send them to the capital. Those who arrived [numbered] several thousand persons.

駕一封軺傳遣詣京師者數千人
五經論語孝經爾雅教授者在所爲
歷算鍾律小學史篇方術本草及以
爲列侯徵天下通知逸經古記天文
使行風俗宣明德化萬國齊同皆封

[9.4] These eight were Wang Yün, Yen Ch'ien, Ch'en Ch'ung, Li Hsi, Ho Tang, Hsieh Yin, Lu P'u, and Ch'en Feng, according to *HS* 19: 30a–31b. This passage is probably composed of quotations from the imperial edicts making these enfeoffments.

[9.5] Cf. *HS* 18: 29a–31b.

[9.6] *HS* 99 A: 19a dates the summoning of these persons in A.D. 4. The dating A.D. 5 here probably is that of their arrival.

Ju Shun remarks, "[According to] the Code, those who are required [to ride] riding quadrigae (*sheng chuan* 乘傳) together with those who [ride] equipages [specially] sent out [for them] (*fa-chia* 發駕) or post-quadrigae (*chih-chuan* 置傳) [cf. *HFHD* I, 107, n. 3 for these types of chariots] must all hold wooden passport credentials (*mu-chuan-hsin* 木傳信), [cf. I, 252, n. 2] one foot five inches [long], sealed with the seal of the Grandee Secretary. Those who [ride] riding quadrigae have [their passports] sealed thrice. When there is a set convocation, the two ends [of the passports] are repeatedly sealed, each end having two seals, [making] altogether four seals. For riding post quadrigae (*chih* 置-*chuan*) and galloping quadrigae (*ch'ih-chuan* 馳傳) there are five seals: each of the two ends has two [seals] and in the center there is one [seal]. For small chariots (*yao-chuan* 軺傳) with two horses, [passports] are sealed twice; for [small chariots] with one horse, [passports] are sealed once." *Han Chiu-yi* A: 6b (by Wei Hung, fl. dur. 25–57) says, "For those who in accordance with an imperial edict are sent to dispose of some matter, the [Grandee] Secretary has yoked [a small carriage and their passports are sealed with] one seal; [for those who] transmit an ordinance of amnesty, he has yoked [a small carriage and their passports are sealed with] two seals." (Reference from Shen Ch'in-han.) Yao Nai (1732–1815) suggests that "equipages [specially] sent out" may be equipages like the comfortable carriage (*an-ch'e* 安車) sent for his excellency Shen, to bring him to the capital, who was accompanied by two disciples riding small chariots (cf. 88: 16a).

閏月立梁孝王玄孫 之耳孫晉爲王冬十 二月丙午帝崩于未 央宮大赦天下有司 議曰禮臣不弔君

In the intercalary month, [Liu] Yin$_{1b}$, a great-great-grandson of a great-grandson of King Hsiao of Liang, [Liu Wu$_3$], was made King [of Liang].[10.1]

**10a**
**June/July**

In the winter, the twelfth month, on [the day] *ping-tzu*,[10.2] the Emperor died in the Wei-yang Palace. A general amnesty was granted to the empire. The high officials discussed and said, "[According to] the rites, 'Subjects do not treat their lord as if he had died before he reached maturity.'[10.3]

**A.D. 6**
**Feb. 3**

"Shih Chou's Fascicles" is the famous word list attributed, in Han times, to a clerk of the eighth century B.C., cf. *HS* 30: 22b.

For Han materia medica cf. *HS* 25 B; 15a, 92: 7b. The latter passage mentions a work containing several hundred thousand words.

[10.1] *HS* 14: 12a dates this appointment in the second month on the day *ting-yu* (Mar. 1).

*HS* 27 A: 16a says, "In Yüan-shih V, vii, on *chi-hai* [Aug. 30], there was a visitation [of fire] to the doors of the Hall in the Second Temple of Emperor Kao, and they were reduced to ashes."

[10.2] The text reads *ping-wu*, but Hoang places no such day in that twelfth month. *HS* 99 A: 24b also reads "twelfth month." *Han-chi* 30: 6b reads, "the twelfth month, [the day] *ping-tzu*," which seems to be correct, for that day occurred in that month.

Yen Shih-ku comments, "A Han commentator says, 'When the Emperor became older and grew up, he had a grudge on account of his mother, the Queen Dowager [nee] Wei, [who had wept day and night for her son, but was nevertheless not allowed to come to the imperial capital to care her child, and all of whose relatives had been killed by Wang Mang], and was unhappy. [Wang] Mang himself knew that [the Emperor] was becoming increasingly estranged from him, and [Wang Mang's] plot to usurp [the throne] and kill [the Emperor] arose from this circumstance. Hence when the *la* day [which that year was Jan. 20, A.D. 6] arrived, [Wang Mang] presented to the Emperor the peppered wine, and put poison into the wine.' Hence Chai Yi sent about a message which said, '[Wang] Mang assassinated Emperor Hsiao-p'ing by poison.'" *HS* 84: 11a records that when in A.D. 7 Chai Yi rebelled against Wang Mang, he sent urgent messages thru the empire with the foresaid words. Wang Ch'ung (*Lun-heng*, Forke's trans., I, 485) repeats this charge. Ch'ien Ta-chao remarks, "[Emperor] Hsiao-p'ing was poisoned by [Wang] Mang, [but a historian] does not record an assassination, [according to] the principle of the *Spring and Autumn*, that one should keep silent about great evils [that occur] within [the court. Pan Ku] merely did not record the day of the burial, in order to point out that it was to be classed with grievous vicissitudes." *Kung-yang Commentary* 3: 8b (Dk. Yin, X, vi) says, "Great evils within [the court] are not mentioned; small evils are recorded"; cf. *ibid.* 2: 2a (Dk. Yin, II, v). The *HS* records the dates of burial for all the rulers except for those of Emperor P'ing and the Empress nee Lü. For the latter it is not even mentioned that she was buried. For a discussion of the evidence for this poisoning, cf. Introduction to this chapter, pp. 57–60.

[10.3] *Huang-ch'ing Ching-chieh* (1813) 1250: 27b quotes the *Wu-ching Yi-yi* by Hsü Shen

*8a*　The Emperor was in his fourteenth year. It is proper that, according to the rites, when he is enshrouded, the bonnet of virility should be put upon him." The memorial was approved. He was buried in the K'ang Tomb.

An imperial edict [from the Grand Empress Dowager nee Wang] said, "The Emperor was benevolent and kindly, and there was nothing that he did not consider or feel distressed about. [But] whenever he became ill, his breath was blocked from coming out, which kept him from speaking.[10.4] Hence he did not get to prepare a testamentory edict. Let his concubines be sent away and all be returned to their homes and be permitted to be married, as in the former case in the time of [Emperor] Hsiao-wen."[10.5]

**10b** 9b　In eulogy we say: In the reign of [Emperor] Hsiao-p'ing, the government proceeded from [Wang] Mang, who recompensed laudable [circumstances] and made meritorious deeds manifest, in order to make himself honorable and prominent. When we consider his literary compositions, [it seems that] of the many barbarians outside the [four] quarters [of the empire], "none failed to think of and submit to him,"[10.6] happy omens, auspicious responses, and eulogizing songs were simultaneously produced. [But] as to the grievous vicissitudes and prodigies that appeared [in heaven] above and the hatreds of the common people[10.7] [on the earth] below, [Wang] Mang was however unable to cover them up.

皇惠出褒頌
帝無滕善聲
年不妾顯並
十顧皆功作
有哀歸以至
四每家自乎
歲疾得尊變
宜一嫁盛異
以發如觀見
禮氣孝其於
斂輒文文上
加上時辭民
元逆故方怨
服害事外於
奏於贊百下
可言曰蠻莽
葬語孝亡亦
康故平思不
陵不之不能
詔及世服文
曰有政休也
皇遺自徵
帝詔莽嘉
仁其出應

(d. 121; a lost book; fragments collected by Ch'en Feng-ch'i, 1771–1834), as saying, "In accordance with the rites, Mr. Hsü said, 'Subjects do not treat their lord as if he had died before he had reached maturity (the twentieth year); a son does not treat his father as if he had died before he had reached maturity. When a lord dies without children and no temple is established for him, this [act] is contrary to moral principles and disdainful of the rules of proper conduct, the greatest of crimes.' "

[10.4] Asthma?

[10.5] Cf. 4: 20b.

[10.6] A quotation from *Book of Odes*, III, i, x, 6 (Legge, p. 463).

[10.7] *T'ai-p'ing Yü-lan* 89: 8b quotes this eulogy, with the word 人 after the 民.

# CHAPTER XII
## APPENDIX

## ECLIPSES DURING THE REIGN OF EMPEROR P'ING

i. An solar eclipse is recorded in Yüan-shih I, v (the fifth month), on the day *ting-szu*, the first day of the month (12: 4a). Hoang equates this day with June 10, 1 A.D., for which Oppolzer calculates his solar eclipse no. 2885. According to calculation, at Ch'ang-an the eclipse reached a magnitude of 0.75 (sun's diameter = 1.00) at 10:44 a.m. local time, so that it was conspicuous. The sun's longitude was 76° = 75° R.A. *HS* 27 Cb: 16a says that the eclipse was "in [the constellation] Tung-ching," whose first star, $\mu$ Gem, was then in 66° R.A. This constellation extends for some 33°.

In the year between this and preceding recorded eclipse, no solar eclipses were visible in China.

ii. A second solar eclipse is recorded in Yüan-shih II, ix, *mou-shen*, the last day of the month (12: 6a). *HS* 27 Cb: 16 adds that it was total. Hoang equates this day with Nov. 23, 2 A.D., for which Oppolzer calculates his solar eclipse no. 2888. Calculation shows that at Ch'ang-an the eclipse reached a magnitude of 0.88, and that the path of totality passed thru the present Ning-hsia, northern Shensi, K'ai-feng, and Shanghai, so that reports of totality could easily be brought to the capital.

It is curious that the totality should be reported in the "Treatise," and not in the Annals; twice previously (ch. II, eclipse ii; ch. X, eclipse ii) differences between the accounts in the "Annals" and "Treatise" showed that the "Treatise" represents observations in the capital. But after 28 B.C., (except for the eclipse of 2 B.C.) the account in the "Treatise" does not as previously give the precise positions of eclipses in the heavens, only stating what constellation it was in and not always that; possibly the detailed account of eclipses, which was made at the capital and was used by Pan Ku as the source for his Treatise, ended with the eclipse of 28 B.C.

In the seventeen months between this and the preceding recorded eclipse, no solar eclipses were visible in China.

# THE HISTORY OF THE FORMER HAN DYNASTY

## CHAPTER XCIX

## WANG MANG

## INTRODUCTION

### Reason for presentation of this chapter here

The "Annals" in the *History of the Former Han Dynasty* recount events only until the death of Emperor P'ing on Feb. 3, A.D. 6. There was no legal Han emperor from that date until Aug. 5, A.D. 25, when Emperor Kuang-wu of the Later Han dynasty took the throne. During the first three of these years, Wang Mang, a maternal first cousin of Emperor Ch'eng (the latter of whom was Emperor P'ing's adoptive father), ruled as Regent and Acting Emperor, with Liu Ying, a descendant of Emperor Hsüan, as Heir-apparent and Young Prince, (*Ju-tzu*, an ancient title, given to King Ch'eng of the Chou dynasty). On Jan. 10, A.D. 9, Wang Mang took the throne as actual Emperor, and ruled until his death on Oct. 6, A.D. 23. Seven months previously, a scion of the House of Han had been set up as Emperor by a group of generals (called, from his reign-period, the Keng-shih Emperor), and, between that time and until Emperor Kuang-wu was seated firmly on the throne, about a dozen other persons were set up or set themselves up as Emperor (cf. Glossary, *sub* Kuang-wu, Emperor). The events in the first part of this period, from A.D. 6 to A.D. 23, are related fully only in this chapter of the *History of the Former Han Dynasty*. These seventeen years belong properly to the Former Han period.

The period of Wang Mang's reign is extremely interesting. Its events result from the tendencies that had previously been operating. The "Annals" in the *HS* constitute a summary of the history during the reigns of the Han emperors; in order to continue that account until the beginning of the Later Han period, there is presented here a translation of the "Memoir of Wang Mang," which is the only extensive primary source for that period. It really constitutes an appendix to the "Annals of Emperor P'ing."

### The form of this Memoir

In its form, the "Memoir of Wang Mang" is that of a sequent memoir (*chuan*); its latter portion, since it is the only extensive account in the *HS* of these seventeen years, is also an annals for those years.

A typical memoir states first the given name and courtesy name of the

88

person treated, then recounts his native place and ancestry, including a notice of those ancestors who were important. If, however, his father or some antecedent relative has been given a separate memoir, the notice of his native place and ancestry is omitted in such a sequent memoir. This section is followed by an account of his education, how he secured office, what offices he held, his distinguished deeds, his titles, etc. Samples of his writings are quoted, if they were important or interesting. Somewhere in the account there is a description of his character (and possibly of his appearance), preceded by the words, "As a man, ...". The notice of his death is followed by a similar account of his descendants, if they were important, and sometimes of other relatives. In general, events are related chronologically, but there are occasional deviations from that chronological order, as when an earlier event is recounted in order to explain or lead up to a later one. (Sometimes in the text there is no indication of a deviation from the chronological order; it is surprising how often a proper understanding of the chronology requires the use of the pluperfect tense).

The account is thoroughly objective; the historian's feelings are rarely allowed to appear until the end of the chapter, where there is appended a "eulogy (*tsan*)", giving the historian's judgment upon the person or persons considered in the chapter. This eulogy is usually a highly polished statement, sententious and pregnant. (Later historians, such as Hsün Yüeh, have not been content with exercising so much self-restraint, and, while keeping the objective form of the account, they have introduced at various places in the text a "discussion (*lun*)" of the events, criticizing or approving the person or deed under consideration, sometimes at considerable length. The term "eulogy" is then reserved for a final polished literary summary.)

A typical annals opens with a brief introductory section, in which are discussed matters concerning the ruler's childhood and the way he came to be selected for the throne. The chapter then relates the events during his reign, by years and months. These recordings are confined to matters of governmental concern; circumstances concerning the private life of even the ruler are relegated to the memoirs of the non-imperial individuals most concerned. Only rarely is there mentioned a matter not of governmental concern, and then only when it is of great importance. Thus Pan Ku did not even mention in his "Annals" the famous poet, Szu-ma Hsiang-ju, although he greatly admired this genius. Matters concerning legal developments are usually summarized briefly, sometimes with a reference to the "Treatise on Punishments and Laws." Matters that can be discussed better in other treatises (*chih*) or memoirs are similarly dealt with. Typical and important imperial edicts are quoted. After recounting the death and burial of the ruler, there is a eulogy, similar to that in a memoir.

The "Memoir of Wang Mang" is preceded by that of his aunt, the Grand Empress Dowager nee Wang (ch. 98), in which there is given an extended account of the Wang clan's ancestry and of the other members of that important clan. (An abstract of that memoir will be found in the Glossary.) Consequently, matters concerning Wang Mang's ancestry and predecessors are to be found in that memoir. His memoir is thus a sequent one, and omits the features with which a typical memoir begins. Since it is a memoir, not an annals, Pan Ku does not confine himself to governmental concerns, and introduces memorials written by Wang Mang and others. He also relates fully the antecedents of events. The part of this memoir devoted to the reign of Emperor P'ing is more than twice as long as the "Annals" of that Emperor.

Pan Ku's problem was how to include properly an account of Wang Mang's reign in a history of the Han period. Before he wrote the *Han-shu*, Pan Ku had prepared an annals for the first of the Later Han emperors, so that he knew where a history of the Later Han dynasty must begin. He did not wish to leave unrecorded the two decades between these two periods. If Wang Mang had been a legitimate emperor, Pan Ku could have written an annals for his reign, with additional memoirs treating of his important officials. Since Wang Mang was a usurper, Pan Ku could not do so. But Wang Mang was a minister to the last emperor of the Former Han line. So Pan Ku could legitimately write a memoir for him and could continue this account down to the beginning of the Later Han period. Thus he cleverly included this interregnal period in his *History of the Former Han Dynasty*.

Since this chapter is a memoir, the accounts of Wang Mang's officials are also included in it and they are not given separate accounts. Thus this chapter contains almost all the information in the *History* about Wang Mang. In addition to what we have here, there is elsewhere material about this usurper in the "Annals of Emperor P'ing" (with brief mentions in those of Emperors Ch'eng and Ai), an important section concerning Wang Mang's economic policies in the "Treatise on Food and Goods" (translated in Appendix I), and a very short notice of his religious activities in the "Treatise on the Suburban and Other Sacrifices." The rebellion of Chai Yi is furthermore treated in detail in this person's memoir (abstracted in the glossary). Thus this account of Wang Mang is more rounded than that in other memoirs, in dealing with which it is necessary, in order to obtain a complete account, to read also the memoirs of the several participants in the series of events, and supplement them by the chronology to be found in the imperial annals and the tables, especially that in part B to the "Table of the Many Offices" (ch. 19). Hence this chapter dealing with Wang Mang is much longer than an annals or an ordinary memoir would be—and also much more satisfying.

Because there is no annals for the reign of Wang Mang, the later portion of this chapter is both an annals and a memoir. A memoir regularly proceeds chronologically, so that Pan Ku could easily combine these two forms.

Since this chapter also contains the only account of Wang Mang's officials, Pan Ku found that he could not end it with the death of the usurper, for he needed to relate the fate of those officials. Then he also summarized the subsequent history down to the accession of Emperor Kuang-wu. This chapter is complicated in its form.

Its division into three parts was probably the work of either Ying Shao or Yen Shih-ku, who made the divisions in the chapters of the *HS*. This division is logical and deserves to stand. Part A deals with the rise of Wang Mang down to his assumption of the throne in A.D. 9. Part B pictures him at the height of his power. It relates his extensive changes in rites and titles and the beginning of his decline. Part C deals with the collapse of his rule, from A.D. 17 to the end. The chapter is so long that these divisions have proved useful as well as logical.

## Its sources

Concerning the sources of this and other chapters, I shall have something to say in the volume of "Prolegomena" to this series. In the main, the sources here are the same as elsewhere: imperial messages and edicts, stenographical reports of imperial conversations (cf. 99 A: 27a), some official annals kept at the palace, memorials to the throne, with their very varied contents, such as even testimony at trials and the reports given by informers. In addition, Pan Ku used the political pamphlets of the day, which probably also formed part of the memorials to the throne, sometimes being presented to the throne by the author of the pamphlet, and sometimes (in the case of those attacking Wang Mang) forming part of the evidence memorialized to justify a condemnation. The material that might have come from the above sources may well account for practically the whole of this chapter.

In this chapter, the amount of direct and extended quotation from primary sources is noteworthy. In Part A, these explicit quotations form 68% of the whole; in Part B, 53%; and in Part C, 41% (exclusive of the eulogy); an average of 55% for the chapter. Pan Ku was himself a poet and literary artist of the first rank, and plainly admired the Confucian literary products of Wang Mang's time, including Wang Mang's own edicts, hence was led to quote them as examples of the age's literary products. The two memorials written by Chang Sung (99 A: 10a–16a; 27b–29a) alone account for 27% of the direct quotations in Part A.

In addition to the direct quotations, there is a very large amount of information that must have come from written documents, such as official appointments, enfeoffments, summaries of official orders concerning economic matters, concerning the redistricting of territory, concerning military expeditions, etc. Much of this material is probably fragmentary direct quotation. Since there is no difference in Chinese style between direct and indirect discourse (except for the personal pronouns, the phrase "your servant," and a few such phrases), a clever compiler, such as Pan Ku shows himself to be, could more easily piece together phrases from earlier documents to produce his own account than himself compose the whole account anew. The peculiar description of the bandits in 99 C: 14b, which makes them out to be beggars going about asking for food, blaming the fighting upon the government officials who come out and get hurt, was very likely part of the report sent in by the Higher Subordinate Official of the Commander-in-chief mentioned immediately afterwards, who was captured by the bandits and freed, probably because he promised to plead for them. Pan Ku used it as his own account of the bandits (without mention of his source), since it came from a man who could speak at first hand about them.

Another noteworthy feature of the age was the number of extensive political documents, chiefly propaganda, that are mentioned in this chapter. Evidently it was an age when there was a large reading public, who eagerly perused such documents and passed them from hand to hand. In A.D. 5, 487,572 persons (probably by groups) turned in memorials at the capital concerning Wang Mang (99 A: 19b). We hear of a work on filial piety written by Wang Mang in eight fascicles (99 A: 17a), of a report by the eight commissioners concerning the people's customs, praising Wang Mang, in 30,000 words (99 A: 23b), of a piece of propaganda, entitled "The Mandate of Heaven Given Through Portents," in 42 fascicles (99 B: 9a), of a remonstrance to Wang Mang written by his general, Chuang Yu, in three fascicles (99 C: 5b), of a book of revelations written by Wang K'uang$_{4b}$ attacking Wang Mang, in over 100,000 words (99 C: 12b), and of Wang Mang's own *apologia*, in more than a thousand words (99 C: 25a). In addition there are mentioned other political documents that must have been extensive, but about whose length we are given no information: Chai Yi's message attacking Wang Mang, sent about the country at the outset of his rebellion (99 A: 30a; 84: 11a); Liu Yin$_{4a}$ Po-sheng's messages (99 C: 20a), and Wei Hsiao's message (*HHS*, Mem. 3: 2a–4a), all attacking Wang Mang. There must have been many more, in addition to the government documents and constant propaganda. Pan Piao's "Discussion of the Mandate to True Kings" (quoted in *HS* 100 A: 7b–11b) was probably a pamphlet passed about the country in support of Emperor Kuang-wu.

Stange (in *Die Monographie über Wang Mang*, p. xxiv) states that this chapter contains many matters which could only have come from oral tradition or court gossip. There are, of course, some matters that did come from oral tradition, such as the opinion about Wang Mang's music (99 C: 4b), which might indeed have come from Pan Chih, Pan Ku's grandfather. But such matters that are traceable to no written sources are very much fewer than one might think, and Stange's own examples are all chosen unfortunately.

Whenever a capital sentence was imposed, the facts upon which that sentence was based were summarized in the form of a memorial and sent to the emperor for his approval before the sentence was carried out. These memorials then formed part of the government records, were preserved, and were available to Pan Ku for the compilation of his *History*. The government archives from Former Han times must have been very extensive. The most surprising case is that in a memorial of A.D. 9 (99 A: 34b), Wang Mang mentions a book of revelation by Kan Chung-k'o as being extant and stored in the Orchid Terrace (the imperial archives). Now this remarkable work (in twelve rolls) had been written some time in the reign of Emperor Ch'eng. It contained a prophecy that the Han dynasty had come to the end of its period and must receive a renewed mandate from Heaven. The famous Liu Hsiang had memorialized that the matter was a fabrication to impose upon the vulgar, and Kan Chung-k'o died in prison. In 5 B.C., a disciple, Hsia Ho-liang, memorialized this book to Emperor Ai, who was impressed by it and changed his own title and year-period in order to conform with this prophecy. (It was evidently this copy that Wang Mang read.) A few months later, when his illness did not improve, Emperor Ai abrogated his change and turned Hsia Ho-liang over to his officials, who decided that he had maliciously deceived the Emperor, which was an inhuman crime; he and his associates were executed. Now if this repudiated prophetic book, forming part of a memorial from a man who was executed for one of the most serious crimes in the code, was preserved in the imperial archives for a period of fourteen years, during three reigns, it is likely that memorials to the throne were generally preserved. Such memorials contained information and advice about all sorts of matters; they must have been an extensive source of information for anyone who had access to them. Pan Ku occasionally quotes such memorials, for example, Chuang Yu's advice about the expedition against the Huns, which advice was rejected (found in 94 B: 19a–b = de Groot, *Die Hunnen*, pp. 273–275).

Now let us examine the examples of supposedly oral tradition mentioned by Stange. The first one, the intrigue of Wang Mang against Shun-yu Chang (99 A: 2a), resulted in the death of Shun-yu Chang, the execution of his family and several dozen other persons, including a former Empress, and the promotion of Wang Mang, so that there must have been official documents recounting the testimony of those examined, requesting the execution of these persons, detailing the culprit's crimes, and indicating the person who reported them (cf. Glossary *sub* Shun-yu Chang). Pan Ku's information about this incident was very likely based upon these written documents.

The account of Wang Mang's wife's economy (99 A: 2a, b) also probably came from a documentary source; some among the hundreds of thousands of memorials praising Wang Mang probably contained this detail, as well as many other details of Wang Mang's early life. A similar memorial was probably the source for his interview with K'ung Hsiu (99 A: 3b–4a). It is even more probable that the statement made by Liu Ch'ung to his Chancellor, Chang Shao (99 A: 27a, b), was taken from a documentary source, either from the report of the magistrate about this rebellion or from a memorial to Wang Mang by Chang Shao's cousin, Chang Sung, excusing himself. In the case of Chao Ming's message to Chai Yi (99 A: 30b), it is quite possible that this message might have been found in Chai Yi's camp after his defeat or in the city of Yü, to which he fled and which was taken by storm.

It is not asserted that these conversations actually occurred, any more than that the Higher Subordinate Official's account of the bandits was true; it is merely pointed out that these conversations, etc., found in the *HS*, could in most cases have been found by Pan Ku in some documentary source, and that he used them as representing what very likely had happened. There are many cases, especially in the *HS* memoirs, in which a conversation would have enlivened the account and in which no conversations are recounted. Hence it is most probable that Pan Ku did not invent the conversations he recounts. He may be criticized for using other people's invented conversations, but it seems rarely the case that he himself invented matters which were not found in documents.

We have considered each of the cases Stange brings forward as supposed instances of oral tradition, and note that, as Pan Ku used them, they were all probably found by him in written form. The accounts of conversations, etc., found in the *HS* are different in their nature from the ones in the *SC* that have been so correctly suspected of having been fabricated by Szu-ma Ch'ien. The latter writer has been known for his lively accounts of events. Pan Ku's *History* has been criticized as being inferior in its literary character—the difference is probably that Pan Ku refused to invent conversations and events to enliven his writings, unless he found them in his sources. Hence the reliability of each case must be judged upon its own merits and any general suspicion of Pan Ku's reliability must be laid aside.

## The sources for the account of Wang Mang's last days

The account of Wang Mang's death is extremely interesting because of the abundant details recounted and their vividness. The number of intimate details are so extraordinary that this account must have come from an eye-witness who had close access to the Emperor. It tells what happened on each day of the siege; how Wang Mang changed the guard at the city gates; how Chang$_2$ Han was killed as he was making the rounds of the gates; how Wang Mang was robed and where he sat in the throne-room, in the direction of the handle to the Great Dipper, performing divination while the Palace was burning (99 C: 27a). We are told by what steps he left the throne-room building—a staircase seemingly not mentioned elsewhere in ancient literature (a detail that would hardly have been invented by a forger)—and that his driver on his final journey was Wang Yi$_6$, a person only mentioned here and among the list of those who died with Wang Mang. At the tower where Wang Mang's followers made their last stand, we are told how Wang Mu, the son of Wang Mang's Heir-apparent, Wang Yi$_5$, was taking off his court robes, preparing to flee, when his father arrived, who made him don them again and stay to die with Wang Mang. Thus part of the account plainly comes from an intimate companion of Wang Mang.

Other features are written from the viewpoint of the attackers. We are told in some detail how Teng Yi and Yü K'uang arose, whom they first attacked, how they effected entrance through the Wu Pass, how Teng Yi marched around the Han-ku Pass—by an obscure path not mentioned elsewhere by Chinese geographers—and how he defeated the Nine Tiger Generals, bottled the remainder of them up in the Capital Granary, left them, and began preparing siege implements.

Then we are told by what gate the attackers entered the palace, what important courtiers died defending the entrance to the Tower Bathed by Water, and which ones died with Wang Mang in the room on top of the Tower; exactly who killed Wang Mang and took his imperial seals and cords; who recognized the cords, evidently by their distinctive color, identified the corpse and took its head; and how Wang Hsien$_4$ lived like an emperor after the death of Wang Mang.

Where did all these details come from? They are too circumstantial to have been invented by a romancer. The "Memoir" gives us two details that seem to solve the problem. In the first place, it says that after

95

the death of Wang Mang, Shen-t'u Ch'ien, a Han general, directed Liu Tz'u$_{4b}$, the Lieutenant Chancellor of the Keng-shih Emperor, to have Ts'ui Fa beheaded, because the latter had written an account of Wang Mang (99 C: 28b). Liu Tz'u$_{4b}$ came to Ch'ang-an before the Keng-shih Emperor arrived, to look over the situation and prepare a residence for the new Emperor, at which time this sentence was probably passed. Ts'ui Fa was an important personage, one of Wang Mang's advisors; a request for his execution would very probably have been prepared in accordance with the regular court procedure—a *dossier* of the evidence accompanied the request. In this case, most of the evidence was probably Ts'ui Fa's written account. The Keng-shih Emperor made Ch'ang-an his capital, so that the whole document found its way into the imperial archives. Thus we can trace back to Ts'ui Fa an important part of the material concerning the death of Wang Mang.

Ts'ui Fa was in a position to know these events, for he belonged to the innermost circle about Wang Mang. Ts'ui Fa appears again and again in the account of Wang Mang's reign, giving successful advice upon various superstitious practises, such as the very interesting wailing at the Altar to Heaven and the wailing in the city of Ch'ang-an to keep off invaders.

Ts'ui Fa seems, after his surrender to Shen-t'u Ch'ien, to have written an *apologia*, recounting his influence over Wang Mang and relating the details of the last days in his master's life. Perhaps he was with Wang Mang in the Tower and, as Wang Mu began to do, he took off his court robes, mixed with the ignorant soldiers who did not even recognize Wang Mang, and escaped. Ts'ui Fa seems to have been the sort of man who would do such a thing, and afterwards attempt to gain glory by writing an account of what had transpired. We know that this *apologia* was preserved, for it is stated that Emperor Kuang-wu had Yin Min rebut "a comparison written in behalf of Wang Mang by Ts'ui Fa" (*HHS*, Mem. 69 A: 10a), which contained prophecies and revelations.

Other features of Pan Ku's account came from separate sources. Someone undoubtedly wrote an account of the capture of Ch'ang-an as a report to the Keng-shih Emperor. We are not told who it was; the account did not come from Wang Hsien$_4$; it is too unfavorable to him. I suspect that Teng Yi was the author of this account, if there were not many such accounts—many of the details in the *HS* are connected with Teng Yi's expedition. Kung-pin Chiu, who secured Wang Mang's head, moreover carried this trophy to the Keng-shih Emperor at Yüan and received a marquisate for his deed. He undoubtedly had someone prepare an account of his exploit for presentation to the Emperor—possibly he wrote it himself. This account might naturally contain a list stating where each of Wang Mang's officials died, for Kung-pin Chiu was familiar with the court and could identify them.

The curious literary addition that several tens of soldiers killed each other in hacking Wang Mang's body to pieces may also come from his account. This incident is strikingly like the occurrence at the death of Hsiang Yü, when several tens of soldiers killed each other in the struggle for his body (*Mh* II, 320); indeed, exactly the same Chinese words are used. In that case, a reward was given to each person who finally secured a member; in the case of Wang Mang, we hear of nothing except the reward to Kung-pin Chiu; indeed, no reward seems actually to have previously been offered for Wang Mang's head, although everyone doubtless expected a reward. This incident looks like a literary embellishment to the account of Wang Mang's death, and might very likely have been added by Kung-pin Chiu in order to make an impression. If it was found in the written report of an eye-witness, we can hardly blame Pan Ku for utilizing it.

The foregoing analysis may indicate something of the nature of the sources used by Pan Ku. Of course, this analysis is wholly hypothetical; Pan Ku left no detailed account of the sources he used. But we know that he had free access to the imperial archives, and we can determine, from a knowledge of Han practises, about what sort of material must have been in those archives. Since Pan Ku spent twenty years working on his *History* while he was an official of the imperial private library and had access to the archives, he would naturally have culled out the material we find in this chapter. Then it is almost entirely a skilful piecing together of documentary material.

### Pan Piao's part in this chapter

It is difficult to determine whether most of this chapter was written by Pan Ku or by his father, Pan Piao. Stange (*ibid.*, xii) thinks that a large part came from the experiences of Pan Piao. But Pan Piao was born in A.D. 3 (*HHS*, Mem. 30 A: 5a), so that he was only twenty years of age when Wang Mang was killed. His father, Pan Chih, was living in retirement as a Gentleman at the tomb of Emperor Ch'eng, because of his tacit opposition to Wang Mang, so that Pan Piao would hardly have been acquainted in court circles. It would thus seem that only a negligible part of this chapter could have come from Pan Piao's own experiences. In a work made up largely of piecemeal quotations from documentary sources, we would hardly expect any differences in style between father and son. Pan Piao became later only a minor official in some of the capital offices; he was sent out to hold office in a city of the present Anhui and later to one in Hopei, so that he hardly had access to the numerous sources available to Pan Ku. The *HHS* says that Pan Ku considered his father's account not to have been sufficiently detailed (*HHS*, Mem. 30 A: 7b), and, in his own preface, Pan Ku does not mention his father's work. I suspect that Pan Piao did not have much to do with the "Memoir of Wang Mang," although it is impossible to prove such a statement.

## The reliability of this account

Pan Ku has often been suspected of bias against Wang Mang. He indeed condemns Wang Mang in the severest terms—his eulogy (99 C: 29a–30a) could hardly have been more drastic. His family, too, suffered from Wang Mang. In the reign of Emperor Ch'eng (during ca. 32–18 B.C.), Pan Ku's clan had for a time been very close to the throne, enjoying an eminence that was said to have shaken the empire (100 A: 6a). About 1 B.C., however, Pan Ku's grandfather had been accused of a capital crime by Wang Mang's associates and compelled to retire from official life (100 A: 5b). Hence the Pan clan was not in sympathy with Wang Mang, although it took no part in the rebellions against him. In the disorder after the death of Wang Mang, Pan Piao fled to the present Kansu, where he finally joined Emperor Kuang-wu's forces, and later returned to the capital with them. Pan Ku was moreover a loyal adherent of the Later Han dynasty; he was highly honored by and intimate with its second emperor (*HHS*, Mem. 30 A: 8b). He thus had ample reason to be prejudiced against Wang Mang.

There is, however, little or no evidence that he actually distorted his *History* because of any such prejudice. In the first place, his method of writing history by extensively quoting sources was itself a safeguard. If there had been any considerable distortion of the facts on his part, the large amount of quotation from contemporary documents would enable us to discover such distortion.

The high literary quality of Wang Mang's edicts and of his courtiers' memorials indeed probably caused Pan Ku to admire them greatly and to quote them extensively. He was actually attracted to this age, because of its Confucian spirit. Yin Min, with whom Pan Ku worked on "The Fundamental Annals of the Epochal Exemplar, [Emperor Kuang-wu]," (*HHS*, Mem. 30 A: 8a), found it impossible to rebut Ts'ui Fa's *apologia* for Wang Mang, probably because it was so thoroughly Confucian in its spirit and sayings. All he could say was that the sages had written no prophetic writings and that the dissection of characters to derive meanings from them was almost the same as vulgarity (*HHS*, Mem. 69 A: 10a). Wang Mang's portents were so Confucian and were presented with so much Confucian learning that probably the only possible refutation was that offered tacitly by Pan Ku—that they were fabrications.

In the second place, Pan Ku seems personally to have cherished a high ideal of historical accuracy. He does not tell good stories for their own sake, as did Szu-ma Ch'ien. His literary style may have suffered thereby; the ambitious Szu-ma Ch'ien seems to have told dramatic stories, whereas Pan Ku clung to what he conceived to be the truth. Pan Ku's spirit was that of the fifty-odd Confucians whom Emperor Wu asked (ca. 110 B.C.) to determine the ancient ceremonies for the imperial sacrifices *feng* and *shan*, which that Emperor proposed to reestablish. Failing to discover any detailed account of these rites, they replied that they could not determine them, and the Emperor himself fixed these rites (*HS* 58: 12a, b).

This spirit of historical accuracy was nourished by the famous story in the *Tso-chuan* (Dk. Hsiang, XXV; Legge, p. 514), concerning the historiographers in the state of Ch'i. When, in 548 B.C., Ts'ui Chu's followers killed Duke Chuang, who had illegally entered the former's house, the Grand Clerk is said to have written on his records, "Ts'ui Chu assassinated his prince." Ts'ui Chu had the clerk put to death, but his younger brother, who succeeded to the position, made the same record. (Official posts were hereditary in the clans of their occupants.) Ts'ui Chu had this brother in turn put to death, but the third brother, on succeeding to the position, made the same record. So Ts'ui Chu forgave the last brother and let the record stand. Meanwhile the Clerk For the South, hearing that the clan of the Grand Clerk had been extinguished, had taken his writing tablets and started for the court, evidently intending to make the same record when he would succeed to the post of Grand Clerk. Upon hearing that the record had been made, he however returned home. This story, whether true or not, must have been a powerful stimulus in ancient times to a correct recording of history, since it was the picture of the ideal clerk.

One of the accusations made against Liu Hsin[1a] was that he had "done away with the traditions about the classics handed down from generation to generation by his teachers"—he seems to have merely changed the principles of portent-interpretation (Cf. 99 C: 14b & n. 14.6). There was thus in certain strains of Confucianism a strong tradition of fidelity to the facts of history. Pan Ku, a thorough-going Confucian, had this strong incentive to give an unprejudiced picture of even a ruler whom he reprobated deeply.

In the third place, the Pan clan had not actually been harmed by Wang Mang, and had good reason to be attached to his aunt, the Grand Empress

Dowager nee Wang. Pan Ku's own great-aunt had become a favorite of Emperor Ch'eng and came to be entitled the Favorite Beauty nee Pan. She retired from the imperial court in 18 B.C., when she became unwillingly involved in an intrigue. She then devoted herself to the care of the Grand Empress Dowager, who became fond of her (100 A: 5b). Wang Mang belonged to the same social group as Pan Ku's grandfather and great-uncles. Wang Mang indeed treated them as his own brothers and wore mourning for Pan Ku's great-uncle (before 1 B.C.; 100 A: 5b). Pan Ku's grandfather, Pan Chih, who was a commandery official during the reign of Emperor P'ing, was impeached by Wang Mang's associates for having failed to forward to the throne a laudatory report, which he probably knew was false. Through the intercession of the Grand Empress Dowager, he was not punished, and retired from active life *with his former salary* to the funerary park of Emperor Ch'eng. Thus Pan Ku's clan was able to remain unmolested in safe obscurity during the reign of Wang Mang and had no reason for any active animosity towards Wang Mang. The family income came from Wang Mang's treasury.

In the fourth place, the popular reaction against Wang Mang was so thorough that the Later Han dynasty did not need to encourage propaganda against him, so that a prejudiced account was not expected. Pan Ku was moreover born nine years after Wang Mang died, so that he came of a generation which was able to view Wang Mang dispassionately. He wrote half a century after Wang Mang's age, when active resentment had had time to die down.

In the fifth place, Pan Ku seems to have clung to a historian's objective valuation of events, and refused to over-value events in order to make an impression. For example, he did not record all the early revolts on the part of the Liu clan against Wang Mang, which he might have done in order to exalt the Han dynasty. He tells merely of Liu Ch'ung (99 A: 27a) and of Liu K'uai (99 B: 7b, 8a); it is only through an incidental mention in a memorial by Sun Chien that we learn of Liu Ts'eng and Liu Kuei, who also revolted (99 B: 13b). Probably these latter two revolts were so ineffective that Pan Ku did not consider them worth recounting. He even gives an outline of Wang Mang's book of propaganda and quotes its conclusion at length (99 B: 9a–11a), without attempting any rebuttal. The coincidences and analogies he quotes are quite adequate to convince a superstitiously inclined person of Wang Mang's legitimacy. Pan Ku does thus seem to try to give a fair view of Wang Mang and to be objective in his presentation of the evidence. I began my study of this chapter with a decided prejudice against Pan Ku (expecting him to be prejudiced) and in favor of Wang Mang, but the weight of the primary sources quoted by Pan Ku and the facts he recounts forced me to reverse my opinion and to agree with Pan Ku in condemning Wang Mang. There is every evidence that Pan Ku really tried and largely succeeded in giving an objective and reliable account of Wang Mang.

## The literary quality of this chapter

The "Memoir of Wang Mang" is a literary masterpiece, in which the author largely succeeds in giving the reader the impression that Wang Mang left upon his contemporaries. Upon first reading it, Wang Mang appears at the outset as an unusually able and upright person, ambitious perhaps, but of uncommon high-mindedness. He outdoes his age in scrupulous morality, and his few off-color deeds, such as his purchase of a slave-girl and the supplanting of Shun-yü Chang, appear as quite excusable in such an unusual person. Even the execution of his son, Huo, appears as sheer uprightness, not ruthlessness. His handling of the crisis at the death of Emperor Ai is magnificent, and the clever way he afterwards disposed of those who might thwart him brings applause. His steady humility and princely generosity fill one with admiration, just as they did the public of his time. As clever intrigues, one after another, bring success and he is praised, rewarded, and raised to heights never before known in Chinese history, a casual reader may well feel approval of this hero, although the approval may not be so whole-hearted when one remembers his ruthless crushing of his oldest son, of the Wei clan, and their associates, and the cruel way he secured settlers for the new Hsi-hai Commandery. (It is not until one has read through the whole account to the end and recognizes Wang Mang's character in its full depth of ruthless self-centeredness and shrewd deception, that these early events take on a sinister, not a benignant aspect. This masterly effect is achieved by the simple expedient of relating facts objectively and leaving their interpretation for the most part to the reader. [Exceptions to this entire objectivity are confined to adjectives and phrases, the condemnatory nature of which are deliberately hightened in the translation, in order to indicate the author's inner attitude. Cf. 99 A: 1b, 4b, 6b, 8b.] It is not, for example, until Wang Mang's last legitimate son has died that we are informed of the four children he begat in his three years of retirement at his estate, just as his public did not know of this fact until that time. Then we realize that he was no high-minded monogamist, but an iron-willed hypocrite, ready to conceal anything from the public.)

As portent follows portent with ever increasing impressiveness, and as rebellions are crushed, we are filled with admiration for this able statesman, and realize that his public approved of his taking the throne. When he attains the height of his power and ascends the throne with seeming reluctance, we feel that he has secured his just deserts. He appears as the conscientious Confucian, bent on obedience to the examples of the ancient sage-kings, determined to perfect his state in all particulars.

Then, as unwise and oppressive measures follow one after another, as he crushes ruthlessly his old followers, Chen Feng and his party, we realize the tremendous force for evil that he incarnated, and we begin to guess something of the tortures in store for the country. When the people are driven to banditry, when his own grandson and his son plot against his life, and when finally even his three highest officials plot to abduct him, we feel that he is getting only his just deserts. When however the collapse comes, and Wang Mang appears as a tired old man, sleeping only on his stool (99 C: 24a), wearing himself out to the end in an iron determination to vanquish even hopeless circumstances, using every means except the right ones, our indignation turns to pity, and the final massacre becomes not merely the inevitable result of his deeds, but a real tragedy, for the whole account constitutes a masterly portrayal of overweening ambition and its inevitable result.

Pan Ku has moreover achieved this wonderful effect, not by a free composition, but by piecing together documents in the right order, clinging to the facts as he found them—a work of extraordinary artistry. Sometimes the machinery does creak, as when we are given the long list of appointments and enactments made when Wang Mang ascended the throne, but such things are inevitable in a history that attempts to be complete. When the edicts and memorials drag out their weary length and the flowery parallels are repeated again and again, we begin to get weary, until we realize that we are being treated to samples of the age's literature. It is rather surprising that the whole account is not dull and long-winded from beginning to end. A lesser artist would have made it so. Pan Ku saw his opportunity for producing an unusually artistic history out of dry-as-dust materials and solved the problem of doing so. Such an achievement is nothing less than a work of genius.

### Historical problems connected with Wang Mang

Because this chapter is not accompanied by memoirs that elaborate the dry facts given in its chronological outline, as was the case with the "Imperial Annals," but is itself a historical unit, it is not necessary in this introduction to present matters omitted from this chapter, as was done previously. The only important matters not presented fully in this chapter are the economic measures adopted by Wang Mang, and they are discussed fully in the appendices.

The important problems concerning Wang Mang up to the time of Emperor P'ing's death have been discussed in the introduction to that Emperor's "Annals." It remains here to discuss two further matters:

102

Why was there so little opposition to Wang Mang's seizure of the throne? and, What were the reasons for his fall?

## How Wang Mang secured general approval for his usurpation

As was pointed out previously, Wang Mang gained his honors by espousing thoroughly the Confucian faith and utilizing its traditions. After Emperor P'ing's death, Confucian principles were used to exalt Wang Mang by persons who believed they would be benefited by his elevation. Thereby they raised him to the throne.

Confucianism has had a curiously ambivalent attitude towards existing rulers. Confucius was himself a legitimist; he tried to strengthen the power of the ruler in his own state of Lu against the noble clans who were usurping that power. The *Spring and Autumn* has been interpreted, from ancient times, as indicating an attempt on the part of Confucius to exalt the position of the Son of Heaven (the Chou King) against the feudal nobles who were usurping that power. Thus Confucianism has stood for loyalty to the titular ruler of the state and the exaltation of his power against other claimants for power. This fact is, I think, the ultimate reason that China has never had any successful line of nobles, such as the Shoguns, who ruled for a succession of faineant emperors.

On the other hand, Confucianism has included the splendid doctrine of Heaven's Mandate, by virtue of whose possession a dynasty rules, but which may be lost by wicked or incapable rulers. This doctrine has been of inestimable ethical benefit to China and has probably been responsible for the generally good character of Chinese rule. The teaching that "Heaven's mandate is not constant" (*Book of Odes*, III, i, i, 5; Legge, p. 430) was dinned into the ears of Chinese heir-apparents by their Confucian tutors and ministers, so that rulers were induced to attempt being models for the empire, for the sake of keeping themselves on the throne and of perpetuating their dynastic lines. In Former Han times at least, the character of the emperors was generally higher than that of their brothers and cousins, who were petty kings. Confucianism has both supported existing dynasties and also, when a dynasty has shown itself feeble, has helped to bring about its fall.

By the end of Former Han times, Confucianism had absorbed and modified the teachings of the Yin-and-Yang school and the school of the Five Powers. The latter school asserted that the coming of each dynasty had been heralded by portents. This belief was accepted by Han Confucianism. The heralding of great rulers by supernatural portents is a widespread ancient belief; it could be justified in Han China by many ancient myths concerning the founders of the Chou dynasty and others, which myths were accordingly incorporated into the Confucian tradition.

103

Wang Mang's many portents were quite Confucian.

In Chou times, divination and magical practises were part of the state religion, and many examples of both are to be found in the *Tso-chuan*, so that the acceptance of magical performances of many sorts became part of the Confucian imitation of ancient practises. The famous Hsün-tzu, whose interpretation of Confucian theory dominated Han Confucianism, had indeed attacked superstition of all sorts, even denying the existence of any spirits whatever, but the anti-superstitious phase of his teaching was not adopted by Han thinkers. Wang Mang's extensive use of magic, especially in the closing phase of his reign, was quite Confucian. His use of the divining-board when the Palace was being attacked (99 C: 27a) was copied directly from the account of the Grand Astrologer in the *Chou-li*. The magical sacrifices, by which he expected to attain immortality, were probably also considered to be Confucian. They were suggested by Su Yo, who is entitled a magician (*fang-shih;* 25 B: 22b). Magic was then probably considered a Confucian practise, for the *Chou-li* includes among the imperial officials such magical offices as the Grand Augur (Biot, II, 69), the Master of Augury (*Pu-shih; ibid.* 74), Diviners (*Chan-jen; ibid.* 78), the Interpreter of Dreams (*Chan-meng; ibid.* 82), the Grand Intercessor (*T'ai-chu; ibid.* 85), the Imprecator (*Tsu-chu; ibid.* 101), the Chief of the Shamans (*Szu-wu; ibid.* 102), the Male and Female Shamans (*Nan-, Nü-wu; ibid.* 103, 104), the Hereditary Magical Chancellor (*Fang-hsiang-shih; ibid.* 225), and the Shaman for Horses (*Wu-ma; ibid.* 259). Indeed, many practises which later became specifically Taoist seem to have been considered Confucian in Former Han times; Liu Hsiang₄ₐ, one of the outstanding Confucians, spent much time and money, in his younger days, in attempting to make alchemistic gold. Since Confucianism stressed the imitation of ancient practises, magic, alchemy, and superstition entered this stream of thought with little hindrance. They seem only later to have been cast out, especially in Sung times.

Wang Mang was such a convinced Confucian that he accepted its superstition and magic, and may never have doubted, even in his last hours, that the careful use of Confucian magic would eventually bring success—at least that is Ts'ui Fa's picture of him. Yet he was so worried during the last few days that he could not eat (99 C: 27a). Confucians could later explain the failure of this magic in the case of Wang Mang by alleging that magic does not work for a usurper.

### Literary noble titles

The use of literary titles for nobles, rather than titles drawn from their fiefs, seems also to have been a specifically Confucian practise. Emperor

104

Kao gave a few such literary titles before he acquired any secure territory, such as that of Baronet Enlarging Our Territory, given to Li Yi-chi. Li Yi-chi was the first Confucian whom Emperor Kao was able to endure. When this emperor later took the throne, with characteristic common sense, he gave only titles taken from some fief. There were a few other literary titles, all of which were similarly unimportant. The first important and permanent literary title in Han times was Emperor Wu's title for the noble he enfeoffed to carry on the sacrifices to the Chou dynasty, the Baronet Baron Descendant of the Chou Dynasty. The practise of enfeoffing a descendant of a supplanted dynasty to carry on the ancestral sacrifices of that dynasty is itself Confucian and this practise is recorded in the Confucian Classics as having been performed by the founders of the Chou dynasty. In the course of time, as Confucian influence became stronger, more and more literary titles appeared. When Emperor Yüan took the throne, he appointed K'ung Pa, a descendant of Confucius who had been this Emperor's teacher, as Baronet in Recompense for [Confucius'] Perfection (81: 15a). He also raised the title for the descendant of the Chou dynasty to be that of marquis. Emperor Ch'eng furthermore appointed a Marquis Continuing and Honoring the Ancestral Sacrifices of the Yin Dynasty, and then raised both these last two marquises to the rank of duke.

Wang Mang at first continued this practise of giving literary titles only to those nobles continuing ancient lines. In A.D. 1, Confucius was posthumously made Duke Hsüan-ni as Recompense for Perfection. As time went on, the Confucian literary flavor of such titles attracted him more and more, and the magical properties of such names made them important. Confucius was said to have emphasized the "rectification of names". That statement was now taken to imply the giving of magically effective titles. After he came to the throne, Wang Mang used almost none but literary titles for his nobles, his officials, and his generals. I have attempted the difficult and dubious task of translating them, in order to indicate their literary and magical flavor.

Wang Mang changed the titles of his officials to phrases found in the Confucian classics. These titles are sometimes curious, but always literary. Since it takes at least two words to make an unmistakable title, and since, in a speech of Shun, the *Book of History* contains the phrase "my forester," Wang Mang entitled one of his officials, the My Forester. The Chinese phrase, because of the cryptic nature of Chinese words, does not openly convey the nonsensical connotation of the English, but the meaning is exactly as I have translated it. In the titles of his generals, magical connotations seem to have overbalanced purely literary ones; Wang Mang seems indeed to have relied largely upon his literary-magical titles for military success. That was a legitimate conclusion from the strain of Confucianism he had imbibed.

Towards the end of his reign, the grandiose tendency of literary titles resulted in the multiplication of generalissimos and commanders-in-chief, a tendency continued in the early days of the Later Han dynasty. Indeed, Wang Mang's literary titles made such an impression on his age that the rebels against him imitated his titles. They were in good Confucian tradition.

## The doctrine of the Five Powers

Two historical circumstances were responsible for convincing intelligent people that Wang Mang should take the throne. These were the philosophical doctrine of the five elements and certain historical events that led people to believe the Han dynasty must inevitably end. This philosophical theory was not the creation of a single person or age, but changed radically during Han times. Its various forms each influenced history, so it deserves careful study.

A cyclical theory of history is natural in any early philosophy. Greece too, in the philosophies of Empedocles and others, possessed such cyclical theories. The five Chinese elements, earth, wood, metal, fire, and water, seem to have come from popular thought. Tsou Yen, in the first half of the third century B.C., made them into a cyclical succession which constituted a philsophy of history. As one element or power becomes victorious over another, the dynasty upheld by that power conquers its predecessor dynasty. Each power has its color, its appropriate month for its New Year's day, its number, its note, etc. The victory of a new power exhibits itself by supernatural portents, so that the dominant power can be determined by historical events. Hsün-tzu had interpreted the Confucian supreme deity, Heaven, as an impersonal Nature; the succession of the elements came to be considered a law of Nature. It explained the succession of dynasties and, like natural laws today, was thought to enable the prediction of future events—in this case, the next dynasty. This doctrine soon became popular and was taught instead of the earlier Confucian doctrine that a dynasty falls because of its moral inadequacies. In a period of constant civil war, this earlier Confucian theory had little empirical confirmation. In Han times, Tsou Yen's theory was taken into Confucian thought and secured wide acceptance.

The Chou dynasty, because of the red crow that appeared to King Wu (*Book of History*, Legge, II, 298) was considered to have had the virtue of fire, hence the Ch'in First Emperor adopted the virtue of water, for water conquers (quenches) fire. He adopted the corresponding month for his New Year's. But the Ch'in dynasty ruled China for only fifteen years, a time much too brief for the period a power rules, if the Chou period is taken as typical. The Han dynasty located its capital near the destroyed Ch'in capital; the last Ch'in ruler surrendered his insignia and authority to the Eminent Founder of the Han dynasty; the latter accordingly assumed that he took over the Ch'in dynasty's power of water, whose color is black. He established a temple to the Black Lord, thus increasing the number of Lords on High to five (25 A: 17b). Down to the end of the Former Han period, Palace Attendants wore black sables (98: 15a). Until the time of Emperor Wen, this theory held the field. It was championed by Emperor Kao's paladin, who became Emperor Wen's learned Lieutenant Chancellor, Chang Ts'ang.

Some other learned men were not however satisfied. A change in the dynasty indicates a change in the ruling power; earth conquers (dykes) water just as the Han dynasty conquered the Ch'in. Hence the Han dynasty should change its New Year's day, the colors of court robes, etc., to those corresponding to earth. So reasoned Chia Yi. Kung-sun Ch'en even predicted that a yellow dragon would appear to manifest what was the dynasty's virtue. Earth is yellow. In 165 B.C., a yellow dragon did appear—Chang Ts'ang was accordingly dismissed and Kung-sun Ch'en was made an Erudit. He however fell into disgrace through being connected with the charlatan, Hsin-yüan P'ing, and his proposed change in the dynastic institutions was dropped. Only in 104 B.C. did Emperor Wu officially adopt the color yellow and the power earth as Han imperial institutions (6:31b).

Meanwhile there had been other developments in this cyclical philosophy of history. Tung Chung-shu (ca. 175 - ca. 105 B.C.) proposed a tripartite succession (*san-t'ung*) of red, black, and white, which three were supposed to succeed each other concomitantly with the five powers. Emperor Wu's New Year's day was fixed in the first month in accordance with this theory.

During the peaceful decades in the early part of the Han period, Confucians moreover came to give more attention to the ancient legendary lords, Fu-hsi, Shen-nung, the Yellow Lord, Chuan-hsü, K'u, Yao, and Shun. These lords did not succeed each other by conquest. Each one was said to have resigned the throne to his successor. A cyclical theory that the powers conquer each other does not fit a history which includes such peaceful changes of dynasties. Tung Chung-shu accordingly suggested a theory by which the five powers each produces its successor: wood produces fire, that produces earth (ashes), that produces (mines) metal, that produces (melts into) water (liquid), that produces (nourishes) wood (vegetation), and so on. His *Ch'un-ch'iu Fan-lu* contains both this theory and the earlier one that each power conquers its predecessor, but he himself plainly favored the other theory of production. Through his influence it came to be accepted widely. It found a place in the "Explanation of the Trigrams (*Shuo-kua*)" (Legge, *Yi King*, App. V), which was "discovered" during 73–49 B.C. Thus it was given classical confirmation. Liu Hsiang₄ₐ developed it and gave it the weight of his great influence, so that it came to be the only one given serious consideration during the latter part of the Former Han period. The Han dynasty was now given the virtue of fire, which was supported by the story of the Eminent Founder being the son of the Red Lord (1 A: 7a). Down to 91 B.C., the imperial credentials were pure red (66: 3b), possibly because Liu Chi, when he first arose, anointed his drums with blood (1 A: 9b). Since the Ch'in dynasty had ruled for such a short period, this dynasty was considered to have achieved its conquest without securing the Mandate of Heaven and without the assistance of a power in the regular cycle. The Ch'in dynasty then constituted an intercalary period. The Han dynasty was considered to have succeeded the Chou dynasty, to the latter of which was now given the virtue of wood. The ancient lords and the three ancient dynasties were each given their appropriate power in the cyclical succession and ancient history was explained thereby. In this way, the succession of dynasties was made to appear as inevitable and natural as the succession of the seasons (cf. Ku Chieh-kang, *Kushih-pien*, V, 404–617).

Liu Hsiang₄ₐ was a loyal member of the imperial clan. He opposed the influence of the Wang clan so strongly that he was never given high office. This theory of dynastic succession was then not originally intended to aid Wang Mang. It however aided mightily in bringing him to the throne.

This theory made intelligent people think that a change in the dynasty was inevitable. The succession of the powers moreover made them think it would be possible to predict the next dynasty. Fire produces earth. The Wang clan claimed descent from the Yellow Lord, who had the virtue of earth. This genealogy almost certainly antedated Wang Mang; it seems to have been merely a noble clan's attempt to exalt itself by claiming divine descent. There were other clans also claiming descent from this mythical ruler. The Wang clan however dominated the government for over three decades, so that it became only natural for people to point to this clan when they talked about the next dynasty.

Astrology and prognostication also played a part in this speculation. Generations before the Wang clan ever appeared at court, Lu Wen-shu's (fl. 73 B.C.) great-uncle had calculated by astrology that after a period of three times seven decades of years, the Han dynasty would end (cf. 99 A: n. 34.5). During the reign of Emperor Ch'eng, Ku Yung, a famous exponent of the *Book of Changes* and interpreter of portents, revived this prediction. This period of 210 years would end in A.D. 4. When, in 12 B.C., there was an eclipse of the sun on New Year's day, followed by thunder without clouds in May and the appearance of Halley's comet in the autumn, the court became greatly exercised. Shun-yü Chang, an imperial maternal relative, was sent to secure Ku Yung's interpretation. The latter replied that the number of portents during the last twenty years was greater than in the *Spring and Autumn* period or during the reigns of all the preceding Han emperors; the period of three sevens of decades was coming to an end; and the lot indicated by the hexagram *wu-wang* (then meaning "hopelessness") was coming up. He went on to intimate that the essence of the power earth was being born (85: 15b–16b). His memorial made a deep impression in the court. Thus in 12 B.C., there was already a general belief among intelligent persons that the Han dynasty's period was coming to an end.

When moreover Emperors Ch'eng, Ai, and P'ing died without natural heirs, people naturally saw in this extraordinary circumstance Heaven's plain intention to end the dynasty. There could indeed be hardly any surer manifestation that the supernatural powers intended to end a dynasty than that three of its rulers should in succession all have left no heir. The death of Emperor P'ing at the end of the Chinese year beginning in A.D. 5 was naturally interpreted as a confirmation of Lu Wen-shu's great-uncle's prophecy. The count of years in Emperor Kao's reign had been begun before he had even become a king (1 A: 26b); it could easily be maintained that he began one year too early. If so, Emperor P'ing died at precisely the end of the dynasty's two hundred and tenth year. People naturally concluded that the virtue of fire had expired and the virtue of earth was arising by the inexorable operation of Heaven's cyclical natural law.

Yao and Shun had each resigned the throne to his greatest minister. Wang Mang came from a clan that had now controlled the government for many decades; he himself had been raised to previously unprecedented honors. He was descended from the Yellow Lord and possessed the virtue of earth. He had done all he could to maintain the Han dynasty on the throne, but nevertheless all these events had happened. He had not been responsible for the succession of coincidences that had occurred or the philosophical theory by which they were interpreted. History runs in cycles. The laws of Heaven cannot be evaded. People naturally drew the conclusion that history was repeating itself and that Heaven had destined Wang Mang to inaugurate a new dynasty under the rule of the power earth.

The depth and sincerity of this political consequence drawn from philosophical principles is shown by the fact that it was shared by members of the Liu imperial clan itself, especially after Wang Mang's victory over Chai Yi's formidable rebellion had given apparent empirical confirmation to the belief that Wang Mang possessed the mandate of Heaven. The famous Liu Hsin$_{1a}$, who was a descendant of Liu Chiao, Emperor Kao's younger brother, actively assisted Wang Mang to take the throne. Liu Ching$_{4b}$, a descendant of Emperor Wu, presented one of the crucial portents, urging Wang Mang to take the throne (99 A: 34a, b). Liu Kung$_2$, a first cousin of Liu Hsin$_{1a}$, also presented a portent (99 B: 14a). When Liu K'uai rebelled against Wang Mang, his brother, Liu Yin$_2$, a descendant of Emperor Ching, resisted and defeated the insurrection (99 B: 7b, 8a). Altogether some thirty-two members of the Han imperial clan either presented portents to Wang Mang, offered congratulatory sayings, or arrested and informed on rebels against him. These persons and their families were granted the new imperial surname, Wang, so that they were continued in their nobilities (99 B: 14a). Some of these persons were, of course, mere sycophants, seeking continued enjoyment of their fiefs, but there were honest persons among them. If then even members of the Han imperial clan were convinced, it is not surprising that intelligent persons generally accepted Wang Mang's legitimacy. The famous writers of the day all accepted Wang Mang. Huan T'an assisted Wang Mang at the time of Chai Yi's rebellion, by publishing abroad Wang Mang's *apologia*, and in reward was enfeoffed as a Vassal (84: 17a). The philosopher, Yang Hsiung$_2$, who cared not for fame or disciples and spent his energy solely in elaborating his philosophy, wrote mandates through portents for Wang Mang (87 B: 22b). Most of the Confucians seem to have approved of Wang Mang's succession, for this seemed to be Heaven's will.

Once there was such a general expectation of Wang Mang's succession to the throne and once portents of that event were expected, it was only natural that those individuals who were bolder than others should have manufactured what was required. The first portent came in the same month that Emperor P'ing died and was offered by an official ranking next to the high ministers (99 A: 25a). After Chai Yi had been defeated, portents began to appear more frequently, until at last there were more than a dozen (99 B: 9a–10b), whereupon Wang Mang finally ascended the throne.

I do not think that Wang Mang instigated any of these portents in even as indirect a manner as he instigated the coming of the white pheasant in A.D. 1. My chief reason is that it would have been quite unnecessary for him to have done so. He had carefully weeded out of his court all those who might oppose him. His courtiers were sensitive to his feelings. They knew he was intensely ambitious and they had helped him by indirect means to secure his unusual honors, being amply rewarded for doing so. After he controlled the government and had attained his unusual titles, there was only one honor really greater than those he had received, so that when the opportunity offered itself, his courtiers, as previously, spontaneously continued to flatter his ambition.

It is furthermore worthy of note that Ai Chang's portent, which was the decisive one, upset Wang Mang's plans considerably. On Jan. 6, A.D. 9, upon the receipt of some portents, he memorialized the Grand Empress Dowager, asking to be entitled Acting Emperor and to change the year-period to Ch'u-shih, saying that he would rear the Young Prince of the Han dynasty, Liu Ying, and return the government to him when he was grown (99 A: 34a–35a). Two days later, on Jan. 8, Ai Chang's portent arrived, and it was accepted on Jan. 9 or 10 (99 A: 35b & n. 35.12), whereupon Wang Mang took the throne. Ai Chang's portent completely upset the whole situation, so that it can hardly have been planned by Wang Mang.

We have no means of knowing Wang Mang's own attitude to these portents, whether he actively welcomed them or whether he was surprised. At least he was not displeased. If he had been a doggedly faithful servant of the Han dynasty, he would have arrested and executed Hsieh Hsiao and Meng T'ung, who presented the first portent (99 A: 25a), as he had treated Tung Hung (99 A: 2b), and there would have been no more portents. When, instead, he had the portent reported to the Grand Empress Dowager, probably without any comment of his own, he let it be known to the court that he was not displeased and gave his courtiers time to make up their minds about such matters. The general opinion in the court undoubtedly became favorable to Wang Mang's advancement, so that other persons were naturally stimulated to present their portents. They knew they had nothing to lose by so doing, and might secure boundless rewards.

It is quite possible that Wang Mang did not at first really want to take the throne. He waited three full years from the time of the first portent until he finally accepted the post those portents declared was his. Confucian sentiment honored the capable minister far more than the prince; Wang Mang had been promoted to the status of a Duke of Chou, the person whom Confucius had taken as his ideal character. If Wang Mang had finally refused the throne and maintained his position as a minister, he might well have come down in history as the greatest of ancient statesman, a man who outshone even Kao-yao, Yi Yin, and the Duke of Chou. But he loved power and knew what it was to have that

111

power completely shorn from him and to be sent away to his estate in the provinces, with no prospects of further advancement. His lack of honors in his youth had made him intensely ambitious. And so, when his courtiers kept urging him, by renewed portents, to take the throne, he at last yielded to their proddings and accepted the dangerous honor. Thus his delay of three years in accepting the throne may have represented, not merely the proper Confucian modesty, but a real hesitation on his own part. Pan Ku says that in the autumn of A.D. 8 he at last plotted to secure the throne; that judgment may well be correct. Ts'ao Ts'ao (155–220 A.D.), in similar circumstances, benefited by Wang Mang's experience and never actually took the throne, although he wielded the imperial power. Wang Mang was a Confucian minister who put his minions into office and allowed them to persuade him, when the opportunity patently offered itself, to take the throne.

## Reasons for Wang Mang's fall

It remains to discuss the reasons for Wang Mang's fall. Undoubtedly the most important cause was the weather. Wang Mang seems to have come upon a period of severe droughts, which were quite as bad as those in 1876–9. The resultant social confusion, brought to fruition by failure in government, caused widespread unrest, rebellion, and his fall.

(1) Wang Mang's whole reign seems to have been a time of poor harvests. In an edict of A.D. 20, he says that since he ascended the throne, there had several times been withering droughts, plagues of locusts and caterpillars, and the harvests of grain had been sparse and lacking, so that the people had suffered from famine (C: 8a). In A.D. 11, there was a famine at the northwestern borders (94 B: 19a). In A.D. 14, there was another famine at the borders, so severe that people took to cannibalism (99 B: 26a). The most severe droughts occurred in the years A.D. 18–22, the years immediately preceding Wang Mang's fall. In A.D. 18, there was a famine in Lang-yeh Commandery (southeastern Shantung), at which time the Red Eyebrows arose (99 C: 4b). This famine continued for several years. By A.D. 20, there was already considerable vagabondage: "In Ch'ing and Hsü Provinces [present Shantung and Kiangsu], many of the common people left their villages and hamlets and wandered about as vagabonds. The aged and weak died on the roads and paths, and the vigorous entered the robber bands" (99 C: 5b). In that year, there was a prolonged rain for sixty days at the capital (99 C: 9b), but in A.D. 21, there was a great famine in Honan and east China (99 C: 12b). In that year, east of Lo-yang, grain was 2000 cash per picul, about twenty-five times its normal price (99 C: 16a). In the spring of A.D. 22, east of Shensi, there was cannibalism (99 C: 17a). In

that summer, the locusts even invaded Ch'ang-an, where they crawled about the palaces (99 C: 18a). Several hundred thousand refugees came to Shensi from the east, but famine relief in Shensi itself was inadequate and mismanaged, so that 70% to 80% of these refugees starved (99 C: 18a). At the same time, there was a famine in the middle Yangtze valley (Nan-yang Commandery; *HHS*, An. 1 A: 2a). Thus the climatic cycle made Wang Mang's later years a period of extreme stress and strain. Had there been consistently good seasons in Wang Mang's reign, as there were during the reign of Emperor Hsüan, he might have kept his throne and successfully founded another dynasty.

At the same time there was famine in the capital region itself (Kuan-chung, central Shensi). The plain in central Shensi north of the Wei River had been irrigated by some famous canals, the first of which was dug by the engineer Cheng Kuo in 237 B.C. This first canal had its intake in the ancient Ku-k'ou prefecture, not far from the place where the Ching River emerges from the mountains. North of that place, the river runs through a gorge cut in limestone; south of it the river runs through soft deep loess. This canal was *planned* to irrigate a region of 40,000 *ch'ing* (186,000 acres, 300 sq. miles), but it is doubtful if the canal was originally built on as large a scale. In 111 B.C., six subsidiary canals were dug, and in 95 B.C. at the suggestion of a Mr. Po (or Pai 白), another canal was dug nearly 200 *li* in length. This canal irrigated an additional 4500-odd *ch'ing* (20,925 acres).[1] These canals were responsible for the strength of the Ch'in state and for the economic importance of Ch'ang-an in Former Han times. It was the one region in northern China where there were no droughts or famines. The grain in the Great Granary at Ch'ang-an was untouched for over a century, so that it became rotten and could not be eaten (*HS* 24 A: 15b).

The Ching River, after it leaves the mountains, flows through soft loess to the place where it joins the Wei River. It has a considerable gradient. Erosion dug the bed of this River deeper and deeper, until the intake of these canals finally drew less and less. At first, they drew an inadequate amount of water or none at all except in times of flood, and finally they drew no water at all. At present the original intake of

[1]Cf. *SC* 29: 6–8 - *Mh* III, 523–525; Bodde, *China's First Unifier*, 59–60; Ch'ao-ting Chi, *Key Economic Areas in Chinese History*, 75–77, 83–84, 87–89; *HS* 29: 11b–12b; M.S. Bates, "Problems of Rivers and Canals," *JAOS*, 55 (1935): 304–305; S. Eliassen and O. J. Todd, "The Wei Irrigation Project in Shensi Province", *China Journal*, 17(1932): 170–180; *Shui-ching-chu* 16: 32b–33a; 19: 30a–31a, 46a; W. C. Lowdermilk & D. R. Wickes, "Ancient Irrigation in China Brought Up to Date", *Scientific Monthly*, 55 (Sept., 1942), 209–225.

these canals is about sixty feet above the river level.[2] The intake for the canal of 95 B.C. was placed somewhat higher up the river than the original intake. But continued erosion caused this intake, too, to become useless.

We are not told when these canals ceased operating. Li Tao-yüan (vi cent.), in his *Shui-ching-chu*, says they were then dry. In all probability, they ceased to draw an adequate supply of water in Wang Mang's time. On June 2, A.D. 16, the banks of the Ching River collapsed at the Ch'ang-p'ing Lodge (99 B: 29b), which was located about half-way between the intake of the canals and the Wei River. (In 35 B.C., an earthquake had previously caused these banks to collapse [9: 12a], and on May 7, 25 B.C., the high bank of this River had collapsed in Ch'ang-ling Prefecture [10: 6a], not far from the junction of this River with the Wei.) At this time, erosion had already dug the bed of the River so deep that its sides caved in—in all probability, the canals were then already useless except when there was a flood on the Ching River. Only forty miles from its junction with the Wei, the Ching River flows through the mountains in a deep gorge cut into the rock, so that the intake of any irrigation canals could not be moved further upstream with the means of digging then available.

The result was bound to be famine in the capital area itself. Hence the Ch'ang-an area became economically less important than the Yellow River area in northern Honan, and Wang Mang talked of moving his capital to Lo-yang (where Emperor Kuang-wu later actually located his capital). Already at the time of Chai Yi's rebellion (A.D. 7), there were robbers in Kuan-chung; in A.D. 21 there was so much trouble in that region that special officers had to be appointed to deal with the robbers (99 C: 12b), and in the summer of A.D. 22, there was famine even in Ch'ang-an itself (99 C: 18a). The failure of this canal, and the impossibility of relocating it, was another cause for Wang Mang's fall.

In A.D. 11, the Yellow River caused a great flood and changed its course; because it seemed to have found an easier outlet to the ocean, no attempt was made to check it (99 B: 18a), especially because Wang Mang's own ancestral area was thus protected from further floods. The climatic cycle and failure in irrigation was the most important factor in Wang Mang's fall.

H. Bielenstein, *The Restoration of the Han Dynasty*, pp. 145–153, argues that Wang Mang's fall was ultimately caused by this change in the course of the Yellow River. He has established the importance of this factor. But other factors were equally and more important.

[2]Lodermilk & Wickes, *op. cit.*, p. 211, 215.

(2) North China is a region of recurrent droughts; it was recognized in ancient times that a drought was to be expected every six or seven years on an average, and the government maintained granaries for such occurrences. Hence ordinary famines would not cause widespread suffering unless at the same time the government was inefficient. A famine year was really a time when the competence of the government was tested. The real cause for Wang Mang's fall was the failure of his government to meet the strains put upon it.

It should not be thought that Wang Mang's time was a period of general decay. There are signs that just the opposite was the case. Indeed, some circumstances seem to indicate that the period of cultural advance during Former Han times was coming to flower in an age of unusual progress. We are told that the study of anatomy was being pushed to the extent of human dissection (99 B: 30b), and that geometrical proportion was used in architectural design (99 C: 9a). Most interesting of all is the brief and cryptic account of an attempt at aviation in A.D. 19 —the earliest account in human history of an actual flight that was not mythology (99 C: 5a). The carriage with flowery baldachins (99 C: 13b, 14a) was an outstanding mechanical achievement. It may well be the case that Wang Mang's Nine Ancestral Temples were more magnificent than anything previously erected (99 C: 9b).

But Wang Mang's government exhibited many signs of widespread corruption. During the reign of Emperor Ch'eng, when his uncles controlled the government, corruption was rife. Wang Mang came to the throne by fraudulent portents, and so needed officials who would countenance fraud, with the result that they countenanced fraudulent reports on the part of their subordinates (99 C: 15b), and the government became permeated with corruption (99 B: 27a). Wang Mang himself publicly confessed that some officials would extort ransoms from innocent persons by illegally condemning them as slaves and removing the sentence upon payment of a bribe. Yet he was powerless to stop this practise (99 B: 17b). That the outrageous T'ang Tsun should have become his minister is only natural.

(3) Wang Mang enacted some very unwise administrative measures. Emperor Wu had established Inspectors of Regional Divisions, ranking at only 600 piculs, who were really spies of the central government, traveling about the commanderies, reporting upon the rule of the Administrators for those commanderies (who ranked at 2000 piculs). The Confucians did not like this unhierarchical arrangement, by which a lower-ranking official supervised a higher-ranking one; in 7 B.C., when

Wang Mang first came to power, the title and rank of these Inspectors were changed to that of Provincial Shepherd (an ancient name), so that names should correspond to reality. Emperor Ai changed these officials' titles back again to Inspector; in 1 B.C., Wang Mang again entitled them Shepherds, ranking them the same as the highest ministers. But now these Shepherds lost much of their incentive for careful supervision of their provinces. Inspectors had previously hoped that they might be promoted to the post of Administrator, if they did careful and honest work; the Shepherds could now be promoted only to one of the ministerial offices, among which there were very few openings. The result was that they were content to do little and merely held their positions (99 C: 10b). Consequently, in A.D. 21, Wang Mang was driven by the inefficiency of the provincial governments to appoint Shepherd's Superintendents and Associate Shepherds, who were to do the work previously done by the Inspectors. But it was now too late to reform a corrupt government.

Wang Mang knew how subordinates could thwart their superior, he had detailed ideas about what should be done in government, and he was suspicious of his associates. Consequently he did not give his ministers the power to decide matters themselves, but had every decision referred to himself. Since the ministers thus found themselves merely executive officers, they ceased to feel any responsibility for their offices and merely transmitted business to Wang Mang, awaiting his orders.

He was especially suspicious of his private secretaries, the Masters of Writing, who could control the government by withholding the information which came to the throne in the form of memorials. Hence he permitted eunuchs and members of his entourage to open and read memorials to the throne, with the result that memorials sometimes never even reached the Masters of Writing and were not dealt with in proper fashion.

The most important feature in government, according to Confucius' supposed teaching, was the rectification of names; if that were done, all governmental difficulties would automatically be solved. Wang Mang hence deliberated long and profoundly on geographical arrangements, rites, and music, endeavoring to make them accord with classical precedents. From dawn to dark, he discussed these matters with his ministers. He himself was a learned Confucian, the first such literatus to be on the throne; he surrounded himself with the best scholars he could find. But the classical precedents were by no means unambiguous, many matters were treated only implicitly in the Classics, and there were good arguments both for and against most decisions. Wang Mang was not like Emperor Wu, a dilettante who could blithely decide out of his own consciousness such a weighty matter as the proper rites for the important imperial sacrifices *feng* and *shan*. Wang Mang was a thoroughly conscientious man, who felt the importance of properly determining each matter. Hence his discussions with his ministers and advisors were interminable. Since no one else could make the final decision about precisely how classical precedents should be applied, Wang Mang had to decide these matters himself. After he had decided, he would change his mind again and again. In the case of some place-names, in his anxiety to get them exactly right, he changed them as much as five times, finally returning to the original name! (99 B: 25a, b) In addition, he had himself to decide on the multifarious details of an autocratic government. He worked all night at his documents, but even then he was unable to keep up with the government business.

The result was, as Pan Ku says (99 B: 26b–27b), that, since Wang Mang had little leisure to examine matters conscientiously, and yet was determined to do so, law-cases were not decided for years, prisoners were not released from prison except when there was an amnesty, vacancies in the government were not filled with permanent occupants for years, and the government in general could do little except routine work. Corruption could not be checked and things went from bad to worse. The ruler was too conscientious and too suspicious to delegate power and the governmental duties were too multifarious for him to manage.

As a result of such an eager concern about general principles, Wang Mang was led to make serious mistakes in particular matters. When the famine in the east was at its hight and the bandits were even capturing cities, Wang Mang decided that they must be put down at all costs. The man he had put over the Shepherds of that region protested (99 C: 16a), but nevertheless, in A.D. 22, Wang Mang sent 100,000 troops into the famine regions. The granaries were empty and could not feed them, so the troops foraged among the people, with dire results. It is not surprising that the people found the troops a greater calamity than the bandits, for the soldiers, under the guise of protecting the people, took what little food was left. The curious verse quoted in 99 C: 17b probably represents a mild version of what the people felt.

Wang Mang furthermore enacted into a systematized law the procedure, begun by Emperor Hsüan, of reducing official salaries at a time of drought or calamity. He made the various officials of the central court and the provinces each guarantors for a certain region. At the end of the year, when the yearly reports from the commanderies were presented, the amount of damage to the crops in each part of the empire was to be reported in percentages, and the number of dishes on the imperial table was to be reduced in proportion. At the same time, the officials guaranteeing the various sections in which there were calamities were to have their salaries reduced in proportion to the suffering in their region (99 B: 28a–29b). It was an idealistic proposal, but the result was that officials could not anticipate the amount of their salaries and income, so that they exacted fees and presents to support themselves. So bribery and corruption became general.

Wang Mang furthermore imitated a practise of Chou times, when official positions were largely hereditary. In A.D. 14, he made all his important provincial offices hereditary in the clans of his nobles (99 B: 24a). Thus he eliminated the incentive to efficient government that had been introduced by the Ch'in dynasty and continued by the Han dynasty, which regimes gave office for merit, not for family connections. Wang Mang probably thought he was doing away with another of the corruptions inherited from the Ch'in regime (6: 39a), but a more unwise measure could hardly have been conceived. As a result, he had to dismiss a noble from his title in order to get rid of a corrupt provincial official, and promotions for merit from one grade to another in the provincial government were made impossible. Wang Mang seems to have removed most of the stimuli to good government that the Ch'in and Han dynasties had laboriously set up. It is not surprising that the government in the provinces degenerated badly.

He furthermore exhibited the conceit that sometimes comes to self-made men. He did not like to listen to admonitions, and became angry when his proposals were opposed, even for the wisest reasons. Hence the people who had the best interests of the country at heart came to avoid him and he failed to learn the truth about things. He dismissed those who explained that undue taxation had produced banditry (99 C: 2b). He removed Feng Ch'ang, his Communicator (the state treasurer), because the latter protested against the state monopolies (99 C: 2a), and he dismissed a newly appointed Shepherd of the central Yangtze region, Fei Hsing, who had plans for reducing banditry by lightening the pressure of these monopolies upon his people (99 C: 3a). He even removed his best general, Chuang Yu, when the latter remonstrated against his unwise plans (99 C: 5b). As a consequence, the eunuchs, such as Wang Yeh₅, merely flattered Wang Mang and deceived him about the condition of the people (99 C: 18b).

(4) Wang Mang seems to have been personally stingy and publicly extravagant with government funds. He hoarded the gold he secured, and would not expend it even in an emergency (99 C: 25b). He liked to give noble titles, and at first did not give fiefs to his nobles, on the pretext that the country's geographical arrangements had not yet been settled, with the result that some of his nobles had to work for a living (99 B: 19b). Within noble estates he set up "reserved fields," nominally

later to be used as fiefs for vassals, but really to economize on the incomes paid to the nobles and to reward or punish them by decreasing or increasing these reserved areas (99 B: 25a).

Wang Mang seems to have furthermore established quite a number of sinecure positions in the court. The Han dynasty had three highest ministers (*kung*) and nine high ministers (*ch'ing*); Wang Mang established four Coadjutors, three highest ministers, and four generals, making eleven officials who ranked as highest ministers (*kung*). The number of important subordinates to the high ministers (*ch'ing*) was also increased. The Han dynasty had only a few such, depending on the amount of business in each office. Such an unsymmetrical arrangement did not however suit literary Confucian ideals; Wang Mang appointed three grandees and nine Officers of the First Rank to each one of the nine highest ministers, making 27 and 81 respectively of these two grades. He also instituted seven grandees whose duty it was to admonish the emperor (99 B: 4a), Directors of Mandates from the Five Majestic Principles, whose duty it was to spread propaganda, and four Masters, four Companions and nine Libation Officers to the Heir-apparent, all of whom ranked the same as the highest of the high ministers. These additional salaries must have been quite expensive.

Outside the capital, Wang Mang increased the number of commanderies from 103 to 125 and the number of prefectures from 1314 to 2203 (28 Bii: 48b; 99 B: 25a), with a corresponding increase in the number of administrative officials and in the cost of administration. He frequently sent out commissioners and others to supervise the administration. In A.D. 11, he sent out 55 Generals of the Gentlemen-at-the Palace and 55 Administrators of the Laws Clad in Embroidered Garments to control the large commanderies along the border (99 B: 17a). His commissioners followed each other on the roads, one after another, sometimes ten chariots-full a day; when the public granaries and post-stations could no longer supply their needs, these commissioners forcibly took horses, carriages, and supplies from the people along the road (99 C: 7a).

Wang Mang also greatly expanded his nobility. In the time of Emperor Wu, before the great purge, there had been some twenty kings and about two hundred marquises (*HFHD*, ch. vi, app. III); in A.D. 12, Wang Mang had already appointed 796 nobles of the first five ranks (who corresponded to the kings and marquises of Han times). In addition there were Baronesses and Vassals (99 B: 19b). Thus Wang Mang's nobility must have been a great drain upon the empire, even though he did not give his nobles the full amount of their allowances.

(5) Perhaps Wang Mang's greatest extravagance was his military expeditions. Emperor Wu had flailed the Huns until, after his death,

119

they were glad to submit and make peace with the Chinese; he had attacked the barbarians in all directions, so that eventually the border peoples recognized the might of the Chinese and kept the peace. Wang Mang upset this peace in the interests of a Confucian imitation of ancient practises. The Han rulers followed the Ch'in practise of calling themselves emperors, consequently they could entitle the rulers of neighboring vassal states kings, just as their own greatest vassals were entitled kings. But, at the beginning of the Chou period, the ruler had entitled himself king and his greatest nobles were only dukes, so Wang Mang followed the Confucian precept, "Heaven has not two suns nor has Earth two kings" (*Mencius* V, i, iv, 1 attributes this saying to Confucius), and degraded all his highest nobles to be dukes. They accepted the change of title without a murmur, for they knew it was a change in name only. When however Wang Mang came to change similarly the titles of his barbarian vassals, trouble ensued. They did not understand the necessity of conforming to Confucian principles, became suspicious, and felt insulted. Eventually the Huns, the Kao-chü-li in the present Manchuria, the petty states in the Western Frontier Regions, and those in Szechuan and Yünnan all revolted, and Wang Mang had to face border raids and war in all directions.

The worst trouble was with the Huns. When *Shan-yü* Hu-han-hsieh had come to submit to Emperor Hsüan, the latter had treated him as a guest, had ranked him above all the Chinese nobles, and had given him an imperial seal as his sign of office, with the word *hsi* (denoting an imperial seal) in its inscription. Emperor Hsüan was not Confucian enough to esteem correct terminology above the establishment of friendly relations with a neighboring state. Wang Mang's envoys carried to the *Shan-yü* a new seal bearing the Hsin dynasty's name, with the word *chang* (which was used for a noble or official seal) in its inscription. The *Shan-yü* unsuspectingly made the exchange; afterwards, when the seal was read to him, he thought the Emperor's intention was to degrade him to be a mere noble, ranking below the Chinese vassal kings, and asked to have his old seal back. But the senior Lieutenant to the Chinese envoy had thoughtfully smashed the old seal. As a result of this deed and some other disagreements, the Huns raided the Chinese borders, capturing countless prisoners (to be sold as slaves) and animals, welcomed and shielded Chinese rebels against Wang Mang, and the *Shan-yü* announced that he owed allegiance to the Han dynasty, not to the Hsin dynasty.

Wang Mang now declared war and planned a grandiose attack, which would send twelve armies by different routes simultaneously into Hun territory, numbering altogether 300,000 men, carrying provisions for

300 days. He would overthrow this *Shan-yü* and divide his territory among fifteen *Shan-yü*. But General Chuang Yu replied, with the carefulness of a staff officer, that 300 days' provisions would require 18 *hu* (10 bushels or 36 liters) of grain per man, which amount could only be transported by oxen; that the border commanderies could not furnish so much grain, so that it would take more than a year to collect and transport it from the parts of the empire from which it could be secured; that an ox would need 20 *hu* more grain; that, since Hun territory was lacking in water and grass, experience had shown that within 100 days all the oxen would be dead, while the balance of the provision could not be carried by men, so that it would be best to send a light expedition in order to come up with the rapidly moving Huns.

Wang Mang would not heed, and in A.D. 10, he ordered the expedition to be formed. The result was that large numbers of men collected at the borders, where they waited for their provisions. Having inadequate shelter and provisions, they foraged among the Chinese of those regions. But there had been a famine and scarcity in the northwestern borders (94 B: 19a); the result was that the farmers of the borders left their homes and scattered. The armies never started out and the men merely encamped at the border. Wang Mang had to maintain some 200,000 guards at the borders, who tyrannized over the people, with the result that the farmers turned robbers and raided neighboring commanderies. It took more than a year to put down these robbers and by that time the border commanderies were practically empty (99 B: 27b). In A.D. 19, he summoned an army and levied taxes for another expedition against the Huns, planning to put Hsü-pu Tang on the Hun throne. Chuang Yu's sound arguments led to the army not being sent out, and Wang Mang had to content himself with dismissing Chuang Yu (99 C: 4b–5b). In A.D. 21, Wang Mang had grain and currency worth millions of cash transported to the borders to prepare for an expedition against the Huns. But the expedition never started out (99 C: 12b). Wang Mang squandered his people's livelihood and lives in an attempt to secure an empty fame.

A similar result eventuated on the southwestern borders, with even greater wastage of men and wealth. By A.D. 16, all the border dependencies had broken from their allegiance to the Chinese. Wang Mang showed the typical learned Confucian's inability to understand peoples who possess a different cultural tradition and he was not sufficiently teachable to learn how to employ military force efficiently.

(6) Like all rulers who think of themselves as great, Wang Mang entertained grandiose plans of various sorts. In A.D. 12, he planned a grand tour to the east, and an order was dispatched that 450,000 rolls of silk

should be collected to defray its cost. Only half of this amount arrived, so the expedition was put off (99 B: 21b). Wang Mang believed he had succeeded to the throne by virtue of the power earth, which was equated, not with one of the four directions, but with the center, so he concluded that he should make his capital at the center of the earth, and fixed upon Lo-yang, the ancient capital of the Chou dynasty. In A.D. 14, he proposed to make four less expensive tours in the four directions, and afterwards go to Lo-yang (99 B: 22a, b). He was again dissuaded from making these tours, and put off the change of the capital to a date seven years later. Meanwhile he sent two ministers to build palaces, temples, and altars at Lo-yang. In A.D. 20, he also spent some ten billions of cash in building his Nine Ancestral Temples near Ch'ang-an (99 C: 10a). In A.D. 23, when rebellion became serious, he exhibited his nonchalance by marrying a second time, sending the bride's family as betrothal presents the sum of 30,000 catties of actual gold (235,347 troy oz. or 7,320,000 g.; 99 C: 20a).

(7) With such heavy and unusual expenses, it is not surprising that Wang Mang should have resorted to depreciating the currency, making government monopolies out of especially profitable enterprises, and increasing the taxes. These and other economic measures are discussed elsewhere (cf. App. II). In so far as they were not soon rescinded, they represented increased burdens upon the people. Wang Mang seems to have drained the country's wealth. The suffering drove great hordes of people to banditry and rebellion, until even the people of the capital hated him so much that they were anxious to kill him and restore the Han dynasty to the throne.

(8) Wang Mang mistreated his own relatives and followers, so that he did not secure the permanent and unchallengeable loyalty of any group. He did not execute his Lieutenant Chancellors, as Emperor Wu had done, but he remained severe towards all, so that no one could permanently count on his favor and he could trust no one completely.

In his own family, he seems to have been the stern and strict father, who sacrifices his family to his own ambition. He executed three of his four legitimate sons: his eldest, Yü, because of an intrigue that opposed his own plans (99 A: 16b); his second, Huo, because he murdered a slave (99 A: 3b); and the third, Lin$_1$, because an unfortunate liaison had put him in the position where the son was afraid he would be executed if he did not first assassinate his father (99 C: 11a, b). The fourth son, An, was not quite right in his mind and died before his father (99 C: 11b). People naturally thought this series of deaths was Heaven's judgment upon Wang Mang.

Wang Mang was equally severe upon his relatives. He executed his own nephew, Kuang, because the latter had been responsible for a judicial murder (99 A: 33b).   He also executed a grandson and a grand-daughter Tsung and Fang, because the first had in a silly fashion anticipated coming to the throne, by having a picture painted of himself in imperial garb and preparing other imperial paraphernalia (99 C: 3a, b), and the latter had performed black magical ceremonies against her mother-in-law and had murdered a slave to hide the matter (99 C: 3b).

In his younger days, Wang Mang, in his intrigues for power, had not spared his relatives.   Shun-yü Chang was his first cousin, and seemed likely to inherit the power Wang Mang wanted; the latter thereupon had no scruples about informing on his cousin's crimes and getting him executed (99 A: 2a).   Wang Mang sent away from the court and later executed his own uncle and another first cousin, Wang Li₅ and Wang Jen, because he feared their influence with the Grand Empress Dowager (99 A: 4b, 16b).

Chen Han and his son, Feng, were Wang Mang's closest intimates, and had assisted most actively in securing for Wang Mang his unusual honors as a minister.   When however Wang Mang advanced to the throne, they were not entirely pleased and were a little frightened at the prospect, for they were not overweeningly ambitious.   Chen Han died in office; when Chen Feng's son, Hsün, ambitiously presented a portent ordering him to marry Wang Mang's daughter, the latter decided it was time to show his power and overawe the court.   He executed Chen Feng and Chen Hsün, together with their associates, who included two sons of the famous Liu Hsin₁ₐ and his own first cousin, Wang Ch'i, a brother of the Wang Yi₅ whom he later made his Heir-apparent (99 B: 16a).   A daughter of Liu Hsin₁ₐ, Yin₃, who was the wife of Wang Mang's third son, was executed with her husband.   Thus Wang Mang executed three of Liu Hsin's children.

Wang Mang in this way antagonized his own clan.   While he gave them wealth and high noble rank, yet none felt secure, for they knew not when the imperial power might uproot and destroy them.   His closest officials felt equally insecure.   Consequently he could trust no one and was constantly suspicious, which made matters worse.   Because he feared a revolt, he would not allow even his provincial Shepherds to maintain armies for bandit suppression.   When he sent his generals to gather troops for use against the bandits he would not allow them to make a move without first consulting the throne.   Thus the bandits and rebels could gain a firm foothold before the imperial forces were allowed to attack them.

It is hence not so surprising that in A.D. 23 another imperial first cousin, Wang Shê, should have been persuaded by astrology that Wang

Mang would inevitably fall, and should have headed a conspiracy to remove the Hsin Emperor and put the Han dynasty back on the throne. He secured the cooperation of Wang Mang's Commander-in-chief and of Liu Hsin₁ₐ. Only the fortunate disclosure of the plot and the pusillanimity of the Commander-in-chief prevented its success. Wang Shê had gone to the extreme of making out that Wang Mang was a bastard (99 C: 22b–23b). The plotters were all executed without trouble, but this plot was a severe shock to Wang Mang. Thereafter he could not eat properly nor sleep comfortably. His severity had recoiled upon his own head.

The greatest suffering of the country came, not directly from Wang Mang, but from the robber bands that came into being as an indirect result of the famine and of his rule. They went through the country, looting, pillaging, and burning. The Red Eyebrows were merely the largest of these many illiterate robber armies. They swept over North China, defeating imperial armies and capturing cities by storm, destroying as they went. At the death of Wang Mang, only the Wei-yang Palace was burnt; the rest of Ch'ang-an was undamaged. In A.D. 25, after the Keng-shih Emperor had established himself in Ch'ang-an, the Red Eyebrows arrived, plundering along their route. They had set up another Emperor; they defeated the Keng-shih Emperor's general, captured Ch'ang-an, and plundered it. The people fled the city; the Red Eyebrows had to leave when the food in the city was exhausted. Then they burnt the remainder of the city, went west and north, digging into the imperial tombs and pillaging the cities. The snow drove them back to Ch'ang-an, where at last they were defeated by a ruse. A great famine now raged in the capital region; Ch'ang-an was itself empty and waste. No one dared to show himself alone for fear of being robbed; honest men gathered in camps and cities, which they defended desperately, so that the Red Eyebrows could secure little. In the winter of 26/27, famine drove them eastwards out of Kuang-chung. Meanwhile, Emperor Kuang-wu had been putting down robbers and rebels in eastern China. He met the remnants of the Red Eyebrows with his great army, overawing them, and they meekly surrendered, transmitting to him the Han dynastic imperial seals. Pan Ku states that the population of the empire had been reduced by half (24 B: 27a). So terrible were the forces that Wang Mang let loose upon his land.

[Chapter] XCIX

## THE SIXTY-NINTH [MEMOIR]

### THE MEMOIR OF WANG MANG

#### PART A

修靡曰與馬聲色佚游相高萆獨孤貧因折節為恭儉

傳唯莽父曼蚤死不侯莽羣兄弟將軍五侯子乘時

元成世封侯居位輔政家凡九侯五大司馬語在元后

王莽字巨君孝元皇后之弟子也元后父及兄弟皆曰

漢書九十九

王莽傳第六十九上

Wang Mang, whose courtesy given name was Chü-chün, was the son of [Wang Wan], a younger [half]-brother of the Empress [nee Wang of Emperor] Hsiao-yüan. The father, [Wang Chin], and the [living] elder and younger brothers of the Empress [nee Wang of Emperor] Yüan were all enfeoffed as marquises during the reigns of [Emperors] Yüan and Ch'eng. They occupied [high] positions and had important influence in the government. In the clan there were nine marquises and five Commanders-in-chief.[1.1] A discussion is in the "Memoir of the Empress [nee Wang of Emperor] Yüan."

His clan.

Ch. 98.

Only [Wang] Mang's father, [Wang] Wan, who had died young, was not made a marquis. The various elder and younger cousins of [Wang] Mang were all the sons of Generals or of the Five Marquises,[1.2] so they took advantage of their opportunities and were extravagant. In their equipages and horses, music and women, idleness and gadding[1.3] they competed with one another.

[Wang] Mang alone was an orphan and in humble circumstances, hence he humbled himself and made himself courteous and temperate.[1.4] In studying the

---

[1.1] *HS* 98: 15b says "ten marquises," but that passage includes Shun-yü Chang in its enumeration. He was merely a relative of the Wang clan on the distaff side.

[1.2] For these Five Marquises (Wang T'an₂ᵦ, Wang Shang₁ₐ Wang Li₅, Wang Ken, and Wang Feng-shih) and similar terms, cf. Glossary *sub vocibus*.

[1.3] "*Yi-yu* 佚游 idleness and gadding" is a phrase from *Analects* XVI, v.

[1.4] *Kung-chien* 恭儉 is a phrase from *Analects* I, x, 2.

Classic of Rites [the *Yi-li*], he rendered to Ch'en Ts'an, [a man] from P'ei Commandery,[1.5] the services due to a teacher. [Wang Mang] fatigued himself and studied extensively, wearing garments like the Confucian masters. He served his mother and the widow of his elder brother, [Wang Yung], and reared [Wang Kuang], the orphaned son of his elder brother. Thus his conduct was quite perfect. Moreover, out-

**1b***
1b†
side [his clan] he associated with eminent persons, and within [his clan] he served his various uncles, paying minute attention to the spirit of the rules of proper conduct.

24-21 B.C.
First
*1b‡*
Positions
During [the period] Yang-so, when his paternal uncle who was the heir of his grandfather, the General-in-chief, [Wang] Feng, became ill, [Wang] Mang waited upon him in his illness, himself tasting the medicine [before administering it]. For successive months, [Wang Mang's] hair was disordered, his face uncleansed, and he did not [even] loosen the girdle to his garments. When [Wang] Feng was

Oct. 4, 22[1.6]
about to die, he therefore confided [Wang Mang] to the Empress Dowager [nee Wang] and Emperor [Ch'eng]. He was installed as a Gentleman of the Yellow Gate and was promoted to be Colonel of the Archers Who Shoot By Sound.

Ennoble-
ment
After a long time, his paternal uncle who was younger than [Wang Mang's] father, the Marquis of Ch'eng-tu_b, [Wang] Shang_1b, memorialized that he

太后及帝拜為黃門郎遷射聲校尉久之叔父成都侯高上書願
將軍鳳病恭侍疾嘗藥亂首垢面不解衣帶連月鳳且死呂託
兄子行甚敕備又外交英俊內事諸父曲有禮意陽朔中世父大
受禮經師事沛郡陳參勤身博學被服如儒生事母及寡嫂養孤

---

[1.5] *HS* 88: 25b states that Ch'en Ts'an's younger brother, Ch'en Ch'in, taught Wang Mang the *Tso-chuan* (cf. also *HHS*, Mem. 26: 9b); Hsü Hsüan taught him the *Book of Changes*, cf. *HHS*, Mem. 34: 4b. (From Yang Shu-ta.) The *Classic of Rites* (*Li-Ching*) is listed in *HS* 30: 10a.

* Bold-face type numbers indicate the paging in Wang Hsien-ch'ien's *Han-shu Pu-chu*, as in previous volumes.

† Light upright numbers indicate the paging in the Ching-yu ed., reprinted in the "Po-na" Series, pub. by the Commercial Press.

‡ Italic numbers indicate the paging in the Palace ed. or Wu-ying Tien ed., pub. in the "Szu-pu Pei-yao Collecteana."

[1.6] *HS* 19 B: 43b.

為激發之行廒之不懲恐莽兄永為諸曹盡死有子光莽使學博士門下

鄉大夫甚眾故在位更推薦之游者為之談說虛譽隆洽傾其諸父兄敢

位益尊節操愈謙散輿馬衣裘振施賓客家無所餘收贍名士交結將相

侯國南陽新野之都鄉千五百戶遷騎都尉光祿大夫侍中宿衛謹敕封

並中郎陳湯皆世名士咸為莽言上由是賢莽永始元年封莽為新都

分戶邑曰封莽及長樂少府戴崇侍中金涉胡騎校尉箕閎上谷都尉陽

wished to divide the households of his estate in order to enfeoff [Wang Mang]. Moreover, the Privy Treasurer of the Ch'ang-lo [Palace], Tai Ch'ung, the Palace Attendant, Chin Shê, the Colonel of Northern Barbarian Cavalry, Chi Hung, the Chief Commandant of Shang-ku [Commandery], Yang Ping, and the Gentleman-of-the-Household, Ch'en T'ang, who were all gentlemen well-known in that age, all spoke in behalf of [Wang] Mang. Because of that, the Emperor esteemed [Wang] Mang. In the first year of [the period] Yung-shih, he enfeoffed [Wang] Mang as Marquis of Hsin-tu₆ with an estate of fifteen hundred households in the Tu District of Hsin-yeh [County] in Nan-yang [Commandery]. He was promoted to be Chief Commandant of Cavalry, Imperial Household Grandee, and Palace Attendant, and was careful as [an imperial] guard. *June 12, 16[1.7]*

*His Treatment of Others.* As his noble rank and position became more and more honorable, his conduct became more and more humble. He distributed equipages and horses, clothes, and fur garments, and bestowed them upon his guests, so that in his household there was no surplus [wealth]. He received and succored well-known gentlemen. He associated with a very large number of generals, chancellors, ministers, and grandees, hence those who occupied official positions in turn recommended him. Travelers talked about him; his empty fame flourished and spread, so that it overwhelmed that of his various uncles. He dared to do affected deeds which created a stir and performed them without shame. *2a*

*Care for his Nephew* [Wang] Mang's elder brother, [Wang] Yung₃, had been a Department Head. He had died young and had had a son, [Wang] Kuang₁. [Wang] Mang sent him to study at the gates of the Erudits. When [Wang] Mang took his leave, [usually once each five

[1.7] *HS* 18: 21a.

days], he led out and arranged his chariots and horse-men and brought sheep and wine to recompense and offer to [Wang Kuang₁'s] teachers; his favor was [also] shown to all of [Wang Kuang₁'s] fellow-students, so

*2a* that the masters all stared at him and the elders admired him.

*2a* [Altho Wang] Kuang₁ was younger than [Wang] Mang's son, [Wang] Yü₃, [Wang] Mang had them [both] married on the same day. [At the wedding feast], when the guests had filled his halls, in a moment a man told him that his Lady Dowager [mother] was suffering from a certain pain and must drink a certain medicine. Up to [the time] when the guests left, he had [thus] arisen several times.

He Refuses to Have any Con-cubines

He once[2.1] privately purchased a waiting-maid. Some of his cousins came to know something about it. Because of that, [Wang] Mang said, "The General of the Rear, Chu [Po] Tzu-yüan, has no sons. I, Mang, heard that this girl's line is fruitful in bearing sons, so I purchased her for him." The same day he presented the slave-girl to [Chu Po] Tzu-yüan. In the foregoing manner he hid his desires and sought for fame.

*2b*

He Supplants Shun-yü Chang.

At this time, Shun-yü Chang, the son of an elder [half]-sister of the Empress Dowager [nee Wang], had, because of his ability, become one of the nine high ministers. He was senior to and ahead of [Wang] Mang. [Wang] Mang secretly[2.2] sought out [Shun-yü Chang's] crimes. [Wang Mang] took ad-vantage of [this information and informed] the Com-mander-in-chief, the Marquis of Ch'ü-yang, [Wang] Ken, who had him speak [to the Empress Dowager

Dec., 8 B.C.[2.3]

nee Wang and the Emperor. Thereupon, Shun-yü] Chang suffered execution. From this [deed, Wang]

---

[2.1] For 為, the Ching-yu ed. (1035) reads 嘗. Wang Hsien-ch'ien (1842–1918) states that the Official edition (1739) and the Southern Academy ed. (1531) also read thus.

[2.2] The Official ed. erroneously reads 因 for the 陰 read by the Ching-yu and other editions.

[2.3] *HS* 10: 15b = *HFHD* II, 416 dates Shun-yü Chang's death in the eleventh month, which began on Dec. 3. Pan Ku is anticipating events. Wang Mang was appointed

直語在長傳根因乞骸骨薦莽自代上遂擢為大司馬是歲綏
和元年也三十八矣恭既拔出同列繼四父而輔政欲令名
譽過前人遂克己不倦聘諸賢良吕為掾史賞賜邑錢悉臣享
卿列侯遣夫人問疾恭逢迎之衣不曳地
士愈為儉約母病公

Mang obtained [a reputation] for straightforwardness. A discussion is in the "Memoir of [Shun-yü] Chang." [Wang] Ken then begged to retire and recommended [Wang] Mang to take his place. The Emperor thereupon selected him to be the Commander-in-chief. This year was the first year of [the period] Sui-ho, and [Wang Mang] had reached his thirty-eighth year.[2.5]

93: 7a–8a.

Nov. 28 8 B.C.[2.4]

When [Wang] Mang had surpassed his equals and succeeded his four uncles, [Wang Feng, Wang Shang₁ₐ, Wang Yin, and Wang Ken], as chief assistant in the government, he wished to make his fame and reputation surpass that of his predecessors, hence he denied himself[2.6] tirelessly and invited[2.7] the Capable and Good [to come to him], making them Division Head Clerks. He bestowed upon [other] gentlemen all of his grants [from the Emperor] and the income from his estate, being even more economical [in his personal expenses].

His Self-Denial

When his mother was ill, the ministers and full marquises sent their Ladies to ask after her illness. When [Wang] Mang's wife received them, her clothes did not trail on the ground [and she wore] a linen apron.[2.8] Those who saw her, thought she was a

His Wife's Economy.

2b

2b

Commander-in-chief before Shun-yü Chang died.

[2.4] *HS* 19 B: 48a dates this event in the xi month, on the day *ping-yin*. This day did not occur in that month; no other cyclical characters seem plausible. Probably the date should be x, *ping-yin*, November 28 (julian). Wang Ken resigned on Nov. 16; the office of Commander-in-chief would not have been left vacant for long.

[2.5] Wang Mang was born in 45 B.C., according to 27 Ba: 26a.

[2.6] An allusion to *Analects* XII, i (Soothill, p. 115).

[2.7] The Sung Ch'i ed. (ca. xii cent.) said that after 聘, for 諸, there should be read 請.

[2.8] The *Fang-yen* (attributed to Yang Hsiung₂, 53 B.C.–A.D. 18; annotated, possibly restored by Kuo P'o, 276–324) 4: 1b, 2a says, "The *pi₁-hsi* 蔽膝 [translated 'apron', lit., 'covering for the knees'], in the region of the Yangtze and Huai [Rivers], is called *hui* 褘. Some call it *fu* 被 [more exactly 韍]; in the region of Wei_h, Sung, and Southern Ch'u, it is called the large napkin 大巾; from [the region] east of the [Han-ku] Pass and westwards it is called *pi-hsi*. In the countryside of Ch'i and Lu it is called *jan* 袡." The *Erh-ya* (before and during the Han period) 5: 7a says, "Clothes that cover (*pi*) the front are called *ch'an* 襜 (aprons)," and Kuo P'o glosses, "They are the present *pi-hsi*." The *Shih-ming* (ca. iii cent. A.D.; attributed to Liu Hsi [fl. dur. Han period]) ch. 16, 5: 1b, servant, and sent someone to ask [who she was]. When they learned that she was the Lady, they were all astonished.

**7 B.C.
Apr. 17**[2.9]     [Wang Mang] had been chief assistant in the government for more than a year when Emperor Ch'eng died. When Emperor Ai ascended the
**May 7**[2.10]  throne, he honored the Empress Dowager [nee Wang] and made her the Grand Empress Dowager. The [Grand] Empress Dowager [nee Wang] issued an
**3a**  imperial edict to [Wang] Mang, [ordering him] to go to his residence and leave [his position vacant for some of] the Emperor's maternal relatives.[2.11] [Wang] Mang [hence] presented to the Emperor a request
**His**  begging to retire. Emperor Ai [however] sent his
**Resigna-**  Prefect of the Masters of Writing, [T'ang Lin], with
**tion**  an imperial edict to [Wang] Mang, saying,
**Refused.**   "The late Emperor entrusted the government to

2a says, "The *pi₂* 韠 is a cover (*pi₁*); it is the means whereby one covers his knees (*pi₁-hsi*) and front. Women's *pi₁-hsi* are also of this sort. The people of Ch'i call them great napkins 巨 巾. When the wives and daughters of people who work in the fields go out to the fields and wilds, they use them to cover their heads. Hence because of that they give them their name. They are also called kneeling aprons 跪襜. When they kneel down, [this apron] covers them and is spread out." A discussion of this garment is to be found in Nieh Ch'ung-yi's *San-li-t'u* (presented 962) 8: 10a, b, also in Ch'en Hsiang-tao's (1053–1093) *Li-shu* 23: 1a–6b, in which it is pointed out that this article was used in ceremonial dress, even by the Son of Heaven. (References from Shen Ch'in-han.) Legge, *Li Ki*, II, SBE, XXVIII, p. 14, n. 1, reproduces pictures of it, but the Chinese phrase *pi₁-hsi* led him and Couvreur to translate it as "knee-covers." The dimensions given in the text should have warned them that this translation is inappropriate.

[2.9] The date of Emperor Ch'eng's death is from 10: 16a. It was only four and a half months after Wang Mang had been made Commander-in-chief. Pan Ku seems to have been careless about this date—he did not compile the "Table" from which the date of Wang Mang's appointment was taken.

[2.10] *HS* 11: 2a.

[2.11] A willingness to retire from office at the proper moment exhibited, on Wang Mang's part, the Confucian virtue of "declining and yielding". Such a virtuous act should properly be met by a similar "declining and yielding," i.e., a refusal of the resignation. The Grand Empress Dowager's edict was very likely instigated by Wang Mang himself, for the purpose of securing from the new Emperor a confirmation of his position as the dominant minister. Ho Kuang had similarly resigned (8: 4a = *HFHD* II, 207).

布蔽媵見之者曰為僮使問知其夫人皆驚
輔政歲餘成帝崩哀帝即位尊皇太后為太
皇太后太后詔莽就第避帝外家莽上疏乞
慨肎哀帝遣尚書令詔莽曰先帝委政於君

書言春秋之義母以子貴丁姬宜上尊號荅與師丹共勸宏謀
令羣視事時哀帝祖母丁姬母丁姬在高昌侯董宏上
皇帝聞太后詔甚悲大司馬即不起皇帝即不敢聽政太后復
又遣丞相孔光大司空何武左將軍師丹衛尉傅喜白太后曰
蓄朕之不能奉順先帝之意朕甚傷焉已詔尚書待君奏事
而棄羣臣朕得奉宗廟誠嘉與君同心合意今君移病來退曰

you, sir, whereupon he departed from his subjects. We have obtained [the opportunity] to uphold the [imperial] ancestral temples and will in truth consider [Ourself] fortunate to be of the same mind and similar opinions with you, sir. Now you, sir, have sent [Us a letter saying that you] are ill and ask to retire. Thereby you make known that We are not able to uphold or follow the intentions of the late Emperor. We are greatly saddened. [We] have already issued an imperial edict to the Masters of Writing to await your memorials, sir, about [government] business."

[The Emperor] also sent the Lieutenant Chancellor, K'ung Kuang, the Grand Minister of Works, Ho Wu, the General of the Left, Shih₁ Tan, and the Commandant of the Palace Guard, Fu Hsi, to speak to the [Grand] Empress Dowager [nee Wang], saying, "The Emperor has heard of the Empress Dowager's imperial edict and is much saddened. If the Commander-in-chief [Wang Mang] does not arise, the Emperor will then not presume to attend to the government." The [Grand] Empress Dowager [nee Wang thereupon] again ordered [Wang] Mang to attend to the [government] business.

At that time, the grandmother of Emperor Ai, the Queen Dowager [nee] Fu of Ting-t'ao, and his mother, the Concubine nee Ting [of the deceased King of Ting-t'ao], were alive, so the Marquis of Kao-ch'ang, Tung Hung, presented to the throne a letter saying, "According to the principles of the *Spring and Autumn* [in the *Kung-yang Commentary*], a mother becomes honorable because of her son, so that the Concubine [nee] Ting should be presented with the imperial title [of Empress Dowager]."[2.12] [Wang] Mang together with Shih₁ Tan impeached [Tung] Hung for misleading the court, which consti-

He
Opposes
the
Elevation
of the
Fu and
Ting Clans.

[2.12] Cf. 11: n. 2.3; Glossary, *sub* Fu, Brilliant Companion nee.

tuted inhumanity.　A discussion is in the "Memoir of [Shih₁] Tan."

86: 17a
3b
He
Demotes
3a
*3a*
the Queen
Dowager
nee Fu.

At a later date, there was a banquet in Wei-yang Palace. The Prefect of the Flunkies spread the canopy and seat for the Queen Dowager [nee] Fu at the side of the seat for the Grand Empress Dowager [nee Wang. Wang] Mang investigated and reproached the Prefect of the Flunkies, saying, "The Queen Dowager of [the kingdom of] Ting-t'ao is a concubine from a tributary [kingdom]. How could she be permitted to be honored equally with the most honorable [lady in the palace]?　Take it away and put the seat [of the Queen Dowager of Ting-t'ao] at a different [place]."

He
Resigns
Again.
Aug. 27,
7 B.C.[3.1]

When the Queen Dowager [nee] Fu heard of it, she was furious and refused to attend [the banquet. She thereupon held] a great hatred against [Wang] Mang.　[Hence Wang] Mang again begged to retire. Emperor Ai granted [Wang] Mang five hundred catties of actual gold, a comfortable carriage and a quadriga of horses, dismissed him [from his position], and sent him to his residence.　Most of the ministers and grandees praised him, so the Emperor added his grace and favor, and established, as [regular] messenger to his home, a Palace [Attendant Within] the Yellow Gate to grant him a meal [from the imperial cuisine] once every ten days.　[The Emperor] sent

公卿大夫多稱之者上乃加恩寵置使家中黃門十日一賜
志恭恭後亡骸肯哀帝賜恭黃金五百斤安車駟馬罷就弟
臣得與至尊並徹去恭索設坐傅太后閤之大怒不肯會重怨
坐於太皇太后坐旁恭索行責內者令曰定陶傅太后藩妾何
朝不道語在卅傳後日未央宮置酒內者令為傅太后張慍

---

[3.1] *HS* 19 B: 48b says, *sub* the year Sui-ho II, "In month xi, *ting-mao*, the Commander-in-chief, [Wang] Mang, was granted gold, a comfortable chariot, a quadriga of horses, and was dismissed.　On *keng-wu*, the General of the Left, Shih₁ Tan, became Commander-in-chief.　In iv, he was moved [to another office]."　On the same page, it says, "In month x, *kuei-yu* [Dec. 30, 7 B.C.], the Commander-in-chief, [Shih₁] Tan, became the Grand Minister of Works.　Within the year, he was dismissed."

Now there were no *ting-mao* or *keng-wu* days in Sui-ho II, xi.　If Shih Tan's appointment as Grand Minister of Works happened in month x and in the fourth month before Wang Mang was dismissed, the dismissal could not have happened in month xi.　Szu-ma Kuang suggests that "month xi" is an error for "month vii" (十 and 七 were written almost alike in the *li* style), hence Wang Mang's dismissal occurred on Aug. 27 and Shih₁ Tan's appointment as Commander-in-chief on Aug. 30.

籤下詔曰新都侯奔憂勞國家乾義墾因朕庶幾與為治太皇太

后詔就第朕甚閔焉其曰黃郵聚戶三百五十益封茀位特進

給事中朝朝望見禮如三公車駕乘綠車從後二歲傳太后丁姬

皆稱尊號丞相朱博奏前不廣尊尊之義抑貶尊號虧損孝道

to his subordinates an imperial edict which said,

"The Marquis of Hsin-tu꜀, [Wang] Mang, has worried and toiled for the state and has firmly held to his fealty. We hoped with him to produce a good government, [but] the Grand Empress Dowager [nee Wang] has issued an imperial edict that [Wang] Mang should go to his residence, for which We are very sorry. Let [Wang Mang][3.2] be additionally enfeoffed with three hundred fifty households in Huang-yu Village; let his position be Specially Advanced, let him [be given the rank of] Serving in the Palace, [be required] to come to court [only] on the first and fifteenth days of the month, and present himself with formalities like those of the three highest ministers. When [the Emperor rides] his chariot of state, [Wang Mang] may follow in the [imperial cortege] riding a green chariot.[3.3]

4a

The second year afterwards, when the Queen Dowager [nee] Fu and the Concubine [nee] Ting had both been given the imperial titles [of Emperor's Great Empress Dowager and the Emperor's Empress Dowager, respectively], the Lieutenant Chancellor Chu Po memorialized,

5 B.C., May/ June[3.4] He is Sent Away From the Court.

"[Wang] Mang has not previously applied broadly [enough] the principle of honoring those [deserving of] honor[3.5] but has humbled and degraded those who should be honored with an imperial title, [thereby] injuring the doctrine of filial piety, so that he ought

---

[3.2] The Sung Ch'i ed. reports that other editions and the Yüeh ed. (xi–xii cent.) lack the word for "Mang." The Ching-yu ed. lacks this word.

[3.3] Chin Shao, in a note to 68: 21b, says, "[According to] a Han commentator, 'Green chariot 綠車' designated the chariot of an Imperial Grandson; if the Heir-apparent has a son, [the son] rides in this [sort of a chariot] when following [in the train of the emperor]." This equipage is described in HHS, Tr. 29: 10a. Yen Shih-ku explains, "When the Son of Heaven rode out, he ordered that [Wang] Mang [should be permitted] to ride this [sort of a chariot] in following him, thereby [granting him] his favor."

[3.4] HS 11: 4b.

[3.5] A phrase from Li-chi XIV, 3 (Couvreur, I, 777; Legge, II, 61).

**3b**
**3b**

to suffer public execution. Fortunately [for him], he has received [the advantage of a general] ordinance of amnesty, [yet] it is not proper that he should possess a noble title or land. I beg that he be dismissed [from his titles] and made a commoner."

The Emperor said, "Because [Wang] Mang is related to the Grand Empress Dowager [nee Wang], let him not be dismissed [from his noble titles], but be sent away to his estate."

**Summer[3.6]**
**He Executes His Son.**

While [Wang] Mang had closed his gates and was keeping to himself, [Wang] Huo_b,[3.7] his son who was neither his eldest nor his youngest, murdered a slave. [Wang] Mang bitterly reproached [Wang] Huo_b and caused him to commit suicide.

**Popular Opinion Leads to (2 B.C., Feb. 5[3.9]) His Recall.**

While he had been at his estate to the third year, officials[3.8] by the hundreds sent letters to the Emperor grieving and pleading for [Wang] Mang. In the first year of [the period] Yüan-shou, when there was an eclipse of the sun, [some persons who had been recommended as] Capable and Good, Chou Huo, Sung Ch'ung, and others, in their written replies to the examination, praised highly [Wang] Mang's achievements and virtue. The Emperor therefore summoned [Wang] Mang [to come to court].

**His Advances to an Unimportant Official.**

When [Wang] Mang had first gone to his estate, because [Wang] Mang was an honorable and important [personage], the Grand Administrator of Nan-yang [Commandery] selected a Division Head from his office, K'ung Hsiu, [a man of] Yüan, to be the acting Chancellor of Hsin-tu_c, [Wang Mang's marquisate. When K'ung] Hsiu went to pay a

---

[3.6] Chu Po was Lieutenant Chancellor from May 9 to Sept. 21, 5 B.C., so that Wang Mang's dismissal from the court occurred between those dates; cf. 19 B: 49a.

[3.7] Yen Shih-ku (581–645) states that some texts write this given name as 護, which he says is "a vulgar change."

[3.8] The Sung Ch'i ed. says that after the word 吏 there should be the word 民. The Ching-yu ed. does not read this character.

[3.9] HS 11: 7a.

詔見莽莽盡禮自納休亦聞其名與相答後莽疾休候之

莽綵思意進其玉具寶劍欲曰為好休不肯受莽因曰誠

見君面有瘢美玉可已滅瘢欲獻其珠耳即解其珠休復

辭讓莽曰君嫌其貴耶遂推碎之自裹曰進休休乃受及

莽傲去欲見休休稱疾不見莽遂京師歲餘帝崩無子

visit to [Wang] Mang, [Wang] Mang [treated K'ung Hsiu] with all possible formalities and in person welcomed him [at the door]. [K'ung] Hsiu had also heard of [Wang Mang's] fame and responded to him in like manner.

Later, when [Wang] Mang was ill, [K'ung] Hsiu attended upon him. Because of his gracious intent, [Wang] Mang presented him with his [own] precious sword having jade furnishings, desiring to make [K'ung Hsiu] a good friend. [But K'ung] Hsiu refused to receive it. [Wang] Mang said therefore, "I verily see that on your face, sir, there is a scar. A fine jade can extinguish a scar. I merely wanted to present you with the ring on the hilt of the sword."[3.10] He immediately loosed its [jade] sword-ring.

When [K'ung] Hsiu again excused himself and refused, [Wang] Mang said, "Do you, sir, dislike [to receive it] because of its [high] value?" Then he pounded it to pieces, himself tied it up, and thereupon presented it to [K'ung] Hsiu. [K'ung] Hsiu then received it.

When [Wang] Mang was summoned [to the court and was about to] leave, he wanted to see [K'ung] Hsiu, [but K'ung] Hsiu pronounced himself ill and did not present himself.

More than a year after [Wang] Mang returned to the imperial capital, Emperor Ai died. He had no

4b

4a *4a*

Aug. 15
1 B.C.[4.1]

[3.10] The Sung Ch'i ed. says that 耳 should be excised. The Ching-yu ed. does not read it.

Fu Ch'ien (ca. 125–195) states that *chuan* 璲 is pronounced the same as *wei* 衛. Su Lin (ca. 160–ca. 240) states that it is the ring at the end of the hilt on a two-edged sword. Yen Shih-ku hence infers that the text originally read *chih* 璏 (which has also the pronunciation *wei* and, with another meaning, is pronounced *chuan*) and that it was later mistakenly altered, for *chuan* means merely "engraved (with raised figures)." *Shuo-wen* 1 A: 4b says that *chih* means the jade ring at the end of the hilt on a sword, using the same words as Su Lin. Cf. Chavannes, *Documents chinois decouverts*, p. 19, no. 39.

It is still believed that a fine jade made into powder and put upon a scar will extinguish the scar.

[4.1] *HS* 11: 8b.

He is
Put in
Control
of the
Govern-
ment.

children and both the [August Grand] Empress
Dowager [nee Fu] and the [Emperor's] Empress
Dowager [nee] Ting had died previously.  On the
same day [as the death], the Grand August Empress
Dowager [nee Wang] rode a quadriga to the Wei-
yang Palace, where she secured the imperial seals
with their seal-cords.[4.2]  She sent a messenger galloping to summon [Wang] Mang.  She issued an imperial
edict to the Masters of Writing, [declaring] that the
various insignia and credentials for mobilizing troops,
the matters memorialized by the various officials, and
the troops of the Palace Attendants Within the

5a Yellow Gate and of the Attendants at the Gates
should all be under the control of [Wang] Mang.

Demotion
of Tung
Hsien.
Aug. 16[4.3]

[Wang] Mang advised [the Grand Empress Dow-
ager] that the Commander-in-chief, the Marquis of
Kao-an, Tung Hsien[2a], was too young and [that his
occupying that position] did not accord with public
opinion, [so that she should] take [away] his [official
and noble] seals and cords.  On the same day,
[Tung] Hsien[2a] committed suicide.

Wang
Mang
is made
Command-
er-in-
chief.

The [Grand] Empress Dowager [nee Wang] in an
imperial edict ordered the ministers to recommend
persons who might become the Commander-in-chief.
The Grand Minister Over the Masses, K'ung Kuang,
and the Grand Minister of Works, P'eng Hsüan,
recommended [Wang] Mang.  The General of the

[4.2] Emperor Ai had given his imperial seals and authority to Tung Hsien[2a] before he
died; Wang Hung took them away from Tung Hsien[2a] and gave them to the Grand Empress Dowager.  Cf. Glossary *sub* Wang Hung.

[4.3] *HS* 19 B : 51a records Tung Hsien[2a]'s dismissal on Yüan-shou III (an error for
Yüan-shou II), vi, *yi-wei*, which is impossible.  Emperor Ai died on vi, *mou-wu*, a day
before the day *chi-wei*, so that Tung Hsien's dismissal occurred on vi, *chi-wei*, Aug. 16;
cf. 99 A : 21b.  *Chi* 己 and *yi* 乙 are frequently mistaken for each other.  This emendation is confirmed by the date for Wang Mang's appointment to succeed Tung Hsien, which
is vi, *keng-shen*, the day after *chi-wei*.

将军何武后将军公孙禄互相举太后拜莽为大司马与议

立嗣安阳侯王舜莽之从弟其人脩饬太后所信爱也莽白

曰舜为车骑将军使迎中山王奉成帝后是为孝平皇帝帝

年九岁太后临朝称制委政于莽莽白赵氏前害皇子傅氏

骄僭遂庆孝成赵皇后孝哀傅皇后皆令自杀语在外戚传

莽以大司徒孔光名儒相三主太后所敬天下信之于是盛

Van, Ho Wu, and the General of the Rear,[4.4] Kung-sun Lu, recommended each other. The [Grand] Empress Dowager installed [Wang] Mang as Commander-in-chief and discussed with him the establishment of an heir [to the throne].    Aug. 17[4.5]

The Marquis of An-yang, Wang Shun$_{4b}$, was a second cousin of [Wang] Mang, was cultivated and self-controlled[4.6] in his person, and was trusted and beloved by the [Grand] Empress Dowager. [Wang] Mang advised her to make [Wang] Shun$_{4b}$ the General of Chariots and Cavalry and send him to invite the King of Chung-shan, [Liu Chi-tzu], to carry on the posterity of Emperor Ch'eng. This was Emperor Hsiao-p'ing.

The Emperor was in his ninth year, so the [Grand] Empress Dowager attended court and pronounced [that she issued the imperial] decrees.[4.7] She entrusted the government to [Wang] Mang.

[Wang] Mang advised her that [the lady] nee Chao had previously killed some imperial sons[4.8] and that [the lady] nee Fu had been proud and arrogant, so she thereupon dismissed the Empress [nee] Chao of [Emperor] Hsiao-ch'eng and the Empress [nee] Fu of [Emperor] Hsiao-ai [from their titles]. Both were ordered to commit suicide. A discussion is in the "Memoir of the [Imperial] Relatives by Marriage."

Because the Grand Minister Over the Masses, K'ung Kuang, was a famous scholar, had acted as chancellor to three lords [of men], was respected by the [Grand] Empress Dowager, and the whole empire trusted him, [Wang] Mang therefore honored [K'ung] Kuang greatly and served him. [Wang

*[Marginal notes:]*

He Summons Emperor P'ing to the Throne.

He is Entrusted With the Government.

The Fu and Chao Empress Dowagers Executed. 97 B: 15b, 16a, 20a.

**4b**
*4b*
He gets 5b Rid of His Opponents.

---

[4.4] *HS* 19 B: 49b (under the date 4 B.C.) and 86: 4b (in recounting the same incident) list Kung-sun Lu as General of the Left, so that "Rear" is probably an error. (Noted by Ch'ien Ta-hsin.)

[4.5] *HS* 19 B: 51a.

[4.6] Yen Shih-ku remarks that 飭 should be read the same as 敕, which means 整.

[4.7] Cf. *HFHD*, I, p. 192, n. 1.

[4.8] Cf. 10: 14a; *HFHD* II, 411; Glossary, *sub* Chao, Brilliant Companion nee.

Mang] introduced [to the court K'ung] Kuang's son-in-law, Chen Han, and made him a Palace Attendant and the Chief Commandant of the Imperial Equipages.

[Wang] Mang attributed crimes to all the various maternal relatives of Emperor Ai, together with [those of] his great officials and those who held office whom [Wang] Mang had disliked, and prepared [unsigned] memorials begging [that they be punished]. He had [Chen] Han take them to [K'ung] Kuang. [K'ung] Kuang was habitually timid and cautious, so did not dare to refuse to send in these memorials [as his own]. Each time [they were received, Wang] Mang advised the [Grand] Empress Dowager to assent to these memorials. In this way, the General of the Van, Ho Wu, and the General of the Rear, Kung-sun Lu, were sentenced for having recommended each other and were dismissed. The relatives of the Ting and Fu [clans], together with [those of] Tung Hsien₂ₐ were all dismissed from their positions and from their noble titles and were exiled to distant regions.

**Wang Li Sent Away from the Court.**    The Marquis of Hung-yang, [Wang] Li₅ₐ, was a younger [half]-brother of the [Grand] Empress Dowager. Although he did not occupy any [official] position, yet because he was one of his uncles who was respected within [the Palace, Wang Mang] dreaded him. He feared [Wang] Li₅ₐ might casually say something to the [Grand] Empress Dowager which would bring it about that [Wang Mang] would not be permitted to follow his own intentions. So [Wang Mang] had [K'ung] Kuang also memorialize [Wang] Li₅ₐ's former evil deeds: that he had previously known that the Marquis of Ting-ling, Shun-yü Chang, had committed the crime of rebellion and he had [nevertheless] received from him a large bribe and

尊事光引光女婿甄邯為侍中奉車都尉諸哀帝外戚及大臣居

位素所不說者莫白太后輒可其奏於是前將軍何武後將軍公孫祿

敢不之莽白太后莽皆免官爵徙遠方紅陽侯立太后

坐互相舉免丁傅及董賢親屬皆免官爵徙遠方紅陽侯立太后

親弟雖不居位莽旦諸父內敬憚之長立從容言太后令已不得

肆意乃復令光奏立舊惡前知定陵侯淳于長犯大逆罪多受其

138

賂為言誤朝俊白曰官婢楊寄私子為皇子衆言曰呂氏少帝俊
出紛紛為天下所疑難呂示來世成緒揉之功請遣立就國太后
不聽恭曰今漢家衰比世無嗣太后獨代幼主統政誠可畏懼力
用公正先天下尚恐不從今曰私恩逆大臣議如此舉下傾邪亂

had falsely[4.9] spoken for him, [thus] misleading the court. Later he had advised that a secret son of a government woman, Yang Chi, [allegedly by Emperor Ch'eng], should be made an Imperial Son, [a **6a** possible heir to the throne. But] the common opinion [in the court was, "It is a case of] the reappearance of the Young Emperor of the Lü clan.[4.10] It is most disturbing. It would be suspicious to the empire, so that it would be difficult to establish [such a babe's legitimacy] to later generations or to achieve anything creditable in behalf of [such a babe] in swaddling clothes." [The memorial] begged that [Wang] Li**5a** should be sent back to his state.

When the [Grand] Empress Dowager would not listen to it, [Wang] Mang said to her, "Now the Han dynasty has decayed and has been without [natural] heirs [to the throne] for successive generations. You alone, [Grand] Empress Dowager, can take the place of the young lord in directing the government. It is sincerely to be dreaded that, even **5a** if you strive hard to use justice and uprightness in leading the empire, it is yet to be feared that [the empire] will not follow [you. But] now if for the sake of your private affection you go contrary to the advice of your highest officials, in this way your **5a** many subordinates will become dangerous and evil;

---

[4.9] Li Tz'u-ming (1829–1894), *Han-shu Cha-chi* 7: 14b, says that 為 should be read as 偽.

[4.10] The "Young Emperor" was Lü Hung; cf. *HS* 3: 3b, 8a; *HFHD*, I, 198, 209. Prof. Duyvendak interprets differently, inserting 王 after the 成, noting that the succession of King Ch'eng, as an infant, to King Wu, and his being presented by the Duke of Chou to the feudal lords is the classical and often mentioned case of a child on the throne, which is later on frequently cited in this Memoir. He translates: "Later he had proposed that a private son of a government slave, Yang Chi, be set up as an Imperial son. The unanimous opinion [of the Ministers] was that a recurrence of the case of the young Emperor from the Lü clan would in a most disturbing way arouse the suspicion of the empire so that it would be difficult to show to later generations the [same] good results [which had been obtained by setting up King] Ch'eng in swaddling-clothes. They begged therefore that [Wang] Li be sent back to his state."

disorder will arise because of this [event]. It is proper to approve [this petition], temporarily send [Wang Li5a] to his state, and, after the situation has become more tranquil, to summon him back." The [Grand] Empress Dowager had no alternative, so sent [Wang] Li5a to his state. The [methods] by which [Wang] Mang compelled and controlled his superiors and inferiors were all of the foregoing sort.

**His Clique.** In this way, those who attached themselves to him and accorded with him were promoted and those who opposed or disliked him were exterminated. Wang Shun4b and Wang Yi5 became his intimate advisers. Chen Feng and Chen Han had charge of making decisions[5.1], P'ing Yen had charge of delicate matters[5.2], Liu Hsin1a[5.3] took care of [classical] literature, Sun Chien was his military assistant.[5.4] [Chen] Feng's son, [Chen] Hsün, [Liu] Hsin1a's son, [Liu] Fen, Ts'ui Fa from Cho Commandery, and Ch'en Ch'ung from Nan-yang [Commandery] were all

**6b** favored by [Wang] Mang because of their ability.

**His Procedure.** [Wang] Mang's appearance was severe and his speech was blunt.[5.5] When he wanted to have some-

---

[5.1] *Han-chi* 30: 1a writes *chüeh-tuan* 訣斷 instead of 擊-*tuan*. I have followed its reading.

[5.2] *Chi-shih* 機事 is a phrase from *Book of Changes*, App. III, I, 47 (Legge, p. 363).

[5.3] Li Tz'u-ming, *ibid.*, remarks that, in A.D. 6, Liu Hsin1a had changed his personal name to Hsiu (cf. Glossary, *sub voce*); but Pan Ku still used Hsin to avoid the taboo on the personal name of Emperor Kuang-wu, which was also Hsiu.

[5.4] The phrase in the text, "talons and teeth, *chao-ya* 爪牙," is used in *Book of Odes*, no. 185; II, IV, i, 1 (Legge, p. 298) as a figure for the king's soldiers. This phrase came to have various meanings. Ku Yung writes (*HS* 70: 14a, b), "A general who is victorious in battle is the talons and teeth of the state 戰克之將國之爪牙." Sun Chien served Wang Mang as a general. This phrase also signified the subordinates who execute their superior's plans. *HS* 90: 7b states that Wang Wen-shu controlled the commandery of Kuang-p'ing by selecting some ten-odd braves as his "talons and teeth," hiding their crimes, and sending them to search out the commandery's thieves and robbers. Prof. Duyvendak suggests that "talons and teeth" denoted the secret police. H. O. H. Stange, *Die Monographie über Wang Mang*, p. 15, l. 5, translates this phrase as "Leibgardist," but the technical term for body-guard was *su-wei* 宿衛 (*HS* 38: 3b[12]).

[5.5] The Official ed. reads *chih* 之 for *fang* 方, and quotes the Sung Ch'i ed. as saying that *chih* should be *fang*. Wang Hsien-ch'ien adds that the Southern Academy ed. (1531) reads *fang*. The Ching-yu ed. reads likewise.

陽陳崇皆曰材能幸於莽莽色屬而言方欲有所為微見
事劉歆典文章孫建為爪牙豐子尋歆子葉涿郡崔發南
恨者誅滅王舜王邑為腹心甄豐甄邯主擊斷平晏領機
就國莽之所已喬持上下皆此類也於是附順者拔擢忤
從此起宜可且遣就國安後浸浸僭召之太后不得已遣立

風采薰與承其指意而顯奏之莽稽首涕泣固推讓焉上曰惑太

后下用示信於眾庶始風益州令塞外蠻夷獻白雉元始元年正

月莽白太后下詔曰白雉薦宗廟群臣因奏言太后委任大司馬

爵邑比蕭相國莽宜如光故事太后問公卿曰誠曰大司馬有大

恭定策安宗廟故大司馬霍光有安宗廟之功益封三萬戶等其

thing done, he subtly indicated it in his bearing; his clique took up his intentions and manifested them in a memorial, [whereupon Wang] Mang bent his head to the earth with tears in his eyes, and firmly declined. On the one hand, he thereby misled the [Grand] Empress Dowager, and on the other, he thereby exhibited faithfulness to the mass of commoners.

First, he had hinted that [the Governor of] Yi Province should induce the barbarians outside the barrier to present a white pheasant,[5.6] and, in the first year of [the period] Yüan-shih, in the first month, [Wang] Mang advised the [Grand] Empress Dowager to issue an imperial edict that the white pheasant should be offered in the [imperial] ancestral temples. The many courtiers therefore memorialized, saying,

"The [Grand] Empress Dowager entrusted to the Commander-in-chief, [Wang] Mang, the duty of planning the imperial enthronement that gave peace to the [imperial] ancestral temples. When the former Commander-in-chief Ho Kuang had the merit of [similarly] having given peace to the [imperial] ancestral temples, his enfeoffment was increased by thirty thousand households, the noble title and estate [of his posterity was ordered] to be the same [as that of the founder of their house,[5.7] and he was ranked] the same as the [former] Chancellor of State Hsiao [Ho]. It would be proper for [Wang] Mang to be [treated] as [Ho] Kuang was formerly [treated]."[5.8]

The [Grand] Empress Dowager questioned[5.9] the ministers, saying, "Is it really that, because the Commander-in-chief, [Wang Mang], has achieved

A.D. 1,
Feb./Mar.
The
White
Pheasant
From the
Yüeh-
shang.

5b
5b
He is
Likened
to Ho
Kuang.

---

[5.6] Cf. 12: 2a; Glossary *sub* Yüeh-shang.

[5.7] Cf. *HS* 8: n. 7.9.

[5.8] Cf. 8: 7b.

[5.9] The Sung Ch'i ed. says that before the word 問 there should be the word 召.

great merit, he ought to be given [high] honors?　Or it is because he is of [Our] flesh and blood that you have wanted to distinguish him?"

Thereupon various courtiers produced long expositions, [saying, "Wang] Mang's achievements and

**7a**
**He is Likened to the Duke of Chou.**
virtuous conduct have brought about the auspicious presage of a white pheasant [as at the time the Duke of] Chou [was minister to King] Ch'eng.　That in a thousand years there are similarities is a law of the sage-kings.[5.10]　When a subject has great achievements, in his lifetime he should have a laudable title. Hence the Duke of Chou, during his lifetime, was given[5.11] a title with [the name of] the Chou [dynasty in it.　Wang] Mang has the great achievement of having given stability to the state and of having given tranquillity to the Han dynasty, so that it is proper

**He is Given a Laudatory Title.**
that he should be granted the title, 'The Duke Giving Tranquillity to the Han [Dynasty],' that the [number of] households [in his noble estate] should be increased, and [his posterity should be given] the same noble title and estate [as the founder of their house]. On the one hand, [this appointment] will be in accordance with ancient principles, and on the other hand, it will take as its model past situations. Thereby it will accord with the mind of Heaven."

**He Refuses It.**
When the [Grand] Empress Dowager, in an imperial edict, ordered a Master of Writing to prepare [an edict for] this matter, [Wang] Mang presented a letter which said, "Your servant planned the enthronement [of Emperor P'ing] together with K'ung Kuang, Wang Shun[4b], Chen Feng, and Chen Han. Now I wish that the achievements and rewards of

功當者之邪將臣骨肉故欲異之也於是羣臣乃盛陳莽功德致

公及身在而託號於周莽有定國安漢家之大功則生有美號故用周成白雉之瑞千載同符聖王之法臣有大功

公益戸疇爵邑上應古制下準行事臣順天心太后詔尚書具其事莽上書言臣與孔光王舜氣豐氣邪共定策今願獨條光等功

---

[5.10] The "law" is found in Mencius IV, ii, i, 3 (Legge, p. 316).　Cf. *HS* 12: n. 2.3.　These Yüeh-shang are also mentioned in Lu Chia's *Hsin-yü* (196 B.C.), cf. *MSOS* v. 33, p. 32. The *Han-shih Wai-chuan* 5: 7a declares that their language must be translated by "nine [successive interpreters]."

[5.11] The Official ed. has 記 for the *t'o* 託 of Wang Hsien-ch'ien's text; he notes that the Southern Academy ed. has *t'o*.　The Ching-yu ed. reads likewise.

賞復置臣莽勿隨羣列靚邸白太后下詔曰無偏無黨王道蕩蕩虜有親

者義不得阿君有安宗廟之功不可以骨肉故薇隱不揚君其勿辭莽復

上書讓太后詔謁者引莽待殿東箱莽稱疾不肯入太后使尚書令怡詔

之曰君呂邁故而辭呂疾君任重不可闕呂時亟起莽迺固辭太后復使

長信太僕閎承制召莽莽固稱疾左右白太后直勿彊莽意但條孔光等

[K'ung] Kuang and the others should alone be listed and that [any rewards for] your servant, Mang, should be abandoned and set aside. Do not list me with them."

Chen Han advised the [Grand] Empress Dowager to issue an imperial edict, which said,

" 'Without deflection and without partiality, Great is the way of [true] Kings.'[5.12] Although a relative should be loved, [yet We] should not be partial to him. [But] you, sir, have achieved the merit of having given tranquillity to the [imperial] ancestral temples. [We] cannot set aside [your merits] and not exalt them just because you are of [Our] flesh and blood. You, sir, must not refuse."

When [Wang] Mang again presented a letter excusing himself, the [Grand] Empress Dowager by an imperial edict ordered an Internuncio to lead [Wang] Mang to await [investiture] in the Eastern Wing of the [Palace] Hall. [But Wang] Mang pronounced *6a* himself ill and would not enter [the Palace Hall, so the Grand] Empress Dowager sent the Prefect of the Masters of Writing, [Yao] Hsün, with an imperial *7b* edict to [Wang Mang], saying, "Because you, sir, *6a* are humble,[6.1] you have refused on account of illness. Your position, sir, is important, and may not be left vacant. Arise promptly at this time."

When [Wang] Mang completely and firmly refused, the [Grand] Empress Dowager again sent the Grand Coachman at the Ch'ang-hsin [Palace, Wang] Hung, with an imperial decree summoning [Wang] Mang. [Wang] Mang [however] insistently pronounced himself ill. Her entourage advised the [Grand] Empress Dowager that it was proper not to force [Wang] Mang's will, and merely to list K'ung Kuang and the

---

[5.12] A quotation from *Book of History* V, iv, 14 (Legge, p. 331); but cf. Karlgren in *BMFEA* 20, p. 237, Gl. 1539.

[6.1] Li Tz'u-ming, *ibid.*, 7: 15a, says that 選 should be read as 巽, with which it was anciently interchanged.

others, whereupon [Wang] Mang would be willing to arise.

**Apr. 10[6.2]**
**His**
**Followers**
**Honored**
**First.**

The [Grand] Empress Dowager [thereupon] issued to her subordinates an imperial edict, saying, "The Grand Tutor, the Marquis of Po-shan, [K'ung] Kuang, has guarded [the throne] for four reigns and from reign to reign has been tutor or chancellor. He is loyal, filial, benevolent, and sincere; his conduct and his fealty have been outstanding. He made the proposal and planned the imperial enthronement. He shall be additionally enfeoffed with [the income of] ten thousand households. [K'ung] Kuang shall become the Grand Master, participating in a government by Four Coadjutors.

"The General of Chariots and Cavalry, the Marquis of An-yang, [Wang] Shun[4b], has repeatedly and continually been benevolent and filial; he was sent to invite the King of Chung-shan, [Liu Chi-tzu, to ascend the throne] and he has 'repulsed [by diplomacy] the attacks of [the enemy at a distance of] ten thousand *li*.'[6.3] His achievements and virtuous conduct are abundant and brilliant. He shall be additionally enfeoffed with [the income of] ten thousand households. [Wang] Shun[4b] shall become the Grand Guardian.

"The General of the Left and Superintendent of the Imperial Household, [Chen] Feng, has guarded [the throne] for three reigns. He is loyal, trust-

肯乃莽起太后下詔曰太傅博山侯光宿衛四世世為傅忠

孝仁篤行義顯著建議定策益封萬戶呂光為太師與四輔之

政車騎將軍安陽侯舜齊績景仁孝使迎中山王折衝萬里功德

茂著益封萬戶呂舜為太保左將軍光祿勳豐宿衛三世忠信

[6.2] *HS* 19 B: 51b supplies this date for the appointing of three Coadjutors, including Wang Mang. The latter declares (99 A: 18a) that on this date he was appointed Grand Tutor, but 99 A: 6a states that when the others had been appointed, Wang Mang had not yet arisen to receive his appointment. Wang Mang hence received his appointment later on in the same day as the others—court was held early in the morning.

[6.3] A quotation from a saying of Confucius in *Han-shih Wai-chuan* 8: 11b, sect. 18, "Without leaving the sacrifical vases or tables, Yen-tzu repulsed the attack [of the enemy] at a distance of a thousand *li*," denoting a diplomatic victory. This saying is in turn taken from *Yen-tzu Ch'un-ch'iu* 5: 14a, sect. 16. A comparison of these two sources shows, in an illuminating fashion, how certain sayings attributed to Confucius arose.

曰時加賞明重元功無使百僚元元失望太后乃下詔曰大司

百戶四人阮受賞莽尚未起羣臣復上言莽雖克讓朝所宜章

奉車都尉邶宿衛勤勞建議定策封邶為承陽侯食邑二千四

千戶臣豐為少傅授四輔之職嚖其將邑各賜第一區侍中

仁萬使迎中山王輔尊共養臣安宗廟封豐為廣陽侯食邑五

worthy, benevolent, and sincere. He was sent to invite the King of Chung-shan [to ascend the throne] and has assisted and guided him and supplied his needs, thereby giving tranquillity to the [imperial] ancestral temples. [Chen] Feng shall be enfeoffed 8a as Marquis of Kuang-yang with the income of a state of 5000 households. [Chen] Feng shall become the Junior Tutor.

"Upon all [these persons] there shall be conferred the position [of being included among] the Four Coadjutors. Their noble ranks and estates shall be the same [for their descendants as for the founders of their houses] and to each shall be given one residence.

"The Palace Attendant and Chief Commandant of Imperial Equipages, [Chen] Han, has guarded the throne and toiled diligently. He made the proposal and planned the imperial enthronement. [Chen] Han shall be enfeoffed as the Marquis of Ch'eng-yang 6b with the income of an estate of two[6.4] thousand four hundred households."

When these four persons had received rewards and [Wang] Mang had not even yet arisen, various courtiers again presented [a memorial to the Grand Empress Dowager nee Wang], saying, "Although [Wang] Mang is able to yield [to others,[6.5] yet] he is one whom the court should properly make illustrious and to whom should be given at [this appropriate] time [suitable] rewards, [thereby] making well-known and important one who has achieved great merits and [thereby] not causing the hopes of the many officials or of the great multitude to be disap- 6b pointed."[6.6]

The [Grand] Empress Dowager thereupon issued an imperial edict, saying, "The Commander-in-chief,

6.4 The Official ed. misprints 三 for 二. The latter reading is confirmed in 18: 28a.

6.5 A phrase from *Book of History*, I, i, 1 (Legge, p. 15), where Yao is said to have been "able to yield to others."

6.6 Note the rimes: 讓，章，賞，望.

He is
Awarded
High
Honors.

the Marquis of Hsin-tu_c, [Wang] Mang, has been one of the three highest ministers for three reigns and has performed the [same] duties [as those performed by] the Duke of Chou. He has established the plan [for the succession to the throne that is to endure for] ten thousand generations. In achievements and virtuous conduct[6.7] he has been a model to palace officials.[6.8] His influence has spread over [all] within the [four] seas, so that people of distant [regions] have thought with affection of right principles; a potentate of the Yüeh-shang,[6.9] [whose speech must be] repeatedly interpreted [from one interpreter to another], presented a white pheasant as tribute.

"Let [Wang] Mang be additionally enfeoffed with [the income of] the twenty-eight thousand households in the two counties of Shao-ling and Hsin-hsi. His heirs who succeed him shall be exempted [from taxes and service] and their noble rank and estate shall be the same [as his].[6.10] His achievements[6.11] shall be [ranked] the same as those of the [former] Chancellor of State, Hsiao [Ho.

8b

Wang] Mang shall be the Grand Tutor and in charge of the business of the Four Coadjutors. His title shall be the Duke Giving Tranquillity to the Han Dynasty. The first residence, that of the former Chancellor of State, Hsiao [Ho], shall become the residence of the Duke Giving Tranquillity to the Han Dynasty. Let [this ordinance] be established and published as a

[6.7] For 能, the Ching-yü ed., the Southern Academy ed., and the Official ed. read 德. I adopt the latter reading.

[6.8] Li Tz'u-ming, *ibid.*, asserts that 忠 is an error for 中; and I follow him. Cf. *HHS*, Mem. 17: 15a, *sub* Chao Wen, where a similar reading is found.

[6.9] The Sung Ch'i ed. notes that the Hsi-ning Academy ed. (1069) and the Yüeh ed. (xi–xii cent.) lack the word 裳. The Ching-yü ed. also lacks it.

[6.10] They were to be exempted from the usual inheritance tax upon noble estates; cf. 8: n. 7.9.

[6.11] Liu Ch'ang (1019–1068) remarks that *feng* 封 is an interpolation. The Sung Ch'i ed. notes that the Shao ed. (xi or xii cent.) reads 加 instead of 功 *gung*. I have followed Liu Ch'ang.

太傅安漢公號讓還益封疇爵邑事云爾須百姓家給然
故賜號曰安漢公輔翼於帝期於致平毋違朕意苾受
位而公韋之功德茂著宗廟呂安益白誰之瑞周成虜焉
危無嗣而公定之回鄙之職三公之任而公幹之韋僚衆
於今傳之無窮於是帝為惺恐不得已而起受策策曰漢

[permanent] ordinance and be transmitted [forever] without end."

Thereupon [Wang] Mang hypocritically[6.12] feared that he had no alternative and so he arose and received his charter [of appointment]. The charter said, **His Charter.**

"The Han [dynasty] was in danger because there was no heir, and your excellency stabilized it. As to the positions of the Four Coadjutors and the responsibilities of the three highest ministers, your excellency controls them. As to the various officials and the many positions, your excellency rules them. Your merits and virtue are abundant and brilliant. Thereby the [imperial] ancestral temples are tranquil. Verily, the auspicious presage of the white pheasant is symbolical of [the way the Duke of] Chou [acted as minister to King] Ch'eng. Hence [We] grant you the auspicious title of the Duke Giving Tranquillity *7a* to the Han Dynasty. When you are the Coadjutor and protector of the Emperor, do you aim at bringing about [a condition of the utmost] tranquillity. Do not disappoint Our intentions."

[Wang] Mang received the titles of Grand Tutor and Duke Giving Tranquillity to the Han Dynasty, [but] he yielded up and returned the matter of his increase in enfeoffment and his noble rank and estate being the same [for his descendants as for himself], saying, "I wish to wait until the people[6.13] have a **He Refuses Some Grants.**

---

[6.12] Su Yü (fl. 1913) remarks that 為 and 偽 were interchanged. I read the latter.

[6.13] H. O. H. Stange, *Die Monographie über Wang Mang*, 22, n. 1 follows the *Tz'u-yüan* in interpreting *po-hsing* 百姓 as denoting the families of officials, stating that this term was first democratized gradually in Han times. I believe that this process had already been completed. The meaning here is explained later (7a), when Wang Mang says that "benefits should be granted to gentlemen and common people and to widowers and widows ... to everyone." That the "families of officials" should be favored moreover implies an aristocratic age, in which descent, rather than ability, brought official position. This was the fact in Spring and Autumn times, but the Han dynasty ushered in a period when not family, but ability was supposed to bring position; the founder of this dynasty and his paladins were commoners; their advent marks the final breakdown of a true hereditary aristocracy (cf. *HFHD*, I, 13–15). Han Confucianism, with the examination

sufficiency in their households and then only should
I be given any rewards." The other highest ministers again argued with him. The [Grand] Empress
Dowager's imperial edict said, "You, Duke, of your
own accord aim at the people having a sufficiency
in their households, because of which [We] listen to

**7a** you. Let it be ordered that your salary, Duke, and
the rewards granted to the members of your suite[7.1]

**9a** shall all be double what they were previously, and
when the people have a sufficiency in their households
so that personally they have enough, the Grand
Minister over the Multitude, [K'ung Kuang], and
the Grand Minister of Works, [Wang Ch'ung], shall
report [the fact] in order that [you may thereupon
be granted the full amount of your reward]."

He has
Others
Honored.

[Wang] Mang again refused and would not receive
[these honors] and proposed that it would be proper
to set up descendants of the vassal kings [as kings]
and to enfeoff the descendants of the more important
of the meritorious courtiers of the Eminent Founder,
[Emperor Kao], and his successors, as marquises or
to grant them the noble rank of Marquis of the Imperial Domain with the income of estates; and thereafter those in office should each have his [full] rank,
[so that there may be] a government making grants to
every one, in which on the one hand, the [imperial] ancestral temples are honored[7.2], by augmenting the

系統 opening even the highest positions to able persons, regardless of their descent,
took an attitude to aristocracy quite different from that of Chou times, when, until its
last centuries, official positions were hereditary in certain families. The *Tz'u-hai*, *sub
po-hsing*, shows that this phrase, even when referring to the most ancient times, in addition to the meaning, "the officials," also meant "the common people." Stange himself
is sometimes forced to translate *po-hsing* as "Volk" (p. 25, l. 4).

[7.1] Yen Shih-ku remarks, "The members of his suite were the regularly authorized
number of officials in his own yamen 舍人私府吏員也."

[7.2] Ho Ch'uo states that the honoring of an imperial ancestral temple refers to the
giving to the Temple of Emperor Yüan the name of the Temple of the Eminent Exemplar;
cf. 12: 8a. But this title was not given until A.D. 4, so that Ho Ch'uo is very likely
mistaken.

孫大者封侯或賜爵關內侯食邑然後及諸在位各有茅序
聞莽復讓不受而建言宜立諸侯王俊及高祖呂宋功臣子
令公奉舍人賞賜皆倍故百姓家給人足大司徒大司空呂
後加賞犖公後爭太后詔曰公自期百姓家給是呂聽之其

碎朕忝秋高精氣不堪殆非所巳安躬體而育養皇帝者也故選忠賢
宜親省小事令太后下詔曰皇帝幼年朕且統政比加元服今眾事煩
二千石及州部所舉茂材異等吏率多不稱宜皆見安漢公又太后不
阮説眾庶又欲專斷知太后猒政乃風公卿奏言往者吏呂功次遷至
上享宗廟增加禮樂下惠士民鰥寡恩澤之政無所不施語在平紀牽

rites and music [employed therein] and on the other hand, gentlemen and commoners are shown kindness and widowers and widows [are given] grace and bounty. A discussion is in the "Annals of [Emperor Hsiao]-p'ing." 12: 2b, 4b–6a.

When [Wang] Mang had pleased the mass of commoners,[7.3] he also wanted the right to decide matters on his own authority. He knew that the [Grand] Empress Dowager had no taste for governing, so he gave a hint to the ministers. They memorialized her, saying, "In the past, officials have been promoted in accordance with the order of their merits to [positions ranking as] two thousand piculs. They, together with minor officials who have been recommended from the provincial divisions as being Abundant Talents of Unusual Degree, are for the most part not worthy [of their positions, so that] it would be proper that they should all interview the Duke Giving Tranquillity to the Han Dynasty, [Wang Mang]. It is also not proper that the [Grand] Empress Dowager should in person supervise unimportant matters." He is Given Plenary Power.

[Thus they] caused the [Grand] Empress Dowager to issue an imperial edict which said, "Since the Emperor is young in years, We are temporarily directing *7b* the government until he puts on the bonnet of virility.[7.4] Now most matters are complicated and detailed, while Our years are many and [Our] bodily *9b* vigor is insufficient. [If We attend to these matters], there is danger that [We] may not have the means of keeping [Our] body in health or of caring for the Emperor. Hence [We] have selected loyal and capable persons and have set up the Four Coadjutors,

[7.3] Ch'ien Ta-chao states that the Southern Academy ed. (1531) and the Fukien ed. (1549) read 意 for 庶; the Official ed. reads likewise. The Ching-yu ed. reads the latter word. I follow it.

[7.4] The Sung Ch'i ed. said that after the word 服 there should be the word 者. The Ching-yu ed. does not have it.

so that [Our] many inferiors should be urged to do their duty and there should perpetually be prosperity and peace.

**7b**　　"Confucius 'said, "How sublime the way Shun and Yü held possession of the country and yet remained indifferent to [the details of government]!" '[7.5] From this time and henceforth, except[7.6] for enfeoffments of noble titles, which shall nevertheless be reported [to Us], in all other matters, the Duke Giving Tranquillity to the Han Dynasty and the Four Coadjutors shall judge and decide. As to Provincial Shepherds, [officials ranking at] two thousand piculs, together with minor officials [who are recommended as being] Abundant Talents, when they are [considered] for their first appointment [to office] and when they memorialize matters, they shall each time be led into an office near [the palace] to answer questions; the Duke Giving Tranquillity to the Han Dynasty, [Wang Mang], shall examine into their former offices and ask about their new duties, in order that he may know whether they are worthy or not."

Thereupon [Wang] Mang received and questioned each one [of the officials], conveyed to them his secret gracious intentions, and bestowed upon them rich parting gifts, while he brought out memorials concerning those who did not suit his purposes and dismissed them, so that his power was equal to that of the lord of men.

*The Grand Empress Dowager Imitates His Humility.*

[Wang] Mang wanted to delight the [Grand] Empress Dowager with vain reputation, so advised her in conversation that since she had herself succeeded to the extravagance of the Ting and Fu [clans

---

[7.5] *Analects* VIII, xviii.

[7.6] Wang Hsien-ch'ien states that *fei* 非 is a mistake; the Official ed. and the Southern Academy ed. (1531) emend it to 惟. The Ching-yu ed. reads *fei*, and I prefer not to alter the text. We cannot always expect perfect Chinese style, even in imperial edicts.

立四輔羣下勸職永曰康寧孔子曰巍巍乎舜禹之有天下而不與
馬自今已來非封爵乃曰閣他事安漢公曰輔平決州牧二千石及
茂材吏初除奏事者輒引入至近署對安漢公考故官問新職曰知
其稱否於是恭人人延問致密意厚加賜送共不合指顯奏免之
權與人主侔矣恭欲臣虛名說太后白言親承前孝哀丁傅奢侈之

下德澤閎者風雨時甘露降神芝生萐莆朱草嘉禾休徵同時並

氣育皇帝安宗廟也臣莽數叩頭省戶下爭未見許今辛賴陛性

馬莽帥群臣奏言陛下吞秋尊久衣重練減御膳誠非所以輔精

願出錢百萬獻田三十頃付大司農助給貧民於是公卿皆慕效

後百姓未贍者多太后宜且衣繒練頗損膳己視天下奉因上書

related to] the deceased [Emperor] Hsiao-ai, while most of the people did not have enough [to live on],[7.7] it would be proper for the [Grand] Empress Dowager temporarily to wear coarse plain silk,[7.8] and to reduce considerably [the expense of] her cuisine, in order to show [her economical spirit] to the empire.

[Wang] Mang thereupon presented a letter, stating that he would pay a million cash and offer thirty *ch'ing*[7.9] of cultivated fields, to be paid to the Grand Minister of Agriculture, for assistance and gifts to the poor people.[7.10] Thereupon the ministers all admired and imitated him.

[Wang] Mang led the various courtiers in a memorial, saying, "Your Majesty is of an honorable age, [yet] you have for a long time worn heavy plain white silk and have reduced your imperial cuisine, which verily is not the way to sustain your bodily vigor, to care for the Emperor, or to give tranquillity to the [imperial] ancestral temples. Your subject, Mang, has several times knocked his head to the ground at the door to your Inner Apartments and has advised and argued with you [concerning this practise, but my request that this practise be discontinued] has not yet been approved. Now, thanks to your Majesty's virtue and beneficence, the wind and rain have recently been timely, sweet dew has descended, the supernatural fungus of immortality has grown, the calendar plant and the red herb,[7.11] auspicious cereals and [other] favorable signs have all appeared simultaneously.

10a
A.D. 2,
Summer[7.10]
A Great
Charity.
8a
He
Lauds
the Grand
Empress
Dowager.

---

[7.7] Reminiscent of *Mencius* I, i, vii, 22 (Legge, p. 148).

[7.8] Yen Shih-ku says, "*Tseng-lien* 繒練 means silk without markings 帛無文."

[7.9] An area totaling about 340 acres or 136 hectares; cf. n. 9.7.

[7.10] Cf. *HS* 12: 5b.

[7.11] The calendar plant 蓂莢 grew in Yao's courts, a new leaf growing each of the fifteen days in the first half of a month and a leaf dropping each of the remaining days in a month. In the *Ta-Tai Li*, "Ming-t'ang," 8: 12a, ch. 67 (not in Wilhelm's trans.) the red herb 朱草 is described in the same terms as the calendar plant is described elsewhere.

"Your servant Mang and the others are not capable of overcoming their great hopes: we wish that

**8a** your Majesty would have compassion upon your energy, rest your spirit, relax your thoughts, conform to the regular imperial robes, and restore the legal cuisine of the Grand[8.1] Provisioner, thereby causing each of your subjects and children to be completely content in his heart and to supply your needs perfectly. We hope that you will sympathetically scrutinize [our request]."

**The Regency Will Terminate when the Emperor 10b Comes of Age.**

[Wang] Mang also caused the [Grand] Empress Dowager to issue an imperial edict which said, "Verily, [We] have heard that [according to] the moral principles for the mother of a ruler, her thoughts should not go outside the threshold of the door.[8.2] Since the state has not received [Heaven's] blessing and the Emperor is of the age when he is in swaddling-clothes and is not yet capable of governing in person, [We] have trembled with apprehension and [guarded Ourself] for fear that the [imperial] ancestral temples would not be tranquil. Except for Us, who can control the general policies of the state?

"It was for such reasons that Confucius interviewed Nan-tzu and that the Duke of Chou acted as regent, which was probably an expedient suited to the time.[8.3] [We] have fatigued [Ourself] and have pondered to the utmost [degree], have toiled and worried, and have not yet become tranquil. Hence 'if the state is prodigal, then [a sage] gives it an example of economy,'[8.4] and 'in straightening a

孔子見南子周公居攝權時也勤身極思憂勞未綏故國奮則視
親政戰戰兢兢懼於宗廟之不安國家之大綱微朕孰當統之是呂
詔曰蓋聞女后之義思不出乎門閫國不蒙佑皇帝年在繈褓未任
太宮之法膳使臣子各得盡驩心備共養唯臣妾省荅荅又令太后下
至臣莽等不勝大願願陛下受精休神闓略思慮遵帝王之常服復

---

[8.1] The Official ed. reads 大 for this 太. The Ching-yu ed. reads the latter.

[8.2] Liu Hsiang₄'s *Lieh-nü Chuan* 1: 17a says, Women "should have their cares inside the women's apartments and should have no thoughts outside that region." (Reference from Shen Ch'in-han.) He is probably quoting from the *Meng-tzu Wai-shu* 1: 5b.

The Sung Ch'i ed. says that the Academy ed. (1005) does not have the word 門.

[8.3] For Nan-tzu, cf. *Analects* VI, xxvi; *Tso-chuan*, Dk. Ting, XV (Legge, 788). Both she and the Duke of Chou controlled the government.

[8.4] A quotation from the *Li-chi*, II, ii, ii, 4 (Legge, I, 175; Couvreur, I, 213).

平惟四天未有吳乃遣使者齎黃金幣帛重賂匈奴單于使上書言閒中

公菜食憂民深矣今秋幸孰公勤於職日時食肉定身為國者念中國己

傳有成其腸之哉每有水旱菲飯惡食左右白白太后遣使者詔菲曰閒

姓家給比皇帝加元服委政而枝焉今誠未皇于輕靡而備朱庶幾與百

之臣僑矯枉者過其正而朕不身帥將謂天下何夙夜憂想五穀豐孰百

curved [piece of wood, it may be spoiled by being bent backwards] beyond a straight [line,'[8.5] so We may have gone too far in economizing], yet if We *8b* do not personally lead [the empire back to correctness], what will [We be able] to say to the empire?

"[We] have hoped morning and night that the five [kinds of] grains should be harvested in abundance and the peoples' households should have a sufficiency. When the Emperor dons the cap of virility, [We] shall entrust the government to him and transfer it to him.

"[We] now verily have had no leisure for light and delicate [clothing] or for perfectly flavored [food] and hope that together with the many officials [We] may achieve [a good government]. Let [us all] make [great] efforts towards this [end]."

Every time there was a flood or drought, [Wang] Mang would eat plain food.[8.6] When her entourage advised her of it, the [Grand] Empress Dowager sent a messenger with an imperial edict to [Wang] Mang, saying, "[We] have heard that you, Duke, have been eating [only] vegetables. Your solicitude for the common people is indeed deep. Since in this autumn there has fortunately been a good harvest, and you, Duke, are so diligent in your duties, at this time you should eat meat and care for your body for the sake of the state."

He Suffers with the People.

[Wang] Mang pondered that the Middle States were already tranquil, and only the barbarians of the four [quarters] were still the same as [before]. So he sent an envoy to give actual gold and valuable silks, as heavy bribes, to the Hun *Shan-yü*, in order to have him send a letter to the Emperor, which said, "I have heard that in the Middle States a

8b 11a
The *Shan-yü* Takes a Single Personal Name.

---

[8.5] A saying attributed to Mencius, found in the *Meng-tzu Wai-shu* 3: 5b.

[8.6] The Grand Empress Dowager's edict shows that "*su-shih*, 素食, plain food," in Han times, meant vegetables without meat. Cf. also *HS* 68: 7a.

double personal name is criticized.[8.7]  My former personal name has been Nang-chih-ya-szu.  Now I change my personal name to Chih, in admiration of and conformity to the regulations of the sages." He also sent [Lüan-ti Yün], the Hun Princess [who had married] Hsü-pu [Tang] and who was the daughter of Wang [Ch'iang] Chao-chün, to enter [the court] and wait upon [the Grand Empress Dowager.  Wang Mang thus used] myriads of methods and stratagems to dazzle deceptively and serve flatteringly the [Grand] Empress Dowager and her inferiors down to her Chief Chamberlain who was at her side.

**The Emperor to be Married.**

When [Wang] Mang had become an important personage, he wanted to mate his daughter to the Emperor, making her the Empress, in order to make his power secure.  [So] he memorialized, saying, "The Emperor has been on the throne to the third year, [yet the occupant of] the Ch'ang-ch'iu Palace, [the Empress], has not yet been established and [the positions of] concubines in the Lateral[8.8] Courts have not yet been filled.  Recently, the difficulties of the dynasty have originated from heirs being lacking and from [imperial] marriages and takings [of concubines] having been incorrect.  I beg that the Five Classics be investigated and discussed in order to establish rites for [the imperial] marriage

国讌二名故名襄知牙斯今，更名知慕従聖制又遵王

昭君女須卜居次入侍所曰諓耀媚事太后下至旁側

長御方故萬端奔院尊重欲曰女配帝為皇后曰固其

椎奏言皇帝即位三年長秋宮未建液廷媵未克乃者

国家之難本従亡嗣配取不正請考論五経定取禮正

[8.7] For this incident, cf. *HS* 94 B: 16a = de Groot, *Die Hunnen*, p. 264.

*Kung-yang Commentary* 26: 1a, Dk. Ting VI, says, "They criticized a double personal name.  A double personal name is contrary to the rites."  Ho Hsiu (129–182) explains, "Because it is difficult to taboo."  (Reference from Shen Ch'in-han.)  From late Chou times onwards, double personal names were unpopular, especially among rulers, whose names had to be tabooed.  But in the V cent. and later, double personal names, even for rulers, appear again.  Emperor Kao, the Grand Founder of the Southern Ch'i dynasty, had the given name 道成, but his successors took single personal names.  Cf. Ch'en Yuan's *Shih-hui Chü-li*, 48b, 49a.

[8.8] Yen Shih-ku remarks that 液 and 掖 have the same pronunciation and were interchanged.

and to fix the principle of [the Emperor's] twelve *9a* women,[8.9] in order to increase his posterity, and that there be a wide selection [for his harem] from the daughters of the principal wives of the descendants from the two [immediately preceding dynasties of true] kings, [the Shang and Chou dynasties], the posterity of the Duke of Chou and of Confucius, and the marquises in Ch'ang-an."

The matter was referred to the high officials and they presented [to the Grand Empress Dowager] the names of a multitude of girls. The girls of the Wang clan were the most numerous of those selected [as candidates for becoming the Empress. Wang] Mang feared that they would compete with his own daughter,[8.10] so he immediately presented [a letter] saying,

Wang Mang Withholds His Own Daughter.

---

[8.9] In a comment to *Chou-li* 7: 7a, sub the *Nei-tsai*, Cheng Chung [ca. 5 B.C.–A.D. 83] says, "The consorts (*fei* 妃) of the king [numbered] 120 persons. There was one queen (*hou* 后), three ladies (*fu-jen* 夫人), nine spouses (*p'in* 嬪), 27 women destined to provide descendants (*shih-fu* 世婦) and 81 female attendants (*nü-yü* 女御)." These same titles are found in the *Book of Rites*, I, ii, ii, 1 (Legge, I, 109; Couvreur, I, 86 f); *ibid.* XLI, 11 (Legge, II, 432; Couvreur II, 648). When Wang Mang married a second time, his concubines were of this number; cf. 99 C: 20a, b. In a comment to *Li-chi* 7: 1b, 2a (to Legge's verse 29 in II, i, i), Cheng Hsüan (127–200) says, "The Lord, K'u, established four consorts [for himself], which typify the four stars of the Empress and Consorts [a constellation in Scorpio and another in Ursa Minor], of which the brightest one is the principal consort, and the other three small ones are the secondary consorts. The Lord, Yao, followed [his example]. Shun did not inform [his parents] when he married, so did not establish a principal consort, and merely had three consorts, calling them the three Ladies. . . . The Sovereign of the Hsia dynasty, [Yü], increased them by three threes, which is nine, so that altogether there were twelve women. The explanation in the *Spring and Autumn* [unidentified] says, 'The Son of Heaven marries twelve [women]', which [speaks of] the regulations of the Hsia [dynasty]. . . . Then the members of the Yin [dynasty] again increased them by three nines, which is twenty-seven, altogether 39 women. The members of the Chou [dynasty] imitated the Lord, K'u, and established a principal spouse and also increased [the King's concubines] by three twenty-sevens, making eighty-one women, altogether 121 women." Shen Ch'in-han remarks that, according to the *Lieh-nü Chuan*, the Son of Heaven had twelve [concubines], nobles had nine, grandees had three, and gentlemen had two. Cf. also *T'ai-p'ing Yü-lan* 135: 1b ff. *Po-hu-t'ung* 9: 5b explains that "twelve women" is "to imitate Heaven, who has twelve months [in a year]." Cf. M. Granet, *La Polygnie Sororale*, p. 67, n. 1.

[8.10] *HS* 97 B: 23a states that Wang Mang wanted, like Ho Kuang, to have his daughter become the Empress, but "the [Grand] Empress Dowager did not wish it."

"I personally am without virtue and my child's abilities are of a low [order], so that it would not be proper for her to be put with the multitude of girls [from whom the Empress] is to be chosen."

The [Grand] Empress Dowager thought that he was completely sincere, so issued an imperial edict [for the Emperor], saying, "The girls of the Wang clan are Our maternal relatives. Let them not be selected [for the imperial harem]."

**9a**
**The People Memori-alize That His Daughter Should Become the Empress.**

The many common people, the [Confucian] masters, the Gentlemen, the lower officials, and [those holding] higher positions, who [thereupon came to] wait at the [Palace] Portals to present letters [to the Grand Empress Dowager, numbered] more than a thousand daily; some of the ministers and grandees went to the middle of the [principal] court and some prostrated themselves outside the doors of the Inner [Apartments]. All said, "The sage virtue of your enlightened edict is as sublime as" that, [or] "The abundant and glorious services of the Duke Giving Tranquillity to the Han Dynasty are as magnificent as" this, [or], "Now that an Empress is to be established, why should the daughter of the Duke be specially excluded? Where would the destiny of the empire be [better] placed? We wish to secure the daughter of the Duke as the mother of the empire."

[Wang] Mang sent his Chief Clerk and subordinates by divisions to instruct and stop the ministers and the [Confucian] masters, but those who presented letters [to the Grand Empress Dowager] were even greater [in number than before, so the Grand] Empress Dowager had no alternative but to listen to the ministers and select the daughter of Wang] Mang [to be the Empress].

[When Wang] Mang again himself advised her

部曉止公卿及諸生而上書者愈甚太后不得已聽公卿采眾女復自
后獨柰何廢公女天下安所歸命願得公女為天下母莽遣長史曰下分
中或伏省戶下咸言明詔聖德巍巍如彼安漢公盛勳堂堂若此今當立
家其勿采庶民諸生郎吏曰上守闕上書者日千餘人公卿大夫或詣廷
亡德子材下不宜與眾女並采太后曰為至誠乃下詔曰王氏女朕之外

156

言公女漸漬德化有窈窕之容宜承
樂少府宗正尚書令納采見女還奏
女臣貳正統莽白願見女太后遣長
白宜博選眾女公卿爭曰不宜采諸

that it would be proper to select widely from among the host of [suitable] girls, the ministers contested with him, saying, "It is not proper to select other girls and thereby alter the proper line of succession, [which can only come through the daughter of the Duke]."

[Wang] Mang [accordingly] advised [the Grand Empress Dowager] that he was willing to have his daughter interviewed. The [Grand] Empress Dowager sent the Privy Treasurer of Ch'ang-lo [Palace, Hsia-hou Fan[9.2]], the Superintendent of the Imperial House, [Liu Hung₃ᵦ], and the Prefect of the Masters of Writing, [P'ing Yen[9.2]], to present the proposal [of marriage][9.3] and to interview the girl. They returned and memorialized, saying, "The daughter of the Duke has been imbued with virtue and culture and has a beautiful and fascinating appearance, so

A.D. 3. Spring[9.1] 12a She is Selected.

9b

[9.1] Cf. *HS* 12: 6b.

[9.2] From *HS* 97 B: 23a, which states that the Privy Treasurer, Tsung-po Feng, was also sent.

[9.3] *Na-ts'ai* 納采 was the first of the five preliminary rites in a marriage. It was the ancient technical term for proposing an engagement, from *Yi-li* 4: 1a (Steele, I, 18), "When the [prospective] bride's [parents] have made known [their willingness], in presenting (*na*) [the announcement that the girl] had been chosen (*ts'ai*), a wild goose is employed." Cheng Hsüan comments, "After the girl's family has agreed, [the boy's parents] send a person to present (*na*) the rites of her choosing and selection (*ts'ai-tse* 擇), using a wild goose as an offering." Chia Kung-yen (fl. 640–655) adds, "*Na* (to present) means that the person who is doing the presenting, [the representative of the boy's parents], fears that the girl's family will not accept [the announcement], similar to the principle of *nei* 內 and *na* [to present a lady to a noble's harem] in the *Spring and Autumn*, when, if [the noble] approves, she is presented. *Ts'ai* (to select) means that the person who is doing the presenting, because [the girl] is newly chosen and selected (*ts'ai-tse*), fears that the girl's family will not agree to [the engagement]. Hence he calls it a *na* (presentation)."

The five preliminary rites in marriage were: (1) "the presentation of the choice [to the girl's parents] (*na-ts'ai*), (2) the request for the [girl's] given name (*ch'ing-ming*), (3) the presentation of the lucky [divination concerning the marriage] (*na-chi*), (4) the presentation of the betrothal presents (*na-cheng*), and (5) the request to fix a date [for the marriage] (*ch'ing-ch'i*)" Legge, *Li Ki*, II, 428; Couvreur, *Li Ki*, II, 641–42. The sixth and final rite was "the [groom] in person fetching [the bride, bringing her to his ancestral home] (*ch'in-ying*)," cf. Steele, *op. cit.*, I, 18ff; *Po-hu-t'ung* 9: 2b–3b.

that it would be proper for her to continue the heavenly[9.4] succession and uphold the [imperial] sacrifices."

There was an imperial edict sending the Grand Master Over the Masses, [Ma Kung], and the Grand Minister of Works, [Chen Feng], to inform in an official document [the imperial ancestors in the imperial] ancestral temples and in various ways to perform divination by the tortoise-shell and by the stalks. They reported unanimously, "The cracks upon the tortoise-shell which occurred were [a prognostic] that metal and water will flourish and assist. The diagram formed by the stalks which occurred was that the father and mother will occupy [their due] positions,[9.5] which may be said to be a response [presaging] prosperity and security, a portent of great good fortune."

所謂康彊之占逢吉之符也信
兆遇金水王相卦遇父母得位
司空策告宗廟雜加卜筮皆曰
大序奏崇祀有詔遣大司徒大

[9.4] Wang Hsien-ch'ien states that the Official ed. is correct in emending 大 to 天. The Ching-yu ed. reads the latter.

[9.5] Fu Ch'ien says, "[According to] the rules for the cracks upon the tortoise-shell, crosswise ones are earth; vertical ones are wood; slanting ones in the direction of the grain are metal; [slanting ones] across [the grain] are fire; those that accomodate themselves to the tortoise-shell and are slightly curved are water." (Quoted by Ch'ien Ta-chao).

*Wang*₂ should here be read as *wang*₄ 旺; these words were interchanged. In his comment on *Mencius* II, ii, i, 1, (Legge, p. 208), "Heaven's times are not as good as Earth's advantages," Chao Ch'i (108–201 A.D.) says, " 'Heaven's times' means the time and the day when the branches and stems and five elements *wang-hsiang* 王相 (flourish and assist), or are absent in that ten-day week or are the two middle days of a ten-day week." (The phrase *wang-hsiang* is also found in *Lun-heng* 1: 12b, ch. 3 [Forke, I, 148] where it is applied to people. For an explanation of *ku-hsü* 孤虛, cf. P'ei Yin's comment on these words in *SC* 128: 29.)

The *Meng-tzu Cheng-yi* (quoted in *Meng-tzu Chu-su* 4 A: 1b), attributed to Sun Shih (compiled before the xii cent.) explains that the element metal flourishes (*wang*₄) for the branches *szu, wu, wei, shen*, and *yu* and the element water flourishes (*wang*₄) for the branches *shen, yu, hsü, hai*, and *tzu*. Hence the prognostication was *shen* and *yu*, for these branches are in both lists. Yet the marriage was performed on the day *ting-wei* (A: 17a), so that there must have been a separate divination to determine the day of marriage.

Chang Yen says, " 'Father and mother' means hexagram [no. 11], *t'ai* (泰), [which

鄉侯佟上言春秋天子將娶於紀則襄
紀子稱侯安漢公國未稱古制事下有
司皆白古者天子封后父百里尊而不
臣呂重宗廟孝之至也佟言應禮可許

The Marquis of Hsin-hsiang, [Liu] T'ung₂ᵦ, presented [to the throne a memorial], saying, "[Accord-
ing to] the *Spring and Autumn*, when the Son of
Heaven was about to take [a bride from the state of]
Chi₆, he rewarded the Viscount of Chi with the title
of Marquis.[9.6]　The estate of the Duke Giving Tranquillity to the Han Dynasty, [Wang Mang], is not
yet conformable to [this] ancient regulation."

The matter was referred to the high officials, and
all advised, "Anciently, the Son of Heaven enfeoffed
the father of his Empress [with a fief] a hundred *li*
[square]; he honored [his father-in-law] and did not
treat him as his subject, in order to give importance
to his ancestral temple.　It was the extreme of filial
piety.　[Liu] T'ung's advice is in conformity with
the rites and may be approved.　We beg that [Wang]

**9b
Confucian
Tradition
Awards
Him
Great
Grants.**

has the trigram] *ch'ien* [male, heaven, etc.] below and [the hexagram] *k'un* [female, earth,
etc.] above.　Heaven is lower than Earth—this is the hexagram for mating and enjoying."　Lin Pin however ridicules this interpretation, "I say that it nevertheless means
'[Her] father and mother [shall] obtain [high] position.'　How could he know that this
was the hexagram *t'ai*?"　Perhaps Chang Yen understood divination better than Liu
Pin did.

9.6 In the *Spring and Autumn*, Dk. Yin, II (721 B.C.), (Legge, p. 8), there is mentioned
a "Tzu-po of Chi₆ 紀子伯."　In a note to *Tso-chuan* 2: 17a, Tu Yü (221–284) declares,
"Tzu-po is the style of Lieh-hsü 裂繻 [a grandee of Chi₆, mentioned in the same chapter
of the *Tso-chuan*]."　But the *Kung-yang Commentary* (iii cent. B.C.) 2: 3b, commenting
upon the same passage, says, "Who was Tzu-po of Chi₆?　It has not been reported."
According to the *Ku-liang Commentary* 1: 6b, the phrase in the *Spring and Autumn*, "*Chi
Tzu-po*," was sometimes interpreted as "The Viscount of Chi treated [the Viscount of Lü]
as his elder."　This latter interpretation underlies the passage in the *HS*.　The *Spring
and Autumn*, Dk. Huan II, vii, (710 B.C.), (Legge, p. 39) mentions "the Marquis of Chi,"
and Ying Shao, in a note to *HS* 18: 1b, explains, "[The ruler of the state of] Chi had
originally the title of Viscount, hence [the Son of Heaven] previously rewarded him and
made him a marquis.　It means that [true] kings do not take a bride from small states."
In a note to the *Kung-yang Commentary* 4: 5a, explaining the latter passage of the *Spring
and Autumn*, Ho Hsiu (129–182) glosses, "That he is entitled a marquis is [because], when
the Son of Heaven was about to take [a bride from the state of] Chi, he gave [this title
to its Viscount] since with her he would uphold his ancestral temple [sacrifices] and transmit them without end, than which nothing is greater.　Hence he was enfeoffed [with a
territory] of a hundred *li* [square]."　There were thus two interpretations of the phase
*Chi Tzu-po*.

12b Mang be additionally enfeoffed with the 25,600 *ch'ing* of cultivated fields in [the county of] Hsin-yeh, [in order that he may have] a full hundred *li*."[9.7]

He
Returns
Hsin-yeh.

[Wang] Mang excused himself, saying, "Your subject Mang's daughter is really not fit to be mated to the most honorable person [i.e., the Emperor]. I furthermore have heard about the discussions of the

足臣配至尊復聽眾議
莽辭曰臣莽子女誠不
六百頃益莽滿百里
請呂新野田二萬五千

[9.7] *HS* 24 A: 2b declares that six feet made a *pu* 步 (double pace) and a hundred *pu* made a *mou* 畝, i.e., an area 1 *pu* wide and 100 *pu* long. This was probably the ancient *mou* and the Han *pu*. Teng Chang (fl. ca. 208), in a note to *HS* 24 A: 18a remarks, "Anciently [cf. also Li Hsien's note to *HHS*, Mem. 39: 17a], a hundred *pu* made a *mou*, [but] in Han times 240 *pu* made a *mou*. 1200 ancient *mou* then made five present [Han] *ch'ing* 頃," i.e., if the ancient and Han foot were of the *same* length, 1200 ancient *mou* were equal to 500 Han *mou*, since the Han *ch'ing* contained 100 *mou*.

Since the Han foot was 9.09 in. (Eng. meas.) long, and the Han *mou* was one Han *pu* wide and 240 Han *pu* long, a Han *mou* contained 0.114 acre or 4.61 ar. A *ch'ing* was then 11.4 acres or 4.61 hectares.

The fields of Hsin-yeh, 25,600 *ch'ing*, were then 291,840 acres or 118,016 ha. "A full hundred *li* [square]" thus refers to the whole of his holdings.

The Han *li* 里 does not seem to have been based on the Han *mou*, but on the *pu*. Anciently, the *li* was the length of one side of a *ching* 井, i.e., 300 *pu*; the Han *li* was 300 Han *pu* long. *HS* 24 A: 2b states that an [ancient] *ching* was one *li* square and contained 900 [ancient] *mou*. The same passage states that a *mou* was one *pu* wide and a hundred *pu* long, so that a *ching* was 300 *pu* square. *Li-chi* III, v, 19 (Legge, I, 244; Couvreur I, 320) and *Han-shih Wai-chuan* 4: 7b (from which *HS* 24 A: 2b probably took its information) declare directly that a *ching* was 300 *pu* square. The latter and the *HS* assert that a *pu* was six feet long. Since the Han foot was 9.094 inches (Eng. measure) long (cf. *HFHD*, I, ch. IV, app. II, p. 279), the *li* was 1364 feet Eng. measure or 415.8 meters long. This length can be confirmed from a study by Ch'ou Tsai-lu in the *Chinese Historical Geography Magazine (Yü-kung)*, Sept. 16, 1935, vol. 4, no. 2, p. 12, in which he points out that the *HS* states the distance from Yarkhand (Sha-ch'ê) to Guma (P'i-shan) to be 380 *li*, while it is measured at 155 km.; from Guma to Yotkan (Yü-tien) is 380 *li*, which is 150 km., so that a *li* must have been 408 or 400 m. Thus our deduction from *HS* 24 A concerning the *li* is confirmed; that conclusion also confirms our figure for the size of a *mou*. Cf. W. Eberhard, "Zur Landwirtschaft der Han-Zeit," *MSOS*, v. 35 (1932), p. 98, and his "Bemerkungen zu statistischen Angaben der Han-Zeit," *T'oung Pao*, 36 (1940), 2–4. This conclusion concerning the size of the *mou* and *li* applies only to Han times, more exactly, to Wang Mang's time. According to *Li-chi* III, v, 21 (Legge I, 246; Couvreur, I, 323), in Chou times the *pu* contained eight feet, so that writers, assuming a foot of the Han length, calculated the Chou *mou* and *li* to have been larger than in Han times; but such need not actually to have been the case.

益封臣奉伏自惟念得託肺腑獲爵
土如使子女誠能奉稱聖德臣恭國
邑足呂共朝貢不須復加益地之寵
願歸所益太后許之有司奏故事聘

many [officials concerning] an increase in my enfeoffment. I, your subject Mang, myself humbly meditate that I have been permitted to rely upon [the fact that I am] a distant relative [of the throne][9.8] and have [thus] attained noble rank and lands. If my daughter is really capable of supporting and according with your sage virtue, the estate of your subject Mang is [yet] sufficient to make offer- *10a* ings for the tribute at the court; it is not necessary again to give me the favor of added territory. I wish to return what was to be added." The [Grand] Empress Dowager approved it.

The high officials memorialized that, [according to] ancient practises, an empress was betrothed [with a

---

[9.8] Wang Nien-sun, in a note to *HS* 36: 17a, states that both the words *fei₁-fu₁* 肺腑 mean bark (or shavings, splinters). *Shuo-wen* 6 A: 3b defines *p'o* 朴 as bark (or shavings) 木皮, and *ibid.* 7b defines *fei₂* 柿 as a scraped wooden writing block. Wang Nien-sun asserts that *fei₁* is borrowed for *fei₂* (giving examples); that 柎, *fu₂* 附 and *p'o* (also pronounced *pu*), all of which are used as the second word of this phrase, are close in pronunciation; and that *fu₁* is used for *fu₂*. The phrase *fei-fu* "means that he considered himself as an unimportant relative of the imperial house, just as bark is a part of a tree (or the shavings were part of a wooden writing block)." Liu Hsiang uses this phrase of himself in 36: 17a; in 36: 29b he speaks of himself as "having fortunately been permitted to attach himself as one of the least of [the imperial] relatives," which passage is parallel to this expression. This phrase *fei-fu* is also used in ch. 52: 5a and *SC* 107: 10 *sub* T'ien Fen; *HS* ch. 53 *sub* King Ching of Chung-shan; ch. 55 *sub* Wei Ch'ing; ch. 80; ch. 86 *sub* Shih₁ Tan; *SC* 19: 3 (*MH* III, 148); *HHS*, Mem. 2 *sub* Lu Fang. The foregoing interpretation follows that of Szu-ma Cheng in *SC* 19: 3, who takes it from Yen Chih-t'ui's (531–ca. 591) *Yen-shih Chia-hsün* B: 23a, b; ch. 17 (q.v.).

It is strongly attacked by Chang Shou-chieh in a note to *SC* 107: 10, where he follows an ancient interpretation quoted by Yen Shih-ku in *HS* 36: 17a and 52: 5a, which states, " '*Fei₁-fu₁*' means that the liver and lungs are close to each other, as if one said, 'heart and spine'. " He quotes Ku Yeh-wang (519–581) "*Fei₁-fu₁* [means the same as] belly and heart." In a note to *SC* 19: 3, Takigawa states that it was an expression peculiar to Han times, not seen in the *Books of Odes, of History*, the *Tso-chuan* or the *Kuo-yü*, and was used to denote close relatives. Cf. *Tz'u-tung*, I, 1313–1314.

But this latter interpretation, which makes Wang Mang boast that he is a close relative, is not at all humble. According to Han Confucian theory, close imperial relatives ought to be given high office (*HFHD*, II, 292). Wang Mang is not claiming a right, but humbly mentioning the favors granted him. Wang Nien-sun must be correct in this case.

He
Distrib-
utes
**10a**
the Dowry
Money
Among the
Families of
the Im-
perial
Concu-
bines-
elect.
He is
Given
Additional
Sums.
Chang
**13a**
Sung's
Laudatory
Memorial
for
Ch'en
Ch'ung.

gift of] twenty thousand catties of actual gold,[9.9] which would be two hundred million cash. [Wang] Mang declined it and asked strongly that it be given to others, [but] received forty million [cash] and gave thirty-three million [cash] of that [sum] to the families of [the Emperor's] eleven concubines, [who were to accompany the Empress].

Various courtiers again said, "Now the betrothal presents received for the Empress barely surpass those for the various concubines." [So] there was an imperial edict again increasing [the gift to Wang Mang] by twenty-three million [cash, making it] altogether thirty million [cash. Wang] Mang again used ten million [cash] of that [sum] to divide among the poor persons in his nine [sets of] relatives.

Ch'en Ch'ung was at that time Director of Justice to the Grand Minister over the Masses, [Ma Kung], and was good friends with Chang Ch'ang's grandson, [Chang] Sung. [Chang] Sung was a gentleman of wide learning, and drafted for [Ch'en] Ch'ung a memorial praising the achievements and virtuous conduct of [Wang] Mang, which [Ch'en] Ch'ung memorialized. It said,

"[According to] the opinion of your unworthy servant, from the time that the Duke Giving Tranquillity to the Han Dynasty first 'brought his bundle of dried flesh [and began studying],'[10.1] he has been placed in an age when customs have been highly

---

[9.9] *Han-chiu-yi* B: 2a declares, "The Emperor bethroths his Empress with ten thousand catties of actual gold." *HHS*, An, 10 B: 6a says, "Thereupon altogether according to the former practice of the presents for an Empress [in the case of] the Empress [nee Chang of Emperor] *Hsiao-hui*, she was betrothed with twenty thousand catties of actual gold." *Sung-shu* 14: 4a states that in A.D. 287, a Master of Writing, Chu Cheng, asserted "According to the regulation of the Empress of [Emperor] Kao of the Han dynasty, an empress is betrothed with two hundred catties of actual gold and twelve horses and Ladies with fifty catties of gold and four horses." Shen Ch'in-han notes this statement and adds that the *Sung-shu* is correct.

[10.1] A phrase from *Analects* VII, vii.

誅管蔡季子鶴叔牙公之謂矣是呂孝成皇帝命公大司馬委曰
及為侍中故定陵侯淳于長有大逆罪公不敢私建白誅討周公
士惠于故舊篤于師友孔子曰未若貧而樂富而好禮公之謂矣
驚馬妃匹無二閨門之内孝友之德衆莫不聞清靜樂道溫良下
意怡然而折節行仁克心履禮拂世矯俗確然特立惡衣惡食隨車
麗之時蒙兩宮厚骨肉之寵被諸父赫赫之光財饒勢足亡所語

extravagent and luxurious, has had the high favor of being allied in flesh and blood to [the occupants of] two palaces, [Emperor Ch'eng and the Grand Empress Dowager nee Wang], and has been covered with the illustrious brilliance of his various uncles. His wealth has been great and his power abundant, so that his will was unopposed.

"Yet he has humbled himself, lived a life of kindness and goodness, vanquished his desires, and walked in the path of proper conduct, resisting the age and correcting its customs, standing firmly alone, [wearing] poor clothes and [eating] poor food, with a shabby carriage and sorry horses, with one consort and no other [woman]. No one of the multitude has failed to hear of [the wonderful conditions] within the doors of his inner apartments and of his virtues of filial piety and friendliness. He is quiescent, rejoicing in the Way, gentle and good, and associating with worthy inferiors. He is kindly to his old friends and servitors and faithful to his teachers and associates. Confucius said, 'No [one] is as good as the man who is poor and yet happy, rich and yet loves the rules of proper conduct,'[10.2] which indeed applies to the Duke.

"When he was a Palace Attendant and the former Marquis of Ting-ling, Shun-yn Chang, committed the crime of treason, the Duke did not presume to keep it to himself [but] advocated that [his cousin] should be punished. The Duke of Chou executed [the King's Uncles] of Kuan and of Ts'ai and Master Chi [Yu] poisoned Shu Ya,[10.3] which [precedent] indeed denotes that the Duke [is like these sages].

"For this reason, Emperor Hsiao-ch'eng gave the Duke a mandate to be his Commander-in-chief, entrusting him with the government of the state.

Chang Sung's Laudatory Memorial. (1) His Self-discipline.

*10b*

(2) His **10b** Impartial 13b Revelation of His Cousin's Crime.

---

[10.2] *Analects* I, xv, 1.
[10.3] For these events, cf. Glossary, *sub* these names.

**Chang Sung's Laudatory Memorial. (3) His Opposition to the Advancement of Natural Imperial Maternal Relatives.**

When [Emperor] Hsiao-ai ascended the throne, the Marquis of Kao-ch'ang, Tung Hung, divined the desires [of the Concubine nee Ting] and sought for her approbation [by suggesting that the Emperor's natural mother, this Concubine nee Ting, should be given the title belonging to his imperial mother, instead of recognizing that Emperor Ai was the adopted son of his predecessor, hence his natural mother could not be his imperial mother. Tung Hung thus actually proposed] creating two lines of [imperial] descent. [But] the Duke in person impeached [Tung Hung] and thereby established a fundamental principle [of government]. He advocated that it was not proper for the Queen Dowager [nee Fu] of Ting-t'ao to have [her canopy and seat beside] the imperial[10.4] canopy and seat [of the Grand Empress Dowager],[10.5] in order to make plain the constitution of the state. The *Book of Odes* says,

> 'The weak he did not devour
> And the powerful he did not eject;
> He did not insult widowers or widows
> Nor fear the strong or resistful,'[10.6]

which indeed applies to the Duke.

**(4) His Unjust Dismissal.**

"He firmly held to humility and expressed his sincerity in yielding his position. When the Queen Dowager [nee Fu] of Ting-t'ao wanted to secure for herself the usurped title [of Empress Dowager], she feared his sense of duty which [made him] rebuke her to her face [for placing] her canopy and seat [next to that of the Grand Empress Dowager]. Flattering

---

[10.4] Ts'ai Yung, in his *Tu-tuan*, A: 2b, explains that *sheng-yü* 乘輿 and *ch'e-chia* 車駕 came to mean merely "imperial" or "Emperor."

[10.5] Cf. 99 A: 2b, 3a.

[10.6] *Book of Odes*, ＊260; III, III, vi, 5 (Legge, p. 544). The Mao text reads 矜 for the *HS's* 鰥. Two other variations are merely substitute characters. The Sung Ch'i ed. remarks that the Academy ed. (1005) and the Yüeh ed. (xi-xii cent.) omit the third line.

女之援皆自知得罪天下結離中山則必同憂斷金相翼蔣假
國多頗公之謂矣當此之時宮亡儲主董賢擅重加呂傅氏有
國朝政崩壞絪紀廢弛危亡之禍不隊如髮詩云人之云亡邦
制度遂成簒號斥逐仁賢誅殘咸屬而公被脅原之訴遠去就
之雄朱博之嚾慼此長宏手劫之事上下壹心讒賊交亂詭辭

and misleading braves, [such as] Chu Po and his
sort, were restrained by the other fact that [Wang
Mang] had in person impeached [Shun-yü] Chang
and [Tung] Hung. [Hence] superiors and inferiors
were united in calumniating, injuring, and causing
confusion, so that they violated and perverted the
regulations, and [the Queen Dowager] succeeded in
usurping the title [of Grand Empress Dowager].
They drove away [men of] stable benevolence and
executed [the imperial] relatives by marriage [who
were related to the preceding emperor, so that]
the Duke suffered the calumny [undergone by
Wu Yüan Tzu]-hsü and [Ch'ü] Yüan, and was
caused to go far away to his state [of Hsin-tu_c]. The
court and the government were collapsing in ruins,
the main and subordinate [dynastic] principles were
going to pieces, and the calamity of the overthrow
[of the dynasty] remained suspended by no more
than a hair. The *Book of Odes* says,

> 'When [capable] men flee,
>     The state is exhausted and at the point
>         of ruin,'[10.7]

which applies indeed to the Duke.

"At this time, [when Emperor Ai had died], there
was no heir in the [imperial] palaces; Tung Hsien[2a]
occupied the most important [position], added to
which the Fu clan had the assistance of their daughter, [who was the Empress]. They all themselves
knew that they had offended the country and had a
feud with [the royal family in the kingdom of]
Chung-shan, so that it would have been necessary
for [the Fu and Ting clans] to be 'one in' their worries,
protect each other by [the power which enables a
person] to 'shatter metal [bars]',[11.1] utilize a forged

Chang
Sung's
Laudatory
Memorial.
*11a*

14a

**11a**
(5) His
Crushing
of
Imperial
Favorites.

---

[10.7] *Book of Odes*, ＊264; III, III, x, 5 (Legge, p. 563). One character there is written
differently from in the Mao text.

[11.1] Phrases from the *Book of Changes*, App. III, Sect. 1, ch. 8, 43 (Legge, p. 362),
    "When two men are one in heart
    Their power shatters metal [bars]."

Chang
Sung's
Laudatory
Memorial.

testamentary edict [of Emperor Ai], make frequent use of rewards and punishments, first eliminate those whom they dreaded and hastily introduce [to office] those who were attached [to them], then make false accusations against [those against whom they had] long standing grudges, [i.e., the clan of Emperor P'ing], and furthermore repress [even] distant [imperial] relatives. If the circumstances had developed and occurred [after this manner], it would not have been difficult [for the Fu and Ting clans to seize the power of the government].[11.2]

"Thanks to the Duke, who at once entered [the court, Tung] Hsien$_{2a}$ was immediately made to retire, together with his clique and relatives. At this time, the Duke acted by his own brilliant insight and

14b *11b* wielded an unprecedented majesty. He lifted his eyebrows with a stern air and disseminated a martial ardor. Taking advantage of the fact that [Tung Hsien$_{2a}$] was not secure [in his position], he crushed him before he could move. Like a thunderbolt he set in motion the mechanism [of government] and his enemies were broken. Even if [Meng] Pen or [Hsia] Yü had been [there], they would not have [had time] to take up [their weapons] and touch him; even if Shu-li [Chi] had been [there], he would not have had time to use his wits; even if [the Master of] the Demon Valley had been [there], he would have been unequal to such rapid [action]. For this reason Tung Hsien$_{2a}$ lost his spirit and committed suicide by strangling. People did not [have time] to turn

**11b** around, the sun did not [have time to] move on the sun-dial, when suddenly on all [sides, the conspirators] were eliminated, [things were] changed and it became a peaceful court.

"Without your Majesty, [Grand Empress Dow-

遺詔頻用賞誅先除所憚急引所附遂誣住冤更徵遠屬事執見其
不難矣賴公立入即時退賢及其黨覩當此之時公運獨見之明曾亡
前之威昕衡屬色振揚武怒乘其未堅厥其未發震起機勳敵人摧折
雖有賁育不及持刺雖有慶里不及回知雖有鬼谷不及造次是故董
賢喪其魂魄遂自絞殺人不遑踵日不移晷雀然四除更為亭朝非陛

[11.2] The Sung Ch'i ed. asserted that 徵 should be 懲, after 其 there should be the word 然, and the 矣 should be excised. The Ching-yu ed. has the first of these changes.

下莫引立公非公莫克此禍詩云惟師尚父時惟鷹揚亮俵武

王孔子曰敬則有功公之謂矣於是公乃白內故泗水相豐纂

令邸與大司徒光車騎將軍莽建定社稷奉節東迎皆曰功德

受封益土為國名臣書曰知人則哲公之謂也公卿咸歎公德

同國公勳皆呂周公為比宜賜號安漢公益封二縣公告不受

ager], no one could have presented [for appointment] and given [office] to the Duke; without the Duke no one could have vanquished this calamity.

The *Book of Odes* says,

> 'Verily, the [Grand] Master was Shang-fu, [Lü Shang].
> He was an eagle, a hawk,
> Assisting King Wu;[11.3]

and Confucius said, 'With promptness you will have success;'[11.4] which indeed apply to the Duke.

"Hence the Duke thereupon advised [the Grand Empress Dowager] to receive the former Chancellor of [the kingdom of] Szu-shui, [Chen] Feng, and the Prefect of T'ai, [Chen] Han, together with the Grand Minister over the Masses, [K'ung] Kuang, and the General of Chariots and Cavalry, [Wang] Shun[4b], [and have them] propose and plan [the enthronement of the Emperor who should care for the dynasty's] altars to the gods of the soils and grains, go eastwards, bearing credentials, and invite [the present Emperor to ascend the throne]. All of them received enfeoffment or additional territory because of their achievements and virtuous conduct and became famous officials of the state. The *Book of History* says, 'One who knows people is wise,'[11.5] which applies to the Duke.

"The ministers all sighed after the Duke's virtue and all honored the Duke's signal services, [saying that] they were equal to those of the Duke of Chou, so that it would be proper to grant him the title of the Duke Giving Tranquillity to the Han Dynasty and to increase his enfeoffment by two counties, [but] the Duke would not accept any of them. A book

*(marginal notes, right column:)* Chang Sung's Laudatory Memorial.

(6) His Selection of Capable Subordinates.    15a

12a

(7) His Refusal of Honors.

---

11.3 *Book of Odes*, ⋕236; III, i, ii, 8 (Legge, p. 436).

11.4 *Analects* XVII, vi.

11.5 *Book of History*, II, iii, ii, 2 (Legge, p. 70).

Chang
Sung's
Laudatory
Memorial.

**12a**

says, 'Shen Pao-hsü would not receive the reward for having preserved [the state of] Ch'u,'[11.6] and 'Yen [Ying] P'ing-chung would not receive the enfeoffment for having acted as [chief] assistant [in the government of the state of] Ch'i.'[11.7] Confucius said, 'If [a prince] is able to rule his state in accordance with the rules of proper conduct and yielding [to others], what [difficulty] will he have?',[12.1] which apply to the Duke.

(8) His
Prelimi-
nary
Refusal to
Let his
Daughter
Become
Empress.

**15b**

"When they were about to determine upon and establish an Empress-consort for the Emperor, the high officials sent up [to the Grand Empress Dowager] the names [of suitable girls], the first of whom was the daughter of the Duke, [and] the Duke declined it strongly and asked that it be given to others. He was constrained and had no resource, and then only did he accept the imperial edict [ordering his daughter to be Empress]. The love between father and child is a Heaven-[endowed quality of human] nature and spontaneous; [a father] desires glory and honor for his [child] much more than for himself. The honor of being Empress is equal to that of being the Son of Heaven. The opportunity [offered to his daughter] at that time is rare [even] in a thousand years. Yet the Duke thought of the great principles of the state and yielded up the favor of the greatest blessing. In all matters he was humble, and, [what-

傳曰申包胥不受存楚之報晏平仲不受輔齊之封孔子曰
能呂禮讓為國乎何有公之謂也將為皇帝定立妃后有司
上名公安為首公深辭讓迫不得已然後受詔父子之親天
性自然欲其榮貴甚於為身皇后之尊侔於天子當時之會
千載希有然而公惟國家之統撰大福之恩事事謙退動而

---

[11.6] For this event, cf. *Tso-chuan*, Dk. Ting, V, (Legge, p. 760). We have not been able to find this quotation.

[11.7] *Yen-tzu Ch'un-ch'iu* 6: 17b, sect. 19, states that when the Duke of Ch'i wanted to enfeoff Master Yen, the latter replied, " 'From [the time of the Foreseen] Grand Duke, [Lü Shang], to your own [time], Duke, there have been several tens of Dukes. If people were able to obtain [noble] estates [merely] by delighting their princes, they would not have waited until your [time], Duke, to hasten to Ch'i and strive [with each other] in seeking promotion and lands [in such great numbers that] it would have been impossible for them to get a foothold or lodging there.' ... Thereupon he did not accept [the enfeoffment]." Perhaps the foregoing is the passage that is loosely quoted here.

[12.1] *Analects* IV, xiii.

卿羣下彌劭執平吕逮公卿敎子尊學吕隆
吕命下國俊儉隆約吕矯世俗割財損家吕
策吕至于今蠢蠢翼翼日新其德增修雅素
固辭書曰舜讓于德不嗣公之謂矣自公受

ever] was done, he firmly refused [honors]. The *Book of History* says, 'Shun [wished to] yield to someone more virtuous, and was not delighted [at the prospect of taking the throne],'[12.2] which applies indeed to the Duke.

Chang Sung's Laudatory Memorial.

"From the time that the Duke received his charter[12.3] down to the present, he has been indefatigable and orderly, daily renewing his virtue. He has added to and cultivated his whole life, so that he might issue the [proper] commands to the nobles; he has followed[12.4] economy and exalted moderation, so that he might correct the customs of the age. He has diminished his wealth and disparaged his family, so that he might lead his many subordinates; he has humbled himself and held firmly to equity, so that he might influence the ministers. He has taught children and has honored scholarship, so that he

*12b*
(9) His Personal Economy.
**12b**

---

[12.2] *Book of History*, II, ɪ, iii, 3 (Legge, 32). Wang Nien-sun declares that the text should read *yi₂* 怡 or 台 instead of *szu* 嗣. Yen Shih-ku explains *szu*. The ancient text of the *Book of History* read *szu* and the modern text read *yi₂*. The *HS* regularly quotes the modern text. *SC* 1: 32 (*Mh* I, 56) quotes this verse from the *Book of History* with the word *yi₅* 懌 (which means the same as *yi₂*), and Hsü Kuang (ca. 352–425) glosses, "The modern text *Book of History* reads *yi₂*. *Yi₂* is *yi₅*." Szu-ma Cheng (fl. 713–742) adds, "The ancient text reads *szu*; the modern text reads *yi₂*." *SC* 130: 30 also quotes this passage with *yi₂*. *HHS*, Mem. 30 B: 11a and the *Wen-hsüan* 48: 24b, in Pan Ku's "Tien-yin," quote this verse with *yi₂*; Li Shan (vii cent.), in his comment, quotes the same verse with *szu* and adds, "Wei Chao (197–273/4) says, '[According to] the ancient text, *yi₂* is *szu*.'" In a note to *HHS*, Mem. 30 B: 11a, b, Li Hsien (651–684) glosses that in the *HS* this verse is written with *yi₂* and the *HS Yin-yi* (probably the one written by Wei Chao) states that *yi₂* is to be read as *szu*. Wang Nien-sun concludes that according to the above evidence, the *HS* text which both Li Shan and Li Hsien saw read *yi₂* and Yen Shih-ku altered it to *szu* to agree with the ancient text of the *Book of History*, explaining the meaning accordingly. Cf. also Karlgren *BMFEA* 20, 76, Gl. 1253.

[12.3] Cf. 99 A: 6b.

[12.4] "Issue commands to the nobles" is a reminiscence of *Book of Odes* IV, ɪɪɪ, v, 4, line 5 (Legge, p. 645; his translation is unsatisfactory). The *Tz'u-hai* defines *hsia-kuo* as "the feudal nobles."

Yen Shih-ku asserts that *ch'ün* 後 means to retire, but Wang Yin-chih (1766–1834) replies that because of the parallelism Yen Shih-ku's interpretation is mistaken; *ch'ün* should be read as *tsun* 遵 (follow); anciently *ch'ün* and *tsun* were interchanged; the *Erh-ya* 1: 6a interprets *tsun* by *hsün* 循 and the *Fang-yen* 2: 6b interprets *ch'ün* by *hsün*. Sun Hsing-yen (1743–1818) in his *Yen-tzu Ch'-un-ch'iu Yin-yi* B: 34b, *sub* ch. 7, states that *tsun-hsün* means *ch'ün*-巡, identifying *ch'ün* and *tsun*.

Chang
Sung's
Laudatory
Memorial.

might raise the development of the state. His slaves have worn plain cloth[12.5] and his horses have not been fed grain, and the expense for his food and drink has not surpassed that of ordinary people. The *Book of Odes* says,

'One must be mild and humble
As if perched upon trees;'[12.6]

and Confucius said, 'In his food he should not seek for satiety and in his dwelling he should not seek for comfort;'[12.7] which indeed apply to the Duke.

16a
(10) His
Generosity

"He has denied his person and was himself frugal, buying food [only] to the point of what has been necessary. For all articles he has depended upon the market-place, daily emptying [his bins] and keeping no stores.[12.8] He furthermore sent a letter to the throne [asking to be permitted] to return the estate with which Emperor Hsiao-ai had additionally enfeoffed him and to pay[12.9] cash [to the government] and to offer his cultivated fields. He entirely exhausted his former possessions in order to lead the many [officials in making contributions]. There-

孝哀皇帝所益封邑入錢獻田驛盡舊業為眾倡始於
矣克身自約羅食建給物物卬市日閱亡儲又上書歸
溫恭人如集于木孔子曰食無求飽居無求安公之謂
國化僮奴衣布馬不秣穀食欽之用不過凡庶詩云溫

---

[12.5] The Official ed. emends by interchanging and reads *pu-yi* 布衣. Wang Wen-pin (xix cent.) however points out that this phrase is from *Tso-chuan*, Dk. Ch'eng, XVI (Legge, p. 394[7], 399b), which states that Viscount Wen of Chi, Chi-sun Hang-fu, "has had no concubines who wore silk (*yi-po*) nor horses who ate grain"; hence, because of parallelism, the phrase should be *yi-pu*, not *pu-yi*.

[12.6] *Book of Odes*, #196; II, v, ii, 6 (Legge, p. 335). Yen Shih-ku repeats the Mao interpretation of this couplet, so I have adopted it as the Han interpretation, although Karlgren's rendering (*BMFEA*, 16, p. 106) is better.

[12.7] *Analects*, I, xiv.

[12.8] Yen Shih-ku explains, "He did not engage in the production of [food or goods], so that he did not take their profits away from the merchants." In this respect, he imitated Tou Tzu-wen; cf. n. 12.11.

[12.9] Wang Hsien-ch'ien notes that the Official ed. and the Southern Academy ed. (1530) have *chin* 金 after the 入. But the Ching-yu ed. does not have the *chin*. The reference is to 99 A: 7b, where only cash and no gold or equivalent of gold (*chin*) is mentioned.

廷士下及白屋裏省朝政綜管衆治親見牧守臣下考迹雅
昔令尹子文朝不及夕魯公儀于不茹園葵公之謂矣開門
同時各竭所有或入金錢或獻田畝曰振貧窮收贍不足者
是小大卿和承風從化外則王公列侯內則惟幄侍御翕然

upon small and great [turned] towards him in harmony, accepting his influence and following his example; outside [the court], kings, the highest ministers,[12.10] and the full marquises, and within [the court, the occupants of the imperial] canopies and the imperial attendants, harmoniously and at the same time, each exhausted his possessions. Some paid gold and cash and some offered cultivated fields and acres to assist the impoverished and exhausted and to provide for and support those who had not sufficient [to live on]. Anciently, what the Chief Governor [Tou] Tzu-wen had in the morning did not last until night,[12.11] and Master Kung-yi [Hsiu] of Lu would not eat mallow from his garden [in order not to deprive gardeners of their profit], which indeed applies to the Duke.

"He opened his gates and invited in gentlemen and [those of lower rank] down to [the occupants of] plain houses.[13.1] He has frequently inspected court affairs, has controlled all the administration, and has himself interviewed the [Provincial] Governors and [Commandery] Administrators and those of lower [rank], investigating their whole life, until he had

*Chang Sung's Laudatory Memorial.*

**13a** *13a*

**(11) His Industry.**

16b

[12.10] That *kung* 公 here means the three highest ministers is shown by the expression 三公 in the similar list in 84: 12a.

[12.11] In *Kuo-yü* 18: 7a, Tou Ch'ieh says, "Anciently Tou Tzu-wen three times resigned [the position of] Chief Governor. He did not have one day's supplies, because he pitied the common people. King Ch'eng [of Ch'u] heard that what [Tou] Tzu-wen had in the morning did not last until night. Therefore every morning he had prepared one bundle of dried flesh and one basket of parched grain, in order to nourish [Tou] Tzu-wen. Down to the present, the Chief Governor has it for his salary."

For Kung-yi Hsiu, cf. Glossary *sub voce.*

[13.1] Yen Shih-ku explains, " 'Plain houses' means the people, who use white grass (quitch-grass) 白茅 to cover their houses." Ch'eng Ta-ch'ang however declares, "Anciently there were regulations concerning [the color of] palace buildings. Officials were not under those requirements, so their buildings exposed the natural [color] of their materials, for it was not necessary to add any colors or ornaments. These were the 'plain houses.' When [Yen] Shih-ku says that white quitch-grass covered the building, he is in error."

Chang Sung's Laudatory Memorial.

made plain those to be promoted and demoted. The *Book of Odes* says,

> 'He never slackened, day or night,
> In serving the ruler,'[13.2]

and the *Book of Changes* says, '[The superior man] all day is active and vigilant, and in the evening still careful and apprehensive of evil,'[13.3] which indeed apply to the Duke.

**(12) His Service to the State.**

"During three successive reigns he has been [one of] the three highest ministers and has twice been in charge of accompanying the imperial funeral cortege. He has held the position of prime minister and has pacified and tranquillized the state. The radii of [all within] the four seas have converged[13.4] [in him] and nothing has failed to be given its [proper] place. The *Book of History* says, '[Shun] was received as the chief director [of the administration], and, amidst violent wind, thunder, and rain, he did not go astray,'[13.5] which indeed refers to the Duke.

**13b**

"All the foregoing have been rare in very ancient times and would be difficult, [even] for Yü and [Prince] Millet, yet the Duke encompassed its entirety, 'containing the one pervading principle.'[13.6] He may indeed be said to be perfect.

**Peroration**

"For this reason, in the course of [these] three years, his influence has affected [people] like that of

終始一臣貫之可謂備矣是曰三年之閒化行如神嘉瑞
不迷公之謂矣此皆上世之所鮮禹稷之所難而公皆其
填安國家四海翕湊靡不得所書曰納於大麓列風雷雨
惕若屬公之謂矣比三世為三公再奉送大行東家宰職
素蕃知白黑詩云凤夜匪解曰事一人易曰終日乾乾夕

---

[13.2] *Book of Odes*, ✳260; III, iii, vi, 4 (Legge, p. 543).

[13.3] *Book of Changes*, Hex. I, 3 (Legge, p. 57; Wilhelm, I, 4).

[13.4] Wang Hsien-ch'ien asserts that 秦 is mistaken; the Official ed. and the Southern Academy ed. instead read 湊. The Ching-yu ed. reads the latter.

[13.5] *Book of History*, II, i, iii, 2 (Legge, p. 32). The use of *Ta-lu* 大麓 in *HS* 99 B: 6b shows that in Wang Mang's time the K'ung An-kuo interpretation of that phrase (which Legge rejects, cf. his trans., p. 32, note, also Karlgren *BMFEA* 20, 75, Gl. 1251) was accepted. Yen Shih-ku prefers it in his comment.

[13.6] Said by Confucius of himself in *Analects* IV, xv, 1. The 'one principle' which unified Confucius' teaching is there stated to have been, "Integrity and reciprocity," i.e., the Golden Rule.

帝
襃
賞
元
功
相
國
蕭
何
邑
戶
既
倍
又
豪
殊
禮
奏
事
不
名
入
殿
不

成
而
賞
不
配
立
而
褒
不
副
誠
非
所
以
厚
國
家
順
天
心
也
高
皇

不
散
擅
天
之
功
也
掛
公
德
行
為
天
下
紀
親
公
功
勳
為
萬
世
基
基

之
生
亦
不
虛
矣
是
呂
伯
禹
賜
玄
圭
周
公
受
郊
祀
益
臣
達
天
之
使

壘
累
豈
非
陛
下
知
人
之
劾
得
賢
之
致
哉
故
非
獨
君
之
受
命
也
臣

a god and auspicious presages have repeatedly succeeded [each other]. Is this not the result of your
Majesty, [Grand Empress Dowager], being able to
know people and having obtained a most capable
[person]? Hence not only has the prince received
the mandate [of Heaven, but] also the lives of your
courtiers have indeed not been in vain.[13.7] For such
a [reason] Prince 'Yü was presented a dark-colored
jade tablet'[13.8] and the Duke of Chou received [the
privilege of] being sacrificed to [after his death] with
the suburban sacrifice.[13.9] Verily, since [these rulers]
reported [to Heaven the great deeds of those] sent
by Heaven, they did not presume to arrogate to
themselves the merit [that came from] Heaven.

"When we estimate the upright character of the
Duke, it is a model for the empire, and when we look
at the achievements of the Duke, they are a foundation for ten thousand generations. If a foundation
has been laid and the reward is not appropriate to it,
and if a model has been established and the recompense is not in accord, [such a condition] is verily not
the way to help the state or to obey the will of
Heaven.

"Emperor Kao rewarded and recompensed [those
persons who had performed] the greatest services.
His Chancellor of State, Hsiao Ho, both [was given]
twice [as many] households for his estate [as others
had] and also received special ritual privileges: of
not [needing to use] his personal name in memorializing matters and of not [being required to] hasten

*Chang
13b
Sung's
Laudatory
17a
Memorial.*

Precedents
for
Rewarding
Govern-
ment
Servants:
Hsiao Ho

[13.7] The point is that good ministers have been able to carry out their conceptions of
good government.

[13.8] Presented by Yao to Yü at the completion of the latter's work upon the waters
(according to the K'ung An-kuo interpretation); *Book of History* III, I, ii, 23 (Legge,
p. 150; Couvreur, p. 89).

[13.9] *Li-chi* XII, 6–9 (Legge, II, 32; Couvreur, I, 729) states that King Ch'eng granted
to the Duke of Chou to be sacrificed to with the ceremonies and songs reserved to the
Son of Heaven.

Chang
Sung's
Laudatory
Memorial.

in entering the [Palace] Hall.[13.10] More than ten of
his relatives by marriage were enfeoffed. Since
[Emperor Kao] rejoiced without satiation in goodness, the recompenses he made were not parsimonious. If [a person propounded] one [good] plan,
[Emperor Kao] invariably [gave that person] noble
rank. For this reason, [although] the position of

17b
Kung-sun
Jung
14a

Kung-sun Jung was [merely] that of a Gentleman,
he was selected from [among] the standard-bearers
when he had once explained [the conduct] of Fan
K'uai, and was enfeoffed [with the income of] two
thousand households.[14.1]

14a
Chou P'o

"Emperor Hsiao-wen rewarded the Marquis of
Chiang, [Chou P'o], by adding to his enfeoffment
[the income of] ten thousand households and granting
him five thousand catties of actual gold. Emperor

Wei Ch'ing

Hsiao-wu favored and recorded military achievements, so allocated thirty thousand households
wherewith to enfeoff Wei Ch'ing; [Wei] Ch'ing's
three sons, some of whom were in swaddling clothes,

Ho Kuang

all became full marquises. Emperor Hsiao-hsüan
made Ho Kuang distinguished and brilliant, adding
to the households [of his estate] and commanding
[that his descendants should have] the same [rank
and estate as the founder of the house]; three persons
[in his clan] were enfeoffed, [enfeoffments] being
extended to the grandsons of his elder [half]-brother
[Ho Ch'ü-ping].[14.2]

"Now at the time of the Marquis of Chiang, [Chou
P'o], because of the firmness of the Han [dynasty's]

[13.10] Cf. *HS* 39: 4b.

[14.1] Cf. Glossary, *sub* Kung-sun Jung.

[14.2] The three enfeoffments in honor of Ho Kuang were: his son, Ho Yü, as Marquis
of Po-lu, on Apr. 27, 68 (*HS* 18: 11a); Ho Shan, grandson of Ho Ch'u-ping, as Marquis
of Lo-ping on May 14, 68 (18: 9a), at the special request of Ho Kuang, in order to continue the ancestral sacrifices of a noble to Ho Ch'ü-ping (68: 11a); and Ho Yün, elder
brother of Ho Shan, as Marquis of Kuan-yang, on Apr. 24, 67 (18: 9b). Cf. A. Jongchell,
*Huo Kuang och hans Tid*, pp. 150, 194, 195, 197, 205.

趙封其親屬十有餘人樂善無厭班賞亡逮苟有一策即必爵

之是故公孫戎位在兗部選諫施頭壹明樊會封二千戶孝文

皇帝襃賞絳侯益封萬戶賜黃金五千斤孝武皇帝卹錄軍功

裂三萬戶臣封衛青青子三人或在繦褓皆為通侯孝宣皇帝

顯著莅光增戶命賜封者三人延及兄孫夫絳侯即因漢藩之

功所因亦易然猶有計策不審過微之累及至青兀揣末
假離朝朝之執事亡非同題剖斷歷久統政曠世難曰有
能達霍光即席常任之重乘大勝之威未嘗遭時不行陷
回扶朱虛之毅依諸將之遲接相扶之甄其事雖醜要不

tributary [kings], thru the obstinate courage of the [Marquis of] Chu-hsü, [Liu Chang₁ₐ,] by the support of the various generals who surrounded [the Empress Dowager nee Lü], and by the aid of the power of mutual assistance [of these persons], altho the project [of the Lü clan] was detestable, they were not able to progress.

Chang Sung's Laudatory Memorial.

"When Ho Kuang entered his position [as Commander-in-chief], the authority of having long held office multiplied the majesty of his great prestige.[14.3] [Different from Wang Mang], he never happened upon a situation that he could not handle and that caused him to fall into disfavor[14.4] and [to be compelled] to leave the court. None of those in charge of matters in the court failed to be of the same [mind as he]; when the break [in the imperial line occurred at the death of Emperor Chao, Ho Kuang had controlled the government] for a long period and his direction of the government had brilliantly illuminated the age. Altho it may be said that he distinguished himself, he had [those circumstances] to rely upon, so that [his achievement] was moreover [comparatively] easy. Yet he suffered the embarrassment of not being discerning in making his plans by erroneously summoning [the King of Ch'ang-yi, Liu Ho, to the throne].

18a Wang Mang's Superiority. 14b

"As to [Wei] Ch'ing and [Kung-sun] Jung, [the one gained distinction] at the point of his sword,[14.5]

*14b*

---

[14.3] The Official ed. reads 媵 for 勝. The Ching-yu ed. however reads the latter.

[14.4] Reading 假 as 瑕 at the suggestion of Wang Nien-sun. These two words were anciently interchanged. The reference is to Wang Mang's resignation; cf. 99 A: 3b.

[14.5] Fu Ch'ien explains, "P'iao 標 has the pronunciation of the p'iao of the tip of a sword"; Shen Ch'in-han points out that in *Huai-nan Tzu*, 19: 8b, "*Hsiu-wu-shun*," Kao Yu (fl. 205–212) also declares, "*P'iao* should be read as the p'iao of a sword," and concludes that in Han times the point of a sword was called p'iao. Hence p'iao is borrowed for 鏢 or 剽, meaning the point of a sword (or the ornament at the tip of a scabbard). Cf. the use of this word in *HHS*, Tr. 30: 12b⁹; *Hsün-tzu*, 18: 16a⁶, ch. 26; and in Ho Hsiu's comment to the *Kung-yang Commentary*, 7: 9b⁶, Dk. Chuang, XIII, winter.

Chang Sung's Laudatory Memorial.

[and the other performed] the service of [saying] one word, yet both received a hill-[high] recompense.

"Examining the merits [of the Duke along] with those of [the Marquis of] Chiang, [Chou P'o], and of Ho [Kuang, the first shows] creativeness and [the others] were followers, when compared with [those of Wei] Ch'ing and [Kung-sun] Jung, [the Duke's merits are as different] as earth is from heaven. The Duke, moreover, also performed the service of controlling the government, hence he ought to be elevated to be equal in greatness and glory with Prince Yü and the Duke of Chou, and should receive the [same] reward and recompense that they did. Why should he be only discussed at the same time as those others just mentioned, [the Marquis of Chiang, Ho Kuang, Wei Ch'ing, and Kung-sun Jung]? Yet he has not yet obtained nor received the generosity [received by Wei] Ch'ing and the others. Your servant is verily mystified by this [circumstance].

He should be given the same Rewards as the Duke of Chou.

15a 18b

"Your servant has heard that, when services are measureless, the recompense should be boundless, and that when virtuous conduct is peerless, rewards should be unrestrained. This is the reason for King Ch'eng's [treatment] of[15.1] the Duke of Chou, which passed beyond the limits of a hundred *li* [of territory] and overpassed the restrictions of the nine distinctions,[15.2] creating a territory of seven hundred *li* [in extent], including both the people of [the states of] Shang and Yen[3a], and granting him to have as his vassals the six clans from [the state of the] Yin [dynasty],[15.3] 'the great chariot,[15.4] the great banner,

[15.1] Wang Hsien-ch'ien remarks that the Official ed. and the Southern Academy ed. correctly read 於 for 與. The Ching-yu ed. reads the former.

[15.2] Cf. *HFHD* II, 47, n. 9.2; 99 A: 22b.

[15.3] *Tso-chuan*, 54: 8b, Dk. Ting, IV, (Legge, p. 754), enumerates these six clans as "the T'iao 條 clan, the Hsü 徐 clan, the Hsiao 蕭 clan, the So 索 clan, the Ch'ang-sho 長勺 clan, and the Wei-sho 尾勺 clan."

[15.4] Cf. *Mh* III, 225.

非劉氏不王然而番君得王長沙下詔稱忠定著於令明
雖亡德不報報當如之不如非報也近觀行事高祖之約
之可謂不偷亡原者共非特止此六子皆封封詩曰言不
壯之牲郊望之禮王曰叔父建爾元子子父俱延拜而受
封父之繁弱夏后之璜祝宗卜史備物典策官司彝器白

[the great bow], Fan-jo, [belonging to] Feng-fu, the semi-circular jade tablet [used by] the Sovereign of the Hsia [dynasty, Yü], a [Grand] Intercessor, a [Master of the Ducal] Clan, a [Grand] Augur, a [Grand] Astrologer, the appendages [of state, a ducal] code and institutes, officials, high and low, vases for offering liquors [in the ancestral temple, and other] utensils,'[15.5] with a white bull as his sacrificial victim,[15.6] and the rites of the suburban [kingly] sacrifices and the sacrifice from a distance. 'King [Ch'eng] said, "My uncle, I will establish your eldest son [as Duke of Lu]." '[15.7] Son and father were both installed in order, and received their [fiefs], which may indeed be called an unrestrained [reward for] measureless [services. But his honors] did not stop merely with these; his six sons were all enfeoffed.[15.8] The *Book of Odes* says,

'No word but has its answer,
'No good deed but has its reward.'[15.9]

The reward must accord with the [deed]; if it does not accord, it is not a reward.

"When we consider matters done in more recent [times], there is the oath of the Eminent Founder, [Emperor Kao], that except for [members of] the Liu clan, no [one] should be made a king. Yet the Baronet of P'o, [Wu Jui], was permitted to be King of Ch'ang-sha and [Emperor Kao] promulgated an imperial edict praising him as loyal, establishing and publishing [his position as a permanent] ordinance,[15.10]

[15.5] The passage in single quotation marks is taken from *Tso-chuan* 54: 8b, Dk. Ting, IV, (Legge, p. 754).

[15.6] Taken from *Li-chi* XII, 9 (Legge II, 32; Couvreur, I, 730).

[15.7] A quotation from the *Book of Odes*, IV, ii, iv, 2 (Legge, p. 623).

[15.8] Chou Shou-ch'ang remarks that the princes of Fan 凡, Chiang 蔣, Hsing 邢, Mao 茅, Tsu 胙, and Ts'ai 祭 were the descendants of the Duke of Chou. His eldest son, Po-ch'in, in addition, succeeded his father as Duke of Lu. Cf. *Mh* IV, 100, n. 2.

[15.9] *Book of Odes*, #256; III, iii, ii, 6 (Legge, p. 514).

[15.10] Cf. *HS* 34: 24b.

Chang Sung's Laudatory Memorial.

[thus] making plain that where great confidence exists, [the Emperor] should not be held by the regulation [restricting vassal kings to the imperial clan].

"[According to] the *Spring and Autumn* [in *Mr. Tso's Commentary*], Duke Tao of Chin employed the plan of Wei Chiang and all of China served and followed him; when the prince of Cheng presented [to Duke Tao] musical [instruments and musicians], Duke Tao thereupon granted half of them to [Wei Chiang. Wei] Chiang declined strongly and asked that they be given to others, [but] the noble [ruler] of Chin said, 'But for you, sir, I, your humble servant,

*15b* would not have been able to cross the [Yellow] River. Verily, rewarding is in the code of the state and cannot be annulled. Do you, sir, receive these [things].' Wei Chiang thereupon possessed musical instruments of metal and stone.[15.11] The *Spring and Autumn* [in *Mr. Tso's Commentary*] praises him. It approves [the fact that] he, a subject, was entirely devoted [to his prince] and therefore refused [a reward for] his services, [but] the prince knew his subject, and accordingly rewarded him.

Conclusion
19b

"Now since your Majesty, [Grand Empress Dowager], already knows that the Duke has the achievements and virtuous conduct of the Duke of Chou,[15.12] if you do not put into effect the rewards and recompenses [granted by] King Ch'eng, and consequently accept the Duke's firm refusals, not considering the plain meaning of the *Spring and Autumn*, then how can the common people and your courtiers praise [your deeds], and how can they be recounted to ten thousand generations? In truth, this is not [the way] the state should be governed.

[15.11] Cf. *Tso-chuan*, Dk. Hsiang, XI, ix (Legge, p. 453).

[15.12] The Sung Ch'i ed. says that after the 德 there should be an 而. The Ching-yu ed. however does not have this word.

顧春秋之明義則民臣何稱萬世何述誠非所呂為國也臣
下既知公有周公功德不行成王之褒賞達聽之固辭不
之樂春秋善之取其臣鴻忠呂辭功君知臣忠呂逐賞也今性
能濟河夫賞國之典不可廢也子其受之魏絳於是有金石
伯獻樂悼公於是呂半賜之絳辭讓晉侯曰微子寡人不
有大信不拘於制也春秋吾悼公用魏絳之策諸夏服從鄭

愚呂為宜恢公國令如周公建立公子令如伯禽所賜之品亦皆如

之諸子之封皆如六子即莽下載然輸忠黎庶昭然感德臣誠輸忠

民誠感德則於王事何有唯陛下深惟祖宗之重敬畏上天之戒儀

形虜周之國敷盡伯禽之賜無遺周公之報今天法有效後世有祖

天下幸甚太后呂視羣公羣公方議其事會呂寬事起初莽欲擅權

"Your stupid subject considers that it would be appropriate to enlarge the Duke's state, causing it to be like that of the Duke of Chou, and to set up and establish the Duke's [eldest] son [as a noble], causing him to be like Po-ch'in. The articles that are granted to him should also be like those [granted to the son of the Duke of Chou]. The enfeoffments of [the Duke's] various sons should all be like those of the six sons [of the Duke of Chou]. Then your many subordinates will openly offer[15.13] their devotion, and the many people will be brilliantly moved by your virtue. If your courtiers really offer[15.13] their devotion and if the common people are really moved by your virtue, then which of the deeds of an [ideal] King would be [lacking]?

"I hope that your Majesty will ponder deeply the weighty [deeds] of your [imperial] ancestors, respect and fear the warnings of High Heaven, imitate[16.1] the gloriousness of Yü [Shun] and of the Chou [dynasty, follow] completely and entirely [the example of] the grants [made] to Po-ch'in, and not be parsimonious [in granting to the Duke] a recompense [similar to that made to] the Duke of Chou, in order that[16.2] this law of Heaven may be established and a model may be [set] for later generations. The whole world would [thus] be favored."

The [Grand] Empress Dowager [nee Wang] thereupon showed [the memorial] to the various highest ministers. [But] just when the various highest ministers were discussing this matter, it happened that the affair of Lü K'uan arose.

Previously, [Wang] Mang had wanted to arrogate

Chang Sung's Laudatory Memorial.

The Honors Recommended.

**16a**

The Affair of Lü K'uan.
*16a*

20a

---

15.13 The Sung Ch'i ed. says that the Chekiang ed. (xi–xii cent.) reads 諭 for the 輸 in this and the next sentence. The Ching-yu ed. reads the latter.

16.1 Wang Hsien-ch'ien notes that the Official ed. reads 刑 for 形, but the Ching-yu and Southern Academy ed. read the latter.

16.2 Ch'ien Ta-chao remarks that 今 should be 令. The Ching-yu ed. reads the latter; Wang Hsien-ch'ien adds that the Official ed. and the Southern Academy ed. read likewise.

Wang
Mang
Had
Denied
Emperor
P'ing's
Natural
Relative
a Place
at Court.

the [imperial] power to himself, so had said to the [Grand] Empress Dowager, "Previously, when Emperor Ai was set up [as Emperor] and went contrary to the favor and beneficence [shown him by you, Grand Empress Dowager, the Emperor] himself raised his maternal relatives, the Ting and Fu [clans], to high rank, who troubled the state, so that they almost destroyed the [dynasty's] gods of the soils and grains, [almost overthrowing the dynasty]. Now, since the Emperor is young and is again upholding the main line [of the dynasty] as the [adopted] child of Emperor Ch'eng, it is proper to make plain the principle of [only] a single line of [imperial] descent, in order to ward off [such a] situation as had previously [arisen] and to make [the new arrangement] a model for later generations."

July/Aug.
A.D. 1[16.3]

Thereupon she had sent Chen Feng, bearing a kingly seal and cord, who had gone to the Emperor's mother, the Concubine [nee] Wei, had installed her as the Queen of King Hsiao of Chung-shan, [the deceased Liu Hsing], and had granted to the Emperor's maternal uncles, Wei Pao and [Wei] Pao's younger brother, [Wei] Hsüan, the noble rank of Marquises of the Imperial Domain. All of them were detained in [the kingdom of] Chung-shan and were not permitted to go the imperial capital.

Wang
Yü
Intrigues
With
Them.

[Wang] Mang's son, [Wang] Yü₃, disapproved [of the fact] that [Wang] Mang had separated the Wei clan [from the Emperor] and feared that when the Emperor grew up, enmity would later appear [between the Wei and Wang clans. Wang] Yü₃ hence sent a man privately to give letters to [Wei] Pao and the others, instructing the Emperor's mother to send a letter to the throne, asking [that she be permitted]

97 B:
21b–22b.

to enter [the imperial palace]. A discussion is in the "Memoir of the Queen [nee] Wei."

16.3 *HS* 12: 4a.

大俊見惡宇即私遣人與賓等通書敕今帝女上書求入語在衛后
玄等開内侯皆囍中山不得至京師恭子宇非茅隔絶衛氏恐帝長
是遠甄豐奉璽綬即拜帝女衛姬為中山孝王后賜帝舅衛寶弟
臣幼年俊奉大宗為成帝後宜明一統之義臣戒前事為後代法於
白太后前袤帝立皆恩義自責外家丁傅撓亂國家幾危社稷今帝

其誅甄邯等白太后下詔曰夫唐堯有丹朱周文王有管蔡此皆上聖

殺之莽奏言宇為呂寬等所詿誤流言惑眾惡與管蔡同罪臣不敢隱

灑莽第門吏發覺之莽執宇送微欽藥死宇妻懷子繫獄須產子已

神可為變怪呂驚懼之章固推類說令歸政於衛氏宇即使寬夜持血

傅莽不聽宇與師吳章及婦兄呂寬議其故章呂為莽不可諫而好鬼

[Wang] Mang did not listen [to this request, so Wang] Yü₃ and his teacher, Wu Chang, together with his own wife's elder brother, Lü K'uan, discussed the circumstances. [Wu] Chang considered that [Wang] Mang could not be admonished, but, since he was fond of spiritual beings, they should make some grevious vicissitudes or portentous happenings,[16.4] in order to terrify him. [Wu] Chang would thereupon explain them by citing parallel [instances from history] and so would cause him to give the government to the Wei clan. [Wang] Yü₃ then had [Lü] K'uan carry blood at night and sprinkle it at the door of [Wang] Mang's residence. When the officials discovered the [plot], [Wang] Mang had [Wang] Yü₃ seized and sent to prison, where he drank poison and died. [Wang] Yü₃'s wife, [Lü] Yen, who was with child, was held in prison until she gave birth to the child; when it had been [born], she was killed.

[Wang] Mang memorialized, saying, "[Wang] Yü₃ has been led into error by Lü K'uan and others, who spread groundless rumors to mislead the crowd, which is[16.6] a crime similar to that of the [King's Uncles of] Kuan and of Ts'ai. Your servant does not dare to hide [the fact that] he has been executed."

Chen Han and others advised the [Grand] Empress Dowager to issue an imperial edict saying, "Verily, T'ang Yao had, [as his son], Tan-chu and King Wen of the Chou [dynasty] had, [as sons, Hsien and Tu, who were known as the King's Uncles of] Kuan and of Ts'ai. These [two rulers] were both sages of the highest [degree], yet they could not

*Marginal notes:* Wang Mang to be **16b** Superstitiously Terrified.

20b

Wang Yü Executed.[16.5]

*16b*

Wang Mang Praised for his Freedom From Partiality.

16.4 For these technical terms, cf. Glossary, *sub* portents.

16.5 *HS* 12: 7a.

16.6 The Sung Ch'i ed. notes that the Yüeh ed. (xi–xii cent.) and the Shao ed. (xi or xii cent.) omit the 惡; the Ching-yu ed. also lacks it; Wang Hsien-ch'ien adds that the Southern Academy ed. (1530/1) omits it. I have not translated it. The King's Uncles of Kuan and of Ts'ai also spread rumors; cf. *Book of History* V, vi, 12 (Legge, p. 357); Glossary, s.v.

prevent their sons from being of the lowest [degree] of stupidity. Why? Because their own [good] natures could not be transplanted [into the hearts of these others]. You, Duke, occupy the position of the Duke of Chou and assist your lord [as he assisted] King Ch'eng. You have also executed [your son as he executed the King's Uncles of] Kuan and of Ts'ai, and have not [allowed] your love for your relatives to injure the honor [due to] those who are honorable, [i.e., the imperial family]. We approve of it most highly.

"Anciently, after the Duke of Chou had executed the descendants of the four states,[16.7] his grand transformation [of the country] was perfected, until even the multilating punishments [could be] established but not employed.[16.8] Do you, Duke, concentrate on attending to the state and aim at bringing about the [utmost] tranquillity."

Hundreds More Executed.

Taking advantage of this [edict, Wang] Mang exterminated the Wei clan and examined exhaustively the case of Lü K'uan. [Wang Mang] involved [in this case] the prominent persons of the commanderies and kingdoms who had in the past criticized him in memorials, and within [the imperial court] even [implicated] the Princess of Ching-wu, the King of Liang, [Liu] Li$_{5a}$, the Marquis of Hung-yang, [Wang] Li$_{5a}$, and the Marquis of P'ing-o, [Wang] Jen. Messengers tortured or guarded them, and they all committed suicide. Those who died were numbered by the hundreds, so that [all] within [the four] seas trembled at it.

The Commissioner Over the Army [subordinate to]

21a

---

[16.7] Yen Shih-ku explains that these four were those of the three Overseers (including the King's Uncles of Kuan and of Ts'ai) and the wild tribes of the Huai region. Cf. Glossary sub Kuan.

[16.8] Cf. HFHD, II, 36, n. 5.1.

比孝經四年春郊祀高祖呂配天宗祀孝文皇帝呂配上帝四月
國令學官呂敦授事下羣公諸令天下吏能誦公戒者呂著官簿
室故不敢顧私惟字遭辜唱然憤發作書八篇呂戒子孫宜班郡
司馬護軍褒奏言安漢公遣子宇陷於管蔡之辜子愛至深為帝

the Commander-in-chief, Pao$_{1b}$, memorialized, saying, "The Duke Giving Tranquillity to the Han Dynasty, [Wang Mang], has suffered from the fact that his son, [Wang] Yü$_3$, has fallen into the [same] crimes [as the King's Uncles of] Kuan and of Ts'ai; his love for his son was very deep, [but], for the sake of the imperial house, [Wang Mang] has not presumed to consider his private [interests. Since], however, [Wang] Yü$_3$ has suffered for his crime, [Wang Mang] has sighed and has been deeply moved, so he has composed a writing in eight fascicles, in order to warn posterity. It would be proper to publish it in the commanderies and kingdoms and order the school officials to teach it."

The matter was referred to the various highest ministers, who begged that it should be ordered that the officials of the empire who were able to recite and explain the Duke's warning should therefore be recorded on the official registers [of meritorious persons preferred for official positions], just as those [who recite and explain] the *Classic of Filial Piety*.[17.1]

In the fourth year, in the spring, the suburban sacrifice (*chiao*) was performed to the [dynasty's] Eminent Founder, [Emperor Kao], making him the coadjutor of Heaven, and the sacrifice to the greatest exemplar (*tsung*) was performed to Emperor Hsiao-wen, making him the coadjutor of the Lords on High.[17.2]

*Wang Mang's Book Added to the* **17a** *Official Curriculum.*

*17a* A.D. 4 Feb./ Mar.[17.2]

---

[17.1] Yen Shih-ku glosses, "*Chu kuan-pu* 著官薄 means that it was used in securing [persons who] were selected and recommended [to the central government as candidates for official position]." Chou Shou-ch'ang adds (in his *HS-chu Chiao-su* 55: 16a), "[Emperor] Hsiao-wen had an Erudit for the *Classic of Filial Piety* and the imperial capital commanderies had Masters for the *Classic of Filial Piety* [12: 7a], which was recording the *Classic of Filial Piety* on the official registers [as a regular study]. Wang Mang's ... edict ... ordering the government schools to teach [his own book] was, it seems, establishing it [too] in the government schools [as a regular subject of study]."

[17.2] This passage is also found in *HS* 12: 7a, cf. 12: n. 7.4 for annotations.

Mar. 16.
His
Daughter
Made
Empress.

He should
Be
Honored
Further.
21b

In the second[17.3] month, on [the day] *ting-wei*, the daughter of [Wang] Mang was established as Empress. A general amnesty [was granted] to the empire and the Director of Justice to the Grand Minister over the Masses, Ch'en Ch'ung, and others, eight persons [in all], were sent to travel separately about the empire, to observe and see [the people's] customs.[17.4]

The Grand Guardian, [Wang] Shun[4b], and others memorialized, saying, "[According to] the principles of grading achievements and meritorious conduct in the *Spring and Autumn* [in *Mr. Tso's Commentary*], 'The highest [degree of celebrity] is to establish [an example of] meritorious conduct, the next [degree] is to establish [a name for] successful achievements, and the next [degree] is to establish [wise] sayings.[17.5] Verily, those of extreme meritorious conduct or of great excellence are alone able to do this. Such persons, if they were courtiers, thereupon [during] their lifetime received great recompenses and [after] their death became [known as] exemplary subjects;[17.6] Yi Yin in the Yin [dynasty] and the Duke

賢然後能之其在人臣則生有大賞終為宗臣殷之伊
之義太上有立德其次有立功其次有立言唯至德大
八人分行天下覽觀風俗太保屏等奏言春秋列功慮
丁未奉女立為皇后大赦天下遣大司徒司直陳崇等

---

[17.3] The text reads "fourth month," but *HS* 12: 7b, *Han-chi* 30: 4b, and *Tzu-chih T'ung-chien* 36: 4b all read "second month." "Fourth month" is an error. The fourth month was the first month of *summer*, but 12: 7b notes, *after* the marriage, "In the *summer*, the Empress [nee Wang] was presented in the Temple of [Emperor] Kao," and 97 B: 23a says, "In the next year, in the *spring*, [the Grand Empress Dowager] sent" various courtiers "with the legal equipage to go and fetch the Empress from the residence and palace of the Duke Giving Tranquillity to the Han [Dynasty, Wang Mang,]" to be married. Cf. Szu-ma Kuang, *Tzu-chih T'ung-chien K'ao-yi* 2: 2a.

[17.4] According to 18: 30a–31b these eight persons were Wang Yün, Yen Ch'ien, Ch'en Ch'ung, Li Hsi, Ho Tang, Hsieh Yin, Lu P'u, and Ch'en Feng.

[17.5] *Tso-chuan*, Dk. Hsiang, XXIV (Legge, p. 507; Couvreur, II, 408).

[17.6] Yen Shih-ku, in a note to *HS* 39: 13b, says of *tsung-ch'en* 宗臣, "It means that they are those whom later generations honor and look up to." Chang Yen (iii cent. A.D.), in a note to 99 A: 21a, states, "A *tsung* subject has performed signal services and becomes a duke of the first class, whom the state takes as an exemplar 國所宗者也." This ancient usage justifies the translation of *tsung* in imperial temple names by the word "exemplar."

尹周之周公是也及民上書者八千餘人咸曰伊尹為阿衡周公為太

宰周公享七子之封有過上公之賞宜如陳崇言章下有司有司請遷

前所益二縣及黃郵聚新野田采伊尹周公稱號加公為宰衡位上公

揆史秩六百石三公言事稱敢言之羣吏女得與公同名出從期門二

十人羽林三十人前後大車十乘賜公太夫人號曰功顯君食邑二千

of Chou in the Chou [dynasty] were such [persons]."

The common people who presented [similar] letters to the Emperor moreover [numbered] more than eight thousand persons. They all said, "Yi Yin became the Supporting Governor and the Duke of Chou became the Grand Ruler. The Duke of Chou enjoyed [the honor of] having his seven sons enfeoffed and had recompenses greater than the highest rank of the highest ministers. It is proper that [it should be done] as Ch'en Ch'ung has said."

Their memorials were referred to the high officials, and the high officials begged that [Wang Mang] be returned the two counties [of Shao-ling and Hsin-hsi, with which his enfeoffment] had previously been increased, [and which he had returned to the government], together with Huang-yu Village and the cultivated fields in Hsin-yeh [County, which he had previously held]; that there be selected [a term] from [each of] the titles of Yi Yin, [Supporting Governor], and the Duke of Chou, [Grand Ruler], so that the Duke should be given the title of Ruling Governor, with his rank in the highest rank of the highest ministers; his division head clerks should be ranked at six hundred piculs; the three highest ministers, when speaking to him of [government] business, should say that they 'presume to speak of it;'[17.7] the various [lower] officials should not be permitted to have the same personal name as the Duke; when he goes out he should be followed by twenty Attendants at the Gates, thirty [members of] the Winged Forest, and that before and after him there should be ten great chariots. The Duke's Lady Dowager, [his mother], should be granted the title, the Baronetess of Apparent Merits, with the income of an estate of

A New Title.

**17b**

---

[17.7] Parallel to the expression used to the emperor, "foolishly risking the commission of a crime worthy of death." Cf. *HFHD*, I, 99, n. 2; Ts'ai Yung's *Tu-tuan*, p. 5b. Yang Shu-ta quotes the *Lun-heng* as saying, "When [the officials of] commanderies speak of matters to the two yamens, they say, 'We presume to speak of it.'"

17b
22a
two thousand households, a golden seal and a red seal-ribbon; the Duke's two sons should be enfeoffed: [Wang] An$_{1a}$ as Marquis in Recompense to [the Marquis of] Hsin-[tu], (Pao-hsin), and [Wang] Lin$_{1a}$ as Marquis in Reward to [the Marquis of Hsin]-tu (Shang-tu); and thirty seven million [cash] should be added to the betrothal present of the Empress, [making it] altogether a hundred million [cash],[17.8] in order to glorify the great rites [of imperial marriage].

June 1[17.9]
He
Refuses
Most
of the
Honors.
The [Grand] Empress Dowager went to the Front Hall [of the Palace] in person to enfeoff [the Duke and his sons]. The Duke Giving Tranquillity to the Han Dynasty was first installed, and his two sons were later installed, as [had happened] in the former case of the Duke of Chou. [But Wang] Mang repeatedly bent his head to the ground, declining and asking that [these honors] be given to others. When he had gone out, he memorialized [the Empress Dowager] concerning these enfeoffments, [declaring that] he wished only to accept the title for his mother and [wished] to return the seals and [ceremonial] aprons of [Wang] An$_{1a}$ and [Wang] Lin$_{1a}$, together with their titles, positions, and the households in their estates.

The matter was referred to the Grand Master, [K'ung] Kuang, and others, who all said, "These rewards are not adequate for the achievements [of him to whom they have been given]. Humility, self-restraint, retiringness, and yielding are the constant moderation of the Duke. [His request] should not be eventually accepted."

[Wang] Mang asked for an audience and firmly declined [these honors, so the Grand] Empress Dow-

戶黃金印赤韍封公子男二人安為褒新侯臨為賞都侯加后
聘三千七百萬合為一萬萬臣明大禮太后臨前敕親封拜安
漢公拜前二子拜後如周公故事莽稽首辭讓出奏封事願獨
受母號還安臨印韍及號位戶邑事下太師光等皆曰賞未足
臣直功謙約退讓公之常節終不可聽莽未見因讓太后下詔

---

[17.8] Wang Mang had previously received 40 million cash (of which he gave 33 million to the families of Emperor P'ing's concubines), then he was additionally granted 23 million cash (99 A: 10a); now he was given 37 million more, making a total of 100 million cash.

[17.9] Cf. *HS* 99 A: 18a.

皇后非為公也功顯君戶止身不傳襲新賞都兩國合三千戶芘

可聽許治平之化當呂時成宰衡之官不可世及納徵錢乃呂尊

黃郵召陵新野之田為入尤多皆止於公公欲自損呂成國化宜

行其賞遣歸就第七光等曰安臨親受印載策號通天其義昭昭

曰公每見叩頭流涕固辭今移病固當聽其讓令眂事郇將當遣

ager issued an imperial edict which said, "Every time that the Duke has an audience, he kowtows with tears falling, as he firmly refuses [his honors]. Now he has sent [Us] a communication [informing Us] that he is ill. Should [We] indeed accede to his yielding so that [We] may order him to attend to his business? Or should [We] indeed put into effect his recompenses and send him home to his residence?"17.10

[K'ung] Kuang and the others replied, "[Wang] An and [Wang] Lin₁ have in person received their seals and aprons, their charters and titles, and it has been communicated to Heaven, so that the justice [of their appointments] is patent. The cultivated fields of Huang-yu, Shao-ling, and Hsin-yeh are extraordinarily great in their income. [Their disposal] altogether rests with the Duke. If the Duke wishes to diminish himself in order to bring about a [moral] transformation in the state, it is proper that [his request to yield up these fields] be approved and acceded to, and it is to be expected that the [moral] transformation [which will bring about a condition of] good government and peace will accordingly be achieved in [due] time.

He is Not to be Allowed to Refuse Everything.

22b

"[But] the office of Ruling Governor cannot be attained by [his heirs in the next] generation, [so that he should not be permitted to refuse it]. The cash [used] in the betrothal presents17.11 [of his daughter] was moreover to honor her as the [future] Empress, and not for the Duke's sake. The households [in the estate] of the Baroness of Apparent Merits will lapse with her [death] and not be transmitted [to her descendants]. The two estates of Pao-hsin and Shang-tu together [amount only to] three thousand

18a

17.10 To "send a minister to his residence" meant dismissing him from his position and from the court. Evidently the Grand Empress Dowager had become tired of Wang Mang's posing.

17.11 The "presentation of the betrothal presents" was the fourth of the rites preliminary to a marriage; cf. n. 9.3. It made the betrothal binding.

households, which is indeed very little. [According
to] the conduct of a loyal official, it is moreover
*18a*   proper that he should humble his own [will] in order
to show his fealty to his lord.

"It would be proper to send the Grand Minister
over the Masses, [Ma Kung], and the Grand Minister
of Works, [Chen Feng], with credentials, bearing
your edict of decree that the Duke must quickly
enter [the court] and attend to business, and give
an edict to the Masters of Writing not again to
receive a memorial from the Duke which yields up
[his honors]." The memorial was approved. [Wang]

June 1   Mang thereupon arose and attended to business.

He presented a letter saying, "Your servant, as the

1 B.C.   Marquis of Hsin-tu₍c₎, in [the year-period] Yüan-shou,

Aug. 15   the second year, the sixth month, on [the day]
*mou-wu*, in a night of haste and confusion, as Marquis
of Hsin-tu₍c₎, was led into the Wei-yang Palace. On

Aug. 17   [the day] *keng-shen*, I was installed as Commander-in-
chief and occupied the position of [one of] the three

A.D. 1,   highest ministers. In [the year-period] Yüan-shih,

Apr. 10.   the first year, the second[18.1] month, on [the day]
*ping-ch'en*, I was installed as Grand Tutor, granted
the title of the Duke Giving Tranquillity to the Han
Dynasty, and merely acted as [one of] the Four Coad-

A.D. 4,   jutors. In the present year, the fourth month, on

June 1.   [the day] *chia-tzu*, I was again installed as Ruling
Governor, being ranked in the highest class of the

He   highest ministers. I, your servant Mang, myself

Reviews   think humbly that my noble rank is Marquis of

23a   Hsin-tu₍c₎, my title is Duke Giving Tranquillity to the

His   Han Dynasty, my offices are those of Ruling Gov-

Honors.   ernor, Grand Tutor, and Commander-in-chief, so that

伏自惟爵為新都侯號為安漢公官為宰衡大傅大司馬爵貴號
賜號安漢公備四輔官今年四月甲子復拜為宰衡位上公臣茶
夫宮庚申拜為大司馬充三公位元始元年正月丙辰拜為太傅
事上書言臣呂元壽二年六月戊午倉卒之夜呂新都侯引入未
節承刑詔公丞入眠事詔尚書勿復受公之讓奏奏可茶乃起眠
少矣忠臣之節亦宜自屈而信主上之義宜遣大司徒大司空持

18.1 The text reads "first month," but Hoang does not list a *ping-ch'en* day in that
month; *HS* 19 B : 51b reads "second month," which checks; I emend the text accordingly.
Cf. also n. 6.2.

尊官重一身家大寵者五誠非鄙臣所能堪攝元始三年天下歲已
後官屬宜皆教授傳曰天子之宰通于四海臣愚呂為宰衡官呂
正百僚平海內為職而無印信名實不副臣莽無兼官之材今聖朝
既過誤而用之臣請御史刻宰衡印章曰宰衡太傅大司馬印成授
臣莽上太傅與大司馬之印太后詔曰可敕如相國朕親臨授馬莽

my noble rank is [too] high, my title is [too] honorable, and my offices are [too] weighty for a single person. That I should have received [these] five great favors, is indeed beyond your humble servant's merits.

"Since in the third year of [the period] Yüan-shih,   A.D. 3. the empire had a good harvest, it is proper that those official subordinate positions which have been abolished should all be [now] reestablished.

"The *Ku-liang Commentary* says, 'The [Grand]   He Ruler of the Son of Heaven should be acquainted with   Requests [all within] the four seas.'[18.2] Your servant stupidly   a Seal considers that the office of Ruling Governor has for   of Office. its duties the correcting of all the officials and the tranquillizing of [all] within [the four] seas. Yet it has no seal or sign, so that its name does not correspond to its reality. [Although] your servant Mang does not have the ability to [hold many] offices concurrently, since now you, the sage court, have through an error and mistake employed me, your servant begs that the Attendant Secretaries should have a seal engraved for the Ruling Governor with the inscription, 'Ruling Governor, Grand Tutor, and Com-   *18b* mander-in-chief,' and, when the seal is completed,   **18b** transmit it to your servant Mang, who will [then] return the seals of the Grand Tutor and of the Commander-in-chief." The [Grand] Empress Dowager's imperial edict said, "It is approved. His [ceremonial] apron[18.3] shall be like that of the Chancellor of State. We will Ourself attend [court] to transmit it to him."

[18.2] *Ku-liang Commentary* 8: 2b; Dk. Hsi, IX, summer.

[18.3] For the apron (fu₁ 韍) as an article of ceremonial attire, cf. 99 A: n. 2.8. Wang Mang seems to have first made it part of a noble's or official's insignia of office, for it is first mentioned in the reign of Emperor P'ing. Its use was in imitation of classical practises—it is mentioned in *Li-chi*, XI, ii, 21–27 and XII, 29 (Legge, II, 14–16, 38; Couvreur, I, 700–702, 740). Cf. also *Po-hu-t'ung* 10: 1a, b.

Yen Shih-ku, both here and in his notes to 14: 4b, 99 B: 1a, and 99 C: 5b, glosses, "The *fu₁* is also called a *tsu* 組," which latter article was the cord by which seals were

A Great
Gift.
[Wang] Mang thereupon again took ten million cash of what had been added to the betrothal present [for his daughter] and left it with the Chief Chamberlain at the Ch'ang-lo [Palace], who had charge of providing for [the Grand Empress Dowager].

23b The Grand Guardian, [Wang] Shun₄ᵦ, memorialized, saying, "The empire has heard that the Duke would not accept a territory [that would furnish] a thousand chariots, has refused a present of [the equivalent of] ten thousand [catties of] gold,[18.4] has

受千乘之土辭萬金之聘
大保舜奏言天下聞公不
遣與長樂長御奉供養者
乃復呂所益納徵錢千萬

suspended from the wearer's girdle. The use of $fu_1$ with the word for seal (e.g. 99 B: 23a) makes this interpretation plausible. The word $fu_1$ was moreover interchanged with $fu_2$ 紱, which latter word later denoted the seal-ribbon.

This interchange between $fu_1$ and $fu_2$ has probably misled Yen Shih-ku. Ch'en Hsiang-tao (1053–1093), in his *Li-shu* 23: 6b, states that from the Wei and Chin periods (iii cent. A.D.) onwards, the $fu_1$, instead of being made of leather, was made of silk gauze, hence the word was sometimes written $fu_2$ (with the silk radical. Such may have been the case already in Pan Ku's time; cf. 99 B: n. 1.1). As a result, people would be likely to confuse $fu_1$ and $fu_2$ and think mistakenly that the $fu_1$ denoted a seal-ribbon— which statement was evidently current in T'ang times and is to be found in the dictionaries today. But Ch'en Hsiang-tao takes his information, according to a note, from Hsü Kuang's (ca. 352–425) "Rites and Institutes Concerning Carriages and Robes 車服儀制" (probably the same as his 車服雜注, listed in the *Sui-shu* bibliography 2: 14a, the *Old T'ang-shu* bibliography 1: 34b, and the *New T'ang-shu* bibliography 2: 21b; the book is now lost), so that this information dates from two centuries before the time of Yen Shih-ku.

Until Wang Mang came into power, the term used along with the word for seal is *shou* 綬, seal-ribbon (8: 22b, 12: 1a, 99 A: 4a). During the time Wang Mang controlled the government, the $fu_1$ is however occasionally mentioned along with the seal as the insignia of noble or bureaucratic rank (14: 4b, 99 A: 18b, 22b, 26b; 99 B: 1a, 23a). In Wang Mang's time, the term *shou* also on occasions accompanies the word for seal (98: 13b, 99 B: 11a, 12b, 18a; 99 C: 27b). The Later Han dynasty also used the *shou* (*HHS*, Tr. 30: 13b–15a). The $fu_1$ (apron) was the first of the nine distinctions (99 A: 22b), so that it was only natural for Wang Mang to have used it as one of his insignia for a high office. Such an article of attire was plainly convenient at a court where the kowtow was common. The $fu_1$ is mentioned under circumstances in which it can only mean "apron" (99 B: 22b, 26b); it would be very strange to have the same word used to denote two very different articles of apparel without any explanation on the part of the author. Yen Shih-ku's change in the meaning of $fu_1$ is unacceptable.

[18.4] A catty of gold was equivalent to ten thousand cash; ten thousand catties of gold were then equivalent to a hundred million cash. This was the amount of the dowry; cf. 99 A: 17b.

故財旋于千萬數莫不鄉化蜀郡男子路建等輟訟慚作而

退雖文王卻虞芮何足加宜報告天下奏可宰衡出從大車

前後各十乘直事尚書郎侍御史謁者中黃門期門羽林軍

衛常持節所止謁者代持之羽衛擽史秩六百石三公稱敢

言之是歲羣秀起明堂辟雍靈臺為學者筑舍萬區作市常

distributed his wealth and has given it away by the ten-millions, so that no one fails to reform himself. A man of Shu Commandery, Lu Chien, and others have stopped their litigation, blushing for shame, and retired. Although King Wen [of the Chou dynasty caused the rulers of the states of] Yü[2a] and Jui to cease [their quarrels],[18.5] how could it be more than [what Wang Mang has accomplished]? It would be proper to inform the empire [of the foregoing facts]." The memorial was approved.

When the Ruling Governor, [Wang Mang], went out, he was both preceded and followed by ten large chariots, with a Specially Serving Master of Writing, Gentlemen, Attending Secretaries, Internuncios, Palace Attendants Within the Yellow Gate, Attendants at the Gates, and [members of] the Winged Forest. The Ruling Governor regularily bore his credentials. When he stopped [anywhere], an Internuncio held them for him. The division head clerks of the Ruling Governor were ranked at six hundred piculs. The three highest ministers, [in speaking to him] said that they "presumed to speak of [their business]."[18.6]

In this year, [Wang] Mang memorialized [the plans for] and built a *Ming-t'ang*, a *Pi-yung*, and a Spiritual Tower, and for the students [in the Imperial University] he erected ten thousand houses and had made a Market and a Regularly Full Granary.[18.7]

*His Train.*

*He Enlarges the 19a Imperial University.*

---

[18.5] For this story, cf. Glossary, *sub* Yü[2a].

[18.6] Liu Pin (1022–1088) remarks that this last sentence is repeated from 99 A: 17b, and declares that it should be excised here; but this whole paragraph seems to be a summary of the ritual, etc. connected with the office of Ruling Governor in the spirit of *HS*, ch. 19 A, in which case this sentence is pertinent here.

[18.7] Li T'zu-ming, *op. cit.*, 7: 15a, states that the *Ch'u-hsüeh Chi* (viii cent.; I cannot find this passage) quotes the *San-fu Huang-t'u* (iii to vii cent.) as saying that in 4 A.D. Wang Mang "built the *Ming-t'ang*, *Pi-yung*, made 30 residences for the Erudits, and made a market-place for meeting," and also, "Seven *li* east of the city he made a Regularly Full Granary. North of the Granary he made the Huai Market-place. The various

**19a**　　His institutions were very grand.　He established
the *Classic of Music*[19.1] [as an imperially approved
classic], and increased the regular number of the
**24a**　Erudits, having five for each Classic.　He summoned
those from the empire who were versed in one classic
and were teaching eleven persons or more,[19.2] together with those who possessed the lost [chapters of]
the *Rites*, the ancient [text of] the *Book of History*,[19.3]

滿倉制度甚絨立樂經
益傅士員經各五人徵
天下通一蓺教校十一
人臣上及有逸禮古書

Huai trees were in several hundred rows and the students would meet and hold market
[there] on the first and fifteenth days of the month."　This passage is not now in the
*San-fu Huang-t'u*, which has suffered losses.　Cf. Glossary *sub* Imperial University.　Li
T'zu-ming accordingly says that in the *HS* text, before the word 市 there has dropped
out the word 會, reading, "a market-place for meeting."

[19.1] This *Classic of Music* has been lost.　Wang Ch'un, in his *Lun-heng* 13: 16a, 29:
9b (Forke, II, 297, I, 88) says twice, "Yang-ch'eng [Heng] Tzu-chang 陽成子長 composed the *Classic of Music*."　Huan T'an (ca. 40 B.C.–A.D. 29), in his *Hsin-lun* (lost,
quoted in *T'ai-p'ing Yü-lan* 815: 11b), says, "Yang-ch'eng Tzu-chang's personal name
was Heng 衡 and he was a man from Shu Commandery.　When Wang Weng and I
were both Libationers Expounding the Classic of Music and [Yang-ch'eng Heng] was in
bed ill, we purchased ahead of time inner and outer coffins [for him]."　Wang Weng took
part in the rebellion of Chai Yi and was burnt to death by Wang Mang in A.D. 7 (cf.
*HHS*, Mem. 35: 10b); the Libationers were not however appointed until A.D. 11 (*HS*
99 B: 18a), so that Huan T'an's memory must have been at fault about his title at that
time.　Yang-ch'eng Heng's death then probably occurred some time during Wang
Mang's reign.　The *T'ung-chih*, ch. 29 (Com. Pr. ed.), p. 479c, *sub* double surnames
quotes the *Feng-su-t'ung* as stating that in Han times there was a Grandee Remonstrant
and Consultant, excellency Yang-ch'eng Heng.

The *Classic of Music* established as canonical by Wang Mang was then written by
Yang-ch'eng Heng and this is probably the one mentioned in the *Chin History*.　(From
Ma Kuo-han's [fl. 1832–1852] "Introduction" to the *Yo-ching* in his "Yü-han Shan-fang
Chi-yi-shu").　*Sui-shu* ch. 32, "Treatise on the Classics and Literature" 1: 21a, lists a
"Classic of Music in four rolls."　But this book is not mentioned in later bibliographies.
What the relation was of this book to the "*Yo-chi* (Record of Music)," now ch. 17 in the
*Book of Rites*, is unknown.　Cf. *Szu-k'u Ch'üan-shu Tsung-mu T'i-yao* 38: 1a (Com. Pr.
ed. p. 789).

[19.2] *HS* 12: 9b dates this summons in A.D. 5; probably that date represents the time
these persons mostly arrived.

[19.3] "The lost [chapters of] the *Rites*" denotes the 39 fascicles (chapters) of the *Book of
Rites* in ancient characters said by Liu Hsin[1a] to have been found by King Kung of Lu, Liu
Yü[2] (d. 129 B.C.), in the wall of Confucius' house and presented to the imperial throne
by K'ung An-kuo after 100 B.C. (*HS* 36: 33a).　These chapters were not the *Chou-li*
(mentioned separately), which is said to have been secured about the same time by King

毛　天　月　文
詩　文　令　字
周　圖　兵　通
官　讖　法　知
爾　鍾　史　其
雅　律　篇　意

the Mao [text of] the *Book of Odes*, the *Chou Offices* [the *Chou-li*],[19.4] the *Erh-ya*, [books on] astronomy, divinations and revelations, the musical tubes, the "Ordinances for the Months,"[19.5] military methods,[19.6] the written characters in Shih [Chou's] *Fascicles*,[19.7] and who were versed in and understood

He Gathers the Learned and Establishes New Classics.

Hsien of Ho-chien, Liu Tê (*HS* 53: 1b).

"The ancient [text of] the *Book of History*" denotes the 16 fascicles (chapters) of that *Book* in ancient characters, said by Liu Hsin[1a] to have been found along with the lost *Rites* and also to have been presented to the throne by K'ung An-kuo (*HS* 36: 33a).

*HS* 36: 31b states that Liu Hsin[1a] "wanted to have made authoritative *Mr. Tso's [Commentary on] the Spring and Autumn* [i.e., the *Tso-chuan*], the Mao [text of the *Book of] Odes*, the lost [chapters of] the *Rites*, and the ancient [text of the *Book of] History*." Hence this order of Wang Mang was instigated by Liu Hsin and constituted a step towards making these classics authoritative, i.e., placed on the curriculum of the government schools and used for government examinations.

[19.4] The "Mao [text of the *Book of] Odes*" is the one at present current. It was made authoritative by Wang Mang during the reign of Emperor P'ing (Legge, *Chin. Clas.* IV, I, p. 11]).

Liu Hsin[1a] also worked on the *Chou-li* and eventually Wang Mang made it authoritative. During the reign of Wang Mang, all the books here listed, from the lost *Book of Rites* to the *Erh-ya*, were probably made authoritative.

[19.5] "Ordinances for the Months, *Yüeh-ling* 月令" is the title of the present chap. IV in the *Li-chi* (Legge, I, pp. 249–310; Couvreur, I, 330–410), which chapter consists of excerpts from chaps. I–XII of the *Lü-shih Ch'un-ch'iu* (Wilhelm's trans. pp. 1–156). Besides this document, there were probably other writings on this popular subject.

[19.6] "The *Art of War, Ping-fa* 兵法," is the title of the military treatise attributed to Sun-tzu 孫子 and translated by L. Giles, *Sun Tzu on the Art of War*. Giles (p. xvii) however points out that the title, "*Sun-tzu* in 82 fascicles, with diagrams in 9 rolls" listed in *HS* 30: 59a, shows that in Han times there were other apocryphal works on this subject, not included in the 13 books of Sun-tzu that we have at present. Wang Mang's call was probably for more than just this one book, for in 99 C: 21b he is said to have employed military men of all the 63 schools mentioned in *HS* 30: 64a (cf. 99 C: n. 21.3). The Han dynasty had its own military methods 軍法, set forth by Han Hsin (*HS* 1 B: 24b; *HFHD*, I, 146 & n. 4). Wang Mang seems to have intended to accumulate the country's learning at the imperial capital and use it for the imperial benefit.

[19.7] *Shih Chou's Fascicles* was the earliest Chinese lexicographical work. It seems to have been a word list of correct forms; cf. D. Bodde, *China's First Unifier*, ch. VIII. This book is listed in *HS* 30: 22b. *Ibid*, 26a, b says, "In [the period] Yüan-shih, [Wang Mang] summoned from the [whole] empire those who were versed in philology. [They arrived] by the hundreds, and each one was ordered to record words in the [Palace] courts. Yang Hsiung[2] took those [writings] that were of use and composed from them his *Hsün-*

their meaning. All went to the [office of the Major in Charge of] Official Carriages, [so that Wang Mang] ensnared and collected [all] the gentlemen of uncommon ability in the empire. Those who came, at former and later [times], were numbered by the thousands. All were ordered to write out their explanations [of the Classics] in his courts, with the intention of making them correct their discrepancies and errors and unify differing explanations.

Various courtiers memorialized, saying, "Anciently, when the Duke of Chou upheld the heir who succeeded his father, although he possessed the honor of being in the highest rank of the highest ministers, yet only in the seventh year were the institutions fixed.[19.8] Verily, the *Ming-t'ang* and *Pi-yung* have fallen into ruins and have been abolished for a thousand years and no one has been able to revive them. Now the Duke Giving Tranquillity to the Han Dynasty has arisen from a great family and has assisted and protected your Majesty for four years down to the present. His achievements and virtuous conduct are brilliant.

Sept. 5    "The Duke, in the eighth month, when the moon began to wax, on [the day] *keng-tzu*,[19.9] received the

*tsuan P'ien* 訓纂篇. He followed the *Tsang Chieh* and also altered the duplicating words in the *Tsang Chieh*. It was in 89 paragraphs."

[19.8] A reference to *Li-chi* XII, 7 (Legge, II, 31), where the Duke of Chou is said to have resigned in the seventh year. Cf. infra, n. 20.1.

[19.9] Wang Mang's action in laying the foundations "when the moon began to wax" was in imitation of the foundation of the city of Lo by the Duke of Chou. The phrase, "when the moon began to wax, *tsai₁-sheng-p'o₂* 載生魄" is a quotation from the account of that foundation in *Book of History*, V, ix, 1 (Legge, p. 381). (That *Book* writes *tsai₂* 哉 for *tsai₁*. These words were interchangeable; so were *p'o₁* and *p'o₂*.)

The meaning of the phrase, *tsai-sheng-p'o*, seems to have suffered a complete reversal due to an inexact writing of the word *p'o*. The correct word was *p'o₁* 霸. Hsü Sheng, in his *Shuo-wen* 7 A: 4a, defines *p'o₁* as follows: "When the moon is first born, it is like a *p'o₁* (new moon). When [in the calendar, we receive] a long month, [*the p'o₁*] is on the second day [of the month; when we] receive a short month, it is on the third day." (In China, months have begun with the new moon, or, more exactly, the day of the moon's conjunction with the sun, when the moon is invisible). Since $p'o_1$ is written with the word for "moon," this is probably the fundamental meaning of the character. *Shuo-wen* 9 A: 7a defines $p'o_2$ quite differently, as "A *yin* spirit." Since $tsai_1$ (and $tsai_2$) means "beginning," $tsai$-$sheng$-$p'o$ then originally meant "When the new moon appears," and denoted the second or third day of the (lunar) month. This interpretation is confirmed by *Li-chi* XLII, i, 4 (Legge, II, 436; Couvreur, II, 655), "Like the third day of the moon, when it produces its $p'o$ (new moon), 象月之三日而成魄也," and *ibid*. 20 (Legge, II, 445; Couvreur II, 667), "The moon, when it is in the third day [of the month] produces its $p'o$ 月者三日則成魄." In a note to the above passage from the *Book of History*, ("*Shih-san Ching Chu-su*," *Shu-ching* 14: 1b), Ma Jung (79–166) moreover glosses, "$P'o_2$ is the new moon 朏. It means that in the third day [of the month] the moon first brings to birth the form of its new moon and its name is called $p'o_2$." Wang Mang used this interpretation, for this date was the second day of a short month, according to Hoang. (Chen Yüan's *Comparative Daily Calendar* is probably in error, for it makes this date the first day of the month).

This meaning of $p'o$ seems to have suffered reversal because it was the ancient practise to interchange many words with their homonyms. Thus $p'o_1$ came to be written $p'o_2$, with the resultant interpretation of $p'o_2$ (which ordinarily means the vital principle of the body, the material soul) to mean "the substance of the moon 月質," i.e. the unilluminated part of the moon, which appears when the moon begins to wane. Hence $tsai$-$sheng$-$p'o$ came to mean, "when the dark part of the moon is first born," i.e., a day after full moon, the sixteenth day of the month and after. This interpretation appears in the K'ung An-kuo gloss to the above passage in the *Book of History*, *ibid.*, "The Duke of Chou established his government in the seventh year, third month, when the $p'o$ (dark part of the moon) was first born, on the sixteenth day of the [lunar] month, when the full moon was waning and the dark part of the moon ($p'o$) was born." To justify his chronological calculations, Liu Hsin$_{1a}$ adopted this interpretation; *HS* 21 B: 60b quotes his *San-t'ung-li* as follows: "When the dark of the moon ($p'o$) dies, it is the day of new moon; when the dark of the moon ($p'o$) is born, it is the day of full moon. 死霸朔也 生霸望也." Meng K'ang, in a note to *HS* 21 B: 60a, interprets likewise, "In the second day of the month and onwards, the moon is born and its dark ($p'o$) dies." K'ung Ying-ta consequently took this interpretation of $p'o$. In a note to *Book of History* V, iii, 3 (*Ibid*. 11: 11b), he explains, "The places in which the circle of the moon have no light are called $p'o$. After the day of new moon, its *ming* 明 (its brilliance or spiritual substance) is born and its $p'o$ (its dark or material substance) dies. After the day of full moon, its *ming* dies and its $p'o$ is born." Here is the pretty conceit that the moon has two souls, like man, which die and are born as the moon waxes and wanes. This interpretation was adopted by Legge (cf. his *Book of History*, p. 307) and Couvreur (*Dict. Class.*, III ed. sub $p'o_2$), so that it influences their translations of the classics, sometimes with curious consequences.

It is interesting that in this case Wang Mang's courtiers deliberately departed from the interpretation given to a passage of the classic by his greatest authority, Liu Hsin$_{1a}$. Wang Mang's court contained other authorities who disagreed with Liu Hsin, and these scholars preserved the correct interpretation of $p'o$. (Cf. *T'zu-hai*, sub $p'o_1$, $p'o_2$, $tsai_2$-$sheng$-$p'o$; Wang Kuo-wei, *Kuan-t'ang-chi-lin*, I:1a-5b.)

**19b** message [authorizing him to] employ [people] for the purposes of the court,[19.10] and he himself attended to the required service and the work of construction.

**24b** And on the next day, [the day] *hsin-ch'ou*, the various
**Sept. 6** masters and common people assembled in great harmony; a great crowd of a hundred thousand [persons] joined together, working with vigor[19.11] for twenty [days], when the great work was all com-
*19b* pleted. When T'ang [Yao] and Yü [Shun] did [great] things or when at Ch'eng-chou [the Duke of Chou] founded the dynasty's [capital], they verily did no better.

"It is proper that the rank of the Ruling Governor should be above that of the vassal kings, that he should be granted bundles of silk to which are affixed jade circlets, one chariot of state [like that for] a large kingdom, one comfortable carriage, and two quadrigae of black horses." The imperial edict said, "It is approved. Let rules for the nine distinctions be discussed."

**Winter** In the winter, a great wind blew off almost all the roof-tiles on [the buildings at] the eastern gates of the city wall of Ch'ang-an.[19.12]

**A.D. 5,** In the fifth year, in the first month, the *hsia* an-
**Jan./Feb.** cestral sacrifice to all the ancestors together was performed in the *Ming-t'ang;* twenty-eight vassal kings, one hundred twenty full marquises, and more than nine hundred scions of the imperial house were

[19.10] Meng K'ang (fl. 220–240) explains, "It is the message taxing [the people] for corvée service 賦功役之書."

[19.11] Yen Shih-ku suggests that *p'ing* 平 might be emended to *p'ei* 不. Ho Ch'uo (1661–1722) quotes *Book of History*, V, xii, 7, (Legge, p. 424) which contains the phrase *p'ei-tso* 作, to substantiate this emendation. Wang Nien-sun (1744–1832) adds that this passage imitates *Book of History*, V, xiii, which uses the unusual word *p'ei* twice, and calls attention to the fact that, in the ancient official form of writing, *p'ing* and *p'ei* were written similarly and were sometimes confused.

[19.12] This sentence is also found in 12: 8b. The next sentence is also found in that passage, q.v. for annotations.

明堂諸侯王二十八人列侯百二十人宗室子九百餘人俱助祭
其議九錫之法冬大風吹長安城東門屋瓦且盡五年正月袷祭
諸侯王上賜呂東吊加壁大國乘車安車各一驪馬二駟詔曰可
平作二句大功畢成唐虞發舉成周造業誠亡已曰加宰衡位宜在
奉使朝用書臨賦營莽越若朒辛丑諸生庶民大和會十萬衆竝集

次備位未能奉稱伏念聖德純茂承天當古制禮曰治民作
皆叩頭言宜亟加賞於安漢公於是奏上書曰臣臣呂外屬越
四十八萬七千五百七十二人及諸侯王公列侯宗室見者
帛之賞各有數是時吏民呂奉不受新野田而上書者前俊
禮畢封孝宣曾孫信等三十六人為列侯餘皆益戶賜爵金

summoned to assist in the sacrifices.[19.13]   After the
rites were ended, thirty-six great-grandsons of [Em-
peror] Hsiao-hsüan, [Liu] Hsin$_{4g}$ and others, were
enfeoffed as full marquises.[19.14]   The other [persons
who assisted in the sacrifices] all had households
added [to their estates] or were granted noble ranks
and rewards of money and silk, to each a definite
amount.

At this time, because [Wang] Mang had not accepted the cultivated fields of Hsin-yeh, the officials
and common people who sent letters to the Emperor,
[including] previous and later [times, numbered]
487,572 persons.  Moreover, the vassal kings, the
highest ministers, the full marquises, and [the members of] the imperial house, when they had audience,
all kowtowed, saying that it would be proper immediately to give rewards to the Duke Giving Tranquillity to the Han Dynasty.

Thereupon [Wang] Mang presented a letter to
the throne, saying, "Because I, your servant, am your
maternal relative, I have overleaped my [due] sequence and occupy my [present] post, [but] I have
not yet been able to be worthy of my position.  I
humbly reflect that your sage virtue is pure and
abundant, you have received [the mandate] of
Heaven and have followed ancient [practises], you
have instituted rites in order to govern the common
people, and you have composed music[20.1] in order to

He
Distributes
Honors
to the
Imperial
Clan.

The People
Memori-
alize
that he
25a
should be
Rewarded.

20a
He will
Rule Like
the Duke
of Chou,
Aided by
the Others
in the
Govern-
ment.

[19.13] The Sung Ch'i ed. said that the Shun-hua ed. (997) had the word *szu* 祠 after
the 祭.  In a loose quotation of this passage in *HHS*, Mem. 4: 10a[1], the *szu* is omitted.

Stange, *Die Monographie über Wang Mang*, 62, n. 9, declares that Wang Hsien-ch'ien's
ed. reads erroneously "1900 members of the imperial house."  My copy (purchased at
Ch'ang-sha, hence probably the original ed.) does not have this error.  It likewise does
not have the variant noticed in *ibid.*, 63, n. 1.

[19.14] *HS* 12: 2b dates this enfeoffment in Mar., A.D. 1.   Cf. 12: n. 2.5.

[20.1] The phrase "instituting rites and composing music 制禮作樂" is an allusion to
the activity of the Duke of Chou, who, when he was acting as regent for the young King
Ch'eng, is said to have "instituted rites and composed music" (*Li-chi* XII, 6; Legge's

improve their customs, so that [all within] the four seas have run and hastened to obey you, [even] the many barbarians have all come to you, and on the days when they had to take leave and go, none have failed to drop tears. If they had not been sincere, how could this [situation] have been gratuitously brought about?

20a

"From the vassal kings on down to the lower officials and common people, all know that your servant Mang on the one hand and your Majesty on the other are related as closely as the pellicle inside a reed is to the reed. Moreover, [now] that I have been permitted to exercise an [important] charge, those who attribute merits and rank virtuous conduct always have some superfluous words about me, your servant Mang, so that when I, your servant, have an audience and the nobles of the imperial house themselves speak of business before me, I never fail to break out in perspiration and be mortified. Although my nature is stupid and rustic, I myself know most sincerely that while my virtue is small and my position honorable, my strength is too little and my duties are too great. Day and night I am fearful and circumspect, continually being afraid that I will sully and disgrace your sage court.

25b

"Now the empire is well-governed and at peace, the [people's] customs are uniform, the many bar-

薄位尊力小任大凡夜讦棐常恐污辱聖朝今天下治平風俗
而言事於前者未嘗不流汗而惡愧也雖性愚都至誠自知德
尊之故又得典職每歸功列德者輒呂臣恭為餘言臣恭見諸侯
豈可虛致自諸侯王巳下至於吏民成知臣恭上與陛下有薆
樂呂移風回海奔走百壘站蕃辭去之日莫不隕涕非有款誠

---

trans. II, 31). On 99 A: 19a, the courtiers, in a memorial, compare Wang Mang to the Duke of Chou and allude to this passage from the *Book of Rites*, saying that the Duke of Chou fixed "his institutions" to the seventh year; on p. 20a, Wang Mang takes up this phrase, stating that the Empress Dowager has "instituted rites . . . and . . . composed music" (through his own instrumentality, of course), and now (p. 20b) he declares that he wishes to use his whole time in "instituting rites and composing music," i.e., in ruling in behalf of the young emperor and, in establishing truly Confucian institutes and government, and, when this task is complete, like the Duke of Chou, he will return to private life. The phrase "instituting rites and composing music" thus implied "ruling for the minor sovereign in the spirit of the Duke of Chou." It occurs frequently in subsequent passages. Since the Duke of Chou was one of the greatest Confucian sages, these rites and music were of course understood to designate Confucian practises.

齊今大禮已行助祭者畢辭不勝至願願諸章下議者皆寢勿上使臣茶得
同大禮已行助祭者畢辭不勝至願願諸章下議者皆寢勿上使臣茶得
百故也陛下不忍眾言瓴下其章於議者臣茶前欲立秦止恐其遂不肯止
雲被無益之辜所呂敢且保首領須史者誠上休陛下銓光而下依羣公之
車右聖詔宣之于下不能得什一叉羣賢之籌畫而上呂閣不能得什伍當
服大夫莫不忠良故能呂五年之閒至致此爲臣茶實無奇策異謀奉承太
皆齊同百雲車服皆陛下聖德所自躬親太師先太保舜等輔政佐治羣瑣

barians obey and have submitted, all of which
[comes] from your Majesty's sage virtue and what
you yourself [have done]. The Grand Master,
[K'ung] Kuang, and the Grand Guardian, [Wang]
Shun₄ᵦ, and others assist you in the government and
aid in ruling. None of the various ministers and
grandees have failed to be sincere and good, hence
it has been possible, in the time of five years, to
attain this extreme achievement.

"I, your servant Mang, have really had no wonderful
plans or extraordinary projects. When I have received the sage edicts of the [Grand] Empress Dowager and have promulgated them to your subjects, I
have not been able to attain one-tenth [of the sageness contained therein]; when I received plans from
various capable [persons] and reported them to the
throne, I have not been able to attain five-tenths [of
the virtue contained therein], so that I ought to suffer
for the crime of being of no benefit [to the empire].
The reason that I temporarily presume to protect my
head and neck for the moment is in reality because
on the one hand I have reposed upon your Majesty's
superabundant glory and [because] on the other hand
I have relied upon my old friends, the highest
ministers.

"Your Majesty could not bear [to refuse] the **20b**
words of the crowd, so their writings were each time
referred to [the officials] for discussion. Your serv- *20b*
ant Mang previously sought immediately to memorialize and stop [their proposals], but I feared
that you thereupon would not be willing to stop the
matter.

"Now that the great rites have already been performed and the assistants at the sacrifices have all
left, I cannot repress my greatest wish. It is my
wish that the various writings which have been referred to those who are to discuss [these matters]
should all be laid aside and not reported to the
throne, [thereby] causing your servant Mang to be

公功德光於天下是呂諸侯王公列侯宗室諸生吏民翁然同辭
者路是臣之私願也惟陛下哀憐財幸甄邯等自太后詔曰可唯
則臣莽當被註上誤朝之罪如無他讁得全命賜散骨歸亰避賢
盡力畢制禮作樂事事成呂傳示天下與海內平之卽有所聞非

26a able to use all his efforts in completing the business of instituting [Confucian] rites and composing [Confucian] music.[20.1] When these matters are completed, I will then transmit and show them to the empire and give them to [all] within the [four] seas to criticize. Supposing that they contain anything traitorous[20.2] or evil, your servant Mang ought accordingly to suffer for the crime of having misled the Emperor and of having deceived the court. If I do not undergo any other impeachments, to be permitted to preserve my life, to be granted to ransom my person and return home, and to make way for a worthier person will be the private wish of your servant. I only hope that your Majesty would have compassion and pity and favor me somewhat."[20.3]

Chen Han and others advised the [Grand] Empress Dowager to issue an imperial edict saying, "It is permitted. Verily, Duke, your achievements and virtuous conduct are [the most] brilliant in the empire. For this reason the vassal kings, the highest ministers, the full marquises, [the members of] the imperial house, the various masters, the lower officials, and the common people were of one accord and

---

[20.2] For this meaning of *chien*, cf. *SC* 29: 7 and *Mh* III, 524[3].

[20.3] Yen Shih-ku asserts that *ts'ai*[1] 財 is the same as "*ts'ai*[2] 裁, to select," but Wang Nien-sun, in a note to *HS* 48: 34a, states that this interpretation does not fit the phrase *ts'ai*[1]-*hsing* 幸. He declares that *ts'ai* means "*shao* 少, somewhat," and that the meaning of this phrase is similar to the expression in 48: 35a[10], "I wish that your Majesty would pay some attention to it 少留計." He also quotes similar cases of the phrase *ts'ai-hsing* from *HS* 77: 5b[7] *sub* Chu-ko Feng, ch. 93, ch. 49 *sub* Ch'ao Ts'o (thrice), 72: 6b[10] *sub* Wang Chi, ch. 59 *sub* Chang An-shih, 75: 31a[3] *sub* Li Hsün, and 86: 19b[4] *sub* Shih[1] Tan. In a note to 54: 14a[11], Yen Shih-ku, seemingly following an ancient comment, declares that *ts'ai* means "*chin*[4] 僅, somewhat"; the *Kuang-ya* interprets *chin*[3] 菫 as *shao*; these two words *chin* are interchanged. In a note to *HS* 4: 9b (cf. *HFHD* I, 242, n. 4) Yen Shih-ku himself asserts that *ts'ai* means *shao*. Cf. also *HFHD* II, 387, n. 6.4. *Ts'ai*[1], *ts'ai*[2], and *ts'ai*[3] 才 are given the same archaic pronunciation in Karlgren, *Grammatica Serica*, # 943 h, ć, a, and were interchanged with *ts'ai*[4] 纔, which latter character seems not to have occurred in Chou literature, but is used in *HS* 49: 13b[11] and 51: 5b[4].

錫禮儀亟奏於是公卿大夫博士議郎列侯富平侯張純等九
定事須公而決故且聽公制作羣公曰開宪于前議其九
公每見輒流涕叩頭言願不受賁賁即加不敢當位方制作事未
罷遣猶不肯去告曰孟夏特行厥賁莫不雝悅稱萬歲而退今
運守闕庭故下其章諸侯宗室辭去之日復見前重陳雖曉喻

said the same things. They continually waited at the gate towers and the great court, hence their writings were referred [by the throne to the proper officials]. On the day when the nobles and the members of the imperial house took their leave and left, they again presented their previously emphasized proposals.[20.4] Although they were plainly instructed to be dismissed and sent off, [yet they acted] as if they were unwilling to leave. When [we] informed them that in the first month of summer your rewards would be put into effect, no one failed to rejoice and be pleased. They called out, 'Long life,' and left.

"Now every time that you, Duke, have an audience, you always drop tears and kowtow, saying that you wish not to receive a reward and that if a reward is given you, you will not presume to occupy your position. Just now [the rites and music] that are being instituted and composed have not yet been fixed upon, so that those matters need you, Duke, to decide upon them, hence for the time being [We] accede to you, Duke. When what is being instituted and composed is all completed, the highest ministers 26b will report it and investigate into the previous proposal [of the nobles, etc.]. Let the ceremonial for *21a* the nine distinctions be promptly memorialized [to Us]."

Thereupon the ministers, grandees, erudits, gentle- **21a** men-consultants, and the full marquis,[21.1] Chang

[20.4] The Sung Ch'i ed. said that the word *chung* 重 should be changed to come after the 復, following the Yüeh ed. (xi–xii cent.). Since the Ching-yu ed. agrees with the present text, I have not adopted the Yüeh ed.'s emendation. Yen Shih-ku reads *chung* with the present fourth tone, meaning "emphasis".

[21.1] At this point, the text contains the words for "the Marquis of Fu-p'ing," necessitating the translation, "erudits, gentlemen-consultants, full marquises, and the Marquis of Fu-p'ing, Chang Shun." The Sung Ch'i ed. however reports that the Yüeh ed. lacks the words for "the Marquis of Fu-p'ing," and the Ching-yu ed. also lacks them. I have followed their reading. It is quite peculiar that one grade of the nobility should be specifically mentioned as all being concerned in a Confucian ritual, along with the erudits and learned persons at the court. The insertion of Chang Shun's marquisate was almost surely a scribal interpolation.

The Nine
Distinc-
tions
to be
Conferred
Upon him.

Shun, and others, nine hundred two persons [alto-
gether], all said, "When the sage lords and glorious
kings beckoned to the capable and urged the able [to
come to them], those whose virtuous conduct was
abundant [were given] high positions and those
whose achievements were great [were given] rich
rewards. Hence when an exemplary subject possessed the honor of being a 'high duke with the nine
conferments,'[21.2] he [also] possessed the favor of hav-

九命上公之尊則有九
功大者貴厚故宗臣有
招賢勸能德盛者位高
百二人皆曰聖帝明王

[21.2] For these conferments, cf. *Li-chi* III, ii, 8 (Legge, I, 215; Couvreur, I, 273), *Book
of History* V, viii, 4 (Legge, 379). The phrase, "a high duke (*shang-kung*) with the nine
conferments" is quoted from *Chou-li* 21: 1a (Biot, II, 1). The conferments (*ming* 命) as
rewards given by the Son of Heaven are seemingly first mentioned in *Book of Odes*, II,
VII, viii, 3; Legge, p. 403.

*Chou-li* 18: 10b–12b (Biot, I, 428–430), *sub* the *Ta-tsung-po*, says, "He uses the conferments in the nine rituals to correct the rankings of states. The first conferment is
investiture with office, the second conferment is investiture with robes, the third conferment is investiture with rank, the fourth conferment is investiture with [sacrificial]
utensils, the fifth conferment is the granting of a *tsê* (cf. 99 B: n. 19.5), the sixth conferment is the granting of [subordinate] officials, the seventh conferment is granting him a
[noble] estate, the eighth conferment is making him a Shepherd (*mu*), and the ninth
conferment is making him a Chief (*po*) [of a quarter of the country]."

Chang Yen (iii cent. A.D.) says, "The nine conferments (*ming*) are the nine distinctions (*hsi* 錫)." In the *Spring and Autumn*, Dk. Chuang, I, 6; Dk. Wen, I, 5; Dk.
Ch'eng, VIII, 7 (Legge, pp. 72, 227, 229, 366), *hsi* is used as a verb, "to impart," in the
phrase, "impart (*hsi*) the conferments (*ming*)." But in the *HS* text here both *hsi* and
*ming* are used as nouns. Very likely in Wang Mang's time *ming* denoted the nine "conferments" mentioned in the *Chou-li* passage quoted above, whereas *hsi* denoted the
"distinctions" enumerated in n. 23.3.

*Chou-li* 21: 1a (Biot, II, 1), *sub* the *Tien-ming* (Officer in Charge of the Conferments)
says "High Dukes (*shang-kung* 上公) have the nine conferments (*ming*) and become
Chiefs [of quarters of the country]. Their states and households (*kuo-chia* 國家), their
palaces and residences, their chariots and banners, their garments and robes, and their
rites and usages all use nine as the limit. Marquises and earls have seven conferments.
Their states and households (*kuo-chia*), their palaces and residences, their chariots and
banners, their garments and robes, and their rites and usages all use seven as the limit.
Viscounts and barons have five conferments. Their states and households (*kuo-chia*),
their palaces and residences, their chariots and banners, their garments and robes, and
their rites and usages all use five as the limit." Cheng Hsüan explains (not too accu-

錫登等之寵今九族親睦百姓既章萬國和

協恭民時寵聖瑞畢秦太平已洽帝者之盛

莫陸於虞唐而陛下任之忠臣茂功英者於

伊周而辛衡配之所謂異時而與如合符者

ing been promoted '[an additional] step,'[21.3] with the nine distinctions.

"Now 'the nine [classes of the imperial] kindred are affectionately harmonious' and 'the official class' is already 'honored,' 'the myriad states' are 'harmonized and united,' and 'the many people have then become harmonious.'[21.4] The auspicious presages of sageness have all arrived and the great peace has become universal. Of the greatest lords, none were greater than T'ang [Yao] and Yü [Shun], yet your Majesty is worthy [of occupying their positions]. Of loyal ministers who had abundant achievements, none were more outstanding than Yi [Yin and the Duke of] Chou, yet the Ruling Governor, [Wang Mang], is equal to them. It is what might be called a revival [of ancient glories] at a different time, '[and is as similar to those great days] as the matching of [the two halves] of a tally.'[21.5]

rately), "The high dukes (shang-kung) are the three highest ministers (san-kung 三公) of the king, [who have only *eight* conferments; cf. n. 21.3]. To those who possess virtue, there is added a conferment and they become the two Chiefs (po). The descendants of the two dynasties, [Hsia and Yin], were also high dukes (shang-kung)." In Wang Mang's time the Shang-kung were the Four Coadjutors, who ranked above the San-kung. In Chou times, office was hereditary, so that the highest ministers were nobles; whereas in Han times such feudalism had disappeared and kung no longer always denoted a noble. Cheng Hsüan continues, "Their state and households (kuo-chia) is where the prince and his followers dwell 國之所居. It means the square which is their [capital] city. The [capital] city of a duke was probably nine li square and his palace was nine hundred paces square. The [capital] city of a marquis or earl was probably seven li square and his palace seven hundred paces square. The [capital] city of a viscount or baron was probably five li square, and his palace five hundred paces square." This scholastic architectonic does not, of course, represent the facts of history.

[21.3] Chou-li 21: 2a (Biot, II, 2) says, "The three highest ministers (san-kung) have eight conferments.... When they are sent out [of the court] and enfeoffed [as feudal nobles with fiefs, going to rule them], one [more] step [in conferments] is added." This passage is referred to in the phrase, "promoted [an additional] step."

[21.4] This sentence uses phrases from the *Book of History*, I, 2 (Legge, p. 17; translated in *HFHD* II, 215, n. 7.6), which passage describes the virtue of Yao. In this passage of the *HS*, as in the *Book of History*, po-hsing means "official class," cf. n. 6.13. The word pang 邦 in the *Book of History*, which was Emperor Kao's given name, is tabooed here and kuo 國 is used instead. Pang was not however always tabooed. It is used in the *Shuo-wen* (A.D. 100).

[21.5] A quotation from *Mencius* IV, ii, i, 3 (Legge, p. 317).

"We have carefully taken the universal principles of the six canons and what is found in the text of the Classics, [especially] in the *Chou Offices* and the *Record of Proprieties (Li-chi)*, and is suitable to the present [time], and have made the distinctions for the nine conferments. Your servants beg [your approval of] the distinctions for the conferments." The memorial was approved.

27a

A.D. 5, June 22. His Charter.

[Wang Mang's] charter said, "Verily, in the fifth year of [the period] Yüan-shih, the fifth month, on [the day] *keng-yin*, the Grand Empress Dowager [nee Wang] came to the Front Hall [of the Palace, had Wang Mang] conducted and [ordered to] mount [the steps to the throne], and in person[21.6] commanded him by this imperial edict, which said,

21b *21b*

" 'Let the Duke approach, empty himself,[21.7] and listen to Our words. Previously you, Duke, have guarded the throne [from the time of] Emperor Hsiao-ch'eng [now] to the sixteenth year. You have presented your plans and have been completely loyal. You advised [the Emperor] to execute the former Marquis of Ting-ling, Shun-yü Chang, in order to repress his rebellion and reveal the evil-doers. You mounted to [the position of] Commander-in-chief and your duties were to assist [the Emperor] at the court.

" 'When Emperor Hsiao-ai ascended the throne, while the proud concubine, [the Queen Dowager nee Fu] watched him furtively [for a chance] to work her will and while his wicked courtiers hatched rebellion,

---

[21.6] Shen Ch'in-han (1775–1832) declares that 請 should be 親. The Ching-yu ed. and the Official ed. read the latter word. Wang Hsien-ch'ien says however that the Southern Academy ed. reads as he does.

[21.7] The connotation of "empty oneself (*hsü-chi* 虛己)," a phrase frequently used in imperial charters to officials (cf. *HFHD* I, 334), is "pay close attention." The *Tz'u-hai*, *sub* this phrase, quotes the *Han-shih Wai-chuan* (by Han Ying, fl. 179–141 B.C.; I have not been able to find this passage), "A superior man who has the highest degree of virtue is yet humble, [so that] he will empty himself and receive [the instructions of] others."

大司馬職在內輔孝哀皇帝卽位騎奏寇姦臣萌亂公手
十有六年納策盡忠白謀改定陵侯浯于長臣媢亂發姦登
于前殿延登請詔之曰公進虛聽朕言前公宿衞孝成皇帝
錫臣請命錫奏可策曰惟元始五年五月庚寅太皇太后臨
也謹呂六藝通義經文所見周官禮記宜於今者為九命之

旱舉禍龍不作輔朕五年人倫之本正天地之位定欽承神祇經緯

安侯董賢轉漏之閒忠策瓶建細紀咸張綏和元壽再遷大行萬事

臣充朝危殆甚矣朕惟定國之計果宜于公列納于朝即日罷退高

復還公長安屬病加劇猶不忘公復持進位是夜倉卒國無儲主姦

不據經呂病辭位歸于第家為賊臣所陷就國之後孝皇帝覺寤

劾高昌侯董宏改正故定陶共王母之僭坐自是之後朝臣論議靡

you, Duke, yourself impeached the Marquis of Kao-ch'ang, Tung Hung, and [at an imperial banquet] changed and corrected the usurped seat of the now deceased [Queen Dowager nee Fu], the mother of King Kung of Ting-t'ao, [Liu K'ang]. From that time on, when the officials of the court discussed [matters], no one failed to accord with the Classics.

" 'When you had resigned your position on account of illness and returned to your great house, you were endangered by brigand-like officials, [but] after you had gone to your estate, Emperor Hsiao-ai awakened [to a comprehension of his error] and again returned you, Duke, to Ch'ang-an. When he became ill and [his illness] became increasingly severe, he still did not forget you, Duke, and again especially advanced your rank.

" 'That night, in [a time of] haste and confusion, the state was without a presumptive heir and wicked courtiers filled the court, so that the peril was indeed great. We reflected that no one was more fitting than you, Duke, [to make] a plan for giving tranquillity to the state, [so We] had you inducted into the court. That same day [We] dismissed the Marquis of Kao-an, Tung Hsien[2a], and within the interval of a turn of the clepsydra, your loyal plans were immediately established and the main and subordinate [dynastic] principles were all set forth in detail.

" '[During the year-periods] Sui-ho and Yüan-shou, when you twice happened upon the death of an emperor, you carried out all things perfectly, so that civil disturbances did not take place. You have assisted Us to the fifth year, [during which time] you have corrected fundamental matters of human relationships and have fixed the altars of Heaven and Earth.[21.8] You have carefully served the gods in

The Charter Bestowing the Nine Distinctions.

27b

8-7 B.C.
2-1 B.C.

---

[21.8] Chang Yen (iii cent.) explains that these two clauses refer to "the rites for capping and marriage and the moving of the Southern and Northern [Altars for] the suburban sacrifices."

The
Charter
Bestowing
the Nine
Distinc-
tions.

*22a*

**22a**

28a

heaven and earth and have disposed of [matters in all] the four seasons. You have restored what had been abolished for a thousand years and straightened out the mistakes of a hundred generations.[21.9] [People from all over] the empire have met in harmony and a great crowd has collected together. The Spiritual Tower [spoken of] in the *Book of Odes*,[21.10] the building of [the city of] Lo in the *Book of History*,[21.11] the institutes of the capital at Hao and the regulations of the Shang [dynasty's] capital[21.12] have been revived by you in the present [age]. You have made glorious and illustrious the supreme achievements of the deceased deified rulers and have made brilliant and manifest the 'excellent virtue'[22.1] of the founder and exemplars [of the imperial line]. You have exalted and made apparent the principle that respect for the father [of a dynasty] consists in [making him] the coadjutor of Heaven. You have restored and established the rites for the suburban sacrifice to the most prominent ancestor of the line anterior to the founder of the house (*chiao*), the sacrifice to the most ancient ancestor of the line (*ti*), and for the sacrifice to the greatest exemplar of the house (*tsung*),[22.2] in order to make glorious the great

[21.9] Chang Yen explains, "He had enfeoffed the descendants of the previous dynasties, established [as official] the ancient text of the Classics, and fixed the rites of successively removing [the shrines of remote ancestors to the shrine of the most ancient ancestor]." For the latter rite, cf. Glossary *sub* Wei Hsüan-ch'eng.

[21.10] Referring to *Book of Odes*, III, I, viii (Legge, p. 456).

[21.11] Referring to *Book of History* V, xiii (Legge, p. 434 ff).

[21.12] Yen Shih-ku explains that when the city of Lo was completed, the stubborn people of Shang were removed to dwell there. The point of this passage is that Wang Mang's achievements were as great as those of the founders of the Chou dynasty.

[22.1] "Excellent virtue" is a phrase from *Book of Odes*, no. 174; II, II, x, 3 (Legge, p. 276).

[22.2] This sacrificial canon was a scholastic adoption of the ancient Chou sacrificial custom as recorded in the *Kuo-yü* and the *Li-chi* XX, 1 (Legge, II, 201–202). There were four ancestral sacrifices: the *ti* 禘 sacrifice to the most ancient ancestor of the line, the *chiao* 郊 (suburban) sacrifice to the most prominent ancestor of the line anterior to the founder of the house, the *tsu* 祖 sacrifice to the founder of the house, i.e., the ancestor

四海雍雍萬國慕義蠻夷殊俗不召自至漸化端
兄奉珍助祭尋舊本道遵術重古勤而有成事得
厥中至德要道通於神明祖考嘉享光耀顯章天
符仍臻元氣大同麟鳳龜龍泉祥之瑞七百有餘

[principle of] filial piety. For this reason [all within] the four seas are concordant, all countries incline towards correct principles, and the barbarians, who have different customs [from the Chinese], have of their own accord come [to the imperial court] without being summoned and are gradually progressing [in civilization] and have corrected their ceremonial bonnets and bring their treasures to assist at the [imperial] sacrifices.

" 'You have searched for old [precedents and have based [yourself] on the [correct] Way [of action], you have obeyed the [Confucian] canons and honored ancient [practices, so that] whenever you acted, you have been successful, and in everything you have attained the mean. Your extreme virtue and essential principles have become known to the gods; the imperial ancestors have esteemed you and rejoiced, so that lights have shone brightly and happy portents from Heaven have arrived repeatedly. The grand [cosmological] principles are universally concordant [and there have been] more than seven hundred auspicious presages of unicorns, phoenixes, tortoises, and dragons.[22.3] You are accordingly in-

The
Charter
Bestowing
the Nine
Distinc-
tions.

who was responsible for the house securing its royal or imperial standing, and the *tsung* 宗 sacrifice to the greatest ruler subsequent to the founder of the house, i.e., the greatest exemplar (for *tsung* as denoting an exemplar, cf. n. 17.6). On these sacrifices, cf. B. Karlgren, "Legends and Cults in Ancient China," *Bull. of the Museum of Far Eastern Antiquities*, no. 18, p. 215.

The previously established imperial ancestral sacrifice to Emperor Kao was evidently considered as the *tsu* sacrifice, so that only the three others are mentioned. By the device of making these ancestors the coadjutors (*pei* 配) of high gods, as on p. 17a, i.e., making them the introducers of the worshipper to, intercessors with, and transmitters of the sacrifice to these high gods, these ancestral sacrifices became at the same time the worship of the highest deities. *HS* 25 B: 21a, b does not mention the sacrificial canon referred to in this passage, merely saying, "In the course of [Wang Mang's] more than thirty years [of rule], the sacrifices to Heaven and Earth underwent five changes."

[22.3] Pan Ku thus omitted all but a very few of Wang Mang's portents. This fact speaks well of Pan Ku's judgment of historical values. The *Lun-heng* (Forke, I, 366) mentions a bird as large as a horse with variegated colors, which roosted in P'ei Commandery.

The
Charter
Bestowing
the Nine
Distinc-
tions.

stituting rites and composing music, so that you will have the great merit of having restored peace to the [imperial] ancestral temples and the [imperial] gods of the soils and grains. All [persons] under Heaven rely upon you alone, Duke. Your office is that of Ruling Governor and your rank is[22.4] in the highest class of the highest ministers.

" '[We] now add [to your honors] the distinctions for the nine conferments. Let them be used in assisting at the [imperial] sacrifices and in performing your civil and military duties. [Their favor] shall moreover be conferred upon your [deceased] ancestors. Oh! How can that fail to be good!' "

*22*

**22b**
The Nine
Distinc-
tions.
28b

Thereupon [Wang] Mang bent his head to the ground, and, bowing repeatedly, received [1] a green apron,[22.5] a tunic embroidered with dragons and other figures and a mortar-board hat, a short tunic and robe, a fine gold mouth for a scabbard and a fine gold tip for a scabbard,[22.6] and ornamented shoes,[22.7]

於是莽稽首再拜受綠韍袞冕衣裳瑒琫瑒珌句
曰助祭共大武之職乃遂及厥祖於戲豈不休哉
惟公是賴官在宰衡位在上公今加九命之錫其
遂制禮作樂有綏靖宗廟社稷之大勳普天之下

[22.4] The *Ching-yu* and the Official ed. read 爲 instead of 在.

[22.5] For this garment, cf. n. 2.8.

[22.6] Meng K'ang glosses, "*Tang₁* 瑒 is the name of a jade. Of the ornaments for the scabbard of a sword, [the one] on the top [of the scabbard] is called a *peng* 琫 and [the one] on the bottom is called a *pi* 珌. The *Book of Odes* [＊213; II, VI, ix, 2 (Legge, p. 383)] says, 'His scabbard has a gem mouth and a gem tip,' which is this [meaning]."

The word here written *tang₁* is not the exactly correct form of the word intended in the text. Meng K'ang seems moreover to have been in part mistaken in his interpretation of its meaning. The *Ching-yu* ed. and the Official ed. read for *tang* the word 瑒 (which I do not find in the *K'ang-hsi Dictionary*), and the latter quotes Liu Pin as declaring that *tang₁* should have the phonetic *yi* 易, with which the Sung Ch'i ed. agrees. But Su Yü (fl. 1913) notes that *Shuo-wen* 1 A: 4b defines the word here pronounced as *tang₁* as "a jade tablet one foot two inches [long], with a spoon, which is used in the sacrifices in the [imperial] ancestral temples. It comes from [the radical for] jade and *yang* 昜 [which latter gives] its pronunciation, 丑亮 [at present pronounced *ch'ang*]." Su Yü points out that the *ch'ang* is accordingly not an ornament for a scabbard, but the same as the libation tablet 祼圭, the description of which in the *Chou-li* 41: 2b, *sub* the *Yü-jen* (Biot, II, 523), is in precisely the same words as that for *tang₁* in the *Shuo-wen*, and of the *ch'ang-kuei* 瓚圭 in *Kuo-yü* 4: 4a. This word thus has the pronunciation *ch'ang* and should be written with the phonetic *yang*, not *yi*; hence the Sung Ch'i ed. was mistaken.

履鸞路乘馬龍斾九旒皮　弨弓矢路乘馬彤弓矢　盧弓矢左建朱鈇右建金　咸甲冑一具秬皂二卣主

[2] a princely chariot with bells and a quadriga of horses,[22.8] with the dragon banner with nine tails and the spotted deerskin cap and white silk pleated robe, a war-chariot with a quadriga of horses, [3] a red bow and arrows and a black bow and arrows,[22.9] [4 a] vermillion axe of authority to be held on his left and a metal (copper) battle-axe to be held on his right, one set of armor and a helmet, [5] two flagons of black millet herb-flavored liquor[22.10] and two jade tablet

The Nine Dictinctions.

Su Yü asserts that $tang_1$ is here probably used for $tang_2$ 璗. *Shuo-wen* 1 A: 6a defines $tang_2$ as "the [most] beautiful [kind of] gold, which has the same color as jade. It comes from [the radical for] jade and *t'ang* 湯 [which latter gives] its pronunciation. For the scabbards of their ceremonial swords, the nobles have $tang_2$ mouths and gem [more probably *liu* (fine gold)] tips." *Erh-ya* 5: 9b says, "Gold is called $tang_2$; the [most] beautiful [kind] of it is called *liu* 鏐." In a note to the passage of the *Book of Odes* quoted above (in *Shih-san Ching Chu-su* 14 ii: 2a), the Mao interpretation (ii cent. B.C.; describing ancient practices) says, "The Son of Heaven has a jade mouth to his scabbard and a mother-of-pearl tip to his scabbard. Nobles have $tang_2$ mouths to their scabbards and gem [more probably *liu* (fine gold)] tips to their scabbards. Grandees have fine silver mouths to their scabbards and *liu* (fine gold) tips to their scabbards. Gentlemen have shell mouths to their scabbards and shell tips to their scabbards." *Shuo-wen* 1 A: 4b, *sub peng*, however says, "The ornament for the tip of a scabbard. The Son of Heaven uses jade and the nobles use metal (gold)." *HHS*, Tr. 30: 12b states moreover that both the Emperor and the vassal kings used gold in their scabbards. Hence $tang_1$ cannot here be the name for a kind of jade and this word should be read as $tang_2$.

[22.7] Meng K'ang explains, "They are the present ornamental tips to fasting and sacrificial shoe clogs. They protrude from the shoe one or two inches." Yen Shih-ku adds, "Their shape is that of a forked [raised] end." The Sung Ch'i ed. says, "Wei Chao says, '*Chü-li* 句履 are ornamented at the end and are in the shape of the hilt of a sword.'" In *Li-chi* II, I, iii, 38 (Couvreur, I, 183) and XI, iii, 12 (Couvreur, I, 710) the first word of this phrase is written 絇. In a note to *Yi-li* 3: 6a (Steele, I, 15), Cheng Hsüan says, "The *chü* . . . are used as guards in walking. In shape they are like the hilt on a scabbard of a sword, and they are at the front of the shoes." For figures of these clogs, cf. Nieh Ch'ung-yi's *San-li T'u* (presented 962) 8: 11a; also the account in *Wen-hsüan* 35: 36a, *sub* P'an Hsü Yüan-mou's (d. 215) "*Chiu-hsi-wen.*"

[22.8] Yen Shih-ku explains, "The *luan-lu* 鸞路 is a princely (*lu*) carriage on which are used little bells (*luan*) . . . Four horses are called a 乘 (quadriga)." The reference is to *Li-chi* XII, 15 (31: 7b; Legge, II, 34; Couvreur, I, 734–35). *Luan-lu* is also used in *HS* 22: 23b, 24a; 25 B: 13a.

[22.9] *Book of History* V, xxviii, 4 (Legge, p. 619) states that "a red bow and a hundred red arrows, a black bow and a hundred black arrows" were awarded to Marquis Wen of Chin.

[22.10] Mentioned in the *Book of History*, V, xiii, 25 (Legge, p. 449).

**23a**
**The Nine Distinctions.**

spoons, [6] two green jade tablets for the nine conferments,[23.1] [7] vermillion doors, [8] inside staircases,[23.2] and [9] the insignia of having an Office of [Superintendancy over] his Clan, an Office of Praying, an Office of Augury, an Office of Recording, three hundred men of [the Gentlemen] as Rapid as Tigers, one Household Steward and one Assistant [Household Steward]. In each of the Offices over his Clan, of Praying, of Divination, and of Recording there

*23a*

were established Bailiffs and Accessory [Officials]. When the Duke Giving Tranquility to the Han Dy-

29a

nasty was in his yamen inside [the Palace] or in his residence outside [the Palace, the Gentlemen] as Rapid as Tigers were to act as the guard at his gates, and those who were qualified to come out or in were to have their names inscribed on a register [at his gates]. From the Four Coadjutors and the three highest ministers [on down, if anyone] had business at his yamen or residence, they were all to use passports. The Prince's Lodge of the Kings of Ch'u was made the residence of the Duke Giving Tranquillity to the Han Dynasty. It was grandly repaired and

---

[23.1] Yen Shih-ku remarks, "*Ch'ing* 青 is the color of spring. The eastern quarter gives birth to, grows, and nourishes all things."

[23.2] Meng K'ang explains, "納 is 內. It means to make an opening at the junction of two walls in the basement of his mansion (*tien*), and make a staircase, so as not to cause [the staircase] to be exposed to the sky." Yen Shih-ku adds, "Meng [K'ang's] explanation is correct. Honored persons do not wish to be exposed to the sky as they go upstairs, hence they [put the stairs] inside beneath the eaves." In *Wen-hsüan* 35: 37a, P'an Hsü writes in his "*Chiu-hsi-wen*" ("Essay on the Nine Distinctions"), "For this reason the prince who possesses the distinctions has an inside staircase to mount up [to the main floor of his house]," and Li Shan quotes Ju Shun's explanation, "The basement of the mansion (*tien*) is cut into to make a staircase in order to have comfort on both sides, above and below [in climbing to the main floor]." Ancient Chinese official residences seem often to have had below the main floor a basement floor for the servants and usually to have had the main floor elevated above the level of the ground. Han funerary pottery shows houses with even five stories; cf. Maspero, "La vie privée a l'époque Han," in *Revue des arts asiatiques*, 7: 188.

公弟大繕治通周衛祖禰廟
及寢皆為朱戶納陛陳崇又
秦安漢公祠祖禰出城門城
門校尉直特騎士從入有門

built and a vacant space [arranged] all around it for the guard. The temples and funerary chambers of his [deceased] grandfather and father were all given vermillion doors and inside staircases.[23.3]

The Nine Distinctions.

Ch'en Ch'ung also memorialized, "When the Duke Giving Tranquillity to the Han Dynasty goes outside of the city gate for the purpose of sacrificing to his [deceased] grandfather or father, it would be proper for the Colonel of the City Gate to accompany [the Duke] at the head of his cavalrymen. Then when [the Duke] enters [the city] he will have the guards

[23.3] There are five ancient lists of these nine distinctions: (I) In *Han-shih Wai-chuan* 8: 9a, sect. 13 (by Han Ying, fl. 174–141 B.C.), "The books say, 'When the nobles are virtuous, the Son of Heaven gives them distinctions. The first distinction is carriages and horses; the second distinction is garments and robes, the third distinction is the As Rapid as Tigers; the fourth distinction is music and [musical] instruments; the fifth distinction is inside staircases; the sixth distinction is vermillion doors; the seventh distinction is bows and arrows; the eighth distinction is ceremonial- and battle-axes; the ninth distinction is black millet herb-flavored liquor." (II) The *Li-wei Han-wen-chia* (prob. end i cent. B.C.), *Yü-han Shang-fang Chi-yi-shu* collection, p. 6a, has a similar list, but in a slightly different order; (III) the passage of the *HS* translated above; (IV) in a note to the *Kung-yang Commentary* 6: 3b, Dk. Chuang, I, x, Ho Hsiu (129–182) quotes the list in the *Han-wen-chia*; (V) Ying Shao (ca. 140–206) has the same list (translated in *HFHD*, II, 47–48, n. 9.2). Fan Ning (339–401) also quotes the list from the *Han-wen-chia* in a note to *Ku-liang Commentary* 5: 2a, Dk. Chuang, I, x. Wang Mang's list is different from all the others in that, instead of musical instruments, he received "jade tablets with the nine emblems." These nine distinctions are not mentioned in the Five Classics. They are mentioned first, seemingly, in the *Han-shih Wai-chuan*, and in a memorial of 128 B.C. to Emperor Wu (*HS* 6: 9a); *Chou-li* 18: 10b ff, *sub* the *Ta-tsung-po* (Biot, I, 428–430) gives a list of the "nine conferments (*ming*)," (trans. here in n. 21.2); *ibid.*, 21: 1a (Biot II, 1) refers to them (also cf. n. 21.2); but this passage of the *Chou-li* may be no earlier than the time of Wang Mang. The *Spring and Autumn* (v cent. B.C.; Dk. Chuang, I, x; Legge, p. 72) uses the phrase 錫桓公命, in which the first word is interpreted by the *Kung-yang Commentary* (iii cent. B.C.) 6: 3a as 賜, but understood as "distinctions" by Ho Hsiu and others. The *Bamboo Annals*, K. Yu, yr. I (Legge, *Shoo-king*, Intro., p. 157) uses the term *hsi* to mean "to grant distinctions." It is thus probable that the tradition concerning these nine distinctions came down to Wang Mang in a slightly different form from that in the *Han-shih Wai-chuan*.

The use of those distinctions was continued after Han times; *San-Kuo-chih*, Wei, 1: 35b–36b, quotes an edict of Emperor Hsien, dated A.D. 213, granting these nine distinctions to Ts'ao Ts'ao and enumerating them in detail.

of his gates [to protect him] and when he goes out of [the city] he will have cavalrymen [following him, by all of which] his state would be made more honorable." His memorial was approved.

Autumn    That autumn, because of the auspicious presage that the Empress [nee Wang] would have descendants,[23.4] [Wang] Mang cut the Tzu-wu Road. The

**23b**

The Tzu-wu Road.    Tzu-wu Road cuts straight across the Southern Mountains from Tu-ling and passes [into] Han-chung [Commandery].

The eight messengers[23.5] [who had been sent to observe and influence the people's] customs had returned and had said that the customs of the empire

29b have been unified. They had falsely invented ac-

A companied and unaccompanied songs from the com-

Flattering manderies and kingdoms to praise [Wang Mang's]

Report achievements and virtuous conduct, in altogether

On the thirty thousand words. [Wang] Mang memorialized

State that [their report] should be established and pub-

Of the lished as a [permanent] ordinance.[23.6] He also me-

Empire. morialized that [because] there existed such [perfect] institutions, in the market-places there were not two

*23b* prices, the offices were without law-cases or litigation, towns were without thieves or robbers, the countryside was without famished people, things dropped on the roads were not picked up, and males and females took separate paths,[23.7] [hence] those who violated

[23.4] Chang Yen (iii cent.) explains, "At that time she was in her fourteenth year and first showed signs of womanhood." For the meaning of this name, cf. Glossary *sub* Tzu-wu Road.

[23.5] They had been sent out in March, A.D. 4; cf. A: 17a. Ch'en Ch'ung was one of these commissioners, so that their return preceded this notice.

[23.6] Chou Shou-ch'ang explains the phrase *ting-chu-ling* 定著令: "When the Son of Heaven of the Han [dynasty] published an ordinance, it was stored in the yamen of the [Grandee] Secretary. The Eminent Founder, [Emperor Kao], and the Empress of [Emperor] Kao employed this practise. When, [in the case of] Emperor Ch'eng, it was ordered that an Heir-apparent should be permitted to cross the imperial pathway [cf. *HFHD* II, 373–74], the ordinance was also published. At this time, [Wang] Mang openly memorialized, begging that [the matter] should be established and published as an ordinance."

[23.7] A condition described in *Li-chi* III, v, 15 (Legge I, 244; Couvreur I, 319).

制犯者衆刑劉歆陳崇等十二人皆曰治明堂宣教化封為列侯

恭阮致太平北化匈奴東致海外南懷黃支唯西方未有加迺遣

中郎將平憲等多持金幣誘塞外羌使獻地願內屬憲等奏言羌

豪良願等種人口可萬二千人願為內臣獻鮮水海允谷鹽池平

地美草皆予漢民自居險阻處為藩蔽問良願降意對曰太皇太

[the institutions should merely suffer] punishments [which portrayed] the likeness [of the mutilating punishments in the criminal's clothing].[23.8]

Liu Hsin[1a], Ch'en Ch'ung, and others, twelve persons [altogether], were all enfeoffed as full marquises because they had built the *Ming-t'ang* or had spread the [imperial] teaching and influence.[23.9]    June 29.[23.9]

Since [in the empire, Wang] Mang had brought about [the condition of] complete tranquillity, in that to the north he had influenced the Huns, to the east he had caused [people] to come [from] beyond the ocean, and to the south he had attracted the Huang-chih, [but] only in the western quarter he had not yet produced [any effects], he therefore sent a General of the Gentlemen-at-the-Palace, P'ing Hsien, and others, bearing much money and silk, to tempt the Ch'iang outside the barriers and have them present their territory [to the throne and to express] a desire to be received by and to be subordinate [to Chinese rule.    The Ch'iang Are Induced To Surrender the Kokonor Territory.

Upon his return, P'ing] Hsien and the others memorialized, saying, "The leaders of the Ch'iang tribes, Liang Yüan, and others, whose number might be twelve thousand persons, wish to be received and to be your subjects. They offer the Hsien-shui Sea, the Yün Gorge, and the Salt Lake. The level land with fine grass is all given to the Chinese people, and [the Ch'iang] will themselves dwell in the narrow and difficult places and act as guards at the frontiers.    **24a**

"When I asked Liang Yüan the reason for his submitting, he replied, saying, 'The Grand Empress

---

[23.8] Cf. *HFHD* II, 123–25, App. II.

[23.9] According to 18: 29a–31b, on June 29, P'ing Yen, Liu Hsin[1a], K'ung Yung, and Sun Ch'ien were enfeoffed because they had built the *Ming-t'ang* and *Pi-yung*; Wang Yün, Yen Ch'ien, Ch'en Ch'ung, Li Hsi[6], Ho Tang, Hsieh Yin, Lu P'u, and Ch'en Feng[1] were enfeoffed because as messengers they had unified and spread the imperial teaching and influence.

Dowager is sage and glorious, the Duke Giving
Tranquillity to the Han Dynasty is most benevolent,
30a and the world is completely peaceful, so that the five
[kinds of] cereals ripen and there are good harvests.
Some stalks of grain are ten feet or more tall, sometimes one spikelet has three kernels, sometimes,
without being sown, [grain] springs up of itself,
sometimes [silk] cocoons form themselves without
any worms having been fed, sweet dew comes down
from Heaven and wine springs come out of the
earth,[24.1] "male and female phoenixes have come
and arrived,"[24.2] supernatural birds have descended
and perched, so that for the [last] four years the
Ch'iang people have had nothing to suffer [from the
government]. Hence "oh! how pleasant"[24.3] to be
admitted [to the Chinese empire] and to become
your subordinates.'

"It would be proper at this time to settle them in
[stationary] occupations and to establish a [Chief
Commandant] of a Dependent State to direct and
protect them."

The matter was referred to [Wang] Mang. [Wang]
Mang memorialized in reply, saying, "You, [Grand]
Empress Dowager, have controlled the rule for several years; your grace and bounty have inundated
and overflowed, so that a filial attitude of submission
[has spread over] the four quarters and not even the
most distant regions with different customs have
24a failed to turn towards correct principles. A Yüeh-
shang potentate, [whose speech must be] successively
interpreted, presented a white pheasant; the Huang-
chih [came] from [a distance of] thirty thousand *li*

塞絕域殊俗靡不慕義越裳氏重譯獻白雉黃支自三萬里貢生
置屬國領護事下奉符俊奏曰太后秉統數年恩澤洋溢和氣回
神爵降集從回歲以來羌人無所疾苦故思樂內屬宜呂時處業
或不種自生或蠒不繅自成甘露從天下醴泉自此出鳳皇來儀
后聖明安溪公至仁天下太平五穀成熟或禾長大餘或一粟三米

---

24.1 Phrases from *Li-chi* VII, iv, 16 (Legge, I, p. 392; Couvreur I, 536), "Hence Heaven
will send down sweet dew and Earth will produce wine springs."

24.2 A quotation from the *Book of History*, II, iv, 9 (Legge, p. 88), cf. Karlgren, *BMFEA*
20, 142, Gl. 1346.

24.3 Quoting the first two words in *Book of Odes* IV, ii, iii, 1, 2, 3, no. 299 (Legge, 616,
617). The use of a phrase from the *Odes* in a quotation of a speech by the barbarian
Ch'iang indicates the artificial classicism of Wang Mang's court.

廣二帝三王凡十有三州名及界多不應經堯典十有二州後

郡臣又聞聖王序天文定地理因山川民俗曰制州界漢家地

有東海南海北海郡未有西海郡請受良願等所獻地為西海

願等俊舉地為臣妾昔唐堯橫被四表亦亡已加之今謹某已

犀東夫王虔大海奉國珍匈奴單于順制作去二名今西域良

to offer a live rhinoceros as tribute; kings of the Eastern Barbarians crossed the Great Ocean to offer the treasures of their states; the Hun *Shan-yü* conformed to [Confucian] institutions and did away with his double personal name. Now at the western boundary, Liang Yüan and the others in turn present their land and [desire to] become your menials. Anciently T'ang Yao's [virtue] 'filled[24.4] and covered [all within] the four extremities of the empire,' but it could not surpass your [virtue].

Oceanic Barbarians.

"Now I have carefully examined that there are already a Tung-hai (Eastern Sea), a Nan-hai (Southern Sea), and a Po-hai (Northern Sea) Commandery, [but] there is not yet a Hsi-hai (Western Sea) Commandery. I beg that you will accept the territory which Liang Yüan and the others are offering and make it the commandery of Hsi-hai.

"Your servant has also heard that when the Sage-kings gave order to the ornaments of Heaven, [the stars], and fixed the principles of geographical [arrangements], they took the mountains, streams, and customs of the common people as the principles for the boundaries of their provinces. The territory of the Han dynasty is broader than that of the two [sage-]lords and three [dynasties of] kings,[24.5] having altogether thirteen provinces. Many of the names of the provinces together with their boundaries do not correspond to those in the Classics. The 'Canon of Yao' [speaks of] twelve provinces;[24.6] later they

30b Geographical Arrangements to be Rectified. **24b**

---

[24.4] Ch'ien Ta-chao (1744–1813) states that 橫 is used for 光, to agree with the *Book of History* I, i, 1 (Legge, p. 15). In a note to *HHS*, Mem. 7: 9b, 10a, Ch'ien Ta-hsin (1728–1804) asserts that the original of both the above words was *kuang* 桄, which in the *Erh-ya*, "Shih-yen," 3: 2b, is said to mean "穎充, to fill."

[24.5] Fu Ch'ien comments, "The domain of restraint [belonging to] T'ang [Yao] and Yü [Shun], [who were the two "sage-lords"], together with that [belonging to] the Chou [dynasty] was seven thousand *li* square; that [belonging to] the Hsia and Yin [dynasties] was three thousand *li* square; the territory of the Han [dynasty] is thirteen thousand *li* from north to south." With this belief that the Han was the greatest of dynasties, it was only natural that the Chinese called themselves "men of Han."

[24.6] *Book of History*, II, i, 10 (Legge, p. 38).

were fixed at nine provinces. The vast territory of the Han dynasty is far-extending. When the Provincial Shepherds go to inspect their divisions, the most distant ones are more than thirty thousand *li* [away], so that there cannot be [only] nine [provinces]. I would respectfully employ the ideas of the Classics in correcting the names of the twelve provinces and make boundaries for them to correspond to the correct original [boundaries]." The memorial was approved.

**Thousands Exiled to Kokonor.** He also added fifty items to the laws. Offenders were transported to Hsi-hai [Commandery]. Those who were transported were counted by the thousands and ten-thousands, so that the common people for the first [time] held grudges [against Wang Mang].

**24b** The Marquis of Ch'üan-ling, Liu Ch'ing₄ᵢ, sent to the imperial court a letter saying, "When King Ch'eng of the Chou [dynasty] was a minor, he was called the Young Prince, and the Duke of Chou acted as Regent. Now that the Emperor is rich in youthfulness, it would be proper to order the Duke Giving Tranquillity to the Han Dynasty to perform the duties of the Son of Heaven like the Duke of Chou." The various courtiers all said, "it would be proper [to do] as [Liu] Ch'ing₄ᵢ has said."

**31a Winter. A Declaration Stored in a Metal-bound Coffer.** In the winter, when [the planet] Mars was occulted by the moon,[24.7] Emperor P'ing became ill. [Wang] Mang made a written declaration [to Heaven] in which he begged for [the Emperor's] life at the altar to the Supreme [One]. He had a jade circlet hung on his person, carried jade insignia, and [declared] that he was willing in person to take the place [of the dying Emperor]. The declaration was stored in a "metal-bound coffer"[24.8] and placed in the

*Marginal labels:*
- It is Suggested that he be made Regent.

[24.7] Mars was occulted by the moon at sunset on Nov. 29 of this year.

[24.8] This term is the title of ch. vi in the *Book of History* V (Legge, p. 351); Wang Mang was imitating the incident therein recorded as performed by the Duke of Chou. The coffer was opened in 24 A.D., cf. 99 C: 22b.

平帝疾莽作策請命於泰畤戴璧秉圭願以身代藏策金縢
漢公行天子事如周公羣臣皆曰宜如慶言冬祭惑入月中
書言周成王幼少孺子周公居攝今帝富於春秋宜令安
徐犯者徙之西海徙者吕千萬數民始怨矣泉陵侯劉慶上
九謹曰經義正十二州名分界吕應正始奏可又增法五十
定為九州漢寠廓地遠遠州牧行部遠者三萬餘里不可為

有見王五人列侯廣戚侯顯等四十八人恭
宗孝平廟曰元宗時元帝世絕而宣帝曾孫
六百石曰上皆服喪三年奉尊孝成廟曰統
赦天下恭儉明禮者宗伯鳳等與定天下吏
置于前殿敢詰公卿敢言十二月平帝崩大

Front Hall [of the Palace]. He ordered the various highest ministers not to presume to speak [to him about government business, in order that he might concentrate on caring for the Emperor's illness].[24.9]

In the twelfth month, Emperor P'ing died. A general amnesty [was granted] to the empire. [Wang] Mang summoned those who understood the rites, Tsung-po Feng and others. With them, [Wang Mang] determined that the officials of the empire [ranking at] six hundred piculs and above should all wear mourning to the third year. [Wang Mang] memorialized, that the Temple of [Emperor] Hsiao-ch'eng should be honored with the title of [the Temple of] the Controlling Exemplar and the Temple of [Emperor] Hsiao-p'ing with the title of [the Temple of] the Primary Exemplar.

At that time, the line of descent from Emperor Yüan had been ended, but of the great-grandsons of Emperor Hsüan there were living: five kings and forty-eight full marquises, [including] the Marquis of Kuang-chi, [Liu] Hsien[3c].[25.1] [Wang] Mang hated it

A.D. 6,
Feb. 3.[24.10]
Emperor
P'ing
Dies.

25a

[24.9] I owe this illuminating interpretation of a very condensed expression to Prof. Duyvendak. He points out that 敢言 denotes the reports made by the highest ministers to Wang Mang; cf. 99 A: 18b.

[24.10] Cf. 12: 10a.

[25.1] These five kings were the King of Huai-yang, Liu Yin[4b] 縯 (*HS* 14: 21b); the King of Chung-shan, Liu Ch'eng-tu (14: 22a); the King of Ch'u, Liu Yü[1a] 紆 (14: 22b); the King of Hsin-tu[a], Liu Ching[3b] (14: 22b); and the King of Tung-p'ing, Liu K'ai-ming (14: 21b). (Listed by Hu San-hsing, [1230–1287].) He also enumerates the following as the marquises referred to: the Marquis of Kuang-chi, Liu Hsien[3c] (*HS* 15 B: 37b); the Marquis of Yang-hsing, Liu Chi-sheng 寄生 (15 B: 41a); the Marquis of Ling-yang, Liu Chia[1n] (15 B: 41b); the Marquis of Kao-lo, Liu Hsiu[2c] 修 (15 B: 41b); the Marquis of P'ing-yi, Liu Min[3d] 閔 (15 B: 42a); the Marquis of P'ing-tsuan, Liu K'uang[4c] 況 (15 B: 42a); the Marquis of Ho-ch'ang, Liu Fu[3b] 輔 (15 B: 42b); the Marquis of Yi[1]-hsiang, Liu K'ai[1b] 開 (15 B: 42b); the Marquis of Chiu-hsiang, Liu Pu-hai[d] 不害 (15 B: 43a); the Marquis of Chiao-hsiang, Liu Wu[3c] (15 B: 43a); the Marquis of Yi[2]-hsiang, Liu K'uei[1f] 恢 (15 B: 43b); the Marquis of Ch'ang-ch'eng, Liu Feng[2a] 豐 (15 B: 43b); the Marquis of Lo-an, Liu Yü[10g] 禹 (15 B: 44a); the Marquis of T'ao-hsiang, Liu Kuei[1e] 恢 (15 B: 52a); the Marquis of Li-hsiang, Liu Pao[1c] 褒 (15 B: 52b); the Marquis of Ch'ang-hsiang, Liu Tan[4d] 且 (15 B: 52b); the Marquis of Hsin-hsiang, Liu Li[7] 鯉 (15 B: 53a); the Marquis of Wu-hsiang, Liu Kuang[1k] 光 (15 B: 53a); the Marquis of Hsin-ch'eng, Liu Wu[3d] (15 B: 53b); the Marquis of Yi-ling, Liu Feng[2b] (15 B: 53b); the Marquis of T'ang-hsiang, Liu

The
Youngest
Descend-
ant of
Emperor
Hsüan
Selected
to Succeed
to the
Throne.
Feb.

31b

that they were adults, so advised, "A cousin is not permitted to be the successor [to his cousin of the same generation]." So he selected the very youngest among [Emperor Hsüan's] great-great-grandsons, [Liu] Ying₁ₐ, the son of the Marquis of Kuang-chi, [Liu] Hsien₃c. He was in the second year of his age. [Wang Mang] took as a pretext that when he was divined about and physiognomized, he was the most auspicious [of all].

In this month, the Displayer of Splendor in the South, Hsieh Hsiao, memorialized that the Chief of Wu-kung [prefecture], Meng T'ung, while a well was being dug, had secured a white stone, round above the square below, with red writing on the stone.

孟通浚井得白石上圓下方有丹書著
卜相最吉是月前煇光謝囂奏武功長
孫中最幼廣戚侯子嬰年二歲託臣為
惡其長大曰兄弟不得相為後迺選玄

Hu₄e 護 (15 B: 54a); the Marquis of Ch'eng-ling, Liu Yu₂c 由 (15 B: 54a); the Marquis of Ch'eng-yang, Liu Chung₆c 眾 (15 B: 54b); the Marquis of Fu-ch'ang, Liu Hsiu₁b 休 (15 B: 54b); the Marquis of An-lu, Liu P'ing₂e 平 (15 B: 55a); the Marquis of Wu-an, Liu Yü₉ 譽 (15 B: 55a); the Marquis of Chao-hsiang, Liu Ch'ung₁c 充 (15 B: 55b); the Marquis of Fu-hsiang, Liu P'u₃c 普 (15 B: 55b); the Marquis of Fang-ch'eng, Liu Hsüan₁f 宣 (15 B: 56a); the Marquis of Tang-yang, Liu Yi₈ 益 (15 B: 56a); the Marquis of Kuang-ch'eng, Liu Chieh₂ 㐱 (15 B: 56b); the Marquis of Ch'un-ch'eng, Liu Yün₃ 允 (15 B: 56b); the Marquis of Lü-hsiang, Liu Shang₄c 尚 (15 B: 57b); the Marquis of Li-hsiang, Liu Yin₂e (15 B: 58a); the Marquis of Yüan-hsiang, Liu Lung₁b 隆 (15 B: 58a); the Marquis of Shou-ch'üan, Liu Ch'eng₅b 承 (15 B: 58b); the Marquis of Hsiang-shan, Liu Tsun₂ 遵 (15 B: 58b); the Marquis of Yen-hsiang, Liu Hsin₄g (15 B: 50a); the Marquis of Wu-p'ing, Liu Huang₅b 璜 (15 B: 50b); the Marquis of Ling-hsiang, Liu Ts'eng_b (15 B: 50b); the Marquis of Wu-an, Liu Shou₅c 慢 (15 B: 51a); the Marquis of Fu-yang, Liu Meng 萌 (15 B: 45a); the Marquis of Hsi-yang, Liu Yen₃j 偃 (15 B: 47a); the Marquis of T'ao-hsiang, Liu Li₅b (15 B: 44a); the Marquis of Li-hsiang, Liu Hsüan-ch'eng 玄成 (15 B: 39b); the Marquis of Chin-hsiang, Liu Pu-hai_c 不害 (15 B: 40a); the Marquis of P'ing-t'ung, Liu Tan₄c 且 (15 B: 40a); the Marquis of Hsi-an, Liu Han₄d 漢 (15 B: 40b); the Marquis of Hu-hsiang, Liu K'ai₁ₐ 開 (15 B: 40b); and the Marquis of Chung-hsiang, Liu Shao-po 少柏 (15 B: 41a). Hu San-hsing enumerates fifty marquises and states that the Marquis of Kuang-chi, Liu Hsien₃c, was the father of the Young Prince (so should not be counted) and the Marquis of Li-hsiang, Liu Hsüan-ch'eng, had previously been dismissed, leaving only forty-eight. But I find no evidence and no date for the dismissal of Liu Hsüan-ch'eng (15 B: 39b). Forty-one of the foregoing fifty. marquisates had been established at the request of Wang Mang in A.D. 1, 2, and 5

石文曰告安漢公莽為皇帝行命之起自此始矣莽使羣公曰

白太后曰此証固天下不可施行太保舜謂太后事已如

此無可奈何沮之力不能止又莽敢有它但欲稱攝曰重其

權填服天下耳太后聽許舜等即共令太后下詔曰蓋聞天生

衆民不能相治為之立君曰統理之君年幼稚必有寄託而居

攝焉然後能奉天施而成地化庶生茂育書不云乎天工人其

The writing said, "An instruction to the Duke Giving Tranquillity to the Han Dynasty, [Wang] Mang, that he should become the Emperor." The coming of mandates [from Heaven] through portents began indeed with this one.

[Wang] Mang had the various highest ministers advise the [Grand] Empress Dowager [nee Wang] of it. The [Grand] Empress Dowager said, "This [thing] is trumped up to deceive the empire. [Its message] cannot be put into practise." The Grand Guardian, [Wang] Shun4b, said to the [Grand] Empress Dowager that when matters have already reached such [a condition as they had], there was nothing that could be done [about it], that if she wished to check it, she did not have the strength to stop it; and also that [Wang] Mang would not presume to have any other [intentions], but merely desired to be entitled[25.2] the Regent, in order to make his power greater and to settle the empire and make it obedient. The [Grand] Empress Dowager listened to him and promised [to do so].

[Wang] Shun4b and others thereupon together had the [Grand] Empress Dowager issue an imperial edict which said, "Verily, [We] have heard that when 'Heaven gave birth to' the crowd of 'common people,' they were unable to govern themselves, so 'He set up princes for them,'[25.3] in order to control them. When a prince is young, there must be someone whom he can rely upon, who should then act as regent. Then only will [the prince] be able to carry out [the duties] given him by Heaven and complete the transforming influence of Earth, so that the various living beings will flourish and be nurtured. Does not the *Book of History* say, 'The work is Heaven's—let men take the place of [Heaven]'?[25.4]

The First Portent that Wang Mang Should

*25a*

Become Emperor

**25b**

He is Made Regent.

---

[25.2] The Official ed. reads 居 for 稱. The Ching-yu ed. reads the latter.
[25.3] A quotation from *Tso-chuan*, Dk. Hsiang, XIV, summer (Legge, 462[7], 466b).
[25.4] *Book of History* II, iii, ii, 5 (Legge, p. 73; Couvreur, p. 47).

"Because Emperor Hsiao-p'ing was young, We temporarily took charge of the government of the state.  [We] hoped to put upon him the cap of maturity and to entrust the government to him and 32a hand it over.  But now his life has been cut short and he is dead.  Alas!  How sad!

"[We] have already had the high officials summon twenty-three great-great-grandsons of Emperor Hsiao-hsüan, to choose an appropriate person to be the heir and successor of Emperor Hsiao-p'ing.  This great-great-grandson is of the age when he is in swaddling-clothes; if [We] are not able to secure [to be his regent] a princely man who has reached the very heart of virtue, who can give tranquillity to [the empire]?

"The Duke Giving Tranquillity to the Han Dynasty, [Wang] Mang, has assisted in the government for three reigns, has repeatedly met with critical times, has tranquillized and made brilliant the House of Han, and has thereupon made [people] of customs differing [from those of the Chinese become] like [the Chinese even] in their institutions, [so that] he 25b has had the same presages as those had at a different age by the Duke of Chou.  Now the Displayer of Splendor in the South, [Hsieh] Hsiao, and the Chief of Wu-kung [prefecture, Meng] T'ung, have presented [a memorial] speaking of a red stone portent. We have thought profoundly that its meaning, which said, '[Wang Mang] should become Emperor,' is however that as Regent he should perform the duties of the Emperor.  Verily if there is a model, accomplishment is easy; [but] if there is no sage, there is no model.[25.5]

"Let it be ordered that the Duke Giving Tranquillity to the Han Dynasty should occupy [the

---

[25.5] Stange, *ibid.*, 82, n. 1, remarks that this sentence refers to the Duke of Chou as the model.

令書曰我嗣事子孫大不克共上下遇失前人光在家不知命

之烈周公攝而居攝則周道成王室安不居攝則恐周隊失天

居攝臣聞周成王幼少周道未成王不能共事天地修文武

禮儀奏於是羣臣奏言太后聖德昭然深見天意詔令安漢公

攝政祚如周公故事臣武功縣為安漢公采地名曰漢光邑其

post of] Regent and should [be permitted to] mount the eastern [master's] steps [at the altar to Heaven], as in the former case [was done by] the Duke of Chou. **26a** Let the prefecture of Wu-kung become the territory whose revenue is allocated to the Duke Giving Tranquillity to the Han Dynasty, and let its name be the town of Han-kuang (the Han [dynasty's] brilliance). Let there be prepared a memorial concerning the ceremonial [for the above]."

Thereupon the various courtiers memorialized, saying, "The sage virtue of the [Grand] Empress Dowager is brilliant. You have seen deeply into the intentions of Heaven and have issued an imperial order that the Duke Giving Tranquillity to the Han Dynasty should act as Regent. Your subjects have heard that when King Ch'eng of the Chou [dynasty] was a minor and the practises of the Chou [dynasty] had not yet been completed, so that King Ch'eng was unable to perform his duties to Heaven and Earth and to renew the illustrious services [performed by Kings] Wen and Wu, the Duke of Chou temporarily acted as Regent and the practises of the Chou [dynasty] were therefore completed and its kingly house was at peace. If he had not acted as Regent, then it is to be feared that the Chou [dynasty] would have lost the mandate of Heaven.

"The *Book of History* [quotes the Duke of Chou as] saying [to Prince Shih, the Duke of Shao], 'If the son or grandson who becomes the heir to and serves our [lord, King Wu], should be altogether incapable of reverencing [the deities] above and below, [Heaven, Earth, the ancestors, and gods], and lose the glory of his predecessors, if we [were retired, living] at home, we would remain ignorant of it.[26.1]

*He is Given the 32b Rites of a Son of Heaven and the Title of Acting Emperor.*

---

[26.1] This translation deviates from that of Legge, who follows the pseudo-Kung An-kuo comment. It is justified by the context in the *HS*, cf. *Shang-shu Chu-su* 16: 11a; Chiang Sheng, *Shang-shu Chi-chu Yin-su* ("Huang-ch'ing Ching-chieh," 397: 11b); Sun Hsing-yen,

The Mandate [of Heaven] is not easy [to retain], and the assistance of Heaven is not sure, so that His mandate may be lost.'[26.2] The explanation says,

26a  'The Duke of Chou wore the tasselled mortar-board bonnet of the Son of Heaven, faced south and held audience for the courtiers, and made proclamations and gave ordinances, constantly calling them the mandates of the King. The Duke of Shao was a worthy person, [but] did not understand the intentions of the sage, [the Duke of Chou], hence was not pleased.'[26.3] The [Record of] Proprieties (Li[chi]), in 'Record of the Ming-t'ang,' says, 'When the Duke of Chou held court for the nobles in the Ming-t'ang, [like] the Son of Heaven, he turned his back to the

33a  axe-embroidered screen, faced south, and stood up.'[26.4] It means that the Duke of Chou occupied the throne of the Son of Heaven to the sixth year,

26b  held court for the nobles, established the rites, and composed the music, so that the empire submitted widely. [But] the Duke of Shao was not pleased. At that time, King Wu had [just] died and the coarse mourning garments had not yet been put off. If we consider it in this way, when the Duke of Chou first became Regent, he then occupied the Son of Heaven's throne and it was not [that he waited] until the sixth year [before] he mounted the eastern steps.[26.5]

廬末陳由是言之周公始攝則居天子之位非乃六年而踐阼也
位六年朝諸侯制禮作樂而天下大服也召公不說時武王崩綠
記曰周公朝諸侯於明堂天子負斧依南面而立謂周公踐天子
發號施令常稱王命召公賢人不知聖人之意故不說也禮明堂
不易天應柴甚乃亡隊命說曰周公服天子之冕南面而朝羣臣

---

*Shang-shu Chin-ku-wen Chu-su* 22:2b ("P'ing-chin-kuan Ts'ung-shu ed."). But Yen Shih-ku and Liu Fung-lu, *Shang-shu Chin-ku-wen Chi-chieh* ("Huang-ch'ing Ching-chieh Hsü-p'ien" 344: 1b) punctuate differently. The point is that just as the sage Duke of Chou knew he needed to be Regent, so Wang Mang must now be Regent.

[26.2] *Book of History* V, xvi, 3, 4 (Legge, p. 476; Couvreur, pp. 298, 299). This quotation differs from the present (ancient) text of the *Book of History*: for 復嗣, this quotation reads 嗣事; for 弗 it reads 不; for 恭 it reads 共; for 佚, it reads 失; the 天 before the 命 is omitted; for 難, it reads 應斐; for 其隊 it reads 亡隊. The *HS* quotes, as usual, the "modern text" of that book (Tuan Yü-ts'ai, *Ku-wen Shang-shu Chuan-yi* ("Huang-ch'ing Ching-chieh" 590: 1b).

[26.3] We have not been able to discover whence this comment was taken.

[26.4] *Li-chi* XII, 1 (Legge, II, 29; Couvreur, I, 725).

[26.5] The eastern steps were reserved for the host or the master of the household and for the Son of Heaven at the altar to Heaven.

書逸嘉禾篇曰周公奉鬯立于阼階延登贊曰假王莅政勤和
天下此周公攝政贊者所稱成王加元服周公則致政書曰朕
俊子明辟周公常稱王命專行不報故言我俊子明君也臣請
安漢公居攝踐祚作服天子敷冕背斧依于戶牖之間南面朝羣

"The lost chapter of the *Book of History*, 'Auspicious Grain,'[26.6] says, 'When the Duke of Chou offered the herb-flavored millet liquor, he stood upon the steps of the eastern staircase and was conducted to mount them, and the presentation speech [at the offering] said, "The Acting King is ruling over the government and diligently harmonizing the world." ' The [foregoing] is how the Duke of Chou was entitled by the person [who read] the presentation speech when [the Duke of Chou] was regent in the government.

"When King Ch'eng put on his cap of maturity, the Duke of Chou thereupon presented the government to him. The *Book of History* [quotes the Duke of Chou] as saying, 'We return [the government to Our] nephew, the intelligent prince.'[26.7] The Duke of Chou constantly called [his orders] the mandates of the King, and acted on his own authority without reporting [matters to the King], hence he said, 'I return [the government] to my nephew, the intelligent prince.'

"Your subjects beg that the Duke Giving Tranquillity to the Han Dynasty should act as Regent, mount the eastern steps,[26.8] wear the apron and tasselled mortar-board hat of the Son of Heaven, turn his back to the axe-embroidered screen[26.9] between the door and window, and face south as he holds

[26.6] The chapter "Auspicious Grain" is one of the lost chapters of the *Book of History*. It seems to have been one of the "lost chapters" made canonical by Wang Mang.

[26.7] *Book of History*, V, xiii, 1 (Legge, p. 434; Couvreur, 269). I have adopted the K'ung An-kuo interpretation of this sentence, discussed and rejected by Legge, but plainly employed in this memorial. *Fu-p'i* has come to mean "restore the monarchy." (Duyvendak.)

[26.8] The Official ed. emends 祚 to 阼. The Ching-yu ed. reads the latter.

[26.9] We would expect the word 立 after the 依, reading, "stand between the door and window," to correspond with 99 A: 26a. *Tzu-chih T'ung-chien* (1084) 36: 13a has this word.

court for the courtiers and attends to the business of government.　When he goes in or out [of the Palace]
33b in his chariot and robes, [the people] should be
26b warned and [the streets] cleared.　The common people and courtiers should call themselves his 'subjects' or 'female servants.'[26.10]　In all [these matters, he should be treated] as in the regulations for the Son of Heaven.

"When he makes the suburban sacrifices to Heaven and to Earth, makes the sacrifice to the greatest exemplar of the house in the *Ming-t'ang*, makes offerings and sacrifices in the [imperial] ancestral temples, and performs worship and makes sacrifices to the many gods, in his presentation speech he should be called, 'the Acting Emperor.'　The common people and courtiers should speak of him as 'the Regent-Emperor'; he should call himself 'I'.[26.11]　In judging and deciding matters [when holding] court, he should regularly employ the imperial edicts of the Emperor and pronounce [that he issues imperial] decrees,[26.12] thereby upholding and obeying the will of August Heaven, assisting and protecting the House of Han, and guarding and tranquillizing the young heir to Emperor Hsiao-p'ing, [thus] carrying out the principle of entrusting [a Regent with the rule] and exalting the development of good government and peace.

"When he pays court at an audience of either the Grand Empress Dowager [nee Wang] or the Empress
27a Dowager [nee Wang], he should reassume the devotion of a subject.　He should in his own person [as a noble] exercise the government and issue 'instructions' to his own palace, his family, his [marquis's] estate, and his special territory [of Han-kuang], as in

[26.10] *Chieh* 妾 is the feminine of *ch'en* 臣; cf. 24 A: 20b[12]; 44: 3a[3].
[26.11] This word *yü* is part of the imperial self-designation 予一人.
[26.12] Cf. *HFHD*, I, 192, n. 1.

朝見太皇太后帝皇后皆復臣節自施政教於其宮家國采如
輔翼漢室保安孝平皇帝之幼嗣遂寄託之義隆治平之化其
帝自稱曰予平決朝事常曰皇帝之詔稱制曰奉順皇天之心
地宗祀明堂共祀宗廟享祭羣神贊曰假皇帝民臣謂之攝皇
臣聽政事車服出入警蹕民臣稱臣妾皆如天子之制郊祀天

為太保俊承又置四少秩皆二千石四月安眾侯劉崇與相張紹謀曰

孫嬰為皇太子號曰孺子曰王舜為太傅左輔甄豐為太阿右拂甄邯

去置柱下五史秩如御史聽政事侍旁記疏言行三月己丑立宣帝玄

恭祀上帝於南郊迎春於東郊行大射禮於明堂養三老五更成禮而

諸侯禮故事臣昧死請太后詔曰可明年改元曰居攝居攝元年正月

his previous practise, [according to] the legal practises of a noble. Your subjects, risking death, make this request." The edict of the [Grand] Empress Dowager said, "It is approved."

The next year, [Wang Mang] changed the year-period and called it Chü-shê (the Regency).

In [the year-period] Chü-shê, the first year, the first month, [Wang] Mang sacrificed to the Lords on High at the Southern [Altar for] the suburban sacrifice, welcomed the spring at the Eastern [Altar for] the suburban sacrifice, performed the rites of the great archery contest in the *Ming-t'ang*, and served food to Thrice Venerable and Fivefold Experienced. He completed the rites, then left.[27.1]

*(margin: I A.D. 6, Feb./Mar.)*

He established the Five Clerks At the Foot of the Pillars, with their rank like that of the [Attendant] Secretaries. When he attended to government business, they attended at his side and recorded and made detailed accounts of his words and acts.

*(margin: Court Steno-graphers. 34a)*

In the third month, on [the day] *chi-ch'ou*, [Liu] Ying[1a], a great-great-grandson of Emperor Hsüan, was set up as the Imperial Heir-apparent and was given the title, Young Prince (*Ju-tzu*). Wang Shun[4b] was made Grand Tutor Assisting on the Left, Chen Feng was made Grand Support Aiding on the Right, and Chen Han was made Grand Guardian Serving at the Rear. There were also established four Junior [Coadjutors] whose ranks were all two thousand piculs.[27.2]

*(margin: Apr. 17. Liu Ying is made Heir-apparent and Young Prince.)*

In the fourth month, the Marquis of An-chung, Liu Ch'ung[2c], plotted with his Chancellor, Chang

*(margin: May/June 27a)*

---

[27.1] He probably followed the ritual in the *Li-chi* XXI, ii, 21 (Legge, II, 231; Couvreur, II, 311). Cf. Glossary *sub* Fivefold Experienced. The last sentence probably means that his attendance was not perfunctory and that he stayed through the whole ceremony.

[27.2] Hu San-hsing states that these four Junior Coadjutors were the Junior Master, the Junior Tutor, the Junior Support, and the Junior Guardian.

Shao, saying, "The Duke Giving Tranquillity to the Han Dynasty, [Wang] Mang, acts on his own authority in holding court and exercizing the government, which will inevitably endanger the Liu clan. No one of those in the empire who disapprove of it has however dared to be the first to make a move. This is a shame to the [imperial] house. I will give an example to the [imperial] house and clan and be the first [to attack. All] within [the four] seas will certainly respond." [Chang] Shao and others, who followed him, [to the number of] more than a hundred persons, thereupon made an assault upon [the city of] Yüan, [but] did not succeed in entering it and were defeated.

**27b**
**Liu Ch'ung's Rebellion.**

[Chang] Shao was a cousin of Chang Sung. [Chang] Sung, with [Liu] Ch'ung's father's cousin, Liu Chia₁ₛ, went to [the palace] portals and surrendered of their own accord, [so that Wang] Mang pardoned them and did not condemn them. Thereupon [Chang] Sung composed a memorial for [Liu] Chia₁ₛ, which said,

**Chang Sung's Memorial for Liu Chia**

"During [the year-periods] Chien-p'ing and Yüan-shou, when the main line [of the Han Dynasty] was in imminent danger of being cut short and the [imperial] house was in imminent danger of being overthrown, thanks to your Majesty [Wang Mang's] sage virtue, you 'crawled on your knees to rescue and save it,'[27.3] you protected and defended, succored[27.4] and guarded it, so that the [heavenly] mandate of the [Han] state was again prolonged and the imperial house opened its eyes [again].

**6-1 B.C.**

**34b**

"When you attended court, controlled the government, put out proclamations, and put forth ordi-

[27.3] A phrase from the *Book of Odes*, I, III, x, 4 (Legge, p. 57).

[27.4] The Official ed. has restored the stroke taken from the word 匡, both here and on p. 30a, which was omitted because of the taboo on the personal name of the Grand Founder (T'ai-tsu) of the Sung dynasty, Chao K'uang-yin, who reigned 960–975.

施令勤呂宗室為始登用九族為先竝錄支親建立王侯
南面之孤計呂百數收復絕屬存亡續廢得比肩首俊為
人者燦然成行所呂藩漢國輔漢宗七建辟雍立明堂班
天法流聖化朝羣后昭文德宗室諸侯咸益土地天下喁

nances, in your every act you made the imperial house the first [and most important consideration] and the promotion and employment of the nine [sets of imperial] relatives as the primary matter. You have had included with them and recorded [upon the registers of the imperial house] cadet branches [of that house] and have established kings and marquises [from among these cadet branches], so that those who face south [in holding court and call themselves by the designation a noble uses for himself], *ku*,[27.5] are numbered by the hundreds. You gathered in and restored those members whose [registration in the imperial house] had been broken off, you preserved those [whose lines of descent as nobles] had died out, and you continued [those lines whose heads] had been dismissed [from their noble ranks], so that they form a numerous company who are able to be shoulder to shoulder and head to head [with the other nobles] and have been restored in their persons. You have thereby defended the Han [dynasty's] state and supported the Han clan.

"You have established the *Pi-yung* and set up the *Ming-t'ang* to propagate the law of Heaven and to spread the influence of the sages. You have held court for the various princes in order to render your 'culture and virtue'[27.6] manifest. You have added to the lands and territory of all the nobles in the imperial house, so that all under Heaven lift up their

Chang Sung's Memorial for Liu Chia.

[27.5] *Ku* 孤 was used by reigning nobles to designate themselves when addressing their subjects. The term means literally, "orphan," and implies therefore, in a patriarchal society, a rightful ruler, indicating that he is no usurper but reigns by right of succession to his father (Duyvendak). For these enfeoffments from and favors to cadet members of the imperial house, cf. *HS* 12: 2b, 3a, 4b, 5a, 8b, 9a; 99 A: 7a, 19b.

[27.6] "Culture and virtue, *wen-tê* 文德" is a phrase from *Book of History* II, ii, 21 (Legge, p. 66). Stange, op. cit., 89, n. 2 remarks that *wen-te* originally referred to a magical dance. That is probably correct, but the gloss on this passage attributed to K'ung An-kuo (*Shih-san-ching Chu-su* 4: 8b) shows that in Han times these words denoted, not magical practises, but civilization and culture.

*27b*  heads, stick out their necks and sigh [with approval], and the sound of their praises is 'magnificent and ear'-filling,[27.7] and enters [the sense of hearing]. The

*28a*  reason that the state has gained this beauty, has

Chang   obtained this fame, has enjoyed these blessings, and

Sung's   has received this glory—is it not [the result of the

Memorial   fact that] the Grand Empress Dowager considers

for   [that she must be diligent until] 'sundown'[28.1] and

Liu Chia.   that 'in the evening' your Majesty is still 'carefully' contemplating [your duties]?[28.2] How [otherwise could it be] explained?

"When there has been disorder, you have controlled it; when there has been danger, you have turned it to tranquillity; when there has been calam-

*35a*  ity, you have led it to happiness; when [lines of descent] have been cut off, you have continued their succession, when[the Emperor] is young, you have taken his place and borne his burdens. Day and night, you have performed detailed labor; in cold and in heat, you have been diligent, without any time for relaxation, with unending unwearied effort. All was for the sake of the empire and to favor the Liu clan.

"The courtiers, whether stupid or wise, and the common people, whether male or female, have all understood your high intentions. But the Marquis of An-chung, [Liu] Ch'ung₂c, alone entertained perverse illusions in his heart and held rebellious thoughts, so that he raised his troops and moved the multitude, intending to endanger the imperial [ancestral] temples. Of his wickedness one cannot endure to hear and for his crime one cannot be patient with [mere] execution. Verily, he was an enemy of [loyal] subjects and [filial] sons,[28.3] a foe of the im-

---

[27.7] A reminiscence of *Analects* VIII, xv.

[28.1] An allusion to *Book of History* V, xv, 10 (Legge, p. 469).

[28.2] An allusion to *Book of Changes*, Hex. 1, 3 (Legge, p. 57).

[28.3] *Chen-tzu* 臣子 is today a compound noun meaning "ministers of state." The

納垢濁焉名曰凶虛雖生菜茹而人不食四牆其社覆上校

詩哉臣聞古者咩迻之國既呂謀討而豬其宮室呂為汙池

子同時斷斬懸竿杪珠珥在耳首飾猶存為計若此豈不

民人潰畔而弃其兵進不跬步退伏其踦百歲之母孩提之

宗室之讎國家之賊天下之害也是故親屬震恐而告其罪

perial house, a rebel against the state, and an injury to the country.

"For this reason, his clan and relatives by marriage quaked, became distant to him and gave information of his crimes; the common people dispersed, rebelled against him, and threw away their arms, so that in advancing he could not [take] a step and when he retired he suffered the calamity [visited upon] him [by Heaven]. His mother, who was near the end of her life, and his smiling babes, carried in [their nurses'] arms,[28.4] were beheaded at the same time with him; their heads were hung on the ends of poles with their pearl earrings [still] in their ears and their hair ornaments still on [their heads]. How can it not be perverse to make a plan such as this?

"Your servant has heard that anciently, when [the head of] a rebellious state had already been punished, then[28.5] they made a pool out of his palace-buildings, making them a stagnant pond, and put filth into it, calling its name, 'The baleful waste,' so that, although it might grow vegetables, yet people would not eat them.[28.6] They put four walls [around] its mound to the gods of the soils, covered it above, and

Chang Sung's Memorial for Liu Chia.

28b *28a*

35b

difference between Han and recent usage is illustrated by this phrase, which is found twice in the *Li-chi* (*Li-chi Chu-su* 50: 2a, b = Legge, *Li Ki*, II, 258, 259), where it plainly means "courtiers [or subjects] *and* sons."

28.4 "Hundred years 百歲" is a phrase from *Book of Odes*, I, xi, 4 (Legge, 187). "Smiling babes carried in arms" is from *Mencius* VII, B, xv, 2 (Legge, 456). Both in the *Mencius* and here 孩 should be read as 咳, "an infantile smile."

28.5 Wang Hsien-ch'ien notes that the Official ed. and the Southern Academy ed. have correctly emended 而 to 則. The Ching-yu ed. reads the latter.

28.6 Li Ch'i (fl. ca. 200) explains, "They dug up his palace to make a pool and used it for storing water." This practise is mentioned in *Mencius* III, B, ix, 5 (Legge, 280) and in *Li-chi* II, ii, iii, 18 (Legge, I, 195). In the latter it is the punishment for parricide. The translation "palace-building" for *kung-shih* 宮室 is suggested by Duyvendak. The *Erh-ya* equates *kung* and *shih*. But after Ch'in times they were distinguished (*Erh-ya Chu-su* 5: 1a).

Chang Sung's Memorial for Liu Chia.

put a mat [on it] below,[28.7] so that spirits of the earth could not communicate [with those of heaven.[28.8] The soil of] its mound was distributed to the nobles' [altars for the gods of the soils], so that when they went out of their gates and saw it, it would be visible to them as a warning.

"Just now, when the empire heard that [Liu] Ch'ung[2c] rebelled, all wanted to raise up [the skirts of] their robes, [take] a two-edged sword in their hand, and rail at him.   Those who first reached him, cut[28.9] his throat, struck his breast, pierced his body,[28.10] and hacked his flesh.   Those who came

**29a** later wanted to pull down his gates, break down his walls, raze his houses, and burn his utensils. [As rapidly as] an echo follows a sound, [their blood] stained the earth, so immediately was a wound created

其門仆其牆夷其屋焚其器應聲淾地則時成創
者則拂其頸衡其勾刃其軀切其肌後至者欲撥
天下聞崇之反也咸欲寨衣手劍而叱之其先至
下示不得通辨社諸侯出門見之著曰為戒方今

[28.7] Wei Chao remarks, "*Chan* 棧 is *ch'ai* 柴 [firewood or a wooden fence]." *Kung-yang Commentary* 27: 5b, Dk. Ai, IV, vi, says, "The mound to the gods of the soils of a destroyed state is covered up; it is covered from above and *ch'ai* below," and Cheng Hsüan, in a note to *Chou-li* 26: 3a, *sub* the *Sang-chu*, quotes the latter part of that sentence, using *chan* instead of *ch'ai*, so that these two words had the same meaning.   Yen Shih-ku explains, "*Chan* means to use a mat 簀 to cover it.   Below, it is *chan*, and above, it is, covered, in order that to block off and prevent the passage of the *yin* and *yang* emanations." Ma Hsü-lun (xx cent.), in his *Tu Liang-HS Chi*, p. 18a, who quotes the preceding passages, states that the text means that the mound was covered by a bamboo framework, citing *Shuo-wen* 6 A: 6b, which explains *chan* by *p'eng* 棚, a scaffold, and adds that it also denotes a bamboo wattled military chariot.   King Wu is said to have levelled the mound of the Yin dynasty's gods of the soils at Po[5] and to have distributed its soil to the nobles to serve as a warning against rebellion; four walls and a roof, with possibly a window only on the north, were built around the place to keep out the *yang* influence (which comes from Heaven with the sun); then the place was covered with a mat of branches, etc., to keep out the *yin* influence.

[28.8] Prof. Duyvendak suggests reading 示 as 祇, interpreting the clause to mean that the *yin* (spirits of the earth) and the *yang* (spirits of heaven) could not intercommunicate.

[28.9] Wang Nien-sun states that 拂 should be read as 刜, to chop, to make it parallel with the other clauses.

[28.10] The Sung Ch'i ed. states that for 刃其軀 there was anciently written 刔其體, but the Ching-yu ed. reads the former.   The *Tzu-lin K'ao-yi* (by Jen Ta-ch'un, 1738–1789), basing itself on the *Tzu-lin* (by Lü Shen, iv cent.; book lost), declares that the first word of the latter phrase means "切, to cut."

而宗室尤甚言必切齒焉何則呂其背畔恩義而不知重德之
所在也宗室所居或遠嘉幸得先聞不勝憤憤之願願為宗室
倡始父子兄弟負籠荷鍤馳之南陽豬崇宮室令如古制及崇
社宜如亳社曰賜諸侯用永監戒願下回輔公卿大夫議呂明
好惡視四方於是恭大說公卿曰皆宜如嘉言恭白太后下詔

[in people's feelings]. [The members of] the imperial house moreover [felt it] especially keenly, so that, when they spoke of him, they inevitably gnashed their teeth. Why so? Because he had gone contrary to and rebelled against your favor and beneficence and did not recognize where the greatest virtue lay.

"The [members of] the imperial house, for the most part, live at places distant [from Yüan]; I, Chia, have been fortunate to have been able to hear of [his rebellion] first and have not [been able] to resist my indignant desire. I wish to take the lead of the imperial house, myself, [with] my sons and my elder and younger brothers, to carry baskets on our shoulders and to bear mattocks,[29.1] gallop to Nan-yang [Commandery], and make a pond of [Liu] Ch'ung2c's palace-buildings, in order to cause them to be according to the ancient institutions. They, together with the mound to the gods of the soils belonging to [Liu] Ch'ung2c, should be like the mound to the gods of the soils at Po5,[29.2] and should be used to grant to the nobles, in order that it may be an eternal lesson and warning. I wish that [this matter] may be referred to the Four Coadjutors, the ministers, and the grandees, for discussion, in order to make plain its right and wrong and to show it [as an example] to the four quarters [of the empire]."

[Wang] Mang was thereupon very much pleased. The ministers all said,[29.3] "It would be proper [to do] as [Liu] Chia1s says," [so Wang] Mang advised the [Grand] Empress Dowager to issue an imperial edict,

*28b*

*36a Chang Sung's Memorial for Liu Chia.*

*Liu Chia and Chang Sung Rewarded.*

[29.1] The official ed. reads *yi* 倚 for *ho* 荷, and quotes the Sung Ch'i ed. as saying that *yi* should be *ho*. The Ching-yu ed. however reads *ho*. Wang Nien-sun adds that anciently *yi* was read like 阿, with the upper tone, quoting in proof a line from the *Lao-tzu* ch. 58 in which *yi* is rhymed with 禍, so that its pronunciation must have been quite similar to that of *ho*.

[29.2] Po5 was the capital of the Yin dynasty; cf. n. 28.7.

[29.3] Su Yü states that 曰皆 should probably be interchanged.

which said, "Verily, although [Liu] Chia₁ₛ, a father and his sons, his elder and younger brothers, are related to [Liu] Ch'ung₂꜀, they did not presume to show partiality to him. Whenever they saw some sprouts [of evil], they led each other in giving information [about it]. Now that this calamity [of rebellion] has come to pass, they unanimously and together [want to] take vengeance upon him. [Their act is] a re-

29b sponse to ancient institutions, so that their loyalty and filial devotion is apparent.

"Let [Liu] Chia₁ₛ be enfeoffed with a thousand households of [the prefecture] of Tu-yen, as the Marquis Leading²⁹·⁴ by the Rules of Proper Conduct, and [let Liu] Chia₁ₛ's seven sons be all granted the noble rank of Marquises of the Imperial Domain."

36b　　Later [Chang] Sung was also enfeoffed as the Marquis of Pure Virtue. In Ch'ang-an there was a saying about him, which said,

> "If you seek enfeoffment,
> 　Go to Chang [Sung] Po-sung.
> Strength in fighting
> 　Is not as good as cleverness in preparing
> 　　memorials."

[Wang] Mang also enfeoffed more than a hundred officials and common people of Nan-yang [Commandery] who had distinguished themselves. He made a stagnant pond of Liu Ch'ung₂꜀'s residence.

29a People who later plotted to rebel all had stagnant ponds [made out of their residences].²⁹·⁵

²⁹·⁴ The text reads *shih* 師, but Ch'ien Ta-chao asserts that the word should be *shuai*₁ 帥, which is interchanged with *shuai*₂ 率. On 99 B: 14a he is called the *Shuai*₂-*li* Marquis; Wang Nien-sun adds that the *T'ai-p'ing Yü-lan*, ch. 201, quoting this passage, reads *shuai*₁ (the Sung ed. reprinted in the "Szu-pu Ts'ung-K'an" and my reprint of a 1807 edition, 201: 4b, both read *shih*).

²⁹·⁵ We are told chiefly incidentally about such subsequent rebellions. *HS* 15 B: 50b mentions Lin Huang₅ᵦ, Marquis of Wu-p'ing, who rebelled in A.D. 7. In 99 B: 13b, Sun Chien also mentions Liu K'uai, Liu Ts'eng₆, and Liu Kuei₆; cf. Glossary, *sub vocibus*.

又封南陽吏民有功者百餘人汙池劉崇室宅後謀反者皆
侯長安謂之語曰欲來封過張伯松力戰鬭不如巧為奏茸
封嘉為師禮侯嘉子七人皆賜爵關內侯後又封竦為淑德
之及其禍成同共釁之應合古制忠孝著焉其曰杜行戶千
曰惟嘉父子兄弟雖與崇有屬不敢阿私或見萌牙相率告

為攝省府為攝殿第為攝宮奏可恭白太后下詔曰故太師光
為攝省府為攝殿第為攝宮奏可恭白太后下詔曰故太師光
廟長丞中府子虎賁旅下百餘人入置衛士三百人安漢公廬
有食之十二月羣臣奏請益安漢公宮及家吏置率更令廟殿
内五月甲辰太后詔莽朝見太后稱假皇帝冬十月丙辰朝日
汙池云羣臣後白劉崇等謀逆者曰莽權輕也宜尊重曰填海

The various courtiers furthermore advised [the Grand Empress Dowager] that Liu Ch'ung[2c] and the others had plotted treason because [Wang] Mang's power was too light, and that it would be proper to honor and make him more powerful in order that he might control [all] within [the four] seas.

**Wang Mang's Power Increased.**

In the fifth month, on [the day] *chia-ch'en*, the [Grand] Empress Dowager issued an imperial edict that when [Wang] Mang comes to a court audience of the [Grand] Empress Dowager, he should be called the Acting Emperor.

**July 1. He is made Acting Emperor.**

In the winter, the tenth month, on [the day] *ping-ch'en*, the first day of the month, there was an eclipse of the sun.[29.6]

**Sept. 11.**

In the twelfth month, various courtiers memorialized, begging to increase the officials in the palace and in the home of the Duke Giving Tranquillity to the Han Dynasty, [Wang Mang], to establish a Chief Leader of Conscripts, Chiefs and Assistants in his Temple, Stable, and Kitchen, Palace Bodyguards, [Gentlemen] As Rapid as Tigers, and those of lower [rank, to the number of] more than a hundred persons, and also establish Guards [for him to the number of] three hundred persons. The rooms, [in the imperial palace], of the Duke Giving Tranquillity to the Han Dynasty should be [called] the Regent's Apartments; his yamen should be [called the Regent's Hall; and his residence should be [called] the Regent's Palace.[29.7] The memorial was approved.

**A.D. 7, Jan./Feb. His Residence is given the Honors of an Imperial Palace.**

[Wang] Mang advised the [Grand] Empress Dowager to issue an imperial edict which said, "Verily when the late Grand Master, [K'ung] Kuang, died

---

[29.6] Cf. Appendix IV. Before this eclipse there appeared the varicolored horse of the constellation San-t'ai, the second portent urging Wang Mang to take the throne; cf. 99 B : 9b.

[29.7] Hu San-hsing explains, "The rooms *lu* 廬 were his habitations *shê* 舍 for stopping and spending the night in the [Palace] Hall 殿; his yamen *fu* 府 was his place for doing business; his residence *ti* 第 was where he lived."

**37a**

previously, his achievements were already made known. The Grand Guardian, [Wang] Shun₄ᵦ, the Grand Minister of Works, [Chen] Feng, the General of Light Chariots, [Chen] Han, and the General of Foot-soldiers, [Sun] Chien, all formed plans for in-

**30a**

**His Associates' [image] Sons Honored.**

ducing the *Shan-yü* [to adopt Chinese customs]. They also had charge of the Spiritual Tower, the *Ming-t'ang*, the *Pi-yung*, and the four [altars for] the suburban sacrifices, and fixed their institutions and regulations. They opened up the Tzu-wu Road, were of the same mind with the Ruling Governor in delighting in virtue, and were in accord with his ideas and of mutual assistance to him, so that their achievements and virtuous conduct are abundant and apparent. [We] enfeoff the sons of [Wang] Shun: [Wang] K'uang₁ₐ as the Marquis of the Same Mind [with the Ruling Governor] and [Wang] Lin₂ as the Marquis Delighting in Virtue; [K'ung] Kuang's grandson, [K'ung] Shou, as the Marquis of Accordance of Ideas; [Chen] Feng's grandson, [Chen] K'uang, as the Marquis of Mutual Assistance; and add [to the enfeoffments of Chen] Han and of [Sun] Chien, to each [the income of] three thousand households."

**The Ch'iang Rebel.**

In this year, P'ang T'ien, Fu Fan, and others of the Western Ch'iang, who had held a grudge [because Wang] Mang had taken away their land and made of it the commandery of Hsi-hai, rebelled and attacked the Grand Administrator of Hsi-hai [Com-

**29b**

mandery], Ch'eng Yung. [Ch'eng] Yung fled hastily, [so Wang] Mang executed [Ch'eng] Yung and sent the Colonel Commissioner for the Ch'iang, Tou K'uang, to attack [the Ch'iang].

**II Spring.**

In the second year, in the spring, Tou K'uang and others attacked and routed the Western Ch'iang.

**June/July. Change of Coinage.**

In the fifth month, [Wang Mang] changed [the coinage] and created as [objects of] exchange, [gold] inlaid knife [coins] (*ts'o-tao*), one of which was worth five thousand [cash], graving knife [coins] (*ch'i-tao*),

難前羌功效已列太保舜大司空豐輕車將軍邯步兵將軍建皆為誘

進舉于善業又興靈臺明堂辟雍回郭定制度開子午道與羌術同心俟林為說德俟先孫壽為

說德合意并力功德茂著封弈子臣為同心俟林為

合意俟豐孫匡為益邯建各三千戶是歲西羌龐恬傅幡等怨

恭寧其地作西海郡反攻西海太守程永永奔走莽誅永遣護羌校尉

賓況摯之二年春賓況等擊破西羌五月更造貨錯刀一直五千契刀

卿侯劉信為天子移檄郡國言莽毒殺平帝攝天子

直九月東郡太守翟義都試勒車騎因發卒命立嚴

者禁列侯臣下不得挾黃金輸御府受直然卒不與

一直五百大錢一直五十與五銖錢並行民多盜鑄

one of which was worth five hundred [cash], and large cash (*ta-ch'ien*), one of which was worth fifty [cash].     Together with the [previous] five-*shu* cash,[30.1] [all of them were to] circulate together. Many common people cast counterfeit [money]. Full marquises and those of lower [rank] were not permitted to possess actual gold; they were to transport it to the Imperial Wardrobe, to receive its value [in money]. Yet in the end he did not give them its value.

37b

In the ninth month, the Grand Administrator of Tung Commandery, Chai Yi, held his [annual] general [military review and] examinations,[30.2] led [out] his chariots and cavalry, and made use of this occasion to mobilize emergency troops. He set up the Marquis of Yen-hsiang, Liu Hsin₄g, as the Son of Heaven, and sent a call-to-arms to the commanderies and kingdoms, saying, "[Wang] Mang murdered Emperor P'ing by poison and, as Regent, [has taken to himself] the throne of the Son of Heaven, intend-

Oct. Chai Yi's Rebellion.

[30.1] Cf. *HS* 24 B: 21a, b (trans. in Appendix I to this chapter) and annotations. From the nature of this coinage, Wang Mang does not seem to have yet been aiming at the imperial throne, for he had to abolish the gilded knife-money when he took the throne. That change may however have been an afterthought. Cf. 24 B: 21b.

[30.2] The parallel passage in 84: 11a (cf. Glossary *sub* Chai Yi) makes it plain that the *tu-shih* 都試 (the annual review and inspection) occurred on a special day; in 76: 9a, when Han Yen-shou was Grand Administrator of the Tung Commandery, it is said that he "*tu-shih* and *chiang-wu* 講武, set up axes and banners and practised archery and driving." Ju Shun, in a note to the former passage, explains, "The Grand Administrator, Chief Commandant, Prefects, Chiefs, Assistant [Prefects and Chiefs], and Commandants assembled to *tu-shih*, and were examined for their ranking [in efficiency]," but Ch'i Shao-nan (1703–1768) declares that this explanation is incorrect, for the *tu-shih* day was the day for *chiang-wu* (which latter term is found in *Li-chi* IV, vi, 20 [Couvreur, I, 396; Legge, I, 300] where it seems to mean, "give instructions on military operations"). He asserts that according to the Han dynasty's Code, in the autumn a *tu-shih* was regularly performed. The phrase *tu-shih* also occurs in *HHS*, Mem. 5: 2a³, where Li Hsien explains, "According to the Han law, on the day of the autumnal equinox, they *tu-shih* the cavalrymen and soldiers, which means that they were examined concerning their relative ranking [in military efficiency]."

ing to cut short [the reign of] the House of Han. Now we should respectfully[30.3] inflict the punishment of Heaven and execute [Wang] Mang."

**Wang Mang's Fearfulness.** In the commanderies and kingdoms he caused a crowd of more than a hundred thousand [persons] to doubt and suspect [Wang Mang].[30.4] [Wang] Mang was frightened and afraid and could not eat. Day and night he held the Young Prince, [Liu Ying], in his arms. He gave information [to the gods] in prayers at [the altars for] the suburban sacrifices and at [the imperial ancestral] temples. He made a document after the model of the "Great Announce-

**30b** ment,"[30.5] and sent the Grandee-remonstrant Huan T'an and others to publish it in the empire and to proclaim the idea that, since [Wang Mang] had [only] the post of regent, he would be obliged to return the government [in due time] to the Young Prince. [Wang Mang] sent Wang Yi5, Sun Chien, and others, eight generals [in all], to attack [Chai] Yi, and distributed [others] to garrison the various passes and guard the barriers in the defiles.

**Rebellion Near the Capital.** Some men of Huai-li, Chao Ming, Ho Hung, and others, raised troops in response to Chai Yi, and plotted with them, saying, "The generals and picked troops have all gone to the east, so that the imperial capital is empty [of troops] and it is possible to

**30a**
**38a** attack Ch'ang-an." Their bands were quite large, reaching almost a hundred thousand persons. [Wang] Mang was afraid and sent the generals, Wang Ch'i and Wang Chi6, leading troops, to resist them. He made the Grand Guardian, Chen Han, the General-in-chief. [Chen Han] received his axe

---

[30.3] I have adopted Yen Shih-Ku's interpretation, that 共 should be read as 恭. The latter character is found in the Ching-yu ed.'s note.

[30.4] Cf. 84: 11a for another phrasing and a parallel account of this rebellion.

[30.5] This phrase is the title of ch. vii in *Book of History* V, (Legge, 362–375), which was supposed to have been written by the Duke of Chou in the name of King Ch'eng on the occasion of the revolt by the King's two Uncles of Kuan, of Ts'ai, and others.

莽恐遣將軍王奇王級將兵拒之曰太保甄邯為大將軍受鉞
與謀曰諸將精兵悉東京師空可攻長安眾稍多至且十萬人
義分屯諸關守阨塞槐里男子趙明霍鴻等起兵呂和翟義相
於天下諭曰攝位當反政孺子之意遣王邑孫建等八將軍擊
能食盡夜抱孺子告禱郊廟放大誥作策遣諫大夫桓譚等班
位欲絕漢室今共行天罰誅莽郡國疑惑眾十餘萬莽惶懼不

聖思始發而反虜仍破詔文始書反虜大敗制書始下反虜畢斬

主應則移氣言則動物施則成化臣崇伏讀詔書下日竊計其時

洪範心合寶龜膺受元命豫知成敗感應兆占是謂配天配天之

十二月王邑等破翟義於圉司威陳崇使監軍上書言陛下奉天

高廟領天下兵左杖節右把鉞屯城外王舜甄豐晝夜循行殿中

of authority in the Temple of [Emperor] Kao [and was ordered] to lead the empire's troops. In his left [hand] he held his credentials and in his right [hand] he grasped his axe of authority. He encamped outside the city walls. Wang Shun4b and Chen Feng day and night patrolled in the [Palace] Halls.

In the twelfth month, Wang Yi5 and the others routed Chai Yi at Yü3.    *Dec./Jan. A.D. 8. Chai Yi Defeated.*

The Director of Majesty, Ch'en Ch'ung, who had been sent to superintend to army, sent [to Wang Mang] a letter, saying,

"Your Majesty has upheld the great plan[30.6] of Heaven and in your heart you have accorded with [the prognostications from] the precious tortoise.[30.7]    *A Flattering Memorial.* You have received the great mandate [of Heaven, so that] you know beforehand [what will] succeed [and what will] fail, and you were influenced by and responded to the auguries by the tortoise-shell and the lots. This means that you are the associate of Heaven. When a lord who is the associate of Heaven reflects, he changes the emanations; when he speaks, he moves [the many] beings and things; when he acts, he brings his transforming influence to success.

"Your subject Ch'ung humbly read of the date when your written imperial edict was issued, and your humble servant compared it with the time [of the victory]. When your sage reflections were first begun, the rebellious caitiffs were then routed; when the words of your edict were first written, the rebellious caitiffs were seriously defeated, and when your written imperial decree was first issued, the rebellious caitiffs were completely beheaded. Before the many

---

30.6 An allusion to the title of *Book of History* V, ch. iv (Legge, p. 320).

30.7 An allusion to *Book of History* V, vii, 3 (Legge, p. 365). The "great mandate" is that of a dynasty (*Book of History* V, xiv, 5; Legge, 456); Ch'en Ch'ung hints that Wang Mang ought to be the actual Emperor.

generals had time to array the sword points [of their troops], and before I, your subject Ch'ung, had time to complete my foolish thoughts, the matter had been already settled." [Wang] Mang was greatly pleased.

**31a 38b**
**III**
**Spring.**

In the third year, in the spring, there was an earthquake, and a general amnesty [was granted] to the empire.

Wang Yi₅ and the others returned to the imperial capital and went west to join with Wang Chi₆ and the others to attack [Chao] Ming and [Ho] Hung, who were all routed and annihilated. A discussion is in the "Memoir of Chai Yi."

**84 : 18b,**
**19a.**
**The**
**Victory**
**Banquet.**

[Wang] Mang held a great banquet in the White Tiger Hall of the Wei-yang Palace to make grants to the generals and leaders for their toil. In an imperial edict, [he ordered] Ch'en Ch'ung to examine and estimate the military achievements [of the leaders] and rank them as high or low.

*30b*

**Five**
**Grades of**
**Nobility**
**Estab-**
**lished.**

[Wang] Mang then sent [to the Grand Empress Dowager] a memorial which said, "In an age of brilliant sages, there are many capable persons in the state, hence at the time of T'ang [Yao] and Yü [Shun], in every house [someone] was capable of being enfeoffed and when their meritorious services had been performed and their work had been done, rewards were given. At the time of the assembly [called by] the Sovereign of the Hsia [dynasty, Yü,] at T'u-shan, those who held jade and silk [at the ceremonies, belonged to] ten thousand states.[31.1] (The nobles held jade and their sub-vassals held silk.) [In the time of] King Wu of the Chou [dynasty, at

---

[31.1] A reference to *Tso-chuan*, Dk. Ai, VII; Legge, p. 814.

Duyvendak remarks that the next sentence in the text, which I have placed in parentheses, is probably an interpolation from some commentary. It is now found in Tu Yü's (222–284) comment to the *Tso-chuan* passage. This sentence may however have been Wang Mang's citation of the classical authority for his establishment of the noble rank of Vassal at this time, in addition to his other five noble ranks, the classical authority for which is cited a little further on.

夏后塗山之會執玉帛者萬國諸侯執玉帛庸執帛用武王
賢人故唐虞之時可比屋而封至功成事就則加賞焉至於
帥詔陳崇治校軍功第其高下奏乃上奏曰明聖之世國多
明鴻皆破滅語在翟義傳莽大置酒未央宮白虎殿勞賜將
說三年春地震大赦天下王邑等還京師西與王級等合擊
眾將未及齊其鋒芒臣崇未及盡其愚慮而事已決矣莽大

高皇帝受命除殘考功施賞建國數百後稍衰做其餘僅存太皇
孝也泰為亡道殘滅諸侯曰為郡縣欲擅天下之利故二世而亡
而況於公侯伯子男乎故得萬國之歡心曰事其先王此天子之
矣禮記王制千七百餘國是曰孔子著孝經曰不敢遺小國之臣
於明堂曰配上帝是曰四海之內各曰其職來祭蓋諸侯千八百
盂津之上尚有八百諸侯用公居攝郊祀后稷曰配天宗祀文王

the assembly] above the Meng Ford, there were still eight hundred nobles. When the Duke of Chou occupied [the post] of Regent, he performed the suburban sacrifice to Prince Millet as the coadjutor of Heaven and performed in the *Ming-t'ang* the ancestral sacrifice to the greatest exemplar, to King Wen, as the coadjutor of the Lord on High. For this reason, when, within the four seas, each person came to [assist in] the sacrifice in accordance with his duty, there were indeed probably 1800 nobles. The *Record of Proprieties* (*Li-chi*), [in the chapter,] 'The Royal Regulations,' [speaks of] more than seventeen hundred states.[31.2] For this reason, when Confucius composed the *Classic of Filial Piety*, he said, '[anciently, the brilliant kings] did not presume to neglect the ministers of [even] small states—then how much more dukes, marquises, earls, viscounts, and barons! Hence they brought it about that the myriad states rejoiced in heart and therefore served [the King's] deceased predecessors.'[31.3] The foregoing [was the result of] the Son of Heaven's filial piety.

39a

"The Ch'in [dynasty] acted contrary to the [right] way, killing the nobles and exterminating their clans, making [their territories] into commanderies and prefectures, with the intention of arrogating to itself [all] the benefits of the whole country. Hence [in the reign of] the Second Emperor, it fell and Emperor Kao received the mandate [of Heaven] to do away with [the Ch'in dynasty's] oppression. He examined [his subjects'] merits, distributed rewards, and established several hundred [kings' and marquises'] states. Later they declined considerably [in number] and the remainder have barely preserved [their noble

---

[31.2] *Li-chi* III, i, 10 (Legge, I, 212; Couvreur, I, 269).

[31.3] *Hsiao-ching* ch. viii; 4: 1a (Legge, 474). The Official ed. of the *HS* lacks the word 其, but the Ching-yu ed. reads it. The Sung Ch'i ed. states that the Shao ed. (xi or xii cent.) has this word.

ranks].

"You, Grand Empress Dowager, have yourself controlled the great fundamental [features of the government] and have extensively enfeoffed meritorious and virtuous [persons] in order to stimulate [people] to goodness. You have revived destroyed [nobilities], and continued [noble houses] that had been ended,
**31b** in order to perpetuate their lines. For this reason your great transforming influence has spread abroad and will be completely effective in a short time.

"It happened that, when the Ch'iang malefactors injured Hsi-hai Commandery, when rebellious caitiffs
*31a* spread lying words in Tung Commandery, and when treasonable robbers misled the crowd [even] in the land west [of the imperial capital], no loyal subjects or filial sons failed to become angry, so that those against whom they made expeditions have been extirpated and have all suffered[31.4] for their crimes, with the result that the empire is altogether peaceful.

"I[31.5] have been instituting rites and composing music, and have verified by investigation that there is an explicit written statement [to the effect that] the noble ranks of the Chou [period] were of five grades and that their lands were of four grades,[31.6] and that there is the saying but no written statement that the noble ranks of the Yin [period] were of three grades.[31.7] Confucius said, 'The Chou [dynasty]

[31.4] Wang Nien-sun asserts that *pei* 備 should be read as *fu₁* 伏 (the usual word in this phrase) and that the word was probably originally *fu₂* 服; anciently *pei*, *fu₁*, and *fu₂* were all read like the second word in the phrase 匍匐, hence were interchanged. Li Tz'u-ming suggests that *pei* should be 犕, which is the same as *fu₂*, quoting the use of this word in *HHS*, Mem. 61: 6b.

[31.5] The Sung Ch'i ed. says that the Yüeh ed. (xi–xii cent.) did not have the word 今. The Ching-yu ed. also lacks it, I have omitted it.

[31.6] Su Lin explains, "The five grades of noble ranks were dukes, marquises, earls, viscounts, and barons. The four grades of lands were: the first grade, those of dukes; the second grade, those of marquises and earls; the third grade, those of viscounts and barons; the fourth grade, those of sub-vassals.

[31.7] Yen Shih-ku glosses, "The first grade were dukes, the second grade were marquises,

盟　者　當　羌　后
於　齊　賜　為　修
二　五　爵　號　功
代　等　關　桅　錄
郁　地　內　里　德
郁　回　侯　以　遠
乎　等　者　武　者
文　秦　更　為　千
武　可　名　號　載
吾　於　曰　崔　近
從　是　附　義　者
周　封　城　臣　當
臣　者　凡　虜　世
請　高　數　為　或
諸　為　百　號　曰
卅　侯　人　犖　文
帥　伯　犖　臣　封
當　次　西　俊　或
受　為　海　奏　曰
爵　子　者　言　武
邑　男　曰　太　爵

surveyed the two [preceding] dynasties. How replete **39b**
was its culture! I follow the Chou [dynasty].'[31.8]
Your subject begs that the various leaders who ought
to receive noble ranks and estates should [be granted]
noble ranks of five grades and lands of four grades."
The memorial was approved.

Thereupon the highest of those who were enfeoffed
were made marquises and earls; the next were made
viscounts and barons; those who would have been
granted the noble rank of Marquis of the Imperial
Domain [had their nobilities] changed and were entitled Sub-vassals. Altogether there were several **32a**
hundreds [of people enfeoffed]. Those who had attacked [the rebels in] Hsi-hai [Commandery] had [the
word] *Ch'iang* used in their titles, [those who had attacked the rebels in] Huai-li had [the word] *Wu* (military) used in their titles; [those who had attacked]
Chai Yi [had the word] caitiff (*lu*) used in their titles.

The courtiers again memorialized, saying, "Of the **His**
persons whose merits the [Grand] Empress Dowager **Sons**
has embellished and whose virtue she has recorded, **Ennobled.**
the greatest ones [will be remembered for] a thousand
years, and the lesser ones for the present generation.
Some were enfeoffed for civil [deeds] and some received noble ranks for military [acts]. None,

and the third grades were earls, viscounts, and barons." Su Yü remarks that the *Po-hu-t'ung* (i or iii cent.) 1: 1b quotes the *Li-wei Han-wen-chia* (end i cent.) as saying that in Yin times there were three grades of noble ranks and in Chou times there were five grades; the *Kung-yang Commentary* 5: 6a states that in the Spring and Autumn period, earls, viscounts, and barons were classed together as one grade, making, with dukes and marquises, three grades (the Ho Hsin [129–182] gloss states that the Spring and Autumn period reverted to the Yin practise); the *Ch'un-ch'iu Fan-lu* (by Tung Chung-shu, ca. 175–ca. 105 B.C.), 7: 7b, chap. 23, "San-tai Kai-chih," states that there were five grades of noble ranks in the Chou period and three grades in the *Spring and Autumn* period. Su Yü concludes, "Probably the explanations of the 'modern text' school were such as [those referred to in the edict and Wang Mang] says, 'There is not this written statement' [because] these words do not appear in the Classics."

[31.8] *Analects*, III, xiv.

[whether their merits were] deep or shallow, great or small, have failed to be presented [for rewards].

"Now the Regent-Emperor, [Wang Mang], turns his back to the screen and mounts the eastern steps, so that it is proper that he should be [treated] differently from at the time when he was [merely] the chief minister of the state. Although his instituting [of regulations] and composing [of music and dances] has not yet been all completed, it is proper that the noble ranks of his two sons should be advanced and that both should be made dukes.

"[According to the principle of] the *Spring and Autumn* [in the *Kung-yang Commentary*], that 'treating well the good should be extended to their sons and grandsons and [treating well] the worthy to' their descendants,[32.1] it is proper that [these persons] should possess lands and territory. King Ch'eng

*31b* gave broad enfeoffments to the sons of the Duke of Chou by concubines, so that all his six sons had soil enveloped in quitch-grass [as a token of their enfeoffment]. So the relatives of the famous Chancellor [of State] and of [the famous] General-in-chief of the Han dynasty, Hsiao [Ho] and Ho [Kuang, respec-

*40a* tively,] were all [enfeoffed] together with their relatives and connections. [Wang Mang's] elder brother's son, [Wang] Kuang₁, might first be enfeoffed as a full marquis. When the institutions and regulations are all completed, the Grand Minister over the Masses and the Grand Minister of Works should present the names of [Wang Mang's various grandsons] to the throne in accordance with the previous written imperial edict."

The [Grand] Empress Dowager's imperial edict said, "[We] promote the sons of the Regent-Emperor: the Marquis in Recompense to [the Marquis of] Hsin-[tu], [Wang] An₁ₐ, to be the Duke Recom-

[32.1] *Kung-yang Commentary*, 23: 7b; Dk. Chao, XX.

司空上名如前詔書大后詔曰進攝皇帝子襃新俟安為新舉公
之屬咸及支庶兄子光可先封為列侯諸孫制度畢已大司徒大
土地成王廣封周公庶子六子皆有茅土及漢家名相大將蕭霍
雖未畢已宜進二子爵皆為公春秋善善及子孫賢者之後宜有
深淺大小靡不畢舉今攝皇帝背踐祚袥宜異於宰國之時制作

蠻天其子太甲幼少不明伊尹放諸桐宮而居攝呂與殷道周武
立天功與崇帝道成就法度安靜海內也昔殷成湯既沒而太子
服少阿義和劉歆與博士諸儒七十八人皆曰居攝之義所旦統
送謀即真之事矣九月莽母功顯君死意不在哀令太后詔議其
白曰封莽孫宗為新都侯莽既滅翟義自謂威德日盛覆天人助
賞都侯臨為襃新公封光為行功侯是時莽還歸新都國羣臣俊

mended by [the Marquis of] Hsin-[tu]; and the Marquis in Reward to [the Marquis of Hsin-]tu, [Wang] Lin₁ₐ, to be the Duke in Recompense to [the Marquis of] Hsin[-tu]; and enfeoff [Wang] Kuang₁ as the Marquis of Vast Merit."

At this time, [Wang] Mang returned his state of Hsin-tuₑ, so various courtiers again advised [the Grand Empress Dowager] and she enfeoffed [Wang] Mang's grandson, [Wang] Tsung, as the Marquis of Hsin-tuₑ.

Since [Wang] Mang had annihilated Chai Yi, he himself considered that his majesty and virtue was increasing daily and that he had secured the assistance of Heaven and of men, so he plotted to ascend [the throne] as the actual [Emperor].　*He Plots to Become Emperor.*

In the ninth month, [Wang] Mang's mother, the Baroneteess of Apparent Merits, died. [Wang Mang's] mind was not upon mourning, so he had the [Grand] Empress Dowager issue an imperial edict [ordering] the discussion of [what] mourning garments [should be worn]. The Junior Supporter, the Hsi-and-Ho, Liu Hsin₁ₐ, with the Erudits and Confucians [to the number of] 78 persons [altogether], all said,　*Oct./Nov. His Mother Dies.*

"The principle of acting as Regent is to direct the performance of the duties established by Heaven, to promote the reverencing of the way of [the ancient Sage]- lords,[32.2] to bring to a successful issue the laws and regulations, and to make tranquil and concordant [all] within [the four] seas. Anciently, when T'ang the Victorious of the Yin [dynasty] had died and his Heir-apparent had died in his youth, his son T'ai-chia was a minor and unintelligent, so Yi Yin banished him to the T'ung Palace and acted as Regent in order to promote the course of the Yin　*32b His Mourning Rites.*　*40b*

[32.2] For this peculiar philosophical concept, cf. Duyvendak, *Book of Lord Shang*, p. 11; Bodde, *China's First Unifier*, p. 43.　Here it means, "the highest ideals."

[dynasty]. When King Wu of the Chou [dynasty] had died, the ways of the Chou [dynasty] had not yet been completed and 'King Ch'eng was young' and a minor, 'so the Duke of Chou protected King Ch'eng'[32.3] and acted as Regent in order to perfect the ways of the Chou [dynasty]. For this reason the Yin [dynasty] had the development of being 'orderly'[32.4] and the Chou [dynasty] had the merit of establishing but not employing the mutilating punishments.[32.5]

32a

"Now the Grand Empress Dowager has frequently 'happened upon untoward circumstances in the state,'[32.6] and has commissioned the Duke Giving Tranquillity to the Han Dynasty to rule and control the various officials, and to govern[32.7] the empire justly. It has happened that since the Young Prince is a minor and has not yet been able to be diligently respectful[32.8] to [the gods] above and below, August Heaven has sent down auspicious presages and has produced the portent of the red stone. For this reason, the Grand Empress Dowager followed the plain mandate of Heaven and issued an imperial edict that the Duke Giving Tranquillity to the Han Dynasty should act as Regent and mount the eastern steps in order that he might perform the duties of the sage Han [dynasty] and make it equally eminent with that of T'ang [Yao], Yü [Shun], and the three dynasties.

王既沒周道未成成王幼少周公屏成王而居攝曰成周道

是曰殷有翼翼之化周有刺錯之功今太皇太后比遭家之

不造委任安漢公宰尹摩像衡平天下遭孺子幼少未能共

上下皇天降瑞出丹石之符是曰太皇太后則天明命詔安

漢公居攝踐祚將曰聖漢之業與唐虞三代比隆也攝皇

[32.3] A quotation from *Hsüntze* 4: 1a, Bk. VIII (Dubs, p. 91). (Reference from Liu Ch'ang.)

[32.4] A quotation from *Book of Odes*, #305; IV, iii, v, 5 (Legge, p. 646). This adjective is applied to Wang Mang in *HS* 99 A: 12a.

[32.5] During the reigns of Kings Ch'eng and K'ang; cf. *HFHD*, II, 36, n. 5.1.

[32.6] A quotation from *Book of Odes*, #286; IV, i, [iii], i, (Legge, p. 569).

[32.7] "Ruling" and "governing" allude to his title of Ruling Governor. Yen Shih-ku states that the phrase translated "govern justly" means literally, "like the beam of a balance."

[32.8] I follow Yen Shih-ku in reading 共 as 恭.

帝遂開祕府會羣儒制禮作樂卒定庶官茂成天功聖心
周悉卓爾獨見發得周禮曰明囚監則天稽古而損益焉
猶仲尼之聞韶日月之不可階非聖哲之至孰能若茲綱
紀成張成在一匡此其所呂保佑聖漢安靖元元之效也

"The Regent-Emperor thereupon opened his private yamen[32.9] and met with various Confucians to institute rites and compose [the proper] music, to assist in fixing the [titles of] the many offices, and to complete beautifully the work of Heaven. His sage mind is in all respects complete, and eminent are his individual insights. The *Chou Rites* (the *Chou-li*) was discovered and secured,[32.10] so that it was made plain what should be 'followed' and 'surveyed'.[32.11] He took Heaven as his model and searched out ancient ways, yet modified them. It was just as when [K'ung Ch'iu] Chung-ni heard [the music] Shao,[32.12] and [just as] 'the sun and moon' 'cannot [be climbed up to by any] stairs.'[33.1] If [Wang Mang] had not the utmost of sage wisdom, how could he have been able to perform these [deeds]? The fundamental and subordinate principles [of government] are all displayed and completed [except for] one basketful.[33.2] These [matters] are the means by which he has devoted himself to protecting and assisting the sage Han [dynasty] and giving tranquillity to the great multitude.

41a

33a
*32b*

[32.9] *Pi-fu* 祕府 is also used in *HS* 30: 1b, "[Emperor] Hsiao-wu ... thereupon had prepared blank fascicles for library writing tablets and set up an office for copying writings. He sent to it [for copying] even the accounts and sayings of the various philosophers. All [those books] were stored in his private courts (*pi-fu*)," i.e., the imperial private library (pi-書). But to interpret the text here as declaring that Wang Mang "opened [to the public] the imperial private library" does not fit the context. We must take *pi-fu* in its generic sense, "private courts" or "private yamen."

[32.10] K'ang Yu-wei, in his *Hsin-hsüeh Wei-ching K'ao*, ch. 6, p. 24, takes this passage to imply that Liu Hsin fabricated the *Chou-li* and deceived Wang Mang by means of it. The *Chou-li* however contains passages that date as far back as the iv cent. B.C.; cf. Karlgren, "The Early History of the *Chou Li* and *Tso Chuan* Texts," *Bull. Mus. Far East. Antiq.*, no. 3 (1931), pp. 1–59.

[32.11] "Followed" is an allusion to *Analects* II, xxiii, 2 and "surveyed" is another allusion to *ibid.*, III, xiv (from Li Ch'i).

[32.12] An allusion to *Analects* VII, xiii.

[33.1] Allusions to *Analects* XIX, xxiv; xxv, 3, which praise Confucius.

[33.2] An allusion to the *Book of History* V, v, 9 (Legge, p. 350) or to *Analects* IX, xviii.

"Now the Baronetess of Apparent Merits has died. The [*Ceremonies and*] *Rites* [*Yi*]-*li* [says], 'The son of a concubine who becomes the heir [of his father] wears the three-month's *szu* mourning for his own mother,' and the explanation says, 'He is in the same position as the most honorable person [in the family, i.e., his father, and so] should not presume to wear [deep] mourning for his own mother.'[33.3]  The Regent-Emperor has, through his sage virtue, obtained the mandate of August Heaven, received the imperial edict of the [Grand] Empress Dowager that he should act

41b as Regent and mount the eastern steps,[33.4] and support the descendant of the great Han imperial family. On the one hand, he has his weighty [duties] to Heaven, Earth, and the gods of the soils and the grains, and on the other hand, he has the care of the great multitude and the multifarious matters [of the government],[33.5] so that he is not permitted to consider his own relatives.  Hence the Grand Empress Dowager has established his eldest grandson [as a noble], causing him to be the marquis at Hsin-tu_c and the successor to Marquis Ai, [Wang Wan], making plain that the Regent-Emperor is in the same position as the most honorable person, [the Emperor], upholds the sacrifices at [imperial] ancestral temples,

33b is in charge of supplying the needs of the Grand Empress Dowager, and is not permitted to wear mourning for his own parents.

"The *Chou Rites* (*Chou-li*) says, 'A king, . . . [in wearing mourning] for his nobles, [wears] the hemp

33a mourning badge and cap,' to which there is added a ring of 'hemp banding.'[33.6]  If [the nobles] are of the

---

[33.3] *Yi-li* 33: 4a, b (Steele, II, 37).  The explanation is said to have been made by Tzu-hsia.

[33.4] The Official ed. emends 袥 to 阼.  The Ching-yu ed. reads the latter.

[33.5] A phrase from *Book of History* II, iii, 5 (Legge, p. 73; Couvreur, p. 47).

[33.6] *Chou-li* 21: 7a *sub* the *Szu-fu*, (Biot, II, 9 f).  The *Chou-li* makes no distinction

共養太皇太后不得服其私親也周禮王為諸侯緦線弁而加環絰
建辰元孫佺侯新都為哀侯後明攝皇帝與尊者為體承宗廟之榮奉
上有天地社稷之重下有元元萬機之憂不得顧其私親故大皇太后
也攝皇帝且聖德承皇天之命定太后之詔居攝踐祚奉漢大宗之後
今功顯君薨禮庶子為後為其母緦傳曰與尊者為體不敢服其私親

同姓則麻其姓則葛攝皇帝當為功顯君緦縗弁而加麻環

經如天子弔諸侯服曰應聖制奉遵行焉几臺弔再會而令

新都侯宗為主服喪三年云司威陳崇奏行功侯先私報執

全吾寶況令殺人況為收繫致其法大怒切責光光毋曰

女自眠載與長孫中孫遂女子自殺及況皆死初莽曰事女

same surname [as the king], then [his mourning garments] are of hemp (Cannabis); if they are of a different surname, then they are of *ke* hemp (Pueraria). The Regent-Emperor ought to wear the hemp mourning badge for the Baronetess of Apparent Merits and a cap to which there has been added a hemp ring of banding, like the mourning garments of the Son of Heaven in condoling his nobles, in order to respond to the institutions of the sages."

[Wang] Mang therefore acted [accordingly]. Altogether he paid one mourning [visit] and a second [time] assembled [the mourners] and ordered the Marquis of Hsin-tu$_c$, [Wang] Tsung, to be in charge [of the ceremonies] and wear mourning to the third year.

The Director of Majesty, Ch'en Ch'ung, memorialized that the Marquis of Vast Merit, [Wang] Kuang$_1$, had secretly sent a message to the Bearer of the Gilded Mace, Tou K'uang, and had ordered him to kill a man,[33.7] and that for this reason [Tou] K'uang had arrested and bound [this person] and had applied the law to him. [Wang] Mang was furious and bitterly reproached [Wang] Kuang$_1$. [Wang] Kuang$_1$'s mother said [to her son], "Do you yourself consider in what way [you are any different from Wang Yü] Chang-sun or [Wang Huo$_b$] Chung-sun, [Wang Mang's dead sons]?" Thereupon [both of them], mother and son, committed suicide; together with [Tou] K'uang they all died.

Previously, because [Wang] Mang had served his

*Wang Mang's Nephew's Execution.*

42a

between mourning for those relatives of the same and of different surnames. Cheng Chung (ca. 5 B.C.–A.D. 83), in a note to that passage, says, "*Szu* 緦 has its woof of fifteen times eighty threads of hemp, half of which are dropped. The threads may be treated [i.e., cleaned]; but the cloth may not be treated." If Liu Hsin fabricated the *Chou-li*, it is curious that he should have quoted it so inexactly.

[33.7] The Official ed. and the Southern Academy ed. read 之 for the 人. But the Ching-yu ed. and *Tzu-chih T'ung-chien* 36: 18a read the latter, so I make no emendation.

mother, had nourished his elder brother's wife, and had raised his elder brother's son, [Wang Kuang₁], he had made a name [for himself]. Then later, his perversity and cruelty were again used to show [that he was actuated by] public spirit and sense of duty.

**34a** He ordered [Wang] Kuang₁'s son, [Wang] Chia₁ᵦ, to inherit [his father's] noble rank and become the Marquis [of Vast Merits].

[Wang] Mang issued a written message,[34.1] which said, "The principle of 'stopping and hushing [instru-

---

[34.1] In this chapter, after Wang Mang is declared to have plotted to become actual Emperor (99 A: 32a), Pan Ku avoids stating that Wang Mang issued any "imperial edicts, *chao* 詔", or "imperial decrees, *chih* 制." (These two terms are equated in 99 A: 30b, altho they were not precisely synonymous; cf. *Mh* II, 126, n. 2.) The full terms for these imperial orders were "written imperial edict, *chao-shu* 書" and "written imperial decree, *chih-shu*" (cf. Yen Shih-ku's statement, quoted in *HFHD* I, 192, n. 1). Pan Ku merely states that Wang Mang issued "written messages, *shu*" or, occasionally, "documents, *ts'e* 策" (99 B: 23a⁸). In this usage and in refusing to call Wang Mang by the title of emperor 皇帝, Pan Ku indicates his loyalty to the Han dynasty. If he had written regularly that Wang Mang issued *chao* or *chih*, he would have implied that Wang Mang was a legitimate emperor. (*Chao* in 99 B: 20b⁵, 99 C: 4a², 10b⁶, 11b⁷, 21a⁴, and *chao-shu* in 99 B: 25b¹ are slips or later emendations, since they are contrary to Pan Ku's regular practise; *chih-chao* in 99 B: 25b¹, *chao-shu* in 99 C: 13a¹¹, and *chao-ling* 令 in 99 C: 19b² are probably quoted from Wang Mang's edicts. In other chapters, Pan Ku is not so careful: Wang Mang is said to issue imperial edicts (*chao*) in 24 A: 21b⁴, 22a³; B: 23a¹⁰, b⁵, and 25b¹¹.)

Pan Ku does not however refrain from quoting statements by others that Wang Mang issued imperial edicts (*chao*, 99 B: 23a¹; C: 5b⁶, 16a²) or that he was the Son of Heaven (99 A: 36a⁸) and Emperor (99 B: 10b²). He allowed to Wang Mang the terms proclamation (號, 99 A: 35a⁴) and ordinance (*ling*, 99 A: 35a⁴; B: 6a⁶). These terms, while used by emperors, could also be used by high nobles. He also allows Wang Mang to issue mandates 命 (99 B: 1a¹²), charters (*ts'e*, 99 B: 1a¹², 2b⁸), royally sealed messages *hsi-* 璽 *shu* (99 C: 16a⁹; *hsi* may denote either an imperial or a royal seal), and commands (敕, 99 B: 2b⁵, 23b¹¹; this last term was not yet commonly used nor was its use as yet an imperial prerogative).

The avoidance of *chao* and *chih* was a courtesy to the reigning Han dynasty and does not imply any perversion of the facts. The term *shu* for an imperial order is moreover unusual, so that any reader who knew the correct terms for imperial orders would immediately understand the reference to *chao-shu* or *chih-shu*. Thus Pan Ku actually preserved the original meaning, while extending to the Emperor, his patron, the proper courtesy. I have accordingly translated *shu* as "message."

子茶上奏大后曰陛下至聖遭家不造遇漢十二世三七之
郡新井雲言巴郡石牛鳴言扶風雍石茶皆迎受十一月甲
饒侯劉京車騎將軍千人扈雲大仟屠蔽鴻秦符命書言齊
八音修各云何其與所部儒生各盡精恩意陳其義是咸廣
義記于李冬正月部記八音當奉王公卿士樂凡幾等五聲

ments' as a sign of mourning for the Emperor][34.2] will end with the last month of [this] winter. In the first month [of the next year], at the suburban sacrifices, the eight [kinds of] musical instruments should be played. Altogether how many grades of music [should be played by their own musicians] for the kings, ministers, and gentlemen? For each of the several ranks, what should be the number of the five [kinds of] notes and the eight [kinds of] musical instruments? Let [the proper officials] with the Confucian Masters under their control each employ their spirits and minds to the utmost and set forth their ideas completely."

*33b*
Mourning Rites for Nobles Ordered Fixed.

In this year, Liu Ching[1a], the Marquis of Kuang-jao, Hu Yün, a Millenary of the General of Chariots and Cavalry, and Tsang Hung, a subordinate of the Grand Guardian, memorialized mandates [from Heaven through] portents. [Liu] Ching[1a] spoke of the new well in Ch'i Commandery, [Hu] Yün spoke of the stone ox in Pa Commandery and [Tsang] Hung spoke of the stone at Yung in the [Yu]-fu-feng [Commandery. Wang] Mang welcomed and accepted all [of them],[34.3] and in the eleventh month, on [the day] *chia-tzu*, [Wang] Mang presented a memorial to the [Grand] Empress Dowager, which said,

More Portents that he Should Become Emperor.

42b
A.D. 9, Jan. 6.

"When your Majesty with your extreme sagacity 'happened upon untoward circumstances in the state,'[34.4] and met with the dangers [at the end of] the twelve reigns of the Han [dynasty, at the end of] the three [times] seven [decades of years],[34.5] you

He asks to be Temporarily Emperor.

[34.2] An allusion to *Book of History*, II, i, v, 13 (Legge, p. 40f), where it is said that the people mourned for Yao to the third year, stopping and hushing the eight kinds of musical instruments. This written (edict) refers to the third year after the death of Emperor P'ing, including A.D. 6 as the first year.

[34.3] For these portents, cf. the subsequent memorial.

[34.4] Another quotation of *Book of Odes*, *286; IV, i, [iii], i (Legge, p. 596). Cf. n. 32.6.

[34.5] Where this phrase occurs in *HS* 51: 33b, Chang Yen explains, "Three sevens is

received a majestic mandate from Heaven, and
issued an imperial mandate that I, your servant
Mang, should act as Regent, should receive the care
of the Young Prince, and should be entrusted with
the charge of the empire.  Your servant Mang was
careful and vigilant, fearing lest I would be unworthy.

"[A member of] the imperial house, the Marquis
of Kuang-jao, Liu Ching[1a], has sent to the throne a
letter saying,

Aug./
Sept.,
A.D. 8.
"'During the seventh month, Hsin Tang, the
Chief of the Ch'ang-hsing Commune in the county
of Lin-tzu in Ch'i Commandery, in one night had a
dream several times, which said,

"'"I am a messenger from his excellency Heaven.
His excellency Heaven sent me to inform you, Chief
of the Commune, saying, 'The Regent-Emperor is
due to be the actual [Emperor].'  If you do not believe me, in this commune there is due to be a
new well."'

**34b**
"'The Chief of the Commune arose at dawn and
looked, and in the Commune there actually was a
new well, which entered into the earth for almost a
hundred feet.'

Dec. 25,
A.D. 8.
"In the eleventh month, on [the day] *jen-tzu*,
[which was a day] for establishing,[34.6] and was the
winter solstice, the stone ox from the Pa Com-

210 years.  From the beginning of the Han [dynasty] . . . to the death of Emperor P'ing
was to the 210th year."  Emperor Kao's first year was 206 B.C.; to the death of Emperor
P'ing in the last month of the year beginning in A.D. 5 was actually 211 years.  But
Emperor Kao did not reign in his first year, so that the period was close enough.  The
text of that passage says that Lu Wen-shu's (fl. 73 B.C.) great uncle had by astrology
calculated that after three seventies of years the Han dynasty would come into dangers.
He memorialized the matter; in the time of Emperor Ch'eng, Ku Yung also made this
prophecy (85: 15b); when Wang Mang wanted to displace the Han dynasty, he published
these prophesies.  Cf. Meng K'ang's note to 85: 15b.

[34.6] Cf. n. 36.1.  But the winter solstice occurred on Dec. 22 about 8 p.m.—illustrating
the inaccuracy in ancient Chinese determinations of the solstice by the gnomen.

班石文告到于未央宮之前殿臣與太保安陽侯舜等視天風起塵冥

風止得銅符帛圖於石前文曰天告帝符獻者封侯承天命用神令騎

都尉崔發等馳說及前孝哀皇帝建平二年六月甲子下詔書更為太

初元將元年景其本事廿忠可夏賀良讖書臧蘭臺臣莽曰為元將元

年者大將居攝改元之文也於今信矣尚書康誥王若曰孟侯朕其弟

mandery [arrived] and, on [the day] *mou-wu*, the
inscription on the stone at Yung arrived at the Front
Hall of the Wei-yang Palace. When your servant,
with the Grand Guardian, the Marquis of An-yang,
[Wang] Shun4b, and others were looking at them, a
wind arose from Heaven and dust obscured things.
When the wind ceased, we obtained a copper portent
and a silk design from in front of the stone. Its
text reads,

Dec. 31,
A.D. 8.

*34a*

43a

> 'A portent by which Heaven [proclaims that
> you should become] Emperor.
> The person who presents it should be en-
> feoffed as a marquis.
> Accept the mandate of Heaven
> And obey the command of the gods.'

A Chief Commandant of Cavalry, Ts'ui Fa, and
others looked at it and explained it.

"Moreover previously, in [the reign of] Emperor
Hsiao-ai, in [the year-period] Chien-p'ing, the second
year, the sixth month, on [the day] *chia-tzu*, [the
Emperor] issued a written imperial edict changing
[the year-period] and making it the first year of [the
period] T'ai-ch'u-yüan-chiang. When the source of
this [matter] is examined, [it is found to be] the
books of revelation by Kan Chung-k'o and Hsia
Ho-liang, which have been stored in the Orchid
Terrace. Your servant Mang considers that the
words, 'the first year of [T'ai-ch'u]-yüan-chiang
(great general)' [mean that] when 'the General
(*Chiang*)-in-chief acts as Regent, he will change the
year-period (*yüan*),' which is a testimony for the
present [time].

July 13,
B.C. 5.

"The *Book of History*, [in the chapter], 'The
Announcement to the King's Uncle of K'ang,' [says],
'[The Acting] King, [the Duke of Chou], speaks in
the following fashion, "The chief of the nobles, Our
younger brother, my little one, Feng, [the King's

Uncle of K'ang]." '[34.7]   The foregoing words [show that] the Duke of Chou, when acting as Regent, was

**35a** entitled King.   In the *Spring and Autumn*, it is not said that Duke Yin ascended the throne, because he was Regent.[35.1]   These two Classics were those fixed by the Duke of Chou and Confucius, indeed to be a model for later [generations].   Confucius said, '[The superior man] fears the Mandate of Heaven, fears the great, and fears the precepts of the Sages.'[35.2] [How can] your servant Mang presume not to obey?

"Your servant begs that in respectfully serving the gods in heaven and earth, in the [imperial] an-

**43b** cestral temples, and in memorializing the Grand Empress Dowager and the Empress [nee Wang] of [Emperor] Hsiao-p'ing, he may call himself 'the Acting Emperor,' [but that] when he gives proclamations or ordinances to the empire or when [anyone in] the empire memorializes him about matters, they should not use [the words] 'Regent' [i.e., should merely say, 'Emperor']; that the third year of [the period] Chü-shê should become the first year of [the

**34b** period] Ch'u-shih,[35.3] and that 120 gradations on the clepsydra [in a day] should be the rule,[35.4] which

---

[34.7] *Book of History*, V, ix, 2 (Legge, p. 383; Couvreur, p. 233).   The Duke of Chou is using phraseology reserved for the ruler.   The foregoing was the interpretation of this disputed passage in Han times.   But cf. Karlgren, *BMFEA* 20, 278, Gl. 1622.

[35.1] In the *Spring and Autumn*, the first year of Duke Yin's reign lacks the statement of his accession which is found for all the other Dukes.   Wang Mang accepts the explanation of the *Tso-chuan*, "It does not state that he took the throne, because he was a regent [for the infant Duke Hui]."   This sentence is not translated by Legge, cf. p. 4–5 of his *Ch'un Ts'ew*.

[35.2] *Analects* XVI, viii, 1.

[35.3] Szu-ma Kuang (1019–1086) in his *Tzu-chih T'ung-chien K'ao-yi* 2: 2b states that Hsün Yüeh's (149–209) *Han-chi* 30: 9a, together with Wei Kuang-mei's (fl. 881–4; book lost) *Chia-hao Lu* and Sung Hsiang's (996–1066; book lost) *Chi-nien T'ung-p'u*, all invert the name of this year-period to read Shih-ch'u.   But the "Szu-pu Ts'ung-k'an" photographic reprint of a 1548 ed. of the *Han-chi*, 30: 9b and a 1696 ed. of the same book, 30: 9a, do not invert these words.   *Tzu-chih T'ung-chien* 36: 17a moreover reads Ch'u-shih; only 36: 19a reads Shih-ch'u.

事毋言攝曰居攝三年為初始元年滿刻曰百二十為度
太皇太后孝平皇后皆假皇帝其號令天下天下奏言
人畏聖人之言臣恭敬不承用臣謹共事神祇宗廟奏言
也此二經用公孔子所定益為後法孔子曰畏天命畏大
小子封此周公居攝稱王之文也春秋隱公不言即位攝

用應天命臣莽夙夜養育隆就孺子令與周之成王比德宣明太

皇太后咸德於萬方期於富而教之孺子加元服復子明辟如周

公故事奏可東庶知其奉行命指意羣臣博謀別奏呂視即真之

漸矢期門郎張充等六人謀共劫莽立楚王發覺誅死梓潼人哀

章學問長安素無行好為大言見莽吾攝即作銅匱為兩檢署其

should be used to respond to the Mandate of Heaven.

"Your servant Mang will day and night rear and raise the Young Prince and bring it about that he will be equal in virtue with King Ch'eng of the Chou [dynasty] and [thus] spread abroad the majesty and virtue of the Grand Empress Dowager to all quarters, hoping to 'enrich and then teach [the people].'[35.5] When the Young Prince is capped, I will 'return [the government] to the intelligent prince,'[35.6] as in the former circumstance the Duke of Chou did." The memorial was approved.

The mass of commoners knew [what was Wang Mang's] motive in receiving respectfully the mandate [given through] the portents. The courtiers discussed it extensively and memorialized separately in order to indicate the gradual [steps] by which he should take [the throne as] the actual [Emperor].

A Gentleman Attendant at the Gate,[35.7] Chang Ch'ung, and others, six persons [in all], plotted together to abduct [Wang] Mang and set up the King of Ch'u, [Liu Yü1a, as Emperor, but the plot] became known and they were executed and died.

**An Abortive Rebellion.**

Ai Chang, a man of Tzu3a-t'ung, had been doing elementary studying in Ch'ang-an. Heretofore he had no distinction but loved to boast. When he saw that [Wang] Mang was acting as Regent, he immediately made a bronze casket with two envelop covers.[35.8] He wrote on one of them, "The design

**35b**

Ch'u-shih might be translated "The original beginning [of Wang Mang's reign as Acting Emperor]."

[35.4] Cf. 11: 5b & n. 5.9.

[35.5] An allusion to Analects XIII, ix, 3, 4.

[35.6] A second quotation of Book of History V, xiii, 1 (Legge, p. 434).

[35.7] Wang Hsien-ch'ien notes that in 1 A.D. the title of the Attendants at the Gate had been changed to the As Rapid as Tigers, and says that this title is a contradiction. Cf. Glossary sub vocibus.

[35.8] Hu San-hsing explains, "Mao Huang (fl. dur. 1131–1163) says, 'A chien 檢 is the

44a
Ai Chang's
Portent
from
Emperor
Kao.

in the metal casket [with] the Seal of the Lord of Heaven's Act." On the other he wrote, "The written metal charter [with] the Seal of the Red Lord's Act,[35.9] which a certain person transmits to the Yellow Emperor, [Wang Mang." (Instead of] "certain person" [there was written Pang], the personal name of Emperor Kao). The writing said that Wang Mang should be the actual Son of Heaven and the [Grand] Empress Dowager [should act] according to the mandate of Heaven. Both on the design and the writing were written [the names of] eight persons who were [Wang] Mang's high officials. It also named two fine names, Wang Hsing (Wang Rises) and Wang Sheng (Wang Prospers); [Ai] Chang, taking advantage [of this opportunity, also] inserted his own surname and personal name amongst [them, so that] altogether there were eleven persons. For all of them there were written official [titles] and

35a

noble ranks as [Wang Mang's] coadjutors and assistants.

Jan.8.[35.10]

When [Ai] Chang heard that the matters of the well in Ch'i [Commandery] and of the stone ox had been referred [to the officials], on that very day, at dusk, he put on yellow clothes, took the casket, went to the Temple of [Emperor] Kao, and thereupon delivered it to the Supervisor [of the Temple].[35.11]

井石牛事下即日昏時衣黃衣持匱至高廟以付僕射
章因自稱姓名凡為十一人皆書官爵為輔佐章閻齊
后如天命圖書皆書莽大臣八人又取令名王興王盛
帝金䇿書某奇高皇帝名也書言王莽為真天子皇太
一曰天帝行璽金匱圖其一署曰赤帝行璽某傳予黃

cover of a letter, which has the cavity for the seal, and the inscription." The *chien* was the ancient wooden envelop top; cf. *HFHD* II, 86, n. 25.1.

[35.9] The legends of these seals imitate the legends on the imperial seals. Cf. *HFHD*, I, 56, n. 3.

The Sung Ch'i ed. reported that the Yüeh ed. (xi–xii cent.) and the Shao ed. (xi or xii cent.) lacked the second 行. The Ching-yu ed. also lacks it.

[35.10] Cf. *HS* 99 B: 10b.

[35.11] Hu San-hsing glosses, "For the Temple of [Emperor] Kao there was a Prefect and a Supervisor," but Wang Hsien-ch'ien answers that according to *HS* 19 A: 7a, *sub* the Master of Ceremonies, the temple had a Prefect, but no Supervisor. According to that passage, such temples had assistants as well as Prefects or Chiefs; possibly, because of Emperor Kao's eminence, a Supervisor had been appointed for his temple.

帝之靈承天命傳國金策之書子甚祇畏敢不欽受臣戊長真定

符契圖文金匱策書神明詔告屬子曰天下兆民赤帝漢氏高皇

庶帝之苗裔而太皇太后之末屬皇天上帝隆顯大佑成命統序

央宮前殿下書曰子曰不德託于皇初祖考黃帝之後皇始祖考

僕射以聞戊辰恭至高廟拜受金匱神禪御王冠謁太后還坐未

The Supervisor thereupon reported it.

On [the day] *mou-ch'en*,[35.12] [Wang] Mang went to the Temple of [Emperor] Kao, bowed, and received the metal casket and the resignation [of the Han dynasty, which] the gods had [commanded]. Wearing the royal hat,[35.13] he visited the [Grand] Empress Dowager, returned, seated himself in the Front Hall of the Wei-yang Palace, and issued a written message, which said:

    *Jan. 10.*
    *He Takes*
    *the Throne*
    *as Actual*
    *Emperor.*

"I possess no virtue, [but] I rely upon [the fact that] I am a descendant of my august deceased original ancestor, the Yellow Lord, and a distant descendant of my august deceased first ancestor, the Lord of Yü, [Shun], and the least of the Grand Empress Dowager's relatives. August Heaven and the Lords on High have made abundantly apparent their great assistance, so that the mandate [of Heaven] has been completed and the succession [to the imperial rule] has been set in order. By portents and credentials, designs and writings, a metal casket and a written charter, the gods have proclaimed that they entrust me with the myriad common people of the empire.

    *His*
    *Announce-*
    *ment.*

    44b

"The Red Lord is the genius of Emperor Kao of the Han dynasty. He has received a mandate from Heaven and has transmitted the state [to me by] a writing on a metal charter. I have been extremely reverent and awed—[how could I] presume not to receive it respectfully? On [the day] *mou-ch'en*, which is a day for founding,[36.1] I wear the royal hat

    36a

    *Jan. 10.*

[35.12] According to 99 B: 10b, Wang Mang received the mandate on the previous day, Jan. 9; but that is possibly a change to suit the theory of the five elements.

[35.13] Wang Mang followed the classical Chou practise, which entitled the monarch, "the King." He also used the title, "emperor." He used the ordinary first personal pronoun and not the special imperial personal pronoun established by the First Emperor of the unclassical Ch'in dynasty.

[36.1] The twelve branches were used to indicate the months, in accordance with the position taken by the handle of the Dipper at dusk, and the days of the month were given

and ascend the throne as the actual Son of Heaven.

真天子位
御玉冠即

astrological significence in accordance with the branch for the month. *SC* 27: 8 (Mh III, 341), in discussing the constellation Po-tou (the Northern Bushel or the Dipper), says, "[The star] used to determine (*chien* 建) [the month] at dusk is Piao 杓 [η U Ma here; elsewhere Piao denotes ε, ζ, and η U Ma]." The astronomical designation for the months, which consists of the word *chien* with one of the twelve "branches," comes accordingly from the direction taken by a line drawn through this star and the tail star in the handle of the Dipper in the various months. At the winter solstice, the handle of the Dipper points to the northern horizon at dusk; due north is called *tzu*; hence the month containing the winter solstice is called the *chien-tzu* month, i.e., the first astronomical month. The other "branches" are distributed about the horizon; cf. de Saussure, *Les origines de l'astronomie chinoise*, p. 237," who indicates that in Han times this method of determining the months was more theoretical than practical. The eleventh month of this year was accordingly the month *chien-tzu*, i.e., "the [month when] the determining stars point north."

The particular branch used to denote a day in naming the day by the sixty cyclical characters (each of which names contains one "branch" and one "stem") is given an astrological significance which depends upon which branch denotes the month. *Huai-nan-tzu*, 3: 12a, "T'ien-wen Hsün," says, "If *yin* is *chien* [which clause means both of two things in accordance with two meanings of the word *chien*: "If the day having the branch *yin* occurs in the month having the branch *yin*," and "The day *yin* is (in that case) the day for establishing"], [the branch] *mao* is to remove; *ch'en* is to fill full; *szu* is to be tranquil, it is in charge of life; *wu* is to determine; *wei* is to grasp, it is in charge of danger; *shen* is to break, it is in charge of yokes; *yu* is to be solicitous, it is in charge of attracting to oneself; *hsü* is to be completed, it is in charge of small virtues; *hai* is to receive, it is in charge of great virtue; *tzu* is to open, it is in charge of the planet Jupiter; *ch'ou* is to close, it is in charge of the retrograde correlate of the planet Jupiter." 寅爲建，卯爲除，辰爲滿，巳爲平，主生，午爲定，未爲執，主陷，申爲破，主衡，酉爲危，主杓，戌爲成，主少德，亥爲收，主大德，子爲開，主太歲，丑爲閉，主太陰。 (The terms used to give the meanings of the various days all have many meanings, so that the above translation is only approximate; diviners doubtless rung the changes on those words.) The *Huai-nan-tzu* is interpreting the meanings of those days for a *chien-yin* month only; in a *chien-mao* month, the meanings would be shifted along; the day *mao* would be the day for establishing, *ch'en* the day for removing, etc. Chou Shou-ch'ang states that today in general, "removing, being solicitous, determining, and grasping are lucky; establishing, filling full, being tranquil, and receiving are the next [lucky days]; to be completed and to open are also lucky; to be closed and to be broken are therefore unlucky. [This is sufficient] to show that this method was already [used] in Han [times]."

Since in this case the eleventh month was the month *chien-tzu*, the interpretations of the branches would accordingly be shifted to mean, *tzu* is to be established, *ch'ou* is to remove, ... *ch'en* is to determine; etc., and thus the interpretation in this passage and on p. 34b above was generated. Wang Mang seems to have made much of this astrological interpretation for the cyclical days.

256

定 之
有 號        It is fixed that the title [of my dynasty] in possessing
天 曰        the empire shall be Hsin.[36.2]
下 新

A calendar for 63 B.C., found by Stein in the limes at Tun-huang (Chavannes, *Docu ments chinois*, p. 10–14) marks these "determining" days by the word 建 after the day containing the "day for establishing" in each month. Chavannes notes that within a month these "days for establishing" (he misunderstands and translates, "points fixes") are twelve days apart, but in two successive months the "days for establishing" are separated by thirteen days. (Since in successive months the sun advances to the next one of the twelve cardinal points, indicated by the twelve branches, the days containing the next branch will be "days for establishing," so that thirteen, not twelve days separate "days for establishing" in successive months.) It is interesting to find this astrological device so popular that it was put into the calendar half a century before the time of Wang Mang.

This precise method of determining lucky and unlucky days seems to have been lost. but the terms, "establishing," "fill full," "be tranquil," etc. are still used; cf. Duyvendak in *T'oung Pao*, v. 32 (1936), p. 297 & n. 3; H. Doré, *Recherches sur les Superstitions en Chine*, Ière partie, tome II ("Var. Sin." no. 34), p. 269; PP. Havret & Chambeau, "Notes Concernant la chronologie chinoise," pp. 29, 30, in *Mélanges sur la chronologie chinoise*, ("Var. Sin.," no. 52).

[36.2] This dynastic title was taken from Wang Mang's previous marquisate of Hsin-tu, just as Emperor Kao's dynastic title came from his previous kingdom of Han.

*Sui-shu* 16: 27a, "The Treatise on the Musical Tubes and the Calendar, Part A," at the end quotes an inscription of the same date as this edict, "In the Later Wei [dynasty], during [the period] Ching-ming [500–503], a man of Ping Province, Wang Hsien-ta, presented one ancient bronze balance, on the top of which there were engraved 81 words. The engraving reads, 'A legal balance in which the picul has the weight of four *chün*.' It said also [the remainder of this inscription is also to be found on Wang Mang's Standard Measure, cf. *Chin-shih-so*, chin, 2: 51b, 52a. It is explained in Ma Heng, *The Fifteen Different Classes of Measures as given in the Lü Li Chih of the Sui Dynasty History*, trans. by John C. Ferguson, p. 5, 6],

" 'The Yellow Lord was my original ancestor. In a cycle, his virtue came to Yü [Shun]. Lord Yü [Shun] was my first ancestor. In a cycle, his virtue came to the Hsin [dynasty]. When the planet Jupiter was in Ta-liang [Taurus] and the [Azure] Dragon [the hypothetical symmetrically placed and retrograding correlate of Jupiter] [was in *mou-ch'en* (these words are omitted in the *Sui History* by a dittographic lapse, but are found in the *Chin-shih-so* and are needed for the rhythm)], on [the day] *mou-ch'en*, which was a day for founding, [Jan. 10, A.D. 9], by the mandate of Heaven, a [certain] commoner [the *Sui History* reads "man" because of the taboo in T'ang times on the word *ming*, "commoner"], who depended upon the virtue of [the element] earth, received his dynastic title, ascended [the throne as] the actual [Emperor], and changed the first [month of the year to be the astronomical] second month. May he have long life, be eminent, and prosperous! "He made uniform the musical tubes, the measures of length, the measures of capacity, and the weights" [a quotation from the *Book of History* II, I, iii, 8 (Legge, p. 35)], investi-

"Let there be a change in the first day of the first month, an alternation in the colors of the [court] robes, a variation in the sacrifical victims, a difference in the standards and pennons, and a diversity in the utensils and institutions.    Let the first day of the

Jan. 15.    twelfth month, [the day] *kuei-yu*, become the first day of the first month in the first year of [the year-period Shih]-chien-kuo,[36.3] and let the crowing of the

36b    cock be the hour.[36.4]    The colors of robes shall match the virtue [of the ruling element, earth, so that] yellow shall be esteemed.    The sacrificial victims

*35b*    shall correspond to the first month, and so shall be

其改正朔易服色變犧牲殊徽
慨異器制已十二月朔癸酉為
建國元年正月之朔已雞鳴為
時服色配德上黃犧牲應正用

gating so that they are in accordance with [those of] the ancients.    When the [Azure] Dragon was in Chi-szu and the planet Jupiter was in Shih-shen [the constellation Pi, i.e., in the next Chinese year, A.D. 9], [this regulation] was first proclaimed to the empire, so that all countries should forever obey it from generation to generation and it should be enjoyed and transmitted for a hundred thousand years.'

"This [balance] was also made under Wang Mang.    At that time the Chief of the Great Music, Kung-sun Ch'ung 公孫崇 [not mentioned in the *HS* or *HHS*], first prepared and evaluated the foot [measure] according to the Han institutions.    Moreover we see that this weight is an evaluation of the Hsin [dynasty], which evaluated it, [so that one picul] should weigh 120 catties.    The evaluation and the weights of the Hsin [dynasty] were according to [Wang Mang's] portents and documents, so that they were entrusted to [Kung-sun] Ch'ung."

[36.3] Liu Pin notes that Wang Mang named this new period Shih-chien-kuo and suggests that the word *shih* 始 has dropped out of the text.

The year was now to begin with the second (*chien-ch'ou*) astronomical month, not, as previously, with the third (*chien-yin*) astronomical month.    This change was made in order to follow Tung Chung-shu's doctrine of triple dynastic beginnings, in accordance with which the Han dynasty ruled by virtue of the black dynastic beginning, so that the next dynasty would rule by virtue of the white dynastic beginning 白統.    Cf. Ku Chieh-kang, *Ku-shih-pien* V, 443, 599.    In A.D. 23, the rebels against Wang Mang changed back to the Han practise of beginning the year with the third astronomical month.    Ho Ch'uo remarks that in A.D. 237, Emperor Ming of the Wei dynasty, Ts'ao Jui, again changed and used the second astronomical month as the first month of the year, but his son Fang changed the first month back to the third astronomical month when he ascended the throne in 240.

[36.4] Hu San-hsing remarks that the second double-hour, *ch'ou* (1–3 a.m.), was now taken as the beginning of the day, just as the *chien-ch'ou* month was taken as the first month. The justification of this change was the same as that for the change in the first month of the year; cf. n. 36.3.

white.[36.5] The pennons and banners of commissioners' credentials shall all be made pure yellow. The writing on them shall be, 'Credentials of the Five Majestic [Principles] for Commissioners of the Hsin [Dynasty],' to accord with the majestic mandate of August Heaven and the Lords on High."

[36.5] Hu San-hsing explains, "[Wang Mang] considered that [the element] earth succeeded to that of fire, [which latter was the element taken by the Han dynasty], hence he took, [as the imperial color], the [color] yellow. All things knot (niu 紐) their sprouts in the ch'ou 丑 ([astronomical] second month, [which was the former calendrical twelfth month]). Its color is white. [Wang Mang] hence responded to the first [month of his calendar year] by employing white." Shuo-wen 14 B: 7a, sub ch'ou (which is the word used to denote the second astronomical month) says, "To knot (niu [a play on words, found in Huai-nan-tzu ch. 3; Mh III, 306; etc.]). In the twelfth [calendrical] month, all things move and [begin to] act. It symbolizes the shape of a fist." The color yellow is that of the element earth, which, according to the Liu Hsiang's theory of the succession of the elements, followed the element fire, the element by virtue of which the Han dynasty ruled; cf. 99 C: n. 24.1; Ku Chieh-Kang, Ku-shih-pien, V, 599. The color of the sacrificial victims, white, was taken from Tung Chung-shu's triple theory; cf. n. 36.3. Wang Mang was using eclectically the theories of both these great Han teachers.

259

## [Chapter] XCIX

## THE SIXTY-NINTH MEMOIR
### The Memoir of Wang Mang

### PART B

I
A.D. 9,
Jan. 15.
The
Dynasty
Changed.

In [the year-period] Shih-chien-kuo, the first year, the first month, on the first day of the month, [Wang] Mang led the highest ministers, marquises, high ministers, and gentlemen to offer the imperial seal and [ceremonial] apron[1.1] of an Empress Dowager and present it to the Grand Empress Dowager [nee Wang,[1.2] in order to] obey the mandate [given through] the portents and do away with her title from the Han [dynasty].

An
Heir-
Apparent
Appointed.

Previously, [Wang] Mang had married a daughter of the Marquis of Yi-ch'un[a], [Wang Hsien[2a]], who was surnamed Wang.[1.3] She was made the Empress.

始建國元年正月朔莽帥公
王莽傳第六十九中
侯卿士奉皇太后璽紱上太
皇太后順符命去漢號焉初
莽妻宜春侯王氏女立為皇

[1.1] Wang Hsien-shen (1859–1922) points out that in the parallel passage, 98: 14a[12], the term $fu_1$ 韍 is written $fu_2$ 紱. Seemingly the Grand Empress Dowager's ceremonial apron was made of silk instead of leather, as befits a lady, and the word for this article, when the article is made of silk, could be written with the silk radical as early as the time of Wang Mang or of Pan Ku; cf. 99 A: n. 18.3.

[1.2] The Grand Empress Dowager bitterly opposed Wang Mang's usurpation of the imperial title; she possessed the Ch'in dynasty's imperial seal, which Chao Tzu-ying had surrendered to Emperor Kao, and which was called "The seal whereby the Han dynasty transmits the state 漢傳國璽." When Wang Mang asked for this important seal, she refused to give it up, saying that Wang Mang was worse than a pig or dog. She was however compelled by threats to give up this seal and she accepted the Hsin dynasty's seal. But secretly she continued certain of the Han dynasty's practises, which Wang Mang had abolished. Cf. 98: 13a–15a; Glossary *sub* Wang, Grand Empress Dowager nee.

Wang Mang made her his Empress Dowager, i.e., instead of being the grandmother of a Han emperor, she became the (adopted) mother of the Hsin emperor. Wang Mang later wore mourning for her as for his own mother; cf. 99 B: 21b.

[1.3] The Wang clan of Yi-ch'un was not related to the Wang clan of Yüan-ch'eng, to which Wang Mang belonged, so that this marriage was considered quite proper; cf. 99 B: 6a & n. 6.4.

又曰其曰平原安德漂陰高重丘凡戸萬地方百里為定安公國立漢祖
命靡常封爾為定安公永為新室賓於戲敬天之休住踐迺位毋慶于命
太祖歷世十二享國二百一十載歷數在于于躬詩不云乎侯服于周天
為功昭公利為功著公大赦天下莽迺策命孺子曰咨爾嬰昔皇天右迺
嘉辟封宇子六人千為功隆公壽為功明公吉為功成公宗為功崇公世
后本生四男字獲安臨二子前誅死安顏荒忽迺曰臨為皇太子安為新

She had originally given birth to four boys: Yü₃, Huo_b, An₁ₐ, and Lin₁ₐ. Two sons had previously been executed. [Wang] An₁ₐ's mind was almost completely gone, so [Wang Mang] made [Wang] Lin₁ₐ the Imperial Heir-apparent, and made [Wang] An₁ₐ the Admirable Prince of the Hsin [House. Wang Mang] enfeoffed the six sons of [Wang] Yü: [Wang] Ch'ien₂ as Duke of Prospering Merits, [Wang] Shou as Duke of Brilliant Merits, [Wang] Chi₅_b as Duke of Perfected Merits, [Wang] Tsung as Duke of Eminent Merits, [Wang] Shih as Duke of Shining Merits, and [Wang] Li₄ as Duke of Marked Merits. A general amnesty [was granted] to the empire.

[Wang] Mang thereupon gave a charter-mandate to the Young Prince [Liu Ying₁ₐ], which said, " 'O thou'[1.4] Ying! Anciently, August Heaven assisted the Grand Founder of your [dynasty, Emperor Kao, so that his descendants] succeeded [each other] for twelve reigns and enjoyed the state for two hundred ten years. 'The [Heaven]-determined order of succession rests upon my person.'[1.5] Does not the *Book of Odes* say, 'They became subject to the Chou [dynasty, for] the mandate of Heaven is not constant'?[1.6] I enfeoff you as the Duke of Established Tranquillity, forever to be a guest of the Hsin House. Alas! Reverence the beneficence of Heaven. Go and take your position and do not neglect my commands."

It also said, "Let a region a hundred *li* square, with altogether ten thousand households in [the prefectures of] P'ing-yüan, An-tê, T'a-yin, Ko, and Chung-ch'iu become the state of the Duke of Established Tranquillity, and let there be set up a temple to his ancestors, [the Emperors] of the Han [dy-

**1b**
1b
The Han
Young
Prince is
Dismissed.
1b

---

[1.4] A phrase from *Analects* XX, i, 1.

[1.5] A quotation from *Book of History*, II, ii, 14 (Legge, p. 61) and *Analects* XX, i, 1.

[1.6] *Book of Odes*, ※235; III, ɪ, i, 5 (Legge, p. 430).

The
Han
Young
Prince.

nasty], at his state, just as [was done] for the descendants of the Chou [dynasty].[1.7] Let him carry on the first day of the [Han] first month and the colors of the robes of that [dynasty],[1.8] from generation to generation serving his ancestors, so that they may eternally, because of their famous[1.9] virtue and abundant achievements, enjoy sacrifices for successive generations. Let the Empress [nee Wang] of [Emperor] Hsiao-p'ing become the Duchess Dowager of Established Tranquillity."

When the reading of the charter was ended, [Wang] Mang himself grasped the hand of the Young Prince, dropped tears, and sighed, saying, "Anciently, when the Duke of Chou had the position of regent, he was finally able to 'return [the government] to his intelligent prince.'[1.10] [But] now, only [because] I am pressed by the majestic mandate of August Heaven, am I unable to follow my intention [to return the government to you]." He sorrowed and sighed for a long time. A Palace Tutor took the Young Prince down below the Hall, faced him north, and pronounced him a subject [of the new dynasty]. None of the many lower officials who acted as assistants to those who had positions [in the court at this ceremony] failed to be moved and influenced.

2a

2a

The
Ministers
Ennobled.

The coadjuting ministers were moreover all enfeoffed and installed according to [the list in] the metal casket. The Grand Tutor Assisting on the Left and General of Agile Cavalry, the Marquis of An-yang, Wang Shun[4b], became the Grand Master and was enfeoffed as the Duke Giving Tranquillity to the Hsin [Dynasty]. The Grand Master over the Masses, the Marquis Conforming to Virtue, P'ing

皆封拜曰太傅左輔驃騎將軍安陽侯王舜為太師封安新公大司徒就
良久中傅將孺子下殿北面而稱臣百僚陪位莫不感動又按金匱輔臣
獻教曰昔周公攝位終得復子明辟今子獨迫皇天威命不得如意哀歎
功享歷代之祀焉呂孝平皇后為定安太后讀策畢親執孺子手流涕
宗之廟於其國與周後並行其正朔服色世世曰事其祖宗永曰命德茂

---

[1.7] Cf. *HS* 6: 19a; 12: 7a.

[1.8] Hu San-hsing remarks caustically, "All these were empty words." Cf. 99 B: 2b.

[1.9] Wang Hsien-ch'ien notes that 命 and 名 were anciently interchanged.

[1.10] A quotation of *Book of History* V, xiii, 1 (Legge, p. 434) for the third time in this chapter.

德侯平晏為太傅就新公少阿義和京兆尹紅休侯劉歆為國師嘉新公

廣漢梓潼哀章為國將美新公是為四輔位上公太保後承陽侯甄邯

為大司馬承新公至進侯王尋為大司徒章新公步兵將軍成都侯王邑

為大司空隆新公是為三公大阿右拂大司空衛將軍廣陽侯甄豐為更

始將軍廣新公京兆王興為衛將軍奉新公輕車將軍武侯孫建為立

國將軍成新公京兆王盛為前將軍崇新公是為四將凡十一公王興者

Yen, became the Grand Tutor and the Duke Con- *2a* forming to the Hsin [Dynasty]. The Junior Supporter, the Hsi-and-Ho and Governor of the Capital, the Marquis of Hung-and-Hsiu, Liu Hsin[1a], became the State Master and the Duke Honoring the Hsin [Dynasty].[2.1] Ai Chang, from Tzu[3a]-t'ung in Kuanghan [Commandery], became the State General and the Duke Beautifying the Hsin [Dynasty]. The foregoing were the Four Coadjutors. Their rank was that of the highest rank of the highest [ministers].

The Grand Guardian Serving at the Rear, the Marquis of Ch'eng-yang, Chen Han, became the Commander-in-chief and the Duke Serving the Hsin [Dynasty]. The Marquis Making Great Efforts, Wang Hsün[3], became the Grand Minister over the Masses and the Duke Ornamenting the Hsin [Dynasty]. The General of Foot-soldiers, the Marquis of Ch'eng-tu[b], Wang Yi[5], became the Grand Minister of Works and the Duke Prospering the Hsin [Dynasty]. The foregoing were the three highest ministers.

The Grand Supporter Aiding on the Right, the Grand Minister of Works and General of the Guard, the Marquis of Kuang-yang, Chen Feng, became the General of a New Beginning and the Duke Extending the Hsin [Dynasty]. Wang Hsing[a], from the im- *2b* perial capital, became the General of the Guard and the Duke Upholding the Hsin [Dynasty]. The General of Light Chariots, the Marquis of Ch'eng-wu, Sun Chien, became the General Establishing the State and the Duke Perfecting the Hsin [Dynasty]. Wang Sheng, from the imperial capital, became the General of the Van and the Duke Exalting the Hsin [Dynasty]. The foregoing were the Four Generals. Altogether there were eleven highest ministers.

[2.1] The Sung Ch'i ed. says that Chin Shao's *HS Yin-yi* reads 陭 for 阿. Wang Hsiench'ien says that the Southern ed. (poss. x cent., or the Southern Academy ed., 1531) reads 林 for 休. The Ching-yu ed. agrees with our text.

Wang Hsing<sub>a</sub> was a former clerk to a Prefect of a

**2b** City-gate,[2.2] and Wang Sheng had been a seller of cakes. In accordance with the mandate [given through] the portent, [Wang] Mang sought out and secured more than ten persons with these surnames and given names. These two persons' features responded to divination and physiognomization, so they were elevated directly from [the condition of] wearing plain clothes and were given [these high] offices, in order to show that it was a supernatural [matter]. The other persons [with these surnames and given names] were all installed as Gentlemen. On this day, altogether several hundred persons were enfeoffed and installed in the offices of high ministers, grandees, Palace Attendants, and Masters of Writing. Those [members of] the Liu [clan] who had been

*2b* Commandery Administrators were all changed to be Grandee-remonstrants.

His Daughter.  [The name of] the Ming-kuang Palace was changed to be the Lodge of Established Tranquillity, and the Duchess Dowager of Established Tranquillity inhabited it.

Liu Ying's Resting.  The yamen of the former[2.3] Grand Herald was made the residence of the Duke of Established Tranquillity, [Liu Ying<sub>1a</sub>]. At both of these [residences] there were established guards for the gates, and commissioners inspected and directed them. It was ordered that [Liu Ying<sub>1a</sub>'s] nurses[2.4] and wet-nurses should not be permitted to talk with him. He was

---

[2.2] Hu San-hsing explains, " 'A clerk to a Prefect of a City-gate' served a Colonel of a City-gate. He had charge of writings."

[2.3] The Sung Ch'i ed. states that the Shao ed. (xi or xii cent.) has not the word 故, but the New ed. (unknown) inserts it. The Ching-yu ed. lacks it.

[2.4] Wang Nien-sun (1744–1832) asserts that the word *pao* 保 should be inserted after the *o* 阿, in accordance with *Han-chi* 30: 10b. He declares that *pao* and *o* are always used together, that without *pao* the phrasing would not be good and the meaning (merely "wet-nurses," omitting the other nurses) would not be complete. In *HS* 75: 26a, a similar phrasing, *pao-o*, is read.

故城門令史王盛者賣餅苯按符命求得此姓名十餘人

兩人容貌應卜相徑從布衣登用呂視神馬餘皆拜為郎

是日封拜卿大夫侍中尚書官凡數百人諸劉為郡守皆

征為諫大夫改明光宮為定安館定安太后居之呂故大

鴻臚府為定安公第皆置門衛使者監領敖阿乳母不得

與　六　宇　司
語　於　于　曰
常　高　妻　歲
在　後　之　星
四　莽　恭　司
壁　呂　萊　肅
中　女　策　東
　　孫　摹

constantly [kept] within the four walls [of his residence, so that] when he grew up, he could not name
the six [kinds of] domestic animals.  Later [Wang]
Mang married him to his granddaughter (a child of    3a
[Wang] Yü₃).[2.5]

[Wang] Mang's charters to his various high offi-    Charters
cials said: "As [the planet] Jupiter presides over    to ▓▓
'respectfulness,'[2.6] so [the Chief of] the Eastern    Ministers.

[2.5] Yang Shu-ta, in his "Examples of Historical Method in the *HS*," *Yenching Jour. of
Chin. Studies*, no. 3, June, 1928, p. 441 f, states that the phrase, "a child of [Wang] Yü,"
is an example of Pan Ku's use of author's explanatory notes—a practise first used by him
in a historical work.  Since the practise of writing annotations in smaller characters was
not invented until a generation later (Ma Jung is said to have first used it in his edition
of the *Chou-li*, A.D. 138–40; cf. Maspero, "Melanges Chinois et Bouddhiques," *Inst.
Belge des Hautes Etudes Chinoises*, I [1931–32], p. 183), Pan Ku had to insert such an
annotation into the text as a phrase in apposition with the term explained, which ap-
pository phrase accordingly interrupts the sentence.  Yang Shu-ta instances seven other
examples from different parts of the *HS*.  Perhaps this use of explanatory notes was taken
by Pan Ku from official documents such as the edict of Wang Mang to be found on
99 B: 25b.

[2.6] This and the next three paragraphs constitute four series of correspondences between (a) four planets (and the corresponding powers or elements), (b) personal qualities,
(c) quarters of the compass, (d) ministers, (e) types of weather, (f) colors, (g) the activities of nature during the four seasons, and (h) measuring instruments:

1. (a) Jupiter (wood), (b) respectfulness, (c) the east, (d) the Grand Master, (e) timely
   rain, (f) cerulean, (g) rising (spring), (h) the sun-dial.
2. (a) Mars (fire), (b) wisdom, (c) the south, (d) the Grand Tutor, (e) timely warmth
   (f) red, (g) enlarging (summer), (h) the musical tubes.
3. (a) Venus (metal), (b) orderliness, (c) the west, (d) the State Master, (e) timely cool
   sunshine, (f) white, (g) taking form (autumn), (h) weighing instruments.
4. (a) Mercury (water), (b) deliberation, (c) the north, (d) the State General (because
   executions [war] were set for the winter), (e) timely cold, (f) black, (g) harmony
   (winter), (h) the clepsydra.

The fifth of these correspondences: (a) Saturn (earth), (b) sageness, (c) the center, (e)
timely wind, (f) yellow, (g) (no season), is omitted, because this series corresponds to
(d) the King, Wang Mang.

Among these correspondences, (b) and (e) are quoted from the "Great Plan," *Book
of History* V, iv, verses 6 & 34 respectively (Legge, 327, 340; Couvreur, 198, 207), as
Prof. Duyvendak points out.  The powers or elements, colors, and directions are those
assigned to these planets, but their order is not the same as that of the corresponding
powers or elements in *op. cit.* V, iv, 5 (Legge, 325; Couvreur, 197), probably in order to

Charters
to
Ministers.

[Sacred] Peak[2.7] and Grand Master has charge of bringing 'timely rains.' As its cerulean splendor enlarges tranquillity, so he investigates [the sun's] shadow by the sundial."[2.8]

"As [the planet] Mars presides over 'wisdom',[2.9] so [the Chief of] the Southern [Sacred] Peak and Grand Tutor is in charge of bringing 'timely

**3a** warmth.'[2.10] As its red spendor enlarges tranquillity, so he investigates sounds by the musical tubes."[3.1]

"As [the planet] Venus presides over 'orderliness,' so [the Chief of] the Western [Sacred] Peak and

平考聲呂律太白司艾西
微太傳典致時奧赤煒頌
平考景呂醫筮怱司怒南
微太師典致時雨青煒登

enable the imperial virtue, sageness, to be coupled with Wang Mang's elemnet, earth Liu Hsiang wrote a "Discussion of the Tradition Concerning the Five Powers in the 'Great Plan' [of the *Book of History*] 洪範五行傳論," which is lost, and most of these correspondences may have come from that book, *SC* ch. 27, or one of the various other works of this sort written in Han times. Cf. the correspondences in Couvreur, *Dict. Classique*, iii ed., p. 1059.

The planet Jupiter was supposed to punish injustice and disrespectfulness; cf. *Mh* III, 356.

[2.7] Chin Shao (fl. ca. 275) explains, "All things are brought to birth in the eastern quarter [spring], hence he warned the Grand Master."

Wang Hsien-ch'ien declares that 獄 is an error; the Ching-yu ed., the Official ed. and the Southern Academy ed. read 嶽 at this point and below.

[2.8] Fu Chien declares that 煒 is pronounced the same as 暉 (*hui*). Ju Shun explains, "[It is] the brilliance of the cerulean [springtime] emanation," and Chin Shao adds, "It means that cerulean is the emanation of the *yang* principle, which first rises and goes upwards in order to complete all things. At the vernal and autumnal equinoxes a gnomen is set up to determine [due] east and west. East is where the sun first rises [at the equinoxes], hence 'its shadow is examined by the sun-dial' belongs to [the planet Jupiter]."

[2.9] Mars was supposed to punish violations of the rites by unusual heat; cf. *Mh* III, 364. Ying Shao glosses, "[Mars] punishes [lack of wisdom] by prolonged heat."

[2.10] Chin Shao comments, "The southern quarter is the seat whence the *yang* principle rises."

[3.1] Chin Shao explains, "*Yung* 頌 is 寬頌 (enlarge, be liberal, pardon). [Yen Shih-ku explains *yung* as 容. These two words are interchanged.] Summer 夏 [archaic pronunciation g'å] [means] 假 (to enlarge [archaic pronunciation kå; an assonance]. Things grow large, whereupon they manifest their tranquillity. The sixth month [is the time for] the beginning of the *yin* emanation, hence the earth is made to rule. 'The middle number of earth is six. Six is the musical tube, [*huang-chung*]. The musical tube has a shape and a color. Its ruling color is yellow.' [A quotation from *HS* 21 A: 5b]. Hence 'investigating the sounds by the musical tubes' belongs to [the planet Mars]."

嚴　考　將　曰
國　量　典　淵
師　呂　致　月
典　銓　時　刊
致　辰　寒　元
時　星　玄　股
陽　司　煒　左
白　謀　和　司
煒　北　平　馬
衆　嶽　考　典
平　國　星　致

State Master has charge of bringing 'timely sunshine.'[3.2] As its white splendor gives form to tran-   *3a*
quillity, so he investigates measures of capacity by
weighing instruments."[3.3]

"As [the planet] Mercury presides over 'deliberation,' so [the Chief of] the Northern [Sacred] Peak
and State General has charge of bringing 'timely   *3b*
cold.'[3.4] As its sombre brilliance harmonizes tranquillity, so he investigates the planets by the clepsydra."[3.5]

"As the Moon [has charge of] punishments, and is
the great limb[3.6] [of the heavenly powers], so the
Commander-[in-chief] on the left has charge of
bringing about military responses [to evil deeds.

[3.2] Ying Shao explains, "When [a person's] words are not in accordance [with the Way],
this is what is meant by not-*yi* 艾. *Yi* makes peaceful 安. The punishment for [failing
to do] this is always [a superabundance of the principle] *yang*. *Yang* brings drought."
Instead of *yang* 陽, *Book of History* V, iv, 34 has 睗, cool sunshine. Yen Shih-ku adds,
"*Yi* should be read as 乂." *Mh* III, 371 states that Venus presides over killing and
punishes murder.

[3.3] Ying Shao explains, "The measures of capacity 量 are the *tou* and *hu*. 銓 are the
steelyard and balances 權衡." Chin Shao adds, "All things perfect their forms in the
western quarter [autumn, so that] their size and weight may all be known. Hence scales
and 'measures of capacity' belong to [the planet Venus]."

[3.4] Ying Shao explains, "To listen to a person [but] without attentiveness, this is what
is meant by not deliberating well. *Mou* 謀 is 圖. The punishment [for failing to do]
this is prolonged cold." Chin Shao adds, "North is to be prostrated. When the *yang*
emanation is prostrate underneath [the earth], the *yin* principle has charge of killing.
Hence he has the State General guard against it." *Mh* III, 379 says that Mercury
punishes for incorrect punishments.

[3.5] Ying Shao explains, "We investigate the courses and degrees of the five planets by
the clepsydra and its divisions." Chin Shao adds, "*Ho* 和 is to unite 合. All things
are all united and stored in the northern quarter [winter]. Mercury is also in charge of
peace, hence he said, 'harmonizes tranquillity.' The regulations for the calendar arise
from [the constellation] Tou [the Bushel, Ursa Major], which distinguishes the revolutions
of the sun and moon by [the constellation] She-t'i [η, τ, ν; ο, π, ς Bootes]. She-t'i occupies
the place where the handle of the Bushel points, and is used to establish the seasons and
the [twenty-four] solar terms, hence 'investigating the planets' belongs to [the planet
Mercury]."

[3.6] I.e., executive; the officials were considered to be the "arms and legs" of the
Emperor.

[Charters ▮▮▮ to Ministers.]

As we] investigate squareness[3.7] by the standard of the try-square, so he has charge of presiding over astrological phenomena, 'reverently in accordance with [the observation] of the vast heavens, to deliver the seasons respectfully to the common people,'[3.8] and to give stimulation and encouragement to agricultural pursuits, in order [to bring about] an abundant harvest of grain."

"As the Sun has charge of virtues[3.9] and is the great arm [of the heavenly powers, so] the [Grand] Minister over the Masses on the right has charge of bringing auspicious presages [concerning] civil [matters]. As a circle is investigated by testing it with the compasses,[3.10] so he has charge of presiding over human ways. The 'five [fundamental] teachings' are to be supported by him. He is to lead the common people, to receive [commands] from the throne, to propagate and beautify the customs and usages, and the five grades [of people will be well] instructed."[3.11]

**3b**

武應考方法矩主司天文欽若
吳天敬授民時力來農事日豐
年敎日德元左右司徒典致文
瑞考圓合規主司人道五敎是
輔卹民承上宣美風俗五品畫

[3.7] The earth was thought to be square and heaven round; both the moon and the earth are *yin*; hence heavenly phenomena that concern the earth (astrology) belong to the commander-in-chief.

[3.8] A quotation from *Book of History* 2: 5b; I, ii, 3 (Legge, p. 18).

[3.9] "Virtue" is to be taken in its ancient meaning of "power." "Arm" denotes "executive"; cf. n. 3.6.

[3.10] Chin Shao explains, "The arms [can be made into the shape of] a circle, [as the limbs form right angles]. When 'the five [things that must be] taught are [taught] with gentleness' [a quotation from *Book of History* II, I, v, 19 (Legge, p. 44; Couvreur, p. 26)], then a filial attitude of submission influences creatures and things and the **four** supernatural animals [probably: unicorn, phoenix, tortoise, dragon] appear. Hence 'auspicious presages [concerning] civil [matters]' belongs to [the Sun]."

[3.11] Yen Shih-ku explains, " 'The five [fundamental] teachings (*wu-chiao* 五敎)' [a phrase from *Book of History* II, I, v, 19 (Legge, p. 44)] means the justice (*yi*) of a father, the kindliness (*tz'u*) of a mother, the friendliness (*yu*) of an elder brother, the respectfulness (*kung*) of a younger brother, and the filial piety (*hsiao*) of a son. [This interpretation comes from *Tso-chuan*, Dk. Wen, XVIII (Legge, 280[8], 283a). *Mencius* III, I, iv, 8 (Legge, p. 251f) has a slightly different list.] The five grades (*wu-p'in* 五品) are the five social usages (*wu-ch'ang* 五常), which means benevolence (*jen*), righteousness (*yi*), proper conduct (*li*), wisdom (*chih*), and trustworthiness (*hsin*)." The K'ung An-kuo

訓斗平元心中司空典致物圖考度呂繩主司地里平治水土

掌名山川衆殖鳥獸蕃草木各策命呂其職如典諮之文置

大司馬司允大司徒司直大司空司若位皆孤卿更名大司農

大理曰作士太常曰秩宗大鴻臚曰典樂

曰義和後更為納言

"[As the constellation of the Northern] Bushel [has charge of] balancing [i.e., judging][3.12] and is the great **heart** [(or center) of heaven], so in the center the [Grand] Minister of Works has charge of preparing designs [i.e., planning] for (animate and inanimate) things. As length is investigated by the [carpenter's] line, so he has charge of presiding over *3b 4a* the principles of geographical arrangements, of balancing and ruling the waters and the earth, and is in charge of [the spirits of] the famous mountains and streams, of multiplying birds and beasts, and of making grass and trees luxurious and abundant."

[Wang Mang thus] gave a charter-mandate to each one according to his duties, [using] words like those in the "Canons" and the "Announcements."[3.13] He established a Director of Confidence in the Commander-in-chief, a Director of Uprightness to the Grand Minister over the Masses, and a Director of Obedience to the Grand Minister of Works, whose positions were those of senior high ministers.

He [had previously] changed the title of the Grand Minister of Agriculture to be the Hsi-and-Ho,[3.14] and later changed it to be the Communicator. The Grand Judge was called the Deciding Judge, the Grand Minister of Ceremonies was called the Arranger of the Ancestral Temples, the Grand Herald was called the Director of Music, the Privy Treasurer

**Titles Changed.**

interpretation of the above passage from the *Book of History* (*Shang-shu Chu-su* 3: 13a) however states that the five grades are the five social usages and K'ung Ying-ta (*ibid.*, 3: 13b) explains that the five grades are "the differences of honor within one family, namely, father, mother, elder, younger brother, and son, who are taught by justice, kindliness, friendliness, respectfulness, and filial piety"—the same list as that for the five fundamental teachings, which accordingly fits better here than Yen Shih-ku's list (which comes from Wang Ch'ung).

[3.12] *SC* 27: 6 = *Mh* III, 341 states that the constellation Po-tou (the Northern Bushel) is the jade balance.

[3.13] "Canon" is part of the title to *Book of History* I, bk. i and II, bk i; "Announcement" is similarly part of the title to *op. cit.* V, bks. vii, ix, x, xii, and xiii.

[3.14] This change had been made in 1 A.D. Cf. 12: 3b.

**New Titles.** was called the Provider of Works, and the Chief Commandant of Waters and Parks was called the My Forester. [These six officials], with the [three senior] high ministers who were directors to the three highest ministers were together [ranked as] the nine high ministers. They were divided and [each] made subordinate to [some one of] the three highest ministers. For each high minister there were established three grandees, and for each grandee there were established three First Officers, so that altogether there were twenty-seven grandees and eighty-one First Officers.[3.15] They were separately put in charge of the various duties in the offices of the imperial capital.

He changed the title of the Superintendant of the Imperial Household to be the Director of Palaces, the Grand Coachman to be the Grand[3.16] Charioteer, the Commandant of the Palace Guard to be the Grand[3.16] Guard, the Bearer of the Gilded Mace to be the Inciter to Military Deeds, and the [Colonel of] the Capital [Encampments][3.17] to be the Chief of the Army. He also established the office of Grand Keeper of the Robes, who had charge of the imperial chariots of state, robes, and imperial articles. Later [this officer] also had charge of troops. The ranks and positions [of the foregoing six officials] were all those of the highest [rank] of the high ministers; they were entitled the Six Superintendants.

[The titles of] Grand Administrators of com-

4a
4b

置大贊官主乘輿服御物後又典兵秩位皆上卿號曰六
太僕曰太御衛尉曰太衛執金吾曰奮武中尉曰軍正又
大夫八十一元士分主中都官諸職更名光祿勳曰司中
三公每一卿置大夫三人一大夫置元士三人凡二十七
少府曰共工水衛都尉曰予虞與三公卿凡九卿分屬

---

[3.15] These titles for the grades and the number of officials in each grade are taken from Tung Chung-shu's *Ch'un-ch'iu Fan-lu*, 7: 10a, ch. 24, "Kuan-chih Hsiang-Tien."

[3.16] Li Tz'u-ming, *HS Cha-chi*, 7: 15b, suggests that the first word in 太御 and 太衛 was originally 大, as in 大贊 (Grand Keeper of the Robes) and 大尹 (Grand Governor). The Ching-yu ed. at this point and on the next page and Wang Hsien-ch'ien's text of *HS* 99 B: 28a actually read 大衛.

[3.17] The text reads,' 'the Commandant of the Capital 中尉," but that title had been changed in 104 B.C. to Bearer of the Gilded Mace, so that it is out of place here. Liu Pin suggests that the text should read 中壘校尉, the two middle characters of which have dropped out. I have followed this emendation.

監改部太守曰大尹都尉曰太尉縣令長曰宰御史曰執法公車司
馬曰王路四門長樂宮曰常樂室未央宮曰壽成室前殿曰王路堂
長安曰常安更名秩百石曰庶士三百石曰下士四百石曰中士五
百石曰命士六百石曰元士千石曰下大夫比二千石曰中大夫二
千石曰上大夫中二千石曰卿車服黻冕各有差品又置司恭司徒

manderies were changed to be Grand Governors, [commandery] Chief Commandants were called Grand Commandants, Prefects and Chiefs of prefectures were called Rulers, [Attending] Secretaries *4a* were called Upholders of the Laws, the Majors in Charge of Official Carriages were called [the Directors of] the Four Gates to the Royal Apartments.

The Ch'ang$_1$-lo Palace was called the Ch'ang$_2$-lo House, the Wei-yang (Never Completed) Palace was called the Shou-ch'eng House (the House Where a Long Life is Perfected), the Front Hall was called the Hall with the Royal Apartments, and Ch'ang$_1$-an was called Ch'ang$_2$-an.

The names of the [civil] ranks were changed: the [occupants of positions ranking at] 100 piculs were called Common Officers, the [occupants of positions ranking at] 300 piculs were called Lower-ranking Officers, the [occupants of positions ranking at] 400 piculs were called Middle-ranking Officers, the [occupants of positions ranking at] 500 piculs were called Mandated Officers, the [occupants of positions ranking at] 600 piculs were called First Officers, the [occupants of positions ranking at] 1000 piculs were called Lower-ranking Grandees, the [occupants of positions ranking at] equivalent to 2000 piculs were called Middle-ranking Grandees, the [occupants of positions ranking at] 2000 piculs were called Upper-ranking Grandees, and the [occupants of positions ranking at] fully 2000 piculs were called High Ministers. The carriages, robes, aprons, and mortarboard hats of each [differed according to] their different degrees.

There were also established [the Grandee] in Charge of Respectfulness, [the Grandee] in Charge of Accordance [with the Way,[4.1] the Grandee] in Charge

---

4.1 The text reads, "Minister over the Masses 司徒." Liu Pin suggests emending the last character to 從, and Ch'i Shao-nan points out that this latter term harmonizes with

New
Officials.

of Clearsightedness, [the Grandee] in Charge of Attentiveness, and the Grandee in Charge of Perspicaciousness,[4.2] who, together with the Musician Chanting the Odes and the Ruler for Removing the Viands were to have charge of [the Emperor's] errors. Their charters said,

5a
4b

"I have heard that the sages of the most [ancient times] wished to make their virtues brilliant, so never failed to cultivate their persons carefully, in order that they might tranquillize [everyone, even those] at a distance. For this purpose I have established you to have charge of your 'five activities.'[4.3] Do not hide my faults and do not assist me in vainglory. 'In your likes and dislikes make no errors'[4.4] and hold to the mean. O! Put forth all your efforts!"

[Wang Mang] ordered that the [Directors of Four Gates to] the Royal Apartments should establish the banner for initiating improvements, the post for speaking ill and criticizing,[4.5] and the drum for those who dare to admonish.[4.6] Four Grandee-remonstrants were regularly seated at the Gates to the

善之雄非謗之木欲諫之鼓諫大夫四人常坐王路門受言
母隱尤母將虛好惡不愆立于厥中於戲勗哉令王路設進
聖欲昭厥德固不慎修厥身用綏于遠是用建爾司于五事
司明司聰司中大夫及誦詩工微膳宰曰司過策曰于闕上

the rest of this passage, for these titles are taken from *Book of History* V, iv, 6, (Legge, p. 326), the same one from which come the correspondences in n. 2.6.

[4.2] Li Tz'u-ming, in his *HS Cha-chi* 7: 15b suggests that 中 should be 睿; in the *Book of History* (*loc. cit.*), the latter character is used. The former character has previously been used for the Director of Palaces, so would not be used here.

[4.3] The "five activities" are, according to *ibid.*: demeanor, speech, seeing, hearing, and thinking, the virtues of which are those mentioned in the first five titles of the preceding paragraph.

[4.4] A quotation from *Tso-chuan*, Dk Chao XV, (Legge 657[10], 659a).

[4.5] For these two articles, cf. *HFHD* I, 243, n. 4; p. 244, n. 1.

[4.6] The text reads 欲; Wang Nien-sun says it should be 敢 in accordance with the Ching-yu ed. (1035) and the parallel phrase in *HS* 48: 23b.

The "drum for those who dare to admonish" is mentioned in the *Ta-Tai Li* (compiled i cent. A.D.) 3: 3a, ch. 48 (Wilhelm, *Li Gi*, p. 219), and Liu Pien (fl. 520–557) glosses, "Shun established it. He had those who would admonish, beat it in order that he might himself hear of them." Chia Yi mentions it in a memorial which alludes to that passage (*HS* 48: 23b). K'ung Kuang-sen (1752–1786) adds, "The ordinance of Yü said, 'Those who would teach Us concerning the Way should strike the drum.'" *Chou-li* 31: 7b, 8a

事者封王氏齊縗之屬為侯大功為
伯小功為子緦麻為男其女皆為任
男呂睦女呂隆為號馬皆授印韍
諸侯立太夫人夫人世子亦受印韍

King's Apartments to receive those who would speak of matters.

The members of the Wang clan who were related [closely enough so that they would wear] the one-year's mourning were enfeoffed as Marquises, [those who would wear] the nine-months' mourning became Earls, [those who would wear] the five-months' mourning became Viscounts, and [those who would wear] the three-months' mourning became Barons. The females all became Baronesses. The males all had Mu (concord) and the females had Lung (prosperous) in their titles.[4.7] All received seals and cords.

*Nobilities for the Wang Clan.*

*4b*

[Wang Mang] ordered that for the nobles there should be appointed Ladies Dowager, Ladies, and Heirs, who would also receive seals and cords.

(Biot, II, 226) declares that the *T'ai-p'u* "places the drum for the royal apartments outside the gate to the main part of the royal apartments and has charge of controlling it [beating it to announce the time]. It awaits those who would communicate their misfortunes and those who transmit ordinances. When [the *T'ai-p'u*] hears the sound of the drum, he then quickly receives [the report of] the *Yü-p'u* or the *Yü-shu-tzu* [which two officials were in attendance upon the drum, to take the complaint or report of the person who had struck the drum]." Cheng Chung (ca. 5 B.C.–83 A.D.) comments, "It is like when those beat a drum who at the present time report matters of grievous vicissitudes to the emperor." Wang Mang, in establishing this drum, is following the teaching of the *Chou-li*.

[4.7] Evidently this rule was not always consistently carried out. Wang Yi₅'s title, Duke Prospering the Hsin Dynasty (*Lung-hsin Kung*) and Liu Fen's title, Marquis Prospering the Majestic Principles (*Lung-wei Hou*) contained the word *lung*, although they were men; Wang Mang's daughters by concubines, Wang Chieh₆ and Wang Yeh₆, were entitled the Baroness of Attained Concord (*Mu-tai Jen*) and the Baroness of Cultivated Concord (*Mu-hsin Jen*), respectively. Wang Mang's grandson, Wang Ch'ien₂ was the Duke whose Merits Prosper (*Kung-lung Kung*). Cf. Glossary *sub vocibus*. Wang Mang's enactments were so multifarious that many were probably forgotten, since card files had not yet been invented. *Mu* and *Lung* were not interchanged, as Stange (p. 126, n. 2) suggests, for Yao Hsün was made Marquis of Original Concord (*Ch'u-mu Hou*), Kuei Ch'ang was made Marquis of the Beginning of Concord (*Shih-mu Hou*), Ch'en Ch'ung was made Marquis of Ruling Concord (*T'ung-mu Hou*), and T'ien Feng was made Marquis of Hereditary Concord (*Shih-mu Hou*), all of whom were considered as imperial relatives, since they were considered descendants of Wang Mang's mythical ancestor, the Yellow Lord.

**Kingly Titles Abolished.**

[His message] also said, " 'Heaven has not two suns, nor has Earth two kings'[4.8]—this is the unchangeable way of all the kings. Some of the nobles of the Han clan were entitled Kings, and even the barbarians [beyond] the four [frontiers] followed [this practise]. It is contrary to the ancient institutions and absurd [in view of the principle that there is only] one sovereign [in the world]. Let it be fixed

**5b**

that the titles of vassal kings shall all be [changed to] Duke, and that those of the barbarians [beyond] the four [frontiers] who have usurped this title and called themselves Kings shall all be changed and become Marquises."

**Ancestral Sacrifices to Ancient Rulers Established.**

It also said: "According to the Way of the [ancient] lords and kings, one followed [the ways of his predecessor, so that [their principles] were transmitted [from one to another]. As a recompense for their abundant virtues for hundreds of generations [after their death] they should enjoy sacrifices. I reflect that the Yellow Lord, the Lord, Shao-hao, the Lord, Chuan-hsü, the Lord, K'u, the Lord, Yao, the Lord, Shun, the Lord, Yü of the Hsia [dynasty],

**5a**

Kao-yao, and Yi Yin all possessed sage virtues and ascended to August Heaven, [becoming gods]. Their achievements were sublime and their brilliance was spread[5.1] to a distance. I esteem them highly and have 'instituted a search'[5.2] for their descendants in order to recompense them by [enfeoffing descendants to] sacrifice to them. Verily, the Wang clan are descendants of the Lord of Yü, [Shun], who was descended from the Lord, K'u, and the Liu clan are descendants of Yao, who was descended from Chuan-hsü."[5.3]

---

[4.8] A quotation from *Mencius* V, I, iv, 1 (Legge, p. 352), where it is said to be a saying of Confucius.

[5.1] The Sung Ch'i ed. states that one text reads 化 for 施.

[5.2] A quotation from *Book of History*, Intro. 28 (Legge, p. 7).

[5.3] According to *SC* 1: 45 = *Mh* I, 71, Shun was a descendant of Chuan-hsü; according to *SC* 1: 21 = *Mh* I, 41, Yao was the son of K'u. Wang Mang is following a different

亦為賓敗俊宋公孔弘運轉次移更封為章昭侯位為恪
漢俊定安公劉嬰位為賓周俊衛公姬黨更封為章平公
帝俊山遵為襄謀子牽皋陶俊伊玄為襄衛子牽伊尹俊
俊國師劉歆子疊為伊休侯奉堯俊嬀昌為始睦侯奉虞
少昊俊皇孫功隆公千奉帝嚳俊劉歆為祁烈伯奉顓頊
顓頊於是封姚徇為初睦侯奉黃帝俊梁護為脩遠伯奉

Thereupon he enfeoffed Yao Hsün as the Marquis of Original Concord to make offerings as the descendant of the Yellow Lord and Liang Hu as the Earl Renewing Distant [Sacrifices] to make offerings as the descendant of Shao-hao. The Imperial Grandson, the Duke of Prospering Merits, [Wang] Ch'ien$_2$, was to make offerings as the descendant of the Lord, K'u. Liu Hsin$_{1b}$ became the Earl of Vast Glories to make offerings as the descendant of Chuan-hsü. [Liu] Tieh, the son to the State Master, Liu Hsin$_{1a}$, became the Marquis of Yi-and-Hsiu, to make offerings as the descendant of Yao. Kuei Ch'ang became the Marquis of the Beginning of Concord to make offerings as the descendant of the Lord of Yü, [Shun]. Shan Tsun became the Viscount as a Recompense for Counsel to make offerings as the descendant of Kao-yao. Yi Hsüan became the Viscount in Recompense to the [Supporting] Governor, to make offerings as the descendant of Yi Yin. The position of the descendant of the Han [dynasty], the Duke of Established Tranquillity, Liu Ting$_{1a}$, was made that of a Guest. [The title of] the descendant of the Chou [dynasty], the Duke of Wei$_8$,[5.4] Chi Tang, was changed, and he was enfeoffed as the Duke of Manifest Peace and was also made a Guest. [The title of] the descendant of the Yin [dynasty], the Duke of Sung, K'ung Hung, whose rank was altered [because of] the change in [the dynasty], was changed, and he was enfeoffed as the Marquis of Manifest Brilliance and his position was made that of a Respected Guest.[5.5] A descendant of the Hsia [dynasty], Szu

5a

6a

---

tradition.

[5.4] Wei$_8$ is here probably an anachronism; the title, Duke of Wei$_8$, was bestowed in A.D. 37 upon Chi Tang's grandson, according to HS 18: 10a; HHS, An. 1 B: 9b. Chi Tang was at this time Duke of Cheng, according to 18: 10a.

[5.5] Yen Shih-ku remarks, "K'o$_1$ 恪 is to be respectful. It means that he treated him with added respect, also like a guest. The Chou [dynasty] took the descendants of Shun, together with [the princes of] Ch'i and Sung, [the descendants of the Hsia and Yin

Feng, [a man] from Liao-hsi [Commandery], was
enfeoffed and made the Marquis of Manifest Merits
**5b** and was also made a Respected Guest. (To the most
ancient examplars of the four dynasties there were
made sacrifices to exemplars in the *Ming-t'ang*, and
they were made the coadjutors of the August First
Deceased Ancestor, the Lord of Yü, [Shun].)[5.6] The
descendant of the Duke of Chou, the Viscount in
Recompense to [the Duke of] Lu, Chi Chiu, and the
descendant of Duke Hsüan-ni [in Recompense for
Perfection, Confucius], the Viscount in Recompense
for Perfection, K'ung Chün, had already been previously appointed.

Sacrifices     [Wang] Mang also said, "When previously I was
to     Regent, I founded a temple for the suburban sacrifices,
Ancestors     established a temple for the distant ancestors, and
of the     set up [an altar for] the gods of the soils and grains.
Wang     The gods in heaven and earth responded by [grant-
*5b*     ing] favors. Sometimes 'lights descended from above,
Clan.     dissolving into a crow';[5.7] sometimes there was a

dynasties], and made them the three Respected Guests (*K'o*)." The *Tso-chuan*, Dk.
Hsiang, XXV (Legge, 516) states that the Chou dynasty treated the descendants of
Yü (Shun), the Hsia, and the Shang dynasties as Respected Guests. Cf. also *Mh* I, 239.
On the meaning of *k'o₁*, Wu Ta-cheng (1844–1902), in his *Ku-chuan Pu, sub Shuo
Chou K'o-ting*, (also included in *Shuo-wen Chieh-tzu Ku-lin Pu-yi* 7 B: 494 b, *sub k'o₃*)
remarks that *k'o₁* was a different writing for *k'o₂* 窖, and that *k'o₂* is merely a different
writing of *k'o₃* 客, which means guest, so that the meaning of *k'o₁* was originally "guest."
In the *Book of Odes*, no. 278; IV, ɪ, [ii], iii, (Legge, p. 585), these Respected Ones of the
former dynasties are called *k'o₃*, and Mr. Mao (ii cent. B.C.) explains, "The *k'o₃* are
the descendants of the two [dynasties] of kings." The *K'ung-tsung-tzu* ch. 21, 6: 18a
(prob. iii cent.), in a discussion of the three Respected Ones, says, "*K'o₁* is to respect.
These [three Respected Guests] were treated with rites like those for a guest *k'o₃*." Cf.
*Tz'u-hai*, sub 三 *k'o₁*.

[5.6] Liu Feng-shih remarks that the passage in parentheses interrupts the account, and
also that since the persons to whom sacrifices were made all had descendants enfeoffed,
the sentence is not appropriate at this point. Furthermore the matter is referred to later.
He said that this sentence is therefore an interpolation. Yang Shu-ta however replies
that these sacrifices are mentioned in connection with the enfeoffment of the descendants
of the persons sacrificed to, and says that the passage seems genuine. The four dynasties
were the Hsia, Yin, Chou, and Han dynasties.

[5.7] A quotation from the "Modern text" of the *Book of History*, V, ɪ, now a fragment.

明堂宜序於祖宗之親廟其立祖廟五親廟四后夫人皆配
濟南曰王子伏念皇初祖考黃帝皇始祖考虞帝臣宗祀于
虞帝之先受姓曰姚其在陶唐曰媯在周曰陳在齊曰田在
王而祖世氏姓有五矣黃帝二十五子分賜厥姓十有二氏
黃氣熏烝昭燿章明旦著黃虞之烈馬自黃帝至于濟南伯

yellow emanation which steamed up[5.8] dazzlingly   6b
clear, thereby making manifest my brilliant [inheri-
tance from] the Yellow [Lord] and Yü [Shun].

"From the Yellow Lord to King Po of Chi-nan,
[Wang Sui], there have indeed been five surnames in
the generations of the founders [of my clan].[5.9] The
Yellow Lord had twenty-five sons, and granted them
twelve separate surnames. My ancestor who was
the Lord of Yü, [Shun], received the surname Yao;
in [the time of] T'ao-and-T'ang [Yao], [my an-
cestors] were surnamed Kuei; in [the time of] the
Chou [dynasty], they were surnamed Ch'en; in [the
state of] Ch'i, they were surnamed T'ien; and in
Chi-nan [Commandery] they were surnamed Wang.

"I have humbly remembered my August Deceased
Original Ancestor, the Yellow Lord, and my August
Deceased First[5.10] Ancestor, the Lord of Yü, [Shun],
and have hence performed to them the sacrifice to
an exemplar (tsung) in the Ming-t'ang. It is proper
that [these ancestors] should be [given the proper]
ranks among the founders and exemplars in my personal ancestral temple. Let there be established five
shrines to founders [of my line] and four shrines to
immediate ancestors,[5.11] and let the queens and ladies

Cf. Legge, p. 298; also *HHS*, Mem. 30 B: n. 14.4.

This portent to the Chou dynasty was then understood as a portent denoting the Han
dynasty, which dynasty was believed to have succeeded to the divine powers upholding
the Chou dynasty.

[5.8] This yellow emanation was then understood to have presaged Wang Mang's new
"yellow" dynasty.

[5.9] Li Tz'u-ming, *ibid.*, suggests that 而 is a copyist's error for *kao* 高. But there is
no grammatical necessity to change the text. If *kao-tsu* 祖 had been originally in the text,
it would have preceded "King Po" as it does on 99 B: 9a and Wang Mang's temple name
for the Yellow Lord would also have been used, and if Yen Shih-ku's text had read *kao-tsu*,
he would not have explained in his note that King Po of Chi-nan was Wang Mang's name
for the Eminent Founder (*kao-tsu*) of his house. This person was named Wang Sui, cf.
*Glossary, sub voce.*

[5.10] The Sung Ch'i ed. says that the Nan ed. (x–xii cent.) had 姓 before the 媯, which
is seemingly a partial dittography. The Ching-yu ed. lacks it.

[5.11] The distinction is between the shrines to the founders of houses 祖廟, which were

6a [of these ancestors] all receive offerings with [their husbands]. In the suburban sacrifice, let the Yellow Lord be the coadjutor of Heaven, and let the Queen of the Yellow [Lord] be made the coadjutrix of Earth. Let the Eastern Residence of the Marquis of Hsin-tu꜀ e become the great clan temple[6.1] where [these ancestors] shall be worshipped yearly and seasonally. Those whom my family esteem shall be sacrificed to for posterity thruout the empire.[6.2]

The New Imperial Clan.

"All [the members of] all the five clans [surnamed] Yao, Kuei, Ch'en, T'ien, and Wang are distant descendants of the Yellow [Lord] and of Yü [Shun], and so are my fellowclansman. Does not the *Book of History* say, 'Effect a generous kindness and nice observance of distinctions among the nine [classes of]

7a

6a kindred'?[6.3] Let it be ordered that in the empire the names [of persons bearing] these five surnames should be entered upon the register of the Arranger of the Ancestral Temples; all are to be made [members of] the imperial house. From generation to

九族其令天下上此五姓名籍于秩宗皆曰為宗室

凡五姓者皆黃虞苗裔子之同族也書不云乎惇序

大祺歲時曰祀家之所尚種祀天下姚媯陳田王氏

食郊祀黃帝曰配天黃后曰配地曰新都侯東弟為

not changed, and the personal shrines to the immediate ancestors 親廟, which were altered as each new generation elevated its father and mother to a place in the ancestral temple. Cf. 99 C: 9b; Stange, 129, n. 5. "Temple" 廟 is ambigious, here as elsewhere, denoting sometimes a particular shrine in a temple building, and sometimes the temple building or buildings themselves. Wang Mang was following the rule in *Li-chi* XIII, i, 9 (Legge, II, 42) = *Li-chi Cheng-yi* 32: 4b.

[6.1] Yen Shih-ku explains, "*Mei* 禖 is 祀 (a sacrifice [for descendants]). He established this great temple 祠 to sacrifice yearly and seasonally to his ancestors regularly." *Mei* is usually used to refer to the god of marriage and birth; here it is the clan temple where sacrifices are made for descendants to continue the clan.

[6.2] Yen Shih-ku glosses, "It means that the state had already established its great clan temple to sacrifice to its deceased founders. Each [ancestor] whom the families of the common people esteem should be given ancestral sacrifices and [these sacrifices] should not be interrupted. All under heaven should follow the same principle." But Liu Feng-shih argues, "This [sentence] refers to the sacrifices for posterity [to those whom Wang] Mang's family esteemed. He ordained that the empire should transmit them and make them its sacrifices for posterity and that they might not fail to be upheld in sacrifice. It was like the mound to the gods of the soils at the Fen-yin (White Elm) [District in Feng] at which [Emperor] Kao of the Han [dynasty sacrificed]." Cf. 25 A: 17b.

[6.3] *Book of History* II, iii, i, 1 (Legge, p. 69).

遣騎都尉嚻等分治黃帝園位於上都橋時虞帝於零陵
另宇為附城又封菩恩戴崇金涉其閒楊並等子皆為男
天下牧守皆呂前有翟義趙明等領州郡懷忠孝封牧為
馬封陳崈為統睦侯奉胡王後田豐為世睦侯奉殷王後
世世後無有所與其元城王氏勿令相娶娶呂別族理親

generation, they shall be exempted and shall not pay anything. Let [the members of] the Wang clan from Yüan-ch'eng be ordered not to intermarry [among themselves], in order to distinguish [this clan] and to regulate relationships."[6.4]

[Wang Mang] enfeoffed Ch'en Ch'ung as Marquis of Ruling Concord to make offerings as the descendant of King Hu [of Ch'en],[6.5] and T'ien Feng as Marquis of Hereditary Concord, to make offerings as the descendant of King Ching.[6.6]

[As to] all those [Provincial] Shepherds and [Commandery] Administrators in the empire, who, because of [the rebellion of] Chai Yi, Chao Ming, and others, had led their provinces or commanderies [to attack these rebels and thus] had cherished loyalty and filial piety, the Shepherds were enfeoffed as Barons and the Administrators as Sub-Vassals. [Wang Mang] also enfeoffed as Barons the sons of all those who had formerly shown him kindness, [the sons of] Tai Ch'ung, Chin Shê, Chi Hung, Yang[6.7] Ping and others.

He sent the Chief Commandant of Cavalry, [Hsieh] **6b** Hsiao, and others in separate parties to prepare funerary parks and altars to the Yellow Lord at the Ch'iao Sacred Place in Shang Commandery,[6.8] to the Lord of Yü, [Shun], at [Mt.] Chiu-yi in Ling-ling

---

[6.4] The Yuan-ch'eng Wang clan was that of Wang Mang's own kindred. He had married the daughter of Wang Hsien[2a], who was of another Wang clan, and wanted to show that other members of the large groups of persons surnamed Wang could intermarry, yet also to make plain that he disapproved of the intermarriage of persons of the same surname. He was thus led to distinguish among those surnamed Wang; cf. n. 1.3.

[6.5] Meng K'ang remarks, "He posthumously gave the title of King to Duke Hu of Ch'en," who founded the state of Ch'en at the Chou conquest.

[6.6] Meng K'ang remarks, "He posthumously gave the title of King to Ch'en [Wan] Ching-chung," who founded the T'ien clan.

[6.7] The Official ed. reads 陽 for 楊 to accord with the reading in 99 A: 1b. The Ching-yu ed. reads the latter.

[6.8] Liu Pin asserts that 都 should be 郡, which statement is confirmed by 28 Bi: 26a, *sub* Yang-chou.

7b

Imperial
Ancestral
Sacrifices.

[Commandery], to King Hu in [the former kingdom of] Huai-yang, to King Ching of Ch'en at Lin-tzu in Ch'i [Commandery], to King Min [of Ch'i] at Chü in Ch'eng-yang [Commandery], to King Po, [Wang Sui], at Tung-p'ing-ling in Chi-nan [Commandery], and to King Ju, [Wang Ho₄ₐ], at Yüan-ch'eng in Wei Commandery. At the four seasons, commissioners were to bring sacrifices to them. Those whose temples had to be built, because the empire had just recently been tranquillized, were temporarily to have [their tablets] gathered together and to be offered sacrifice in the Grand [Ancestral] Temple of the *Ming-t'ang*. [The temple of Emperor] Kao of the Han [dynasty] was made the Temple of the Accomplished Ancestor.[6.9]

6b

[Wang] Mang said [in a message], "My August Deceased First Ancestor, the Lord of Yü, [Shun], received [the throne] by the abdication of T'ang [Yao]. In the age of the original ancestor of the Han dynasty, the Lord of T'ang, [Yao], there was the model for transmitting the state [to another dynasty]. I myself in turn received the metal charter from the genius of Emperor Kao of the Han [dynasty]. When I ponder recompensing the generosity of previous dynasties, how could there be a time when I should forget [the Han dynasty]? There are seven Founders or Exemplars[6.10] in the Han dynasty. According to the proprieties, there should be established temples for them in the state of [the Duke of] Established Tranquillity. Let their funerary parks,

---

[6.9] Yen Shih-ku remarks that Wang Mang was imitating the action of Shun, who "received Yao's retirement from the imperial duties in the Temple of the Accomplished Ancestors," a quotation from *Book of History* II, i, iii, 4 (Legge, p. 32).

[6.10] Emperors Kao, the Eminent Founder; Hsiao-wen, the Great Exemplar; Hsiao-wu, the Epochal Exemplar; Hsiao-hsüan, the Central Exemplar; Hsiao-yüan, the Eminant Exemplar; Hsiao-ch'eng, the Dynastic Exemplar; and Hsiao-p'ing, the Supreme Exemplar. The last three titles had been conferred by Wang Mang.

The Official ed. reads, "Exemplars or Founders," but the Ching-yu ed. does not invert thus.

九疑胡王於淮陽陳敬王於齊臨淄愍王於城陽莒伯王於濟南東

平陵瑞王於魏郡元城使者四時致祠其廟當作者曰天下初定且

祫祭於明堂太廟曰漢高廟為文祖廟恭曰子之皇始考虞帝受

煊于唐漢氏初祖唐帝世有傳國之東子復親受金策於漢高皇帝

之靈惟思襄厚前代何有志時漢氏祖宗有七曰禮立廟于定安國

其圜寢廟在京師者勿罷祠焉如故子曰秋九月親入漢氏高元

成平之廟諸劉更屬籍京兆大尹勿解其侵各終厥身州牧數存

悶勿令有侵冤又口于前在大麓至于攝假似深惟漢氏三七之院

赤德氣盡思索廣求所曰輔劉延期之述廉所不用曰故作金刀

之利幾曰濟之然自孔子作春秋曰為後王法至于哀之十四而

funerary chambers, and temples at the imperial capital be not abolished, and let sacrifices and oblations [be made] as formerly. In the autumn, the ninth month, I will myself in person enter the temples of [Emperors] Kao, Yüan, Ch'eng, and P'ing of the Han dynasty.

"The various [members of] the Liu [clan] will be changed to be enregistered with the Grand Governor of the imperial capital,[6.11] and not be relieved from their exemption [from taxes], but each one shall [continue to be exempted] to the end of his life. The Provincial Shepherds shall frequently visit and ask after them, and shall bring it about that they should not [undergo] any encroachments or injustices."

The Liu Clan. 8a

He also said, "When I previously was in [the position of] the chief director [of the administration,[6.12] and became Regent and Acting [Emperor], I pondered deeply the dangers [at the end of] the three [times] seven [decades] of the Han dynasty,[7.1] that the emanation of virtue from the Red [Lord] was exhausted, and I thought and sought, searching widely for means whereby I might support the Liu [house] and lengthen its period [on the throne]. There was nothing that I failed to do. For that reason, I made the beneficial metal knife-[money], hoping thereby to assist [the dynasty].[7.2] Nevertheless when Confucius wrote the *Spring and Autumn* to make it a model for later kings, [he continued it] until the fourteenth year of [Duke] Ai [of Lu], when

7a Change in the Coinage.

[6.11] Wang Hsien-ch'ien remarks that after a change in the dynasty the members of the former imperial house should not continue to be subordinate to the Superintendent of the Imperial House.

[6.12] A phrase from the *Book of History*. Cf. A: n. 13.5.

[7.1] Cf. A: n. 34.4.

[7.2] Fu Ch'ien explains, "The metal knife-[money] was the cash cast by [Wang] Mang." Yen Shih-ku comments, "Because in the word Liu 劉 there is above 'mao 卯,' below 'metal 金,' and on the side there is also 'knife 刀,' [Wang] Mang prohibited the kang-mao [amulets] together with the metal-knife-[cash]." The metal knife-money was supposed by the magic of its rebus to strengthen the Liu house, hence Wang Mang did away with it.

7a
Change
in
Coinage.

one age ended. Comparing it with present [times], it was also fourteen years [after Emperor] Ai [ascended the throne that the Han dynasty ended its rule].[7.3] Since the calculated [number of years allotted] for the age of the Red [Lord] was exhausted, I could not eventually have the power to save [that dynasty]. August Heaven made plain its majesty, so that the virtue of the Yellow [Lord] was due to arise and to make [Heaven's] great mandate abundantly apparent, entrusting me with the empire. Now the people all say that August Heaven has dethroned the Han [dynasty] and set up the Hsin [dynasty], that he has dismissed the Liu [clan from the throne] and caused the Wang [clan] to rise.

"Verily the word for Liu is made up of *mao*, metal, and knife. [The wearing of] the first-month *kang-mao* [amulets] and the convenience of the metal-knife-[money] cannot now be permitted to occur.[7.4]

8b
7b

[This matter] was widely debated by the ministers and gentlemen, and they all said, 'That Heaven and men respond alike is brilliantly apparent. Let the *kang-mao* [amulets] be done away with, and let no one wear them at their girdles; let the knife-cash be abrogated, and let them not be used as a convenience [for exchange], in order to respond to and accord with the will of Heaven and to rejoice the minds of the people'."

Thereupon [the coinage] was changed and there

[7.3] The *Spring and Autumn* ends with the fourteenth year of Duke Ai, although he reigned for 13 years more; Chang Yen remarks that Emperor Ai reigned to his sixth year, Emperor P'ing to his fifth year, and Wang Mang acted as Regent to the third year, which makes fourteen years.

[7.4] For the *Kang-mao* amulets, cf. App. I.

In a note to the *History of the Three Kingdoms* (*San-kuo-chih*) 57: 6a, Pei Sung-chih (372–451) quotes a memorial of Yü Fan (164–233), in which the latter states that in the ancient seal character, *mao* 卯 was written for *liu* 柳 (willow). Chou Shou-ch'ang concludes that the words 劉, 留, 聊 and 柳 were interchanged with and were written the same as *mao*, although distinguished by different pronunciations. Hence the *Kang-mao* amulets also connoted the Liu house, so were forbidden.

更品黨兵子奇
作並數攻之謀
小行千即祖獲
錢欲人墨濟殺
徑防起閉南燕
六民兵城愍將
分盜於門王復
重鑄其自困定
一乃國繫於齊
銖榮快獄燕國
文不兄吏寇今
曰得故民自即
小挾漢距齊墨
錢銅膠快臨士
直炭東快淄大
一是王敗出夫
與歲時走保俊
前四改至于同
大月為長莒心
錢徐扶廣宗殄
五鄉崇死人滅
十侯公莽田反
者劉快曰單虜
為快舉昔廣子
二結　　　殺甚

were made small cash, 6 *fen* in diameter, weighing one *shu*. Their inscription said, "A diminutive cash, worth one [cash]." Together with the preceding large cash, [which were worth], fifty [of the smaller cash], there were two denominations [of coins] circulating at the same time.[7.5] [Wang Mang] wanted to prevent the common people from counterfeit casting [of cash], so issued a prohibition that they were not to be allowed to possess copper or charcoal.[7.6]

In[7.7] the fourth month, the Marquis of Hsü-hsiang, Liu K'uai, formed a cabal of several thousand persons and raised troops in his state. [Liu] K'uai's elder brother, [Liu] Yin₂ₐ, had been the former King of Chiao-tung under the Han [dynasty], and had at this time been changed to be the Duke Supporting and Rendering Homage [to the Hsin Dynasty. When Liu] K'uai mobilized his troops and attacked Chi-mo, [Liu] Yin₂ₐ closed the city gates and had himself bound in prison. The officials and common people resisted [Liu] K'uai, so that [Liu] K'uai was defeated and fled to Ch'ang-kuang, where he died.

[Wang] Mang said [in a message], "When anciently my ancestor, King Min [of Ch'i, who reigned over territory which is the present] Chi-nan [Commandery], was distressed by the robber [state of] Yen and left Lin-tzu (in [the state of] Ch'i) to take refuge at Chü, a man of his clan, T'ien Tan₁, made extensive and clever plans, captured and killed a general of Yen, and re-established the state of Ch'i. Today the gentlemen and grandees of Chi-mo have again been of the same mind [with me] and have extirpated rebellious caitiffs. I commend most highly those

*Apr./May*
*Liu K'uai's Rebellion.*
*7b*
*9a*
*8a*

---

[7.5] These two denominations were later (A.D. 10; 99 B: 15a) supplemented by 26 others, all of which were still later discontinued, except for these two; cf. *HS* 24 B: 21b–23b (in App. I), *Chin-shih So*, "Chin," 4: 28b.

[7.6] This ordinance was repealed in A.D. 13; cf. 99 B: 22a.

[7.7] Before the words for "the fourth month," the present text has the words "是歲 in this year." The Ching-yu ed. lacks them; the Sung Ch'i ed. declares that the Yüeh ed. (xi–xii cent.) lacked them. I have not translated this interpolation.

who have been loyal and have compassion upon those who are guiltless.

**Rewards for Loyalty.** "Let [Liu] Yin$_{2a}$ and the others be pardoned. Except for [Liu] K'uai's wife and children, his blood relatives and relatives by marriage, who ought to be sentenced, are not to be tried. In making consoling inquiries about those who have died, the person in charge of these inquiries shall grant to those who have died fifty thousand [cash] per person for burial money. [Liu] Yin$_{2a}$ understood the great mandate [of Heaven] and deeply hated [Liu] K'uai, for which reason [the latter] suffered immediately for his crimes.[8.1] Let the state of [Liu] Yin$_{2a}$ be made a full ten thousand households, with a territory a hundred *li* square."

[Wang Mang] also enfeoffed the more than ten courtiers [who had been concerned with] the mandates [from Heaven given by means of] portents.[8.2]

**The Ching System Restored.** [Wang] Mang said [in a message], "When the ancients established the cottages of eight families on the *ching* [system][8.3] and one husband and one wife had a hundred *mou* of cultivated land and paid one-tenth in taxes, then the state had enough and the common people were opulent and composed songs of praise. The foregoing was the way of T'ang [Yao] and of Yü [Shun], and that which the three dynasties **9b** practised obediently.

**8a** "The [state of] Ch'in was inhuman and made the taxes heavy, in order that [the ruler] might himself have [a large] income. [The ruler] exhausted the strength of the common people in order to satisfy his desires to the utmost. He destroyed the institutions of the sages and did away with the *ching*

---

[8.1] Prof. Duyvendak points out that the common phrase, "suffered for their crimes" is taken from *Book of Odes*, no. 194; II, IV, x, 1 (Legge, p. 326).

[8.2] The persons concerned with the portents noted on A: 25a, 34a–35b; B: 9a–10a.

[8.3] For this system, cf. Duyvendak, *The Book of Lord Shang*, p. 41 f; Eberhard, "Zur Landwirschaft d. Han-Zeit," *MSOS* 35: 78ff.

三代所遵行也秦為無道厚賦稅曰自供奉罷民力曰極欲壞聖制
家一夫一婦田百畝什一而稅則國給民富而頌聲作此唐虞之道
其滿殷國戶萬地方百里又封符命臣十餘人奉曰古者設廬井八
弔問死傷賜亡者葬錢人五萬殷知大命深疾惡快曰故輒伏厥辜
嘉其忠者慉其無辜其赦殷等非快之妻子宂親屬當坐者皆勿治

284

爇後被此辜矣漢氏減輕田租三十而稅一常有更賦罷
於天地之性人為貴之義書曰予則奴戮女唯不用命者
命姦虐之人因緣為利至略賣人妻子逆天心詩人倫繆
立鍰之居又置奴婢之市與牛馬同蘭制於民臣顓斷其
廢井田是已兼并起貪部生強者規田曰千數弱者曾無

[system of] cultivated fields. For this reason the taking posesssion of and joining together [of fields by the wealthy] arose and avarice and vileness was born. The strong made designs to secure cultivated fields by the thousands [of *mou*] and the weak [even] lacked [enough of] a habitation in which to stand up an awl.

Criticism of the Han Land System.

"[That state] also established market-places for male and female slaves, putting [human beings] in like enclosures with those for cattle and horses. In their rule over their common people and subjects, [the Ch'in rulers] arbitrarily cut short their [very] lives, and villainous and oppressive persons took advantage of the opportunity to make profits, even kidnapping and selling other peoples' wives and children, going contrary to the will of Heaven and disordering human relationships, which is contradictory to the principle that 'of all living things, [i.e., animals and plants, produced by] Heaven and Earth, man is the noblest.'[8.4] The *Book of History* says, '[If you do not obey my commands], I will thereupon enslave and dishonor you,'[8.5] [according to which passage] only those who did not obey [the king's] commands should indeed suffer this punishment[8.6] [of being enslaved].

**8b**

"The[8.7] Han dynasty reduced and lightened the land tax, taking [only] one-thirtieth, [but in addition] there were regularly [required] conscript service and capitation-taxes, which [even] the sick and aged

[8.4] A saying attributed to Confucius in the *Classic of Filial Piety* 5: 1a; ch. 9 (Legge, *SBE* III, p. 476).

[8.5] *Book of History* III, ii, i, 5 (Legge, p. 155). That *Book* reads "wives & children 孥" instead of the *HS*'s "enslave 奴"; Yen Shih-ku attacks that interpretation of this word in this passage, saying that in view of *ibid.* V, i, iii, 3 (Legge, p. 295), "He has imprisoned and enslaved upright gentlemen," the meaning "wives & children" cannot be maintained. Wang Mang certainly took it to mean "enslave." Cf. Karlgren, *BMFEA* 20, 170f, Gl. 1403.

[8.6] The Official ed. emends 辜 to 皋. The Ching-yu ed. reads the former.

[8.7] From this point on, this edict is also found (with omissions) in *HS* 24 A: 21a, b (App. I).

were all required to pay,[8.8] while powerful common people encroached upon [the poor, letting their own]

**10a**

**Criticism of the Han Land System.**

fields [out on] shares, robbing [people] by the rentals [required for their land, so that while] in name they were taxed only one-thirtieth, in reality they are taxed or pay as rent five-tenths of their produce.[8.9] Fathers and sons, husbands and wives plowed and weeded for a whole year, [but] what they got was insufficient to keep themselves alive. Hence the horses and dogs of the rich had surplus beans and grain and [the rich] were proud and did evil, while the poor could not satiate themselves with brewer's

**8b**

grains, became destitute, and acted wickedly. Both [rich and poor] fell into crime, so that the punishments had to be employed and could not be set aside.

"When previously I was the chief director [of the administration], I first ordered that the empire's public cultivated fields [should be organized on] the *ching* [system according to the number] of persons, and consequently at that time there were happy presages of auspicious [large-eared] cereals. [But] there happened to be rebellious caitiffs and treasonable rebels, so that [the scheme] was temporarily stopped.

**Sale of Cultivated Fields and Slaves Forbidden.**

"Now I change the names of the cultivated fields in the empire to be 'the King's fields,'[8.10] and of male and female slaves to be 'private adherents.' All are not to be permitted to be bought or sold. Let it be that those [rich families with] less than eight males,

更名天下田曰王田奴婢曰私屬皆不得賣買其男口不盈八
麓始令天下公田口井時則有嘉禾之祥遭反虜逆賊且止今
為邪貧者不厭糟糠而為姦俱陷于辜刑用不錯于前在大
于夫婦終年耕芸所得不足呂自存故富者犬馬餘菽粟驕而
癃咸出而豪民侵陵分田劫假厥名三十稅一賣什稅五也父

---

[8.8] In a note to 24 A: 21a, Chin Shao explains, "Although they might be old or ill, all had yet to pay the poll-tax (*suan*)."

[8.9] This figure for the rate of rentals was taken from a memorial by Tung Chung-shu, now in *HS* 24 A: 16b.

[8.10] In *Mencius* V, I, iv, 2, (Legge, p. 352), Mencius quotes from *Book of Odes* II, VI, i, 2; no. 205 (Legge, p. 360), the phrase "王土 the king's (or sovereign's) land," which is the source of this term:

"All under the wide heaven
Is the king's land."

Wang Mang took the title of King, hence applied this saying to himself.

而田過一井者分餘田于九族鄰里鄉黨故無田今當受田

者如制度敢有非井田聖制無法惑衆者投諸四裔曰禦魑

魅如皇始祖考虞帝故事是時百姓便安漢五銖錢曰奢錢

大小兩行難知又數變改不信皆私已五銖錢市買謂言大

錢當罷莫肯挾棄忠之後下書諸挾五銖錢言大錢當罷者

who have more cultivated fields than those in one
*ch'ing*, shall divide the cultivated fields that are in
excess [of those in one *ch'ing*] and give them to their
nine [classes of] relatives or to [people in] their
neighborhood.[8.11]  Those who formerly had no cultivated fields and who ought now to receive cultivated
fields [shall be treated] in accordance with the regulations.   If there are any who presume to speak evil
of the sage institution of the *ching* [system of] cultivated fields, and mislead the crowd lawlessly, 'they
shall be thrown out to the four frontiers [and be　**9a**
made] to resist the elves and goblins,'[9.1] as in the
former case my August Deceased First Ancestor, the
Lord of Yü, [Shun], did."

At this time, the people had considered the Han　**10b**
[dynasty's] five-*shu* cash convenient, and, because
Wang Mang's cash coins had been put out in two
[denominations], large and small, and so were difficult
to tell [apart], and moreover had been changed and
altered several times, so that they were not to be
trusted, [therefore the people] all privately used the
five-*shu* cash at the market and in purchases, saying
falsely that the large cash are due to be abolished
and that no one is willing to keep them.

[Wang] Mang was troubled by it and again issued
a written message that all those who hoard five-*shu*
cash and say that the large cash are due to be
abolished are similar to those who criticize the *ching*
system of cultivated fields and should be "thrown out
to the four frontiers."[9.1]  Thereupon farmers and

[8.11] A phrase from *Analects* VI, iii, 4.

[9.1] A quotation from *Tso-chuan*, 20: 10b, Dk. Wen, XVIII (Legge, p. 280[13,14], 283a).
Yen Shih-ku explains, "*Ch'ih* 魑 are the mountain spirits and *mei* 魅 are the essences
of aged things."   Cf. App. I, *HS* 24 B: 23a.   "Being made to resist the elves and goblins"
was a circumlocution for a death sentence.   In 24 A: 21b, the punishment for  violating
the ordinance establishing the *ching* system is said to have been death.   Stange (140, n. 1)
suggests that it meant banishment to frontier military colonies, but Tu Yü, in a note
to the *Tso-chuan* passage, explains "*t'ou* 投, to be thrown out" as "*ch'i* 弃, to be executed" (cf. *HFHD*, I, 319, n. 6.4) and K'ung Ying-ta adds that *t'ou-ch'i* means "至害 the
extreme penalty."

Economic Sufferings.

merchants lost their occupations, food and goods were both rendered useless, and the common people even wept in the marketplaces and highways.   Moreover those who were tried for buying or selling fields or residences, male or female slaves, or for casting cash, from the nobles, high ministers, and grandees down to ordinary common people, and who suffered punishment, could not be counted.

Autumn.

In the autumn, [Wang Mang] sent twelve Generals of the Five Majestic [Principles], Wang Ch'i

*9a*

Propa-

ganda

Sent

Out.

and others, [each with his five Lieutenant Generals],[9.2] to publish through the empire the *Mandate [of Heaven Given Through] Portents*, in 42 fascicles. There were five matters of "Happy Presages of Virtues," twenty-five of "Mandates Through Portents," and twelve of "Responses of Heavenly Favors," forty-two fascicles in all.

[The chapters on] "Happy Presages of Virtues" said that in the reigns of [Emperors] Wen and Hsüan, yellow dragons appeared at Ch'eng-chi and Hsin-tu[b],[9.3] that a catalpa pillar at the gate to the grave of the Deceased Eminent Founder [of Wang Mang's clan], King Po,[9.4] [Wang Sui], had sprouted a branch with leaves, and the like.   [The chapters on] "Mandates Through Portents" spoke of the well, the stone, the metal casket, and the like.[9.5]   [The

*11a*

chapters on] "Responses of Heavenly Favors" spoke

[9.2] *HS* 99 B: 11a mentions five Lieutenant Generals for each of these twelve Generals; 99 B: 12b states that "the Generals . . . and their Lieutenants, seventy-two persons [in all], returned."   Hence the Lieutenant Generals should also be mentioned here.

[9.3] Cf. 4: 15b; 8: n. 23.5.

[9.4] Wang Hsien-ch'ien asserts that the words 王伯 should be interchanged, to conform to the usual writing of his name.   He is probably correct, but this reading is also found in 27 Bb: 6a, where this event is dated in 45 B.C., the year Wang Mang was born.   Liu Hsiang is said to have declared that it symbolized the replacing of the Liu by the Wang clan on the throne.

[9.5] Cf. 99 A: 34a-35b.

比非井田制挍四裔於是農商失業食貨俱廢民人至涕泣於市道及

坐賣買田宅奴婢鑄錢自諸侯卿大夫至于庶民抵罪者不可勝數秋

遣五威將王奇等十二人班符命四十二篇於天下德祥五事符命二

十五福應十二凡四十二篇其德祥言文宣之世黃龍見於成紀新都

高祖考王伯墓門梓柱生枝葉之屬符命言井石金匱之屬福應言雌

難化為雄之屬其文爾雅依託皆為作說大歸言
荅當代漢有天下云總而說之曰帝王受命必有
德祥之符瑞協成五命中呂福應然後能立巍巍
之功傳于子孫永享無窮之祚故新室之興也德
祥發於漢三七九世之後肇命於新都受瑞於黃

of a hen having been metamorphosed into a cock and the like. The language [of the book] was like the Classics,[9.6] accorded with them and made use of them in making its interpretations. Its final conclusion was that [Wang] Mang was due to have taken the place of the Han [emperors] and to possess the empire.[9.7]

**9b**

In sum it said, "When lords or kings are to receive the mandate [of Heaven], there inevitably are portents and auspices concerning the presages of the virtues [and powers through whose dominance they rule], which assist and complete the mandate to the five [powers],[9.8] and make this circumstance known by responses of heavenly favor. Then only can [a dynasty] achieve sublime merit and transmit it to its descendants, who will eternally enjoy boundless prosperity. Hence, when the Hsin dynasty arose, the happy presages of the virtue [of its power] came forth after the three sevens [of decades] and the nine generations [of emperors] of the Han [dynasty had elapsed].[9.9]

"The mandate [to the Hsin dynasty] commenced when [Wang Mang was the Marquis of] Hsin-tu. and received an auspicious presage from [the state

**The Book of Propaganda.**

---

[9.6] *Erh-ya* 爾雅 has here the same meaning as in *SJ* 121: 11[7] = *HS* 88: 5a[8], which quotes from a memorial by Kung-sun Hung, flattering Emperor Wu for his edicts, "Whose literary beauty is like the classics (*erh-ya*) and the expressions whose instructions are extremely effective." Yen Shih-ku explains, "*Erh-ya* [means] approaching the classics 近正 *chin-cheng*. It means that the expressions in his edicts are elegant (*ya*) and classical (*cheng*) and are extremely effective." (Reference from Prof. Duyvendak.)

[9.7] Wang Hsien-shen remarks that this book has not been transmitted, and that *HS* 27 Bb: 6a, b quotes a few sentences from it, concerning the catalpa pillar.

[9.8] Yen Shih-ku comments, "*Wu-ming* 五命 means the order in which the five (*wu*) powers or elements succeed each other and in which the mandate (*ming*) [of Heaven] is transmitted."

[9.9] Ho Ch'uo explains, "[Emperors] Hsiao-hui and Hsiao-wen were of the same generation and [Emperors] Ai and P'ing were of the same generation." The Empress of Emperor Kao is also omitted in this count of nine generations in the Former Han Dynasty. For "three sevens of decades," cf. A: n. 34.4.

The
Book of
Propa-
ganda.

of] Huang-chih.[9.10] His kingship began [with the stone] at Wu-kung.[9.11] The mandate was fixed [upon him by the portent from the man of] Tzu$_{3b}$-t'ung.[9.12] The mandate was completed by [the happening] at Tang-[ch'ü] in Pa [Commandery.[9.13] The gods] expressed their favor by twelve responses, [so that] the method which Heaven has used to [show that it] protects and blesses the Hsin dynasty is indeed deep and indeed substantial.

9b

Feb.,
A.D. 6.[9.11]

11b

"The red stone at Wu-kung appeared in the last year of Emperor P'ing of the Han dynasty, when the virtue of fire had been completely dissipated and the virtue of earth was due to take the place [of the virtue of fire]. August Heaven was solicitous [on account of this circumstance] and so rejected the Han [dynasty] and gave [His mandate] to the Hsin [dynasty], using the red stone as its first mandate to the Emperor. The Emperor, [Wang Mang, however] humbly refused to accept [this title] and hence occupied [the throne] as regent.

Aug./
Sept.,
A.D. 6.

"[But that action] did not accord with the will of Heaven, hence in that autumn, the seventh month, Heaven again used the varicolored horse of[9.14] [the

9.10 Cf. 12: 4b.

9.11 Cf. 99 A: 25a.

9.12 Cf. 99 A: 35a. Tzu $_{3b}$-t'ung was the name to which Wang Mang changed Tzu$_{3a}$-t'ung.

9.13 Cf. 99 A: 34a.

9.14 *Shuo-wen* 10 A: 2a, sub *wen* 馼 (Chin Shao quotes this passage in a summary form) says, "A horse with a red mane, a white body, and eyes like actual gold is named *wen*. It is auspicious for the chariot of the emperor. In the time of King Wen of the Chou [dynasty], the Dog Jung presented one.... The comment on the *Spring and Autumn* [*Tso-chuan*, Dk. Hsüan, II, (Legge, p. 289b)], says, 'The hundred quadrigae of *wen* horses', which are horses with more than one color 畫馬. The Chief of the West, [later King Wen], presented Chou with one in order to save himself."

The *Yi-wen Lei-chü* (compiled by Ou-yang Hsün, 557–641), 93: 3b, quotes the Grand Duke's *Liu-t'ao* (prob. iv or v cent. B.C. or later) as saying (this passage is not found in the present *Liu-t'ao*), "When the King of Shang arrested the Chief of Chou, [Chi] Ch'ang, [later known as King Wen], at Yu-li, the [Foreseen] Grand Duke, [Lü Shang], with San Yi-sheng, took a thousand *yi* of gold and sought for the [most] precious things in the

帝皇帝謀讓曰攝居之未當天意故其秋七月天重曰三能
火德銷盡土德當代皇天眷然去漢與新曰丹石始命於皇
所曰保祐新室者深矣固矣武功丹石出於漢氏平帝末年
支開王於武功定命於子同成命於巴宕中福於十二應天

非皇天所目鄭重降符命之意故是目天復決其目勉書又
就猶尚稱假改元為初始欲目承塞天命克厭上帝之心然
十二目昭告新皇帝皇帝深惟上天之威不可不畏故去攝
十一目大神石十二目銅符帛圖中命之瑞嶷目嶬著至于
六目文圭七目玄印八目茂陵石書九目玄龍石十目神井
文馬皇帝復謙讓未即位故三目鐵契四目石龜五目虞符

constellation] San-t'ai. The Emperor, [Wang Mang], again humbly refused, and did not yet ascend the throne, hence [there came] a third [mandate] by an iron contract, a fourth [mandate] by a stone tortoise, a fifth [mandate] by a portent from Yü [Shun], a sixth [mandate] by an inscribed sceptre, a seventh [mandate] by a black seal, an eighth [mandate] by a stone message at Mou-ling, a ninth [mandate] by a dark dragon stone, a tenth [mandate] by a supernatural well,[10.1] an eleventh [mandate] by a great supernatural stone, and a twelfth [mandate] by a copper portent and a design on silk.[10.2] The happy presages which expressed the mandate [of Heaven] gradually became [more and more] outstanding until they reached [the number of] twelve, in order to announce plainly that the Emperor of the Hsin [dynasty should ascend the throne].

"The Emperor pondered deeply that the majesty of Heaven Above could not but be feared. Hence he did away with the title of Regent, yet still called himself the Acting [Emperor], and changed the year-period to Ch'u-shih, intending thereby to stop the mandate of Heaven and yet to carry out and satisfy the will of the Lords on High. Yet that was not the purpose for which August Heaven had so carefully[10.3] sent down his mandate through portents. Hence on that [very] day Heaven again settled [his hesitancy] by a tortoise letter.[10.4] A Gentleman-in-attendance,

10a
The Book of Propaganda.

Aug./ Sept., A.D. 8.

Dec. 31.

*10a 12a*

world to ransom the crime of their lord. Thereupon they obtained from the clans of the Dog Jung *wen* horses with fine hair, red manes, and eyes like actual gold, and named [the chariot drawn by] them, 'The quadriga with *chi-szu* 雞斯之乘' [the name of a supernatural variety of horse; *Huai-nan-tzu* 12: 12b (Morgan, p. 125) states that San Yi-sheng "secured a quadrigae with *tsou-yü* (herbivorous white tigers with black stripes) and *chi-szu*"] and presented it to the King of Shang."

[10.1] Cf. 99 A: 34a.

[10.2] Cf. 99 A: 34b.

[10.3] Yen Shih-ku glosses, "*Cheng-chung* 鄭重 is as if he said 頻煩."

[10.4] Meng K'ang says that this letter refers to the written charter fabricated by Ai Chang (cf. 99 A: 35a) and that *mien* 勉 means to urge, with which Yen Shih-ku agrees.

Wang Hsü, moreover saw a man clothed in a white plain cloth thin garment with a square collar of red ribbon, wearing on his head the small bonnet, standing in front of the Hall With the Royal Apartments.  He said to [Wang] Hsü, 'Today, in heaven [everyone] is of the same mind to confide the people of the world to [Wang Mang] as Emperor.'[10.5] While [Wang] Hsü was marvelling at it and walked more than ten double-paces, the man was suddenly not seen.

**10b**
**The Book of Propaganda.**

**Jan. 8, A.D. 9.**

"On the evening of [the day] *ping-yin*, at the Temple of [Emperor] Kao of the Han dynasty, there was a metal casket with a design and a charter, [stating that] Emperor Kao had received the mandate of Heaven to transmit the state to the Emperor of the Hsin [dynasty].  The next morning, the Elder of the Imperial House, the Marquis of Loyalty and Filial Piety, Liu Hung[3b], reported it.  Thereupon the ministers were summoned to discuss it.  When they had not yet reached a decision, the great supernatural stone man spoke, saying, 'Hasten the Emperor of the Hsin [dynasty] to the Temple of [Emperor] Kao, [where he is] to receive the Mandate.  Do not delay.'

**Jan. 9**

"Thereupon the Emperor of the Hsin [dynasty,

侍郎王盱見人衣白布單衣赤繢方領冠小冠立于王路殿
前謂盱曰今日天同色呂天下人民屬皇帝盱怪之行十餘
步人急不見至丙寅喜漢氏高廟有金匱圖策高帝承天命
呂國傳新皇帝明旦宗伯忠孝侯劉宏呂聞乃召公卿議未
決而大神石人談曰趣新皇帝之高廟受命毋需於是新皇

But Ai Chang's "metal casket, design, and charter" is referred to later as another portent (99 B: 10b).  Chin Shao asserts that *mien* should be *kuei* 龜 (tortoise), and Li Tz'u-ming, ibid., 7: 16a, points out that *kuei* is similar to *min* 䖝 and that anciently *mien* and *min* were interchanged, so that *kuei* was misread as *min*, and *min* exchanged for *mien*.

The Sung Ch'i ed. notes that other editions lack the three words 復決其, and that the Shao ed. (xi or xii cent.) has not the last of these, *ch'i*.  Wang Hsien-ch'ien adds that the Official ed. and the Southern Academy ed. have 所 after the *ch'i*.  Li Tz'u-ming suspects the *ch'i* to be an interpolation, probably from the same word in Meng K'ang's comment.  The Ching-yu ed. reads as the text does, but its *ch'i* is plainly a correction, being substituted for two words.

[10.5] Yen Shih-ku explains, "同色 means that the heavenly gods of the five quarters had united in their plans and agreed in their colors.  The word should perhaps be *pao* 包. *Pao* means that Heaven as a whole had wrapped up the crowds of people of the world and had given them to [Wang] Mang.  Both these interpretations are meaningful."

問公侯卿大夫僉曰宜奉如上天威命於是乃改元定號海內更

可濟虁虁在左右之不得從意為之三夜不御寢三日不御食延

備固讓十二符應迫著命不可辭懼然祇畏韋然閔漢氏之終不

卯劉姓所呂為宇也明漢劉火德盡而傳於新室也皇帝謙謙睆

帝立登車之漢氏高廟受命受命之日丁卯也丁火漢氏之德也

Wang Mang], at once mounted his chariot and went to the Temple of [Emperor] Kao of the Han dynasty and received the mandate. The day of receiving the mandate was *ting-mao*.[10.6]  *Ting* is fire, which is the virtue of the Han dynasty; *mao* is that whereby the [Han dynasty's] surname, Liu, becomes this written character.[10.7]  It makes plain that the virtue of fire, [which was that of] the Han [dynasty] and of the Liu [clan], is exhausted, and that [the state] has been transmitted to the house of Hsin.

"Since the Emperor was perfect in 'humility,'[10.8] he renounced firmly [the honors indicated by] the twelve responses [from the gods] by portents, [but] he was compelled by the plain mandate [of Heaven] and could not refuse.  He was startled and reverently awed, and worried[10.9] and sad that the ending of the Han dynasty could not have been arrested.  He was indefatigable in assisting[10.10] [the Han dynasty, but] he could not carry out his purposes, and, because of that, for three nights he did not go to his bed and for three days he did not touch food.  He invited and questioned the highest ministers, marquises, high ministers, and grandees, and all said, 'It is proper that you should receive [the rule] according to the majestic mandate of Heaven Above.'  Thereupon he changed the year-period, fixed upon his title, and [gave[11.1] the opportunity for] a new beginning to [all] within [the four] seas.

A.D. 9,
Jan. 9.
12b
The
Book of
Propa-
ganda.

10b

11a

---

[10.6] According to 99 A: 35b, Wang Mang received the mandate on the next day, *mou-ch'en;* cf. A: n. 35.12; B: n. 7.2.

[10.7] The written character Liu 劉 is formed by adding *mao* to the word *chao* 釗, to round off.

[10.8] A quotation from *Book of Changes*, Hex. 15 (Legge, p. 89; Wilhelm I, 47).

[10.9] Ma Hsü-lun, p. 18b, suggests that 韋 be read as 愇, which latter word is said by *Yü-p'ien* 8: 2a (by Ku Ye-wang; preface dated 543; reconstructed 1013) to mean 怨恨.

[10.10] Yen Shih-ku states that 左右 should be read as 佐佑.  Wang Hsien-ch'ien remarks that 在 is accordingly superfluous and could not have been in Yen Shih-ku's text; Yang Shu-ta suggests that it is dittography for the 左.

[11.1] Wang Hsien-ch'ien suspects there should be a 與 before the 海.

The
Book of
Propa-
ganda.

"When the House of Hsin had been fixed [upon the throne], the gods in heaven and earth were glad and rejoiced, and emphasized it by responses of [celestial] favor. Their fortunate presages were continuous and reiterated. The *Book of Odes* says,

> When [the sovereign] orders aright his people
> and orders aright his officers,
>   He receives blessings from Heaven,
> Who protects and aids him and gives him his
>   mandate.
>     By [this mandate] from Heaven he issues
>       his imperial mandates[11.2]—

which refers to the present case."

13a
New
Seals
Distrib-
uted.

The Generals of the Five Majestic [Principles], in respectful obedience to the mandate [given by] portents, brought seals and cords and gave them to the kings, the marquises, and those of lower [rank], down to the lower officials whose official titles had been changed, and, outside [the country], to the Huns, to the Western Frontier Regions, and to the barbarians outside the borders.   From all [of these persons], immediately that [the Generals] had given out the seals and cords of the House of Hsin, they thereupon took up the seals and cords of the former Han [dynasty]. There were granted, to the lower officials, two steps in noble rank per person, to common people, one step in noble rank per person, to the women of a hundred households, a sheep and wine, and to the barbarians, currency and silk, to each proportionately.   A general amnesty [was granted] to the empire.

The Robes
of the
Generals
of the

The Generals of the Five Majestic [Principles] rode in chariots [emblazoned] with the lines of [the hexagram] *Ch'ien*, [representing Heaven], yoked to [the hexagram] *K'un* [in the shape of] six mares.[11.3]   On

---

[11.2] *Book of Odes*, #249; III, ii, v, 1 (Legge, p. 481).   In translating the last line I have followed the interpretation of Cheng Hsüan (A.D. 127–200).

[11.3] Mr. Cheng (fl. dur. 220–317) remarks that six is the number of Earth.   The word

者至西域盡改其王為侯北出者至匈奴庭授單于印改漢印文

菟樂浪高句驪夫餘南出者踰徼外厤益州貶句町王為侯西出

帝之使奉策命曰普天之下迄于四表靡所不至其東出者至玄

冠車服駕馬各如其方面色敦將持節稱太一之使帥持幢稱五

背負鷩鳥之毛服飾甚偉每一將各置左右前後中帥凡五帥衣

their backs they bore the feathers of the golden
pheasant,[11.4] and their robes were decorated very
extraordinarily.    For each General there were established Lieutenants of the Left, of the Right, of the
Van, of the Rear, and of the Center, five Lieutenants
in all.    Their clothes and hats, chariots and robes,
and the horses yoked [to their chariots] were severally
like the colors and numbers of their directions.[11.5]
The Generals carried credentials with the title, "A
Messenger of the Supreme One" and the Lieutenants
bore banners with the title, "A Messenger of the Five
Lords [on High."    Wang] Mang's charter-mandate
to them read, "In the whole world, go to its four
extremities and do not leave any place unvisited."

Those who went out eastwards reached Hsüan-t'u
[Commandery], Lo-lang [Commandery], the Kao-
chü-li, and the Fu-yü.    Those who went out to the
south passed over [the border] beyond Yi Province,
where they degraded the King of Kou-t'ing and made
him a marquis.    Those who went out to the west
reached the Western Frontier Regions and changed
all the kings there to be marquises.

Those who went out to the north reached the court
of the Huns and gave the *Shan-yü* a seal which
changed the words in the Han [dynasty's] seal, doing
away with the word "imperial seal" and reading

*Five
Majestic
Principles.*

*11a*

**11b** 13b

*Revolts
on the
Northern
and*

used for heaven, *ch'ien*, is the name of the first hexagram in the *Book of Changes;* the word
used for mares, *k'un*, is the second hexagram.    This equipage represented Heaven and
Earth.

[11.4] Yen Shih-ku explains, *"Pieh-niao* 鷩鳥 is of the pheasant family and is the 鵔鸃
(golden pheasant).    Today it is commonly called the 山雞, which is erroneous."

[11.5] Yen Shih-ku explains, "Their colors were: in the eastern quarter, cerulean, and in
the southern quarter, red, [etc.].    Their numbers were: as the number of [the power]
wood is three, the number of fire is two, and the like."    A polychrome painting on silk,
dated 897, representing a Buddha seated on a chariot surrounded by the deities of the
five planets (which may be equated with the five directions) is reproduced in A. Stein,
*Serindia*, vol. IV, pl. LXXI, with an inadequate description in *ibid.* II, 1059, liv. 007.
A much better description with a key is found in W. C. White, *Chinese Temple Frescoes*,
p. 99 & fig. 26.

Western
Frontiers.
94 B:
16b–17b.

[instead], "official seal." When the *Shan-yü* desired and asked for his former seal, Ch'en Jao had broken it to pieces. A discussion is in the "Memoir on the Huns."[11.6] The *Shan-yü* became furious. Kou-t'ing and the Western Frontier Regions moreover later finally all revolted because of this [change of titles]. When [Ch'en] Jao returned, he was installed as General-in-chief and was enfeoffed as Viscount of Majestic Virtue.

In the winter it thundered and the *t'ung* trees blossomed.

[Wang Mang] established [as regular officials] Directors of Mandates from the Five Majestic [Principles, Generals] of the Central City [of the Five Majestic Principles], and four Generals of the [respective] Passes [in the four directions for the Five Majestic Principles]. The Directors of Mandates were directors to the officials [ranking] in the highest class of the highest ministers and to those [ranking] lower. [The Generals of] the Central City [of the Five Majestic Principles] were in charge of the twelve city gates [of Ch'ang-an].

Mandates
to
Officials.

The charter-mandate to the Marquis of Ruling Concord, Ch'en Ch'ung, read, "O thou Ch'ung![11.7] Verily, [1] disobedience to mandates is the source of sedition. [2] Great wickedness and knavishness is the origin of rebellion. [3] The casting of counterfeit gold[11.8] and cash is a means whereby obstacles are put [in the circulation of] the valuable currency. [4] Pride and extravagance overpassing the regulations is the beginning of evil and disaster [to oneself].

*11b*

[5] Divulging matters [discussed in] the Inner Apartments and [matters] concerning the Masters of Writing is [what is called], 'When the delicate govern-

去置曰章單于欲求故印陳饒椎破之語在匈奴傳單于大怒而匈

盯西域後卒曰此皆畔饒還拜為大將軍封威德子冬蠹桐華置五

睦侯陳崇曰咨爾崇夫不用命者亂之原也大姦猾者賊之本也統

威司令中城四關將軍司令司上公曰下中城主十二城門策命統

偽金錢者妨寶貨之道也騎奢踰制者兄吝之端也滿池省中及尚

11.6 Cf. Glossary, *sub* Ch'en Jao; de Groot, *Die Hunnen*, p. 266–68.

11.7 Reminiscent of *Book of History* I, ii, 8 (Legge, p. 21).

11.8 Probably a reference to alchemy; cf. *HFHD* I, 323, & n. 7.8.

書事者機事不密則言成也拜爵王庭謝恩私門者

祿去公室政從亡矣凡此六條國之綱紀是用建備

作司命柬亦不茹剛亦不吐不侮鰥寡不畏強圉帝

命帥誅統睦于朝命說符侯在發曰重門擊柝呂待

暴客女作五威中城将軍中德既成天下說符命明

ment affairs are not kept secret, injury will result.'[11.9]
[6] When those who are installed in noble ranks at
the court of a [true] king [nevertheless] give thanks
at the doors of private [persons] for the grace [shown
them, it is what is called] 'blessings leave the public
halls'[11.10] and the government goes to ruin.  All these
six matters are fundamental principles of the state.
For this reason I establish you as Director of Commands [of the Five Majestic Principles].[11.11]

14a
Mandates
to
Officials.

" 'If a thing is soft, he does not devour it.
　If it is hard, he does not spit it out.
He does not insult widowers or widows
　Or fear the strong or oppressive.'[11.12]
The mandates of the Emperor are to be 'followed
and observed,'[12.1] and to control the concord in[12.2]
the court."

12a

His [charter-] mandate to the Marquis Delighting
in Portents, Ts'ui Fa, read, " 'The double gates and
the beating of night watches are a preparation against
violent visitors.'[12.3]  You are to serve as General of
the Central City of the Five Majestic [Principles].
When the central virtue[12.4] is perfected, all the world
will delight in [Heaven's] portents."

[11.9] A quotation from *Book of Changes*, App. III, sect. I, verse 47 (Legge, p. 363).

[11.10] A quotation from *Analects* XVI, iii.  Ho Ch'uo remarks, "[Wang] Mang feared deeply and took precautions against his subordinates, hence [wrote] this sixth sentence."

[11.11] Ch'ien Ta-chao suspects that before the words 司命 there have dropped out the words 五威, and Chou Chou-ch'ang adds that Ch'en Ch'ung had previously been a Director of Justice, so was newly established as Director of Mandates of the Five Majestic Principles.   Hence the full title must have been in the original document, whether Pan Ku copied it out in full or not.

[11.12] A quotation from *Book of Odes*, ♯260; III, iii, vi, 5 (Legge, p. 544).

[12.1] A quotation from *Book of History* V, viii, 4 (Legge, p. 379).

[12.2] Prof. Duyvendak remarks that the use of *yü* 于 instead of 於 is an imitation of the style in the *Book of History*.

[12.3] A quotation from *Book of Changes*, App. III, ii, 18 (Legge, p. 384).

[12.4] The "central virtue" is that of the power earth, by which Wang Mang was believed to rule.

Mandates
**to**
Officials.

His [charter]-mandate to the Marquis Making the Majestic [Principles] Brilliant, Wang Chi₆, read, "The fastnesses of the twists and overhangings[12.5] are at the south facing [the part of the ancient state], Ch'u [in Yü's province of] Ching.[12.6] You are to serve as the General of the Southern Passes for the Five Majestic [Principles]. Invigorate your military [power] and make efforts in guarding [the capital], making the majestic [principles] brilliant at my front."[12.7]

14b His [charter]-mandate to the Marquis the Commandant of Concord, Wang Chia₁c, read, "The narrow places of [Mount] Yang-t'ou are at the north facing [the former feudal states of] Yen and Chao.

王嘉曰羊頭之阮北當燕趙
武舊衛明咸于前命尉睦侯
荊楚女作五威前闢將軍振
威侯王級曰繞䔖之固南當

---

[12.5] Fu Ch'ien remarks, "A narrow and important road," and Yen Shih-ku adds, "Its location is in the present Shang Province, where the 'seven coils and twelve twists' is that place." The *Ch'ang-an Chih* (by Sung Min-ch'iu, 1019–1079) 16: 4a, *sub* Lan-t'ien, says, "The Cheng 絣 slope is southeast of the prefectural city. What the *T'ung-tien* [by Tu Yu, 735–812 (I have not been able to find this passage)] calls, 'The seven coils and twelve bends' is the difficult road of the Lan-[t'ien] Pass," so that Yen Shih-ku probably wrote 'bends 絣' for the 'twists 繞' at present in his note. Shen Ch'in-han declares that the *T'ai-p'ing Huan-yü Chi* preserves Yen Shih-ku's note with the former word (we have not been able to find it). He quotes a note to *Yi-li*, chap. 12, saying that *cheng* 絣 means 屈. (I have not been able to find it.) The reference seems to be to the road from Lan-t'ien south through the Yao Pass and Wu Pass.

*Shui-ching Chu* (by Li Tao-yüan, d. 527) 14: 19b, *sub* the Ju River, says, "The precipitous and rocky slopes of Lu-lung 盧龍 [which Yang Shou-ching (1839–1915), in his *Shui-ching-chu T'u*, N. 1, E. 1, b, locates in the present Jehol, on the Luan River, just north of the Great Wall] are sinuous and broken, hence they have the name of 'the nine bends,' " so that there was another place with this name. (Reference from Shen Ch'in-han.)

[12.6] "Ching-Ch'u" is a phrase used in *Book of Odes* IV, III, v. 1, 2, no. 305 (Legge, 643, 644), so that in Han times this term was eminently classical. The ancient state of Ch'u had its best-known capital at Ying, near the present I-chang. But this state spread until it included the lower Yangtze region and extended northwards along the sea-coast to the present Shantung. The legendary province of Ching was smaller, being supposed to have included roughly the present Hupeh, Hunan, and Kiangsi. "Ching-ch'u," i.e., "the part of Ch'u in Yü's province of Ching," was then a classical phrase denoting the middle Yangtze region below the gorges.

[12.7] The reference is to the position of the emperor on his throne, where he always faces south.

女作五威後關將軍壼口挫抵尉睦于後命壼威侯王奇曰有電
之隙東當鄭衞女作五威右關將軍鬴口批難掌咸于左命懷羌
子王福曰洴隴之阻西當戎狄女作五威右關將軍咸固擄宇懷
羌于右又遣諫大夫五十人分鑄錢於郡國是歲長安狂女子碧
呼道中曰高皇帝大怒趣歸我國不者九月必殺汝茀收捕殺之
治者掌寇大夫陳成自免去官真定劉都等謀舉兵發覺皆誅真

You are to serve as the General of the Northern Passes for the Five Majestic [Principles]. At the Hu-k'ou [Pass], strike [the enemy] and occupy [strategic positions], commanding concord at my rear."

His [charter]-mandate to the Marquis Grasping[12.8] the Majestic [Principles], Wang Ch'i, read, "The difficult places of [Mounts] Hsiao and Mien-[ch'ih] are on the east, facing [the former states of] Cheng and Wei$_s$. You are to serve as the General of the Eastern Passes for the Five Majestic [Principles]. At the Han-ku [Pass], strike down dangers, grasping the majestic [principles] at my left."

His [charter]-mandate to the Viscount Cherishing the Ch'iang, Wang Fu$_{5b}$, read, "The obstacles of the Ch'ien$_1$ [River and Mount] Lung are on the west, facing the barbarians. You are to serve as the General of the Western Passes for the Five Majestic [Principles]. Make them secure, guard them vigilantly and cherish the Ch'iang at my right."

[Wang Mang] also sent Grandee-remonstrants [and others], fifty persons [in all], by divisions to cast cash in the commanderies and kingdoms.

In this year, a mad woman of Ch'ang-an, Pi, called out in the roads, saying, "Emperor Kao is furious [and says], 'Quickly return my state. If not, in the ninth month I will inevitably kill you.'" [Wang] Mang had her arrested and killed. The Grandee in Charge of Brigands, Ch'en Ch'eng, who had to punish her, resigned of his own accord and left his office.

Liu Tu$_{1b}$ and others of [the former kingdom of] Chen-ting plotted to raise troops. [The plot] was discovered and all were executed, and in Chen-ting

*Mandates to Officials.* 12a

12b

The Mad Woman.

Abortive Rebellion.

---

12.8 Wang Nien-sun observes that *t'ang* 堂 is here a copyist's error for *ch'ang* 掌, which latter word is found at the end of this paragraph. The Sung Ch'i ed. however thinks both should be *t'ang*. Cf. Glossary *sub voce*.

and in Ch'ang-shan [Commandery] there was a great rain of hail.

15a
II
A.D. 10,
Feb./Mar.
12b

In the second year, the second month, an amnesty [was granted] to the empire. The Generals of the Five Majestic [Principles] and their Lieutenants, 72 persons [in all], returned and memorialized their reports. The vassal kings of the Han [dynasty] who had become Dukes had all given up their kingly seals and cords, had become common people, and none had disobeyed [Wang Mang's] commands. [Wang Mang] enfeoffed the Generals as Viscounts and the Lieutenants as Barons.

The Six Monopolies.

The ordinances for the six monopolies [lit., "controls"] were first established. It was commanded that the imperial government should [1] dispense liquors, [2] sell salt and [3] iron implements, [4] cast cash, and that all those who picked or took the various things from [5] famous mountains or great marshes were to be taxed.

The Five Equalizations.

13a

It was also ordered [6] that the offices [in charge of] the market-places should collect [things when they are] cheap and sell them [when they are] dear, and should lend on credit to the common people, taking three [cash per] month as interest for a hundred [cash].[12.9] The Hsi-and-Ho, [Lu K'uang], established one Officer for Liquor in each commandery, with a riding quadriga, to oversee the profit from the liquor.

A prohibition was made that the common people were not allowed to possess crossbows or cuirasses. [Those who violated this prohibition][13.1] were to be exiled to Hsi-hai [Commandery].

[12.9] Ju Shun glosses, "They put out a hundred cash and gave it to common people to use, and collected three cash interest for it per month." For these controls, cf., App. I, HS 24 B: 23a–25b. That passage however says that interest was not to be more than 10% of the borrower's income.

[13.1] Tzu-chih T'ung-chien 37: 9a has at this point the words 犯者, which Wang Hsien-ch'ien thinks have dropped out of the HS text.

月三犧和置酒士郡一人乘傳酤酒利禁民不得挾弩鎧徒
山大澤衆物者稅之又令市官收賤賣貴賒貸予民收息百
為男初設六筦之令縣官酤酒賣鹽鐵器鑄錢諸采取名
事漢諸侯王為公者悉上璽綬為民無違命者封將為子帥
定常山大雨雹二年二月赦天下五威將帥七十二人還奏

西　將　殺　不
海　軍　校　知
匈　建　尉　何
奴　奏　刁　一
單　西　護　男
于　域　劫　子
㩻　將　略　遮
故　欽　吏　臣
墨　上　士　建
芬　言　自　車
不　九　稱　前
與　月　廢　自
遂　辛　漢　稱
寇　巳　大　漢
邊　戊　將　氏
郡　己　軍　劉
殺　校　亡　子
略　尉　入　輿
吏　史　匈　與
民　陳　奴　成
十　良　又　帝
一　終　今　下
月　帶　月　妻
立　共　癸　子
國　賊　酉　也
　　　　　　劉

When the Hun *Shan-yü's* [envoy, who had come to the imperial capital,] had asked for [the *Shan-yü's*] former imperial seal, [Wang] Mang had not given it to him, consequently [the Huns had] raided the border commanderies, killing and kidnapping officials and common people.[13.2] — **Hun Raids.**

In the eleventh month, the General Establishing the State, [Sun] Chien, memorialized, "A general in the Western Frontier Regions, [Tan] Ch'in, has sent [to the court a message] which says, 'In the ninth month, on [the day] *hsin-szu*, Ch'en Lang and Chung Tai, officials of the Mou-and-Chi Colonel, joined together, murdered their Colonel, Tiao Hu, and coerced officials and soldiers, calling themselves Generalissimos of the fallen Han [dynasty], and fled to the Huns.'[13.3] — **Nov./Dec. Rebellion in the Western Frontier Regions. Sept. 15. 15b**

"Moreover in the present month, on [the day] *kuei-ch'ou*,[13.4] a man of unknown provenance obstructed the front of your servant Chien's chariot, calling himself Liu Tzu-yü of the House of Han, a son of Emperor Ch'eng by a low-[class] wife,[13.5] — **Dec. 16. A Han Pretender.**

---

13.2 Cf. *HS* 94 B: 17b = de Groot, *Die Hunnen*, p. 268, 269, where the Hun raid on So-fang Commandery is dated in A.D. 9. It is mentioned here to introduce the incident at Turfan.

13.3 For this incident at Turfan, cf. *HS* 94: 17b, 18a = de Groot, p. 270.

13.4 The text reads *kuei-yu*, but there was no such day in that month. *Yu* might easily have been mistaken for *ch'ou*. It seems the only plausible and suitable emendation.

13.5 Yen Shih-ku glosses, "Low-[class] wife *hsia-ch'i* 下妻 is like saying that she was an inferior wife 小妻." But Hung Yi-hsüan (1765-ca. 1830/1840), in his *Tu-shu Ts'ung-lu* 21: 18a, objects that an inferior wife is a concubine 妾, while a low-class wife is not an inferior wife. He notes that *HHS*, An. 1 B: 4b quotes an order of Emperor Kuang-wu stating that slaves and low-class wives who have been kidnapped may leave freely, that *ibid.* 1 B: 10b quotes another order to the effect that people who have been kidnapped and made slaves are to be freed, and those who have become people's low-class wives and want to leave shall be freely permitted to go, that *Shuo-wen* 12 B: 4a, defines *hsü* 嬬 [which is used to denote a wife or a concubine] as follows, "Weak; it also denotes a low-class wife," and that *HHS*, Mem. 2: 1a states that Wang Ch'ang later pretended to be the real Liu Tzu-yü, "saying that his mother was a singer of the former Emperor Ch'eng." Hence Hung Yi-hsüan concludes that a low-class wife was not a regular concubine but a slave-woman who was used as a mistress. The mothers of Wang Mang's illegitimate sons (99 C: 11b) were

[saying that] the Liu clan is due to be restored and that the palaces should quickly be emptied. I arrested and bound the man,[13.6] and he was [found to be a man of] Ch'ang₂-an, surnamed Wu, with the courtesy name Chung.

*13a*

"All of them have gone contrary to Heaven and disobeyed[13.7] His mandate, which is treason and inhumanity. I beg that you will pass sentence upon [Wu] Chung, together with [Ch'en] Liang and the others, and upon their blood relatives and relatives by marriage who are due to be sentenced with them." The memorial was approved.

**13b**

The Han Ancestral Temples Abolished and the Han Nobles Dismissed.

[He also memorialized],[13.8] "Emperor Kao of the Han dynasty frequently made known a warning saying, 'Dismiss the officials and soldiers [in the Han Ancestral Temples] and make [the Han emperors] guests at the sacrifice [in the temples of the present dynasty],' sincerely desiring to accord with the will of Heaven and to preserve his descendants. His ancestral temple ought not to be inside the city-walls of Ch'ang₂-an, and, together with the [members of] the Liu [clan] who are nobles, they should all have been dismissed at the same time that the Han [dynasty was overthrown]. Your Majesty is most benevolent and for this long time has not settled [this matter].

"Previously, the former Marquis of An-chung, Liu Ch'ung₂c, the [former] Marquis of Hsü-hsiang, Liu K'uai, the [former] Marquis of Ling-hsiang, Liu Ts'eng_b, and the [former] Marquis of Fu-ên, Liu

定前故安眾侯劉崇徐鄉侯劉快陵鄉侯劉曾扶思侯劉賁
在常安城中及諸劉為諸侯者當與漢俱廢陛下至仁久未
蓍戒云罷吏卒為賓食誠欲承天心全子孫也其宗廟不當
逆無道請論仲及陳良等親屬當坐者奏可漢氏高皇帝比
氏當復趣宮收繫男子即常安姓武字仲皆逆天違命大

then low-class wives.

Such a distinction between a concubine and a slave-woman mistress is likely to be blurred in practise; Chang Yi (fl. dur. 227–232), in his *Kuang-ya* ["Huang-ch'ing Ching-chieh" 672 B: 5b), says, "A wife 妻 is called a *hsü*," and Tuan Yi-ts'ai (1735–1815) identifies "low-class wife" and "inferior wife." Cf. also Wang Nien-sun's *Kuang-ya Su-cheng Pu-Cheng*: 34b ("Kuang-ts'ang Hsüeh-kuan Ts'ung-shu" ed.)

[13.6] The Sung Ch'i ed. suggests emending 男 to 妻. The Ching-yu ed. reads the former. I have not followed this suggestion.

[13.7] The Sung Ch'i ed. states that one text omits the 違.

[13.8] Wang Hsien-ch'ien observes that the words 又奏 should be in the text at this point.

等更聚眾謀反今狂狡之虜或妄自稱亡漢將軍或稱成帝子子興　至犯夷滅連未止者此聖恩不蚤絕其萌牙故也臣愚呂為漢高皇　帝為新室賓享食明堂成帝異姓之兄弟平帝壻也皆不宜復入其　廟元帝與皇太后為體聖恩所隆禮亦宜之臣謹漢氏諸廟在京師　者皆罷諸劉為諸侯吾呂戶多少就五等之差其為吏者皆罷待徐　於家上當天心稱高皇帝神靈塞狂狡之萌莽曰可嘉新公國師曰

Kuei[b], and others, one by one collected a crowd and plotted to rebel. Now some perverse and treacherous caitiffs have falsely called themselves generals of the fallen Han [dynasty] and one person has called himself [Liu] Tzu-yü, a son of Emperor Ch'eng, so that they have committed [crimes punishable by] being executed and their relatives being annihilated. The reason that these continual [rebellions] have not stopped is that your sage grace has not sooner cut off the early growths [of such events].   16a

"Your servant stupidly considers that Emperor Kao of the Han [dynasty] should become a guest of the House of Hsin and enjoy sacrifices in the *Ming-t'ang*. Emperor Ch'eng wàs your cousin with a different surname and Emperor P'ing was your son-in-law. For all of them it is not proper that they should again enter their temples. Emperor Yüan became of one flesh with the Empress Dowager [nee Wang], and the rites by which your sage grace has exalted her are appropriate also for him.

"Your servant begs that the various temples of the Han dynasty in the imperial capital should all be abolished, that the various [members of] the Liu [clan] who are nobles should be put into the hierarchy of five degrees [of nobility] in accordance with the number of households [in their estates], and that those [members of the Liu clan] who are officials should all be dismissed and await new appointments at their homes. On the one hand, [this procedure] will accord with the will of Heaven and agree with the supernatural manifestations from Emperor Kao, and [on the other hand],[14.1] it will stop the beginnings of perverseness and treachery."   **14a** *13b*

[Wang] Mang said [in his message], "It may be done. The Duke Honoring the Hsin [Dynasty], the State Master, [Liu Hsin[1a]], who, because of the man-

14.1 The word 下 has probably dropped out at this point.

303

date [given by] portents, has been made [one of] my
Four Coadjutors, the Marquis of Brilliant Virtues,
Liu Kung₂, the Marquis Leading by the Rules of
Proper Conduct, Liu Chia₁ₛ" and others, "thirty-two
persons in all, all understood the mandate of Heaven;

16b   they either presented portents from Heaven or offered
congratulatory sayings or arrested or informed upon
rebellious caitiffs, so that their merits are abundant.
The [members of] the Liu [clan] who are of the same
clan and have the same grandfathers as these thirty-
two persons are not to be dismissed and are to be
granted the [imperial] surname, Wang."

Only the State Teacher, [Liu Hsin₁ₐ], was not
granted this surname, because his daughter had been
married to [Wang] Mang's son. The title of the
Duchess Dowager of Established Tranquillity, [Wang
Mang's daughter], was changed, and she was called
the Princess of the Yellow Imperial House, in order
to cut her off from the [house of] Han.

Dec./Jan.,   In the winter, the twelfth month, it thundered.
A.D. 11.   The title of the *Shan-yü* of the Huns (*Hsiung-nu*)
was changed, and he was called the Submitted
Capture (*Fu-yü*) of the Surrendered Slaves
(*Hsiang-nu*).

War   [Wang] Mang said [in a message], "The Submitted
Declared   Capture of the Surrendered Slaves, [Lüan-ti] Chih,
Against   has 'despised and insulted the five powers,'[14.2] has
the Huns.   turned his back upon and rebelled against the four
articles,[14.3] has invaded and violated the Western
Frontier Regions, and has extended himself to and
reached the frontiers [of China], where he has made
himself injurious to the great multitude.   His crimes

[14.2] A quotation from the *Book of History* III, ii, 3 (Legge, p. 153).

[14.3] These four articles are enumerated in *HS* 94 B: 15b, 16a = de Groot, *Die Hunnen*,
264, as follows: "[1] Chinese who escape to the Huns, [2] Wu-sun who escape and surrender
to the Huns, [3] those in the various states of the Western Frontier Regions who have
worn Chinese seals and cords [officials] and surrender to the Huns, and [4] Wu-huan who
surrender to the Huns shall all not be permitted to be received."

将軍王萌出代郡相威將軍李棽遠鎮遠將軍李翁出西河誅貉將軍陽俊討穢將軍
虎貫將軍王況出五原厭難將軍陳欽震狄將軍王巡出雲中振武將軍王嘉平狄
之塞下召拜當為單于者諸匈奴人當坐虜知之法者皆赦除之遣五威將軍苗訢
分匈奴國土人民呂為十五立稽侯狦于孫十五人為單于遣中郎將藺苞戴級馳
祖故呼韓邪單于稽侯狦累世忠孝保塞守徼不忍呂一知之罪滅稽侯狦之世今
滅命遣立國將軍孫建等凡十二將十道並出共行皇天之威罰于知之身惟知先

are such that he ought to be executed and his relatives annihilated. I command and send the General Establishing the State, Sun Chien," and others, "twelve generals [in all], to go out simultaneously by ten routes, and respectfully perform the majestic punishment of August Heaven upon the person of [Lüan-ti] Chih.

"But I ponder that the ancestor of [Lüan-ti] Chih, the former *Shan-yü* Hu-han-hsieh, [Lüan-ti] Chi-hou-shan, was loyal and filial during successive *14a* reigns, protecting the barriers and guarding the frontiers. I cannot bear, because of the crime of one [Lüan-ti] Chih, to destroy the posterity of [Lüan-ti] **17a** Chi-hou-shan. Now I divide the state, territory, and **14b** people of the Huns and make of it fifteen [states], setting up fifteen descendants of [Lüan-ti] Chi-hou-shan as *Shan-yü*."

He sent a General of the Gentlemen-at-the-Palace, Lin Pao, [with] Tai Chi, to gallop just outside the barrier, summon, and install those who ought to become *Shan-yü*. Those people of the Huns who ought to be sentenced because of the law [against] the caitiff [Lüan-ti] Chih were all [granted] amnesty and set free.

[Wang Mang] sent the General of the Five Majestic [Principles], Miao Hsin, and the General of the as Rapid as Tigers, Wang K'uang$_{4a}$, to go out of Wu-yüan [Commandery], the General Repressing Difficulties, Ch'en Ch'in, and the General Making Barbarians Quake, Wang Hsün$_2$, to go out of Yün-chung [Commandery], the General Invigorating His Military [Power], Wang Chia$_{1c}$, and the General Tranquillizing the Barbarians, Wang Meng$_2$, to go out of Tai Commandery, the General Assisting the Majestic [Principles], Li Shen, and the General Maintaining Order in Distant [Places], Li Weng, to go out of Hsi-ho [Commandery], the General Executing the Mo, Yang Chün, and the General Expelling Filth, Chuang Yu, to go out of Yü-yang [Commandery], the General Inciting to Military Deeds, Wang Chün₄c, and the General Settling the Hu, Wang Yen₄, to go out of Chang-yi [Commandery], to-

**Prepara-** gether with their lieutenant-, major-[generals], and
**tions** subordinates, 180 persons [in all].   They enlisted the
**for** convicts, freemen, and armed soldiers of the empire,
**War.** 300,000 persons [in all], transporting the taxes from
**17b** many commanderies,[14.4]—clothes and furs, military implements, and provisions, escorted by the Chief Officials [of the prefectures].   From the seacoast, the Yang-tze, and the Huai [Rivers] to the northern borders, commissioners, [riding in] galloping quad-rigae, supervised and urged them, and acted in
*14b* accordance with the law for levying an army.   The empire was disturbed.   Those who arrived first en-camped in the border commanderies, waiting for them all to arrive, and then go out at the same time.[14.5]

**Five** Because his cash and [other] currencies finally did
**Kinds of** not circulate, [Wang] Mang again issued a written
**Money.** message, which said, "The common people consider their food as their life and their goods as their wealth. For this reason among the eight [objects of] govern-ment, food is given the first place.[14.6]   If the valuable
**15a** currency is all of large [denominations], when one needs a small amount [of money], it is not available; if it is all of small [denominations], then transporting it is troublesome and expensive; if large and small [denominations], big and little [coins], are each of different kinds, then their use is convenient and the common people rejoice."   Therefore [Wang Mang]

---

[14.4] At this point the text has 五大夫; Liu Feng-shih (1041–1113) declares that it is inexplicable and probably an interpolation.   I have omitted it.

[14.5] This expedition was planned on so grandiose a scale, (the armies were to take along provisions for three hundred days) that its requirements could not all be collected and it never set out.   Cf. Chuang Yu's admonition against the plan in *HS* 94 B: 18b–19b = de Groot, *Die Hunnen*, 273–5.

[14.6] A reference to *Book of History* V, iv, 7 (Legge, p. 327).

便而民樂於是造貨貨五品話在食貨志百姓不從但

行小大錢二品而已盜鑄錢者不可禁迺重其法一家

鑄錢五家坐之沒入為奴婢吏民出入持布錢以副符行

傳不持者廚傳勿舍關津苛留公卿皆持以入宮殿門

欲民重而行之是時爭為符命封侯其不為者相戲曰

created valuable currency of five kinds. A discussion is in the "Treatise on Food and Goods."[15.1]

The people did not accord, and only used merely two denominations of cash, the large and the diminutive [cash]. Since those who cast counterfeit cash could not be stopped, [Wang Mang] made the penalties [against counterfeiting] heavy. When one family cast cash, the five [neighboring] families were to be sentenced for it, [their property was to be] confiscated, and they were to be enslaved.

When officials and common people went in or out [the barriers], they were to carry spade-money as an adjunct to their passport credentials.[15.2] For those who did not carry [spade-money], the [post]-kitchens and relay stations were not to house them, and at the barriers and fords they were to be investigated and detained.[15.3] The ministers were all to hold them when they entered the gates of the palaces and halls. The intention was to make them valuable and circulate.

At this time, [many persons] strove to make mandates [from Heaven by means of] portents in order to be enfeoffed as marquises. Those who did not

24 B: 21b–23a.

The People Oppose the New Currency.

18a Officials Forced to Carry Spade-money.

New Portents Prohibited.

[15.1] Cf. App. I, *HS* 24 B: 21b–23a. This passage enumerates six kinds of money, of 28 denominations altogether. In the present passage, round cash and spade-money are grouped together because they were made of the same material, bronze, hence there are said to be only five kinds. The peculiarity of this bronze coinage was that as the denominations of the coins became greater, the proportionate amount of metal became progressively less, so that while the one-cash coin contained 1 *shu* of bronze, the thousand-cash spade coin contained only 24 *shu* of bronze, 0.024 *shu* per cash. Cf. 24 B: n. 22.11. No wonder Wang Mang had to compel people to use them! His purpose seems to have been to facilitate the transport of large sums of money, as well as to profit from the depreciation of the coinage.

[15.2] Yen Shih-ku explains, "[According to] the old laws, those who travelled carried passport credentials and were then not delayed or detained. Now [Wang Mang] changed [the law] and ordered that they should carry spade-money to be with their credentials, and thus only were they permitted to pass."

[15.3] Yen Shih-ku explains, "The kitchens *ch'u* 廚 were the places for eating and drinking in traveling along the roads. The *chuan* 傳 were the hostelries established at the posts. *Ho* 苛 is to question 問."

make them, made sport, saying, "Were we alone without letters of appointment from the Lord of Heaven?" A Director of Mandates [from the Five Majestic Principles], Ch'en Ch'ung, advised [Wang] Mang of it, saying, "This [matter] is opening the way for wicked 'subjects to confer [kingly] favors [upon themselves],'[15.4] and to bring confusion upon the mandate of Heaven. It would be proper to cut away its source." [Wang] Mang also had had his fill of it, and thereupon had a Grandee Master of

*15a*  Writing, Chao Ping, investigate and try [such offenders]. Those who [made known portents] which were not those published by the Generals and Lieutenants of the Five Majestic [Principles] were all sent to prison.

Chen Feng  Previously, Chen Feng, Liu Hsin₁ₐ, and Wang
Discarded.  Shun₄ᵦ had been [Wang] Mang's intimate advisors and had led those who were in office in making known

**15b**  [Wang Mang's] achievements and virtuous conduct for rewards.[15.5] His titles of [Duke] Giving Tranquillity to the Han [Dynasty] and Ruling Governor, together with the enfeoffment of [Wang] Mang's mother and his two sons and a nephew,[15.6] were all planned by [Chen] Feng together with the others. [Chen] Feng, [Wang] Shun₄ᵦ, and [Liu] Hsin₁ₐ had moreover received grants from him and had all become indeed wealthy and honorable.

They did not in addition want to bring it about that [Wang] Mang should become Regent. The first beginnings of his becoming the Regent came from the Marquis of Ch'üan-ling, Liu Ch'ing₄ᵢ, the Displayer of Splendor in the South, Hsieh Hsiao, and the Prefect of Ch'ang-an, T'ien Chung-shu.

[15.4] A phrase from the *Book of History* V, iv, 19 (Legge, p. 334).

[15.5] *HHS*, Mem 2: 8b, quotes Chu Fou as saying, "When Wang Mang was Ruling Governor, Chen Feng went in to him at dawn and at dusk to plan and discuss [matters]. At that time, people said, 'The midnight guest is Chen [Feng] Chang-po.'" (Reference from Yang Shu-ta.)

[15.6] Cf. *HS* 99 A: 32a.

令莽居攝也居攝之萌出於泉陵侯劉慶前輝光謝囂長安令田終術
莽母兩子兄子皆豐等所共謀而豐舜亦受其賜並富貴矣非復欲
初甄豐劉歆王舜為莽腹心倡導在位褒揚功德安漢宰衡之號及封
絕其原莽亦厭之遂使尚書大夫趙並驗治非五威將率所班皆下獄
獨無天帝除書乎司命陳崇白莽曰此開姦臣作福之路而亂天命宜

莽羽翼已成意欲稱攝豐等承順其意莽後封舜歆兩子及豐孫豐等

爵位已盛心意既滿又實畏漢宗室天下豪桀而疏遠欲進者並作符命

莽遂據呂即真舜歆内懼而已豐素剛强莽覺其不説故徙大阿右拂大

司空豐託記符命文為更始將軍與賣餅兒王盛同列豐父子黙黙時子尋

為侍中京兆大尹茂德侯即作符命言新室當分陝立二伯曰豐為右伯

When [Wang] Mang's wings had grown and he desired to be entitled Regent, [Chen] Feng and the others accepted and agreed with his intentions. [Wang] Mang immediately enfeoffed in addition the two sons of [Wang] Shun₄ᵦ and of [Liu] Hsin₁ₐ, together with [Chen] Feng's grandson.  **18b**

When the noble rank and official position of [Chen] Feng and the others had been received, their ambitions were satisfied.  They moreover really feared the Han imperial house and the prominent persons in the empire.  But those who had been distant from [Wang Mang] and wanted to advance, simultaneously made mandates [from Heaven given through] portents.  When [Wang] Mang thereupon employed them in order to ascend [the throne as] the actual [Emperor, Wang] Shun₄ᵦ and [Liu] Hsin₁ₐ merely became inwardly fearful.

[Chen] Feng was ordinarily resolute, [so Wang] Mang became conscious that [Chen Feng] was not pleased.  Hence [Wang Mang] removed him from being Grand Support Aiding on the Right and Grand Minister of Works,[15.7] and, taking advantage of a writing on a mandate by a portent, he made him the General of a New Beginning, ranking him the same as the seller of cakes, Wang Sheng.  [Chen] Feng and his son kept silent [but were dissatisfied].[15.8]

At this time, [Chen Feng's] son, [Chen] Hsün, was a Palace Attendant, Grand Governor of the Capital, and Marquis of Abundant Virtues.  He now made a mandate [from Heaven by means of a] portent, saying that the House of Hsin ought to divide [its territory at] Shan and set up two Chiefs [to govern that territory], making [Chen] Feng the Western   *15b*

Chen Hsün and Associates Executed.

---

15.7 Li Tz'u-ming, *ibid.* 7: 6a, suggests that 豐 is here an interpolation.  It interrupts the sentence.

15.8 In *SC* 84: 24, where this phrase is written *mo-mo* 嘿嘿, Ying Shao interprets it as 不自得也.

Chen Hsün
and his
Associates
Executed.

19a

16a

Chief and the Grand Tutor, and P'ing Yen, the Eastern Chief, as in the former circumstances [was done for the Dukes of] Chou and of Shao.[15.9]

[Wang] Mang thereupon followed this [mandate] and installed [Chen] Feng as the Western Chief. [Chen Feng] was to "report on his duties"[15.10] and go out to the west, but had not yet gone, when [Chen] Hsün again made a mandate [from Heaven by means of] a portent, which said that the Empress [nee Wang] of the former Emperor P'ing of the Han clan, the Princess of the Yellow Imperial House, was [to be] the wife of [Chen] Hsün.

[Wang] Mang had been set [on the throne] by fraud, so he suspected in his heart that his great officials would hate and malign him. He wanted to terrify them in order to make his inferiors fear him. Because of these [feelings], he burst out in anger and said, "The Princess of the Yellow Imperial House is a mother of the empire. What means this [statement] [about her becoming the wife of Chen Hsün]?" He [ordered Chen] Hsün arrested. [Chen] Hsün fled and [Chen] Feng committed suicide.

[Chen] Hsün followed a gentleman versed in the magical arts and entered [the solitudes of] Mt. Hua. After more than a year he was siezed. His confession implicated [1] the Palace Attendant, Supernaturally [Influencing] General [Whose Influence] Penetrates Eastwards, Grandee in Charge of the Five Behaviors, and Marquis Prospering the Majestic [Principles], Liu Fen, the son of the State Master and Duke, [Liu] Hsin[1a], [2] Liu Fen's younger brother, the Senior Department Head, Colonel of the Ch'ang River [Encampments], and Marquis Attacking Caitiffs, [Liu] Yung[4], [3] the General of the

太傅平晏為左伯如周召故事莽即從之拜豐為右伯當述職西出未

行尋俊作行命言故漢氏平帝后黃皇室主為尋之妻莽呂詐立心疑

大臣怨謗欲震威臣懼下因是發怒曰黃皇室主天下母此何謂也收

捕尋尋亡豐自殺尋隨方士入華山歲餘捕得辭連國師公歆子侍中

東通靈將五司大夫陵威侯棻棻弟右曹長水校尉代虜侯泳大司空

---

[15.9] *SC* 34: 2 (Mh IV, 133 f) recounts that at the time of King Ch'eng of the Chou dynasty, the Duke of Shao supervised the country west of Shan and the Duke of Chou that east of Shan.

[15.10] A phrase from *Mencius* I, B, iv, 5 (Legge, p. 159).

邑弟左關將軍堂威候奇及歙門人侍中騎都尉丁
隆等牽引公卿業親列候呂下死者數百人尋手理
有天子字莽解其臂入視之曰此一大子也或曰一
六子也六者殺也明尋父子當殺也迺流㚄于幽
州故尋于三危殛鯀于羽山皆驛車載其屍傳致云

Eastern Passes[16.1] [for the Five Majestic Principles] and Marquis Grasping[16.2] the Majestic Principles, [Wang] Ch'i, the younger brother of the Grand Minister of Works, [Wang] Yi₅, together with [4] a disciple of Liu Hsin₁ₐ, the Palace Attendant and Chief Commandant of Cavalry, Ting Lung, and others. They involved ministers, their cabals, and their relatives. The full marquises and those [ranking] lower who died were numbered by the hundreds.

In the lines of [Chen] Hsün's hands there were the words, "Son of Heaven." [Wang] Mang had his arms untied, had him enter [the palace], and looked at [his hands]. He said, "These [words] are 'one big fellow.' "[16.3] Some one said, "[It is] 'one *lu* fellow.' '*Lu*' is to put to death.[16.4] It makes plain that [Chen Feng and Chen] Hsün, father and son, must be put to death and die." Thereupon [Wang Mang] executed and banished [Liu] Fen to Yu Province, executed and expelled [(Wang) Ch'i to Mt. Ch'ung, executed and drove away Chen] Hsün to [Mt.] San-wei, and executed and killed [Ting] Lung on Mt. Yü.[16.5] The corpses of all were transported in post-chariots to their destinations.

*16a*

19b

16.1 Ch'ien Ta-chao remarks that 闕 should be 關 to accord with the phrase on 99 B: 12a. The Ching-yu ed. reads the latter. Wang Hsien-ch'ien notes that the Official ed. and the Southern Academy ed. read likewise.

16.2 Wang Hsien-ch'ien notes that 堂 should be 掌 to agree with the reading on 99 B: 12a.

16.3 The Official ed. reads *t'ien* 天 for *ta* 大, with the note, "The Sung Ch'i [ed.] says, '*T'ien* should perhaps be *ta*.' " But the Ching-yu ed. (1035) reads *ta*.

16.4 Chen Hsün was said to have had on his hand the words 天子. Wang Mang said they were 一大子. Another person said they were 一六子. The words '六 (six)' and '戮 (put to death)' must have then been pronounced alike; cf. Karlgren, *Grammata Serica*, ∦1032a & 1069v; *Analyt. Dict.* ∦546 & 563.

16.5 He was imitating Shun's treatment of his four criminals as related in the *Bk. of Hist.* II, i, 12 (Legge, p. 39 f). Wang Mang evidently interpreted this passage, not as Yang Shu-ta and Legge do, but as the K'ung An-kuo tradition did, which says,"殛，竄，放 and 流 all [mean] execution 誅. Their difference is in the character of the language used." Even if the K'ung An-kuo commentary is a later forgery, yet it probably contains early statements. *Mencius* V, A, iii, 2 (Legge, p. 349), repeating this passage

**16b**
**Wang**
**Mang's**
**Terrifying**
**Appear-**
**ance.**

As a man, [Wang] Mang had a large mouth and a receding chin, bulging eyes with brilliant[16.6] pupils, and a loud voice which was hoarse. He was seven feet five inches tall,[16.7] loved thick-[soled] shoes and tall bonnets, and used clothes padded with felt.[16.8] He stuck out his chest and made himself look tall, [so that he could] look down on those who were around him.[16.9]

At this time, there was a person skilled in medical and allied arts who was an Expectant Appointee at the Yellow Gate. Someone asked him about [Wang] Mang's figure and countenance, and the Expectant Appointee replied, "[Wang] Mang is a person who may be said to have owl's eyes, tiger's jaws, and a wolf's voice. Hence he is able to eat people and is also due to be eaten by people." The person who questioned him gave information about [his reply, and Wang] Mang exterminated the Expectant Ap-

之聲者也故能食人亦當為人所食問者告之莽誅滅待
詔黄門者或問曰莽形貌待詔曰莽所謂鴟目虎吻豺狼
應高冠呂鷺褏衣反脣高視瞰臨左右是時有用方技待
莽為人侈口蹙頤露眼赤精大聲而嘶長七尺五寸好厚

from the *Book of History*, states that Shun "slew 殺 [the prince of] the San-miao, [one of these four criminals], on [Mt.] San-wei." *Han Fei-tzu* 13: 7b, 8a; ch. 34, furthermore states, "Yao, ... using military weapons, executed 誅殺 K'un in the wilderness of Mt. Yü, ... and, using military weapons, executed 誅 the Provider of Works at the capital of Yu Province." There is thus ample evidence to substantiate the K'ung An-kuo interpretation as ancient. Wang Mang certainly understood this passage to denote execution. Cf. Chung Feng-nien, "The Four Banishments in the *Shu-ching*," in *Yenching Journal of Chinese Studies*, no. 27, June 1940, pp. 211–232, Karlgren, *BMFEA* 20, 91ff, Gl. 1272; *Shang-shu Chu-su* 3: 8b.

The *Bk. of Hist.* records the punishment of *four* criminals; Li Tz'u-ming, *ibid.*, 7: 16a, accordingly suggests that a clause has dropped out of the text. After 放 I accordingly insert the words 奇于崇山竄. (Li Tz'u-ming's own emendation does not follow the *Book of History* closely enough.)

[16.6] 赤 (red) and 赫 (fiery) were anciently interchanged.

[16.7] About 5 ft. 7 in. Eng. measure.

[16.8] For the shoes and hats, cf. Eberhard, *Die Mode der Han-und Chin-Zeit*, pp. 87, 49–55. *Erh-ya* (Han period) 3: 5a, says, "*Li* 氀 is *chi* 罽 (wool or felt)," and Hsing Ping (932–1010) says, "People of honorable clans say that *li* means felt (*mao* 毛 -*chi*). The Hu connect sheep's hair and make clothes. Then *chi* is made of woven hair like the present hairy rug 毛氍毹." K'ung Ying-ta (574–648), in a note to *Book of History* 6: 11a (in "The Tribute of Yü"; cf. Legge, p. 122), quotes Sung Yen (fl. ca. 220) as saying, "*Mao-li* becomes wool (*chi*), which is woven hair."

[16.9] Stange, p. 165, translates differently, "Selbst wenn er (scheinbar) abgewandt war, behielt er doch, von oben sehend, seine Umgebung im Auge."

詔而封告者俊常爵雲母屏面非親近莫得見也是歲吕初睦侯姚

恂為寧始將軍三年莽曰百官改更職事分移律令儀法未及悉定

通政事能言語明文學者各一人詣王路四門遣尚書大夫諸侯二千石舉吏民有德行

勞北邊還言五原北假膏壤殖穀異時常置田官乃吕並為田禾將

軍發戊卒屯田北假吕助軍糧是時諸將在邊須大衆集吏士敢縱

pointee [and his relatives] and enfeoffed the informer. Afterwards [Wang Mang] regularly screened himself with a mica fan, so that, except for his intimates, no one was permitted to have an audience with him.

In this year, the Marquis of Original Concord, Yao Hsün, was made the General of a Peaceful Beginning.

In the third year, [Wang] Mang said, "The many offices have been changed and altered and their duties have been redistributed, but the code, ordinances, ceremonies, and laws have not yet been all determined upon, [hence] temporarily the Han [dynasty's] code, ordinances, ceremonies, and laws should be followed and applied in [government] business." **III A.D. 11. 20a The Han Code Continued.**

He ordered that the ministers, grandees, nobles, [and officials ranking at] 2000 piculs might recommend one official or commoner each who showed an upright character, who was experienced in administrative matters, who was gifted in speech, and who was intelligent in literary studies.[16.10] [Such] persons were to go to the [Directors of] the Four Gates to the Royal Apartments.

[Wang Mang] sent the Grandee Master of Writing, Chao Ping, to bring encouragement to the northern borders. He returned and said that in Po-chia of Wu-yüan [Commandery the soil] is fertile and produces grain, and that at other times offices for cultivated fields had regularily been established there. Thereupon [Wang Mang] made [Chao] Ping the General of Cultivated Fields and Grain to send frontier troops to garrison farms in Po-chia, in order to assist the army with provisions. **16b 17a Trouble At the Northern Borders.**

At that time, while the various generals who were at the border were waiting for the large bands [of soldiers] to be collected, their officers and soldiers

16.10 The four qualifications are taken from *Analects* XI, ii, 2.

Disorder at the Northern Borders.

did as they pleased, while the inner commanderies were troubled with levying [troops] and collecting [materials]. The common people left the cities and suburbs and became vagrants, becoming thieves and robbers. In Ping Province[17.1] they were especially numerous. [Wang] Mang ordered that the seven highest ministers and the six high ministers[17.2] should all be concurrently entitled Generals, and sent the General Outstanding in Military Affairs, Lu Ping, and others to control the famous cities, together with 55 Generals of the Gentlemen-at-the-Palace and 55 Upholders of the Laws Clad in Embroidered Garments separately to control the large commanderies along the border, to correct the greatly cunning

20b　villains who were taking it upon themselves to make

法各五十五人分填緣邊大郡督大姦猾擅
遣羨武將軍逯並等填名都中郎將繡衣執
州平州尤甚恭令七公六卿號皆兼稱將軍
而內郡愁於徵發民棄城郭流亡為盜賊并

---

[17.1] At this point the text has the words "and in the P'ing Province 平州." Hu San-hsing remarks that P'ing Province did not exist until the third century, when the kingdom of Wei divided P'ing Province off of Yu Province and says that the word "P'ing" is an error. He notes that at the end of the Later Han period, Kung-sun Tu set himself up as the Shepherd of P'ing Province, which was in the southern part of the present Manchuria.

Ch'ien Ta-hsin however remarks that *HS* 55: 19b states that Lu Po-tê was a man from "P'ing-chou₁ 平州 in Hsi-ho [Commandery]," so that "P'ing-chou₁ was the name of a county belonging to Hsi-ho Commandery within the section [called] Ping department (*chou*)." (A *chou* contained 2500 families; cf. 24 A: 4a). *HS* 28 Bi: 29a writes this name P'ing-chou₂ 平周, so that probably *chou*₁ and *chou*₂ were anciently interchanged. But Shen Ch'in-han suggests that P'ing Province was probably established by Wang Mang out of part of Yu Province, so that Kung-sun Tu took his title from this occurrence, and that if P'ing-chou was merely the name of a county, disorder confined chiefly to part of one department would hardly have been worth mentioning.

This latter remark seems quite conclusive as a reply to Ch'ien Ta-hsin's suggestion. There is moreover no classical precedent for the name "P'ing Province" and no other notice of Wang Mang having established it, so that this name is itself very doubtful. *HS* 16: 53b and 17: 20b list a Marquisate at P'ing-chou₁, but this place was in the present Shantung, not where these disturbances would be expected. Perhaps the best solution of the difficulty is that of Hu San-hsing; I have consequently omitted this name, since it is uncertain what province was originally mentioned instead of P'ing Province.

[17.2] Hu San-hsing remarks that the "seven highest ministers" were the four Coadjutors with the previous "three highest ministers"; the "six high ministers" were the Hsi-and-Ho, the Deciding Judge, the Arranger of the Ancestral Temple, the Director of Music, the Provider of Works, and the My Forester.

作農民離散司監若此可謂稱不自今日來敢犯此者輒捕繫呂
正也今則不然各為權勢恐揭良民妄封人頸得錢者去毒蠚並
内置司命軍正外設軍監十有二人誠欲曰司不奉命令軍人咸
虜知罪當夷滅故遣猛將分十有二部將同時出一舉而決絕之矣
弄兵者皆便為姦於外梳亂州郡貨賂為市侵漁百姓莽下書曰

dupes of the troops. They all found it convenient to do evil in [the regions] outside [the capital], and caused confusion in the provinces and commanderies, making a business of bribes, taking advantage of the people for their own profit.

[Wang] Mang issued a written message, saying, "The caitiff [Lüan-ti] Chih's crimes are such that he is due to be annihilated [with his relatives]. Hence I sent my fierce generals, with separate [commands as] twelve divisional generals, to set out simultaneously and destroy him utterly at one stroke. Within [the capital], I established Directors of Mandates [from the Five Majestic Principles] and Chiefs of Armies; outside [the capital] I set up Superintendants of Armies, twelve persons [in all] verily intending that they should have charge over those who do not uphold my mandate and should cause the soldiers all to be upright.

"But now they are not so. Each uses his power and influence to intimidate good people, illegally putting seals upon common peoples' necks. When [these officials] secure [a bribe of] cash, they take [the seal] off.[17.3] Poisonous and venomous stings are simultaneously performed [at various places], so that the peasants have left [their homes and have become] scattered. If the Directors and Superintendants are as the foregoing, can they be said to be suitable [for their offices]? From this time and henceforth, those who presume to offend in this [manner] will be immediately arrested and held [in prison] and their names shall be reported to me." [The officials] how-

Corruption
**17b**

*17a*

---

[17.3] Ju Shun explains, "Powerful officials illegally used the law to do injustice to good people, making them slaves by putting a seal upon their necks in order to distinguish them. When they secured cash for the hire [of these condemned persons], they then took off their seals." According to this passage, some sort of a sealed cord about the neck seems to have been used instead of the iron collar also used in the Former Han period to distinguish slaves and criminals; cf. 99 C: 12b. If merely a seal-mark had been used instead of branding, there would have been little reason for putting it on the neck.

ever did as they liked just as before.

**A New**
**Shan-yü**
**Set Up.**

When Lin Pao and Tai Chi reached [the region] just outside the Barrier, they summoned and allured [Lüan-ti] Hsien, the younger brother of the *Shan-yü*, [Lüan-ti Chih], and [Lüan-ti] Hsien's son, [Lüan-ti] Teng, to enter through the Barrier. By force they installed [Lüan-ti] Hsien as the *Shan-yü* Hsiao, granting him a thousand catties of actual gold, and very

21a　much brocade and embroidery. They sent him away and brought [Lüan-ti] Teng to Ch'ang-an, [where he was] installed as the *Shan-yü* Shun and retained in the [Hun] princes' quarters.[17.4]

**Wang**
**Shun**
**dies.**

From the time that [Wang] Mang usurped the throne, the Grand Master, Wang Shun[4b], had been ill with [asthma and][17.5] palpitation of the heart, which gradually became worse, so that he died. [Wang] Mang said [in a message], "Anciently the [Foreseen] Grand Duke of Ch'i, [Lü Shang], became the Grand Master of the Chou dynasty because of his purity and virtue during successive reigns—verily this is what I have perceived [in Wang Shun]. Let [Wang] Shun[4b]'s son, [Wang] Yen[2], succeed to his father's noble rank and become the Duke Giving Tranquillity to the Hsin [Dynasty]; let [Wang] Yen[2]'s younger brother, the Marquis As Recompense to [the House of] Hsin, [Wang] K'uang[1a], become the Grand Master and General; and [let his house] forever be Coadjutors to the Hsin dynasty."[17.6]

[17.4] *HS* 94 B: 18b, 20a = de Groot, *Die Hunnen* p. 272, 276 states that Lüan-ti Teng's brother, Lüan-ti Tsu, was first made *Shan-yü* Shun and was taken to Ch'ang-an with Lüan-ti Teng, where Lüan-ti Tsu died, and then Wang Mang appointed Lüan-ti Teng as *Shan-yü* Shun in place of his brother.

[17.5] The Sung Ch'i ed. states that the Old text (before vi cent.) writes *ch'uan* 喘 for *chi* 悸. Wang Nien-sun accordingly concludes that this passage originally read both words, *ch'uan-chi*. These two words are unlike, so that they would not be confused for each other; probably the Old text and later editions had each dropped out one of these two words. *T'ai-p'ing Yü-lan* (978–983) 741: 4a, quotes this passage with both words. Wei Chao, in a note to *HS* 90: 15a, says, "When in one's heart he pants and sighs (*ch'uan-息*), it is called *chi*." Stange, p. 169, n. 2, suggests angina pectoris.

[17.6] This practise was in imitation of that in the ancient state of Lu, where the highest

講書沛郡陳咸為講禮崔發為講樂祭酒遣謁者持安車印綬即拜楚國
卿琅邪左咸為講春秋潁川滿昌為講詩長安國由為講易平陽唐昌為
是為四友又置師友祭酒及侍中諫議六經祭酒各一人凡九祭酒秩上
唐林為胥附博士李充為奔走諫大夫趙襄為先後中郎將廉丹為禦侮
伯鳳為傅丞博士袁聖為阿輔京兆尹王嘉為保拂是為四師故尚書令
輔為太子置師友各四人秩曰大夫曰故大司徒馬宮為師疑故少府宗

For the Heir-apparent, there were established four Masters and four Companions, who were ranked as Grandees. The former Grand Minister over the Masses, Ma Kung, became the Master of Doubts; the former Privy Treasurer, Tsung-po Feng, became the Assistant Tutor; the Erudit Yüan Sheng became the Supporting Coadjutor; the Governor of the Capital, Wang Chia$_{1c}$, became the Aiding Guardian. The foregoing were the Four Masters.

The former Prefect of the Masters of Writing, T'ang Lin, became the Attacher of the Indifferent, the Erudit Li Ch'ung$_1$ became the Hastener to Submission, the Grandee-remonstrant Chao Hsiang became the Guide, the General of the Gentlemen-at-the-Palace, Lien Tan, became the Defender. The foregoing were the four Companions.

There was also established one Libationer for the Masters and Companions, together with one [Libationer] for the Palace Attendants, one [Libationer for] the Remonstrants and Consultants, and one Libationer [to expound] each of the six Classics, nine Libationers altogether. They were ranked [the same as] the highest ranking of the high ministers. Tso Hsien, from Lang-ya [Commandery], became the [Libationer] Expounding the *Spring and Autumn;* Man Ch'ang, from Ying-ch'uan [Commandery], became the [Libationer] Expounding the *Book of Odes;* Kuo Yu, from Ch'ang-an, became the [Libationer] Expounding the *Book of Changes;* T'ang Ch'ang, from P'ing-yang, became the [Libationer] Expounding the *Book of History;* Ch'en Hsien, from P'ei Commandery, became the [Libationer] Expounding the *Book of Rites;* and Ts'ui Fa became the Libationer Expounding the *Book of Music.* [Wang Mang] sent an Internuncio, bringing a comfortable chariot, seal, and cord, to go to [the home of] and install Kung

New Officials.

18a

17b

21b

A Heroic Refusal.

bureaucratic posts were held hereditarily by the descendants of Duke Huan and were relatives of the ruler.

Sheng, of the [former] kingdom of Ch'u, as the Libationer for the Masters and Companions of the Heir-apparent. [Kung] Sheng would not respond to the summons, refused to eat, and died.[18.1]

The General of a Peaceful Beginning, Yao Hsün, was dismissed and the Palace Attendant, the Marquis of Eminent Blessings, K'ung Yung, became the General of a Peaceful Beginning.

Ominous Portents.
In this year, in the prefecture of Ch'ih-yang, there were shadows of dwarfs, a foot and more tall. Some rode in quadrigae with horses, some walked on foot, holding[18.2] all sorts of things. The size [of these shadows in each group] were all proportionate to each other. On the third day, it stopped.

In the commanderies on the banks of the [Yellow] River, locusts sprang up, and the [Yellow] River broke its banks in Wei Commandery, overflowing several commanderies from Ch'ing-ho [Commandery] eastwards. Previous to this [time, Wang] Mang had feared that the [Yellow] River would break its banks and injure the tumuli and graves [of his great-grandfather, Wang Ho, and his descendants], at Yüan-ch'eng, [but] when it broke its banks, it went eastwards and Yüan-ch'eng was not troubled by the

22a **18b**
IV
A.D. 12
Feb./Mar.
Summer
Lüan-ti
Teng
Executed.
water. Hence he therefore did not dike it.

In the fourth year, the second month, an amnesty [was granted to] the empire.

In the summer, a red emanation came out in the southeast, reaching to heaven.

The General Repressing Difficulties, Ch'en Ch'in,[18.3] said that he had captured some caitiff [Huns] alive, and that [they had told] that violations

----

[18.1] For this heroic loyal refusal to take office under Wang Mang, cf. Glossary *sub* Kung Sheng.

[18.2] Ch'ien Ta-chao notes that the Southern Academy ed. and the Fukien ed. read 操 for 據. The Ching-yu and Official ed. read similarly.

[18.3] In 99 B: 14b and 94 B: 20a this man's given name is written 欽 so that 歆 is an error here.

----

襄回年二月秋天下夏赤氣出東南竟天厭難將軍陳欽言捕虜生口
數郡先是茫恐河決為元城眾墓害及決東去元城不憂水故遂不隄
行據持萬物小大合相稱三日止瀕河郡蝗生河魏郡泛清河巨東
祿侯孔永為亭始將軍是歲池陽縣有小人景長尺餘或乘車馬或步
贊勝為太子師友祭酒勝不應徵不食而死亭始將軍姚恂兌侍中榮

正域曰美風俗追監前代炎綱炎紀惟在堯典十有二州衛有五服詩
芽土下書曰子曰不德襲于聖祖為萬國主恩安黎元在于建侯分州
恭每當出輒先授索城中名曰橫授是月橫授五日恭至明堂授諸侯
大司馬甄邯死寧始將軍孔永為大司馬侍中大贅侯輔為寧始將軍
虜犯邊者皆孝單于咸子角所為莽怒斬其子登於長安曰視諸蠻夷

of the border by the caitiffs had all been done by [Lüan-ti] Chio, the son of *Shan-yü* Hsiao, [Lüan-ti] Hsien. [Wang] Mang became angry and decapitated *18a* [Lüan-ti Hsien's] son, [Lüan-ti] Teng, at Ch'ang-an, in order to make him an example to the barbarians.

The Commander-in-chief, Chen Han, died, and the General of a Peaceful Beginning, K'ung Yung, became the Commander-in-chief. The Palace Attendant and Grand Keeper of the Robes, Hou Fu, became the General of a Peaceful Beginning.

Every time that [Wang] Mang had to go out [of the palace], immediately preceding there was a search in the city, which was called a "general search." In this month there was a general search for five days.[18.4]

When [Wang] Mang reached the *Ming-t'ang* and A New gave the nobles their clods [enveloped in] quitch- Capital grass[18.5] [as a sign of enfeoffment], he issued a written Ordered. message which said, "Although I am not virtuous, because I have inherited [the merits accumulated by] my sage ancestors, I have become the lord of the ten-thousand states. Now the tranquillizing of the great multitude consists in establishing a nobility, dividing up [the country into][18.6] provinces and correcting their frontiers, in order to beautify [peoples'] customs, and so I have sought out and surveyed the fundamental and subordinate principles of the earlier dynasties.

"Verily, in the 'Canon of Yao' [it speaks of] twelve provinces and [concerning] defences [it speaks of] five domains;[18.7] the *Book of Odes* [speaks of] fifteen

---

[18.4] For the "search," cf. *HFHD*, II, 113, n. 36.6. Wang Mang changed its name from *so* 索 to *heng-sou* 橫搜.

[18.5] Cf. Glossary, *sub* Marquises.

[18.6] The Sung Ch'i ed. states that after 分 there should be the word 九. But its insertion would break the rhythm.

[18.7] The nine provinces are mentioned, not in the present "Canon of Yao," but in the next chapter, where Shun is said to have made this division. (Anciently these two

22b
19a
18b

states, distributed among nine provinces;[18.8] the 'Sacrificial Odes of Yin' have the saying, '[T'ang the Victorious] grandly possessed his nine possessions';[19.1] and the 'Tribute of Yü' [speaks of] nine provinces, not having a Ping or Yu [Province],[19.2] while the *Chou Offices*, [*sub*] the Commander-[in-chief], has however no Hsü or Liang [Province].[19.3] The lords and kings changed [the arrangements] of their [predecessors]. Each one [distinguished himself] by his words or actions, some making their deeds brilliant and some enlarging their foundations, [but] their purposes were outstanding and their intentions were the same.

"Anciently, two sovereigns of the Chou [dynasty] received the mandate [of Heaven], hence [the dynasty] had dwelling-places at the Eastern Capital, [Lo], and at the Western Capital, [Feng]. Since I have received the mandate [of Heaven], I should verily also be like them. Let Lo-yang become the Eastern Capital of the House of Hsin and let Ch'ang₂-an become the Western Capital of the House of Hsin, [two] royal domains with the appropriate organizations, each [royal domain] including territory for the estates of high bureaucrats and baronesses. The provinces shall accord with those in the 'Tribute of

國十五拂徧九州殷頌有奄有九有之言禹貢之九州
無幷幽圉司馬則無徐梁帝王相改各有云為或昭
其事或大其本厥義著明其務一矣昔用二后受命改
有東都西都之交命蓋亦如之其曰洛陽為新
室東都常安為新室西都邦畿連體各有采任州從焉

chapters formed one.)　Cf. *Book of History* II, ɪ, iii, 10 (Legge, p. 38).　The five domains are mentioned in *ibid.* II, ɪv, i, 8 (Legge, p. 85).

[18.8] Yen Shih-ku enumerates these fifteen as follows: Chou and the south, Shao and the south, Wei₈, the Chou kingly state, Cheng, Ch'i, Wei₈, T'ang, Ch'in, Ch'en, Kuei, Ts'ao, Pin, Lu, and Shang; and alternatively as Chou and the south, Shao and the south, Pei, Yung, Wei₈, the Chou kingly state, Cheng, Ch'i, Wei₈, T'ang, Ch'in, Ch'en, Kuei, Ts'ao, and Pin. The second list is taken from the names of the "Lessons from the States"; cf. Legge, *She-king*, I, vii ff.

The Sung Ch'i ed. states that the 國 should be 曰.

[19.1] *Book of Odes*, IV, ɪɪɪ, iii (Legge, p. 636).

[19.2] *Book of History* III, ɪ, i (Legge, pp. 92–151).

The Sung Ch'i ed. states that the Shun-hua ed. (994–997) omitted the words 無幷.

[19.3] *Chou-li* 33: 6a–8b (Biot, II, 265–275) contains this list of provinces, which are enumerated *sub* the *Chih-fang-shih*, a subordinate of the Commander-in-chief. The three different lists of the nine provinces are discussed in the *Tz'u-hai, tzu*, p. 106 *sub* 九州.

貢為九爵從周氏有五諸侯之員千有八百附城之數亦
如之呂侯有功諸公一同有眾萬戶土方百里侯伯一國
東戶五千土方七十里子男一則眾戶二千有五百土方
五十里附城大者食邑九成眾戶九百土方三十里自九

Yü' and shall be nine [in number].

"The noble ranks shall follow those of the Chou dynasty and shall be five [in number]. The number of the nobles shall be [limited to] 1800, and the number of the Sub-Vassals shall in addition be the same [as that of the nobles, which positions] shall await those who distinguish themselves. The various dukes shall [each] have the territory of one *t'ung*,[19.4] the multitude in ten thousand households, a territory a hundred *li* square. The marquises and earls shall [each] have one *kuo*, the multitude in five thousand households, a territory seventy *li* square. The viscounts and barons shall [each] have one *tsê*,[19.5] the multitude in 2500 households, a territory fifty *li* square. Great Vassals shall have as their estates nine *ch'eng*,[19.6] the multitude in 900 households, a territory 30 *li* square. From nine [*ch'eng*] on down, [the

         An Ordinance for Noble Ranks.

         23a

[19.4] The Official ed. has mistakenly emended *t'ung* 同 to 國. The Ching-yu ed. reads the former.

    *Chou-li* 42: 1b, sub the *Chiang-jen* (Biot, II, 566) defines a *t'ung* as "a square of a hundred li." This term is also found in the *Tso-chuan*, Dk. Hsiang, XXV, (Legge, 512[11], 516b).

    *HS* 23: 2b elaborates this passage from the *Chou-li* and says, "A territory one *li* square is a *ching* 井; ten *ching* make a *t'ung₁* 通; ten *t'ung₁* make a *ch'eng* 成 (a *ch'eng* is ten *li* square); ten *ch'eng* make a *chung* 終; ten *chung* make a *t'ung₂* 同 (a *t'ung₂* is a hundred *li* square); ten *t'ung₂* make a *feng* 封; ten *feng* make a *ch'i* 畿 (a *ch'i* is a thousand *li* square)."

[19.5] The *Chi-chung Chou-shu* (the lost *Book of History;* possibly written after Han times and taken from earlier material) 5: 8b, 9a, chap. 48, "Tso-Lo Chieh," says, "For those who received a mandate [enfeoffing them as nobles] from the Chou [dynasty, the Chou King had] established a large altar to the gods of the soils in the center of their states [read 國 for 周] . . . and for the nobles who were about to be established, [the King] dug into and took of its soil from the side in the direction of their [territory], covered it with yellow earth, enveloped it with white quitch-grass, and used it for the earth [given them for] their enfeoffment. Hence it is said that they received *tsê* 則-earth from the House of Chou." (One text reads 削 [cut off] instead of *tsê*). Shen Ch'in-han suggests that the term used by Wang Mang for the estates of viscounts and barons is taken from the above passage. The reception of a *tsê* is mentioned as the fifth appointment in *Chou-li* 18: 11b, sub *Ta-tsung-po* (Biot I, 429); cf. 99 A: n. 21.2. This passage of the *Chou-li* also mentions a *kuo* as the seventh appointment.

[19.6] Ju Shun explains, "Ten *li* [square] make a *ch'eng* 成," which is quoted from *HS* 23: 2b; cf. n. 19.4.

**Noble Ranks.**

estates of Vassals] shall decrease [by stages of] two [*ch'eng*], down to one *ch'eng*. When [the position of these] five degrees [of Sub-Vassals] are all filled, [their territories] will together be equal to one *tsê*.[19.7]

**19b** "Those who have now already received their clods [enveloped in] quitch-grass are: fourteen dukes,[19.8] 93 marquises, 21 earls, 171 viscounts, and 497 barons, altogether 796 persons. [There are also] 1511 Sub-Vassals and 83 women among the nine [classes of royal] relatives who have become Baronesses. Moreover the female descendants of the Han dynasty, the Baroness Serving the Rules of Proper Conduct, the Baroness Obedient to Virtue, and the Baroness Cultivating Moral Principles, in [the former kingdom of] Chung-shan, have been changed and made Baronesses. For the eleven highest ministers, the nine high ministers, the twelve grandees, and the twenty-four First Officers, their states, estates, or the places from which they draw their revenues have been fixed.

[19.7] Wang Wen-pin (xix cent.) explains that it means estates of 9, 7, 5, 3 and 1 *ch'eng*. This passage is reminiscent of *Tso-chuan*, Dk. Hsiang, XXVI, (Legge, 519[14], 524b), "It is the regulation that from the greatest to the least, [rewards] should be increased or diminished by two." The areas of these five ranks of Sub-Vassals were, respectively, 900, 700, 500, 300, and 100 square *li*, the sum of which is 2500 square *li*, which is the area of a *tse* (50 *li* square).

[19.8] Ch'ien Ta-hsin comments, "These fourteen persons were: [1] the Duke Giving Tranquillity to the Hsin Dynasty, Wang Yen[2], [2] the Duke Advancing the Hsin Dynasty, P'ing Yen, [3] the Duke Honoring the Hsin Dynasty, Liu Hsin[1a], [4] the Duke Beautifying the Hsin Dynasty, Ai Chang, [5] the Duke Serving the Hsin Dynasty, Chen Han, [6] the Duke Ornamenting the Hsin Dynasty, Wang Hsün[3], [7] the Duke Prospering the Hsin Dynasty, Wang Yi[5], [8] the Duke Upholding the Hsin Dynasty, Wang Hsing[a], [9] the Duke Perfecting the Hsin Dynasty, Sun Chien, [10] the Duke Exalting the Hsin Dynasty, Wang Sheng, [11] the Duke of Manifest Peace, Chi Tang, [12] the Duke Promulgating the Majestic Principles, Lin Pao, [13] the Duke Spreading the Majestic Principles, Tai Chi, and [14] the Duke of Established Tranquillity, Liu Ying[1a]. The Duke Extending the Hsin Dynasty, Chen Feng, had committed a crime, and his state had been abolished, so he is not in this number. The dukes of [Wang] Mang's imperial house, like the Duke Recommended by [the Marquis of] Hsin-[tu], [Wang] An[1a], the Duke in Recompense to [the Marquis of] Hsin-[tu], [Wang] Lin[1a], the Duke of High Merits, [Wang] Ch'ien[2], the Duke of Brilliant Merits, [Wang] Shou, the Duke of Perfected Merits, [Wang] Chi[5b], the Duke of Eminent Merits, [Wang] Tsung, the Duke of Shining Merits, [Wang] Shih, and the Duke of Apparent Merits, [Wang] Li[4] are also not among these fourteen persons."

一公九卿十二大夫二十四元士定諸國邑采之處
氏女孫中山承禮君遵德君修義君更名為任十有
千五百一十一人九族之女為任者八十三人及漢
七十一人男四百九十七人凡七百九十六人子百
受茅土者公十四人侯九十三人伯二十一人附城
臣下降敕曰兩至於一成五差備具合當一則今已

使侍中講禮大夫孔秉等與州部衆郡曉知地理圖籍者共挍治于壽

成朱鳥堂于數與羣公祭酒上卿親聽視成已通矣夫襃德賞功所曰

顯仁賢也九族和睦所曰襃親親也予永惟匪恩稽前人將章點陟

曰明好惡安元焉曰圖簿未定未授國邑且令受都內月錢數千

諸侯皆困之至有庸作者中郎區博諫曰井田雖聖王法其廢久矣

"I have caused the Palace Attendant and Grandee Expounding the *Book of Rites*, K'ung Ping, and others, with [the people] in the provincial divisions and the many commanderies who understand and know the principles of geographical arrangements, maps, and tax registers, together to examine them carefully and study them in the Vermillion Bird Hall of the Shou-ch'eng [House] and determine upon [the division of the empire into nine divisions]. I and the various highest ministers, Libationers, and high ministers of the highest rank have several times in person considered [this matter], so that I have already comprehended it all.

*19a*
Nobles
Given
Salaries.

"Verily, the recompensing of virtuous conduct and the rewarding of achievements are the means of making illustrious men of virtue and stability. Harmony among one's nine [classes of] relatives is their way of making a return for one's love of one's relatives. Since for a long time I have pondered unremittingly and have thought and investigated [the deeds of] persons in previous [generations], I shall make brilliant the demotions and promotions, so as to make plain the good and evil [of officials] and tranquillize the great multitude."

23b

Because the maps and tax registers [for the new division of the country] had not yet been completed, [Wang Mang] had not yet given [these appointees] any states or estates and temporarily ordered that they should receive several thousand cash per month as salary from the [income of] the capital and inner [commanderies]. The nobles were all miserably poor, and there were even some who hired themselves out.

A Gentleman-of-the-Household, Ou Po, admonished [Wang] Mang, saying, "Although the *ching* [system of] cultivated fields was a law of the sage-kings, it has already been abolished for a long time.

20a

The *Ching* System Abolished.

When the practises of the Chou [dynasty] had decayed, so that the common people did not follow them, the Ch'in [dynasty] knew how to accommodate itself to the common peoples' minds so as to be able to make great profits. Hence [this dynasty] did away with the cottages of the *ching* [system] and established [salable] subdivisions [of cultivated fields], and therefore came to rule over all China.

"Down to the present, [all] within [the four] seas have not yet had their fill of the perversity of the [Ch'in dynasty in removing the *ching* system]. If now you wish to go contrary to the desires of the common people and restore the lost practises of a thousand years ago, even though Yao and Shun should arise again, [yet] without a hundred years of gradual [training], they would be unable to put [these ancient practises] into effect. The empire has recently been tranquillized and the many common people have newly attached themselves [to you, so that the *ching* system] cannot yet be really put into practise."

Sale of Land and Slaves Permitted.

24a

[Wang] Mang knew that the common people hated [his arrangements],[20.1] so he issued a written message, which said, "Those who own or enjoy the income from the King's Fields are all permitted to sell them and are not to be restricted by the law.[20.2] Those who

---

[20.1] *T'ung-tien* (by Tu Yu, 735–812) 1: 13b, quotes this sentence with the word *ch'ou* 愁 instead of *yüan* 怨. (*HS* 24 A: 21b, in repeating this sentence, also uses *ch'ou*). Wang Nien-sun declares that someone who did not understand the ancient meaning of *ch'ou* changed the *ch'ou* originally in the text of the *HS* to *yüan*, and that *ch'ou* and *yüan* meant the same. *Shou-wen* 10 B: 8a defined *wen* 慍 as *yüan*, meaning to hate. (The present text of the *Shou-wen* writes *nu* 怒 for *yüan*, but that is an emendation; in the *Shih-san Ching Chu-su, Book of Odes*, no. 238; 16 ii: 13b, K'ung Ying-ta [574–648], quotes the *Shuo-wen* as saying that *wen* means *yüan*. The *Yi-ch'ieh Ching Yin-yi* in 25 chapters, written by the monk Yüan-ying [737–790], 5: 6a, 13: 8a, 19: 11a, however quotes the *Shuo-wen* as defining *wen* by *nu*.) *Kuang-ya* (by Chang Yi; in "Huang-ch'ing Ching-chieh" 668A: 8a) defines both *wen* and *ch'ou* as *hui* 恚, to hate. *HHS*, An. 2: 3b uses *ch'ou-yüan* as a phrase. The Ching-yu ed. however here reads *yüan* and I see no need to change the text.

[20.2] *HS* 24 A: 21b (cf. App. I), in quoting this edict, adds that it applied also to 'private

324

犯私買賣庶人者且一切勿治初五威將帥出改句町王呂為侯　王邯怨怒不附莽諷柯大尹周歆詐殺邯邯弟永起兵攻殺歆　先是莽發高句驪兵當伐胡不欲行部郡張迫之皆亡出塞因犯法　為寇逆西大尹田譚追擊之為所殺州郡歸咎於高句驪侯騶嚴　尤奏言貉人犯法不從騶起正有亡心令州郡且尉安之今猥

violate [the law against] private buying and selling of ordinary people [as slaves] will moreover temporarily not be punished."

*19b*

When previously the Generals and Lieutenants of the Five Majestic Principles had gone out, they had changed [the title of] the King of Kou-t'ing to be that of Marquis. The King, [Wu] Han, was resentful and angry and would not be subordinate [to Chinese nobles, so Wang] Mang hinted to the Grand Governor of Tsang-k'o [Commandery], Chou Hsin, to kill [Wu] Han by a ruse. [After this had been done, Wu] Han's younger brother, [Wu] Ch'eng, raised troops, attacked, and killed [Chou] Hsin.

Trouble at the Southwestern Borders.

Previous to this [time, Wang] Mang [ordered] the troops of Kao-chü-li to be put into the field and they then would have made an expedition against the northern barbarians (Hu), [but] they did not wish to go. When the commandery [authorities tried to] compel and force them [to move], they all fled, went out of the barrier, and thereupon violated the laws and engaged in robbery. When the Grand Governor of Liao-hsi [Commandery], T'ien T'an, pursued and attacked them, he was killed by them. The provincial and commandery [authorities] put the blame upon a marquis of the Kao-chü-li, Tsou.

Trouble at the Northeastern Borders.

**20b**

Chuang Yu memorialized, saying, "The violations of the law by the Mo people did not arise from Tsou. Even if [Tsou] had evil intentions, it would be proper to order the provincial and commandery [authorities] temporarily to soothe him. If now he is suddenly[20.3]

adherents,' i.e., slaves.

[20.3] Yen Shih-ku explains that *wei* 猥 means "many, heavily," but Wang Nien-sun, in a note to *HS* 47: 9a, asserts that *wei* means suddenly, *ts'u* 猝. "In a note to *Li-chi* 17: 2a (quoted in the *Shih-san Ching Chu-su*; the same passage as in Couvreur, I, 386), Cheng Hsüan says, "*Tsung* is like *wei-ts'u* 總猶猥卒" (the last word should be read as 猝), so that *wei* and *ts'u* were used to form a binom. The *Kuang-ya* ("Huang-ch'ing Ching-chieh" 671 B: 23b) defines *wei* as "suddenly 頓," which word means the same as *ts'u*. Ho Hsiu (129–182), in a gloss to *Kung-yang Commentary* 18: 8b, Dk. Ch'eng

**Trouble in the Northeast.**

adjudged [guilty of] a serious crime, it is to be feared that he will thereupon rebel. Some of the Fu-yü and their like would certainly respond to him. Since the Huns have not yet been conquered, if the Fu-yü and the Wei-mo arise again, there would be serious trouble."

[Wang] Mang did not [direct the officials] to console and calm [Tsou], and the Wei-mo accordingly revolted. By an imperial edict, [Wang Mang] ordered [Chuang] Yü to attack them. [Chuang] Yü lured Tsou, the marquis of the Kao-chü-li, to come, and beheaded him.

24b

When his head had been transmitted to Ch'ang-an, [Wang] Mang was greatly pleased, and issued a written message which said, "Recently, I have commanded and sent my fierce generals to perform respectfully[20.4] the punishment [directed by] Heaven, to execute and annihilate the caitiff [Lüan-ti] Chih. They are divided into twelve regiments.[20.5] Some are to cut off his right arm, some to cut thru his left arm-pit, some to break thru his chest and abdomen, and some to pull out his ribs. In this year punishments are in the eastern quarter,[20.6] so the regiments who were to punish the Mo set out first, arrested and beheaded the caitiff Tsou, and tranquillized and made secure the eastern frontiers. The destruction and annihilation of the caitiff [Lüan-ti]

20a

XVIII, says, "Duke Li *wei* killed four grandees," where *wei* means "suddenly." Ma Yung's (79–166) "*Fu* on the Long Flute" (*Wen-hsüan* 18: 3a) likewise says, "The water from the mountains *wei* arrived," with the same meaning of *wei*.

[20.4] I follow Yen Shih-ku in reading 共 as 恭, a common exchange of characters.

[20.5] The reference is to the twelve divisional generals who were to attack the Hun empire simultaneously, as is made plain by 94 B: 20a[8], 18b[10] = de Groot, 276, 273; cf. 99 B: 14a.

[20.6] Chang Yen comments, "In this [year], the year-star [Jupiter] was in *jen-shen* [the cyclical notation for A.D. 12], so punishments were in the eastern quarter." *SC* 27: 33 = *Mh* III, 356 says, "When there are deficiencies in fealty, the punishment comes from the Year-star." *SC* 27: 36 = *Mh* III, 360 notes that when Jupiter is in *shen*, "It is favorable for military [enterprises]."

六宗望秩于山川徧于羣神巡狩五嶽羣后回朝敷奏以言明試
始祖考虞帝受文祖在璇璣玉衡曰齊七政遂顉于上帝禋于
方威曰為回夷不足吞滅專念稽古之事復下書曰伏念予之皇
告天下令咸知焉於是貉人愈犯邊東北與西南夷皆亂云恭志
民同心將率虎之力也予甚嘉之其更名高句驪為下句驪布
珍滅在于徧刻此乃天地羣神社稷宗廟佑助之福公卿大夫士

Chih will come in a moment.

"This [success] was a blessing through the aid and assistance of Heaven, Earth, the many gods, the gods of the soils and grains, and the [royal] ancestral temples, and through the power [coming from] the Ministers, Grandees, Officers, and common people being of the same mind and from the generals and lieutenants being [like] roaring tigers. I approve most heartily of them. Let the name of the Kao (high)-chü-li be changed to be Hsia(low)-chü-li, and let it be published to all the world in order that everyone shall know of it." Thereupon the Mo people violated the borders all the more and the northeastern together with the southwestern barbarians were both in rebellion.

[Wang] Mang's intentions were then grand, and he did not consider the barbarians of the four [quarters] worth destroying, but concentrated his mind on searching out ancient ways. He again issued a written message, which said, "I humbly think that my August Deceased First Ancestor, the Lord of Yü, [Shun], 'received [Yao's] retirement [from the royal duties in the temple of] the Accomplished Ancestor,' and that he 'examined the Fine Jade [Turning] Mechanism and the Jade Balance, in order that he might bring into accord the seven Governors.' Thereupon 'he performed the sacrifice *lei* to the Lords on High, performed the sacrifice *yin* to his six exemplars, performed the sacrifice from a distance (*wang*) and arranged in order the mountains and streams, made a universal sacrifice (*pien*) to the many gods,' 'made tours of inspection to' the five sacred peaks, and 'held four courts for the various princes, at which they set forth and presented [matters] by word of mouth and were clearly tested by their deeds.'[21.1]

21a
25a
An
Imperial
Progress
An-
nounced.

---

[21.1] Quotations from *Book of History* II, i, iii, 4, 5, 6, 8, 9 (Legge, pp. 32, 33, 34, 35, 37). There are certain differences in the *HS* text: For the *Book of History*'s 璿 (also read by

"[From the time that] I received the mandate [of
Heaven] and ascended [the throne as] the actual

命即真到于
曰功子之受

the Official ed. of the *HS*), the *HS* reads 璇; for 肆, it reads 遂; the sixth clause, concerning "the mountains and streams," is quoted at the place given it in the *Book of History's* v. 6, but has the additional word now in the doublet of that clause in v. 7. On the *lei* sacrifice, cf. Karlgren, *BMFEA* 20, pg. 80, Gl. 1256. For the "exemplars," cf. *ibid.*, 81f, Gl. 1257.

In Wang Mang's time, there were two interpretations for the phrases from the *Book of History, hsüan-chi* 璿璣 or 璇璣 (translated here as "the Beautiful Jade [Turning] Mechanism") and *yü-heng* 玉衡 (translated as "the Jade Balance"). Legge, in his translation (*Shoo King*, p. 33) adopts the interpretation by the pseudo-K'ung An-kuo, as does Couvreur (*Chou King*, p. 14–15). It interpreted these two phrases as denoting an armillary sphere and its viewing tube, respectively, the whole forming a spherical astrolabe. If such is the correct interpretation, this chapter of the *Book of History* cannot be very ancient, for the armillary sphere was quite probably a late importation into China. W. Eberhard, "Das Astronomische Weltbild im alten China" (*Die Naturwissenschaften*, 1936, 24 Jahrg., Heft 33, p. 518) states that this instrument was known in China about 100 B.C. Ma Jung (A.D. 79–166), in his comment to this passage (preserved in *Shangshu Chu-su* 3: 3b, 4a), describes a spherical astrolabe.

There was also a quite different interpretation. The *Wen-yao-kou* 文耀鉤 *Woof Exposition to the Spring and Autumn* (fragments collected in the *Yü-han-shan-fang Chi-yi-shu*; this passage is also quoted by Wang Hsien-ch'ien in a note on *HS* 26: 5a) said, "The Bushel 斗 [the Dipper in Ursa Major] is the throat of Heaven. From ancient [times], the Jade Balance (*yü-heng*) has belonged with Piao 杓 [the three stars in the tail of the Dipper: $\epsilon$, $\zeta$, $\eta$ Ur Ma, or, as here, only one of them, $\eta$, cf. *MH* III, 341, n. 5; i.e., the Jade Balance has been the tail of the Dipper] and K'uei 魁 [the four stars in the body of the Dipper, $\alpha$, $\beta$, $\gamma$, $\delta$ Ur Maj, or merely $\alpha$] has been the Beautiful Jade [Turning] Mechanism (*hsüan-chi*)."

In *HS* 21 A: 19b, Pan Ku quotes Liu Hsin concerning "the weights [used with] the balance (*heng*):" "The one [i.e., the balance] in heaven assists the Beautiful Jade [Turning] Mechanism (*hsüan-chi*). [The ruler] consults where it points 'in order that he may [discover whether he] brings into accord the Seven Governors (*ch'i-cheng*).' Hence it is called the Jade Balance (*yü-heng*)."

*SC* 27: 6 = *MH* III, 341 (this passage is also quoted in *HS* 26: 4b by Ma Hsü, a brother of Ma Jung, who compiled this chapter of the *HS*) says, "The seven stars of the Northern Bushel [the Dipper] are what are referred to [in the passage of the *Book of History* which says, 'He examined] the Beautiful Jade [Turning] Mechanism (*hsüan-chi*) and the Jade Balance (*yü-heng*), so that he might bring into accord the Seven Governors (*ch'i-cheng*).' " These passages make clear that Wang Mang interpreted the Beautiful Jade Turning Mechanism and the Jade Balance as the stars of the Dipper and not as any human astronomical instrument (cf. Chavannes' translation in *MH* I, 58–65 and 48, n. 2; Karlgren, *BMFEA* 20, 77ff, Gl. 1255).

堂倉龍癸酉德在中宮
已過歲在壽星填在明
九之院既度百六之會
建國五年已五載矣陽

[Emperor], down to the fifth year of [the period A.D. 13. Shih]-chien-kuo, will be already five years. Since the distresses of the nine dry years will have already been crossed and the [untoward] occurrences in 106 [years] will have already been passed,[21.2] [the planet] Jupiter will be in Shou-hsing, [the planet] Saturn will be in the [heavenly] *Ming-t'ang*, the Azure Dragon will be at *kuei-yu*, the [ruling] virtue will be in the Central Palace,[21.3] [the hexagrams] *Kuan* and *20b*

The Seven Governors (*ch'i-cheng*), according to both schools, were the Sun, the Moon, and the five planets. The K'ung An-kuo gloss (*Shang-shu Chu-su* 3: 3a) states (this interpretation was accepted by both schools): "When Yao did not permit Shun to refuse [the rule] and had him take the throne as regent, Shun examined the Ornaments of Heaven [the stars] and inspected and brought into accord the Seven Governors. When he [found that he had] suited the mind of Heaven, he hence performed his [governmental] duties." The underlying conception was that the sun, moon, and planets moved correctly or incorrectly in harmony with the good or evil character of the government, so that Shun, by observing the motion of the stars, was able to determine whether his assumption of the throne did or did not please Heaven. It did, and so his virtue harmonized the stars.

The two "constellations" sometimes placed on their court robes by the Ch'ing emperors as symbols of imperial rank are almost surely the Beautiful Jade Turning Mechanism and the Jade Balance. According to the passage in the *Book of History*, these constellations were the means whereby Heaven confirms the right of an emperor to occupy the throne. The Jade Balance is the "pointer"—the direction in which it points at dusk is supposed to move around the horizon one-twelfth of the circumference each month, so that it points out the months of the year, and, with the months, the duties of the ruler in each month (given in the "Yüeh-ling," ch. IV of the *Li-chi*). The Jade Balance reminded the emperor of his governmental duties. It was sometimes worn just below the collar in front.

[21.2] Liu Hsin, in his *San-t'ung-li*, calculated that the first 106 years in a *yüan* of 4617 years would contain nine years of drouth; cf. *HS* 21 A: 42a ff.

[21.3] Fu Ch'ien asserts, "The Azure Dragon 蒼龍 is the *T'ai-sui* 太歲 [the hypothetical dextrorotary correlate of the planet Jupiter]." Chang Yen declares, "When the *T'ai-sui* arises in the *chia* and *yin* [parts of the ecliptic], it is the dragon. The eastern quarter is the Azure [part]. In *kuei* its virtue is in the central palace [i.e., the circumpolar stars]." Chin Shao however explains, "Shou-hsing is [the constellations] Chio and K'ang. The Eastern Palace [the eastern part of the ecliptic] is the Azure Dragon. Of [the constellations] Fang and Hsin, Hsin is the [heavenly] *Ming-t'ang*.' [A quotation from *HS* 26: 7a. 'Hsin' here is an allusion to the Hsin dynasty, Wang Mang]. Wherever [the planet] Saturn is located, that state will be prosperous. [Wang] Mang himself said [he ruled through the virtue of the element] earth. The lord of the element earth is [the planet] Saturn. In *kuei*, the [ruling] virtue is in the central palace. The palace is also [the element] earth."

*Chin* will control the year,[21.4] and [divination by] the
tortoise-shell and the milfoil have given information
**21b**   that they approve, let there be prepared a levy and
collection of taxes for the rites and ceremonies of a
tour of inspection eastwards for that year, in the
Feb. 5,  second month, at the conjction inaugurating the
A.D. 13,  second astronomical month."[21.5]
**25b**     The various highest ministers memorialized begging that there should be solicited from the officials
and common people, men, horses, linen cloth, silk
cloth,[21.6] and brocade.  It was also begged that the
twelve inner commanderies and kingdoms should buy
horses and dispatch 450,000 rolls of silk, transporting
them to Ch'ang₂-an.  Those which were to be sent
earlier and later were not to wait for each other.

帛四十五萬匹輸常安前後毋相須至者
民人馬布帛綿又請內郡國十二買馬發
之節東巡狩具禮儀調度羣公奏請募更
觀晉掌歲龜策告從其日此年二月建寅

For an account of the position of Jupiter and its Chinese hypothetical dextrorotary
correlate, cf. Chavannes, *Mh* III, App. III.  He remarks that because the revolution of
Jupiter is accomplished in 11.86 years, instead of in exactly 12 years (in which latter period
the Chinese dextrorotary correlate of Jupiter was supposed to make its revolution, thereby
generating the cyclical date for a year), for *Spring and Autumn* times two years must be
added to the date as given by the position of Jupiter to get the position of its dextrorotary
correlate.  From the above dating, it is evident that for Wang Mang's time, two years
are similarly to be subtracted.

This seems to have been one of the first cases in which the cyclical terms were used
to denote a year.  Previously they had been confined to the days.

[21.4] Meng K'ang explains, "He observed (*kuan* 觀) the advance and retreat of the
sun, moon, stars and their controlling lords."  He would translate this clause: "Observa-
tion of their advance [reading *chin* 晉 as 進] will control the year."  Chin Shao adds,
"The observation [i.e., imitation of Duke Wen of] Chin [*kuan-Chin;* a phase used in
*Kuo-yü* 10: 1a] is to find out where the *T'ai-sui* is, in what degree and constellation of the
Zodiac it is located."  He also declares that Wang Mang was imitating Duke Wen of
Chin in that his movements were timed to those of the *T'ai-sui* (cf. *Kuo-yu*, 10: 1a, b).
But Ch'ien Ta-hsin points out that Meng K'ang is mistaken, for Kuan and Chin are
both hexagrams (nos. 20 & 35 respectively).  In *HHS*, Mem. 20 A: 3b, Su Ching (fl.
A.D. 1–29) is quoted as saying that the hexagram *Pi* controlled a certain year.  The
*Yi-wei Chi-lan T'u* (anonymous, annotated by Cheng Hsüan, 127–200) and the *Yi-wei
Ch'ien-k'un Tso-to* (prob. Han period) discuss what hexagrams control what years.

[21.5] Wang Mang is following the procedure in *Li-chi* III, ii, 13–16 (Legge, I, 216–8;
Couvreur I, 275–8) and the practise of Shun (*Book of History* II, ı, 8, 9; Legge, 35–37).

[21.6] The Official ed. omits the 帛, but the Ching-yu ed. reads it.

過半莽下書曰文母太后體不安其且止待後是歲改十一公號曰新為

心後又改心為信五年二月文母皇太后崩葬渭陵與元帝合而溝絶之

立廟於長安新室世世獻祭元帝配食坐於牀下莽為太后服喪三年大

司馬孔永乞骸骨賜安車駟馬呂特進就朝位同風侯遂並為大司馬是

時長安民聞莽欲都雒陽不肯繕治室宅或頌徹之莽曰玄龍石文曰定

When [only] more than half arrived, [Wang] Mang issued a written message which said, "Since the person of the Empress Dowager the Mother of Culture [nee Wang] is not in good health, let [the transportation] be temporarily stopped and await a future [order]."

In this year, [Wang Mang] changed the titles of the eleven highest ministers, [altering] *hsin*₁ to be *hsin*₂. Later he again changed *hsin*₂ to be *hsin*₄.[21.7]

**Titles Changed.**

In the fifth year, the second month, the Empress Dowager the Mother of Culture [nee Wang] died. She was buried in the Wei Tomb with [her husband], Emperor Yüan, but separated from him by a ditch.[21.9] A temple for her was established at Ch'ang-an, at which the House of Hsin was from generation to generation to offer sacrifices, which Emperor Yüan was [also] to partake as her spouse, seated below her couch. [Wang] Mang wore mourning for the Empress Dowager [nee Wang] to the third year.

**V A.D. 13, Feb. 3[21.8] The Empress Dowager nee Wang dies.**

The Commander-in-chief, K'ung Yung, begged to retire, and he was granted a comfortable chariot with a quadriga of horses, and as [a person who ranked as] Specially Advanced, he took his place at court. The Marquis Unifying the Customs, Lu Ping, was made the Commander-in-chief.

At this time, the common people of Ch'ang-an heard that [Wang] Mang wanted to make his capital at Lo-yang, so they were unwilling to repair their residences, and some [people] destroyed their [houses] considerably. [Wang] Mang said [in a message], "The inscription on the dark dragon stone said,

**The Change of the Capital Postponed. *21a***

---

21.7 The change was from Hsin₁ 新 the name of Wang Mang's original marquisate, to Hsin₂ 心 (heart), and from Hsin₂ to Hsin₄ 信 (faithful). Anciently *hsin*₁ and *hsin*₂ were interchanged; the name of the Hsin dynasty was indifferently written *hsin*₁ or *hsin*₄.

21.8 *HS* 98: 15a.

21.9 Ju Shun explains, "She was buried within the Major's Gates [at the tomb] and a ditch was made to separate her [from her husband's grave]."

26a

A.D. 16.

22a

'Fix the virtue of the emperor [as that of earth and locate] the capital at Lo-yang.'[21.10] The mandate [of Heaven by means of] portents is manifest and clear. Could I presume not to uphold it reverently? Because in the eighth year of [the period] Shih-chien-kuo [the planet] Jupiter will move to [the constellations of] Hsing-chi, [which is equated] with the capital at Lo-yang, let the capital at Ch'ang$_2$-an be carefully put in repair, and let it not be spoilt. Those who presume to violate [this order] shall immediately have their names reported and [the officials] shall beg [the throne to ratify appropriate punishment for] the crimes [of those people]."

Trouble at the Northwestern Frontiers.

In this year, the Greater and Lesser K'un-mi of the Wu-sun sent envoys to offer tribute. The Greater K'un-mi, [Yi-chih-mi], was a grandson of the Chinese [House of Han] on the distaff side.[22.1] His son by a wife who was a northwestern barbarian (Hu) had become the Lesser K'un-mi, to whom the Wu-sun had turned and adhered. [Wang] Mang saw that the Huns were simultaneously invading the various borders, so, with the intention of seeking to obtain the affection of the Wu-sun, he sent a commissioner to lead the envoy from the Lesser K'un-mi and place him [in the court at a station] above that of the envoy of the Greater K'un-mi.

The Libationer for the Masters and Companions [of the Heir-apparent] Guarantor of His Perfection, Man Ch'ang, memorialized, impeaching [Wang Mang's] commissioner, saying, "The barbarians consider that China has [a knowledge of] what is right and proper, hence they submit and are obedient to [China]. The Greater K'un-mi is the prince [and the Lesser K'un-mi is his subject]. Now to rank the

帝德維雒陽符命著明敢不欽奉臣始建國八年歲纏星紀在
雒陽之都勿令壞敗敢有犯者輒白名聞者也
請其罪是歲烏孫大小昆彌遣使貢獻大昆彌中國外孫
其胡婦子為小昆彌而烏孫歸附之莽見匈奴諸邊並侵意欲
得烏孫心迺遣使引小昆彌使置大昆彌上保成師友祭
酒滿昌劾奏使者曰天狄曰中國有禮誼故誅而服從大昆彌

[21.10] Chou Shou-ch'ang remarks, "This was an omen that [Emperor] Kuang-wu would establish his capital [there]."

[22.1] Cf. Glossary sub Wu-sun.

君也今序臣使於君使之上非所宜有天故也奉使大不敬
莽怒免昌官西域諸國呂莽積失恩信焉耆先畔殺都護但
欽十一月彗星出二十餘日不見是歲呂犯挾銅炭者多除
其法明年改元曰天鳳天鳳元年正月赦天下莽曰予二
月建寅之節行巡狩之禮太官齎糗乾肉內者行張坐臥所

envoy of a subject above the envoy of his prince is not the way to hold [the affection of] the barbarians. The commissioner was seriously disrespectful." [Wang] Mang became angry and dismissed [Man] Ch'ang from his office.

The various states of the Western [Frontier] Regions considered that [Wang] Mang had repeatedly broken [the ties of] grace and faithfulness [binding them to China. The state of] Karashahr (Yen-ch'i) revolted first, murdering the Protector-General [of the Western Frontier], Tan Ch'in. *(26b)*

In the eleventh month, a broom-star appeared. In twenty-odd days it disappeared.[22.2] *(Nov./Dec. Prohibition of Copper and Charcoal Abolished.)*

In this year, because those who violated [the law against] possessing copper and charcoal were too many, this law done away with.

For the next year, [Wang Mang] changed the year-period, calling it T'ien-feng.[22.3] *(I)*

In [the year-period] T'ien-feng, the first year, the first month, an amnesty [was granted] to the empire, and [Wang] Mang said [in a message], "In the second month, at the conjunction inaugurating the second astronomical month, I will perform the rites of a tour of inspection. The Grand Provisioner [will take care of] the dry provisions for traveling and the dried meat and the [Prefect of] the Flunkies[22.4] [will take care of] the traveling curtains for my sitting and *(A.D. 14, Jan./Feb. Feb. 19. An 21b Imperial Progress Announced.)*

[22.2] This is no. 54 in Williams, *Observations of Comets*. Dion Cassius (*Hist. Roman.*, lvi, 29) also mentions comets at this time. Cf. Chambers, *Descriptive Astronomy*, p. 557.

[22.3] The *Han-chi* mentions Wang Mang's first year-period, *Shih-chien-kuo*, but it neglects the others entirely, continuing the enumeration of years from the first to the fifteenth year of Wang Mang's reign. *Sub* 20 A.D., it merely mentions that every six years the year-period was to be changed, but does not give the name of the next year-period.

Sung Hsiang (996–1066) in his *Chi-yüan T'ung-p'u* (lost) remarked that he suspects that there had been a happy auspice of phoenixes, from which this reign-period was taken. (Noted by Wang Hui [1321–1373] in the *HS P'ing-lin* 99 B: 24b.)

[22.4] The Sung Ch'i ed. states that the Shun-hua ed. (997) omitted the word *nei* 內, and that the New ed. (unknown) omits *nei-*者行. The Ching-yu ed. reads these words.

sleeping-[places, so that the localities] by which I pass will not be permitted to furnish anything.

**22b**
**The**
**Imperial**
**Progress.**

"When I tour eastwards, I must in person carry a plow,[22.5] and every county shall thereupon plow, in order to encourage 'the beginning [of the work of ploughing] at the eastern [season, spring].'[22.6] When I tour southwards, I must in person carry a hoe, and every county shall thereupon weed, thereby encouraging 'the development[22.7] in the southern [season, summer].[22.6] When I tour westwards, I must in person carry a sickle, and every county shall thereupon reap, thereby encouraging 'harvesting in the western [season, autumn].'[22.6] When I tour northwards, I must in person carry a flail, and every county shall thereupon garner [their grain],[22.8] thereby encouraging covering up and storing [the harvest]. When I have completed the rites of the tour of inspection northwards, I will thereupon go to the center of the earth and dwell in the capital at Loyang. If any [people] presume to run and make a noise, violating the law, they will immediately be dealt with according to military law."[22.9]

**27a**
The various highest ministers memorialized, saying, "You, Emperor, are most filial. In the last year,

---

[22.5] Wang Mang is following teh procedure in the *Li-chi*, IV, i, 13 (Legge, I, 254f; Couvreur, I, 335). The Sung Ch'i ed. asserts that the word 耜 (plowshare) should be added after the word 耒 (plow-handle), to agree with that passage in th e *Li-chi*, but Wang Hsien-shen (1859–1922) replies that this remark is mistaken, for the insertion would break the rhythm of 4-character phrases.

[22.6] These phrases are taken from the *Book of History*, I, ii, 4, 5, 6 (Legge, pp. 18–20); cf. also *HFHD* II, 392, n. 8.2.

[22.7] Yen Shih-ku points out that 僞 should be read as 譌; Ch'ien Ta-chao adds that the former character was anciently written 譌. Cf. also Karlgren, *BMFEA* 20, 52, gl. 1219.

[22.8] The text reads *su* 粟, grain, and Yen Shih-ku declares it means 治粟, to thresh. Li Tz'u-ming however objects that this interpretation does not fit in with the last words of the sentence, "covering up and storing [the harvest]," and states that *su* is probably a copyist's mistake, made before the T'ang period, for 稟, which in ancient times was used for 廩 (to store in granaries), since the latter character did not exist in ancient times.

[22.9] When the Emperor was inspecting, people were supposed to keep quiet in reverence.

聖體不豫躬親供養衣冠稱解因遭菜摩臣悲哀顏色未復飲食損
少今一歲回巡道路萬里春秋尊非柟乾肉之所能堪且無巡狩須
關大服曰安聖體臣等盡力養牧兆民奉稱明詔莽公庫牧庫
司諸侯庶尹願盡力相帥養牧兆民欲曰舜于縣此敬聽其勤之哉
母食言焉更曰天鳳七年歲在大梁倉龍庚辰行巡狩之禮厥明年
歲在實沈倉龍辛巳即土之中雒陽之都迺遣太傅平晏大司空王

when the sage person of the [Empress Dowager] the Mother of Culture [nee Wang] was not in good health, you yourself in person supplied her needs, rarely taking off your clothes or bonnet. When thereupon it happened that she left her subjects, you became melancholy. The color of your features has not yet returned, and you have eaten and drunk too little.

"Now for you to make four tours in one year, [to travel] a road ten thousand *li* [in length]—your age is honorable, so that you cannot endure [living on] dry provisions and dried meat. For the time being, do not make [these] tours of inspection. You need to end your deep mourning in order to rest your sage person. Your subjects will use all their power to care for and shepherd the myriad common people and will support and accord with your brilliant edicts."

23a *22a*

[Wang] Mang replied, "If the highest ministers, the [Provincial] Shepherds, the high officials, the nobles, and 'the heads of offices'[23.1] are willing to use all their power, leading each other in caring for and shepherding the myriad common people, and wish thereby to assist me and in this way to obey respectfully,[23.2] let them make [all possible] efforts in this [direction], and not swallow their words. I will change [my plans] and in the seventh year of [the period] T'ien-feng, when [the planet] Jupiter will be in Ta-liang and the Azure Dragon will be at *keng-ch'en*, I will perform the rites of a tour of inspection. The next year Jupiter will be in Shih-ch'en and the Azure Dragon at *hsin-szu*, when I will go to the center of the earth at the capital in Lo-yang."

A.D. 20.

A.D. 21.

The Capital to be changed.

[Wang Mang] thereupon sent the Grand Tutor, P'ing Yen, and the Grand Minister of Works, Wang

---

23.1 *Shu-yin* 庶尹 is a phrase from the *Book of History*, II, ɪᴠ, iii, 10 (Legge, p. 89), where the pseudo-K'ung An-kuo explains it as 官長.

23.2 For 聽, the Official ed. mistakenly reads 德. The Ching-yu and Mao. ed. read the former.

27b

Yi₅, to Lo-yang to plan and perform divination for [making] a map of the pomeria for [future] graves, and to build the [imperial] ancestral temple, the altars to the gods of the soils and grains, and the pomeria for [the altars for] suburban sacrifices.

Apr. 18
A Solar
Eclipse.

In the third month, on [the day] *jen-shen*, the last day of the month, there was an eclipse of the sun, and a general amnesty [was granted] to the empire. The document to the Commander-in-chief, Lu Ping, said, "The sun has been eclipsed so that it had no light, since the shields and spears had not been gathered in. Let the Commander-in-chief transmit to the emperor his seal and [ceremonial] apron [in token of his dismissal] and take the position of a marquis of a noble clan in the court. The Grand Tutor, P'ing Yen, shall not be Intendant of Affairs of the Masters of Writing. Let the Palace Attendants and Department Heads who concurrently hold other positions be dispensed with. Let Miao Hsin, an advantageous male,[23.3] become the Commander-in-chief."

Disorderly
Officials.

When Wang Mang had taken the throne as actual [Emperor], he took special precautions against his great officials and restrained and took away the power of his subordinates. If a court official said anything about the faults of [the high officials, Wang Mang] each time promoted [the speaker]. Because K'ung Jen, Chao Po, Fei Hsing, and others dared to

23b

attack the great officials, [these daring critics] were

[23.3] The text now reads, "A man of Li-miao, Hsin," and Ju Shun declares that Li-miao is the name of a town. It is listed in the Tung Commandery. But Li Tz'u-ming (7:16b) remarks that, from the previous mention on B:14b and the subsequent notice of his dismissal from the post of Commander-in-chief on B:26a, this name is undoubtedly Miao Hsin; the surnames of Wang Mang's officials are always given; when he enfeoffed people or gave them titles, he always picked lucky names and did not employ the names of towns. Hence 苗 and 男 have probably been interchanged, and after 利 a word or words have probably dropped out. This textual error then antedates the third century, for it was in Ju Shun's text. *Nan* or *nan-tzu* 男子 is occasionally used with the meaning, "a man," cf. *SC* 6:16[1] = *MH* II, 118, *HS* 8:10b, 10:10a, 99 A:18b, 30b.

家上書朱曰亭長奉公勿逐大司空邑斥士曰謝圖將哀章頒不
亭長醉曰寧有符傳邪士曰馬箠擊亭長亭長斬士七邵縣送之
太傅府捕士即時死大司空士夜過奉常亭亭長奇之告曰官名
僕射苟問不遜戊曹士收繫僕射莽大怒使執法發車騎數百圍
任擇名官而居之公卿入宮吏有常數太傅平晏從史過例披門

trusted, were selected for outstanding positions, and held [such positions].

When the ministers entered the palaces, there was a regular number of officials [for their suite]. When the officials accompanying the Grand Tutor, P'ing Yen, were greater [in number] than the regulation [allowed], a Supervisor at a side-gate minutely questioned [P'ing Yen about it] without showing any *22b* deference to him. A Mou Department Head and Officer [in his train] arrested and bound the Supervisor. [Wang] Mang was furious and sent an Upholder of the Laws to send out several hundred chariots and horsemen, surround the yamen of the Grand Tutor, and arrest the Officer, who thereupon died.

An Officer of the Grand Minister of Works passed *28a* at night by a commune [under the control of] the Master of Ceremonies. When the Chief of the Commune was severe with [the Officer and the latter] made known the name of his office, the Chief of the Commune said drunkenly, "Surely you have passport credentials?" The Officer beat the Chief of the Commune with his horsewhip, and the Chief of the Commune beheaded the Officer and fled. The commandery and prefectural [authorities] pursued him, and his household sent to the Emperor a letter [explaining the matter. Wang] Mang said, "The Chief of the Commune was upholding the public [good]. Do not pursue him," and the Grand Minister of Works, [Wang] Yi₅, had his Officer's [body] mutilated[23.4] in order to excuse himself.

Since the State General, Ai Chang, was considerably

---

[23.4] The text reads 斥 (to reprimand); Liu Pin remarks that this official had previously been beheaded and so the word should probably be 斫 (to cut). Stange (p. 187 & n. 4), and Duyvendak prefer not to emend the text. But Wang Yi plainly wanted to inflict additional punishment upon his Officer. After the Emperor, Wang Mang, had condemned the Officer, a posthumous reprimand by a minister could add nothing. "Cutting," i.e., mutilating the body, was a severe additional punishment, quite in harmony with the practises of the age.

lacking in purity, [Wang] Mang selected and established for him a Third Brother Ho.   His [imperial] command said, "Do not only protect the doors of the State General's female apartments; it is necessary to protect his blood relatives and relatives by marriage in the western provinces."[23.5]   The various highest ministers were all light-[weight] and of little worth, [Ai] Chang especially so.

**24a**
**Apr./May.**

In the fourth month, there was a fall of frost which killed the vegetation, especially at the sea-shore.

**June/July.**
**Jul./Aug.**

In the sixth month, a yellow fog [filled up everything within] the four quarters.   In the seventh month, a great wind uprooted trees and blew off the roof-tiles

**Ominous**
**Portents.**
**23a**

on [the buildings at] the Northern Portal [of the Palace] and at the Chih-ch'eng gate [of Ch'ang-an] and hail fell, killing cattle and sheep.

**New Titles**
**for**
**Provincial**
**Officials.**

In accordance with the text of the *Chou-li* and the "Royal Regulations," [Wang] Mang established Directors of Confederations, Leaders of Combinations, and Grand Governors, whose duties were to be the same as those of [the former] Grand Administrators,

**28b**

and [established] Prefects of Associations and Chiefs of Associations with duties the same as those of [the former] Chief Commandants.   He established [nine] Provincial Shepherds who were to be received in audience with [the same] formalities as those [shown] to the three highest ministers, and twenty-five Superintendents of Regional Divisions,[24.1]

[23.5] Ch'ien Ta-chao remarks that Ai Chang came from Tzu-t'ung in Kuang-han Commandery (in the present Szechuan), hence Wang Mang said, "in the western provinces."

[24.1] The suggestion that Provincial Governors (the title previously given to Shepherds) should rank higher than Commandery Administrators had been made by Ho Wu, who represented it as a conception of the *Spring and Autumn;* cf. *HS* 83: 14b, 15a.

The text is difficult to understand as it stands.   After *chou-mu* 州牧, I insert tentatively 十二人, at the suggestion of T'an Ch'i-hsiang (K'ai-ming Bookstore's *Erh-shih-wu-shih Pu-p'ien*, I, p. 1747), to parallel the next clause, *pu-chien erh-shih-wu jen* 部監二十五人.   I also place these last six characters after the clause *chien-li ju san-kung* 見禮如三公, and drop the word *chien* 監 that now comes after this *kung*.   (*Chien* is superfluous as a result of the last change.   It is not in the quotation of this passage in *Han-chi* 30: 13b).

屬令屬長職如都尉置州牧部監二十五人見禮如三公
殺牛羊菶曰周官王制之文置卒正連率大尹職如太守
六月黃霧四塞七月大風拔樹飛北闕直城門屋瓦而雹
州者諸公皆輕賤而章尤甚四月隕霜殺少木海瀕尤甚
清菶為遷置和叔敕曰非但保固將閣門當保親屬在西

監 各
位 主
上 五
大 郡
夫 公

who were to rank as Upper-ranking Grandees.   Each
one was to have charge of five commanderies.   Dukes

The ranking of *san-kung*, the three highest ministers, can hardly refer to the *pu-chien*,
the Superintendents of Regional Divisions, for they are here stated to have had a lower
rank.   In *HS* 99 C: 10b, it is moreover stated that the Provincial Shepherds (*chou-mu*)
had the rank of highest ministers (*san-kung*).   In the transfer of these six characters, I
follow Wang Nien-sun.

He would emend more drastically, following *Han-chi* 30: 13b, and reading, "He established Provincial Shepherds, the formalities for whom (*ch'i-li* 其禮) were to be like those
of the three highest ministers, and twenty-five Superintendents of Commanderies (*chün*
郡-*chien*).   The rank of the Superintendents (*chien*) was to be that of Upper-ranking
Grandees.   Each was to have charge of five commanderies."

Wang Nien-sun eliminates any mention of Superintendents of Regional Divisions (*pu-
chien*) and changes the *chien-li* of the *HS* text to *ch'i-li* as in the *Han-chi*.   As evidence
for his emendations he has only the *Han-chi's* text.   Chu Yi-hsien (1846–1894) however
protests that it is quite unnecessary to change *chien-li* to *ch'i-li; chien-li* is often found
in the *HS* [as in 99 A: 3a], so that there is no reason for emending it.   Yang Shu-ta
approves this refusal to emend.

T'an Ch'i-hsiang (*op. cit.*, pp. 1746–47) argues that Wang Nien-sun is furthermore
mistaken in emending *pu-chien*, Superintendents of Regional Divisions, to *chün-chien*,
Superintendents of Commanderies.   For (1) the Regional Divisions (*pu*) are mentioned
again in *HS* 99 B: 29a.   (2) In *HHS*, Mem. 3: 2a, Wei Ao: is quoted as having sent
out in A.D. 23 a broadcast to Wang Mang's "Shepherds of Provinces (*chou-mu*), Superintendents of Regional Divisions (*pu-chien*)," and minor officials.   (3) T'an Ch'i-hsiang
also quotes Chang Hsüan's (fl. 1582) *Hui Erh-ya* (also called the *Hui-p'ien*) as listing an
impression of an ancient seal with the five words: "東 *pu-chien* 之印.   The Seal of the
Superintendent of the Eastern Regional Division."   There is then ample evidence that
Wang Mang actually had Regional Divisions (*pu*) with Superintendents (*chien*).   T'an
Ch'i-hsiang however finds it difficult to explain how twenty-five regional divisions could
have been arranged into nine provinces and how the word *pu* could have also been used
with the title of Shepherd (*mu*), as in the phrase, "the Shepherd of Yung Regional Division" (99 B: 30a & C: 4b).

The word *pu*, in addition to its other meanings, had, in Han times, certain technical
uses.   For example, it denoted a "regiment" of 1000 men and 111 officers (*HS* 69: 11b).
It was also used for the administrative areas assigned in 106 B.C. to each of the twelve
Inspectors of Regional Divisions (*pu* 刺史; *HS* 19 A: 27a, b).   After this title had been
changed to that of Shepherd (*mu*) in 1 B.C., the term *pu* or regional division naturally
still clung to these Shepherds.   In a memorial dated A.D. 5, Wang Mang remarks (*HS*
99 A: 24b), "When the Shepherds of Provinces (*chou-mu*) go to inspect their regional
divisions (*pu*)," and 99 C: 18a states that K'ung Jen was sent in A.D. 22 "to be in charge
of the division (*pu*), Yü Province."

Something of Wang Mang's districting of China may be inferred from the way he had
his highest ministers "guarantee" the empire (*HS* 99 B: 29a).   The four Chiefs of the

**Changes in Offices.** with noble clans occupied [the positions of] Shepherds, marquises with noble clans [occupied the posi-

氏 侯
作 氏
牧 卒

Sacred Peaks in the four quarters guaranteed 100 commanderies, which were grouped into a total of eight provinces plus five regional divisions. The other three highest ministers guaranteed twenty-five commanderies in the central and neighboring regional divisions. These commanderies were not however assigned to them by regional divisions. The Grand Minister over the Masses guaranteed five commanderies from two different regional divisions. Each of these three highest ministers was assigned commanderies from the areas about both the two imperial capitals, Ch'ang-an and Yi$_4$-yang$_b$ (Lo-yang).

There were in the empire or kingdom (Wang Mang used both the titles of "emperor" [99 B: 22b] and "king") nine provinces, 125 commanderies (99 B: 25a), making twenty-five regional divisions (99 B: 24a). A regional division was composed of five commanderies (99 B: 24a). How many commanderies were there in a province? The three provinces guaranteed by the Grand Master averaged less than seven commanderies each. The two guaranteed by the Grand Tutor and the two guaranteed by the State General averaged ten commanderies each. The province guaranteed by the State Master contained fifteen commanderies. Then a province might have from five to fifteen commanderies or more. In addition to these eight provinces there were five other regional divisions (making twenty-five commanderies) guaranteed by these four ministers, plus twenty-five more commanderies guaranteed by the three other ministers. How could the remaining fifty commanderies form only one province?

In the former Han empire, the commanderies about the imperial capital had formed an administrative area under the Colonel Director of the Retainers (*Szu-li-hsiao-wei*), which was not entitled a province (*chou*), altho it actually functioned as one. Wang Mang almost surely followed this precedent, both for security reasons and in order to exalt the majesty of his arrangements. He had two capitals, Ch'ang-an and Lo-yang, about each of which he would accordingly have established a group of commanderies not included in any province. This arrangement is implied by the edict concerning the areas neighboring the two capitals quoted in 99 B: 24a, b and is practically stated in Wang Mang's enactment of two "royal domains" (99 B: 19a). We know the names of twelve commanderies in these royal domains (the Western Capital had about it the six Commandants' commanderies and the Eastern Capital had about it the six Neighboring commanderies mentioned in 99 B: 29a; cf. also 99 B: 24a, b, 25a, 99 C: 16a, and T'an Ch'i-hsiang *op. cit.*, pp. 1734–1737). It is moreover not likely that Wang Mang could have considered an area of only seven commanderies, about the size of a *small* province, adequate to express the dignity of the Son of Heaven. His two royal domains might well have each been larger than any province, being composed of twenty commanderies each, leaving ten commanderies for the ninth province. His kingdom then contained nine provinces *plus* two large royal domains.

It is unlikely that a single regional division included parts of *two* provinces, since it would be difficult for a single superintendant to investigate two different Shepherds. Then the number of commanderies in a province was five or a multiple thereof—an arrangement that was justified by the current doctrine of "*five powers (wu-hsing)*" accepted by Wang Mang. The actual size of commanderies could be adjusted to such a rigid arrangement by varying the number of counties in a commandery. This supposi-

正伯氏連率于氏屬令男氏
屬長皆世其官其無爵者為
尹分長安城旁六鄉置帥各
一人分三輔為六尉郡河東

tions of] Rulers of Confederations, earls with noble clans [occupied the positions of] Leaders of Combinations, viscounts with noble clans [occupied the positions of] Prefects of Associations, and barons with noble clans [occupied the positions of] Chiefs of Associations. All those offices were made hereditary. Those who did not have any noble ranks were made [Grand] Governors.

The neighborhood of the city of Ch'ang-an was divided into six districts, and one Leader was established for each [district]. The capital commanderies were divided and made into six commandants' commanderies.[24.2] [The commanderies of] Ho-tung, Ho-    **24b**

tion is substantiated by the size of the province guaranteed by the State Master (fifteen commanderies) and by those guaranteed by the Grand Tutor and the State General (either ten commanderies to each province or else five to one and fifteen to the other). The three provinces guaranteed by the Grand Master totalled twenty commanderies. Then some provinces contained only five commanderies and were identical with a single regional division. This conclusion explains and is justified by the phrase, "the Shepherd of the Yung Regional Division" (99 B: 30a). Meng K'ang (fl. A.D. 220–280) glosses (*HS* 95: 7a), "[Wang] Mang changed Yi Province to be the Yung Regional Division." (He probably economized by appointing the same person concurrently Shepherd and Superintendent.) Such an area could be called by the name of either the province or the regional division, as in Ch'ing times a city could be called by its name as a prefecture (*fu*) or as a county (*hsien*).

There is then no reason to follow Wang Nien-sun in his latter two emendations. Some copyist of the *Han-chi* may not have understood Wang Mang's districting of the country, so changed *pu* to the more familiar *chün*, whereupon Wang Nien-sun was misled.

[24.2] *San-fu Huang-t'u* (iii–vi cent.) 1: 2a describes this division: "Wang Mang divided the neighborhood of the city of Ch'ang-an into six districts and established one Leader for each [district]. He divided the capital districts and made them into six [Commandant's Commanderies] with Chief Commandants. The ten prefectures: Wei-ch'eng and An-ling, and northwest to Hsün-yi and Yi-ch'ü, were put under the Capital Commandant Grandee, with his yamen at the former Ch'ang-an official building. The ten prefectures, Kao-ling and northwards, were put under the Metropolis Commandant Grandee, with his yamen at the former Commandant of Justice's yamen. The ten prefectures, Hsin-feng and eastwards to Hu were put under the Supporter Commandant Grandee with his yamen at the east of the city. The ten prefectures, Pa-ling, Tu-ling, and eastwards to Lan-t'ien, and westwards to Wu-kung and Yü-yi, were put under the Commandant of Splendor Grandee, with his yamen at the [south] of the city. The ten prefectures, Mou-ling, Huai-li, and westwards to Ch'ien, were put under the Sustainer Commandant Grandee, with his yamen at the west of the city. The ten prefectures, Ch'ang-ling, Ch'ih-yang,

**Changes in Geographical Names.**

nei, Hung-nung, Jung-yang,[24.3] Ying-ch'uan, and Nan-yang became the six Neighboring Commanderies, and Grandees were established [for them] with duties like those of the [former] Grand Administrators, and Directors of Associations with duties like those of the [former] Chief Commandants. The title of the Grand Governor of Ho-nan [Commandery] was changed to be the High Minister Protecting and devoted to the Hsin$_4$ [Dynasty]. The counties subordinate to Ho-nan [Commandery] were increased to be a full thirty, and six suburbs were established with a Chief of a Deparment for each [suburb], each [Chief of a Department] having charge of five

河內弘農河南潁川南陽為六隊郡
置大夫職如太守屬正職如都尉更
名河南大尹曰保忠信卿益河南屬
縣滿三十置六郊州長各一人人主

and northwards to [Yün-yang and] Tai-hsü, were put under the Commandant of Magnificence Grandee, with his yamen at [the north of the city]." (The words in square brackets are not in the present text of the *San-fu Huang-t'u*, and are supplied from Yen Shih-ku's quotation of this passage, which represents a superior text.) In addition to the six Commandant's counties, the city of Ch'ang-an formed a separate administrative district called "The Western Capital of the House of Hsin" (99 B: 19a).

[24.3] Liu Feng-shih (1014–1113) asserts that the "Ho-nan" in the text should be Jung-yang, for on this page a little farther on, the title of the Grand Governor of Ho-nan is changed to a different title. Lo-yang (renamed Yi-yang), the headquarters of the Ho-nan Commandery, was to be an imperial capital, hence Jung-yang and other prefectures of the Ho-nan Commandery were separated to be a Neighboring Commandery. The Jung-yang Commandery is mentioned on 99 B: 25b.

Chou Shou-ch'ang points out that in this passage Wang Mang is following in general and with changes the account in the *Chou-li*, according to which the region within 100 *li* of the capital was called the suburbs, *chiao* 郊, in which were established six districts, *hsiang* 鄉, and the region beyond the suburbs was called the neighborhood, *sui* 遂, in which were established six administrations over the six Neighborhoods. In a note to *Chou-li* 9: 1b (Biot, I, 172, n. 2), *sub* the *Hsiang-lao*, Cheng Chung (ca. 5 B.C.–A.D. 83) says, "Within 100 *li* [from the capital] are the six *hsiang*: without it are the six Neighboring [Commanderies] (*sui*)."

The *Chou-li* 15: 8a (Biot, I, 336 ff) has an official called the *Sui-jen* 遂人. The term *sui* seems to come from the *Book of History* V, xxix, 5 (Legge, p. 625) where Po-ch'in is made to say, "You men of Lu, from the three *chiao* and three *sui*, prepare forage." *Sui* and *tui* 隊, the word in the text, were anciently interchanged; *SC* 33: 20 (*Mh* IV, 103), which quotes the above passage from the *Book of History*, reads 隊 (actually written in *HS* 99 B: 25b), of which *tui* (here pronounced *sui*$_4$, according to Yen Shih-ku), is a more cursive writing. The six neighboring commanderies were the Capital, Western, Eastern, Southern, Ch'i, and Northern Neighboring Commanderies. Cf. 99 B: 29a.

六尉義陽東都曰六州眾縣曰六陳粟米之內曰內郡其
閑田為黜陟增減云莽下書曰常安西都曰六鄉眾縣曰
百六十曰應行命文也緣邊又置竟尉曰男為之諸侯國
五縣及它官名悉改大部至分為五郡縣曰亭為名者三

counties.

Moreover the names of the other offices were all **29a**
changed.  The large commanderies were divided into *23b*
even as many as five [commanderies],[24.4] and three **25a**
hundred sixty commanderies and counties were given
the names of communes, in order to accord with the
words of the mandates [of Heaven as transmitted by]
portents.  At the borders there were also established Commandants of the Frontiers.  Barons were
given [these offices.  The numbers of] reserved fields
within nobles' estates were increased or decreased in
order to promote or demote [these nobles].[25.1]

[Wang] Mang issued a written message, which
said, "At the Western Capital, Ch'ang₂-an, [the
capital commanderies] shall be called the Six Districts and the various counties shall be called those
of the six Commandants; at the Eastern Capital,
Yi₄-yang_b, [the capital commanderies] shall be called
the Six Departments,[25.2] and the various counties
shall be called [those of] the six Neighboring [Com-
manderies].  Within [the area which] 'contributes
grain in the husk and cleaned grain,' [the com-
manderies] are to be called the Contributing Commanderies.[25.3]  Outside of them, [the commanderies]

[24.4] Ch'ien Ta-hsin remarks that many of these new names are listed in *HS* ch. 28,
the "Treatise on Geography," but the new delimitations of commanderies are not all
indicated there.

"Three hundred sixty" has an astrological significance, being the number of days in an
ancient Chinese solar year.

[25.1] *Hsien-t'ien* 閑田 is a term taken from *Li-chi*, III, i, 8 (Couvreur, I, 268; Legge,
I, 212), of which pseudo-K'ung Ying-ta (quoted in the *Shih-san Ching Chu-su, Li-chi* 11:
5b) says, "If [fields in nobles estates] are not given in enfeoffment to people [who will be
their vassals], they are called reserved fields (*hsien-t'ien*)."

[25.2] Liu Feng-shih remarks that *chou* 州 (Department) should be 郊 (Suburb).  According to 99 B: 24b, however, *chou* is correct, for Wang Mang entitled the heads of the
commanderies nearest Lo-yang (then named Yi₄-yang_b) Chiefs of Departments.

[25.3] *Book of History* III, ɪ, ii, 18 (Legge, p. 144) says, "From the fourth [hundred *li*
from the capital, they contributed] grain in the husk, and from the fifth [hundred *li*,
they brought] cleaned grain."  The first five hundred *li* from the capital constituted the
royal domain.

Classical
Districts.

are to be called the Attached Commanderies. Those [commanderies] which contain barriers or palisades are to be called Border Commanderies. Altogether there are one hundred and twenty-five commanderies in nine provinces with two thousand two hundred and three counties.

"Those who do public service in the imperial domain are those 'constituting fortified walls.' Those in the Domain of the Nobles are those 'securing repose.' Those in the territories allotted to high bureaucrats, baronesses, and the patrols are those 'constituting buttresses.'[25.4] Those in the Domain of

為惟寧在采任諸侯是為惟翰在賓
三公作旬服是為惟城諸在侯服是
十有五郡九州之內縣二千二百有
外曰近郡有郭徼者曰邊郡合百二

---

[25.4] The terms, *ts'ai, jen, chu-hou₂* 采任諸侯 are taken from *Book of History* III, I, ii, 19 (Legge, 144–45), except that it uses *nan* 男 instead of *jen*. Yen Shih-ku interprets *ts'ai* as "the *ts'ai* domain," i.e., the region allotted for the estates supporting ministers and grandees. *Jen* he interprets as "the domain of the barons (*nan*)." Wang Mang had however given the title of *jen* to baronesses (99 B: 4b). The K'ung An-kuo gloss to the above passage (*Shang-shu Chu-su* 6: 18a) says, "*Nan* is *jen*." K'ung Ying-ta explains, "The pronunciation of *nan* is near to that of *jen*, hence [the former] is explained by *jen*." He interprets *jen* as "to be employed on the king's business," seemingly denoting those who hold office. The archaic pronunciation of *nan* (*Grammata Serica*, ✳649) was *nam* and that of *jen* (*ibid.* ✳667f) was *niǝm*. The K'ung An-kuo gloss may have been a mere explanation by an assonant word, so that K'ung Ying-ta interprets it correctly. But by using this gloss, *jen* may be exchanged with *nan*. Indeed in a note to *HS* 99 B: 4b, Yen Shih-ku says, "*Nan* is also *jen*." This circumstance explains Wang Mang's use of *jen* as his title for baronesses. Wang Mang here however uses *jen* instead of the *nan* in the *Book of History*. Did he mean something slightly different? He may have meant (a) baronesses, (b) barons, or (c) those who hold office. I have preferred the first meaning, for he very likely included the barons along with the nobles in the preceding domain. The words *ts'ai jen* are also used on 99 B: 19a, where I have interpreted them likewise.

*Chu-hou₂* may denote "the nobles." But Wang Mang's nobles were located elsewhere, so that this meaning would introduce disorder into his architectonic scheme. The K'ung An-kuo gloss says, "*Hou₂* is *hou₄* 侯. They patrol (*ch'ih* 斥 -*hou₄*) and serve. . . . In their 300 *li* they all alike patrol (*ch'ih-hou₄*) for the king." K'ung Ying-ta explains, "*Ch'ih-hou₄* means that they patrol 檢行 strategic places, watching for bandits." (*Ch'ih-hou₄* today means "sentry.") Wang Mang almost surely had this Han interpretation in mind.

The Sung interpreters were probably correct about this passage in the *Book of History*: the greatest nobles were said to have been located farthest from the king and the smaller ones nearer him, in order to have powerful defenders at the borders, ready to repel an invasion. This passage probably reflects the actual situation during the latter part of

服是為惟屏在撲文教奮武衛是為惟垣在

九州之外是為惟藩各曰其方為稱總為萬

國馬其後歲侵變更一郡至五易名而還復

其故吏民不能紀每下詔書輒繫其故名曰

Submission[25.5] are those 'constituting screens.' Those in [the regions where they] 'cultivate the lessons of learning and moral duties [and where they] show the energies of war and defence'[25.6] are those 'constituting [unfortified] walls.' Those outside the nine provinces are those 'constituting fences.'[25.7]   29b Each one is to be styled in accordance with the region [in which his fief is located]; altogether they constitute the myriad states."

In subsequent years, [Wang Mang] again changed [names], even changing the name of a single commandery five times, returning and restoring its former [name], so that the officials and common people could not keep records of [these names], and whenever a written imperial edict was issued, the former names [of places mentioned therein] were each time

Multiple
Renaming.
**25b**
*24a*

the Chou period: Lo-yang was the capital and the large feudal states were at the periphery of the Chinese orbit. Wang Mang established a feudal nobility, because it was in accordance with classical precedents. He ennobled the members of his clan. But he was an autocrat who intended to rule the whole country, instead of depending upon his nobles for defence. He turned the classical scheme upside down, placing the greatest noble estates nearest the ruler. This arrangement he doubtless felt was more in accordance with the Confucian principle of exhibiting a due gradation of affection as between his closer relatives (the great nobles) and the more distantly related ones (the minor nobles), by placing his closest relatives nearest himself.

25.5 The "domain of submission" is not in the usual lists of domains; this term is taken from the brief list in *Kuo-yü* 1: 2a, b. Yen Shih-ku asserts it is the same as the domain of garrisons 衛服 in *Chou-li* XXXIII, 52 (Biot, II, 276).

25.6 A quotation from *Book of History* III, ɪ, ii, 20 (Legge, p. 145), where, in discussing the region constituted by the five hundred *li* beyond the domain of the nobles, which former is the second domain beyond the innermost one, it says, "In the first three hundred *li* they cultivated the lessons of learning and moral duties; in the other two hundred *li* they showed the energies of war and defence."

25.7 The six phrases, "constituting fortified walls," "securing repose," "constituting buttresses," "constituting screens," "constituting walls," and "constituting fences" are taken from the *Book of Odes*, III, ɪɪ, x, 7 (Legge, II, 503), where they refer to the king's relatives, the cherishing of virtue, great families, great states, the multitudes of people, and good men, respectively. This stanza is quoted in full in *HS* 14: 1a. Wang Mang is using this stanza as the authority for his own system of domains which shall harmonize the two systems in the *Book of History* and the *Chou-li*.

attached.

**Confusing Changes of Names.**

[For example], he said, "An imperial edict of decree to the Grand Governor and Grand Commandant of Ch'en-liu [Commandery]. Let [the territory] from Yi-sui and southwards be transferred to Hsin-p'ing [commandery]. (Hsin-p'ing [commandery] is the former Huai-yang [Commandery].) From Yung-ch'iu and eastwards [the territory] is to be transferred to Ch'en-ting [Commandery]. (Ch'en-ting [Commandery] is the former Liang Commandery.) From Feng-ch'iu and eastwards [the territory] is to be transferred to the Chih Commune [Commandery]. (The Chih Commune [Commandery] is the former Tung Commandery.) From [the city of] Ch'en-liu and westwards, [the territory] is to be transferred to the Imperial Domain Neighboring [Commandery]. (The Imperial Domain Neighboring [Commandery] is the former Jung-yang [Commandery].) Ch'en-liu is now not any more to be a commandery. Its Grand Governor and Grand Commandant are both to go to the place where the [Emperor] is." The changes and alterations in [Wang Mang's] ordinances regarding names were all of the foregoing sort.

**The First Day of the Sexagenary Cycle Changed.**

[Wang Mang] ordered that in the primary schools of the empire [the day] *mou-tzu* should take the place of [the day] *chia-tzu* as the first day of the sixty-[day] cycle.[25.8] In capping [boys at maturity], *mou-tzu* should be considered as the best day. For marriages, the decade [beginning with the day] *mou-yin*[25.9]

[25.8] *Li-chi*, IX, i, 20 (Legge, I, 424; Couvreur, I, 586) says, "For the day, a *chia* [day] is used [for the sacrifice, in order to] employ the first of the days [in the cycle]." *Mou* and *chi* are the stems corresponding to the power earth, which Wang Mang considered to be the ruling power during the time of his dynasty. To the names of his year periods there seem to have been added the phrase *shang-mou* 上戊 (exalting [the stem] *mou*); cf. C: n. 17.5.

[25.9] Ch'ien Ta-hsin remarks, "In the decade [beginning with] *mou-yin* there is no *tzu* [day (*tzu* means son)], hence it is avoided."

戊子代甲子為六旬首冠呂戊子為元日昏呂戊寅之旬為
大尹太尉皆詣行在所其號令變易音此類也令天下小學
東郡呂陳畱呂西付析隄故滎陽陳畱已無復有郡矣
雍丘呂東付陳定故梁郡呂封丘呂東付治亭治亭故
制詔陳畱大尹太尉其呂益歲呂南付新平新平故淮陽呂

忌使等大相
日者付飢瞻
百厚使人今
姓賂者相單
多之檻食于
不詐車諫新
從許詣大和
者遣長夫宜
匈其安如因
奴侍莽普是
單子燒行罷
于登良邊兵
知因等兵校
死購於還尉
弟求城言韓
咸陳北軍威
立良令士進
為終吏久曰
單帶民屯日
于等會塞新
求單觀苦室
和于之邊之
親即緣郡威
莽執邊無而
遣良　已吞

should be considered as days to be avoided. [But] most of the people did not obey [this order].

When the Hun *Shan-yü*, [Lüan-ti] Chih, had died, and his younger brother, [Lüan-ti] Hsien, had been set up as *Shan-yü*, he asked for peace and alliance by marriage [with the Chinese imperial house. Wang] Mang sent an envoy to give him rich presents and to promise falsely to return his son, [Lüan-ti] Teng, who had been an Attendant [at the Chinese court]. Thereupon [Wang Mang] offered rewards for Ch'en Liang, Chung Tai, and the others [of their group] and the *Shan-yü* immediately siezed [Ch'en] Liang and the others, and delivered them to the envoys. In carts with cages they went to Ch'ang-an, where [Wang] Mang had [Ch'en] Liang and the others burnt [to death] at the north of the city, and ordered the officials and common people to gather in order to see it.[26.1]

At the borders there was a great famine, so that people ate each other. The Grandee-remonstrant, Ju P'u, [was sent to] inspect the border troops and returned, saying, "The soldiers have encamped at the barriers for a long time and have suffered [because] the border commanderies have no means of furnishing supplies for them. Now that the *Shan-yü* has newly made peace, it would therefore be proper to dismiss the troops."

Colonel Han Wei came forward and said, "For the majesty of the Hsin House to swallow the northern

*Side notes, right margin:*
30a

Vengeance on Traitors.

26a

Trouble at the Northern Border. *24b*

---

[26.1] *HS* 94 B: 21a = de Groot, *Die Hunnen*, 281 says, "[Wang] Mang created the punishment of burning *fan-ju* 焚如, and burnt to death Ch'en Liang and the others." The term *fan-ju* is a quotation from the *Book of Changes*, Hexagram 30, 4 (Legge, p. 121; Wilhelm I, 89). Ying Shao says that Wang Mang made this punishment in accordance with that passage of the Classic, which reads, "How sudden is his coming; it is burning, dying, and being done away with [in execution]." Ju Shun adds, This line "refers to unfilial children, who do not care for their parents and do not maintain a proper deportment to their friends, hence they are burnt to death and done away with. [Wang] Mang made the name of the punishment in accordance with this [passage]."

**Vain Boasting Rewarded.** barbarian (*Hu*) caitiffs is no harder than [to swallow such small things as] fleas or lice in one's mouth. Your servant wishes to take five thousand brave and daring gentlemen, and, without taking along a bushel of food, in hunger to eat the flesh of the caitiffs and in thirst to drink their blood, so that I shall be able to traverse [their territory freely.'' Wang] Mang admired his words and made him the Majestically Acting General.

But he adopted [Ju] P'u's words and summoned the various generals who were at the border to re-
**30b** turn, dismissing Ch'en Ch'in and others, eighteen persons [in all]. He also abolished the various garrisons of soldiers [belonging to] the Chief Commandants posted at the four passes [to the imperial capital].[26.2]

[But] it happened that when the Hun envoy returned, the *Shan-yü* came to know that his son, [Lüan-ti] Teng, who had been an Attendant, had previously been executed, so he mobilized his troops and raided the borders, [hence Wang] Mang had again to mobilize the military garrisons. Thereupon the people of the border wandered into the inner commanderies and became slaves and slave-women of those people. Then a prohibition was made, that if officials or common people should presume to possess people from the borders, they should be publicly executed.

**Trouble At the Southwestern Borders.** The barbarians in Yi-chou [Commandery] killed their Grand Governor, Ch'eng Lung, so that the whole of the three borders [to the province] were in rebellion. [Wang Mang] sent the General Tranquillizing the Southern Barbarians, Feng[26.3] Mou, lead-

胡虜無異口中蝨蝨臣願得勇敢之士五千人不齎斗糧飢食虜肉渴
飲其血可曰橫行莽壯其言呂威為將軍然米普言徼還諸將在邊者
克陳欽等十八人又罷四關填都尉諸屯兵會勾奴使遷單于知侍子
登前誅死發兵寇邊復發軍屯於是邊民流入內郡為人奴婢迺禁
吏民敢挾邊民者棄市益州蠻夷殺大尹程隆三邊盡反遣平蠻將軍

26.2 Hu San-hsing explains that Wang Mang had established at each of the four passes a Chief Commandant of the Post, with garrison soldiers.

26.3 Ch'ien Ta-chao remarks that 馬 should be 馮, to agree with *HS* 95: 7a and 99 B: 30a. The Ching-yu ed. reads the latter; Wang Hsien-ch'ien adds that the Official ed. and the Southern Academy ed. also read it.

馬　侯　宁　王　大
茂　輔　始　路　赦
將　免　將　堂　天
兵　講　軍　公　下
擊　易　二　卿　是
之　祭　年　大　時
寧　酒　二　夫　日
始　戴　月　皆　中
將　參　置　佐　見
軍　為　酒　酒　星

ing troops, to attack them.

The General of a Peaceful Beginning, Hou Fu, was dismissed, and the Libation Officer Expounding the *Book of Changes*, Tai Ts'an, was made the General of a Peaceful Beginning.

In the second year, the second month, a banquet was held in the Hall with the Royal Apartments, and all the ministers and grandees were present at the feast. A general amnesty [was granted] to the empire.

At this time a star was visible at noon,[26.4] and the

II
A.D. 15,
Feb./Mar.

[26.4] If "at this time" refers to the second month of this year (Feb. 8 to Mar. 9, A.D. 15, Julian), this "star" must have been a nova or comet, not Venus. It is not likely that it was an imaginary object, since its appearance was considered a portent sufficiently great to require one of the high ministers to be dismissed.

Mr. R. B. Weitzel of Washington, D.C. reports: "From experimental observations made under favorable conditions, I would assign for daylight visibility of Venus without optical aid a limiting value of 110 days before inferior conjunction, the planet having then a magnitude of $-3.7$ and on elongation approximately $42°$ east. On Mar. 9, A.D. 15, 160 days before inferior conjunction, Venus with magnitude $-3.4$ and elongation $31°$ east evidently was not visible to the unaided eye at midday." It did not attain its greatest brightness until June 11th, when its magnitude was $-4.25$, before and after which date, during a period of several weeks, it was visible at noon to anyone who knew where to look.

Unfortunately, we cannot be sure that "at this time" refers to the second month. Pan Ku does not in this chapter furnish the month for any of the events in this year, except for the banquet and amnesty, which are mentioned immediately before the "star." Very likely most of the records for this year perished when the palace was burnt in A.D. 23. "At this time" may mean "in this part of the year," in which case this "star" may indeed have been Venus.

Chinese astronomers may however not, in Han times, have been aware that Venus may regularly be seen crossing the sky. *SC* 27: 53 = *Mh* III, 374 states: "When it [Venus] appears, it does not cross the sky. When it crosses the sky, the country changes its government." The above statement is repeated in *HS* 26: 23a and much later in *Sui-shu* 20: 14b. Thus the appearance of Venus in daytime was considered a great sign, portending a change in the dynasty. It was accordingly expected to occur only once every few centuries. Meng K'ang glosses the above passage: "['Crossing the sky'] means when [Venus] rises in the east and sets in the west or when it rises in the west and sets in the east. Venus is a *yin* [weak] star, so that when it rises in the east [as a morning star] it is due to disappear in the east, and when it becomes visible in the west [as an evening star] it is due to set in the west. [The text is emended, following the suggestion of Dr. A. Pogo, to fit the facts of observation. This last clause reads in the present text, "When it rises in the west it is

A Portent.   Commander-in-chief, Miao Hsin, was transferred to a
lower position to be Director of Mandates.   The

左遷司命曰
大司馬苗訢

due to disappear in the west."]   Going across the meridian [i.e., being visible at noon]
is 'crossing the sky'."   Chin Shao adds: "The sun is *yang* [strong].   When it rises, the stars
are due to be submerged.   When Venus is visible in daytime on the meridian, it is 'crossing
the sky'."

The facts of observation are the following: When Venus is a morning star, it rises in
the east, either when the sky is still dark, if its western elongation (the apparent distance
between it and the sun) is sufficient, or, if not, just at dawn.   Then it disappears in the
rays of the sun soon after sunrise before reaching the meridian, or even at sunrise, depending on its elongation.   When Venus is an evening star, it becomes visible in the west
shortly before sunset, while the sky is still illuminated, or just at sunset, depending on
its elongation.   Then it sets in the west soon (possibly three hours) after sunset, depending upon its elongation.   These two phenomena are stated correctly in Meng K'ang's
gloss (with the emendation mentioned above).

Venus is also visible in daylight at the time of its maximum brilliance, which circumstance occurs about five weeks before and after inferior conjunction, twice in each revolution of the planet, in each case lasting for a period of a few weeks.   Venus is not conspicuous, because of the sun's light.   But anyone who has noted the distance of Venus
from the sun at its previous morning (or evening) appearance (which distance is 39° at
its maximum brightness) can easily pick it out in the daylight sky.   At such times, in
addition to its setting, when an evening star (or rising, when a morning star), Venus has
also a real and visible rising (or setting), so that Meng K'ang is quite correct in saying
that Venus may rise in the east and set in the west.

It is not easy to understand how the ancient Chinese could have failed to recognize
this daylight visibility of Venus or to identify this "star visible in daytime" with the
planet.   By following such a star for a few hours, it will be found to be identical with the
"evening star" Venus, which will be very conspicuous in the evening sky by its unusual
brightness.   Or the unusually brilliant "morning star" Venus will be found, when followed,
to be identical with this "star visible in daytime."   So all doubt about the identity of a
"noon star" can easily be dissipated.   These periods of daylight visibility recur regularly
at intervals of 584 days.   In Han times, such a "star visible in daytime" was recorded in
182 B.C. (cf. *HFHD*, I, 198; II, 425), but is not identified with Venus, although that
planet was then visible in daytime.

The reason that Venus was not recorded under that name when it was visible in daytime is very likely the astrological interpretation given that visibility.   Anyone identifying this "noon star" with Venus thereby proclaimed himself a revolutionist, so that his
life might be seriously endangered.   When however a revolution was expected by powerful
persons in the imperial court at the time that the Chou dynasty was being replaced by
the Sui, Venus is recorded as appearing in daytime.   *Sui-shu* 1: 14a, b, 21a states, "Venus
appeared in daytime" on the dates, March 24, 25, May 21, 581 and on Nov. 2, 584.
Jupiter is also said to have been visible in daytime on May 21, 581.   During the next
decade, however, although periods of Venus' daytime visibility occurred almost every

大　延
司　德
馬　侯
訊　陳
言　茂
黃　為

Marquis Extending Virtue, Ch'en Mou, was made the Commander-in-chief.

[Some common people][26.5] falsely said that a yellow

*The Yellow Dragon.*

year, there is no notice of that fact. The dynastic revolution had been completed, so that Venus as a portent was no longer useful.

These appearances have been checked by calculation from the tables in K. Schoch, *Planeten-Tafeln für Jedermann.* The records for Venus on May 21, 581 and Nov. 2, 584 are probably correct, for that planet then had a magnitude of −4.0 and −4.40 respectively. But the times of Venus' greatest brightness were on June 18, 581 and Nov. 8, 584, on which days Venus had a magnitude of −4.23 and −4.44, respectively. Then this planet was not reported when it was brightest. We may infer that, on the days Venus was reported, someone in the court bethought himself of the astrological significance to the appearance of Venus, asked some astrologer about this planet, and reported Venus' daytime visibility to the throne, whereupon this entry was placed on the records.

The reported appearances of Venus in daytime on Mar. 24 and 25, 581 are doubtful. While the planet had an elongation of 39°, its magnitude was only −3.6. Jupiter's magnitude on May 21, 581 was only −1.6. It is not a noon object, but its elongation was 101°, so that it could have been seen when the sun was very low in the west.

We may conclude that, while some time during or after the Han period, Chinese astronomers became aware of the fact that Venus is occasionally visible in daytime, the astrological interpretation of this circumstance prevented it from becoming known to the public, except at times when the court wished a portent known presaging a change in the dynasty.

Meng K'ang's statement that Venus sometimes "rises in the west and sets in the east" raises the interesting question whether he knew that this unusual phenomenon may actually happen. It does not occur at Chinese latitudes, but only near or within the Arctic (or Antarctic) Circles. At the infrequent times when the greatest brightness or the inferior conjunction of this planet occurs in the months of April or May, if an observer is far enough north, he will sometimes see Venus traverse the northern sky from west to east. For example, on May 30, B.C. 85, when Venus was at its greatest brightness with a magnitude of −4.3, an observer north of China in latitude 65.3° could have seen Venus due north on the horizon, 2 hours 45 minutes before midnight, while the sun at midnight was just 3.3° below the horizon. On May 1 of that year, Venus, with a magnitude of −4.1, was on the northern horizon 3 hours 7 minutes before midnight for an observer at 63.2° north, and at midnight the sun was 12.7° below the horizon. The famous Chinese envoy, Su Wu, was in captivity of the Huns during 100 to 81 B.C., for most of which time he was near Lake Baikal, which extends from about 52° to 56° north. It is possible that some nomad told Su Wu or some other Chinese traveler of having seen Venus at midnight and that this report was taken to China.

[26.5] The word 民 seems to have dropped out at this point; *Han-chi* 30: 14a and *Tzu-chih T'ung-chien* 38: 1a both have this word. Wang Nien-sun remarks that without it the meaning is not complete, and that the ancients did not avoid such repetitions as the use of this word here and 百姓 in the next clause.

**26b**

**25a**
An
Awkward
Portent.

**31a**
The
*Shan yü's*
Son's
Corpse
Returned.

May/
June.[26.8]

dragon had fallen down and died in the Huang-shan Palace, and [many] people hastily ran there. Those who went to see it numbered by the ten-thousands. [Wang] Mang hated it, and arrested and bound [some of those people], in order to ask whence this saying arose. He was not [however] able to trace [its source.][26.6]

Since the *Shan-yü*, [Lüan-ti] Hsien, had made peace and an alliance by marriage [with the Chinese imperial house], he asked for the corpse of his son, [Lüan-ti] Teng. [Wang] Mang wanted to send envoys to bring it to him, [but] he feared that because of his grudge [Lüan-ti] Hsien would kill the envoys. So he arrested the former General [Repressing Difficulties], Ch'en Ch'in, who had previously said that [Wang Mang] ought to execute [Lüan-ti Teng,] the son [of the *Shan-yü*], in attendance [upon the Chinese Emperor], and had him bound in prison for another crime.[26.7] [Ch'en] Ch'in said, "This [act is because Wang Mang] wants to use me to excuse [himself] to the Huns," and thereupon committed suicide.

Wang Mang selected [as envoys] Confucian masters who were "able to answer [questions] unassisted."[26.9] Wang Hsien₂c from Chi-nan [Commandery] was made the Chief Envoy and the General of the Five Majestic [Principles]; Fu₅ Yen, [a man of] Lang-yeh Commandery], and others, were made Lieutenant Envoys to accompany the corpse of [Lüan-ti] Teng. [Wang Mang] ordained that they were to dig up the tomb of the *Shan-yü* [Lüan-ti] Chih, and to whip his corpse with thorns. He also ordered the Huns to withdraw their frontiers north

---

[26.6] Yen Shih-ku remarks that since Wang Mang held he ruled by virtue of the yellow principle, this evil auspice was directed against him.

[26.7] Cf. 99 B: 18b.

[26.8] Cf. *HS* 94 B: 21a = de Groot, *op. cit.*, 293.

[26.9] A phrase from *Analects* XIII, v.

漢北責單于馬萬匹牛三萬頭羊十萬頭及稍所略邊民生口

在者皆還之苓好為大言如此咸到單于庭陳苓威德責單于

背畔之辠應從橫單于不能詘送致命而還之入塞成病死

封其子為伯伏黯等皆為子苓意曰為制定則天下自平故銳

思於地里制禮作樂講合六經之說公卿旦入暮出論議連年

of the [Gobi] Desert, and imposed as an indemnity upon the *Shan-yü* ten thousand head of horses, thirty thousand head of cattle, and a hundred thousand head of sheep. Moreover of the few people and livestock from the borders who had been kidnapped, insofar as they were still alive, [the *Shan-yü*] should return them all. [Wang] Mang loved to talk grandly, as in the foregoing [order].[26.10]

When [Wang] Hsien[2c] reached the court of the *Shan-yü*, he set forth [Wang] Mang's majestic virtue and reprimanded the *Shan-yü* for his crimes of rebellion. In his replies, [Wang Hsien[2c]] responded to his opponents in every way, so that the *Shan-yü* was not able to argue him down. Thereupon [Wang Hsien[2c]] carried out [Wang Mang's] mandate and brought back these [people and livestock].[26.11] When he entered through the barrier, [Wang] Hsien[2c] had been ill and died. [Wang Mang] enfeoffed his son as an earl. Fu[5] Yen and the others were all made viscounts.  Dec.[26.11]

[Wang] Mang's notion was that if institutions were fixed, the empire would naturally become tranquil. Hence he thought in detail concerning geographical arrangements, the institution of rites, and the composition of music. In discussing the harmonization and matching of the explanations to the six Classics, the ministers entered [his presence] at dawn and left at dusk. He discussed[27.1] for successive years with-  31b  **27a**  *25b*

[26.10] Liu Pin remarks that the existing text does not make sense, so proposes to emend *shao* 稍 to *ch'ao* 鈔 and invert, reading *so* 所 *ch'ao-lio* 畧. Duyvendak agrees. He also reads 牲 for 生, a common interchange of characters, which latter reading I adopt. But Chou Shou-ch'ang objects to Liu Pin's emendation, "[The text is] not in error. This was just Wang Mang's 'grand talk,' that the Huns had not dared to rob recklessly and had merely kidnapped 'a few' of the people at the borders." P. van der Loon agrees, so do I.

[26.11] Liu Pin asserts that *chih* 之 is an interpolation. But if we accept Chou Shou-ch'ang's interpretation (n. 26.10), this *chih* is needed (here meaning "them," referring to the people and live-stock).

The date of Wang Hsien[2c]'s return is found in *HS* 94 B: 21b = de Groot, *op. cit.*, 283.

[27.1] Wang Hsien-ch'ien states that the Official ed. and the Southern Academy ed.

Officials
Take
Advantage
of
Wang
Mang.

out coming to [final] decisions, so that he did not have leisure to examine law-cases, decide complaints of injustices, or to settle the urgent business of the common people, and when there were vacancies among the rulers of the counties, [Wang Mang left] for several years [officials as] acting [magistrates or as magistrates] concurrently [holding other positions, with the result that] the covetousness and injuriousness of all [his officials] alike daily became greater.

The
Corruption
of the
Bureauc-
racy.

The[27.2] Generals of the Gentlemen-at-the-Palace and Administrators of the Laws Clad in Embroidered Garments who were in the commanderies and states all took advantage of their authority and opportunities, and in turn[27.3] recommended each other in memorials. Moreover when the Officers of the eleven highest ministers were dispersed to encourage agriculture and sericulture, to proclaim the ordinances for the [various] seasons, and to examine into various documentary matters, the [official] bonnets and [chariot] coverings of one [set of officials] could [almost] be seen by the succeeding [set],[27.4] and they jostled one another on the roads. They would summon meetings of the officials and common people and arrest eye-witnesses. When the commanderies and counties [gathered] capitation-taxes, [these officials] exchanged bribes and presents, so that [even] white and black were confused and those who watched at the [palace] portals [to intercept] accusations were many.

吏民逮捕證左郡縣賦斂皆遞相賕賂白黑紛然守闕告訴者多

一公士分布勸農桑班時令案諸章冠蓋相望交錯道路召會

殘日甚中郎將繡衣執法在郡國者並乘權執傳相舉奏又十

不決不暇省獄訟冤結民之急務縣宰缺者數年守兼一切貪

have inverted to read 議論.　The Ching-yu ed. does not invert.

[27.2] The Sung Ch'i ed. declares that at this point there should be the words 是時, "at this time."

[27.3] The Official ed., for 傳 reads 傅 and quotes the Sung Ch'i ed. to the effect that the former word should be read. But the Ching-yu ed. reads the former and Chou Shou-ch'ang remarks that this word should be read as 轉 and that a little further on this same page there is the phrase 遞相賕賂 and on 99 C: 15b there is 傳相監趣 so that the former word is here both the original and correct.

[27.4] A phrase also found in 4: 17b = HFHD, I, 264.

政令煩多當奏行者輒質問乃己從事前後相乘憒眊不

左右開發尚書不得知其畏備臣下如此又好變改制度

諸寶物名帑藏錢穀官皆宦者領之吏民上封事書宦官

恭自見前顓權曰得漢政故務自攬眾事有司受成苟免

[Wang] Mang himself knew that he had previously usurped the [imperial] power, and had thereby obtained the government from the Han [dynasty], hence he took care to control the multitude of [government] affairs himself and when the high officials received [orders directing] the detailed disposition [of cases], they merely did enough to avoid [punishment]. The various offices [in charge of] the valuable objects, the famous treasuries, and the taxes were all in charge of eunuchs. When officials or common people presented to the Emperor matters in sealed letters, the eunuchs serving in the palace offices or [members of the imperial] entourage broke the seals, so that the Masters of Writing did not get to know about them.[27.5] Such were [Wang Mang's] fear of and precautions against his courtiers and subordinates.

32a

27b
Delays in
Decisions.

He also loved to change and alter the institutions and regulations, so that the government ordinances were numerous, and those which needed to be put into practise[27.6] had each time to be asked about, before anything could be done. When earlier and later [documents] succeeded each other, they became unclear, confused, and could not be cleared up.[27.7]

[27.5] Hu San-hsing explains, "Anciently when matters were presented to the Emperor in sealed [envelopes], they first went to a Master of Writing, who then memorialized [the matter] to the Emperor. [Wang] Mang feared that the Masters of Writing would block or hide things, so ordered the eunuchs and his entourage to break the seals and [then] he himself examined them."

[27.6] Wang Hsien-ch'ien states that 奏 is an error; the Ching-yu ed., the Southern Academy ed., and the Official ed. all read 奉.

[27.7] Yen Shih-ku declares that *hsieh* 渫 means 散也徹也. Wang Nien-sun replies that this meaning does not fit into the passage, and asserts that *hsieh* means *chih* 治. In a note to *Book of Changes*, Hex. 48, 3 ("Yü-hen Shan-fang Chi-yi-shu," *Chou-yi Hsün-shih Chu* B: 14a), Hsün Shuang (128–190) says, "*Hsieh* had the meaning of doing away with dirt and turbidity and making it clear and clean." Lu Tê-ming (ca. 560–627), in his *Ching-tien Shih-wen* 2: 19a, "Chou-yi," quotes Huang Ying (fl. iv cent.), as saying, "*Hsieh* is to *chih*." In *SC* 84: 9, *sub* the above line from the *Book of Changes*, P'ei Yin quotes Hsiang Hsiu (d. ca. 280) as saying, "*Hsieh* is to dig (*chih*) deeper and do away

*26a* [Wang] Mang constantly employed the light of a lamp until daylight, but nevertheless he was not able to accomplish his work. Taking advantage of this [circumstance], the Masters of Writing did evil and laid matters aside, so that those who had sent letters to the throne and awaited replies [at the Palace Portals] did not get to leave for successive years. Those who had been arrested and bound [in prison] in the commanderies or counties could only get out when it happened that there was an amnesty, and the soldiers of the [palace] guard were not changed even in the third year.[27.8]

Banditry
At the
Northern
Border.

Grain was constantly expensive. More than two hundred thousand border troops depended for their clothes and food upon the imperial government. They were discontented and bitter. Wu-yüan and Ta Commanderies suffered especially from them, [so that people in these commanderies] arose and became thieves and robbers, several thousand persons becoming a troop, turning around and entering the neighboring commanderies. [Wang] Mang sent the General Siezing Robbers, K'ung Jen, with troops, to join with the commandery and county [authorities] to attack [the robbers]. Only after more than a year were [the robbers] put down. The border commanderies were moreover almost on the point of being emptied [of people].

*32b* North of Han-tan there was a great rain and fog, and the waters rose. The deepest [places] were several tens of feet [deep]. It carried away and killed several thousands of persons.

The General Establishing the State, Sun Chien, died, and the Director of Mandates [from the Five Majestic Principles], Chao Hung, became the General Establishing the State. The General of a Peace-

*28a*

with mud and turbidity."

[27.8] They usually served one year only. Cf. Glossary, *sub* Guard.

殺數千人立國將軍孫建死司命
擊歲餘迺定邊郡亦略將壹邴郭呂北大雨霧水出深者數丈流
盜賊數千人為輩轉入旁郡莽遣捕盜將軍孔仁將兵與郡縣合
貴邊兵二十餘萬人仰衣食縣官愁苦五原代郡尤被其毒起為
連年不得去拘繫郡郡縣者遇赦而後出衞卒不交代三歲尤殺常
漢莽常御燈火至明猶不能勝尚書因是為姦寖事上書待報者

356

参歸故官南城將軍廉丹為寧始將軍三年二月乙酉地震大

而雪關東尤甚深者一丈竹柏或枯大司空王邑上書言視事

八年功業不劾司空之職尤獨慶領至迺有地震之變願乞骸

骨莽曰夫地有動有震震者有害動者不害春秋記地震之變願乞骸繫

坤動動靜辟翕萬物生焉災之變合有云為天地動威吕戒

于躬公何辜焉而乞骸骨非所以助予者也使諸吏散騎司祿

ful Beginning, Tai Ts'an, was returned to his former office [of Libation Officer Expounding the *Book of Changes*], and the General of the Southern City Wall [of Ch'ang-an], Lien Tan, became the General of a Peaceful Beginning.

In the third year, the second month, on [the day] *yi-yu*, there was an earthquake and a great fall of snow, which was especially severe east of the [Han-ku] Pass. The deepest [places] were ten feet [deep]. The bamboos and arbor vitae trees all[28.1] withered.

III<br>A.D. 16,<br>Feb. 20.

The Grand Minister of Works, Wang Yi[5], presented a letter, saying, "I have overseen my affairs to the eighth year, and my efforts have not been successful. In my duties as [Grand] Minister of Works, I have [moreover] been more especially useless, so that recently there has even been the grievous vicissitude of an earthquake. I wish to beg to retire."

Wang Yi's<br>Resigna-<br>tion<br>Refused.

[Wang] Mang replied, "Verily, Earth has movements and has quakes. The quakes cause injury, [but] the movements do not cause injury. The *Spring and Autumn* records earthquakes and the *Book of Changes*, in the "Great Appendix," [says] that [the hexagram] *k'un*, [representing Earth], moves. When [Earth] moves it opens, and when it rests, it closes, and [in this way] all things are brought to birth.[28.2] Each grievous vicissitude of visitation or prodigy has its message and action, so Heaven and Earth move majestically in order to warn me. What crime have you, Duke, committed that you beg to retire? [This] is not the way to assist me. I send the Inspector of Officials, Cavalryman Without Specified Appointment, Director of

*26b*

33a

28.1 Wang Nien-sun says, "或 must be an error for *hsien* 咸. *Han-chi* 30: [14b] and *Po-t'ang Shu-ts'ao* [152: 3b, (completed ca. 618)] "Section on Heaven," [ch.] 4, quote this "Memoir" and read correctly, '*hsien*.' "

28.2 A free quotation from *Book of Changes*, App. III, ch. VI, i, 2(34), (Legge, p. 358; Wilhelm, I, 229).

Emoluments, and Grand Guard, the Baron Cultivating Tranquillity, Tsun₂, to inform you of my
will."

**Apr./May**
**Regula-**
**tions**
**for the**
**Salaries of**
**Officials.**

In the fifth month, [Wang] Mang issued regulations for the salaries of officials, saying, "I have met
with the distresses of the nine dry years and the
[untoward] occurrences in the 106 [years.[28.3] The
revenues for] the expenses of the state have been
insufficient, so that the common people are in disturbance. For the ministers and those of lower
[ranks], the emolument for one month has been two
**28b**  rolls of 800-thread linen cloth[28.4] or one roll of silk.
Every time I think of it, I never fail to be sad.

"Now that the distresses and [untoward] occurrences have already been overpassed, although the
government treasuries have not yet been able to be
filled, [yet] something can be taken out to supply
[what is needed]. On the first day of the sixth
**June 24.**  month, [the day] *keng-yin*, let all the salaries of
officials be for the first time distributed all according
to the regulations. The four coadjutors, the ministers, the grandees, the officers, and on down to the
lower officials [constitute] altogether fifteen grades.
The salary of the lower officials for one year shall be
66 *hu*. [This amount] shall be gradually increased
by steps up to [the rank of] the four Coadjutors, [for
whom] it shall be made 10,000 *hu*."

Wang Mang also said,

" 'Under the vast Heaven
      There can be nothing but the King's lands.

---

[28.3] Cf. 99 B: 21a & n. 21.2.

[28.4] Meng K'ang explains, "A *tsung* 緵 is [cloth woven with] 80 threads [in the warp
of a standard 50 cm. width]." (The Southern Academy ed. and the Chi-ku Ko ed. [1642]
read, "is 80 *tsung*," but the Ching-yu ed. [1035] and the Official ed. read "is 80 threads 縷).
*Shou-wen* 13 A: 1b defines *tsung*ᵦ 綜 as "the threads in [the warp on] a loom." The
*Yen-tzu Ch'un-ch'iu* (iv cent. B.C.; fundamentally retouched in xiii cent.), "Tsa-p'ien, B,
par. 18; 6: 17a, says, "Ten-*tsung*₀ (800 thread) 總 linen cloth and one *tou* of food are
enough to cause a person to escape inner [cold or hunger]." (From Shen Ch'in-han.)

歲六十六斛稍曰差增上至四輔而為萬斛云莽又曰普天之下莫非王
庚寅始賦吏祿皆如制度回輔公卿大夫士下至輿儓凡十五等僚祿一
每念之未嘗不戚焉今朝已度府帑雖未能充略頗給其呂六月朔
會國用不足民人騷動自公卿已下一月之祿十緵布二匹或帛一匹子
大衛脩寧男遵諭子意焉五月莽下吏祿制度曰予遵陽九之阸百六之

太官膳羞備其品矣即有災害呂什率多少而損膳焉東岳
所損與百姓同憂喜也其用上計時通計天下幸無災害者
食其采多少之差咸有係品歲豐穰則充其禮有災害則有
品今諸侯各食其同國則辟任附城食其邑公卿大夫元士
土率士之賓莫非王臣益呂天下養焉周禮膳羞百有二十

The dependents in all lands
    Must not fail to be subjects of the King.'[28.5] Verily [the King] 'is nourished by all under Heaven.'[28.6] The *Chou-li* [says that] in the imperial cuisine, 'one hundred and twenty kinds of meat dishes [are furnished].'[28.7]   *27a*

"The nobles shall now each receive the income of their *t'ung, kuo,* or *t'sê*;[28.8] princesses, baronesses, and vassals shall receive the income of their estates; ministers, grandees, and first officers shall receive the income of the territory allocated to them. There are regulations for all the differences in the amount of their [revenues]. When the harvests are abundant, the rites [regarding the amounts given them] shall be fully carried out; when there are visitations or disasters [to the crops, their revenues] shall be decreased, so that they shall suffer and rejoice along with the people. Let it be that at the time when the [yearly] accounts [from the commanderies] are presented, [there shall be made] a general account for the empire. If there happily have been no visitations or disasters, the Grand Provisioner [shall provide] the complete number of imperial dishes. [But] if there have been visitations or disasters, the amount shall be calculated in percentages, and the dishes [at the imperial table] shall be reduced [proportionately].[28.9]   *33b*

28.5 *Book of Odes,* ☆205; II, vi, i, 2 (Legge, p. 360).

28.6 *Mencius* V, A, iv, 3 (Legge, p. 353), where the clause refers to a filial son. Filial piety includes the duties of a subject to his lord.

28.7 *Chou-li* 4: 1a, *sub* the *Shan-fu* (Biot, I, 70).

28.8 Yen Shih-ku explains, "It means that dukes received the income of *t'ung*, marquises and earls received the income of *kuo*, and earls and barons received the income of *tse.*" For these terms, cf. 99 B: 19a.

The Official ed. has emended 今 to 令, which I have adopted.

28.9 The practise of reducing the imperial table and official salaries in time of poor harvests had been inaugurated by Emperor Hsüan (8: 6b), but had not been systematized, as Wang Mang now proposes. This practise seems first to have been suggested by Mo-tzu; cf. Mei's trans., p. 18 f.

**29a**

**Officials'
Salaries
To be
Reduced
in Times
of
Disaster.**

"[The Chief of] the Eastern [Sacred] Peak and Grand Master and the General Establishing the State shall act as guarantors for twenty-five commanderies of three provinces and one regional division in the eastern quarter; [the Chief of] Southern Sacred Peak and Grand Tutor and the General of the Van shall act as guarantors for twenty-five commanderies of two provinces and one regional division in the southern quarter; [the Chief of] the Western [Sacred] Peak and State Master and the General of a Peaceful Beginning shall act as guarantors for twenty-five commanderies of one province and two regional divisions in the western quarter; [the Chief of] the Northern [Sacred] Peak and State General and the General of the Guard shall act as guarantors for twenty-five commanderies of two provinces and one regional division in the northern quarter.   The Com-

**34a** mander-in-chief shall act a guarantor for ten commanderies in the eastern and southern [parts of] the central regional divisions [subject to] the Communicator and high minister, the Deciding Judge and high minister, the Capital Commandant [Grandee], the Sustainer Commandant [Grandee], the Metropole Neighboring Commandery, and the Western Neigh-

*27b* boring Commandery.[29.1]   The Grand Minister over the Masses shall act as guarantor for five commanderies in the central regional divisions and western regional division [subject to] the Director of Music and high minister, the Arranger of the Ancestral Temples and high minister,[29.2] the Supporter Commandant

太師立國將軍保東方三州一部二十五郡南嶽太傅前將軍保

南方二州一部二十五郡西嶽國師嚳始將軍保西方一州二部

二十五郡北嶽國將衛將軍保北方二州一部二十五郡大司馬

保納卿言卿仕卿作卿京尉扶尉兆隊右隊中部左泊前七部大

司徒保樂卿典卿宗卿秩卿翼尉光尉左隊前隊中部右部有五

---

[29.1] The text has been disarranged.   Liu Pin suggests omitting the first and third 卿, and inverting to read 作仕, thus obtaining known title of officials.   Liu Feng-shih (1041–1113) suggests emending the second 部 to 郡 to agree with the other sentences. Wang Nien-sun suggests emending 七 to 十 to make up the full number of 25 commanderies for these three officials.

[29.2] Liu Pin suggests omitting the first and third 卿 and inverting the others to read 典樂卿秩宗卿 thus obtaining known titles of officials.

郡大司空保于卿廩卿共卿
工卿師尉列尉祈隊後隊中
部洎後十郡及六司六卿皆
隨所屬之公保其災害亦曰

[Grandee], the Commandant of Splendor [Grandee], the Eastern Neighboring Commandery, and the Southern Neighboring Commandery. The Grand Minister of Works shall act as guarantor for ten commanderies in the central regional divisions and northwards [subject to] the My Forester and high minister, the Provider of Works and high minister,[29.3] the Master Commandant [Grandee], the Commandant of Magnificence [Grandee], the Imperial Domain Neighboring Commandery, and the Northern Neighboring Commandery. The directors and high ministers[29.4] shall all join with the highest ministers to whom they are subordinate in acting as guarantors against visitations and disasters [in the regions for which] their [superiors act as guarantors].

"If there have been calamities or injuries to the

[29.3] Liu Pin suggests omitting the first and third 卿 to obtain known titles of officials. This passage seems to have been disarranged in the time of Yen Shih-ku, for his comment misunderstands it; Hu San-hsing in the xiii cent. quotes it in its present form in a note to *Tzu-chih T'ung-chien* 38: 3a.

[29.4] The text says, "The six (*liu* 六) directors (*szu* 司) and the six (*liu*) high ministers (*ch'ing* 卿)." But there are only three directors (*szu*) mentioned in Wang Mang's central bureaucracy, cf. 99 B: 3b. Liu Feng-shih remarks, "This [passage] should say merely *szu-ch'ing*, which were those called 'the high ministers who were directors (*szu-ch'ing*) to the three highest ministers' [a phrase quoted from 99 B: 3b], namely the Director of Confidence [in the Commander-in-chief], the Director of Justice [to the Grand Minister over the Masses], and the Director of Obedience [to the Grand Minister of Works, all of whom are mentioned on 99 B: 3b]. Later persons did not understand [this reference] and erroneously interpolated the two characters *liu*." Hu San-hsing however declares that the "six directors (*liu-szu*)" are the "six superintendents" mentioned on 99 B: 4a. He does not emend the text. But he leaves unexplained who were the "six high ministers."

The exact denotation of the phrase *liu szu liu ch'ing* is not clear, but Wang Mang's intention is plain: the reduction in salaries consequent upon disasters was to be spread among the whole bureaucracy. I have therefore followed Liu Feng-shih in dropping the two characters *liu*, but have differed from him in interpreting the words *szu* and *ch'ing*, making them refer to all officials of those grades without attempting to indicate particular ones.

**29b**

crops in the regions for which they act as guarantors], the amount shall also be calculated in percentages, and their salaries shall be reduced [proportionately]. Gentlemen, the Imperial Retinue, and officials of the imperial capital offices, who receive their salaries from the receipts within the [imperial] capitals, shall take the amount of the imperial dishes [provided by] the Grand Provisioner as the measure [for their salaries]. Nobles, princesses, baronesses, vassals, and minor officials shall also each act as guarantors against visitations and disasters [in] their [districts]. I hope that [thus] superiors and inferiors will be of the same mind and will encourage the advancement of agriculture and tranquillize the great multitude." [Wang] Mang's regulations were as complicated and detailed as the foregoing.

**Corruption Increases.**
**34b**

The calculations of the taxes could not be made out, so that the officials did not eventually obtain any salaries. Each one took advantage of the duties of his office to do evil, receiving and exacting bribes and presents in order to support himself.

**June 2.[29.5]**

**28a**
**Ominous Portents.**

In this month, on [the day] *mou-ch'en*, the western bank of the Ch'ang-p'ing Lodge collapsed, blocking up the Ching River, so that it could not run, was cut off, and flowed northwards.[29.6] [Wang Mang] sent the Grand Minister of Works, Wang Yi₅, to inspect it. When he returned and memorialized a description [of the occurrence], the courtiers offered congratulations, considering that it was what the

[29.5] There was no *mou-ch'en* day in the fifth month, according to Huang. He however follows that month by an intercalary fifth month, which has such a day. I have assumed that this was the month concerned.

[29.6] Hu San-hsing explains, "The Ch'ang-p'ing Lodge was on the plain south of the Ching River. The Ching River flows southeastwards and enters the Wei [River]. It was blocked by the bank, hence was cut off and flowed northwards." The courtiers' actions, interpreting as a happy portent what was actually an indication of a very serious and irretrievable irrigation failure, indicates well the inaccessibility of Wang Mang to unpleasant facts and their own sycophancy and deception of their ruler (cf. Introduction to this chapter, p. 113–114).

十率多少而損其祿郎從官中都官吏食祿都內之委者曰太官

膳羞備損而為節諸侯辟任附城羣吏亦各保其災害幾上下同

心勸進農業安元元焉莽之制度煩碎如此謀計不可理吏終不

得祿各回官職為姦受取賕賂曰自共給是月戊辰長平館西岸

崩邑涇水不流毀而北行遣大司空王邑行視還奏狀羣臣上壽

曰為河圖所謂曰土填水匈奴滅亡之祥也乃遣并州牧宋弘游擊都
尉任萌等將兵擊匈奴至邊止屯七月辛酉霸城門災民間所謂青門
也戊子晦日有食之大赦天下復令公卿大夫諸侯二千石舉四行各
一人大司馬陳茂曰日食免武建伯嚴尤為大司馬十月戊辰王路朱
烏門鳴盡夜不絕崔發等曰虞帝闢四門通四聰門鳴者明當修先聖

*Diagrams From the River* had said, that earth pressing upon water is a happy auspice of the Huns being destroyed. [Wang Mang] thereupon sent the Shepherd of the Ping Province, Sung Hung, the Scouting and Attacking Chief Commandant, Jen Meng,[29.7] and others, leading troops, to attack the Huns. They went to the border, and stopped to garrison it.

In the seventh month, on [the day] *hsin-yu*, there was a visitation [of fire] to the Pa City-gate, which among the common people is called the Cerulean Gate, and on [the day] *mou-tzu*, the last day of the month, there was an eclipse of the sun. A general amnesty [was granted] to the empire, and [Wang Mang] again ordered the ministers, grandees, nobles, and [officials ranking at] 2000 piculs each to recommend one person with the four [types of virtuous] conduct.[29.8] The Commander-in-chief, Ch'en Mou, was dismissed because of the eclipse of the sun, and **30a** the Earl Establishing Military Power, Chuang Yu, was made the Commander-in-chief.

In the tenth month, on [the day] *mou-hsü*,[30.1] the Vermillion Bird Gate to the Royal Apartments cried out for a day and night without ceasing. Ts'ui Fa and others said, "The Lord of Yü, [Shun], 'opened the gates to the four [quarters] to hear with the ears in the four [quarters].'[30.2] The crying out of the gate makes plain that you ought to cultivate the rites of

July 25.

Aug. 21.

Oct. 30.

35a

---

[29.7] The Official ed. reads 明 for 萌, but the Ching-yu ed. reads the latter.

[29.8] Liu Feng-shih remarks that these four types of conduct were probably those mentioned in 99 B: 16b and taken from the *Analects*: moral character, gifts in speaking, administrative ability, and scholarship.

The mention of "[officials ranking at] two thousand piculs" is probably an anachronism for the sake of clearness; Wang Mang had renamed this rank the Upper-ranking Grandees; cf. 99 B: 4a.

[30.1] There was no *mou-ch'en* day in this month; seemingly the only serviceable emendation is from *ch'en* to *hsü* (also made in 11: 8a).

[30.2] A quotation from *Book of History* II, I, 15 (Legge, p. 41; Couvreur, p. 23), cf. Karlgren, *BMFEA* 20, 94ff, Gl. 1274.

the ancient sages in order to attract gentlemen from the four quarters." Thereupon [Wang Mang] ordered that the courtiers should all felicitate him. Those who were recommended for the four [types of virtuous] conduct entered by way of the Vermillion Bird Gate in order to take the examinations.

*28b*
The Southwestern Borders.

The General Tranquillizing the Southern Barbarians, Feng Mou, had attacked Kou-t'ing, and six or seven-tenths of his soldiers had died from pestilence. As a levy for military purposes upon the common people's wealth he had taken five-tenths, so that the Yi Province was empty and waste, yet [the rebellious barbarians] were not vanquished. [Wang Mang] summoned him to return and sent him to prison, where he died.

In his place, [Wang Mang] sent the General of a Peaceful Beginning, Lien Tan, together with the [Provincial] Shepherd of Yung Regional Division, Shih Hsiung, to attack Kou-t'ing.[30.3] When they had cut off a considerable [number of] heads and had had a victory, [Wang] Mang summoned [Lien] Tan and [Shih] Hsiung [to come to the capital. Lien] Tan and [Shih] Hsiung wanted [instead] to increase the taxes, [whereupon] they would be certain to conquer.

Thereupon they returned and again made a great levy for military purposes. The Grand Governor of Chiu-tu [Commandery], Feng Ying, was not willing to furnish [anything], and sent [a memorial] to the throne, saying, "From the time that Chou Niu of Sui-chiu [county] and Hsieh-tou of T'ung Commune and the like in Yüeh-sui [Commandery] revolted, it has been almost the tenth year, in which [time] the commanderies and counties have been resisting the attacks of [the barbarians] without cessation. When, in succession to [Ch'eng Lung], Feng Mou was em-

---

[30.3] Hu San-hsing remarks that previously there were Shepherds of Provinces and Superintendents of Divisions; here a Division and a Province seem to have been the same; cf. n. 24.1, paragraph 9.

ployed, he temerariously put into practise a temporary policy, which was that, altho south of P'o-tao
the mountains are high and defiles are deep, [Feng] 35b
Mou many times expelled their bands from distant
places, so that the expense has been counted by the
hundred-thousands [of cash] and officers and soldiers
have suffered from poisonous emanations,[30.4] seven-
tenths of them dying.

"Now [Lien] Tan and [Shih] Hsiung are afraid
that they themselves would be reprimanded [for not 30b
having completed their task] in the appointed time,
and [seek to] levy and mobilize the troops and grain
of the commandery, to re-appraise [the property of]
the common people and take four-tenths of it. They
have impoverished and ruined Liang Province, but
their efforts will not eventually meet with success.
It would be proper to dismiss the troops and garrison
farms and openly offer rewards [for the rebels]."

[Wang] Mang became angry and dismissed [Feng]
Ying from his office. [But] later he awakened considerably to [the truth] and said, "[Feng] Ying
should not however be severely condemned," and
rewarded [Feng] Ying by making him the Leader of
the Combination in Ch'ang-sha [Commandery].

Wang-sun Ch'ing, [who belonged to] the faction of　　Human
Chai Yi, was arrested and secured, and [Wang] Mang　Dissection.
sent the Grand Physician and the Master of Recipes,
with a skilled butcher, all together to dissect and flay
[Wang-sun Ch'ing], to measure and examine his five 29a
viscera, and to use fine bamboos to trace out his
arteries, so as to find out their beginnings and ends,
saying that [thereby] they would know how to cure
illness.[30.5]

In this year, [Wang Mang] sent as the Chief

[30.4] Was this malaria?

[30.5] No more official dissections seem to be recorded until A.D. 1106; cf. Maspero in
JA 229 (Apr.–June, 1937), p. 188.

**The Silk Route Blocked.** Envoy, the General of the Five Majestic Principles, Wang Chün4c, with the Protector General of the Western Frontier Regions, Li Ch'ung2, leading the Mou-and-Chi Colonel, [Kou Ch'in], to go out to the Western Frontier Regions. All the various states welcomed [the envoys] at their suburbs and offered tribute.

36a   The state of Karshahr (Yen-ch'i)[30.6] had previously murdered the Protector General Tan Ch'in, so [Wang] Chün4c wanted to make a surprise attack upon it. He ordered his Associate Lieutenant, Ho Feng, and the Mou-and-Chi Colonel, Kuo Ch'inb, to separate their commands [from his]. Karshahr (Yen-Ch'i) made a pretense of surrendering, and and ambushed troops, who attacked [Wang] Chün4c and the others, so that all [his company] died. [Kuo] Ch'inb and [Ho] Feng reached [Karshahr shortly] after [Wang Chün4c had been killed, before the troops had returned], and made a surprise attack upon its aged and weak [people, massacring them]. They returned by way of Turfan (Chü-shih) and entered the [Chinese] barrier. [Wang] Mang installed [Kuo] Ch'inb as the General Maintaining Order in Foreign Parts, and enfeoffed him as the Viscount Exterminating Northwestern Barbarians.

31a   Ho Feng was made the Baron Quieting the Northwestern Barbarians. From this time on, the Western Frontier Regions were cut off [from China].

自此絕
恭拜欽為塡外將軍封剝胡子何封為集胡男西域
兵擊駭等皆厄欽封後到襲擊老弱從車師還入塞
襲之命佐帥何封戊己校尉郭欽別將馬著詐降伏
西域諸國皆郊迎貢獻馬諸國前殺都護但欽駭欷
遣大使五威將王駿西域都護李崇將戊己校尉出

[30.6] *Chu* 諸 is very probably a copyist's error for *ch'i* 耆. *Ch'i* was misread as *che* 者 and the following *kuo* 國 caused *che-kuo* to be transcribed as *chu-kuo*. I emend accordingly. There is no reason for a final particle *yen* 焉 at the end of the preceding sentence. *HS* 96 B: 35b states, "The state of Karashahr (*Yen-ch'i-kuo*) was nearest the Huns and revolted first, murdering the Protector-General Tan Ch'in." Then the other states had nothing to do with this murder. Here there is moreover the same group of three words that almost surely originally stood in this passage—*yen-ch'i-kuo*. Pan Ku probably used the same original document in writing both passages. A cursively written *ch'i* in his original draft could easily have caused this mistake. *Chu* is found in the Ching-yu ed., so that this mistake occurred early.

## [Chapter] XCIX

## THE SIXTY-NINTH [MEMOIR]

### THE MEMOIR OF WANG MANG

## PART C

萬校兀枝馬六月更授諸侯茅土於明堂曰予制作地理建封五

為建德侯逸為封德侯位皆特進見禮如三公賜第一區錢三百

忠恕敬上愛下博通舊聞德行醇備至於黄髮靡有愆失其封林

四年五月莽曰保成師友祭酒唐林故諫議祭酒琅邪紀逸孝弟

王莽傳第六十九下

漢書九十九

In [the period T'ien-feng], the fourth year, in the fifth month, [Wang] Mang said [in a message], "The Libationer for the Masters and Companions [to the Heir-apparent] Guarantor of His Perfection, T'ang Lin, and the former Libationer for the Remonstrants and Consultants, Chi Ch'ün, ([a man] from Lang-yeh [Commandery), have shown] filial devotion, brotherly respectfulness, loyalty, and reciprocity; they have been respectful to their superiors and have loved their inferiors; they have been extensively learned in ancient traditions; their upright characters have been excellent and perfect; and even to old age they have not committed any errors. Let [T'ang] Lin be enfeoffed as the Marquis Established Through Virtue and [let Chi] Ch'ün [be enfeoffed as] the Marquis Enfeoffed Through Virtue; the rank of both shall be a Specially Advanced and they shall be received in audience with rites like those of the three highest ministers. They are [each] to be granted one residence,[1.1] three million cash, and are to be given stools and canes."

In the sixth month, when [Wang Mang] changed [the rites, removing to] the *Ming-t'ang* the bestowal of earth [enveloped in] quitch grass to nobles [as a token of enfeoffment], he said [in a message], "I have instituted the geographical arrangements and have established and enfeoffed [nobles] in five grades.

A.D. 17,
May/June.
Enfeoff-
ments
Made

June/July

---

[1.1] The Official ed. has erroneously emended 弟 to 第.

I have examined them by the canonical books and harmonized them with the written traditions [concerning the classics] and the records, and pervaded them by the principles of right relationships.

"I have discussed them and pondered over them again and again, from the beginning of the first [year] in [the period] Shih-chien-kuo down to the present, [which is] the ninth year.   Now they have however been indeed fixed upon.   I have myself established the [inclined] plane of ornamented stones,[1.2] I have arranged the three-ribbed quitch-grass and the four-colored earth,[1.3] and have respectfully given informa-

A.D. 9

1b*

1b†

1b‡

設文石之平陳菁茅回色之土欽
元曰來九年于茲畫今定矣子親
論之思之至於再三自始建國之傳記通於義理
等考之經蓺合之

---

* Light upright numbers indicate the paging in the Ching-yu ed., reprinted in the Po-na Series, pub. by the Commercial Press.

† Bold-face numbers indicate the paging in Wang Hsien-ch'ien's *Han-shu Pu-chu*, as in volumes I and II.

‡ Italic numbers indicate the paging in the Official ed. or Palace ed. or Wu-ying Tien ed., pub. in the "Szu-pu Pei-yao Collecteana."

[1.2] Pan Ku in his "Fu on the Western Capital" (*HHS*, Mem. 30 A: 12a), speaking of the Front Hall in the Wei-yang Palace at Ch'ang-an, says, "On the left was the staircase and on the right was the [inclined] plane."   This statement is repeated in *San-fu Huang-t'u* 2: 3a.   Li Hsien quotes Chih Yü's (fl. ca. 270–310) *Chüeh-yi-yao-chu* (lost) saying, "The [inclined] plane with ornamented bricks paralleled [the staircase up to the Front Hall]."   This inclined plane was probably for the imperial chariot.   Since the Eastern Steps (on the right) were reserved for the Emperor, Wang Mang added a ramp made of ornamented blocks, so that it might be possible to ride down from the hall in the Hall with the Emperor's Apartments (the audience hall).   Cf. the plan of a palace Hall in the *T'zu-yüan*, sub 寢.

[1.3] The "three-ribbed rush, *ching-mao* 菁茅" was used to envelop the clod of earth from the imperial mound altar of the gods of the soils used in enfeoffing nobles.   This rush is mentioned in *Book of History*, III, i, vii, 52 (Legge, p. 115; *Mh* I, 124).   Bretschneider, *Botanicum Sinicum*, no. 459, p. 279, finds it impossible to identify exactly.   In *Kuan-tzu* (iii cent. B.C.) 24: 6b, ch. 83, it is mentioned as growing between the Yangtze and Huai Rivers.

The Imperial mound altar of the gods of the soils contained five colors of soil; here only four are mentioned.   The *Chi-chung Chou-shu* (found in a tomb in 280–289 A.D.; extant in Former Han times) 5: 8b–9a, ch. 48, says, "[The Duke of Chou] established the great mound altar to the gods of the soils in the midst of the [Chou] state [capital at Lo]. Its low ridge around the edge [probably enclosing a ribbon of water encircling the mound] on the east was of cerulean earth, on the south was of red earth, on the west was of white earth, on the north was of black earth, and in the center [the mound] was sprinkled with

告于岱宗泰社后土先祖先妣曰班授之各就厥國養牧民
人用成功業其在緣邊若江南非詔所召遣侍于帝城者納
言掌貨大夫且調都內故錢于其祿公歲八十萬侯伯四十
萬子男二十萬然俊不能盡得莽好空言暴古法多封爵人
性實遒嗇託曰地理未定故且先賦茅土用慰喜封者是歲

tion [of the enfeoffments] to Mount T'ai,[1.4] to the Grand [Imperial] Mound Altar to the Gods of the Soils, to Sovereign Earth, to my deceased male and female ancestors, in order to publish and transmit [these classical practises]. [Let] each [noble] go to his state to care for and shepherd his common people in order to accomplish meritorious achievements. For those whose [estates] are on the borders or in Chiang-nan, except for those who are summoned by an imperial edict to be sent to wait upon [the Emperor] in the imperial capital, the Grandee in Charge of Goods [subordinate to] the Communicator shall temporarily collect the old [style] cash from the capital treasuries [in order to] pay them their allowances: to dukes, 800,000 [cash] per year; to marquises and earls, 400,000 [cash per year]; to viscounts and barons, 200,000 [cash per year]."[1.5]

Yet even then they could not receive the full amount. [Wang] Mang loved bombastic speeches and admired ancient practises. He enfeoffed very many people as nobles, [but] in his nature he was in reality niggardly. He took as a pretext that the geographical arrangements had not yet been determined upon, hence temporarily in advance distributed clods with quitch-grass [in token of enfeoffment], using them to console and delight those whom he enfeoffed.

In this year, [Wang Mang] again published ordi-

yellow earth. When he was about to establish a noble, he dug into and took the earth from one side in that direction [in which the fief of the noble was to be located], enveloped it with yellow earth, and bound it with quitch-grass, using [the whole] for the earth [employed] in the enfeoffment. Hence [the recipient] said, 'I have received my sliced [clod of] earth from the house of Chou.'" Since Wang Mang was following ancient practises, he undoubtedly followed this precedent.

[1.4] This name for Mt. T'ai is taken from the *Book of History* II, i, iii 8 (Legge, p. 35).

[1.5] Under the Han dynasty, each household in a noble estate paid 200 cash per year (91: 6a), hence the allowances of dukes were the same as those previously enfeoffed with an estate of 4000 households; of marquises and earls, 2000 households; and of viscounts and barons, 1000 households.

**The Six Monopolies**

nances for the six controls.[1.6]  For each control he established regulations to restrain violators [of the monopoly]; the penalties were as great as capital [punishment.  Yet] the officials and common people who suffered for crime became increasingly[1.7] numerous.

**2a**

**Tax on Slaves**

He moreover temporarily made a levy [even] upon the highest class of the highest ministers [and those ranking] lower, that whoever possessed male or female slaves should pay a tax of 3600 cash per [slave], so

**2a**

that the empire became even more discontented and thieves and robbers arose.[2.1]

When the Communicator, Feng Ch'ang, remonstrated against the six controls, [Wang] Mang became furious and dismissed [Feng] Ch'ang from office.

**Supervisors for Commandery**

**2a**

**Officials**

[Wang Mang] established Administrators of the Laws at [the Emperor's] Right and Left for the Extirpation of Wickedness, and selected for employment [in this office] capable officials, Hou Pa and others, dispersing them to supervise the six Commandants' [Commanderies] and the six Neighboring Commanderies, like the Inspectors of the Han [dynasty], with one Officer of the three highest ministers for a commandery as an Attendant official [to the Administrator of the Laws for the Extirpation of Wickedness].

**Bandit Bands**

Kua-t'ien Yi of Lin-huai [Commandery] and others became thieves and robbers, relying upon [the fastnesses in] Ch'ang-chou of K'uai-chi [Commandery].  Mother Lü, a woman of Lang-yeh [Commandery], also arose.  Previously, Mother Lü's son had been an official of the county and had been killed on a false charge by its Ruler.  His mother dispersed the wealth of her household on [the pretext] of dealing

邪女子呂母亦起初呂母子為縣吏為宰所寃殺母散家財呂
三公士郡一人從事臨淮瓜田儀等為盜賊依阻會稽長州琅
執法左右刺姦遣用能吏侯霸等分督六尉六隊如漢利史與
六百天下愈愁盜賊起納言馮常呂六筦諫爭大怒免常官置
罪者浸衆又一切調上公吕下諸有奴婢者率一口出錢三千
俊明六筦之令每一筦下為設科條防禁犯者罪至死吏民抵

---

[1.6] Cf. 99 B: 12b.

[1.7] For 浸, the Official ed. and the Southern Academy ed. read 濅; the Ching-yu ed. reads 浸.

[2.1] The Sung Ch'i ed. asserts that before 起 there should be a 興.

370

酤酒買兵弩陰厚貲窮少年得百餘人遂攻海曲縣殺其宰呂祭

子墓引兵入海其衆浸多後皆即赦盜賊還言盜

賊解輒復合問其故皆曰慈法禁煩苛不得舉手力作所得不足

呂給貢稅閉門自守又坐鄰伍鑄錢挾銅姦吏因呂慈民民窮惡

起為盜賊芣大怒免之其或順指言民驕黠當誅及言時運適然

in liquor, by purchasing arms and crossbows, and privately treating poor youths liberally. When she had obtained more than a hundred men, she thereupon attacked the county-seat of Hai-ch'ü and killed its Ruler. She used [his corpse] as a sacrifice at the grave of her son. She led her troops into the sea. These bands gradually became greater. Later both [bandit bands] were numbered by the ten-thousands.[2.2]

[Wang] Mang sent commissioners to go to and pardon the thieves and robbers. When [the commissioners] returned, they said, "Whenever the thieves and robbers disperse, they immediately reunite." When he asked them the reason for this [action], they all said, "They are grieved at the laws and prohibitions, which are vexatious and tyrannous, so that they can do nothing, and what they obtain by hard work is insufficient to pay the taxes, while if they close their doors in order to guard themselves, they are moreover sentenced because their group of five neighboring [families] might be casting cash or possessing copper. Wicked officials take advantage of that to afflict[2.3] these common people. When common people are impoverished, they all arise and become thieves or robbers." [Wang] Mang [became] furious and dismissed them.

Some of them fell in with his ideas and said that the common people were perverse and crafty and ought to be executed and also said that the revolution of the seasons was opportune and [the robbers] would

2b

**2b**

[2.2] At this point *Tzu-chih T'ung-chien* 38: 7a, b adds the names of other robber bands: Wang K'uang[1b] and Wang Feng[4a] 王鳳 from Hsin-shih [in the present central Hupeh; cf. *HHS*, An. 1 A: 3a]; Ma Wu 馬武 in Nan-yang Commandery [cf. *HHS*, Mem. 12: 10a–12a]; Wang Ch'ang and Ch'eng Tan in Ying-ch'uan Commandery; Chang Pa of Nan Commandery; Yang Mu of Chiang-hsia Commandery, each of whose bands increased to be ten thousand in number; cf. Glossary *sub vocibus*.

[2.3] Wang Nien-sun shows that anciently *chou* 愁 and 擎 were interchanged, and suggests reading the latter word here. But *chou* makes quite good sense.

before long be annihilated, [whereupon Wang] Mang was pleased and immediately promoted them.

Aug./Sept.     In this year, in the eighth month, [Wang] Mang in person went to the place for the suburban sacrifice at the south [of the Capital] to have the majestic *tou* [measures] cast.[2.4]  For making the majestic *tou*

鑄作威斗威斗
月奉親之南郊
瓶邐之是歲八
且滅不久莽說

[2.4] Couvreur (*Dict. Class.*, III ed., p. 915), followed by Stange, (p. 214, n. 1) says that these *tou* 斗 were bronze tablets on which the Northern Bushel (北斗, i.e., the Great Dipper) was represented, but I cannot find any other authority for this statement.  It is quite true, as Stange remarks, that ancient Chinese tablets bearing a representation of the Northern Bushel have come down to us, but that fact does not constitute any evidence that these articles were made by Wang Mang.  The only description seems to be the one in the text.  This account furthermore contains some details which indicate that the *tou* were measures rather than tablets.  (1) It says they "were like the Northern Bushel 若北斗," not that they were inscribed with the Northern Bushel.  *T'ai-p'ing Yü-lan* 765: 4b, in quoting this passage, moreover begins the above clause with the word 形, making it say, "Their *shape* was like the Northern Bushel."  I take this to mean that they had handles, like Chinese *tou* measures.  (2) Wang Mang ordered his Directors of Mandates to "bear them on their shoulders 負之."  Tablets are carried in the hands or worn at the girdle, not borne on the shoulders or back.  (3) Their size, 2 ft. 5 in. (58 cm. or 22½ in. Eng. measure) is quite in accord with their being measures and containing a *tou* (cf. *HFHD*, I, 279).  This length was then that of the utensil with its handle.  If its bowl was shallow, like the one dated 65 B.C. and pictured in *Chin-shih-so*, "Chin," 3: 42a, its over-all length was just right to contain a *tou*.  I therefore conclude that a ladle-like shape was much more probable than a tablet-like shape.

The Northern Bushel (the Dipper) was among the most important of Chinese constellations.  Near it is the Pole Star, where resides the Supreme One (*T'ai-yi*), the supreme God who rules the universe.  "The [Northern] Bushel is the chariot of the Lord [i.e., the Supreme One], whereby he moves around at the center [of the heavens], visits and controls the four quarters, separates the *yin* and *yang*, determines the four seasons, proportions [the influences of] the five powers [or elements], and gives information concerning the divisions [of time] and the revolutions [of the stars, thereby] fixing [epochs for all] records.  All this depends upon the [Northern] Bushel" (*SJ* 27: 8 = *Mh* III, 342; cf. also *HFHD* 99 B: n. 21.1).  This constellation is the vehicle whereby the supreme God exerts his authority.  The emperor of China, as the Son of Heaven, was the earthly deputy of this supreme God.  The Heavenly Bushel accordingly represented, more than any other, the imperial authority.  It was a god, to whom sacrifices were made at Yung (*Mh* III, 444, 491).  In 112 B.C., Emperor Wu placed it on his supernatural standard, along with a flying dragon to represent the Supreme One (*Mh* III, 493).  "The southern [side] of the city-wall [of Ch'ang-an, built 194–190 B.C.] had the shape of the Southern Bushel and the northern [side] had the shape of the Northern Bushel, [in order that this city should be a proper habitation for an emperor].  This is [the reason that], down to the present, people call the capital of the [Former] Han [dynasty], 'the Bushel City' " (*San-fu Huang-*

者 之 尺 勝
曰 若 五 眾
五 北 寸 兵
石 斗 欲 阨
銅 長 吕 成
為 二 厭 令

[measures], five [colors of] minerals were used with bronze.[2.5]　They were like the Northern Bushel [in shape], two feet five inches long.　[Wang Mang] intended to use them to repress various military forces by incantations.　When they were completed, he ordered the Directors of Mandates [from the Five

*2b*

The
Majestic
*Tou*
Measures

*t'u* 1: 6a).　When Wang Mang was besieged in his palace in A.D. 23, he sat in the direction occupied by the handle of the Bushel, turning about as this constellation turned in the heavens, by sympathy with it, securing its assistance (*HS* 99 C: 27a).　These majestic *tou*-measures accordingly denoted this divinity, who would naturally exert his authority in behalf of the emperor on earth.　By sympathy with the god, they would draw the god's attention to happenings in their vicinity and would exercise his power to assist and protect the emperor.　Cf. also 99 B: 6b & n. 6.9.

*Nan-shih* 33: 24a–b, *sub* Ho Ch'eng-t'ien, says, (this event is dated between 442 and 447), "Chang Yung was once digging the Hsüan-wu Lake [north of the Shou-tu Metropolis 首都市 i.e., present Nanking, Kiangsu, according to the *Shina Redikai Chimei Yoran*, p. 194a], when he happened upon an ancient tomb.　Above the tomb he secured a bronze *tou* [measure] with handles.　Emperor Wen [of the Sung Dynasty] asked the gentlemen of his court about it, and [Ho] Ch'eng-t'ien replied, 'This is a majestic *tou* [measure] of the fallen Hsin [Dynasty.　When any of his] three highest ministers died, Wang Mang always granted [such measures] to them: one for the outside of the tomb, and one for the inside of the tomb.　At that time, the only one of his highest ministers who lived near the mouth of the Yangtze River [i.e., east of the present Nanking] was Chen Han, who became Grand Minister over the Masses.　It must be [Chen] Han's tomb.'

"Soon [Chang] Yung opened the tomb, and from inside it, he again secured a *tou* [measure], and also there was a stone with the inscription, 'The tomb of the Grand Minister over the Masses, Chen Han.' "

This account must however be mistaken.　Shen Ch'in-han points out that Chen Han died in 12 A.D.　His son, Chen Feng, was executed in 10 A.D., before these majestic *tou*-measures were made.　When he died, Chen Han was moreover Commander-in-chief, not Grand Minister over the Masses.　*San-kuo-chih* 5: 4b, *sub* the Empress nee Chen, who was a descendant of Chen Han, says that her home was in Wu-chi 無極 of Chung-shan Commandery, and *T'ai-p'ing Huan-yü Chi* 60: 10b locates Chen Han's tomb and those of other members of the Chen clan 35 *li* southwest of Wu-chi, which place was located, according to *Ta-ch'ing Yi-t'ung-chih* 27: 5b, at the present place by the same name, in Honan.

[2.5] Li Ch'i explains, "Mineral medicines of five colors, together with bronze [or copper] were used in making them," but Su Lin glosses, "Copper ore of five colors was used in smelting [metal] for them."　Yen Shih-ku adds that Li Ch'i is correct and that "It was like the process of making the present *t'ou-shih* 鍮石 [a gold-appearing copper-zinc alloy, made by smelting together two parts of copper with one part of smithsonite, the present 'yellow copper']."　Dr. Duyvendak remarks that the number five must refer to the five elements.

Majestic Principles] to carry them on their shoulders. When [Wang] Mang went out, they went before him; when he had entered [the palace], they waited upon him at his sides.[2.6]   On the day that these *tou* [measures] were cast, there was a severe cold [spell], so that some men and horses of the various offices froze to death.

**V**
**3a**
**A.D. 18**
**Jan. 6**
**The**
**Monopolies**
**Upheld**
**3a**

In the fifth year, the first month, on the first day of the month, there was a visitation [of fire] to the southern gate of the Northern Army [Encampment].

Fei Hsing, the Director of Confidence in the Commander-in-chief, was made the Shepherd of Ching Province.   When he was asked at an audience what would be his plans of action when he reached his regional division, [Fei] Hsing replied, "The common people of Ching and Yang[3.1] [Provinces] generally take advantage of their mountains and marshes in making fishing and the picking [of wild fruits] their occupations.   Recently the state has set up the six controls, which tax [the products of] the mountains and marshes and have interfered with and taken away the profits of the common people.   For a long time in successive years there have been droughts, so that the people are hungry and impoverished.   Hence they have become thieves or robbers.

"When I, Hsing, reach my regional division, I intend to order and to make it clearly known and inform the thieves and robbers that they should return to their homes and I will lend them oxen for plowing, seed, and food, and exempt them from the land and capitation-taxes.   I hope that thereby I may be able to disperse and tranquillize them."

令明曉告盜賊歸田里假貸犁牛種食闊其祖賦幾可呂解釋安
笼稅山澤妨棄民之利連年久旱百姓飢窮故為盜賊與到部欲
部方略興對曰荊楊之民率依阻山澤以漁采為業閭者國張六
五年正月朔北軍南門災曰大司馬司允費與為荊州牧見問到
司命負之莽出在前入在御旁鑄斗日大寒百官人馬有凍死者

---

[2.6] Wang Nien-sun says that this sentence originally read as it now is in *T'ai-p'ing Yü-lan* 486: 5a, i.e., with the word 則 after the 出 and the last clause reading 入則御旁. He says that people did not understand that 御 means "wait upon," so dropped out the two words 則 and changed one word.   *Tzu-chih T'ung-chien* 38: 6b and *T'ai-p'ing Yü-lan* 765: 5a (with another difference, showing a poorer text) read as the text does here.

[3.1] The Official and Southern Academy ed. emend 楊 to 揚.

自畫容貌被服天子衣冠刻印三一曰維祉冠存已夏處南山藏薄冰二
考覈貪饕開吏告其將奴婢告其主幾曰姦姦愈甚皇孫功崇公宗坐
利增產致富者收其家所有財產五分之四曰助邊急公府士馳傳天下
詔曰詳考始建國二年胡虜擾夏已來諸軍吏及緣邊吏大夫已上為姦
集茶恐免興官天下吏已不得奉祿並為姦利郡尹縣宰家累千金茶下

[Wang] Mang became incensed [at this proposal] and dismissed [Fei] Hsing from his office.

Because the officials of the [whole] empire did not receive their salaries, they all did evil for profit. **Rich Officials Mulcted** The personal property of [Grand] Governors of commanderies and Rulers of counties [amounted to] a thousand [catties of] gold. [Hence Wang] Mang issued an imperial edict which said, "Investigate carefully [the deeds of] the military officials and the officials of the borders, from the grandees and upwards, beginning with the second year of [the period] Shih-chien-kuo, when the northern barbarian (Hu) **A.D. 10.** caitiffs troubled China.[3.2] If any, have done evil for profit, so that they have increased their property and have become rich, [let] four-fifths of the property in their families be taken and used to aid the distress of the borders." Officers from the highest ministers' yamens [rode] galloping quadrigae [all over] the empire, examining and investigating avaricious [persons]. They persuaded officials to inform on their generals, and male and female slaves to **3a** inform on their masters, hoping thereby to stop the **3b** evil, [but] the evil became very much more serious.

An Imperial Grandson, the Duke of Eminent **An** Merits, [Wang] Tsung, was sentenced for having had **Ambitious** a picture of himself painted, wearing the robes and **Imperial** bonnet of the Son of Heaven, and having had three **Grandson** seals engraved. One read, "Because of celestial **Executed** blessings, my official hat is prepared and ready. In the summer [I] dwell in the Southern Mountains, where there is stored up thin ice."[3.3] The second **3b**

[3.2] A phrase from *Book of History* II, i, 20 (Legge, p. 44). This reference is to the events recorded on 99 B: 14b.

[3.3] It is impossible to be sure about the translation of such brief and condensed expressions as these seal inscriptions. Wen Ying glosses, "*Chih* 祉 [means] celestial favors and prosperity. 'The hat is prepared and ready' [means that] he wished to succeed to [the imperial throne]." Ying Shao adds, " 'In the summer to dwell in the Southern Mountains' [means] going to a shady and cool place. 'To store up thin ice' also [means] thereby to avoid the heat."

read, "Revering the Sages and holding precious the heritage."[3.4]　The third said, "[To be] enfeoffed because of virtue and made glorious by the [imperial] documents."[3.5]

The household of [Wang] Tsung's maternal uncle Lü K'uan, which had previously been exiled to Ho-p'u

寬家前徒合
圍又宗勇呂
三曰德封昌
曰肅聖寶繼

Stange (p. 216) translates, "O Glück, die Krone ruht auf mir.　Im Sommer wohne ich im Nan-shan und ziehe mich nach Pao-ping zurück."　He states that according to the commentary Pao-ping was the imperial summer residence.　I have been unable to discover any evidence for this interpretation.　Duyvendak understands, "[So long as] the Cap of Binding Celestial Blessings is preserved, [that is, so long as I possess it], [it is] already [like] living in the southern mountains and appreciating [even] thin ice."　He explains, "That is, even as in extreme heat even thin ice is appreciated, so in this desperate enterprize even the mere possession of the imperial cap gives me courage."　He takes *wei* 維, not as an exclamatory particle (as does Stange), but as meaning "to bind [the blessings] together," probably alluding to the *wei-tou* 斗 "the Great Bushel" [another name for the Northern Bushel constellation], which is an imperial emblem.

I prefer however to take *wei* in its meaning of 以.　Wen Ying does not interpret this word, so that he seems not to have thought it contained any substantial content and almost surely recognized it as an "empty" particle.　The phrase "thin ice" comes from a famous line in *Ode* no. 196 (Legge, II, v, ii, 6, p. 335), and was commonly used to denote the way a true king should act, as if he were treading upon thin ice, i.e., carefully and circumspectly, from fear of Heaven.　Then in the Southern Mountains, Wang Tsung was practising being emperor, by magically treading upon thin ice.　This explanation is however far from certain.

[3.4] Ying Shao explains, "[Wang] Mang himself said that he had inherited descent from the Sage, Shun, and that he had been able to be respectful and to secure the Heavenly treasure, the tortoise, and thereby was set up [as emperor.　Wang] Tsung wanted to be the successor to his line."

Stange (p. 217) translates, "Wenn man ehrfürchtig gegen die Heiligkeit ist, werden sich die Kostbarkeiten [d.i. kostbare Schildkröte des Himmels] forterben."　Duyvendak points out that the vague parallelism with the third seal inscription makes it necessary to take these four characters two by two.　I have adopted his interpretation.

[3.5] Su Lin explains, "[Wang] Tsung himself said that he would be enfeoffed [as emperor] thru his [magical?] virtue and so must advance to [this] glorious and brilliant [position] and receive the documents and registers of the empire."

Stange (p. 217) translates, "Durch magische Wirkungskraft [mir] verliehenes strahlendes [d.i. kaiserliches] Siegel."　Duyvendak interprets, "[Having the empire] conferred [upon me] by virtue, making glorious the Plans [reference to the *Tzu-ko T'u*?]."　I have followed Su Lin more closely.

崇終伯曰諸伯之禮葬于故同
穀城郡宗妙妙為衛將軍王興夫
本名會宗曰制作去二名今復
名會宗貶厥爵改厥號賜謚為功
春秋之義君親母將將而誅焉
迷惑失道自取此辜焉呼哀哉宗
等叛逆族類而與交通刻銅印
三文意甚喜不知厭足竊窺非望
浦私與宗通發覺按驗宗自殺
莽曰宗屬為皇孫爵為上公知寬

[Commandery], had moreover privately communicated with [Wang] Tsung. When [this matter] became known, an examination was made and [Wang] Tsung committed suicide.

[Wang] Mang said, "[According to] his relationship, [Wang] Tsung was an Imperial Grandson; [according to] his noble rank, he was [among] the highest of the dukes. He knew that [Lü] K'uan and the others belonged to rebellious clan, but communicated with them. He had three bronze seals engraved whose inscriptions and intentions were extremely pernicious. He did not know how to be contented, and was watching for and desiring what he should not have hoped for.

"[According to] the principle in [the *Kung-yang Commentary* on] the *Spring and Autumn*, 'A relative of the prince should not have had such an intention, [but] since he had that intention, he should have been executed,'[3.6] [Wang Tsung] was deluded and went astray, so that he brought this punishment upon himself. Alas! It is sad!"

[Wang] Tsung's personal name was originally Hui-tsung; according to the [imperial] institutions, he had done away with there being two words in his personal name [and used only Tsung as his name].[3.7] He was now again named Hui-tsung, and his noble   **4a** rank was degraded and his title was changed. He was granted the posthumous name of the Erring Earl of Eminent Merits, and was buried with the rites of an earl in his former *t'ung* in Ku-ch'eng Commandery.

[Wang] Tsung's elder sister, [Wang] Fang, who was the Lady (wife) of the General of the Guard,

[3.6] A quotation from *Kung-yang Commentary*, Dk. Chuang, XXXII, vii, & Dk. Chao, I, i; 9: 5a & 22: 1b; in each of which cases it is applied to a person attempting to succeed to the throne by assassinating a ruler's son.

[3.7] As a prospective Emperor, he had done away with his other personal name, just as Wang Mang had the Hun *Shan-yü*, Lüan-ti Nan-chih-ya-szu change his personal name to Chih (99 A: 8b).

3b Wang Hsing[a], had made [magical] imprecations against her mother-in-law and had killed a slave-woman in order to stop up her mouth. The matter became known and [Wang] Mang sent the Regular Palace Attendant Tai Yün to interrogate [Wang] Fang under torture and also to flog [Wang] Hsing[a]. Both committed suicide.

The matter also involved the wife of the Director of Mandates [from the Five Majestic Principles], K'ung Jen. She also committed suicide. [When K'ung] Jen had audience with [Wang] Mang, and doffed his bonnet in acknowledging [his fault, Wang] Mang had a Master of Writing impeach [K'ung] Jen [saying that the fact of his] "having ridden in a heavenly chariot [drawn by] earthly mares, 'having on his left the Azure Dragon [Standard], on his right the White Tiger [Standard], in front the Vermillion Bird[3.8] [Standard], and in his rear the Dark Warrior [Standard],' in his right hand grasping the majestic credentials and on his left [shoulder] bearing the majestic *tou* [measure], and being called the Red

4a Planet, was not in order to make [K'ung] Jen proud, but to honor the majestic mandate of the Hsin house, [and yet K'ung] Jen has presumed to doff his astro-logical bonnet, which constitutes [the capital crime] of being extremely disrespectful." [Then] there was an imperial edict [ordering that K'ung Jen] should not be impeached and exchanging his bonnet for a new one. [Wang Mang's] love for marvels was like the foregoing.

The Marquis of the Straight Path, Wang Shê, was made the General of the Guard. [Wang] Shê was the son of the Marquis of Ch'ü-yang, [Wang] Ken. In the reign of Emperor Ch'eng, [Wang] Ken had

---

[3.8] The Official ed. has emended 雀 to the more usual 鳥. But the Ching-yu ed. reads the former.

The sentence in quotation marks is from *Li-chi*, I, I, v, 8 (Legge, I, 91; Couvreur, I, 55).

Doffing the bonnet indicates resigning the office denoted by the bonnet.

下書曰紫閣圖曰太一黃帝皆倦上天張樂崑崙虔山之上後
見盜賊多乃令太史推三萬六千歲歷紀六歲一改元布天下
邪轉鈔掠眾皆萬數遣使者發郡國兵擊之不能克六年春莽
讓公涉嗣其爵是歲赤眉力子都樊崇等呂飢謹相聚起於琅
大司馬薦莽自代莽思之曰為曲陽非令稱乃追謚根曰直道

been Commander-in-chief, and, [when he had been about to retire], he had recommended [Wang] Mang to take his place [as Commander-in-chief,[4.1] so that Wang] Mang was grateful to him.　[The latter] had considered that Ch'ü-yang (crooked phallus) was not a good designation, so had posthumously [granted Wang] Ken the posthumous name, Duke Jang (Ceding) of the Straight Path. [Wang] Shê had inherited this noble title.

4b Wang Ken's Title Changed

In this year, Li Tzu-tu, Fan Ch'ung, and others of the Red Eyebrows gathered together because of the famine and arose in Lang-yeh [Commandery].　They moved about and robbed.　Their bands all numbered in the ten-thousands.　[Wang Mang] sent commissioners to mobilize the troops of the commanderies and kingdoms to attack them, [but these troops] were unable to vanquish [the robber bands].

The Red Eyebrows Arise

In this sixth year, in the spring, [Wang] Mang saw that the thieves and robbers were so many, hence ordered the Grand Astrologers to calculate a calendar for thirty-six thousand years, with one change of the year-period [every] six years, and to publish it to the empire.

VI A.D. 19 Spring 4a

[Wang Mang] issued a message, saying, "The *Tzu-ko T'u*[4.2] says, 'The Supreme One and the Yellow Lord both [became] immortals and [then][4.3] ascended to heaven, [where they] made music on top of the K'un-lun and Ch'ien Mountains.[4.4]　A sage lord who

[4.1] Cf. *HS* 99 A: 2a.

[4.2] Repeated search has failed to discover any listing of this book, either in the lists of books in the standard histories or the bibliography of the *T'ai-p'ing Yü-lan*.　The Tzu-kung (lit. the Purple Palace) was the Chinese name for the circumpolar constellations, at the center of which was the Supreme One, the heavenly emperor.　*Tzu-ko T'u* may then be translated, "The Plan of the Purple [Heavenly Imperial] Pavilion."

[4.3] Wang Nien-sun says that after the 僊 there was originally the word 而, as it now is in the quotation of this passage in *T'ai-p'ing Yü-lan* 16: 9b; and that this insertion improves the phrasing.　(Repeated search has not discovered this passage in the *Ch'u-hsueh Chi*, contrary to what he says.)

[4.4] The *Mu T'ien-tzu Chuan* (pos. iii cent.) 2: 1b (Cheng's trans. in *JNChRAS.*, 64:

is of their later generations and is to secure auspicious presages is due [similarly] to have music made upon the top of the Chung-nan Mountains in [the state of] Ch'in.'

**4b**    "Because of my lack of penetration, my performance of [Heaven's] commands has not been intelligent, yet now I have been informed [of the correct procedure]. I restore [a former title, changing] the General of a Peaceful Beginning to be the General of a New Beginning, in order to conform to the Mandate [of Heaven given through] portents. Does not the *Book of Changes* say, 'The daily renewing [of nature] is what is called the flourishing of its virtue; its pro-

**5a**    duction of what is produced is what is called its change.'[4.5]    May I receive [Heaven's protection]." He wished thereby to deceive and dazzle the people and to scatter and disperse the thieves and robbers, [but] the vulgar all laughed at him.

**The Hsin Dyansty's Music**    Previously when the music of the Hsin [House]had been offered in the Grand [Ancestral] Temple of the *Ming-t'ang*, when the courtiers had first worn the female unicorn-skin caps,[4.6] someone who heard the sound of this music said, "It is limpid and inspiring, but plaintive,[4.7] not the music that will make a state

[1933] 133) says, "On the lucky day *hsin-yu*, the Son of Heaven ascended a mount of the K'un-lun [Mts.] and thereupon gazed upon the palace of the Yellow Lord."

The *Shan-hai Ching* (prob. ii & i cent. B.C.) 2: 11a, locates the Yellow Lord upon Mt. Mi 崟. Shen Ch'in-han suggests that 虗 is an error for Mi. *T'ai-p'ing Yü-lan* 16: 9b reads Ch'u 處.

[4.5] *Book of Changes*, App. III, ɪ, v, 28, 29, (Legge, p. 356).

[4.6] Li Ch'i (fl. ca. 200) declares that these were "deerskin hats." *Shuo-wen* 10 A: 3b defines *lin* 麟 (usually translated 'unicorn') as, "A large female deer." Lu Chi (261–303), in a note to Ode 11, "Lin-chih-chih," in *Mao-shih Cheng-yi* 1, iii: 7b (same as the *Fu-shih-yin Mao-shih Chu-su*), remarks, "At present, in the borders of Ping Province there are *lin*, like deer in size, which are not the *lin* (unicorns) that are auspicious responses [from Heaven]." (From Shen Ch'in-han). Thus these caps were probably made of female deer skins from this later Ping Province; Wang Mang was probably nevertheless glad to call them unicorn caps.

[4.7] This "someone" might very likely have been Pan Chih, Pan Ku's grandfather,

一切税天下吏民訾三十取一練帛皆輸長安令公卿已下至

乃大募天下丁男及死罪囚吏民奴名曰豬突狶勇曰為鋭卒

若豆等太傅犧叔士孫喜清潔江湖之盜賊而匃奴寇邊甚姦

能克儆還復位後大司馬護軍郭興庸部牧李曅擊蠻夷

關東饑旱數年力子都等黨眾浸多更始將軍廉丹擊益州不

flourish."

At this time, east of [Han-ku] Pass there had been **A** a famine and drought for several years, so that the **Grand** partizan bands of Li Tzu-tu and the others became **Levy** gradually larger. When the General of a New Beginning, Lien Tan, had attacked [the rebels] in Yi Province, he had not been able to vanquish them, hence he was summoned to return in order that someone might be sent in his place. He was [however] restored to his [former] position [as General of a New Beginning]. Afterwards when Kuo Hsing, [the Commissioner Over] the Army [subordinate to] the Commander-in-chief, and the Shepherd of the Yung Regional Division, Li Yeh, [were sent to] attack the barbarian Jo Tou and others, and the Third Brother Hsi, Sun Hsi, a higher subordinate official of the Grand Tutor, [was sent to] purify the Yangtze valley[4.8] from thieves and robbers, and when moreover the Huns raided the borders very seriously, [Wang] Mang made a great solicitation of the empire's freemen together with those imprisoned for capital crimes and the slaves of the officials and common people. *4b* [Those who responded] were called "Boar braves who are porcupines rushing out,"[4.9] and were considered as ardent troops.

[Wang Mang] temporarily taxed the officials and **Special** common people of the empire, taking one-thirtieth of **Taxation** their property. Their close-woven waterproof and other silks were all transported to Ch'ang-an. It was ordered that the ministers and those of lower [rank *5b*

who had been a high official and was living in retirement as a Gentleman at Emperor Ch'eng's tomb; cf. 100 A: 5b.

The Official ed. emends 哀 (plaintive) to 衰 (enfeebling), seemingly without any authority.

4.8 Cf. Glossary *sub* Chiang-hu.

4.9 Fu Chien, in a note to 24 B: 26b, explains this phrase thus, "Hogs 豬 [also porcupines] by nature rush against men impetuously. Hence [Wang Mang] took them for a metaphor." Yen Shih-ku adds, "People in the eastern quarter [of the empire] called pigs 豕 *hsi* 狶. Another [explanation] is that *hsi* are pigs running."

down] to the [officials] in the commanderies and counties who wore yellow seal-cords[4.10] should all

**5a** guarantee[4.11] the rearing of horses for the army, the number of which [horses] should be proportionate to each [official's] rank.

[Wang Mang] also made a wide solicitation for those who possessed extraordinary skills that could be used to attack the Huns, [saying that] they would be treated [extraordinarily by being given a high] ranking [at once and] not be [promoted only] by degrees. Those who said that [their arts] would be advantageous were numbered by the ten-thousands. One said that he was able to cross streams without using boats or oars; that by joining horses and connecting their riders he could cause an army of a million to ford [rivers]. One said that without carrying a measure of grain and by taking drugs, the three [divisions of] an army would not become hungry.

**Aviation** One said that he was able to fly a thousand *li* in a day and so could spy out the Huns. [Wang] Mang immediately had him try out [his invention]. He took the quills of a large bird to make his two wings; on both his head and his body he stuck feathers. He connected them by pivots.[5.1] He flew several hundred double-paces [and then he] fell.

[Wang] Mang knew that these [people] could not be useful, [but] he merely wished to make use of their fame, so he installed them all as Directors of

皆著毛通引環紐飛數百步墮苯知其不可用苟欲復其名皆拜

言能飛一日千里可窺匈奴莽輒試之取大鳥翮為兩翼頭與身

弁捍連馬接騎濟百萬師或言不持斗糧服食藥物三軍不飢或

攻匈奴者將待召不次之位言便宜者曰萬數或言能度水不用

郡縣黃綬皆保養軍馬多少各曰桄為差又博募有奇技術可曰

---

[4.10] *HHS*, Tr. 30: 15a, states that officials ranking at 400, 300, and 200 piculs wore yellow seal-cords. Cf. App. I, *HS* 24 B: 26b.

[4.11] Yen Shih-ku, in a note to the parallel passage in 24 B: 26b, explains, "To guarantee means to promise that they will not die or be injured," i.e., to provide another animal in case anything happened to these animals. Probably they also paid for rearing them. For these pastures, cf. *HFHD*, *II* 304, n. 2.8.

[5.1] This is perhaps the earliest authentic account of human flight. He probably set off from a height, so that a flight of several hundred yards was possible. B. Laufer, *Prehistory of Aviation*, does not notice this incident.

There were also other technical developments in Wang Mang's time; cf. the human dissection in 99 B: 30b.

不聽既得當欲遣尤與廉丹擊匈奴皆賜姓徵氏號二徵將軍
大助也于今迎當置長安槀街一胡人耳不如在匈奴有益薺
諫曰當在匈奴右部兵不侵邊單于動靜輒語中國此方面之
詣長安既立呂為須卜善于後安公始欲誘迎當大司馬嚴尤
女也嘗內附來遣君兄子和親侯王歙誘呼嘗至塞下脅將
為理軍賜呂車馬侍發初匈奴右骨都侯須卜當其妻王昭君

the Army and granted them chariots and horses while they waited [until the army should] set out.

Previously, the Hun *Ku-tu* Marquis of the West, Hsü-pu Tang, whose wife, [Lüan-ti Yün], was the daughter of Wang [Ch'iang] Chao-chün, had been attached to [the Chinese. Wang] Mang sent the Marquis of Peace and Alliance By Marriage, Wang Hsi₆, the son of [Wang Ch'iang] Chao-chün's elder brother, to allure and summon [Hsü-pu] Tang[5.2] to the foot of the barrier and by force made him go to Ch'ang-an, where he was compelled to be set up as the *Shan₄-yü* Hsü-pu and the Duke of Future Peace.[5.3]

*Hsü-pu Tang Brought to Chang-an*

**6a**

[When Wang Mang] first wanted to allure and receive [Hsü-pu] Tang, the Commander-in-chief, Chuang Yu, had remonstrated, saying, "[Hsü-pu] Tang is in the western section of the Huns where his troops do not invade [the Chinese] borders. Whenever the *Shan-yü* moves or remains quiet, he immediately [sends] word [of it] to China. [Thus] he is of the greatest assistance in this quarter. If now you receive [Hsü-pu] Tang and establish him on Kao Street[5.4] in Ch'ang-an, he will be merely an individual northern foreigner (Hu) and would not be as helpful as if he were among the Huns." [But Wang] Mang did not listen [to him.

*5a*

When Wang Mang] had secured [Hsü-pu] Tang, he wanted to send [Chuang] Yu with Lien Tan to attack the Huns. He granted both of them the surname Cheng (to make a military expedition), entitling them the Two Generals Making a Military

**5b**

---

[5.2] For 嘗, the Ching-yu ed., the Southern Academy ed., and the Official ed. read 當, which I adopt.

[5.3] According to *HS* 94 B: 21a = de Groot, *Die Hunnen*, p. 283, Hsü-pu Tang had been made Duke of Future Peace in A.D. 15, whereas he was made *Shan-yü* after A.D. 18 (*HS* 94 B: 21b = de Groot, *ibid.*, 286), so that at this time only the Hun title was additionally conferred upon him.

[5.4] On Kao Street was located the government lodge for barbarians, cf. 70: 10b & Glossary *sub voce*.

Expedition. They were required to execute the *Shan-yu* [Lüan-ti] Yü, and set up [Hsü-pu] Tang to take his place. They were to start out[5.5] from the Kuang Stables at the west of the city.

**Chuang Yu Dismissed**    Before they started out, [since Chuang] Yu had usually had wise plans and had opposed [Wang] Mang's [project of] attacking the barbarians in the four [quarters],[5.6] and had remonstrated several times, but [his advice] had not been followed, he composed [a work] in altogether three fascicles, [dealing with] the conception that ancient famous generals, [such as] Yo Yi and Po Ch'i, were [eventually] not employed [by their lords] and also discussing matters [concerning the Chinese] borders, and memorialized [the book] in order to remonstrate with [Wang] Mang. When they were due to start out, in a conference at court, [Chuang] Yu said firmly that the Huns could be temporarily considered as secondary and that the most important concern

6b    [of the ruler] should be the thieves and robbers east of the mountains [of Kuang-chung].[5.7]

[Wang] Mang became furious and [wrote] a dismissal notice for [Chuang] Yu, which said, "You have overseen affairs to the fourth year, [but when] 'the barbarians became troublesome to the Chinese,' you have not been able to stop or destroy them; when 'robbers and brigands have caused disorder outside and inside [the government]',[5.8] you have not been

曰視事四年蠻夷猾夏不能遏絕寇賊姦宄不能珍滅
回言匈奴可且為後先憂山東盜賊芃大怒乃策尤
用之意及言邊事凡三篇奏曰風諫芃及當出廷議尤
智略非芃攻伐西芃數諫不從著古名將樂毅白起不
當誅單于與而立當代之出車城西橫廐未發尤素有

---

[5.5] Wang Hsien-ch'ien suggests that 車 is probably a mistake for 軍. Chariots were then used only in military ceremonies; cavalry and footmen made up the army. *Ch'u-ch'e* is moreover the title of *Book of Odes*, #168; II, I, viii; Legge, p. 261, which ode is stated in the "Little Preface" (Legge, "Introduction," p. 64) to treat of "rewarding the returning troops," with the result that *ch'u-ch'e* has taken this meaning.

[5.6] For 西 (west), the Ching-yu ed., the Southern Academy ed., and the Official ed. read 四 (four); the former is not appropriate for an expedition against the Huns to the north.

[5.7] A previous admonition by Chuang Yu, against the expedition planned in A.D. 11, showing how carefully Chinese generals planned matters, is to be found in 94 B: 19a, b = de Groot, *Die Hunnen*, 273–5.

[5.8] The clauses in single quotation marks are a quotation from the *Book of History* II,

路壯者入賊中凤夜連率韓博上言有奇士長丈大十圍來至臣府

將為伯賜錢二百萬眾庶皆曰之青徐民多棄鄉里流亡老弱死道

翼平連率田況奏郡縣訾民不實荅俊三十稅一曰況忠言憂國進

致于理其上大司馬武建伯印載歸故郡白降符伯董忠為大司馬

不畏天威不用詔命免很自城持必不移懷執異心非沮軍議未忍

able to extirpate them; you have not been awed by the majestic [mandate] of Heaven and have not carried out my mandates in imperial edicts. Your visage has been harsh, [yet] you have approved of yourself. You insist that what you think is right and never change. In your bosom you have cherished inclinations toward rebellion, so that you have condemned and ruined [my plans] in the deliberations on military [matters]. I cannot bear to apply the law to you. You shall deliver up your seals and aprons of the Commander-in-chief and of the Earl Estab- *5b* lishing Military Power and return to your former commandery. [Let] the Earl Making Portents Descend, Tung Chung₁ᵦ, become the Commander-in-chief."

**Double Taxation** T'ien K'uang, the Leader of a Combination at Yi-p'ing [Commandery], memorialized that the commanderies and counties had not appraised the common people's [property] according to the facts, so [Wang] Mang again taxed [their property at the rate of] one-thirtieth. Because of [T'ien] K'uang's faithful words and his solicitude for the state, he was advanced in noble rank, made an earl, and granted two million cash. The mass of commoners all reviled him.[5.9]

In Ch'ing and Hsü [Provinces], many of the common people left their native villages and became vagrants. The aged and weak died on the roads, and the vigorous entered the robber [bands].

The Leader of a Combination at Su-yeh [Commandery], Han Po, sent a message to the emperor, **6a** saying, "There is a marvellous gentleman, ten feet **Chü-wu** tall and ten spans [in circumference], who came to **Pa, the** your subject's yamen and said, 'I am desirous with **Giant**

---

I, v, 20 (Legge, p. 44); cf. also *HFHD, II*, 320, n. 8.3.

[5.9] The Sung Ch'i ed. states that 訾 should be 罵, which suggestion looks very much like a "boner" on the part of an ignorant scholar, thus illustrating the spurious character of the Sung Ch'i ed. Cf. *HFHD*, P., "Editions of the *History of the Former Han Dynasty*."

all my energy to attack the caitiff northern foreigners
7a (Hu).'  He calls himself Chü-wu Pa and comes from
the shore of the Chao-ju Sea northwest of the five
cities southeast of P'eng-lai.  A small chariot is not
able to bear him, and three horses are not able to
transport him, so, on the same day, in a large quadriga
with four horses, on which is erected a tiger flag,
bearing [Chü-wu] Pa, [I have sent him] to go to the
[palace] Portal.  When [Chü-wu] Pa lies down, he
pillows [his head] upon a drum.[6.1]  He eats with iron
chopsticks.

"This [man has been sent] by August Heaven as a
means of assisting the House of Hsin.  I wish that
your Majesty would have a large cuirass made, with
a high chariot and garments for a [Meng] Pen or a
[Hsia] Yü, and send a generalissimo and a hundred
of the [Gentlemen] As Rapid As Tigers to meet him
on the road.  The gates and doors in the imperial
capital which will not admit him should be enlarged
and made taller and larger, in order to show him to
the barbarians and settle down the world."

[Han] Po's intention was that he wanted thereby
to offer a hint to [Wang] Mang,[6.2] [but when Wang]
Mang was informed of it, he disliked it and detained
6a [Chü-wu] Pa at the place where he was in Hsin-feng.
He changed his surname to be Mr. Chü-mu (Chü's
Mother), saying, "Because of the Empress Dowager
the Mother of Culture there has been this portent
[that Wang (Mang) Chü-(chün) should be] a lord
protector (pa) and a [true] king."[6.3]  [Wang Mang]

慾之留霸在所新豐更其姓曰巨母氏謂因文母太后而霸王
戶不容者開高大之呂視百蠻鎮安天下博意欲呂風莽莽開
甲高車賁育之衣遣大將一人與虎賁百人迎之於道京師門
闚霸臥則枕鼓呂鐵箸食此皇天所呂輔新室也願陛下作大
頻詔車不能載三馬不能勝即曰曰大車四馬建虎旗戴霸詣
曰欲奮擊胡虜自謂巨母霸出於蓬萊東南五城西北昭如海

---

[6.1] The Sung Ch'i ed. notes that the Southern ed. (ca. x–xii cent.), instead of 鼓呂,
reads 數尺, "his pillow is several feet [high]," and that this reading is mistaken.  In a note
to HHS, An. 1 A: 5a, Li Hsien (fl. 674–676) quotes this passage, reading as the text does.
(Reference from Ma Hsü-lun.)

[6.2] The hint is conveyed in the man's name, which means literally, "Chü should not be
a tyrant."  Chü was the first word of Wang Mang's courtesy name and is used in Pan Ku's
"Fu on Penetrating Obscurities" (100 A: 12a) to denote Wang Mang.  Chin Shao glosses,
"The hint said, 'It is not permitted to be a usurper and thief and become a tyrant!'"

[6.3] Yen Shih-ku explains that "it means that the Mother of Culture sent this man to

符<br>
也<br>
徼<br>
愽<br>
下<br>
獄<br>
曰<br>
非<br>
所<br>
宜<br>
言<br>
粢<br>
市<br>
明<br>
年<br>
改<br>
元<br>
曰<br>
地<br>
皇<br>
從<br>
三

萬<br>
六<br>
千<br>
歲<br>
歷<br>
也<br>
地<br>
皇<br>
元<br>
年<br>
正<br>
月<br>
乙<br>
未<br>
赦<br>
天<br>
下<br>
下<br>
書<br>
曰<br>
方

出<br>
軍<br>
行<br>
師<br>
敢<br>
有<br>
趨<br>
讙<br>
犯<br>
法<br>
者<br>
輒<br>
論<br>
斬<br>
毋<br>
須<br>
時<br>
盡<br>
歲<br>
止<br>
於<br>
是

春<br>
夏<br>
斬<br>
人<br>
都<br>
市<br>
百<br>
姓<br>
震<br>
懼<br>
道<br>
路<br>
目<br>
目<br>
二<br>
月<br>
壬<br>
申<br>
日<br>
正<br>
黑<br>
希

summoned [Han] Po [to court], sent him to prison, and had him publicly executed, because he had said things that were not proper.

In the next year, the year-period was to be changed to Ti-huang, which was a title taken from the calendar for thirty-six thousand years.[6.4]

In [the period] Ti-huang, the first year, in the first month, on [the day] *yi-wei*, an amnesty [was granted] to the empire. [Wang Mang] issued a message, saying, "At the time when the army is being sent out and the troops are being put into motion, those who presume to run and shout, violating the law, should immediately be judged and beheaded. It is not necessary [to wait for] the season [for executions, winter]. When the year is up, [this order] shall cease." Thereupon during the spring and summer people were beheaded in the market-places of the capitals; the people were terrified and afraid and 'on the highroads and paths, they indicated their hatred [of Wang Mang] in their eyes.'[6.5]

In the third[6.6] month, on [the day] *jen-shen*, in the center of the sun there was a blackness.[6.7] [Wang]

6b     7b<br>
I<br>
A.D. 20<br>
Feb. 9<br>
Executions<br>
Permitted<br>
At All<br>
Seasons

Mar. 17

cause me to be a lord protector and king." *Pa* means both "tyrant" and "Lord Protector."

[6.4] *T'ai-p'ing Yü-lan* 78: 1a quotes Hsiang Chün's (fl. dur. 222–280) *Shih-hsüeh Chi* as saying, "When Heaven and Earth had been set up, there were twelve Heavenly Sovereigns 天皇, called *T'ien-ling* 天靈, who rule over 18,000 years. Because their virtue was wood, they ruled." *Ibid.*, 1b, quotes the same source, "The twelve Earthly Sovereigns 地皇 rule over 18,000 years." These two groups of gods seem to cover the 36,000 years referred to. (Reference from Su Yü.)

[6.5] A famous phrase from *Kuo-yü* 1: 4b, where the peoples' anger is directed against the tyrannous King Li, who was subsequently overthrown. In accordance with the "Ordinances for the Months," executions had previously been confined to the winter months.

[6.6] The text reads "second month," but there was no *jen-shen* day in that month, and there seems to be no servicable emendation of the cyclical characters. Probably "two' was mistakenly written for "three," a common copyist's error.

[6.7] Stange (p. 228) translates *jih cheng* 日正 as, "wurde die Sonne ganz (dunkel)." It might be, "At midday there was (a blackness)," to parallel *jih-chung* 中 below, which may be translated, "At midday (we saw a dusk)." While "midday" is the correct translation for *jih-chung* in the quotation from the *Book of Changes*, yet this line may

An
Ominous
Portent

Mang disliked it, and issued a message which said,
"Recently, 'in the sun an obscurity has appeared.'[6.8]
The Yin [principle] is pressing upon the Yang [prin-
ciple, and has produced] the grievous vicissitude of a
black emanation.   None of the people have failed to
be startled by the marvel.   The Generalissimo of the
Northern City-wall [of Ch'ang-an],[6.9] Wang K'uang$_{1d}$,

兆域大將軍王匡遣
為變百姓莫不驚怪
中見昧陰薄陽黑氣
惡之下書曰廼者日

have been used by Wang Mang without bothering about its exact meaning, just as verses
from the Bible were frequently used as proof-texts with a quite different meaning from
that in the original.   *Jih-chung* furthermore need not necessarily mean "midday," cf.
*HS* 27 Cb: 17b[1], *jih chung yang* 央, "in the center of the sun."   The important circumstance is the Pan Ku does not himself write *jih chung*, but *jih cheng*, and *cheng* means
"the center of a target."   I conclude that Pan Ku writes exactly in his phrase *jih cheng*,
meaning "the middle of the sun," and quotes Wang Mang as fitting to the situation a
classical quotation by wresting it from its original meaning.

A blackness at midday might be a solar eclipse, a heavy cloud, or a dust-storm.   There
was no eclipse at this time.   Heavy clouds and dust-storms were so well-known that
they would hardly have been considered "grievous vicissitudes."   I cannot make the
translations of Stange or the other one physically plausible.   Large sun-spots are however
visible to the naked eye at sunrise or sunset, when the sun's brilliance is dimmed.   Such
a sun-spot would cause as much consternation in ancient China as they did in Europe
when Galileo first saw them.   One had previously been noticed in 28 B.C.   (*HFHD* II,
384, n. 5.6) and was called a "black emanation," like the present one.

[6.8] A quotation from *Book of Changes*, Hex. 55, 3, with *mei*$_a$ 昧 instead of the *mei*$_b$ 沬
in the present text of that classic.   Legge (p. 185) translates this sentence, "At midday
he can see (the small) Mei star."   But Cheng Hsüan, in his comment on the *Book of
Changes*, gives the same interpretation of *mei* as that employed here.

[6.9] I read *po-ch'eng* 北城 instead of the *chao-yü* 兆域 in the text, at the suggestion
of Liu Feng-shih (1041–1113).   While *chao-yü* ("Generalissimo of the Pomoerium for the
Tumuli") is not impossible, as Stange points out (p. 228, n. 4), it is nevertheless un-
paralleled.   Liu Feng-shih says it does not make sense.   *HS* 99 C: 7a states that each
Shepherd of a province was made a generalissimo.   On 99 B: 28a, Lien Tan is said to
have been General of the Southern City-wall [presumably of the imperial capital].   Since
there was a Major (*Szu-ma*) in charge of each city-gate at Ch'ang-an (19 A: 22b), Wang
Mang may well have considered that the dignity of the imperial capital required a generalissimo for each side of its city-wall.

Liu Feng-shih points out that this Wang K'uang$_{1d}$ must have been a different person
from the Grand Master, Wang K'uang$_{1a}$, for Wang K'uang$_{1a}$ is always mentioned by his
highest title of Grand Master.   This cannot also have been Wang K'uang$_{1b}$, who arose
later from obscurity in the Yangtze region, nor can it have been Wang K'uang,$_{1c}$ a son
of Wang Mang who was not publicly acknowledged or brought to the capital until A.D.

吏考問上變事者欲蔽上之明是日適見于天曰正于理蔽

大異馬莽見四方盗賊多復欲厭之下書曰子之皇初祖

考黃帝定天下將兵為上將軍建華蓋立斗獻内設大將外

置大司馬五人大將軍二十五人偏將軍百二十五人禅將

軍千二百五十人校尉萬二千五百人司馬三萬七千五百

人侯十一萬二千五百人當百二十二萬五千人士吏四十

has sent an official to examine and question those who have presented [to the ruler] matters [concerning] grievous vicissitudes, [to examine] whether they intend to blind the throne's intelligence. For this reason, a reprobation has appeared in Heaven, in order that I might correct [matters by right] principles, and stop these great prodigies."

When Wang] Mang saw that the thieves and robbers in the four quarters were many, he again wanted to repress them, and so again sent out a message, saying, "When my August Deceased Original Ancestor, the Yellow Lord, tranquillized the world, he led his troops as a First [Ranking] General and established the flowery baldachin and set up the Bushel Bowl [Standard].[6.10] Within [the imperial court] I[6.11] establish a General-in-[chief]; outside [the court I also] establish five Commanders-in-chief, 25 Generalissimos, 125 Lieutenant Generals, 1250 Major Generals, 12,500 Colonels, 37,500 Majors, 112,500 Captains,[7.1] 225,000 Centurions, 450,000 Petty Offi-

*Military Regulations* 6b

7a
8a

21 (99 C: 11b). It was most likely some other person by the same name.

[6.10] Ts'ui Pao, in his *Ku-chin-chu*, ch. 1: A: 4b, states, "The Flowery Baldachin was created by the Yellow Lord. When he fought with Ch'ih-yu in the wastes of Cho-lu [a mountain located, according to the *Ta-ch'ing Yi-t'ung Chih* 39: 7a, southeast of the present Cho-lu, the Ch'ing dynasty's Pao-an, Chahar], a many-colored cloud emanation with golden branches and jade leaves constantly stopped above the Lord, having the likeness of the corolla to a flower. Hence he followed this pattern and created the Flowery Baldachin." This legendary account probably gives a description of the covering.

Yen Shih-ku explains, "*Hsi*₁ 獻 is pronounced like *hsi*₂ 犧. It means the [constellation] K'uei of the [Northern] Bushel [the bowl of the Dipper, cf. 99 B: n. 21.1], together with [the constellation] Piao [the handle of the Dipper]. Its end is like a handle in shape." Here again the Bushel (cf. n. 2.4) is used as an imperial emblem and protection.

[6.11] Stange (p. 229) makes the Yellow Lord the subject of this sentence, not Wang Mang. But sudden unannounced changes in the unexpressed subjects of verbs are by no means uncommon in Chinese. The *Book of Changes* was moreover not believed to have existed in the time of the Yellow Lord, so that he could not have been the subject of this sentence.

[7.1] The Official ed. and the Southern Academy ed. write 侯 (marquis) for 候 (captain).

cers, and 13,500,000 soldiers, in order to respond to and accord with [the saying in] the *Book of Changes*, '[This gave] the benefit of bows and arrows, whereby they might [awe] the world by their majesty.'[7.2] I have obtained the writings of the mandate [of Heaven given through] portents and have examined [my enactments by the deeds] of earlier persons, since I desire that [my enactments] may be complete in detail."

Thereupon there were established the positions of Commander-in-chief at the Van, at the Rear, at the Left, at the Right, and at the Center. [Wang Mang] granted to the various Provincial Shepherds the title of Generalissimo; Directors of Confederations,[7.3] Leaders of Combinations, and Grand Governors of commanderies became Lieutenant Generals; Prefects and Chiefs of Associations [became] Major Generals; and Rulers of counties became Colonels. Almost ten [groups of] commissioners in riding quadrigae daily passed through the commanderies and king-

**8b 7a** doms. The granaries had no grain ready for supplying [their needs] and the chariots and horses in the post-stations could not be sufficient [for these many messengers, so the officials] levied and seized chariots and horses on the roads and requisitioned supplies from the common people.

**July/Aug.** In the seventh month, a great wind damaged the Hall With the Royal Apartments, [so Wang Mang] again issued a message, saying, "Recently, on [the **July 25** day] *jen-wu*, at the time for eating the afternoon meal, **7b** there was the grievous vicissitude of a strong wind, with thunder and rain, which unroofed houses and

---

The Ching-yu ed. reads the latter.

[7.2] *Book of Changes*, III, ii, ii, 20 (Legge, p. 384). The passage says, "They bent wood by means of a string to make bows and sharpened sticks to make arrows; [this gave them] the benefit of bows and arrows, whereby they might [awe] the world by their majesty."

[7.3] The Sung Ch'i ed. again "pulls a boner" in suggesting that 卒 should be emended to 萃. Hereafter such notations will be neglected.

之變子甚升焉子甚栗焉子甚恐焉伏念一句迷迴解
矣昔符命文立安為新遷王臨國雖陽為統義陽王是
時子在攝僞諫不敢當而曰其後金匱文至議者
皆曰臨國雖陽為統謂攄土中為新室統也宜為皇太
子自此後臨久病雖瘳不平朝見掔百輿行見王路堂

broke down trees. I was greatly excited. I was inspired with great fear. I was greatly terrified. I humbly reflected and after ten days the riddle was then solved.[7.4]

An Ominous Portent

"Previously, the words of a mandate [granted by] portents [said, '[Wang] An[1a] should be set up as the Hsin-hsien[7.5] King [(the King, the Immortal of the Hsin House); Wang] Lin[1a] should have Lo-yang as his state and should be the T'ung-yi-yang King [the King Controlling-the-line in which Right-principles Shine].[7.6] At that time, I was occupying [the post of] Regent and Acting [Emperor], so deferred and did not presume to [accept these titles], but made [my sons] Dukes. After that, there arrived the writing in the golden coffer. Those who discussed [these matters] all said, '[Wang] Lin[1a]'s state should be Lo-yang; to be *t'ung* means to occupy the center of the Earth,[7.7] to be [the continuer of] the dynastic line (*t'ung*) of the Hsin [House, (i.e., *T'ung-yi-yang* means to live in the center of the Earth and continue the dynastic line by which the right principles of the Hsin House shine)]. It is proper that he should be the Imperial Heir-apparent.'

The Heir-Apparent Changed

"After this [time, Wang] Lin[1a] was ill for a long time, and, altho he recovered, he was not entirely well, so that when he appeared at court, he traveled borne suspended on a mattress.[7.8] When he came

9a

7b

---

[7.4] Yen Shih-ku points out that Wang Mang is alluding to the *Book of History* II, i, iii, 2 (Legge, p. 32), "[Shun] was received as the chief director [of the administration], and, amidst violent wind, thunder, and rain, he did not go astray." Cf. 99 A: n. 13.5.

[7.5] For the pronunciation of 遷, cf. Glossary *sub* this title. This word and 僊 were interchanged. Li Tz'u-ming, 7: 16b, suggests that possibly the first word was always written in the *HS* and later changed to the second in most places but not all.

[7.6] *Yang* 陽 is the opposite of "shadow," i.e., "light." Wang Mang renamed Lo-yang to be Yi-yang[b]. Cf. also n. 11.5; Glossary *sub* this title.

[7.7] Cf. *HS* 99 B: 23a. Wang Mang asserted he ruled by virtue of the element earth.

[7.8] *Han-chiu-yi* B: 1b says, "The Empress and Favorite Beauties travel in imperial chariots; all others [of the harem] travel by being carried by four men holding up a mattress 以茵四人舉以行." Chin Shao quotes the above passage and remarks, "Could that

to an audience in the Hall With the Royal Apartments, he set up his bed in the Western Lateral Apartments together with the Central [Room] for

**8a** Changing Garments in the Rear Pavilion.[7.9] Because moreover the Empress was ill, [Wang] Lin[1a] temporarily left his original [rooms] and went to her dwelling. His Crown Princess and concubines were in the Eastern Long Lane.

July 25 "[On the day] *jen-wu*, a strong wind did violence to the Western Lateral Apartments of [the Hall] With the Royal Apartments and the Central Room for Changing Garments in the Rear Pavilion; an elm tree, ten spans [or fathoms] in circumference, southeast of the pool at the Hall of Brilliant Peace, fell eastwards, striking the Eastern Pavilion. This Pavilion is the western wall of the Eastern Long Lane. All [these places] were destroyed. Tiles were broken, the roofs were taken off, and trees were uprooted. I was very much frightened.

An "The Office for Watching [the Heavens] moreover
Ominous memorialized that the Moon has invaded the front
Portent stars of [the constellation] Hsin, which has an interpretation.[8.1] I was very much worried by it.

"I humbly considered the writing in the *Tzu-ko-t'u*, 'The Supreme One and the Yellow Lord both ob-

者張於西廂及後閣更衣中又曰皇后被疾臨且去本就

室昭寧堂池東南榆樹大十圍東僵擊東閣閣卽東永巷壬午列風毀王路西廂及後閣更衣中

犯心前星歷有占子甚憂之伏念紫閣圖文太一黃帝皆之西垣也皆破折瓦壞發屋扶木予甚驚焉又侯官奏月含妃妾在東永巷

---

have been the present sedan chair and it have been spread with a mattress?" Yen Shih-ku replies that he is mistaken, "This [passage] says directly that he sat on top of a mattress [or cushion] and had four men in pairs hold up the four corners of the mattress, and so traveled." Prof. Duyvendak suggests that this was some sort of a stretcher.

[7.9] Chin Shao explains, "*Keng yi shih* 更衣中 means the name of the room (*shih*) and building to which one goes for changing one's robes at the time of court felicitations." Cf. also 97 A: 11b[4]. The first two words of this phrase also mean "go to the toilet."

Chou Shou-ch'ang suggests that the word (*shih*) 室 has dropped out at the end of this phrase; it is read in the comment and in the repetition of the phrase a few lines further on.

[8.1] *Hsin* 心 was one of the names Wang Mang gave to his dynasty. The star Antares in that constellation was moreover called the Heavenly King [*Mh* III, 343], so that this portent meant that the Yin principle (the Moon, the principle of decay) was invading the Hsin dynasty's virtue. The moon passed within a degree of Antares in the early morning of Mar. 3, A.D. 20.

蝗為災穀稼鮮耗百姓苦飢蠻夷猾夏寇姦亢人民正營無
民無所錯手足惟即位呂來陰陽未和風雨不時數遇枯旱螳
而稱太子名不正宣尼公曰名不正則言不順至於刑罰不中
之後也統義陽王乃用五統曰禮義登陽上遠之後也臨有兄
得瑞曰優後世襲主當登終南山所謂新遷王者乃太一新遷

tained auspicious presages and thereby became immortals, and among their later generations a magnificent lord [Wang Mang] is due to ascend the
Chung-nan [lit., he comes to his end to the south]
Mountains.' What is meant by the Hsin-hsien King
is that he is a descendant of the Supreme One and of       9b
the Immortal of the Hsin [House] (*Hsin-hsien*).
[What is meant by] the T'ung-yi-yang King is that
he is a descendant of [the one] who uses the five
dynastic principles (*t'ung*)[8.2] and by means of the
rules of proper conduct (*li*) and moral principles (*yi*)
mounts up to the sunny side (*yang* [the south]) and
becomes an immortal.

"[Wang] Lin[1a] has an elder brother, but is called
the Heir-apparent, so that his title is not correct.
Duke Hsüan-ni [As Recompense for Perfection (of
Pao-ch'eng), Confucius,] said, 'If titles are not correct, then speech will not be in accordance with
[reality,' and so on], even to 'punishments will not be
appropriate' and 'the common people will not know
how to move their hands or feet.'[8.3]

"Verily, since I have ascended the throne, the *Yin*
and *Yang* [principles] have not been harmonious, so
that the wind and rain have not been timely, and [the
country] has several times met withering drought,       *8a*
locusts and caterpillars, which became [calamitous]
visitations. The harvests of grain have been sparse
or lacking, so that the people have suffered from
famine. 'The barbarians have troubled the Chinese
and robbers and brigands have caused disorder outside and inside [the government,'[8.4] so that] the
common people are fearful and disturbed[8.5] and 'do

[8.2] Referring here probably to the five powers, each of which was supposed to set
up a dynasty.

[8.3] *Analects* XIII, iii, 5, 6.

[8.4] *Book of History* II, I, v, 20 (Legge, p. 44), again quoted.

[8.5] *Tzu-chih T'ung-chien* 38 : 12b emends 正 to 征. Yen Shih-ku interprets the phrase
as meaning, "Fearful and not at peace." The subsequent quotation is from *Analects*

not know how to move a hand or foot.'

**8b**     "I have pondered deeply that the blame for this [lies] in titles not being correct.   Let [Wang] An$_{1a}$ be set up as the Hsin-hsien King and [Wang] Lin$_{1a}$ be the T'ung-yi-yang King.   I hope that thereby I may protect and preserve my two sons, that my descendants [may be numbered] by the thousands and millions, and that, without [the country], the barbarians of the four [quarters] may be driven away and within [the country] the Central States may be pacified."

Another Ominous Portent 10a    In this month, the imperial tiger-striped [grave]-clothes [of Emperor Hsüan] in the Side Hall at the Tu Tomb, which had been set aside and stored in the coffers of the [inner] chamber, went out and planted themselves upright outside [the inner chamber] in the Hall above.[8.6]   After a quite long time they however fell to the ground.   The officers and soldiers who had seen them therefore reported it [to the throne.   Wang] Mang disliked it and so issued a message which said, "For the precious [throne] there is yellow and for the servitors there is red.[8.7]   Let it be ordered that the Gentlemen and the Imperial Retinue shall all wear carmine."

Many of those who watched the [cloudy] emanations and made divinations said that there were phenomena of some signal achievements [to be done

XIII, iii, 6.

[8.6] The Tu Tomb was that of Emperor Hsüan; cf. Glossary *sub voce*.   For a similar incident, cf. 12: 3b.

*HHS*, Tr. 30: 10b, says: "[The Gentlemen] As Rapid As Tigers and the cavalrymen all [wear] the dark yellow pheasant cap and tiger-striped unlined clothes.   [The county of] Hsiang-yi yearly offers woven and completed tiger-striped [cloth]."   Shen Ch'in-han remarks that these garments were probably those used in the Emperor's funeral and had all been stored in the funerary chamber at his tomb.

[8.7] Yellow was the color of earth, the power by virtue of which Wang Mang asserted he ruled; red was the color of fire, the power of the Han dynasty.   He was exalting earth (the Hsin dynasty's virtue) and degrading fire (the Han dynasty's virtue).   Yellow was then used for the robes of higher officials and red for those of lower rank.

黃廊赤其令郎從官皆衣絳望氣為數者多言有土功家
立外堂上良久乃安地更卒見者呂闓莽惡之下書曰寶
馬是月杜陵便殿乘輿虎文衣廢臧在室匣中者出自樹
統義陽王戲已保全二子子孫千億外攘四夷內安中國
所錯手足深惟厥咎在名不正焉其立安為新遷王臨為

莽又見四方盜賊多欲視為自安能建萬世之基者乃　下書曰于受命遭陽九之戹百六之會府帑空虛百姓　匱乏宗廟未修且拾祭於明堂太廟夙夜永念非敢寧　息深惟吉昌莫良於今年予乃卜波水之北郎池之南　惟玉食予又卜金水之南明堂之西亦惟玉食予將新

by the virtue] of the Earth.　[Wang] Mang more-over saw that the thieves and robbers in the four quarters were many and wanted to make it appear that he himself was tranquil and was able to be the founder [of a dynasty enduring for] ten thousand generations, so issued a message which said, "I have received the Mandate [of Heaven] and am meeting with the distresses of the nine dry years and the un-toward occurrences in the 106 [years],[8.8] when the government treasuries are empty and the people are exhausted.　The [imperial] ancestral temples have not yet been prepared, [hence] I have temporarily made common ancestral sacrifices in the Grand [An-cestral] Temple of the *Ming-t'ang*.　Day and night I have reflected long and have not presumed to rest. I pondered deeply that no blessing or prosperity is better than that to be had in the present year.　I then divined by the tortoise-shell [concerning the region] north of the Po River and south of the Lang Pool, and it was [divined as fit to produce] imperial sustenance.　I also divined by the tortoise-shell [concerning the region] south of the Chin River and west of the *Ming-t'ang*, and it was also [divined as fit to produce] imperial sustenance.[9.1]　I will now in

The Hsin Dynasty's Nine Ancestral Temples Begun

*8b*

*9a*

10b

[8.8] Cf. 99 B: n. 21.2.

[9.1] These two sentences are in imitation of *Book of History*, V, xiii, 3 (Legge, p. 436f), where the Duke of Chou reports the divination concerning the location of the city he built, Lo.　For the locations herein mentioned, cf. Glossary, *sub vocibus*.

Legge (op. cit.) follows the K'ung An-kuo interpretation of the *shih* in the foregoing passage; for *shih* Wang Mang uses the phrase *yü-shih* 玉食, and Yen Shih-ku adopts the aforesaid interpretation in his comment to the present passage, stating that it means that the ink, smeared on the back of the tortoise-shell used in divination, was dried up by the heat, which was a favorable prognostication.

K'ung Ying-ta, in a note to the *Mao-shih Chu-su* 4, i: 1b, quotes a gloss by Cheng Hsüan (127–200), to the above-mentioned passage of the *Book of History*, in which the latter paraphrases and explains this passage as follows: "On [the day] *yi-mao*, I, [the Duke of Chou], arrived at the [future] capital at the city of Lo and looked at the places which the Duke of Shao [had determined upon as a result of] divination by the tortoise-shell.　They are all able to be permanent homes for the common people and will make them devote

person[9.2] [begin to] build." Thereupon he accordingly made plans [for buildings] south of the city of Ch'ang-an with a total acreage[9.3] of a hundred *ch'ing*.

築 蓬 城 百
馬 營 南 頃
於 長 提 九
是 安 封 月

themselves to cultivating the fields, from which [they and the ruler may secure] food (*shih*)." The last sentence is Cheng Hsüan's paraphrase of the word *shih* in the text of the *Book of History*, hence he did not connect it with "ink" but with food.

Chou-li 24: 13a (Biot, II, 79) *sub* the *Chan-jen*, says moreover, "Whenever [the *Chan-jen*] divines by the tortoise or by the stalks: for the prince, he divines by the form; for a grandee, he divines by the color; for a [low] official, he divines by the ink [Cheng Hsüan says that "ink 墨" means the width of the cracks in the tortoise-shell]; and when he divines by the tortoise for [ordinary] persons, he divines by the cracks." Thus divination by "ink" was only for common officials, and would not be employed by an emperor such as Wang Mang.

The phrase *yü-shih* moreover occurs in the *Book of History* V, iv, 18. Legge (p. 334) translates it "the revenues of the empire." Ma Jung (79–166) in a note to the quotation of that passage in *SC* 38: 15, declares, "*Yü-shih* is fine food 美食," and Cheng Hsüan adds, "*Yü-shih* is all [composed of] unusual delicacies 備珍美也." In the *Shang-shu Chu-su* 12: 9a, K'ung Ying-ta (574–648) quotes what were probably ancient notes to this passage of the *HS*, which Yen Shih-ku (581–645), a contemporary of his, omitted from his edition, because he disagreed with these interpretations: "Chang Yen [prob. iii cent.], in a note to the *HS*, says, '*Yü-shih* is unusual dainties 珍食.' Wei Chao [197–273] says, 'The nobles have nothing but unusually fine food.' " Sun Hsing-yen (1743–1818) in his *Shang-shu Ku-chin-wen Chu-su*, in "Huang-ch'ing Ching-chieh" 752: 5a, concludes, "*Yü-shih* is as if it said good food 好食.... Whenever in the Classics it says a *yü* woman or a *yü* color, the meaning is always that it is good 好." Hence *yü-shih* denoted primarily the fine food of a prince, and secondarily land that was fit to produce such food. Cf. also *Shang-shu Ku-chin-wen Chu-su*, "Huang-ch'ing Ching-chieh" 759: 2a, b.

[9.2] For 新, the Ching-yu ed., the Southern Academy ed. and the Official ed. read 親.

[9.3] The meaning of *t'i-feng* 提封 has been debated. The first word of this phrase is also written 隄 and 堤. In a note to *HS* 23: 3a, Su Lin asserts that *t'i* is pronounced the same as *ti*ᵦ 祇 (the Ching-yu and the Official ed. read *ch'i* 祇 for *ti*ᵦ throughout) and that "the people of the Ch'en-liu [Commandery] say that all its fields are its *ti*ᵦ 舉田為祇." Li Ch'i declares, "*T'i* is *chü* 舉, to *chü* all within four boundaries (*feng*) 舉四封之內." Yen Shih-ku adds that Li Ch'i is correct and Su Lin's pronunciation is erroneous. But Wang Nien-sun states that all the preceding explanations are mistaken, for the *Kuang-ya* (by Chang Yi, fl. dur. 227–232) asserts that *t'i-feng* is *tu-fan* 都凡, which Wang Nien-sun declares is like the present 大凡, "generally," and is merely another phrase with about the same pronunciation. Cf. also the discussion in the *Tz'u-t'ung*, I, 1104.

But "generally" does not appear to express the full meaning of the phrase *t'i-feng*, for this phrase is invariably used referring to some area of land, which fact is excellently illustrated by Wang Nien-sun's examples. For *t'i-feng*, Karlgren, *Grammata Serica*, nos. 866n & 1197i, moreover gives the archaic and T'ang pronunciations *d'ieg* or *tieg-piung* and *d'iei-* or *tiei-piwong*, respectively, and for *tu-fan*, (*ibid.*, 456 & 625a), *to-b'iwăm*

甲申莽立載行視親擧築三下司徒王尋大司空王邑持

節及侍中常侍執法杜林等數十人將作崔發張邯說莽

曰億盛者文縟宜崇其制度宣視海內且令萬世之後無

呂俊加也莽乃博徵天下工匠諸圖畫呂望法度算及吏

In the ninth month, on [the day] *chia-shen*, stand-    Sept. 25
ing in a chariot, [Wang] Mang went to inspect [the
work], and in person began it by pounding three
times [on the earth in the forms for walls]. The
Minister Over the Masses, Wang Hsün₃, and the
Grand Minister of Works, Wang Yi₅, bearing credentials, together with the Palace Attendant, Regular
[Palace]⁹·⁴ Attendant, and Upholder of the Laws, Tu
Lin, and others, several tens of persons [in all],
were to oversee the work.

Ts'ui Fa and Chang₂ Han spoke to [Wang] Mang,
saying, "For those upon whom the virtue [of Heaven
is bestowed] abundantly the ritual practises are
elaborate. It would be proper to make the arrangements [of these temples] magnificent and to make
[that fact] plainly known [to all] within [the four]
seas, so as to bring it about that [even] after ten
thousand generations, nothing in them should be
changed around or despised."⁹·⁵ Thereupon [Wang]
Mang summoned widely the artisans of the empire,
and plans were calculated by means of geometry.⁹·⁶

and *tuo-biwɒm*, respectively, so that the two phrases had different pronunciations. *T'i-feng* has moreover something to do with acreage. Cf. *HS* 23: 4a; 24 A: 7a; 65: 7a; *HHS*, Mem. 30 A: 11a.

The crucial passage is *HS* 28 B ii: 49a, b, where the census totals of China are given, "The land is 9302 *li* [*Han-chi* (ii cent.) 30: 25a, reads 19,302 *li*] from east to west and 13,368 *li* from south to north, with a *t'i-feng t'ien* 田 of 145,136,405 *ch'ing*, of which 102,528,889 *ch'ing* are towns, dwellings, highways, roads, mountains, streams, forests, and marshes, all of which cannot be cultivated, and 32,290,947 *ch'ing* are cultivatable [but] not cultivated [omitting the second 可], and definitely cultivated *t'ien* of 8,270,536 *ch'ing* [*Han-chi, ibid.*, reads 8,270,567 *ch'ing*]." (Of the total, 2,026,023 *ch'ing* are omitted from the itemization.) In this passage, *t'i-feng t'ien* must mean "total acreage." In a note to Pan Ku's "*Fu* on the Western Capital" in *Wen-hsüan* (Szu-pu Ts'ung-k'an ed.) 1: 10a, Fu Tsan is moreover quoted as follows: "In my opinion, an old explanation says, '*T'i* is "to pick it all up." It means, "A grand total of its acreage" 提撮凡也言大擧頃畝也.' " Hence I have translated *t'i-feng* as "total acreage."

⁹·⁴ A second 中 has probably dropped out after the first one, since the full title re-quires it.

⁹·⁵ A reminiscence of Hsiao Ho's remark in *HS* 1 B: 12b (*HFHD*, I, 118).

⁹·⁶ *Wang-(fa)* 望 (法) is a term frequently employed in the *Chou-pi Suan-ching* (ii cent. B.C. to i cent. A.D.) and refers to the method of calculating heights by geometri-

The officials and people who voluntarily paid cash or grain [into the government treasury] to assist the work, moreover came and went on the roads and highways without interruption.[9.7]

　　[Wang Mang] tore down Chien-chang [Palace], Ch'eng-kuang [Palace], Pao-yang [Palace], Ch'üan-

**9b** t'ai [Palace],[9.8] Ch'u-yüan Palace, together with P'ing-lo [Lodge], Tang-lu [Lodge], and Yang-lu Lodge in [Shang-lin] Park west of the city [of Ch'ang-an], in all more than ten places, and took their materials

*9a* 11a and tiles to build the Nine [Ancestral] Temples. (In these months there was a great rain for more than sixty days.) It was ordered that common people who paid six hundred *hu* of grain might become Gentlemen, and that those who were Gentlemen or officials might be increased in rank or given a noble rank, [as high] as that of Sub-Vassal.

　　The first of the Nine [Ancestral] Temples was called the Temple to the Aboriginal Founder [of the Hsin Dynasty], the Yellow Lord; the second was called the Temple Facing South to the First Founder [of the Hsin Dynasty], the Lord, Yü [Shun]; the third was called the Temple Facing North to the Dynastic Founder [of the Hsin Dynasty], King Hu of Ch'en, [Kuei Man]; the fourth was called the Temple Facing South to the Epochal Founder [of the Hsin Dynasty], King Ching of Ch'i, [Ch'en Ching-chung]; the fifth was called the Temple Facing

祖昭廟三曰陳胡王統祖穆廟四曰齊敬王世祖昭廟五曰
吏增秩賜爵至附城九廟一曰黃帝太初祖廟二曰帝虞始
呂起九廟足月大雨六十餘日令民入米六百斛為郎其郎
包陽大臺儲元宮及平樂當路陽祿館凡十餘所取其材瓦
民呂義入錢穀助作者駱驛道路壞微城西苑中建章承光

---

cal means.　Cf. *op. cit.* A: 17b.　(Biot, in *Jour. Asiat.*, 1841, p. 601, translates *wang* as *mesurer*.)

　　[9.7] 駱驛 and 絡繹 were interchanged; Yen Shih-ku explains the latter phrase. Cf. *Tz'u-t'ung*, II, 2614.

　　[9.8] The "Kuang-han Wei Ts'ung-shu" and the "Lung-hsi Ching-han Tsung-shu" ed. of the *San-fu Huang-t'u* 5: 8b and 5: 6b respectively, in discussing the imperial ancestral temples, in quoting this passage, write *ch'üan* 犬 instead of *ta* 大.　The "Szu-pu Ts'ung-k'an" anastatic reprint of a Yüan ed., 5: 6b and the 1792 "Han-Wei Ts'ung-shu" ed., 5: 7b, however read *ta*.　The "Szu-pu Ts'ung-k'an" ed., 3: 6b moreover mentions a Ch'üan-t'ai Palace in the Shang-lin Park.　This Palace is also mentioned in *HS* 45: 11b. *Ta* is here an error for *ch'üan*.

七丈餘廟半之為銅薄櫨飾曰金銀琱文窮極百工之巧帶高

顯王戚禰穆廟殿皆重屋太初祖廟東西南北各四十丈高十

七曰元城孺王尊禰穆廟八曰陽平頃王戚禰昭廟九曰新都

濟北愍王祖穆廟凡五廟不墮云六曰濟南伯王尊禰昭廟

North to the Kingly Founder [of the Hsin Dynasty], King Min of Chi-po, [T'ien An]; (all [the foregoing] five temples were not to be discontinued [as succeeding generations of emperors included their immediate ancestors among the nine ancestors who are given separate fanes]); the sixth was called the Temple Facing South to the Honored Ancestor [of the Hsin Dynasty], King Po of Chi-nan, [Wang Sui]; the seventh was called, the Temple Facing North to the Honored Ancestor [of the Hsin Dynasty], King Ju of Yüan-ch'eng, [Wang Ho₄ₐ]; the eighth was called, the Temple Facing South to the Close Ancestor [of the reigning Hsin Emperor], King Ch'ing of Yang-p'ing, [Wang Chin]; and the ninth was called, the Temple Facing North to the Close Ancestor [of the Reigning Hsin Emperor], King Hsien of Hsin-tuₑ, [Wang Wan].

The [main] halls [of these temples] were all many-storeyed buildings;[9.9] that in the Temple to the Aboriginal Founder, [the Yellow Lord], from east to west and from south to north, in each [direction] was four hundred feet [long] and one hundred seventy feet high. The other Temples were half [that size]. They had bronze brackets,[9.10] and were adorned with gold, silver, and carved tracery, which reached the limit of the workmen's skill. Because they sat[9.11] upon a high [place, the earth] around

[9.9] *Shuo-wen* 6 A: 5a defines 樓 as a *ch'ung-wu* 重屋 (a storeyed building). *Chou-li* 41: 15b, quoting the *K'ao-kung Chi* (Biot, II, 559) says, "The Yin dynasty had a *ch'ung-wu*" and Cheng Hsüan glosses, "The *ch'ung-wu* was the main hall 堂 of the King's Palace, like the Great [Imperial] Apartments. . . . *Ch'ung-wu* is a double [set of] rafters 複笮." Ancient Chinese important buildings seem generally to have had more than one story.

[9.10] Yen Shih-ku explains, "*Po-lu* 薄櫨 are the brackets 枅 on top of pillars, [on which cross-pieces the beams are supported]."

[9.11] Wang Nien-sun suggests emending *tai* 帶 to *hsi* 席. In *HS* 36: 25b[11] and 45: 3a[7], where the word *hsi* is used, Yen Shih-ku each time interprets *hsi* by "*yin* 因; it is as if one sat upon a mat (*hsi*)." In his interpretation of the present passage, he likewise interprets this *tai* by *yin*, so that his text of this passage must have read *hsi*. Wang Nien-sun remarks that in the *li* style, *hsi* is sometimes written 㡯, which is vulgarly written

**10a** them was raised. The expense of the work was several ten thousand millions [of cash] and the con-
**11b** scripts and criminals who died [on this work] were numbered by the ten-thousands.

**An Abortive Rebellion** A man of Chü-lu [Commandery], Ma-shih Ch'iu, and others plotted to raise the troops of [the region comprised in the ancient feudal states of] Yen and Chao in order to execute [Wang] Mang. Wang Tan$_a$, an Officer to the Grand Minister of Works, discovered and reported it. [Wang] Mang sent some Grandees to the three highest ministers to apprehend and punish the cabal. Several thousand prominent persons in the commanderies and kingdoms were
*9b* involved. All were executed. [Wang] Tan$_a$ was enfeoffed as the Marquis Supporting the State.

From the time that [Wang] Mang acted out of accord with the ordinances for the seasons,[10.1] the people hated him, [yet Wang] Mang [acted] as if he was undisturbed by that [hatred. So] he again issued a message, saying, "Verily, ever since these temporary laws have been established, in the capital, Ch'ang$_2$-an, with its six districts and great city, the warning drums have rarely sounded and robbers and bandits have decreased and become few. The people are satisfied with their habitations and yearly there have been [good] harvests. The foregoing [circumstances have been due to] the strength [coming from] the establishment of my authority.

"[But] now the caitiff northern foreigners (Hu) have not yet been annihilated and executed, the southern and southwestern barbarians have not yet stopped burning [with rebellion], the Yangtze valley and the marshes of the sea-[coast] are boiling [with disturbance],[10.2] and the thieves and robbers have

---

帶 (*Yen t'ieh Lun*, 9: 7b[6], ch. 52, writes it thus): by omission of the radical, *tai* was written.

[10.1] Cf. *HS* 99 C: 6b.

[10.2] *Tz'u-t'ung*, II, 1729, asserts that here *ma* 麻 is cursive for 靡. It then means

不發舉皆沒入為官奴婢太傅平晏死呂子虞廖尊為
五銖枚直一兩品並行敢盜鑄義及偏行貨任人知
布長二寸五分廣一寸直貨錢二十五貨錢徑一寸重
盡二年止之百全元妖惡姦是歲罷大小錢更行貨
又興奉宗廟社稷之大作民眾動搖今復壹切行此令

not yet been completely routed and exterminated.
I have moreover taken in hand the great work of
upholding the [imperial] ancestral temples and the
altars to the gods of the soils and grains, so that the
multitude of common people have been agitated.
Now I again temporarily put these ordinances in
effect, [but this practise] will stop with the end of
the second year [of the period Ti-huang], in order
that I may preserve the great multitude and save the   12a
ignorant and wicked."

In this year, the large and small cash were dis-   **The Third**
continued and in their place there were put into   **Change in**
circulation currency spade money, which was two   **Coinage**
inches five *fen* in length, one inch broad, and was
worth 25 currency cash. The currency cash were
one inch in diameter, five *shu* in weight, each of
which was worth one [cash].[10.3] The two kinds [of
money] were to circulate together. When anyone
presumed to cast cash illicitly or only partly accepted
the spade money as currency, [if any person] in a
group of five [neighboring families] knew of it but
did not discover and report it [to the authorities],
all [of the five neighboring families were to have their
property] confiscated[10.4] and to become government
slaves or slave-women.

The Grand Tutor, P'ing Yen, died, and the My   **10b**
Forester, T'ang Tsun_b, was made the Grand Tutor.

"bubbling up like rice-gruel." From this passage, *ma-fei* has now become a set phrase.

[10.3] "Currency spade-money 貨布" and "Currency cash 貨泉" were the names of
Wang Mang's third coinage. Cf. App. I, *HS* 24 B: 26a.

[10.4] The Sung Ch'i ed. states that the Shun-hua ed. (994–997) and the Ching ed. (probably the Ching-te Chien ed., 1004–1005) have the word 官 after the 入. The Ching-yu
ed. does not have it and Chou Shou-ch'ang declares that this word should not be inserted.
*HS* 24 B: 26a (q.v. in App. I) dates this order in 14 A.D., and adds that by the sixth
year after, the people should not be any more allowed to possess the former large cash.
In this "Memoir", Pan Ku is hence recording this order for the change in the currency
on the date when the old currency was finally outlawed, rather than on the date when the
new currency was authorized. Penalties for counterfeiting were at the same time lightened.

T'ang
Tsun's
Pose

10a

[T'ang] Tsun_b said, "The state [treasury] is empty and the people are impoverished, the reason [for which is] prodigal extravagance." Consequently, he personally [wore] short clothes with small sleeves, rode on a chariot with stakes [and drawn by] mares,[10.5] slept upon a couch [made of] straw, [and ate from] tile dishes. He also used earthen dishes[10.6] to send [food] to the ministers. When he went out, if he met any men and women who did not travel separately on the roads, [T'ang] Tsun_b himself would get down from his chariot and, in accordance with [the principle of inflicting] punishments by altering the clothing, he would defile and dye their garments, [using] an ochre-red cloth.[10.7] [When Wang] Mang heard of it, he was delighted with him, so issued an imperial edict instructing the ministers "to think of making themselves equal" with him,[10.8] and enfeoffed [T'ang] Tsun_b as the Marquis Equalizing Culture.

12b

At this time, Chang Pa_c from Nan Commandery, Yang Mu and Wang K'uang_1b from Chiang-hsia

與廄齊封尊為平化侯是時南郡張霸江夏羊牧王匡等
車呂象刑緒幡污染其衣芣闍而說之下詔申敕公卿思
車輮槀瓦器又呂歷遺公卿出見男女不異路者尊自下
太傅尊曰國虛民貧咎在奢泰乃身短衣小褎乘牝馬柴

---

[10.5] Yen Shih-ku says, "A chariot with stakes 柴車 is a wattled chariot 棧車 [used by common soldiers]." It was despized by aristocrats and literati; *Han-shih Wai-chuan* 10: 9a, par. 11, says, "Coarse food and bad meat may be eaten; a jade for a horse and a chariot with stakes may be ridden."

Hu San-hsing adds, "While the Han dynasty flourished, those who rode on mares were prohibited and not allowed to gather together. If in the villages and lanes there was the same [custom, what was true about] the court and market-places can accordingly be inferred. [T'ang] Tsun belonged to the highest class of the highest ministers, yet he rode [a chariot drawn by] mares, which was in order to correct [the modernistic customs of] his age." Cf. *HS* 24 A: 15b = *Mh* III, 545, & n. 4.

This tabu on riding mares is probably connected with the very ancient Chinese belief that the mare was closely connected with the gods of the soils (*shê*). *Book of Changes*, App. I, ii, 3 (Legge, p. 214) says, "The mare is like the earth." Erkes (in *T'oung Pao* 36 [1940], 58) argues that the Chinese Earth-goddess originally had the shape of a mare.

[10.6] Li Tz'u-ming, *op. cit.* 7: 16b, suggests that $li_1$ 歷 should be $li_2$ 曆. Where this passage is repeated in *HS* 72: 25a, b, Fu Ch'ien explains $li_1$ as "earthenware dishes."

[10.7] Ochre-red was the color of clothes used for condemned criminals. Yen Shih-ku explains that he soaked a strip of cloth with ochre-red liquid; cf. *HFHD*, II, 123-5.

[10.8] A phrase from *Analects* IV, xvii, 'When we see men of worth, we should think of equalling them."

起雲杜綠林號曰下江兵衆皆萬餘人武功中水鄉氏三舍墊為
池二年正月呂州牧位三公剌舉怠解更置牧監副秩元士冠法
冠行事如漢剌史是月莽妻死諡曰孝睦皇后葬渭陵長壽園西
令永侍文女名陵曰億年初莽妻呂莽數殺其子湅泣失明莽令

[Commandery], and others arose in the Lu-lin [Mountains] of Yün-tu [County] and called themselves Troops from the Lower Yangtze [Region]. Their bands were all of more than ten thousand men. — **Bandit Armies Arise**

In the Chung-shui District of Wu-kung [County[10.9]] three houses of the common people fell [in a subsidence of the earth and] became a pool. — **Portents**

In the second year, the first month, because the Provincial Shepherds had been given the rank of the three highest ministers,[10.10] and so had become remiss in inspecting and recommending [concerning matters in their provinces], Shepherds' Superintendents and Associate [Shepherds] were established in addition [to the Shepherds], with the rank of First Officers, who were to wear the Bonnet of the Law and whose duties were to be like those of the Han [dynasty's] Inspectors. — **II A.D. 21 January Provincial Inspectors Established**

In this month, [Wang] Mang's wife died. Her posthumous name was the Filial and Harmonious Empress. She was buried west of the Ch'ang-shou Park at the Wei Tomb. It was ordered that she should forever attend upon the [Empress Dowager] the Mother of Culture [nee Wang]. The name of her tomb was called Yi-nien (a hundred thousand years). — **Wang Mang's Wife Dies**

Previously, because [Wang] Mang had more than once killed her sons, [Wang] Mang's wife had wept until she lost her sight, [so Wang] Mang had ordered — **11a**

---

[10.9] According to *HS* 28 Ai: 33b, Chung-shui District was in Mei-yang County. But the text of ch. 99 reads "Chung-shui District *of* Wu-kung." There were reasons that Wu-kung should have been enlarged. It bordered upon Mei-yang; in A.D. 6 it had produced a white stone portent, advising Wang Mang to take the throne. It had consequently been made the private estate of Wang Mang, and its name was changed to Han-kuang (the Han [dynasty's] brilliance); cf. 99 A: 26a. Under such circumstances it would naturally have been enlarged. Wang Mang later changed its name to Hsin-kuang (the Hsin [Dynasty's] brilliance), but probably kept the enlarged boundaries. Pan Ku is naming it, not by its name at the time of this incident, but, for clearness' sake, by its previous (and later) name.

[10.10] Cf. 99 B: 24a.

Wang Lin's
Plot and
Execution

his Heir-apparent, [Wang] Lin₁ₐ, to live at the palace and care for her.　An attendant to [Wang] Mang's wife was [named] Yüan-pi.　[Wang] Mang had favored her and later [Wang] Lin₁ₐ also had relations with her.　They were afraid that the matter would leak out, so plotted that they would together kill [Wang] Mang.

[Wang] Lin₁ₐ's wife, [Liu] Yin₃, was the daughter of the State Master and Duke [Honoring the Hsin

*10b* Dynasty, Liu Hsin₁ₐ].　She knew how to interpret the stars.[11.1]　She told [Wang] Lin₁ₐ that soon there would be a meeting of [people wearing] plain clothes in the palace.[11.2]　[Wang] Lin₁ₐ rejoiced, thinking that what he had planned would soon be achieved.

*13a* Later he was degraded to be the T'ung-yi-yang King and went out [of the palace] to his residence outside. He was [then] all the more apprehensive.

It happened that when [Wang] Mang's wife became seriously ill, [Wang] Lin₁ₐ sent her a letter which said, "The Emperor has been extremely severe with his descendants.　Previously when his sons, [Wang Yü] Chang-sun and [Wang Huo_b] Chung-sun, were each in their thirtieth [year], they were [put to] death.　Now your servant Lin₁ₐ has in turn come upon his thirtieth [year, and so I] truly fear that if some morning I am no [longer] protected by you, the Empress,[11.3] I shall not know whether I shall die

太子臨居中養莽妻旁侍者原碧莽幸之後臨亦通焉

事洩謀共殺臨臨妻愔國師公女能為星語臨宮中且有白

恐會莽妻病因臨子書曰上於子孫至嚴前長孫中孫年俱衣會臨喜曰為所謀且成後貶為統義陽王出在外弟愈愛

三十而死今臣臨復適三十誠恐一旦不保中室則不知死恐

11.1 Chou Shou-ch'ang points out that *wei* 爲 here has the meaning of 治, and quotes parallel passages from *HHS*, Mem. 32: 18b[8] and 33: 16b[9].

11.2 Chou Shou-ch'ang explains that in Han times the garments of those who did not have official position were called *po-yi* 白衣 (plain clothes), which phrase is found in *HHS*, Mem. 42: 10a[11].　He states that Wang Lin₁ₐ was delighted because he thought that "plain clothes" meant mourning clothes, i.e., mourning for Wang Mang, not knowing that it really meant that the common people would congregate in the palaces, an omen of the turmoil when Wang Mang would be defeated.　*Chin-shu*, 12: 3a, declares that when there is a conjunction of Jupiter and Venus, or of Saturn and Venus, there will be a meeting of people in plain clothes.　There was a conjunction of Saturn and Venus on the evening of Feb. 13, A.D. 21.

11.3 Li Ch'i glosses, "*Chung-shih* 中室 [refers to Wang] Lin₁ₐ's mother."　Yen Shih-ku

命所在莽侯妻疾見其書大怒疑臨有惡意不令得會
喪斂葬收原碧等考問具服姦謀殺狀莽欲祕之使殺
素事使者司命從事埋獄中家不知所在賜臨藥酢不
肯飲自刺死使侍中票騎將軍同說侯林賜魂衣璽載

or live."

[When Wang] Mang was waiting upon his wife in her illness, he saw this letter and became greatly incensed, suspecting that [Wang] Lin$_{1a}$ had some evil purpose. [Consequently Wang Mang] did not permit [Wang Lin$_{1a}$] to join in the mourning ceremonies. After [Wang Mang's wife] had been buried, [Wang Mang] had Yüan-pi and others arrested. They were examined and questioned, and they confessed everything about the adultery and the plans for [Wang Mang's] murder. [Wang] Mang wanted to have it kept secret, so sent to kill the commissioner [who had charge of] the case, who was an Attendant Officer of a Director of Mandates [from the Five Majestic Principles], and had him buried in the jail, so that his family did not know where he was. **11b** [Wang Mang] granted poison to [Wang] Lin$_{1a}$, but [Wang] Lin$_{1a}$ was unwilling to drink it, so he stabbed himself and died.

[Wang Mang] had the Palace Attendant, the General of Agile Cavalry and the Marquis of Like Delight, [Wang] Lin$_2$, grant the ghost garments and the Kingly seal and apron [for the deceased].[11.4]

declares he is mistaken, but Chou Shou-ch'ang replies that Li Ch'i is correct, saying that in Wang Mang's time the female members of the imperial family were called *shih* instead of *kung* 宮 as previously. Before the time of Wang Mang, the Empress was called the Inner Palace (*chung-kung*; cf. Glossary *sub voce*); here she is called the *chung-shih*, which has the same meaning as the former *chung-kung*.

[11.4] *Shuo-wen* 8 A: 9b, sub *jung* 襚, defines it as "ghost garments (*kuei-yi* 鬼衣)"; *Yü-p'ien* 28: 3a (by Ku Yeh-wang, 519–581) defines *hsüeh* 祻 as ghost garments (*kuei-yi*)." (Shen Ch'in-han declares that *kuei* should probably be *hun* 魂, the word in the text here.) *Chou-li* 21: 9a, sub the *Szu-fu* (Biot, II, 12) states that at a grand mourning ceremony [for kings], the *Szu-fu* provides "the garments for making offerings 奠衣服," and Cheng Hsüan glosses, "The garments for making offerings are the present ghost garments (*hun-yi*), [which are put] upon the seat [prepared for the ghost of the deceased when sacrifices are made to him]." *Ibid.* 21: 9b, 10a, *sub* the *Shou-t'iao*, (Biot, II, 14) says, "Those garments that remain are stored away. When they are about to offer sacrifices, for each [ancestor], his garments are given to the representative of the deceased." Cheng Hsüan glosses, "The garments that remain are those left over from the final enshrouding [of the deceased]." Thus the "ghost garments" were those used for

[Wang Mang's] funeral eulogy[11.5] [for Wang Lin[1a]] said, "[According to] the writing in the mandate [of Heaven given through] portents, [Wang] Lin[1a] should have been set up as the T'ung-yi-yang King. This [phrase] means that 36,000 years after the House of Hsin had taken the throne, one who is a descendant of [Wang] Lin[1a] is then due to rise up

13b　as the dragon sun.[11.6]

"Previously, when I erroneously listened to those who discussed [this matter] and made [Wang] Lin[1a] my Heir-apparent, there was the grievous vicissitude of a violent wind, so I immediately obeyed the mandate [from Heaven given by] portents and set him up as the T'ung-yi-yang King. Previous to this

11a　[time] and after this [time], he did not act [in accordance with] sincerity and obedience and so did not receive any assistance from this [title], and at an untimely age his life was destroyed. Alas! How sad! [According to] his deeds and acts, I grant him a posthumous name; his posthumous name shall be King Miu (erring)."

enshrouding the corpses of kings, together with those remaining over after the enshrouding, which were preserved and later used by the representatives of the deceased at sacrifices made to him.　(References from Shen Ch'in-han.)

[11.5] The *ts'e-shu* 策書 was a special imperial document used at the appointment and death of vassal kings and the three highest ministers and at the dismissal of highest ministers for crime.　At the death of vassal kings or of highest ministers in office, such a document contained a funeral eulogy and granted them a posthumous name.　Special stationary, composed of tablets alternately two feet long (18 in. Eng. meas.) and one foot long, were used.　(From Ts'ai Yung's *Tu-tuan*, quoted by É. Chavannes in "Les livres chinois avant le papier," *Journal Asiatique*, ser. X, vol. 5, 1905, pp. 24–25).　Ying Shao, in a note translated on *HFHD* I, 318, n. 5.7, also mentions these documents.　In that note I mistakenly followed Ch'ien Ta-hsin in denying the meaning of "funeral eulogy" to *ts'e*.　It means "charter of appointment," "funeral eulogy," or "dismissal notice." The inclusion of the highest ministers with the vassal kings is probably a Later Han practise.　It is not mentioned in HS 5: 5b, 6a.

[11.6] A reference to *Tso-chuan*, Dk. Wen, IV, (Legge, p. 238[14], 239b) "The Son of Heaven being the sun (*yang*)."　This phrase probably explains the meaning of *yang* in the peculiar title given Wang Lin[1a]; *yang* = *t'ai-yang* = the sun = the emperor.

安友于兄弟宜及春夏加封爵於是曰王車遣使者迎興等封興為
安作奏使上言興等女雖微賤屬猶皇子不可呂棄章祝羣公皆曰
開明生女捷皆留新都國曰其不明故也及安疾甚苯自病無子為
為侯就國時幸侍者增秩懷能開明懷能生男興與增秩生男匡女華
國師公臨本不知星事從惜起惜亦自殺是月新遷王安病死初苯

There was also an imperial edict to the State
Master and Duke, [Liu Hsin₁ₐ, to the effect that
Wang] Lin₁ₐ did not originally understand the stars;
the matter arose from [Liu] Yin₃, [so Liu] Yin₃ also
committed suicide.

In this month, the Hsin-hsien King, [Wang] An₁ₐ,
died of an illness.

Previously, [when Wang] Mang had been [a mere]
marquis and had gone to his state, he had favored
[some] attendants, Tseng-chih, Huai-neng, and K'ai-
ming. Huai-neng had given birth to a boy, [Wang]
Hsing_b; Tseng-chih had given birth to a boy, [Wang]
K'uang₁c, and a girl, [Wang] Yeh₆; and K'ai-ming
had given birth to a girl, [Wang] Chieh₆. All had
been detained at [Wang Mang's] state at Hsin-tuc,
for the reason that he did not want to make it
known [that he had had relations with any women
besides his wife].

When moreover [Wang] An₁ₐ had become seriously ill, [Wang] Mang was himself pained that he
would have no sons [remaining, so] he wrote a memorial for [Wang] An₁ₐ and had him send it to the
throne. It said, "Although the mothers of [Wang]
Hsing_b and the others are humble in status, yet in
their relationship [to you, my father, these young
people] are still your Imperial Sons and Daughters,
and so should not be discarded." The document was
shown to the various highest ministers and they all
said that [Wang] An₁ₐ was "fraternally loving to his
[half]-brothers and sisters,"[12.1] so that it would be
proper, when the spring or summer arrived, to give
them enfeoffments and noble titles. Thereupon
kingly chariots were sent with commissioners to go
and bring [Wang] Hsing_b and the others [to the

Wang
Mang's
Last
Legitimate
Son Dies.

5–2 B.C.[11.7]

His
Children
By
Concubines

12a

14a

---

[11.7] Cf. 99 A: 3b.

[12.1] A quotation from *Book of History* V, xxi, 1 (Legge, p. 535). In Han times, the
term frequently used for a younger sister was *nü-ti* 女弟, so that *ti* could stand for both
brothers and sisters.

court. Wang] Hsing<sub>b</sub> was enfeoffed as the Duke of Cultivated Merits, [Wang] K'uang<sub>1c</sub> as Duke of Established Merits, [Wang] Yeh<sub>6</sub> as Baroness of Cultivated Concord, and [Wang] Chieh<sub>6</sub> as Baroness of Attained Concord.

Four Funerals in One Month
[Wang Mang's] grandson, the Duke of Brilliant Merits,[12.2] [Wang] Shou, became ill and died, so that within a full month [Wang Mang] had four funerals.[12.3] [Wang] Mang destroyed the Temples of [Emperors] Hsiao-wu and Hsiao-chao of the Han [dynasty] and buried his sons and grandsons separately among these [temples].

Li Yen's Rebellion
Li Yen, the Grand Governor of Wei-ch'eng [Commandery], had plotted with a diviner, Wang K'uang<sub>4b</sub>. [Wang] K'uang<sub>4b</sub> had said to [Li] Yen, "Since the time that the House of Hsin took the throne, the cultivated fields and slaves of the common

11b
people were not allowed to be bought or sold, the cash and currencies have been changed several times, there have been numerous levies [of troops] and collections [of supplies], the armies have caused disturbances, the barbarians of the four [quarters] have simultaneously invaded, the people have cherished hatred [for Wang Mang], and thieves and robbers have simultaneously arisen [in various localities, so that] the Han dynasty is due to be restored. Your surname, sir, is Li. Li [rimes with] *chih* and [the note] *chih* is [equated with] fire.[12.4] You are due to become a coadjutor to the Han [Dynasty]."

[12.2] The first 公 should be 功, to accord with the name of this dukedom.
[12.3] Wang Mang's wife, his sons, Lin<sub>1a</sub> and An<sub>1a</sub>, and Wang Shou.
[12.4] The Official ed. correctly emends 者 to 晉.

*Li* 李 had the archaic and the T'ang pronunciations *liəg, lji, while *chih* 徵 had the pronunciations *təig, ti; cf. Karlgren, *Grammata Serica*, ＃980a, 891a. *Chih* was the name of the fourth musical note. The *Feng-su-t'ung* (by Ying Shao, ca. 140–206), 6: 3a, says, "I have carefully examined that Liu Hsin<sub>1a</sub>'s *Book of Bells and Musical Pipes* 鐘律書 [says], '*Chih* is a blessing (*chih* 祉). When things become large and numerous, it is a blessing (*chih*). [Among] the five powers or elements, [*chih*] is [equated with] fire; [among]

輔因為馬作讖書言文帝發怒居地下趣軍北告匈奴南告越人江

中劉信執敵報怨侵續古先四年當發軍江湖有盜自稱樂王姓為

劉氏萬人成行不受赦令欲動秦雄陽十一年當相攻太白揚光歲為

呈入東井其覚當行又言莽大臣吉凶各有日期會合十餘萬言馬

令吏寫其書吏亡告之奔道使者即捕馬獄治皆死三輔盜賊麻起

Hence [Wang K'uang4b] composed a book of revelations for [Li] Yen. It said, "Emperor Wen has become indignant and is dwelling on the earth below where he is urging on armies: To the north, he has instructed the Huns and, to the south, he has instructed the people of Yüeh [to attack]. In the center of the Yangtze [region], Liu Hsin4g will sieze his enemy, [Wang Mang], revenge [the Han dynasty], and restore and continue the ancient [line; in] the fourth year he is due to set his army in motion. Among the rivers and lakes there will be a robber **12b** 14b who will call himself a tributary king [of the Han dynasty], his family name will be Liu. Ten thousand men will form ranks and will not accept an ordinance of amnesty, [because they] intend to disturb [the region comprising the former feudal state of] Ch'in and [the region of] Lo-yang. By the eleventh year, they are due to attack. When Venus scatters its light and Jupiter enters [the constellation] Tung-ching, [Liu Hsin4g's] commands are due to be obeyed." He also told of the good and evil fortunes of [Wang] Mang's great ministers, that each had his fated date. Altogether [the writing comprised] more than a hundred thousand words.

[Li] Yen ordered a minor official to write out this book, [but] the official fled and gave information of it, [so Wang] Mang sent a commissioner immediately to arrest [Li] Yen [and his confederates], imprison them, and punish them. They all died.

Robbers and bandits made trouble and arose in the three capital commanderies,[12.5] [so Wang Mang]

---

the five social usages, it is [equated with] the rules of proper conduct (*li*); [and among] the five actions it is [equated with] looking. As a whole it is concerned "with [state] affairs." ' " The last phrase is a quotation from *Li-chi* XVII, I, 5 (Legge, II, 94; Couvreur, II, 48).

[12.5] Cf. p. 364.

"Three capital commanderies" is here an anachronism, for Wang Mang established six such commanderies. But this was a set phrase for the region about Ch'ang-an and

established the office of the Chief Commandant Siezing Robbers and ordered the Upholders of the Laws and the Internuncios to pursue and attack [the robbers] within Ch'ang-an. He established the banner for "beating the drum and attacking" thieves,[12.6] with a commissioner following after it.

He sent Ching Shang, the Second Brother Hsi to the Grand Master, and Wang Tang, the Commissioner Over the Army to the General of a New Beginning, with troops, to attack [the rebels] in Ch'ing and Hsü [Provinces, sent] Ts'ao Fang, the Second Brother Ho to the State Master, to assist Kuo Hsing in attacking Kou-t'ing, and had the
*12a* empire's grain and currency transported to Hsi-ho, Wu-yüan, So-fang, and Yü-yang commanderies, to each by the millions [of cash worth], with the intention of attacking the Huns.

Autumn　In the autumn, a fall of frost killed the beans. There was a great famine and [a plague of] locusts
15a　east of [Han-ku] Pass.

Counter-　When the common people violated [the law
feiters　against] casting cash, the people of five neighboring
Sentenced　families were sentenced together, [their property] was
to the　confiscated by [the government], and they were
Mint　made government slaves and slave-women, their men [went with] carts having cages and the children and women [went] on foot. They had iron locks and chains on [the rings about] their necks.[12.7] [Such

probably continued to be used, in spite of the change in their number.

[12.6] A quotation from *Analects* XI, xvi, 2.

[12.7] *Shuo-wen*, 14 A: 4a, says, "A *lang-tang* 鋃鐺 is a *so* (chain or lock) 瑣." Yen Shih ku says it is "a long chain (*so*)." But Wang Nien-sun points out that the phrase *lang-tang* is here used as a verb. He thinks the *so* should be omitted, but Wang Hsien-ch'ien replies that the *so* is necessary. *T'ai-p'ing Yü-lan* 644: 5a quotes this passage with the *so;* the *Liu-tieh*, the part by Po Chü-yi (772–846), 45: 22b, quotes it without the *so*. Where this passage is repeated in *HS* 24 B: 26b, *so* is used without the *lang-tang*. Slaves commonly wore iron collars in token of servitude. Cf. *HFHD*, I, 122, and n. 3. These convicts were chained to the prison carts they dragged.

其頸傳詣鍾官曰十萬數到者易其夫婦愁苦死者什六七孫喜榮為尚曹

放等擊賊不能克軍師放縱百姓重困奔呂王況議言荊楚當興李氏為

輔欲擊之迺拜侍中掌牧大夫李棽為大將軍揚州牧賜名聖使將兵奮

擊上谷儲夏自請願說瓜田儀奔呂為中郎使出儀儀文降未出而死奔

未其尸葬之為起冢祠室諡曰瓜寧殤男幾曰招來其餘然無肯降者閭

persons] were transported to the Office for Coinage by the hundred thousands. When they arrived, **13a** their husbands or wives were changed, and six or seven-tenths of them died of grief and suffering.

When Sun Hsi,[13.1] Ching Shang, Ts'ao Fang, and the others attacked the robbers, they could not vanquish them. Their armies were allowed to do as they pleased, so that the people were doubly distressed. Since Wang K'uang~4b~'s revelation had said that [the Han dynasty] is due to revive [in the region of the former state of] Ch'u in [Yü's province of] Ching, and that a Mr. Li would be the coadjutor [who brought about this revival,[13.2] Wang] Mang wanted to repress [this belief], so installed the Palace Attendant and Grandee in Charge of Pasturing [Sacrificial Animals], Li Shen, as Generalissimo and Shepherd of Yang Province, granted him the given name Sheng (sage), and sent him, leading troops, to attack [the bandits] with all his energy.

Ch'u Hsia, [a man] of Shang-ku [Commandery], in person begged [Wang Mang] that he wanted to persuade Kua-t'ien Yi [to surrender, so Wang] Mang made him a Gentleman-of-the-Household, and sent him to get [Kua-t'ien] Yi to leave [his banditry. Kua-t'ien] Yi wrote that he surrendered, but before he left [his banditry], he died. [Wang] Mang asked for his corpse, buried it, and built for him a gravemound and a sacrificial temple, with the posthumous name, Baron Shang of Kua-ning. He hoped thereby **15b** to induce the other [bandits] to come [and surrender]. But none were willing to surrender.[13.3]

In the intercalary month, on [the day] *ping-ch'en*, Oct. 22

**Bandits Attacked**

---

[13.1] Chou Shou-ch'ang remarks that the Sung editions read *hsi*~1~ 憙 for *hsi*~2~ 喜. The Official ed. 99 C: 12a accordingly reads *hsi*~1~. But the Ching-yu ed. (1035), p. 15a, the *HS P'ing-lin*, (1581) p. 15a, the Chi-ku-ko ed. (1642), p. 9b, and *HS* 99 C: 4b all write *hsi*~2~.

[13.2] This prophecy seems to have become widespread; it is mentioned in *HHS*, An. 1 A: 2b[5,6] and *Mem.* 5: 1b[1].

[13.3] Possibly they suspected that Kua-t'ien Yi had been done to death.

a general amnesty [was granted] to the empire.

*12b* The heavy mourning of the empire [for Wang Mang's wife was done away with] and those common people who had been mourning for their own [relatives] previous to this written imperial edict were also freed [from their mourning].

A    A Gentleman, Yang-ch'eng Hsiu, presented a man-
Second    date [from Heaven by] a portent saying, "In succes-
Marriage    sion to [Wang Mang's wife] a mother should be set
Ordered    up for the people, [i.e., an Empress]." He also said, "Because the Yellow Lord had 120 women, he be-
**13b**    came a supernatural immortal." [Wang] Mang hence sent Palace Grandees Without Specified Appointments and Internuncios, forty-five of each, by divisions, to inspect the empire and select widely from [families] that were esteemed highly in their native villages, who had "virtuous young ladies,"[13.4] and send up their names [to the throne].

The Han    [Wang] Mang dreamed that five of the bronze
Spirits    [statues of] men in the Ch'ang-lo Palace arose and
Attacked    stood up. [Wang] Mang hated it, and reflected that in the inscription on the bronze [statues of] men, there were the words, "The August Emperor has first taken possession of the whole world." [Wang Mang] immediately sent workmen from the Master of Recipes to chisel out and destroy the writing on the breasts of the bronze [statues of] the men, about whom he had dreamt.[13.5]

He was also excited against the supernatural spirits in the Han [dynasty's] Temple to [Emperor] Kao,[13.6]

---

[13.4] A phrase from *Book of Odes*, I, i, 1 (Legge p. 1).

[13.5] These bronze statues had been cast in 221 B.C. by the First Emperor of the Ch'in Dynasty; the inscription was his. In Han times they were set at the gate of the Ch'ang-lo Palace. For an account of these statues and their history, cf. *Mh* II, 134, n. 1. K. Shiratori, in *Memoirs of the Toyo Bunko*, no. 5 (1930), pp. 39–44, also has an account of them, which must however be used with caution.

[13.6] Probably because of the incident of the mad woman recounted in 99 B: 12b. (Suggested by Chou Shou-ch'ang.)

月丙辰大赦天下天下大服民私服在詔書前亦釋除郎陽成偹

獻符命言繼立民母又曰黃帝曰百二十女致神僊乃遣中

散大夫謁者各四十五人分行天下博采鄉里所高有淑女者上

名莽夢長樂宮銅人五枚起立莽惡之念銅人銘有皇帝初兼天

下之文即使尚方工鐫滅所夢銅人膺文又感漢高廟神靈遣虎

羽葆載曰秘機回輪車駕六馬力士三百人黃衣幘車上
帝時建華蓋曰登僊奔乃造華蓋九重高八丈一尺金瑵
屋壁令輕車校尉居其中又令中軍北壘居高寢蔵或言黃
貢武士入高廟拔劍四面提擊谷壞戶牖桃湯赭鞭鞭灑

and sent [Gentlemen] As Rapid as Tigers and Men of War to enter the Temple of [Emperor] Kao, draw their swords, throw and strike in all directions, destroy its doors and windows with axes, whip the walls of the building with ochre-red whips[13.7] and sprinkle them with peach-water. He ordered a Chief Commandant of Light Chariots to dwell in its midst and also ordered the [Colonel of] the Northern Encampment of the Capital Army[13.8] to dwell in the funerary chamber of [Emperor] Kao.    16a

Someone said, "At the time of the Yellow Lord, he established the flowery baldachin in order that he might mount up [to become] an immortal." So [Wang] Mang had made a flowery baldachin in nine layers, eighty-one feet tall, with a golden claw-tip and feather covering, and had it borne by a carriage with a hidden mechanism and four wheels[14.1] yoked to six horses and three hundred strong men with yellow clothes and [red] turbans.[14.2] On the carriage    The Flowery Baldachin Chariot   **14a**   *13a*

[13.7] The last clause is chiastic. The peach is supposed to have the property of expelling demons. Ochre-red is the color of condemned criminals' clothes. On the apotropaic use of peach-wood and its extract, cf. App. III, *ad finem*.

[13.8] Wang Hsien-ch'en declares that *chung* 中 and *po* 北 have been interchanged here. Yen Shih-ku's note speaks of the "Northern Army." *HS* 19 A: 22b says that the Colonel of the Capital Encampment (*Chung-lei Hsiao-wei* 中壘校尉) had charge of the gates and the walls of the Northern Army's [*Po-chün* (軍) *lei*] encampment; cf. Glossary *sub voce*. But this same phrase *Chung-chün po-lei* appears again on 99 C: 19a, where it can hardly be interpreted as referring to the Colonel of the Capital Encampment; it is quite possible that Wang Mang changed the name of the Northern Army to the Northern Encampment of the Capital Army, a quite logical name, and Yen Shih-ku refers to it by its previous name, the Northern Army. This interpretation is confirmed by the phrase "the Capital Army *Chung-chün*" in 99 C: 23a. The term "Northern Army" is however used on 99 C: 3a; but that may merely be an anachronism. I do not therefore emend the text.

[14.1] Fu Ch'ien explains, "The baldachin was 80 feet tall and on the shaft all [nine covers] had pivot hinges, so that they could be raised and lowered, bent and straightened." Evidently it was an umbrella-like arrangement. Yen Shih-ku adds, "It says that the mechanism was hidden and from outside people could not see it." Bishop White mentions an umbrella-like canopy top in the Han tombs at Lo-yang. Cf. his *Tombs of Old Lo-yang*, p. 37. Such umbrella tops are pictured on Han chariots in the Han grave sculptures.

[14.2] Wang Nien-sun declares that the word 赤 has dropped out before the 幘, making

there was a man beating a drum. Those who pulled it all called out, "He will mount up to be an immortal." When [Wang] Mang went out, he ordered [this carriage] to go before him. The many officials [however] said secretly, "This is like a funeral cart, not a thing for an immortal."[14.3]

Bandits Increase

In this year, the band of Ch'in Feng in Nan Commandery [numbered] almost ten thousand persons. Ch'ih Chao-p'ing, a woman of P'ing-yüan [Commandery], was capable at explaining the *Classic on the Playing Blocks*,[14.4] using eight [blocks] to a throw. She also collected several thousand men in the diffi-

it read, "Red turbans." *T'ai-p'ing Yü-lan*, 772: 9a, quoting this passage, says, "Wang Mang invented a chariot with four wheels drawn by 6 horses and 300 strong men with yellow garments and red turbans and yokes," and the *HHS*, Tr. 30: 11b, says, "Military officers regularly [wear] red turbans to make them awe-inspiring." Chu Yi-hsin (1846–1894) replies, "[Wang] Mang despised the Han [dynasty's] practises; I fear that he did not use red turbans. The [*T'ai-p'ing*] *Yü-lan* is insufficient evidence [for Wang Mang's usages]. The *HHS* Treatises moreover [contain] the Han dynasty's institutions." Nevertheless Wang Mang continued the use of red for his Gentlemen and retinue (99 C: 8b), so that the *T'ai-p'ing Yü-lan's* quotation is probably correct.

[14.3] In a note to *Chou-li* 15: 12a (Biot, I, 349, n. 4), *sub* the *Sui-shih*, Cheng Hsüan says, "The funeral cart . . . has four wheels. It hugs the ground when it moves," and Chia Kung-yen adds, "It is a cart with solid wheels [used as a hearse], which has two axles that pass through four wheels." Shen Ch'in-han explains, "This [carriage of Wang Mang's] also had four wheels, hence they said it was like a funeral cart."

The magical means Wang Mang used to make himself an immortal are recounted in *HS* 25 B: 22b–23b.

[14.4] Fu Ch'ien (ca. 125–195) glosses, "The *Classic on the [Wei-ch'i] Playing Blocks* (*po-yi-ching* 博奕經), which used eight sticks to throw." The present text reads *ching-po*, but Wang Nien-sun infers from the above gloss that Fu Ch'ien's text read *po-ching*, and suggests emending accordingly. Then the word *yi* was probably an interpolation in the gloss. *Po-yi* is mentioned in *Analects* XVII, xxii, whence this interpolation might have come.

*Po* (translated, "playing blocks") was an ancient game analogous to dice. Six sticks and twelve blocks were employed, half of them by each player. This variety of the game seems to have used eight blocks. The classical accounts of this game (which is not clearly understood) are to be found in the notes to *HS* 64 A: 14a and *HHS*, Mem. 24: 9b. The

說經博呂八投亦聚數千人
且萬人平原女子遲昭平能
非優物也是歲南郡奏豐眾
令在前百官犕言此似輀車
人擊鼓輀者皆呼登僊乘出

學士疑惑明學男張邯地理侯孫陽造井田使民棄土業
曰諭名位賊夫人之子國師嘉信公顛倒五經毀師法令
歷侯氣變呂凶為吉亂天文誤朝廷太傅平化侯飾虛偽
漏刻故左將軍公孫祿倖與議祿曰太史令宗宣典星
在河阻中犇召問韋臣禽賊方略宣曰此天曰行尸命在

cult places of the [lower reaches of the Yellow] River. [Wang] Mang summoned and questioned his various courtiers about stratagems for capturing the bandits, and [the courtiers] all said, "These [people] are Heaven's [condemned] criminals and walking corpses. Their lives will [last] only an instant."

The former General of the Left, Kung-sun Lu, was summoned to come and participate in the deliberations. [Kung-sun] Lu said, "The Chief Grand Astrologer, Tsung Hsüan, has had charge of prognostications by the heavenly bodies, and of interpreting the mutations in the emanations [and weather]. He has called the baneful fortunate, has in a disorderly fashion [reported] the astrological [phenomena], and has misled the court. The Grand Tutor, the Marquis Equilizing Culture, [T'ang Tsun b], has covered [his faults] by false pretenses, so that he has been able to treat lightly [the duties of] his title and his position and 'has done ill turns to other men's sons.'14.5 The State Master, the Duke Honoring the Hsin [Dynasty, Liu Hsin 1a,] has overturned the five Classics, has done away with the traditions [about the classics handed down from generation to generation] by his teachers, and has caused his students to doubt and be misled.14.6 The Baron of Brilliant Scholarship, Chang 2 Han, and the Marquis of Geographical Arrangements, Sun Yang, have instituted the *ching* [system] of cultivated fields, [thus] causing the common people to neglect their occupation [in cultivating] the earth. The

16b
Biting
Criticism
of the
Ministers

14b

Roman *astragalen* seems to have been a similar game; cf. H. Blümner, *Die Romischen Privataltertümer*, "Handbuch d. Klassische Altertums-Wissenschaft," 4 Bd., 2 Abteil, 2. Teil, 1911, pp. 412–419.

14.5 A quotation from *Analects* XI, xxiv, 2.

14.6 *HS* 27 Ba: 2b, 3a seems to explain this charge when it says that, concerning the doctrine of the five powers or elements, Hsia-hou Shih-ch'ang transmitted his explanation to Hsia-hou Sheng, he to Hsü Shang, and on to Liu Hsiang 4, whose account was similar to that of his predecessors; but Liu Hsin 1a's account was different. Thus Liu Hsin 1a had changed the traditional explanation of portents, probably to favor Wang Mang, and is here criticized for having done so. An example of his interpretation is quoted in *HS* 27 Ba: 3b (trans. in W. Eberhard, *Beiträge z. kosmolg. Spekulation Chinas*, p. 22, par. 2) where it is declared to be incorrect.

Hsi-and-Ho, Lu K'uang, has set up the six monopolies and has thereby impoverished the artisans and merchants. The Marquis Delighting in Portents, Ts'ui Fa, has truckled and flattered in order to curry your favor and has brought it about that the feelings of inferiors have not been communicated to the throne. It would be proper to execute these several

*13b* persons in order to calm the empire."

He also said, "The Huns should not be attacked, but peace and an alliance by marriage ought to be made with them. Your subject fears that the [proper] cause for the House of Hsin's anxiety does not lie with the Huns, but lies within the borders." [Wang] Mang became incensed and had a [Gentleman] As Rapid as Tigers assist [Kung-sun] Lu to leave.

Nevertheless [Wang Mang] adopted his ideas to a certain [extent]. He demoted Lu K'uang to be the Director of a Confederation at Wu-yüan [Commandery], because the people hated and maligned

*17a* him. [Although] the six monopolies had not been set up by [Lu] K'uang alone, [yet Wang] Mang [wanted to] satisfy the ideas of the crowd, so sent [Lu K'uang] out [of the court].

**Bandit Extermination Ordered** Previously, because the four quarters [of the country] had all [suffered from] famine and cold, [the people] were impoverished and troubled, and so had arisen and become thieves and robbers, until gradually crowds gathered. They constantly thought that if the harvest would be good,[14.7] they would be able to return to their native villages. Although their bands were numbered by the ten-thousands, [their leaders] only called themselves attendants upon great persons, Thrice Venerables, or Libationers. They did not presume to take or to possess cities

---

[14.7] The Southern Academy ed. and the Official ed. p. 13b change 熟 to 孰 to conform to the usual writing of this word in the *HS*. The Ching-yu ed. however reads the former.

盜發不輒得至成羣黨遂略乘傳宰士得脫者又妄自言我責數賊
德明恩呂牧養民仁之道也抑強督姦捕誅盜賊義之節也今則不然
上書具言狀莽大怒下獄呂為誣固因下書責七公曰夫吏者理也宣
而莽終不諭其故是歲大司馬士按章掾州為賊所獲賊送付縣士還
掠求食日閱而已諸長吏牧守皆自亂關中兵而死賊非敢欲殺之也

or towns and went about foraging and seeking for merely what food they would use up daily. When various Chief Officials, Shepherds and Administrators all themselves fought with them in a disorderly manner, were wounded by weapons, and died, it was not because the bandits presumed to intend to kill them.[14.8] But [Wang] Mang to the end did not understand the purposes of these [bandits].

In this year, an Officer of the Commander-in-chief **15a** was in Yü Province, examining [into what had been reported in] a document, and was captured by the bandits, [whereupon] the bandits escorted and sent him to the county-seat. When the Officer returned and memorialized [his report], he wrote out the whole circumstance. Wang] Mang became greatly incensed, and sent him to prison because he considered [that the man] was falsifying [the situation] to deceive [his superiors].

Thereupon he issued a message reproving the seven highest ministers, which said, "Verily, to be an official [means] to bring about order.[15.1] To diffuse virtue and make favors manifest in order to shepherd the common people is the principle of benevolence. To repress the strong, control the wicked, and arrest and execute thieves and robbers are components of justice.

"Now however [the situation] has been otherwise. **17b *14a*** When thieves appeared, they were not immediately apprehended, so they were able to form cliques and intercept and kidnap Ruling Officers from [government] riding quadrigae. An Officer who succeeded in getting free from them moreover himself said senselessly, 'I questioned and reprimanded the rob-

---

[14.8] This paragraph is very likely taken from the report of the Officer of the Commander-in-chief; cf. next paragraph.

[15.1] Here Wang Mang is giving his own etymology for *li* 吏 (*liəg, lji, Karlgren, *Gram. Ser.* ≠ 975g) by a pun with *li* 理 (also *liəg, lji, *ibid.*, ≠ 978d).

bers, [saying], "Why do you do this [robbing]?" and the robbers replied, "Merely because we are impoverished and in need." [Then] the robbers protected and sent me away. At present, vulgar people who discuss [banditry say that the bandits] for the most part are like these [ones].'

"I reflect [that, when people], out of distress from famine or cold violate the laws and do evil, the greater ones become groups of thieves and the lesser ones steal [by making] holes [in people's walls]. There are no more than these two kinds. But now they have conspired together and joined to form gangs of thousands and hundreds. This is the greatest disobedience and rebellion; how could it be spoken of as [due to] famine or cold?

"Let the seven highest ministers strictly order the High Ministers, Grandees, Directors of Confederations, Leaders of Combinations, and 'the heads of offices'[15.2] carefully to shepherd the good common people and hurriedly arrest and exterminate the thieves and robbers. If there are any who do not, with one mind and with mutual assistance, hate and drive out the bandits, and, if they say unreasonably that [the bandits] have been caused by hunger or cold, they shall immediately be arrested and held in prison, and [the officials] shall beg [me to pass sentence upon] their crime."

**Unwise Policies**  Thereupon the numerous subordinates [of the ruler] feared all the more and none presumed to speak of the bandits' circumstances. They also were not permitted to mobilize troops unauthorizedly. Because of this, the bandits were not restrained.

Only the Leader of a Combination at Yi-p'ing [Commandery], T'ien K'uang, had for some time

**18a**  past dared to mobilize the common people who were in their eighteenth year and above, [to the number

---

[15.2] Cf. 99B: n. 23.1.

萬餘人授曰庫兵與刻石為約赤糜聞之不敢入界況自劾奏奔

讓況未賜虎符而擅發兵此弄兵也廢皋之興臣況自說必禽滅

賊故且勿治後況自請出界擊賊所響皆破莽曰璽書令況領青

徐二州牧事況上言盜賊始發其原甚微非部吏伍人所能禽也

咎在長吏不為意縣畏其郡郡畏朝廷實百言十實千言百朝廷

of] more than forty thousand persons, had furnished them arms from the arsenals, and had given them **15b** engraved stones as [signs of their] convenant. The Red Eyebrows had heard of it and had not presumed to enter his borders. [T'ien] K'uang impeached himself in a memorial, and [Wang] Mang reprimanded [T'ien] K'uang: "You have not been granted a tiger credential,[15.3] yet have unauthorizedly mobilized troops. This is playing with weapons. This crime is that of negligence in raising [troops].[15.4] Because you, K'uang, have reproved yourself [and *14b* have said that you would] certainly capture and destroy the robbers, you are [however] temporarily not to be punished."

Later [T'ien] K'uang himself begged to go out of the boundaries [of his commandery] and attack the robbers, [saying that] those against whom he turned would all be routed. [Wang] Mang used a message [stamped] with the imperial seal to order [T'ien] K'uang to be put in charge of the affairs of the Shepherds in the two provinces of Ch'ing and Hsü.

[T'ien] K'uang [memorialized] the throne, saying, "Although when thieves and robbers first start out, in the beginning they are very unimportant, yet they cannot be captured by the divisional officers and [the organization of] people in groups of five.[15.5] The fault lies [in the fact that] the Chief Officials [of counties] do not give it a thought. The counties deceive the commanderies, and the commanderies deceive the [imperial] court. When in reality there are a hundred [robbers], they say ten; and when in reality there are a thousand, they say a hundred.

---

15.3 Cf. *HFHD* I, 245, & n. 2.

15.4 This passage is probably a quotation from Wang Mang's decree. For this crime, cf. *HFHD*, II, 392, n. 7.11.

15.5 Hu San-hsing explains that by "divisional officials" were meant the officials of a commandery division who were in charge of bandits, such as the commandery Department Head for Bandits, the county Commandant, and the Chiefs of Districts and Communes.

Then the court is negligent and does not immediately supervise and punish[15.6] [the bandits], so that they even spread over adjoining provinces.

"When moreover generals and lieutenants are sent, and many commissioners are sent out continuously to supervise and urge each other on, [the officials of] the commanderies and counties serve their superior
18b officials energetically, in answering and excusing themselves, in replying to questions, in offering wine and food, and in furnishing necessaries, in order to save themselves from being sentenced and beheaded, and so do not have [the time] again to think of the thieves or robbers or to perform their official business. The generals and lieutenants moreover are not able in person to lead their officers and soldiers, and so, when a battle [is fought, their troops] are routed by the bandits, their officers gradually [become] dispirited, and [the expedition] is merely an expense upon the people.

"When previously [the bandits] fortunately received an order of amnesty and the bandits wanted to disband and scatter, some [of them] on the contrary were prevented [from returning home] and were attacked, so from fear they entered the mountains and valleys, and in turn told the others [about
16a it]. Hence the bandits in the commanderies and counties who had surrendered all changed [their attitudes] and became terrified, fearing that they would be destroyed by trickery. Because of the famine, they were easily moved, and within ten days there were again more than a hundred thousand men [in the bandit troops]. The foregoing is the reason

----

[15.6] *Tu-tsê* 督責, "supervising [the acts of one's subordinates] and punishing [their delinquencies]" was a technical term from the Legalist School; cf. D. Bodde, *China's First Unifier*, p. 38 & n. 3, 205–6. While I agree with his interpretation, I prefer "punishing" instead of "holding responsible" as a translation of *tsê*. Szu-ma Cheng, in a note to SC 87: 28, interpets *tsê* as "責之以刑罰, punishing them by the [statutory] punishments."

休息郡縣委任臣況吕二州盜賊必平定之
之則滅今空復多出特率郡縣苦之反甚於賊宜盡徵還乘傳諸使者吕
并力固守賊來攻城則不能下所過無食就不得羣聚如此招之必降擊
以下明其賞罰收合離鄉小國無城郭者徒其老弱置大城中積藏穀食
軍二人爪牙重臣多從人衆道上空竭少則亡吕威視遠方宜急選牧尹
盜賊所吕多之故也今雒陽吕東米石二千竊見詔書欲遣太卸更始將

that the thieves and robbers are so numerous.

"At present, east of Lo-yang, grain is two thousand   *15a*
[cash per] picul. Your humble servant has seen a
written imperial edict that it is intended to send the
Grand Master, [Wang K'uang$_{1a}$], and the General
of a New Beginning, [Lien Tan, to attack the ban-
dits]. They are important courtiers who are your
military assistants. If their crowds of followers are
multiplied, [these followers] will become exhausted
[from lack of food] on the way; whereas if [their
followers are] reduced [in number, these ministers]
will have no way of overawing the distant quarters
[of the empire].

"It would be proper to select promptly Shepherds
and Governors or those [ranking] below them, make
plain the rewards and punishments that they [can
deal out], and [have them] collect together those
people from scattered villages and small states [of
nobles] that have no city walls, transport their old
and weak [persons], putting them inside the large
cities, [then] collect and store foodstuffs and mutually   *19a*
assist in firmly guarding [these centers]. When the
bandits come to attack the cities, they will then be
unable to take them and [the places] by which they
pass will have no food, so that their circumstances
will not permit them to collect in bands. Under such
[a situation], when they are summoned, they will
certainly surrender, and when they are attacked, they
will be annihilated.

"If now generals and lieutenants are vainly sent
out in numbers, the commanderies and counties will
suffer from them more severely than from the bandits.
It would be proper to summon back all the commissioners in riding quadrigae in order to give rest to
the commanderies and counties, and entrust to your
servant K'uang the thieves and robbers of [these]
two provinces, for I will certainly tranquillize them."

[Wang] Mang feared and dreaded [T'ien] K'uang,
so secretly sent a substitute for him, and [also] sent a

commissioner to grant [T'ien] K'uang a message with the imperial seal. When the commissioner arrived and had audience with [T'ien] K'uang, he thereupon ordered the substitute to superintend [T'ien K'uang's] troops. [T'ien] K'uang followed the commissioner westwards. When he reached [the court], he was installed as the Metropolis Commandant Grandee. When [T'ien] K'uang had left, the region of [the former feudal state of] Ch'i was thereupon lost [to the bandits].

**III**
**A.D. 22**
**The Hsin Ancestral Temples Dedicated**

In the third year, the first month, the roofing of the Nine [Ancestral] Temples was completed and the spirit tablets were installed. [When Wang] Mang [went] to be presented [to the divinities there, he rode] in the grand carriage of state,[16.1] to which were yoked six horses, [on which] were robes with dragon stripes made of vari-colored feathers, to which were affixed three-foot long horns. The carriage with a flowery baldachin and "ten large war chariots"[16.2]

**16b** went before him. Thereupon he granted to the Minister Over the Masses, [Wang Hsün₃], and the Grand Minister of Works, [Wang Yi₅], who had built the temples, to each ten million [cash]. The Palace Attendants, Regular Palace Attendants, and

**19b 15b** those of lower [rank] were all enfeoffed. He enfeoffed the Chief Workman, Ch'iu Yen, as the Sub-Vassal of Han-tan Hamlet.

**Mar./Apr.** In the third month,[16.3] there was a visitation [of fire] at the Pa [River] Bridge. Several thousand

---

[16.1] For a description of the grand carriage of state, cf. *HHS*, Tr. 29: 11a–12b.

[16.2] A line from *Book of Odes* #177, (Legge, II, iii, iii, 4, p. 283.)

[16.3] The text reads "second month," but this date may be mistaken, for in that month there were no days such as those mentioned in the edict, according to the calendars of P. Hoang and Ch'en Yüan. Such days occurred only in the first and third months. *Han-chi* 30: 18b dates this fire in the intercalary [second?] month, but Hoang and Ch'en have no intercalary month in this year. The mention of the vernal equinox fixes the fire in March, but March 30 (julian) is much too late for the equinox (cf. n. 16.6). Possibly there was an intercalary second month in this year, instead of the preceding year, as Huang and Ch'en have it.

常侍臣下皆封封都匠仇延為邸淡里附城二月霸橋災數
元戎十乘在前因賜治廟者司徒大司空錢各千萬侍中中
謁見大駕乘六馬曰五采毛為龍文衣著角長三尺華蓋車
師尉大夫況去齊地遂敗三年正月九廟蓋構成納神主莽
賜況重書使者至見況因令代監其兵況隨使者西到拜為

千人呂水沃救不滅恭惡之下書曰夫三皇泉春五帝泉夏三王

泉秋五伯泉冬皇王德運也伯者繼空績之臣成歷數故其道駃

惟常安御道多呂所近為名逼二月癸巳之夜甲午之辰火燒霸

橋從東方西行至甲午夕橋盡火滅大司空行視考問或云寒民

含居橋下疑呂火自燎為此災也其明旦即乙未立春之日也子

people sprinkled water to save it, [but the fire was] not [thereby] extinguished. [Wang] Mang hated it, so issued a message which said, "Verily, the three August Ones typify spring, the Five Lords typify summer, the three [dynasties of] Kings typify autumn, and the five Lords Protector typify winter. The virtues of the August Ones and the Kings followed [one another] in a cycle. The Lords Protector [including the Ch'in dynasty] succeeded [to the rule of the world in] the vacancy and continued in the gap [between the periods ruled by the elements wood and fire][16.4] in order to complete the [full] number in a cycle; hence their ways were disorderly.

"Verily, in Ch'ang$_2$-an most of the imperial highways have taken their names from recent [events].[16.5] Recently in the third month,[16.3] in the night of [the day] *kuei-szu* and on the morning of [the day] *chia-wu*, fire burnt the Pa [River] Bridge from the eastern side going westwards. By the evening of [the day] *chia-wu*, the Bridge was completely destroyed by the fire. When the Grand Minister of Works, [Wang Yi$_5$], went to inspect it, he examined and questioned [persons], and someone said that shivering people dwelt below the bridge, and he suspected that they warmed themselves by a fire, which became this visitation [of fire].

"The next day was [the day] *yi-wei*, which was the day of the vernal equinox.[16.6] [From the time that]

*The Pa River Bridge Burns*

Mar. 28
Mar. 29

Mar. 29

Mar. 30

[16.4] According to Liu Hsiang's theory of the succession of the five powers, by virtue of which successive dynasties ruled, between the period dominated by the powers wood (T'ai-hao, K'u, the Chou dynasty) and fire (Shen-nung, Yao, the Han dynasty), there was an intercalary period, during which there were disorderly rulers (Kung-kung, Chih, the Ch'in rulers); cf. n. 24.1; Ku Chieh-kang, *Ku-shih-pien* V, 452, diagram B.

[16.5] *Shui-ching-chu* 19: 16b states that the Pa River "was anciently called the Tzu 滋 River. When Duke Mu of Ch'in [ruled 659–621 B.C.] was the Lord Protector (*Pa*), he changed the name of the Tzu River to be the Pa River, in order to exhibit his glory as a Lord Protector."

[16.6] The vernal equinox occurred at Ch'ang-an in the evening of March 22 (julian),

I received the mandate [of Heaven] through the line of succession transmitted from the gods my sage ancestors, the Yellow [Lord] and Yü [Shun], down to the fourth year of [the period] Ti-huang, it will be the fifteenth year. Exactly at the end of winter in the third year [of the period Ti-huang], the bridge

20a which is [named] Pa ('tyrannical' or 'Lords Protector') and [therefore] disorderly has been broken and destroyed. [Heaven] thereby intends to prosper and perfect the way the House of Hsin is to be unified in control [of the country] and preserved for a long [time].

"This is also a warning [from Heaven in that the breaking of] this bridge has placed a gap in the highway to the eastern quarter [of the empire]. Now in the eastern quarter the harvest has been lacking, the common people are starving, and the highways and roads are impassible [because of bandits. The Chief of] the Eastern Sacred Peak and Grand Master, [Wang K'uang$_{1a}$], shall promptly [make] regulations

17a for opening the various granaries in the eastern quarter and giving or lending to the distressed [people, in order] to apply the principle of benevo-

16a lence.[17.1] Let the name of the Pa Lodge be changed to be the Ch'ang-ts'un (Long-preserved) Lodge, and let the Pa [River] Bridge become the Ch'ang-ts'un Bridge."

In this month, the Red Eyebrows killed Ching Shang, the Second Brother Hsi to the Grand Master. East of the [Han-ku] Pass, people ate each other.

Apr./May　　In the fourth month, [Wang Mang] sent the Grand Master, Wang K'uang$_{1a}$, and the General of a New Beginning, Lien Tan, eastwards. When, outside the

眉殺太師犧仲景尚闋柬人相食四月遣太師王匡更始將軍廉丹
賑貸窮乏曰施仁道其更名霸館為長存館霸橋為長存橋是月赤
方之道今東方歳荒民飢道路不通東岳太師丞科條開東方諸倉
冬絶滅霸駁之橋欲呂與成新室統壹長存之道也又戒此橋空東
呂神明聖祖黄虞遺統受命至于地皇四年為十五年正呂三年終

eight days before this date. Wang Mang's astronomers would hardly be so much in error about such an event; Wang Mang probably post-dated the equinox for the sake of giving a favorable interpretation to the fire.

[17.1] Prof. Duyvendak points out that "benevolence 仁" here is opposed to "*pa* (tyrannical)" in the preceding paragraph.

東祖都門外天大雨露衣止長老歎曰是為泣軍莽曰惟陽
九之阣與喜氣會兌于去年枯旱霜蝗飢饉薦臻百姓困之
流離道路于春尤甚予甚悼之今使東嶽太師特進褒新侯
開東方諸倉賑貸窮之太師公所不過道分遣大夫謁者並
開諸倉全元元太師公因與廉丹大使五威司命位右大

Capital Gate, they were sacrificing to the gods of the roads, Heaven [sent] a great rain which dampened their clothes,[17.2] and the elders sighed and said, "This is because [Heaven] weeps for the army."[17.3]

[Wang] Mang said, "Verily, the distresses of the nine dry years conjoined with disastrous emanations have come to a climax in the past years, when withering droughts, frosts, locusts, and famines came as previously, so that the people are miserably poor, and wander scattered along the roads. In this spring, [the calamity] is especially pitiable. I have been very much saddened by it.

"Now I am sending [the Chief of] the Eastern [Sacred] Peak and Grand Master, [Wang K'uang1a], who is a Specially Advanced and the Marquis as Recompense to [the House of] Hsin, to open the various granaries in the eastern quarter and give or lend to those in distress. On those highways along which the Grand Master and Highest Minister does not pass, he shall separately send a Grandee or Internuncio to open the granaries simultaneously, in other to preserve the great multitude.

"The Grand Master and Highest Minister, [Wang K'uang1a], shall thereupon, with the Chief Envoy and Director of Mandates from the Five Majestic [Prin-

*An Expedition Against the Bandits*

20b

---

[17.2] The Official ed. has emended 止 to 上; the other editions read the former. It may be a mistake for 裳.

[17.3] *T'ai-p'ing Yü-lan* 328: 7a quotes the *Liu-t'ao* (iv or v cent. B.C.; this passage is not in the present *Liu-t'ao*, but is quoted in its appendix of fragments, p. 15b) as saying, "When rain dampens their clothes, it means they will be favored [lit. wetted 潤] weapons; when it does not dampen them, it means that it weeps silently for the weapons." *Ibid.* 11: 1b, 2a quotes Ts'ao Ts'ao's (155–220) *Ping-shu Chi-yao* as saying, "When a Generalissimo marches and the rain wets his clothes and bonnet, this means that he will spatter his weapons [with the enemy's blood] and that his army will secure felicitations.... If when a Generalissimo first marches, it rains but lightly, not dampening his clothes or bonnet, this means that Heaven weeps silently and that this general will have a great misfortune and his soldiers will be defeated and lost."

Shen Ch'in-han accordingly remarks that the prognostications in this "Memoir" are different from those in the books on military affairs.

ciples], ranking as Commander-in-chief of the Right, the General of a New Beginning and Marquis of Equalization and Standards, Lien Tan,[17.4] go to Yen Province, to pacify [the region] of which he, [the Grand Master], is in charge. Moreover those who formerly have been lawless and the bandits in Ch'ing and Hsü [Provinces] who have not yet completely

**17b** dispersed or have later again assembled shall all be purified. I hope that thereby the myriad people may be pacified."

The Grand Master, [Wang K'uang$_{1a}$, and the General] of a New Beginning, [Lien Tan], together led more than a hundred thousand ardent soldiers, and wherever they went they did as they liked, so that the eastern quarter said about them,

> "It would be better to meet the Red Eyebrows,
> And not to meet the Grand Master.
> The Grand Master can however [be endured],
> [But the General of] a New Beginning

*16b*
> would kill me."

[Thus] it was eventually as T'ien K'uang had said.

Famine　　[Wang] Mang also sent out many Grandees and

Relief　Internuncios by divisions to teach the common people to boil grasses and [parts of] trees to make a vegetable juice,[17.5] [but] the vegetable juice could not be eaten, and [the sending merely] made much trouble and expense.

---

[17.4] Wang Hsien-ch'ien suggests that the words "Lien Tan" should be transferred to come after the word *hou* (Marquis). According to 99 B: 29a, the General of a Peaceful Beginning (which title had been changed to General of a New Beginning, cf. 99 C: 4b) was in charge of the western provinces, not the east. The subject of the phrase "to rule and control the region of which he is in charge" must be "the Grand Master," who was in charge of the east (99 B: 2b, 29a). As a matter of fact, both these officials went on this expedition (99 C: 17b). I accordingly transfer these two words, as does Stange (p. 259).

[17.5] In a note to *HS* 24 A: 21b, Fu Ch'ien says, "They boiled the fruits of trees. Someone says it was something like the present thistle cakes 餌朮." Ju Shun adds, "They

惟民困之雖
費恭下書曰

[Wang] Mang issued a message which said, "Verily, the common people are miserably poor, so that al-

made something like an almond drink (*hsing-lo* 杏酪)." Yen Shih-ku approves Ju Shun's interpretation. Chou Shou-ch'ang however objects that these things are scarce, and adds, "It was probably like in the present famine years when the common people cut up [the leaves and bark] of elm trees and made a gruel and take the juice of millet stalks to make soup, etc."

Prof. Duyvendak has called my attention to the importance of this passage for the meaning of *lo* 酪, mentioning the occidental literature. Karlgren (*Philology & Ancient China*, p. 138) states that *lo* had the archaic pronunciation *glak*, which he uses as evidence for an ancient Turkish (Hunnish) stem, *arak-* or *rak-*, denoting kumyss or its forerunner, an alcoholic drink made of fermented milk, for which stem there is also good evidence in many modern Turkish dialects. Karlgren derives the English word "arrack," the Japanese *sake*, and cognate words in other languages from this stem word. (Cf. also his discussion of *lo* in *Deutsche Literaturzeitung*, 47 [1926], 1960–1962.)

The relationship of this ancient Turkish stem *rak-* to the Chinese archaic *glak*, the present *lo*, is however not one of simple derivation, as Karlgren recognizes. The word *lo* was used by the Chinese with a more generalized meaning, seemingly before they became acquainted with kumyss. In ancient China, *lo* denoted three different kinds of drinks:

First, *Li-chi* VII, i, 9; XVIII, ii, ii, 38; & XXI, ii, 5 (Legge, I, 369; II, 160, 222 [he twice mistranslates *lo* as "cream"]; Couvreur, I, 504; II, 176, 293; Karlgren admits the first of these chapters as written in the iv cent. B.C.) uses *lo* to denote some kind of a sour cereal drink, possibly a sour alcoholic drink or a vinegar (Karlgren, *Grammata Serica*, 766 p., defines it as "A kind of acid soy made of rice or millet," which statement may however be merely an over-literal translation of one Chinese glossator's description of a sour liquor). *Lo* is used with *li* 醴, in the phrase *li-lo*, which phrase is most naturally interpreted as "sweet and sour liquors." The aforesaid is the most ancient literary use of the word *lo*, and was its original meaning in Chinese literature.

Secondly, the word undoubtedly denoted kumyss or some similar drink. Karlgren states that *lo* came to be used with this meaning because of the similarity in its ancient pronunciation and its first meaning with the ancient Turkish word from the stem *rak-* (archaic Chinese had no initial *r-* with the ending *-ak*). In 104 B.C., Emperor Wu established the office of Mare Milker (*T'ung-ma* 挏馬; *HS* 19 A: 13a), whose function, according to Ying Shao and Ju Shun, was to prepare a kind of kumyss. *Shuo-wen* 12 A: 6a, sub *t'ung*, defines it as "擁引" (lit. "grab and pull," easily understood as an attempt, in a language unfamiliar with herdsmen's vocabulary, to express the notion, "to milk"), and adds, "The Han [dynasty] had the office of Mare Milker, who made *ma-chiu* (馬酒, kumyss)." Possibly kumyss was introduced to the Chinese in the time of Emperor Wu, when intercourse with the Huns became more frequent. *HS* 22: 36b moreover quotes a memorial by K'ung Kuang and Ho Wu, dated 7 B.C., which mentions "seventy-two apprentices who furnish the Grand Provisioner with kumyss (*t'ung-ma-chiu*)," of whom seventy were dismissed (probably because kumyss was not a classical drink). This beverage, according to the glossators, was anciently made from goat's and cow's milk as

A
Monopoly
Revoked

21a

A.D. 49

though the granaries have been universally opened to give relief to them, I fear that nevertheless it will not be sufficient. Let the interdiction on the mountains and marshes of the empire be temporarily lifted, and let those who are able to take things from the mountains or marshes and [who do so] in accordance with the ordinances for [the various] months [of the year] be freely allowed to do so, and let them not be ordered to pay any taxes [for doing so]. In the thirtieth year [of the period] Ti-huang, [the restric-

聽之勿令出稅至地皇三十年
取山澤之物而順月令者其恣
其且開天下山澤之防諸能采
傅聞諸倉曰賑贍之猶恐未足

well as mare's milk. The *Shuo-wen* does not list the word *lo*; it is however found in *Shih-ming* 4: 6b, ch. 13 (by Liu Hsi, ca. 200 A.D.), where it is interpreted as kumyss. The word *lo* is used with this meaning in the lament of Liu Hsi-chün, the Chinese Princess who became the Wu-sun Queen (in *HS* 96 B: 4a; written between 110 and 104 B.C.) and in Li Ling's letter to Su Wu (in *Wen-hsüan* 41: 2a = G. Margoulies, *Le Kou-wen chinois*, p. 94; possibly written 81 or 80 B.C.; but its authenticity is debated).

There are various ancient Chinese names for this beverage: in addition to *lo*, *ma-lo*, *ma-chiu*, and *t'ung-ma-chiu*, there are *ju* 乳 *-lo*, *lo-su* 酥, and *ti-hu* 飿餬 or 酏醐 (the last two names are found in a quotation from the *T'ung-su-wen* [by Fu Ch'ien, ca. 125–195] in *TPYL* 858: 1a [which chapter deals largely with kumyss and contains interesting quotations]). Of these names, the last, *ti-hu* (for which Karlgren, *Gram. Ser.*, 590e & 49 l', gives the archaic pronunciation *tiər-g'o*), seems a purely phonetic reproduction of a foreign name, for its component words in this phrase are otherwise meangingless.

Thirdly, *lo* was used to denote a drink made from fruits, etc., such as the "apricot drink (*hsing-lo*)" mentioned by Ju Shun in his gloss to the *HS* passage, and to denote gruel made from bark recommended by Wang Mang. On the above meanings, cf. the *Tz'u-hai*, *sub lo*. The *P'ei-wen Yün-fu*, *sub lo* and the other phrases mentioned here, contains many interesting quotations.

*Lo* was originally the name of a sour fermented liquor; when the Chinese came to know kumyss (which the glossators mention specifically as being sour), the Chinese naturally applied the native word for a sour fermented liquor to it, calling it *lo*. They likewise called other similar fermented beverages, such as those made from apricots and from bark, etc. *lo*. Whether this ancient word, *glak*, can be used as evidence for an ancient Hun word with a similar pronunciation, is however not by any means sure, since there was anciently a quite different word meaning kumyss, *tiər-g'o*, which seems more likely to have been the phonetic reproduction of its foreign name. There is however also the possibility that the Chinese took their word for sour liquor, *glak*, from the ancient Hun name for kumyss, but that hypothesis would push the Chinese knowledge of kumyss much farther back than the literary evidence carries us. (Cf. also A. Conrady, "Alte westöstliche Kulturwörter," in *Berichte ü. d. Verhandl. d. Sächs. Akad. d. Wiss. zu Leipzig*, Phil.-hist. Kl., v. 77 (1925), H. 3, pp. 9–10; W. Eberhard, "Çìn de kimiz ve yoğurdum yapilmasi (Ueber die Herstellung von Kumys in China)" in *Ülkü*, Nov. 1940 [in Turkish].)

損上益下民説無疆書云言
民弗蒙非于意也易不云乎
如今豪吏猾民革而權之小
如故是王光上戊之六年也

tions shall be reapplied] as formerly. This [year] will be the sixth year of [the period] Wang-kuang-shang-mou.[17.6]

"If powerful and unruly officials or common people have committed crime and monopolized the [mountains and marshes, so that] the uninfluential common people have not received [any advantages], this has not been my intention. Does not the *Book of Changes* say,

'When the superior's [privileges] are lessened and the inferior's are increased, The common people are boundlessly delighted'?[17.7]

The *Book of History* says that when speech is not **18a**

[17.6] Meng K'ang states that this is "the name of [a year-period in] the calendar made by [Wang] Mang." *Mou* is equated with earth, the element by virtue of which Wang Mang declared he ruled. He had his Grand Astrologer prepare the titles of year-periods for 36,000 years, with one change of the year-period every six years (99 C: 4a), so that names had been invented for all these year-periods.

Chavannes, *Documents chinois découverts par Aurel Stein*, p. 128 ff, no. 592, lists a tablet in which the date A.D. 20 is written with the ten words, *Hsin Shih-chien-kuo Ti-huang-shang-mou*, first year 新始建國地皇上戊元年." He also lists tablets with the date for A.D. 14 written, *Shih-chien-kuo T'ien-feng*, first year (nos. 307, 482) and for A.D. 17, *Shih-chien-kuo T'ien-feng*, fourth year (nos. 368, 369). *Li-hsü* 2: 1b (by Hung Kua, 1117–1184) lists a captain's bell with the date, "*Hsin Shih-chien-kuo Ti-huang-shang-mou*, second year." *Yung-chai Sui-pi* 6: 1a, b (by Hung Mai (1123–1202) says, "In the family of Han [Tien] Chuang-min [lived 815–893] there was a bronze *tou* [measure] with the inscription, '*Hsin Shih-chiew-kuo T'ien-feng-shang-mou*, sixth year.' In [the period] Shao-hsing [1131–1162], Kuo Ching-chou secured a bell with the inscription, '*Hsin Shih-chien-kuo Ti-huang-shang-mou*, second year.' " Lo Chen-yü's *Cheng-sung-t'ang Chi Ku-yi-wen* 15: 2a lists a captain's bell with the inscription "a captain's bell 鉦, weighing six catties five taels, made in *Hsin Shih-chien-kuo Ti-huang* VI." Here is evidence that, in Wang Mang's time, "*Hsin Shih-chien-kuo*" or "*Shih-chien-kuo*" (i.e. "[the House of] Hsin [having for the] first [time] established its state") was prefixed to the two words distinguishing a year-period, and *shang-mou*, lit. "[the dynasty that] exalts [the stem] *mou* [i.e., the element earth]" was added at the end. Wang Mang began the sexagenary cycle with the term *mou-tzu* (99 B: 25b). The names of the reign-periods that are listed in the *HS*, T'ien-feng and Ti-huang, are then cursive forms of the full names found in these contemporary documents.

[17.7] *Book of Changes*, App. I, ii, Hex. 42, 1 (Legge, p. 247; Wilhelm, II, 173.)

practical, this means that there will not be order [in the state].[18.1]  Alas, that you, various highest ministers, should fail to be solicitous [concerning these matters]!"

An Expedition Against the Bandits in the Yangtze Valley

At that time the Troops From the Lower Yangtze [Region] were powerful, and Chu Wei, [a man from] Hsin-shih, Ch'en Mu, [a man from] P'ing-lin, and others had all again collected bands and were attacking villages,[18.2] so [Wang] Mang sent the Director of Mandates [from the Five Majestic Principles] and Generalissimo, K'ung Jen, [to be in charge of] the division, Yü Province, and the Communicator and Generalissimo, Chuang Yu, and the Arranger of the Ancestral Temples and Generalissimo, Ch'en Mou, to attack [the rebels] in Ching Province.  Each one was followed by more than a hundred officers and soldiers.  They rode in boats down the Wei [River]

17a
21b

into the [Yellow] River to Hua-yin, then left [the boats and took] riding quadrigae.

When they reached their divisions, they solicited soldiers.  [Chuang] Yu said to [Ch'en] Mou, "To send a general and not to give him the credentials [for levying] troops, so that he must first beg [the emperor] and then only can he make a move, is like tying up a Han(h) black hunting-dog[18.3] and yet demanding it to catch [game]."

Summer

In the summer, there was [a plague of] locusts which came from the eastern quarter.  In flying they

---

[18.1] Wang Mang is alluding to *Book of History* V, iv, 6 "[The virtue of] speech is practicality" and "Practicality produces good government."  (Reference from Yen Shih-ku.) Legge, pp. 326, 327 translated ts'ung 從 as "accordance with [the Way]."  But the K'ung An-kuo gloss is, "This then *can* be followed (k'o 可 ts'ung)," with which Cheng Hsüan and Ma Jung agree.  K'ung Ying-ta explains, "The second [activity] is speech, of which [the important circumstance] is that it can be used [in practise] k'o 用."  [*Shang-shu Chu-su* 12: 4b.])

[18.2] Cf. *HHS*, An. 1 A: 3a; Glossary *sub* Kuang-wu, Emperor.

[18.3] Yen Shih-ku explains that han-lu 韓盧 was "the name of a dog in the ancient state of Han(h).  A black color is called lu."  This breed of dog is also mentioned in *K'ung Ts'ung-tzu*, ch. 17, sect. 8; 5: 20b.

符必先請而後動是猶紲韓盧而責之獲也夏蝗從東方來蜚蔽
船從渭入河至華陰迺出乘傳到部募士尤謂茂曰遣將不與兵
納言大將軍嚴尤秩宗大將軍陳茂擊荊州各從吏士百餘人乘
平林陳牧等皆復聚衆攻擊鄉聚莽遣司命大將軍孔仁部豫州
之不從是謂不文咨庳韋公可不憂哉是時下江兵盛新市朱鮪

流民也乃市所賣梁飰肉羹持入視莽信曰居民食咸如此莽信
惠之業呂省賣為功賜爵附城莽聞城中飢饉呂問業業曰皆
者十七八先是莽使中黃門王業領長安市買賤取於民民甚
十萬人迺置養贍官稟食之使者監領與小吏共盜其稟民死
穀貴欲厭之為大倉置衛交戟名曰政始掖門流民入闗者數
天至長安入未央宮緣殿閤發吏民設購賞捕擊莽曰天下

covered the sky. They came to Ch'ang-an, entered the Wei-yang Palace, and crawled in its Halls and Pavilions. [Wang] Mang sent out officials and common people and established bounties for those who seized and killed them.    **Locusts in Ch'ang-an**

Because the empire's grain was expensive, [Wang] Mang wanted to depress [its price].[18.4] For the Great Granary he established a guard with joined lances and named them Supporters of the Smaller Gates to the Beginning of Public Authority.[18.5] The vagrant people who had entered the passes [of Kuan-chung numbered] several hundred thousand persons, so [Wang Mang] established an Office for Maintenance and Relief, to feed them. [But] the commissioners who supervised and had charge of [the matter], together with the minor officials, together stole their grain allowances, so that seven- or eighth-tenths of them died of hunger.    **Futile Famine Relief**

Previous to this [time, Wang] Mang had sent a Palace Attendant Within the Yellow Gate, Wang Yeh₅ᵦ, to have charge of buying at the Ch'ang-an markets, and he took things at a low price from the common people, so that the common people suffered severely from it. [Because Wang] Yeh₅ᵦ had achieved the merit of having economized expenses, he had been granted the noble rank of Sub-Vassal. [When Wang] Mang heard that in the city there was a famine, he asked [Wang] Yeh₅ᵦ about it, and [Wang] Yeh₅ᵦ replied, "These all are vagrants." Then he brought some millet mush with meat and thick meat and vegetable soup which were being sold at the market, and showed them to [Wang] Mang, saying, "The food of all the resident commoners is like this," [and Wang] Mang believed him.    **Wang Mang Deceived**

    **18b**

    **22a**

18.4 *HHS*, An. 1 A: 21a states that, towards the end of Wang Mang's reign, when there were drouths and plagues of locusts, a *hu* of grain cost one catty of actual gold.

18.5 The establishment of this guard seems to indicate that there had been disturbances by hungry people outside the government granaries even at the imperial capital.

Winter

In the winter, So-lu Hui of Wu-yen and others raised troops and siezed their city.[18.6] Lien Tan and Wang K'uang[1a] attacked and took it by storm, cutting off more than ten thousand heads, [so Wang] Mang sent a General of the Gentlemen-at-the-Household, bearing a message with an imperial seal, to congratulate [Lien] Tan and [Wang] K'uang[1a]. Their noble ranks were advanced and they became Dukes. More than ten of their officers and soldiers who had distinguished themselves were enfeoffed.

*17b*
A Rebel
City
Taken
by Storm

A detached Colonel of the Red Eyebrows, Tung Hsien[4a], and others, with a band of several tenthousand men, were in Liang Commandery. Wang K'uang[1a] wanted to advance and attack them, [but] Lien Tan considered that [their own troops] had but newly taken a city by storm, so were utterly weary, and their men ought temporarily to be rested, in order to increase their prestige. [Wang] K'uang[1a] would not listen, so alone led his troops to advance, and [Lien] Tan followed after him. Battle was joined at Ch'eng-ch'ang. [The imperial] troops were defeated and [Wang] K'uang[1a] fled. [Lien] Tan sent an official bearing his seals, apron, and tally credentials, to give them to [Wang] K'uang[1a] and say, "You, boy, may flee, but I cannot." Thereupon he stayed and died fighting.[18.7] When his Colonels, Ju Yün,

The Red
Eyebrows
Defeat
an
Imperial
Army

Lien Tan
Dies

走丹使更持其印韍符節付匡曰小兒可走吾不可逃止戰死校
罷勞當且休士養威匡不聽引兵獨進丹隨之合戰成昌兵敗匡
別校重憲等眾數萬人在梁郡王匡欲進擊之廉丹以為新拔城
遠中郎將奉璽書勞丹匡進爵為公封吏士有功者十餘人赤眉
之冬無鹽索盧恢等舉兵反城廉丹王匡攻拔之斬首萬餘級莽

[18.6] Yen Shih-ku explains *fan₃-ch'eng* 反城 as "to sieze a city in order to [start] a rebellion (*fan₃*). It is also said that *fan₃* is pronounced *fan₁* 幡. When today rebels are spoken of, they still say *fan₁-ch'eng*."

[18.7] *HHS*, Mem. 18 A: 6a (which may have been taken from Pan Ku's account of the Later Han dynasty's rise) states that when Lien Tan, on his way east, "had reached Ting-t'ao, [Wang] Mang had sent an imperial edict after [Lien] Tan, which said, 'The granaries are exhausted and the government arsenals are empty. You must now indeed "become enraged"* and must now indeed fight. You, General, have received the weightiest duty in the state. If you do not leave your body "in the midst of the waste,"** you will not be able to repay [the state's] favors or to escape a reprimand.'" Thus Wang Mang drove Lien Tan to his death. (The phrase marked * is an allusion to *Mencius* I, II, iii, 6 (Legge, p. 156). "King Wen, in one burst of rage, gave repose to the common people of the world." That marked ** is a quotation from *Book of Changes*, App. III,

王尋將十餘萬屯雒陽填南宮大司馬董忠養士習射中軍北壘大司空
王邑願平山東奔馳東與太師匡并力又遣大將軍陽淡守敖倉司徒
哀章謂奔曰皇祖考黃帝之時中黃直為將破殺蚩尤今臣奉中黃直之
急於詔筞離其威節騎馬訶諫為狂刃所害烏呼哀哉賜謚曰果公國將
戰死恭傷之下書曰惟公多擁選士精兵衆郡駿馬倉穀帑藏皆得自調
尉汝雲王隆等二十餘人別圍闎之皆曰康公已死吾誰為生馳犇賊皆

Wang Lung, and others, more than twenty persons [in all], who were fighting separately, heard of it, they all said, "Duke Lien is already dead. For whom should we live?" So they galloped rapidly at the bandits and all died fighting.

[Wang] Mang was afflicted by it, so issued a writ-    22b
ten message which said, "Verily, you, Duke, [Lien Tan], controlled many select gentlemen and picked troops. From all the fine horses, the grain in the storehouses, and the stores in the treasuries of the many commanderies, you might have made your own selection, but you cared not for documentary imperial edicts and separated yourself from the majestic credentials [of power]. Mounting a horse you shouted and [your followers] yelled and were killed by wild swords. Alas! How sad! I grant him the    19a
posthumous name of Duke Kuo (Intrepid)."

The State General, Ai Chang, spoke to [Wang] Mang, saying, "In the time of your August Deceased Original Ancestor, the Yellow Lord, when Chung-huang Chih was his General, he routed and killed Ch'ih-yu. Now your servant is occupying the post of Chung-huang Chih, and wishes to tranquillize [the region] east of the mountains." [Wang] Mang [accordingly] sent [Ai] Chang to gallop eastwards and join his forces with the Grand Master, [Wang] K'uang₁ₐ. He also sent Generalissimo Yang Chün to    *18a*
guard the Ao Granary. The Minister Over the Masses, Wang Hsün₃, leading more than a hundred thousand [men], encamped at Lo-yang, where he garrisoned the Southern Palace. The Commander-in-chief, Tung Chung₁ᵦ, instructed soldiers and practiced archery in the Northern Encampment of the Capital Army.[19.1] The Grand Minister of Works, Wang Yi₅, [was given] concurrently the duties of

II, ii, 22 (Legge, 385), which passage discusses methods of burial.)
[19.1] Cf. n. 13.8.

計迫迺議道風俗大夫司國憲等分行天下除井田奴
千石已下太師王匡等戰數不利恭知天下潰畔事窮
自劾去莽擊殺揚四方盜賊往往數萬人攻城邑殺二
銖尉士房揚素狂直迺呉曰此經所謂喪其齊斧者也
王邑兼三公之職司徒尊初發長安葿昌廄亡其黃

[all] the three highest ministers.

**An Ominous Portent**

When the [Grand] Minister Over the Masses, [Wang] Hsün₃, first started out from Ch'ang-an and spent the night at the Pa-ch'ang Stables, he lost his yellow battle-axe. [Wang] Hsün₃'s Officer, Fang Yang, was ordinarily impetuously outspoken, but he wept and said, "This is what the Classic means [when it says], 'He has lost his sharp axe.'"[19.2] He accused himself [of the loss] and left [the army. Wang] Mang had [Fang] Yang killed with a battle-axe.

23a

**More Defeats**

The thieves and robbers in the four quarters, [whose bands] frequently [numbered] several ten-thousands of men, attacked cities and towns, killing [officials ranking at] two thousand piculs and under. The Grand Master, Wang K'uang₁ₐ, and others fought several battles, but unsuccessfully.

19b

[Wang] Mang knew that the empire had got out of his control and rebelled, that matters were at a last extremity and some expedient was urgent, so he discussed sending the Grandee In Charge of Customs and Morals, Szu-kuo Hsien, and others, by divisions, to inspect the empire and to do away with the prohibitions against the *ching* [system of] cultivated

---

[19.2] *Book of Changes*, Hex. 57, 6 (Legge, p. 191; Wilhelm, I, 168). The conclusion of this passage is, "Firmness of mind will bring misfortune." No wonder Fang Yang left!

Yellow was the color of Wang Mang's power, hence his ceremonial axes were yellow.

For the *HS*'s *ch'i* 齊, the Book of Changes reads *tzu* 資. Legge and Wilhelm translate differently, interpreting *tzu* as "property," as they also do in *ibid.*, Hex. 56, 4 where the phrase *tzu-fu* 斧 recurs (Legge, 188, Wilhelm, I, 163). Yü Hsi (ca. 285–360) in his *Chih-lin Hsin-shu* ("Yü-han Shan-fang Chi-yi-shu" ed., p. 6a) declares, "*Ch'i* should be *chai* 齋; whenever an army leaves, [its commander] must fast and purify himself, enter [the imperial ancestral temple], and receive his axe. Hence it says *chai* (fast)."

But Ying Shao, in a note to this passage of the *HS*, defines *ch'i* as *li* 利 (sharp), and interprets, "He has lost his sharp axe (*li-fu*)." Ch'ien Chan (1744–1806) points out that *tzu* and *ch'i* were anciently interchanged. *Erh-ya* ch. 2 (*Erh-ya Chu-su* 3: 2b) says, "*Chi* 劑 (to cut) and *chien* 翦 (to cut off) are *ch'i*," and Kuo P'o (276–324) comments, "The people of the southern quarter call a *chien*-knife a *ch'i*-knife." Shen Ch'in-han quotes the above explanations, concluding that Yü Hsi is mistaken and says, "The words *ch'i-fu* take their meaning from beheading and cutting off." Cf. also *Tz'u-hai, hai*, 154b, sub *ch'i-fu* and *ibid.*, *yu*, 99d, sub *tzu-fu*. Ying Shao's interpretation must be accepted.

羣賊且滅弄差呂自安四年正月漢兵得下江王常等呂為助兵
五日不見弄數召問太史令宗宣諸術數家皆繆對言天文安善
成丹王常等數千人別走入南陽界十一月有星孛于張東南行
致新市平林朱鮪陳牧等合攻拔棘陽是時嚴尤陳茂破下江兵
發會世祖與兄齊武王伯升宛人李通等帥舂陵子弟數千人招
婢山澤六莞之禁即位呂來詔令不便於民者皆收還之待見未

fields, [private] slaves and slave-women, [free use of] mountains and marshes, and the [other] six monopolies, and that all the imperial edicts and ordinances since [Wang Mang] had ascended the throne, which were inconvenient to the common people, should be recalled.

[While the messengers] awaited an audience, and had not yet been sent out, it happened that the [future] Epochal Founder, [Emperor Kuang-wu, Liu Hsiu₄ₐ]; with his elder brother, [Liu Yin₄ₐ] Po-sheng, [later] King Wu of Ch'i; Li T'ung, a man from Yüan; and others led several thousand followers from Ch'ung-ling and induced Chu Wei and Ch'en Mu from Hsin-shih and P'ing-lin, and others to come. Together they attacked and took Chi₅-yang by storm. At this time Chuang Yu and Ch'en Mou routed the Troops from the Lower Yangtze [Region, under] Ch'eng Tan, Wang Ch'ang₂, and others, [to the number of] several thousand men, and they separately fled into the borders of Nan-yang [Commandery].

In the eleventh month, a comet appeared in [the constellation] Chang. It traveled southeastwards for five days and disappeared.[19.3] [Wang] Mang several times summoned and questioned his Chief Grand Astrologer, Tsung Hsüan, and various diviners. They all answered falsely, saying, "The astrological phenomena are peaceful and good, so that the many bandits will soon be destroyed." Thereupon [Wang] Mang [felt] a little more tranquil.

In the fourth year, the first month, the Han troops secured [the Troops from] the Lower Yangtze [under] Wang Ch'ang and others, and made them auxiliary

Wang
Mang's
Economic
Measures
to be
Repealed
The Han
Army
Arises.

18b

Nov./Dec.
23b
A
Comet

IV
A.D. 23
Jan./
Feb.[19.4]

19.3 This is no. 55 in Williams, *Observations of Comets*. It is also listed in *HHS*, Tr. 10: 4a.

19.4 Wang Mang had taken the second astronomical month for the first month of the year, whereas the Han dynasty took the third astronomical month as their first month, so that Wang Mang's first month was the same as the thirteenth month of the preceding year according to the Han calendar. The months of this year in this chapter are thus

The Defeat of Chen' Fou

troops. They [together] attacked the Southern Neighboring Commandery Grandee, Chen Fou, and his Director of an Association, Liang-ch'iu Tz'u, and beheaded them both, killing several ten-thousands of their forces.[19.5]

The Illiterate Red Eyebrows

Previously, the imperial capital had heard that the bands of bandits from Ch'ing and Hsü [Provinces] numbered several hundred-thousands of men, and yet that they had absolutely no written orders, banners, or marks of identification. [The people of the capital] all considered it a portentious prodigy and those who loved [strange] things[19.6] said furtively, "Are not they like the three ancient August Ones, who had no written messages or titles?"

20a

[Wang] Mang also [considered] in his heart that it was wonderful and asked his various courtiers about it. None of the various courtiers answered, only Chuang Yu said, "This [circumstance] is not sufficient [to be considered] wonderful. From the time that the Yellow Lord, T'ang [the Successful] and [King] Wu led their armies, [armies] have always been provided with regiments, companies,[20.1] banners, and orders. These [people] who now do not have them are merely a crowd of thieves [produced by] hunger and cold, [like] dogs or sheep that have gathered together, who merely do not know how to formulate [such institutions." Wang] Mang was

24a

greatly pleased and the various courtiers acquiesced completely.

However later, when the Han troops [under] Liu [Yin4a] Po-sheng arose, [their leaders] all called [themselves] Generals. They attacked cities and

犬羊相聚不知為之耳莽大說羣臣盡服及後漢兵劉伯升起皆稱將
怪也自黃帝湯武行師必待部曲旌旗號令此無有者直飢寒羣盜
三皇無文書號諡邪莽亦心怪曰問羣臣莫對唯嚴尤曰此不足
賊衆數十萬人訖無文號旌旗表識咸怪異之好事者竊言此豈如古
擊前隊大夫甄阜屬正梁丘賜皆斯之殺其衆數萬人初京師聞青徐

---

one month earlier than the corresponding months of the Han calendar, which latter is given in Hoang, *Concordance*.

[19.5] For this famous battle, cf. *HHS*, Mem. 4, and Glossary, *sub* Liu Yin4a.

[19.6] A phrase from *Mencius*, V, I, viii, 1 (Legge, p. 365). For the ancient belief concerning the literacy of the Three Sovereigns, cf. *HFHD*, I, 124, paragraph 3.

[20.1] Cf. Glossary, *sub* Captain.

杜陵史氏女為皇后聘黃金三萬斤車馬奴婢雜帛珍寶巨萬
百官茀聞之愈恐欲外視自安迺染其鬚髮進所徵天下淑女
下江兵將王常朱鮪等共立聖公為帝改年為更始元年拜置
宛城初世祖族兄聖公先在平林兵中三月辛巳朔平林新市
軍攻城略地既殺甄阜移書稱說莽聞之憂懼漢兵乘勝遂圍

overran territory. When they had killed Chen Fou, they sent letters about, giving an account of [Wang Mang's crimes.[20.2] When Wang] Mang heard of it, he was worried and fearful.

The Han troops took advantage of their victories and thereupon besieged the city of Yüan.

Formerly, [Liu Hsüan 2a] Sheng-kung, a second cousin of the Epochal Founder, [Emperor Kuang-wu], had previously been among the P'ing-lin Troops, and, in the third month, on [the day] *hsin-szu*, the first day of the month,[20.3] the P'ing-lin and Hsin-shih [Troops] and the Troops from the Lower Yangtze [Region], led by Wang Ch'ang 2, Chu Wei, and others, together set up [Liu Hsüan 2a] Sheng-kung as the Emperor. He changed the year-[period] to be the first year of [the period] Keng-shih and installed and established a bureaucracy.

*19a*
Mar. 11
The Keng-shih Emperor Set Up

When [Wang] Mang heard of it, he was all the more afraid. He wanted to show to the world that he himself was calm, so he dyed his beard and hair[20.4] and promoted the "virtuous young ladies"[20.5] whom he had summoned from the empire, setting up[20.6] a daughter of the Shih clan at Tu-ling as his Empress. He sent her [family] as betrothal presents 30,000 catties of actual gold, [together with] chariots and horses, slaves and slave-women, variegated silks, and precious things, which were valued by the hundred

Wang Mang Marries Again.

20.2 Hu San-hsing in *Tzu-chih T'ung-chien* 39: 1b explains 稱說 as "recounting [Wang] Mang's crimes."

20.3 *HHS*, An. 1 A: 4a dates this event in the second month; the difference is due merely to the fact that the *HHS* here uses the Han calendar, while this "Memoir" here uses Wang Mang's calendar; cf. n. 19.4.

20.4 Chou Shou-ch'ang remarks that this is the first time dying the beard and hair appeared in Chinese history.

20.5 Cf. 99 C: 13b and n. 13.4.

20.6 Wang Nien-sun declares that before 杜 there was originally the word 立; *T'ai-p'ing Yü-lan* (978–983) 89: 11a and *Tzu-chih T'ung-chien* 39: 2a, in quoting this sentence, have this word.

millions [of cash.[20.7]　Wang] Mang in person welcomed her between the two stairs to the Front Hall and completed the ceremonies of the common [marriage] meal above in the Western Hall.[20.8]

[The prescribed number of] Harmonious Ladies, Spouses, Beauties, and Attendants were all complete. The Harmonious Ladies were three [in number]; their **20b** rank was equal to that of the highest ministers. The Spouses were nine [in number; their rank] was equal to that of the high ministers. The Beauties were twenty-seven [in number; their rank] was equal to that of Grandees. The Attendants were eighty-one [in number; their rank] was equal to that of First **24b** Officers. Altogether there were a hundred twenty women. All wore seals with aprons at their girdles, and held bowcases.[20.9]

[Wang Mang] enfeoffed [Shih] Shen, the father of the Empress, as Marquis of Harmony and Peace, and installed him as General of a Peaceful Beginning. [Shih] Shen's two sons were both [made] Palace Attendants.

On that day, a great wind blew [off] roofs and broke trees. When the many courtiers offered congratulations, they said, "Verily, on [the day] *keng-* **Mar. 30** *tzu*, rainwater sprinkled the highways, and on [the **Mar. 31** day] *hsin-ch'ou*, they were clean and pure, without any dust. That evening, the life-giving valley

---

[20.7] The gold alone was worth (at the standard rate, 10,000 cash per catty, cf. 24 B: 22a) 300,000,000 cash, so that "hundred millions of cash" must refer to the other presents. The gold amounted to 235,343 oz. troy or 7,320,000 g.

[20.8] For the ceremonies, cf. the *Yi-li*, ch. III (J. Steele, trans.). For these parts of the ancient house, cf. plan in *T'zu-yüan*, sub 寢.

[20.9] In accordance with *Li-chi* IV, i, ii, 9 (Legge, I, 259; Couvreur, I, 341 f), "In this month [the second month of spring, Wang Mang's third month], the swallows arrive. On the day of their arrival, a *suovetaurilia* is sacrificed to the Eminent Deity of Marriage and Birth. The Son of Heaven attends in person, and the Queen Consort leads the nine Spouses and the Attendants. Then a ceremony is performed for those [ladies] who have attended [in person] upon the Son of Heaven. They carry bowcases and are given bows and arrows before the Eminent Deity of Marriage and Birth."

折木靡臣上壽曰迺庚子雨水灑道辛丑清靚無塵其夕歙
為和平侯拜為宰始將軍謚子二人宦侍中是日大風發屋
八十一視元士凡百二十人皆佩印韍執弓鞬封皇后父謚
美御和人三位視公嬪人九視卿美人二十七視大夫御人
萬計莽龍迎於前殿兩階閒成同牢之禮于上西堂備和嬪

風迅疾從東北來辛丑吳之宮日也吳為風為順后誼
明母道得溫和慈惠之化也易曰受茲介福于其王母
禮曰承天之慶萬福無疆諸欲依廢漢火劉皆沃灌雪
除殄滅無餘雜矣百穀豐茂庶草蕃殖元元驩喜兆民
賴福天下幸甚莽日與方士涿郡昭君等於俊宮考驗

wind[20.10] blew swiftly and promptly from the northeast. *Hsin-ch'ou* is the day of [the musical note] *kung* belonging to [the hexagram] *sun*.[20.11] *Sun* [indicates] wind and [indicates] obedience. [Thus] the principles of an Empress are made plain and the way of motherhood is secured. [The whole is due to] the influence of your geniality and kindness. The *Book of Changes* says, 'He will receive this great blessing from his [Queen], the Royal Mother [of the country].'[20.12] The [*Yi-li*] says, 'May you receive Heaven's blessing and myriad happinesses without bounds.'[20.13] Those who intend to attach themselves to the abolished Han [dynasty], the Liu [clan, which depends upon the virtue of] fire, shall all be flooded, disappear like melting snow, and extirpated, without any remaining fragments. All the grains shall be bountiful and plants shall grow abundantly. The great multitude will be glad and rejoice and the myriad common people will have the blessings that come from being good,[20.14] so that the world will be greatly favored [because of you]."

[Wang] Mang was daily in the harem with persons versed in the magical arts, Chao-chün, from Cho Commandery, and others, testing magical and techni-

*19b*

*25a*

[20.10] An allusion to *Book of Odes*, I, III, x (Legge, I, 55); the phrase denotes the east wind. The valley wind was supposed to blow gently and bring all genial influences.

[20.11] *Ch'ou* was connected with the note *kung*. Chu Chen (1072–1138), in his *Han-shang Yi-kua T'u*, B: 23b, basing his calculations on the *Yi-chuan* of Ching Fang (B.C. 77–37), asserts that the hexagram *sun*, in the cyclical combination *hsin-ch'ou*, is equated with the power earth (which is equated with the note *kung*). The same equation is found in *San-yi Pei-yi* 6: 5b (by Chu Yüan-sheng; fl. 1211; in *T'ung-chih-t'ang Ching-chien*, vols. 14 & 38). Thus this equation was based upon earlier documents and has passed into the stream of interpretation for the *Book of Changes*. Sun-erh 巽二 was the ancient god of the wind, and the hexagram *sun* was itself equated with wine.

[20.12] *Book of Changes*, Hex. 35, 2 (Legge, p. 132; Wilhelm, I, 103). Yen Shih-ku explains *wang-mu* 王母 as *chün-mu* 君母, i.e., the principal wife, which is a case of tecnonymy become a set title; cf. *HS* 99 A: 9a³, C: 13a¹².

[20.13] *Yi-li* I, ii, 17, c (Steele, I, p. 15). That text has however "受 receive" for the *HS*'s "萬 ten-thousand."

[20.14] An allusion to *Mencius* VI, A, vii, 1 (Legge, p. 404): "With good harvests most people are good."

cal arts and giving himself up to lustful pleasures.

A Price
Put Upon
the Head
of
Liu Yin
Po-sheng

21a

A general amnesty [was granted] to the empire. [Wang Mang] however said [in a message], "The descendants of the Marquises of Ch'ung-ling [under] the former Han dynasty, Liu [Yin₄ₐ] Po-sheng, with the members of his clan, his relatives by marriage, and his cabal, have falsely spread groundless rumors to delude the crowd into a treasonable rebellion against Heaven's mandate. They have by their own hands killed the General of a New Beginning, Lien Tan, the Southern Neighboring Commandery Grandee, Chen Fou, and his Director of an Association, Liang-ch'iu Tz'u. [To them], together with the northern barbarian caitiff,[21.1] the rebel [Lüan-ti] Yü, and the southwestern barbarian caitiffs Jo Tou and Meng Ch'ien, this message [of amnesty] shall not apply. Whoever are able to sieze these persons [Liu Yin₄ₐ Po-sheng, etc.], will all be enfeoffed among the highest ranking of the dukes, will be given the income of an estate of ten thousand households, and will be granted fifty million [cash] of the valuable currency."

Expedi-
tions
Ordered
Against
the Rebels

20a

There was also an imperial edict [saying], "The Grand Master, Wang K'uang₁ₐ, the State General, Ai Chang, the Director of Mandates [from the Five Majestic Principles], K'ung Jen, the Shepherd of Yen Province and Director of the Confederation at Shou-liang, Wang Hung, and the Shepherd of Yang Province, Li Sheng, shall quickly send forward the troops of the provinces and commanderies in the regional divisions which are their charge; altogether a force of three hundred thousand [men], in order to

方術縱淫樂馬大赦天下然猶曰故漢氏香陵侯韋子劉伯升與其族人

婚姻黨與妄流言惑眾悖畔天命及手害更始將軍廉丹前隊大夫甄阜

屬正梁丘賜及北狄胡虜逆與洎南焚虜若孟遷不用此書有能捕得

此人者皆封為上公食邑萬戶賜寶貨五千萬又詔太師王匡國將衰章

司命孔仁兗州牧壽良卒正王閎揚州牧李聖丞進所部州郡兵凡三十

---

²¹·¹ *Ti* 狄 was the classical (Chou period) general designation for the barbarians in the present northern China and north of it, while *hu* 胡 was the general designation in the Han period for the barbarians outside the northern border. Wang Mang, imitating classical models, here uses *ti* in order to be classical and has to add *hu* to make his meaning clear to his contemporaries.

Yen Shih-ku explains 洎 as meaning "and"; the Ching-yu ed., the Southern Academy ed., and the Official ed. read 洎.

宣威虜前呂虎牙將軍東指則反虜破壞西擊則逆
惑不解散皆并力合擊殄滅之兵大司空隆新公宗
十萬眾迫措前隊醜虜明告呂生活丹青之信倍迷
車騎將軍王巡左隊大夫王吳亟進所部州郡兵凡
萬眾迫措青徐盜賊納言將軍嚴尤秩宗將軍陳茂

pursue and arrest the thieves and robbers in Ch'ing and Hsü [Provinces]. The Communicator and General, Chuang Yu, the Arranger of the Ancestral Temples and General, Ch'en Mou, the General of Chariots and Cavalry, Wang Hsün2, and the Eastern Neighboring Commandery Grandee, Wang Wu2, shall quickly send forward the troops of the provinces and commanderies in the divisions which are in their charge, a force of altogether a hundred thousand men, to pursue and arrest the band of caitiffs in the Southern Neighboring Commandery, [Liu Yin4a, Liu Hsiu4a, etc.]. Inform them clearly with trustworthiness [like that of a painting done in] cinnabar and azurite,[21.2] that [if they surrender, they shall] live, [but] if they are again deluded and do not disperse, [these leaders] will all join forces, attack unitedly, and extirpate them. 25b

"Previously, when the Grand Minister of Works, the Duke Prospering the Hsin [Dynasty, Wang Yi5], a relative and member of the imperial clan, as the Tiger Teeth General, went east and pointed [at them], rebellious caitiffs were routed and ruined; when he went west and attacked, seditious bandits 21b

---

[21.2] The phrase *"tan-ch'ing-chih-hsin* 丹青之信*"* was a set expression in Han Times. *Shuo-wen* 5 B: 1a, *sub ch'ing*, says, *"Tan-ch'ing-chih-hsin* [means] certainly 必然." Juan Chi's (210-263) *"Yung-huai Shih"* (*Wen-hsüan*, 23: 3b, not trans. by von Zach) has the lines,

"[Like a painting done in] cinnabar and azurite, our oath has been made plain,
    Which for an eternity of ages we shall never forget."

Li Shan comments, "[A painting done in] cinnabar and azurite does not change, hence he used it to liken to his oath." Li Shan moreover quotes an edict of Emperor Kuang-wu from the *Tung-kuan Han-chi* (lost), "Establish plainly with trustworthiness [like that in a painting done in] cinnabar and azurite and open wide the road which restricts Our action." This edict is also referred to with this phrase in *HHS*, Mem. 3: 19a.

Yang Hsiung, in his *Fa-yen*, 12: 2a, b, ch. *"Chün-tzu,"* uses this phrase similarly: "Someone asked, 'Are the words of a sage as brilliant as [a painting done in] cinnabar and azurite?' I replied, 'Ha! What kind of words are that? At first [a painting done in] cinnabar and azurite is brilliant; after a long time it changes. [Do a sage's words] change?'" The fact that a phrase from painting had already become widely used as a set phrase in Former Han times illustrates the prevalence and antiquity of Chinese painting.

were ground to powder. He is thus a majestic and precious minister of the Hsin House. If the crafty bandits do not disperse, I will send the Grand Minister of Works, leading an army of a million [men], to make a punitive military expedition [against them and] exterminate them."

Wei Ao Flees.

[Wang Mang] sent Wei Ao, an Executive Officer of one of the Seven Highest Ministers, [Liu Hsin₁ₐ], and others, seventy-two persons [in all], by divisions, to issue the ordinance of amnesty and plainly instruct [the people. When Wei] Ao and the others had left [the court], availing [themselves of this opportunity], they escaped.

Apr./May

In the fourth month, the Epochal Founder, [Liu Hsiu₄ₐ], with Wang Ch'ang₂ and others, separately attacked Ying-ch'uan [Commandery] and caused

26a

K'un-yang, Yen, and Ting-ling to surrender. When [Wang] Mang head of it, he was all the more fearful,

20b

and sent the Grand Minister of Works, Wang Yi₅,

Wang Yi's Great Army Gathers.

riding a galloping quadriga, to go to Lo-yang, with the [Grand] Minister Over the Masses, Wang Hsün₃, to mobilize the troops of numerous commanderies, [to the number of] a million [men], calling them the Tiger Teeth [Troops and] the Troops of the Five Majestic [Principles], in order to tranquillize [the region] east of the [Kuan-chung] mountains. [Wang Yi₅] was permitted on his own authority to raise [persons] to the nobility. [The power of] making final decisions concerning government [business was also given] to [Wang] Yi₅. [Wang Mang] appointed to office the [various] persons skilled in methods of the sixty-three schools of military arts whom he had summoned.[21.3] Each one bore his charts and writ-

---

[21.3] *HS* 30: 64a lists "altogether books on military matters from 53 schools, in 790 fascicles," and Pan Ku's note adds, "I have omitted [and transferred to another place the books of] 10 schools, in 271 fascicles." Wang Hsien-ch'ien accordingly concludes that Liu Hsiang's *Ch'i-lüeh Pieh-lu* (now lost) recorded 63 schools of military methods. *HHS*, An. 1 A: 4b also says, "63 schools."

兵平定山東得顒封爵政決於邑除用做諸明兵法六十三家術者各持
遣大司空王邑馳傳之洛陽與司徒王尋發衆郡兵百萬號曰虎牙五威
出因逃亡兵四月世祖與王常等別攻潁川下昆陽郾定陵莽聞之愈恐
征伐剿絕之矣遣七公幹士隗囂等七十二人分下赦令曉諭云囂等阮
賊靡碎此畫室威寶之臣也如黠賊不解散將遣大司空將百萬之師

圖書受器械備軍吏傾府庫呂遺邑多齎珍寶猛獸欲視鋭富用

怖山東邑至雒陽州郡各選精兵牧守自將定會者四十二萬人

餘在道不絕車甲士馬之盛自古出師未嘗有也六月邑與司徒

尋發雖陽欲至宛道出頴川過昆陽昆陽時已降漢漢兵守之嚴

尤陳茂與二公會二公縱兵圍昆陽嚴尤曰稱尊號者在宛下宜

丞進彼破諸城自定矣邑曰百萬之師所過當滅今屠此城喋血

ings, received military implements and armor, and acted as a military officer. [Wang Mang] emptied the government storehouses in order to send out [Wang] Yi₅ provided abundantly with precious things and wild beasts, with the purpose of showing the exceeding wealth [of the imperial forces,] in order to frighten [the region] east of the [Kuan-chung] mountains.

When [Wang] Yi₅ reached Lo-yang, the provinces and commanderies each selected their picked troops, led by their Shepherds and Administrators in person. Those for whom a rendezvous had been appointed [numbered] more than four hundred twenty thousand men and [marched] on the highways in a continuous [stream]. From the [most] ancient [times] that armies had set forth, [such] magnificence in chariots, armor, men, and horses had never before been [seen].

In the sixth month, [Wang] Yi₅ and the [Grand] **22a** Minister Over the Masses, [Wang] Hsün₃, started **June/July** from Lo-yang, intending to go to Yüan. Their road **The** went out of Ying-ch'uan [Commandery] past K'un- **Rout at** yang. At that time, K'un-yang had already sur- **K'un-yang** rendered to the Han [troops], and the Han troops were defending it. Chuang Yu and Ch'en Mou had joined [their troops] with [those of] the two highest ministers. When the two highest ministers [were about to] launch their troops to besiege K'un-yang, Chuang Yu said, "[The rebel] who has been called by the imperial title, [Liu Hsüan₂ₐ Sheng-kung], is below [the walls of] Yüan, [besieging it]. It would **26b** be proper to hasten and advance [to that place]. If he is routed, the various [other] cities will of their own accord be tranquillized." [Wang] Yi₅ replied, "Wherever an army of a million passes, it is due to annihilate [the enemy]. We will now massacre [the defenders of] this city, trample in blood,[22.1] and then

---

[22.1] I take here meaning (1) for this phrase from *HFHD* I, 222, n. 2, since meaning (2) does not seem to fit this case.

advance [to Yüan]. The van will sing and the rear will dance; would not that be enjoyable?"[22.2]   Thereupon they surrounded the city several tens [of men] deep.

[The defenders] in the city begged [for permission] to surrender [on terms], but [permission] was refused. Chuang Yu also said, " 'When an army [wishes] to return [home], do not stop it; in besieging a city, [leave] an opening for them.'[22.3]   In accordance with the *Military Methods* you might cause them to be permitted to escape and leave [the city], and thereby frighten [the attackers of] Yüan."[22.4]   Again [Wang] Yi[5] would not listen.

It happened that when the Epochal Founder, [Liu Hsiu[4a]], mobilized all the troops in Yen and Ting-ling, to the number of several thousand men, and came to rescue [the defenders of] K'un-yang, [Wang] Hsün[3] and [Wang] Yi[5] made light of it. They themselves led more than ten thousand men and reviewed their battle-array. They ordered that the various encampments should all to be retained and that the regiments [therein] should not to be permitted to move.   [Then Wang Hsün[3] and Wang Yi[5]] by themselves [went to] meet the Han troops. When they were not successful in battle, their great army did

*21a* (margin)

將萬餘人行陳敕諸營皆按部毋得動獨迎與漢兵戰兵不利大
又不聽會世祖悉發郾定陵兵數千人來救昆陽尋邑易之自
又曰歸師勿遏圍城為之闕可如兵法使得逸出因佈宛下邑
而進前歌後舞顧不快邪遂圍城數十重城中請降不許嚴尤

---

[22.2] *HHS*, An. 1 A: 5b gives a different and less bombastic explanation for Wang Yi's refusal to advance, namely that Wang Yi[5] had previously been tried and reprimanded because, when he had surrounded Chai Yi, he had not taken him alive. *Tzu-chih T'ung-chien* 39: 3b adopts this explanation.   Cf. Glossary, *sub* Kuang-wu, Emperor.

[22.3] Yen Shih-ku asserts that this sentence is a saying from the standard Military Methods. Ts'ao Ts'ao, in his comment to *Sun-tzu*, 7: 40a, quotes the *Szu-ma Fa* (iv. cent. B.C., later added to; this passage is not in the present text of that book) as saying, "Surround three sides of it, and open one side of it, as a means of showing them that there is a way [to save their] lives."

[22.4] *Hsia* 下 is sometimes a meaningless suffix, used to make a binom out of a place-name composed of only one word; cf. *HFHD*, I, 310, n. 33.   But *hsia* can also mean "below [the walls of]," cf. HS 99 C: 26a[10-11], 28b[3], or "just outside [a wall, door, or gate]," cf. 99 A: 1b[11], 9a[2], B: 14b[2], 17b[4], C: 23a[12], 26b[7].

平帝請命金縢之策泣曰視羣臣命明學男張邯稱說其德及符

又聞漢兵言莽鴆殺孝平帝莽迺會公卿已下於王路堂開所為

邑獨與所將長安勇敢數千人還雒陽關中聞之震恐盜賊竝起

蜚瓦雨如注水大眾崩壞號嘑虎豹股栗士卒各走還歸其郡

軍不敢擅相救漢兵乘勝殺尋昆陽中兵出竝戰莽走軍亂天風

not presume on its own authority to rescue them.[22.5]
The Han troops took advantage of their victory and
killed [Wang] Hsün₃. Simultaneously the [Han]
troops inside K'un-yang came out and fought.
[Wang] Yi₅ fled and the army was in confusion. A
great[22.6] wind blew away tiles, and the rain was as if
water were being poured down, so that the great band
[of soldiers] collapsed in ruin. The shouting [made
even] the tigers and leopards tremble with fear in
their haunches. [Wang Mang's] soldiers fled hastily,      27a
each returning to his own commandery. [Wang] Yi₅,
with only the several thousand brave and daring men      22b
from Ch'ang-an whom he commanded, returned to
Lo-yang. When [the people] in Kuan-chung heard
of it, they quaked with fear and thieves and robbers
arose simultaneously.

Since it was moreover reported that the Han troops
said that [Wang] Mang had murdered Emperor      The Metal-
Hsiao-p'ing by poison, [Wang] Mang thereupon as-      Bound
sembled, in the Hall With the Royal Apartments,      Coffer
the ministers and those [ranking] below and opened      Opened
the metal-bound document in which he had begged
[to substitute his own] life for that of Emperor
P'ing.[22.7] He wept silently as he showed it to his
various courtiers.

He commanded the Baron of Brilliant Scholarship,
Chang₂ Han, to state and explain the virtue [of the      A Clever
power, earth, which brought] him, [Wang Mang, to      Augury
the throne], together with the mandates [given him

[22.5] *Hsiang* 相 cannot here have the meaning found in the dictionaries, "mutual;
reciprocal; direction towards." *Hsiang* can only be equivalent to a pronoun object. It
very often has this meaning, frequently being equivalent to a preposition plus a pronoun
object. Cf. 99 C: 29a³, "*hsiang* 食," which cannot mean "ate each other," but only
"ate them," i.e., "others."

[22.6] The present text reads, "Heaven's wind blew tiles off," which is the reading of the
important texts. The Official ed., which I here follow, has emended 天 to 大, in accordance with *HHS*, An. 1 A: 6b.

[22.7] Cf. 99 A: 24b.

through] portents. Thereupon [Chang₂ Han] said, "The *Book of Changes* says,

'He hides his weapons in a thicket (*mang*),
Mounts (*sheng*) a high mound (*kao-ling*),
And in the third year he will not prosper.'[22.8]

*Mang* is the personal name of the Emperor; *sheng* means Liu [Yin₄ₐ] Po-sheng; *kao-ling* means Chai Yi, the son of the Marquis of Kao-ling♭, [Chai Fang-chin]. It means that Liu [Yin₄ₐ Po]-sheng and Chai Yi will have troops with "hidden weapons in" [the reign of Wang "Mang"],[22.8] the Emperor of the Hsin [House], but yet will be extirpated and "will not prosper."[22.8] The courtiers all called out, "Long life!"

*21b*

Pretended Execution of the Rebels

[Wang Mang] also ordered carriages with cages to transport several men from the eastern quarter [of the empire], saying that [these men] were Liu [Yin₄ₐ] Po-sheng and the others. All of them underwent the grand exposure [of their corpses. But] the common people[22.9] knew that it was false.

*27b*

Previous to this, the General of the Guard, Wang Shê, had kept a gentleman versed in the ways of magic,[22.10] Hsi-men Chün-hui. [Hsi-men] Chün-hui loved astrology and prophetic accounts. He said to [Wang] Shê, "A comet has swept in the [Heavenly] Palace,[22.11] [hence] the Liu clan is due to be restored.

[22.8] *Book of Changes*, Hex. 13, 3 (Legge, p. 86; Wilhelm, I, 42).

[22.9] The Ching-yu ed., the Southern Academy ed. and the Official ed., for Wang Hsien-ch'ien's "臣 courtiers," read "民 common people," which latter reading I adopt.

[22.10] *Tao-shih* 道士 did not yet mean predominately a Taoist practicioner. Huan T'an (ca. 40 B.C.–A.D. 29), in his *Hsin-lun* (lost; quoted in *T'ai-p'ing Yü-lan* 720: 5b), calls Hsi-men Chün-hui a "gentleman possessing magical recipes, *fang-shih* 方士," and states that Wang Ken (the father of Wang Shê) had kept him in order to cultivate methods of securing longevity. Hence *tao-shih* at this time denoted a *fang-shih*. Cf. *Tz'u-hai*, *sub tao-shih*.

[22.11] This comet is not mentioned in Williams' list.

The constellation Ying-shih is meant. This reference is confirmed by the sentence below, referring to it as a zodiacal constellation. *Chin-shu*, 11: 14b, says, "The two stars

師公姓名是也涉信其言曰語大司馬董忠數俱至國師殿中
應道語星宿國師不應俊涉將住對歆涕泣言誠欲與公共安
宗族奈何不信涉也歆因為言天文人事東方必成涉曰新都
哀侯小被病功顯君素耆酒疑帝本非我家子也董公主中軍
精兵涉領宮衛伊休侯主殿中如同心合謀共劫持帝東降南

[The next emperor] will have the surname and given name of the State Master and Highest Minister."[22.12] [Wang] Shê believed his words, and spoke of them to the Commander-in-chief, Tung Chung[1b], who urged that they both go to the private apartments of the State Master, [Liu Hsin[1a]], in the [Palace] Hall and talk to him about the zodiacal constellation. [But] the State Master did not respond.

Later [Wang] Shê went alone to him. He wept silently before [Liu] Hsin[1a] and said, "I really wish with you, Duke, to bring peace to our clans. Alas, why will you not believe me, [Wang] Shê?" Thereupon [Liu] Hsin[1a] said to him that, [according to] the astrological phenomena and human affairs, [the insurgents] in the eastern quarter, were bound to succeed.

[Wang] Shê said, "Marquis Ai of Hsin-tu[c], [Wang Wan, Wang Mang's father], suffered from illness when he was young, and the Baronetess of Apparent Merits, [Wang Mang's mother], habitually loved wine. I suspect that the Emperor was not in his origin a child of my clan.[23.1] His excellency Tung [Chung[1b]] has charge of the picked troops in the Palace Encampments. I, [Wang] Shê, command the Palace Guard; the Marquis of Yi-and-Hsiu, [Liu Tieh], is in charge inside the [Palace] Hall. If we unitedly cooperate in the plot, together sieze the Emperor by force, and surrender to the Son of

An Astrological Portent and Prophecy for Liu Hsin

23a Wang Shê's Plot

of [the constellation] Ying-shih are the palace of the Son of Heaven."

[22.12] The State Master was Liu Hsin[1a], who had previously changed his name to Liu Hsiu[4a], which name is not used in the HS, since it was the same as the tabooed personal name of Emperor Kuang-wu, Liu Hsiu[4a]. Hsi-men Chün-hui was prophesying that a Liu Hsiu (which may mean either Liu Hsin[1a] or Emperor Kuang-wu) would come to the throne.

[23.1] Ju Shun's judgment upon this incident is interesting: "He said that [Wang] Mang's mother was in decayed circumstances, loved wine, and gave herself lascivious liberty, so conceived [Wang] Mang, [hence] he was not a child of the Wang clan. [Wang Shê] put forth this fraud in order to separate himself [from Wang Mang, with the aim of] not receiving execution [when Wang Mang would be destroyed]."

22a  Heaven in Nan-yang [Commandery] to the east, [Liu Hsüan₂ₐ Sheng-kung, we] will be able to pre-
28a  serve our clans.  If not, we will all be executed and our clans annihilated."

涉忠謀欲發敢曰當侍太白星出迺可忠
愛之敢怨莽殺其三子又長大禍至遂與
侯者敢長子也為侍中五官中郎將莽素
陽天子可曰全宗族不者俱夷滅矣伊休

The Marquis of Yi-and-Hsiu, [Liu Tieh], was [Liu] Hsin₁ₐ's eldest son.  He was a Palace Attendant and General of the Fifth Rank Gentlemen-at-the Palace. [Wang] Mang habitually loved him, [but Liu] Hsin₁ₐ held a grudge [because Wang] Mang had killed three of his children,[23.2] and also feared that the great calamity [of execution] would come upon him.  Consequently he plotted with [Wang] Shê and [Tung] Chung.

When they wanted to act, [Liu] Hsin₁ₐ said, "We must wait until [the planet] Venus appears,[23.3] and then only may we [act]."  Because the Director of

[23.2] In 11 A.D., Wang Mang had executed two of Liu Hsin's sons, cf. 99 B: 16a; in 21 A.D. he also executed Liu Hsin's daughter, cf. C: 11b.

[23.3] According to SC 27: 50 = Mh III, 371, Venus "presides over executions.  When a person who has done wrong is killed, that punishment is initiated by Venus."  SC 27: 57 = Mh III, 378 moreover declares: "When Venus is invisible and troops are put into the field, the troops will suffer calamity."  This astrological interpretation explains Liu Hsin₁ₐ's reluctance to act until Venus again became visible.

According to calculation by the tables in K. Schoch, Planeten-Tafeln für Jedermann, Venus had been in superior conjunction on Oct. 25, A.D. 22 (Julian) and became visible as an evening star at Ch'ang-an on Dec. 4, 22.  Venus was last visible as an evening star on Aug. 2, 23 and first became visible as a morning star on Aug. 20, 23.

What evidently happened was that, when the conspirators finally decided to act, Venus had become invisible.  Liu Hsin₁ₐ, who accepted the above astrological interpretation of Venus' influence and who knew that at inferior conjunction this planet is only invisible for a few days, consequently suggested they wait until Venus reappears.  He probably did not know that, at this time, Venus would be invisible for the longest period of time in which it can remain invisible at this latitude—eighteen days.  While awaiting its reappearance, possibly expecting the period would not be long (sometimes Venus does not disappear at inferior conjunction), Tung Chung₁ᵦ took Sun Chi into his confidence, with the result that the plot was revealed and the conspirators, including Liu Hsin₁ₐ, lost their lives.

Pan Ku's dating of the plot is not exact.  He does not mention any date until he notes the revelation of the plot and includes in the events before the seventh month Liu Hsin₁ₐ's proposal to delay acting until Venus reappears.  Evidently Pan Ku knew only the date the plot was memorialized to the throne, that this event occurred during the seventh

呂司中大贅起武侯孫俊亦主兵俊與謀俊歸家
顏色變不能食妻怪問之語其狀妻呂告弟雲陽陳
邯邯欲告之七月俊與邯俱告莽遣使者分召忠等
時忠方講兵都肆護軍王咸謂忠謀久不發恐漏泄
不如遂斬使者勒兵入忠不聽遂與歆會省戶下

the Palace and Grand Keeper of the Robes, the Marquis Raising Military Power, Sun Chi, also controlled troops, [Tung] Chung[1b] also plotted with [Sun] Chi. When [Sun] Chi returned to his home, the color of his face had changed and he could not eat. When his wife marvelled and asked him about it, he told her the circumstances. His wife told it to her younger brother, Ch'en Han, a man from Yün-yang, and [Ch'en] Han wanted to give information about it. In the seventh month, [Sun] Chi and [Ch'en] Han together gave information [about the plot. Wang] Mang sent commissioners separately to summon [Tung] Chung[1b] and the others.

*July/Aug. The Plot is Revealed.*

[Tung] Chung[1b] was just at that time teaching military [methods] at a grand review [of his troops]. His Commissioner Over the Army, Wang Hsien[2d], said to [Tung] Chung[1b], "Your plot has been made for some time but no action has been taken, so that I fear it has been divulged. It would be better immediately to behead the commissioner, take command of your troops, and enter [the Palace to carry out the plot." But Tung] Chung[1b] did not listen [to him], and consequently joined [Liu] Hsin[1a] and [Wang] Shê outside the gate of the inner [Palace] apartments.

month, which was July 7 to Aug. 5. But Venus was still visible as an evening star during most of the sixth month. (The possibility is excluded, with great probability, that Pan Ku's source was using the Han dynasty's months, which set the seventh month a month later, i.e., Aug. 6 to Sept. 3. For Pan Ku's information about the plot and its revelation could hardly have come elsewhere than from Wang Mang's court. It was most probably taken from Sun Chi's memorial, giving information about the plot.)

Since Venus disappeared first on Aug. 3, Liu Hsin[1a]'s proposal to delay could only have been made during the last three days of the seventh month, i.e., Aug. 3, 4, or 5. Sun Chi hence was persuaded by his wife and brother-in-law to reveal the plot on the same or the next day after that on which he was taken into Tung Chung[1b]'s confidence and acted immediately. This inference is confirmed by the circumstance that only by revealing such a plot immediately that he knew of it could Sung Chi have escaped implicating himself in the plot. It is thus not surprising that the conspirators did not suspect they had been betrayed and obeyed Wang Mang's order to come to the Palace.

[Wang] Mang ordered Tai Yün to interrogate them under torture, and all confessed. Palace Attendants Within the Yellow Gate, all with swords

**23b** drawn, conducted [Tung] Chung₁ᵦ and the others to an antechamber. [Tung] Chung₁ᵦ drew his sword with the intention of cutting his own throat. A Palace Attendant, Wang Wang, reported that the

**28b** Commander-in-chief, [Tung Chung₁ᵦ], had rebelled. [The Palace Attendants Within] the Yellow Gate had drawn their swords, and jointly fought with and

Tung killed [Tung Chung₁ᵦ. The people in] the inner [pal-

Chung ace] apartments frightened one another by the report

Killed that troops under a command would arrive. [The Gentlemen] in the Gentlemen's quarters all drew their swords and cocked their crossbows. The General of a New Beginning,²³·⁴ Shih Shen, visited the various quarters and informed the Gentlemen and officials, saying, "The Commander-in-chief, [Tung Chung₁ᵦ], had [a spell] of insanity come upon him;

*22b* he has already been executed. All are ordered to unbend their weapons." [Wang] Mang wanted to repress any baneful influence, so had the [Gentlemen] As Rapid As Tigers use a sword for beheading horses²³·⁵ to cut off [Tung] Chung₁ᵦ's [head], put it in a bamboo vessel, and sent it about [the empire, with a label] saying, "A rebellious caitiff who has

---

²³·⁴ Previously (p. 20b), Shih Shen was made General of a Peaceful Beginning; Liu Feng-shih states that the text may be in error here; Wang Ming-shen thinks that the text should be emended. Lien Tan had been General of a New Beginning and had been killed in the winter of 22 A.D.; the title of General of a New Beginning seems to have been the higher title (cf. Glossary); possibly Shih Shen had been promoted. He is again noted with this title on p. 26b, so that I see no need to emend the text.

²³·⁵ Professor Duyvendak calls my attention to the mention of this sword in *HS* 67: 6a, b, where Chu Yün, in a memorial to Emperor Ch'eng, dated during the decade beginning 20 B.C., declares, "Your servant would be willing to be granted a sword for beheading horses from the Master of Recipes, to cut off the head of one flattering courtier, in order to stimulate the others." The name of this article, which seems originally to have been merely a large sword, accordingly acquired the connotation of an article specially used to behead flatterers.

虜出下書敕大司馬官屬吏士為忠所

註誤謀反未發覺者收忠宗族呂醇醢

毒藥尺白刀叢棘并一坎而埋之劉歆

王涉皆自殺莽曰二人骨肉舊臣惡其

left [his office]."

[Wang Mang] issued a message of amnesty to the officers and soldiers belonging to the office of the Commander-in-chief, who had been led into error by [Tung] Chung[1b], had plotted to rebel, and had not yet been discovered. He had the clan and relatives of Tung Chung[1b] arrested, and buried them together in one pit with strong vinegar, poisonous drugs, foot-[long] naked two-edged blades,[23.6] and a thicket of thorns.[23.7]

Liu Hsin[1a] and Wang Shê both committed suicide. [Wang] Mang considered that [one] of these two persons was [of the same] flesh and blood [as himself and the other was] a minister [who had been in office] for a long [time, so,] because [Wang Mang] disliked [it to be known] that these [persons] within

Liu Hsin Executed

[23.6] Professor Duyvendak suggests emending *ch'ih-po₁-ren* 尺白刃 to *ch'ih-po₂* 尺帛, which latter Couvreur, *Dict. Class.*, defines as short for *san* 三 *-ch'ih po₂-ch'ou* 綢, the cord granted by the throne to erring officials by which to strangle themselves. While this emendation is attractive and has the advantage of not breaking the rhythm of two-word phrases, the phrase *ch'ih-po₂* does not seem to have been used in ancient times, nor can I find any ancient example of this practise. *Ch'ih-po₂* is moreover used in *Chan-kuo-ts'e*, ch. 20, sect. 14 ("Szu-pu Pei-yao" ed., 20: 11a; "Szu-k'u Ts'ung-k'an" ed., 6: 74b) and denoted "a foot of silk cloth," used for making a cap, which meaning is clearly unsuitable here. Professor Duyvendak also suggests rendering *ch'ih* separately by "footrule," perhaps in the sense of the footrule used to bastonnade criminals. He doubts the whole passage.

In Han times, the requirements of parallelism and rhythm were not yet strict, so that a three-character phrase might be allowed to occur along with a series of two-character phrases. *Ch'ih* is used in various compounds to denote a "one-foot long" article; cf. *Tz'u-hai sub ch'ih*. *Ch'ih-tao* 刀 is used in *HS* 54: 12b¹⁰. This phrase still denotes a dagger. *Po₁-ren* is used in the *Doctrine of the Mean*, ix (Legge, p. 389). *Ch'ih-po₁-ren* represents merely the combination of these two anciently well-known phrases.

The ancient Chinese sword was three feet long; cf. *HFHD* I, 142 & n. 3. Since the ancient Chinese conceived ghosts as quite small beings, dagger-blades would naturally be sufficient to put into a grave with the bodies of dangerous criminals, along with poisonous drugs and thorns, in order to prevent their ghosts from rising. For a parallel to the magical use of vinegar, cf. *HS* 100 A: 14b & n. 14.5 (in the Preliminary Volume).

[23.7] The Ching-yu ed., the Southern Academy ed., and the Official ed. read 棘 instead of 棗, which reading I adopt. The phrase "thicket of thorns" is from *Book of Changes*, Hex. 29, 6; Legge, p. 119; cf. also *HS* 45: 18b. For the use of thorns, cf. *HS* 97 B: 19b.

[the court] had been infected [with evil], he kept their execution secret. Because moreover the Marquis of Yi-and-Hsiu, [Liu] Tieh, had constantly been circumspect and [Liu] Hsin₁ₐ had finally not informed [Liu Tieh of the plot], he was merely dismissed [from his posts as] Palace Attendant and General of the Gentlemen-at-the-Palace, and was changed to be a Palace Grandee Without Specified Appointment.

**Liu Hsin's Ghost Appears.**
**29a**
**24a**

A day later, in the [Palace] Hall, beside the palm [of the hand] of the immortal on the hill of earth [in the park under the charge of] the Intendant of the Imperial Palace Parks,²³·⁸ there was a white-headed old man in cerulean clothes. The Gentlemen and officials who saw it said privately that it was the State Master and Highest Minister, [Liu Hsin₁ₐ].

The Marquis of Vast Merit, [Wang] Hsi₃ₐ, was usually good with the hexagrams, [so Wang] Mang had him to interpret its divination. He said, "One should be careful about weapons and fire."²⁴·¹

---

²³·⁸ Mr. Cheng (fl. dur. 220–317) glosses, "The immortal held in his palm a vessel for receiving dew." Professor Duyvendak calls attention to the fact that *HS* 25 A: 25a mentions "the bronze pillar and the immortal's palm for receiving dew [on] the Po-liang [Tower]" (q.v. in Glossary) made at the order of Emperor Wu about 120 B.C. Su Lin glosses, "The immortal held in the palm of his hand an uplifted basin to receive sweet dew." The Po-liang Tower however burnt down in 104 B.C., so that in Wang Mang's time this was another statue. The *San-fu Ku-shih* (iii–v cent.; lost) is quoted by Yen Shih-ku as saying, "The basin for receiving dew in the Chien-chang Palace was 200 feet high [the hight of the Po-liang Tower; the *San-fu Ku-shih* seems to have confused the location] and seven spans in circumference. It was made of bronze. Above it there was an immortal's palm to receive dew, which [latter] was mixed with jade powder and drunk [as an elixir of immortality]." This tradition was derived largely from some lines in Chang Heng's (78–139) "*Fu* on the Western Capital" (in *Wen-hsüan* 2: 15b), which refer to the immortal's palm on the Po-liang Tower (this passage was quoted in the *San-fu Ku-shih* passage):

"He set upon a stalk [referring to the Tower] an immortal's palm
　For receiving the pure dew from the tips of the clouds,
[Which, with] fine jade powder, was used for a morning drink at the con-
　clusion of the meal,
　　[So that the Emperor] would certainly be able to transfer his life [from this
　　world to the next, i.e., become an immortal]."

²⁴·¹ Professor Duyvendak remarks that fire is the power or element of the Han dy-

小兒安得此左道是迊子
我也莽軍師外破大臣內之皇祖叔父子僑欲來迎
哞左右亡所信不能復遠

[Wang] Mang replied, "How did you, boy, get this erroneous explanation? This is indeed my august ancestor's younger uncle, [Wang] Tzu-ch'iao, who has wanted to come and invite me [to become an immortal]."

When, outside [the court, Wang] Mang's armies had been routed and, inside [the court], his greatest ministers had rebelled, so that none of those about him could be trusted, he could no longer deliberate [with them] about matters at a distance in the com-

Wang Yi Made Heir-Apparent

nasty. But red was not *officially* adopted as the color of the Han dynasty until A.D. 26 (Teng Chan, fl. ca. 208, in a note to *HS* 25 B: 23b).

In the time of Emperor Kao down to the time of Emperor Wen, the Han dynasty was supposed to have succeeded to the virtue of the Ch'in dynasty, whose virtue was the element water. Its color, black, is however nowhere said to have been adopted. However, down to the end of the Former Han period, Palace Attendants wore black sables (*HS* 98: 15a).

Kung-sun Ch'en and Chia Yi argued that because earth overcomes water, the Han dynasty's virtue was earth, whose color is yellow. The appearance of a yellow dragon at Ch'eng-chi in 165 B.C. caused the dismissal of Chang Ts'ang, who upheld the theory that water was the Han dynasty's virtue. Yellow was not however adopted as the official Han color until 104 B.C. (*HS* 6: 31b).

Liu Hsiang and Liu Hsin[1a] later argued that the order of the powers (and consequently the succession of the dynasties) was not to be considered as that in which one overcomes the other 相勝, but rather that in which they produced each other 相生, since the ancient (legendary) rulers did not conquer their predecessors, but each one yielded to and resigned in favor of his successor. This theory was supported by verses in *Book of Changes*, App. V, 8, 9 (Legge, 425; in the "Explanation to the Trigrams," a section which was "discovered" during 73–49 B.C.) and so became widely accepted. According to this theory, the virtue of the Han dynasty was that of fire, whose color is red. The Ch'in dynasty was not given any virtue in this succession of powers, merely being counted as an intercalary dynasty, with the intercalary virtue of water, placed between the rule of the virtues wood (the Chou dynasty) and fire (the Han dynasty). The brevity of the Ch'in period was accounted for by the fact that it had no real virtue, only an apparent virtue. Wang Mang and his time (including Pan Piao) accepted this theory, hence thought of the Han dynasty's virtue as being fire and its color as being red, although that view was not officially adopted until the Later Han period under Emperor Kuang-wu. The story of the Eminent Founder having killed the snake (*HFHD* I, 34–36) clinched the acceptance of this theory. But it was probably invented in the first century B.C., so that it was interpolated into the *SC* (*Mh* II, 331). Cf. *HS* 25 B: 23b; Ku Chieh-kang in *Ku-shih-pien* V, 423–500, 560–636.

For Wang Tzu-ch'iao, cf. Glossary, *s.v.*

manderies and kingdoms.  When he wanted to summon [Wang] Yi₅ and make plans with him, Ts'ui Fa said, "[Wang] Yi₅ is habitually cautious.  Now that *23a* he has lost a large force, if he is summoned, I fear that he will grasp his credentials and commit suicide. It would be proper that you should in some great manner console his feelings."  Thereupon [Wang] Mang sent [Ts'ui] Fa in a galloping quadriga with verbal instructions for [Wang] Yi₅, [saying], "I am aged and have no[24.2] son by my legitimate wives.  I wish to transmit the empire to you, Yi.  It is ordered that you shall not need to beg pardon [for your defeat] and when I receive you in audience you shall not again speak [of the past]."

[When Wang] Yi₅ arrived, he was made the Commander-in-chief.  The Grand Prolonger of Autumn, Chang₂ Han, became the Grand Minister Over the Masses.  Ts'ui Fa became the Grand Minister of Works.  The Director of the Palaces and Shelterer *29b* of Long Life, Miao Hsin, became the State Master. The Marquis of Like Delight, [Wang] Lin₂, became the General of the Guard.

[Wang] Mang was so distressed and worried that he could not eat.  He only drank wine, ate shellfish,[24.3] and read books on military matters.  When he was tired, he would rest [his head] upon his stool and sleep without again seeking his pillow.

*Magical Defenses*  By nature, [Wang Mang] loved the numerology of lucky times and days.[24.4]  When moreover matters

---

[24.2] The Official ed. has emended 毋 to 無.

[24.3] Ts'ao Ts'ao also liked to eat shellfish.  Su Shih (1036–1101), in his "Shellfish Song (*Fu-yü Hsing*)" (in the *Tung-p'o Hsien-sheng Shih-chi-chu* 30: 33b) has the apt couplet,
> "Two strong men who alike robbed the Han dynasty
> In what they liked were also shoulder to shoulder."
(Reference from Wang Hsien-ch'ien).

[24.4] The phrase *hsiao-shu* 小數 is also used in *HS* 30: 40a, which says, "But when those who restricted themselves to [the school of Yin and Yang] concerned themselves with [this subject], they tied themselves to prohibitions and abstentions, and became mired in numerology (*hsiao-shu*)."

食豈飲酒嗜鰒魚讀軍書倦因馮几寐不復就枕性好時日小數及
發為大司空司中壽容苗訢為國師同說俟林為衛將軍莽憂憑不能
天下救亡得謝見勿復道邑到呂為大司馬大長秋張邯為大司徒在
決宜有呂大慰其意於是莽遣發馳傳諭邑我年老毋適子欲傳邑呂
念郡國欲謀邑與計議崔發曰邑素小心今失大眾而徵恐其執節引

事迫急宣為厭勝遣使壞渭陵延陵園門景惡曰
毋使民復思也又曰墨涔色其周垣號將至曰歲
宿中水為助將軍右庚刻木校尉前丙耀金都尉
又曰執大斧伐枯木流大水滅發火如此屬不可

became urgent, he merely repressed them by incantations. He sent a commissioner to destroy the screening walls at the gates to the parks of the Wei Tomb and the Yen Tomb, saying, "Do not cause the common people to think of the Han [Dynasty] again."[24.5] **24b** He also used black to defile the color of their surrounding walls.[24.6] He entitled his generals,[24.7] "The general for whom [the planet] Jupiter rests in [the cyclical sign] *shen* and [the element] water is an assistant,"[24.8] "the Colonel who honors [the cyclical sign] *keng* and injures [the element] wood,"[24.9] and "the Chief Commandant who sets [the cyclical sign] *ping* in front and glorifies [the element] metal."[24.10] He also [gave titles] reading, "[The military leader] holding a great axe to chop down withered wood," [and, "The military leader] causing great waters to run, extinguishing any fire that has arisen."[24.11] The things of this sort [that he did and said are too many] to be recorded completely.

[24.5] A magical play on words. 復思 "think again" was another writing for 罘罳, "screening wall"; cf. *HFHD*, I, 250, n. 3.
Wang Nien-sun points out that after 思 there has dropped out the word 漢, which is still read in *T'ai-p'ing Yü-lan* 89: 11b & 185: 8a, *Han-chi* 30: 19a, and *Shui-ching Chu* 16: 17b, *sub* the Ku River.

[24.6] Prof. Duyvendak remarks that this blackening of the walls was to remove the red color of the Han dynasty.

[24.7] Chou Shou-ch'ang says that a Sung ed. in small characters (xii or xiii cent.) reads 軍 for 至. The Southern Academy ed. also has this good reading. The Ching-yu ed. reads the latter.

[24.8] This seems to be one of the first times the cyclical characters were used to denote a year. But A.D. 24, not A.D. 23, has the cyclical character *shen*. Professor Duyvendak remarks that *shen* corresponds to the power metal, so that the emphasis was upon the power, rather than upon the year.

[24.9] Professor Duyvendak points out that *keng* also corresponds to the power metal.

[24.10] Professor Duyvendak remarks that *ping* corresponds to the power fire, the Han dynasty's virtue.

[24.11] Professor Duyvendak notes that "axe" is also metal and that "fire" denotes the Han dynasty. The emphasis throughout these titles is on the power metal, which was believed to govern the sending out and movements of the imperial army, the punishment of rebels and traitors, and the ending of violence and disturbance; cf. *HS* 27 A: 17b; W. Eberhard, "Beiträge zur kosmologischen Spekulation der Chinesen der Han-Zeit," p. 19.

Autumn

In the autumn, Venus moved into [the constellation] T'ai-wei, and lighted the earth like the light of the moon.[24.12]

Rebellion
in the
West
*23b*

*30a*

Wei Ts'ui and his elder brother, [Wei Yi, men from] Ch'eng-chi, together kidnapped the Grand Governor [of T'ien-shui Commandery], Li Yü[5a]. They made their elder brother's son, Wei Ao, their General-in-chief, and attacked and killed the Shepherd of Yung Province, Ch'en Ch'ing, and the Director of a Confederation at An-ting [Commandery], Wang Hsün[1],[24.13] and joined his force [with their own]. They sent a letter to the commanderies and counties enumerating [Wang] Mang's crimes and wickednesses, [saying that they were] ten thousand [times the number of those committed by] Chieh and Chou.[24.14]

Attack
from the
South

In this month, Teng Yeh and Yü K'uang, men from [the prefecture of] Hsi[5], raised troops at Nan-hsiang [to the number of] more than a hundred men. At that time, the Ruler of Hsi[5] led several thousand troops and garrisoned the Ch'iao Commune to defend the Wu Pass.   [Teng] Yeh and [Yü] K'uang said to

勝記秋太白星流入太微熛地如月光成紀隗崔
兄弟共劫大尹李育呂兄子隗囂為大將軍攻殺
雍州牧陳慶安定卒正王旬并其眾移書郡縣數
恭罪惡萬於桀紂是月析人鄧曄于匡起兵南鄉
百餘人時析宰將兵數千屯鄚亭備武闗嘩匡謂

---

[24.12] *HHS*, Tr. 10: 5a, b lists this circumstance and interprets it, "Venus carries out military deeds; [the constellation] T'ai-wei is the court of Heaven.  Venus was victorious and went north, entering T'ai-wei—this [circumstance] is the general-in-chief entering the court of the Son of Heaven."

The first star of T'ai-wei, $\delta$ Leo, was then in R.A. 141°; Venus reached this R.A. on the evening of July 4 and again on Sept. 29, according to calculation by the tables in C. Schoch, *Planeten-Tafeln für Jederman*.  At that time it had attained a declination of 13.9° north of the equator, confirming the phrase "went north."  It had a magnitude of −4.2—so bright that it could easily be seen in daytime by anyone who knew where to look for it, hence it is not surprising that it was said to have lighted the earth like the moon.  "Autumn" began with the first day of the seventh month, which was Aug. 6 of this year, so that "autumn" is confirmed.  Venus was again in T'ai-wei when Wang Mang was killed and with an even greater brilliance—it is not surprising that this apt astrological interpretation should have made an impression.

[24.13] *HHS*, Mem. 3: 4b names this man, "the Grand Governor of An-ting [Commandery], Wang Hsiang 向."

[24.14] This letter is quoted in *HHS*, Mem. 3: 2a–4b.  Cf. Glossary *sub* Wei Hsiao.

456

the Ruler, "An Emperor of the Liu [clan] has already been set up. Why do you, sir, not recognize the mandate [of Heaven]?" The Ruler [thereupon] begged [permission] to surrender, [and so Teng Yen and Yü K'uang] secured all of his band.

[Teng] Yeh called himself the General of the Left Supporting the Han [Dynasty] and [Yü] K'uang [called himself] the General of the Right [Supporting the Han Dynasty]. They took Hsi₅ and Tan-shui by storm. When they attacked the Wu Pass, the Chief Commandant [of the Pass], Chu Meng, sur-    **25a**
rendered. They advanced and attacked the Western Neighboring Commandery Grandee, Sung Kang, and killed him. Then they went west and took Hu₂ by storm.

[When Wang] Mang was all the more worried and did not know what to do, Ts'ui Fa said, "[According to] the *Chou Offices* and *Mr. Tso's [Commentary on] the Spring and Autumn*, whenever a state has a great visitation, [the ruler] should weep, in order to repress [the evil].²⁵·¹ Hence the *Book of Changes* says, 'He at first wails and cries out, but later laughs.'²⁵·²    It    **30b**
would be proper to cry out and sigh, in giving information to Heaven, in order to seek for rescue."

[Wang] Mang himself knew that he would be defeated, but he led his courtiers to the Southern Place

---

²⁵·¹ *Tso-chuan*, Dk. Hsüan, XII, (Legge, p. 311, 316), says, "When the Viscount of Ch'u had besieged Cheng to the seventeenth day, the people of Cheng divined by the tortoise whether they should end their struggle, [and the reply] was unfavorable. Then they divined by the tortoise whether they should lament in the Grand [Ancestral] Temple and set out their chariots in the streets, [and the reply] was favorable, so the people of the state held a great lamentation and the defenders of the parapets all wept." *Ibid.*, Dk. Chao, XXI, (Legge, 686¹¹, 689) records that in the state of Lu, Shu Ch'ê wept for the eclipse of the sun in 520 B.C.

*Chou-li* 26: 6b, *sub* the Female Shaman (*nü-wu*) (Biot, II, 104) says, "Whenever in the country there is a great visitation, [the Female Shamans] sing and weep in order to beg [the divinities]," and Cheng Hsüan explains, "Some sing and some weep. They hope to move the gods in heaven and earth to pity."

²⁵·² *Book of Changes*, Hex. 13, 5 (Legge, p. 86; Wilhelm, I, 42).

陳其符命本末仰天曰皇天既命授臣莽何不殄滅眾賊即令

臣莽非是願下雷霆誅臣莽因搏心大哭氣盡伏而叩頭又作

告天策自陳功勞千餘言諸生小民會旦夕哭為設餐粥甚悲

哀及能誦策文者除曰為郎至五千餘人重澤將領之萃拜將

軍九人皆曰虎為號號曰九虎將北軍精兵數萬人束內其妻

子宮中曰為質時省中黃金萬斤者為一匱尚有六十匱黃門

24a
Wang
Mang
Appeals
to the
Gods and
Weeps.

for the Suburban Sacrifice [to Heaven], set out his mandates [by means of] portents from first to last, looked up to Heaven, and said, "Since thou, August Heaven, hast given thy mandate to thy subject, Mang, why doest thou not immediately order extirpated the bands [of troops] and the robbers? But if thy servant Mang has done wrong, I wish that thou wouldst send down thy thunderbolt to execute thy servant Mang." Thereupon he struck his heart with his palm and wept loudly. When his breath was exhausted, he prostrated himself and knocked his head [upon the ground].

He also composed a document giving information to Heaven, setting out his own important achievements, in more than a thousand words. The various Masters and uninfluential common people met in the mornings and evenings to weep, and for them he established repasts of congee. Those who were [really] melancholy, together with those who were able to recite the words of his document, were made Gentlemen.[25.3] [They numbered] more than five thousand persons. Tai Yün led them.

[Wang] Mang installed nine persons as Generals, all of whom had "tiger" as their title. They were called the Nine Tiger [Generals]. They led several ten-thousand picked soldiers from the Northern Army and went eastwards. Their wives and children were taken into the palaces, to serve as hostages.

His
Stinginess
and
Wealth

At this time, in the inner apartments [of the Wei-yang Palace], ten thousand catties of actual gold were put into one chest and there still remained sixty chests.[25.4] In each of [the offices] of the Yellow

[25.3] *Han-chi* 30: 19a says that these persons were entitled Crying and Sighing Gentlemen 呼嗟郎.

[25.4] Gold was cast into square cake-shaped ingots an inch on a side, weighing a catty (24 B: 1b) and worth ten thousand cash. At 244 g. per catty (*HFHD*, I, 280) a chest contained 2,440,000 grams or 78,448 oz. troy, worth, at present prices, U. S. $2,745,680. Sixty chests, if full, contained 146,400,000 g. or 4,706,880 oz. troy. With this huge treasure may be compared the amount of gold brought to Spain from the Americas between 1503 and 1660, which E. J. Hamilton (*American Treasure and the Price Revolution in Spain*, p. 42) finds to have been 181,333,180 g., or 5,829,996 oz. troy. For the reliability of this statement, cf. App. II, p. 479ff.

作姑破其一部北出九虎後擊之六虎敗走史熊王況詣闕

匡持數千弩乘堆挑戰鄧曄將二萬餘人從閿鄉南出棗街

錢眾重怨無鬭意九虎至華陰回谿距隘北從河南至山于

平準邴矜藏錢帛珠玉財物甚眾莽愈愛之賜九虎士人四千

鈞盾藏府中尚方處度各有數匡長樂御府中御府及都內

Gate and of the Intendant of Palace Parks in the storehouses, and [in the workshop of] the Empress's Master of Recipes, there were [also] several chests. In the Imperial Wardrobe at the Ch'ang-lo [Palace], the Empress's Wardrobe and the storehouses of the [Bureau of] Equalization and Standards in the capital[25.5] there was [in addition] very much cash, silk, pearls, jade, and valuables. [Wang] Mang became [even] more parsimonious with them, and granted [only] four thousand cash to each of the soldiers of the Nine Tiger [Generals].[25.6] Their troops were greatly discontented, so that they had no intention of fighting.    **25b** 31a

The Nine Tiger [Generals] reached the Hui Gorge at Hua-yin and blocked the defiles to the north along the [Yellow] River and south to the mountains. Yü K'uang, with several thousand crossbow [men], mounted the [Feng-ling] mound to provoke a battle. Teng Yeh, leading more than twenty thousand men, went south from Wen-hsiang Highroad and came out of the Tsao-[hsiang] Highroad and the Tso-ku [River valley], routed one division [of soldiers], went north, came out behind the Nine Tiger [Generals], and attacked them. Six Tiger [Generals] were defeated and fled. [Of these six], Shih Hsiung and Wang K'uang[4a] came to the [Palace] portal [and asked for pardon and permission] to return home to die.[25.7]    Kuan-chung Invaded    *24b*

25.5 Yen Shih-ku remarks that the Imperial treasury was under the Privy Treasurer. The Empress was called the Inner Palace; cf. Glossary *sub voce*. Yen Shih-ku explains, "The 中御府 was the treasury of the Empress."

The Bureau of Equalization was under the Grand Minister of Agriculture (the state treasurer), called by Wang Mang the Communicator.

25.6 Contrast the thousand catties of actual gold given to Tou Jung a little later under similar circumstances, probably at the solicitation of Wang Yi[5]; cf. *HHS*, Mem. 13: 1b.

25.7 For this phrase, cf. *Tso-chuan*, Dk. Hsiang, III, (Legge, 419[5], 420b); *HHS*, Mem.

[Wang] Mang sent a messenger to reproach [them, saying], "How is it that those who should be dead are [still] alive?" so they both committed suicide. Four [defeated] Tiger [Generals] fled. Three Tiger [Generals], Kuo Ch'in<sub>b</sub>, Ch'en Hui, and Ch'eng Chung, collected the scattered troops and took refuge in the Capital Granary.

26a  Teng Yeh opened the Wu Pass and invited in Li Sung, the Han [dynasty's] Director of Service to the Lieutenant Chancellor. He led more than two thou-
31b  sand men and came to Hu<sub>2</sub>. With [Teng] Yeh and the others, they together attacked the Capital Granary.

When it did not surrender, [Teng] Yeh made a Division Head of Hung-nung [Commandery], Wang Hsien<sub>4</sub>, his Colonel. [The latter] led several hundred men north, crossed the Wei [River], and entered the territory of Tso-p'ing-yi [Commandery], making cities surrender and overrunning territory. Li Sung sent a Lieutenant General, Han Ch'en, and others, to go across westwards to Hsin-feng, where [Han Ch'en] fought a battle with [Wang] Mang's General of the Po River, [Tou Jung. The General of] the Po River fled.²⁶·¹

Another
Defeat

Han Ch'en and the others pursued the fleeing [troops], and so they came to Ch'ang-men.²⁶·² Wang Hsien<sub>4</sub> went north to P'in-yang, and wherever he passed, [the people came out] to welcome him and

波水將軍戰波水走韓臣等追奔逐至長門宮王憲北至頻陽所過
渭入左馮翊界降城略地李松遣偏將軍韓臣等徑西至新豐與苯
與曄等共攻京師倉未下曄曰弘農椽王憲為校尉將將數百人北度
故卒保京師倉鄧曄開武關迎漢丞相司直李松將二千餘人至湖
歸死苯使使責死者安在皆自殺其回虎亡三虎郭欽陳翬成重收

5: 2a⁹.

²⁶·¹ According to *HHS*, Mem. 13: 1b, Tou Jung had been installed as General of the Po River and was stationed at Hsing-feng. Ch'ien Ta-hsin remarks that when Pan Ku was preparing his *History*, the Tou clan was very powerful, hence he did not mention this name. Cf. Glossary, *sub* Tou Jung.

²⁶·² The present text reads, "Ch'ang-men Palace." But this Palace was inside the city of Ch'ang-an (cf. Glossary *sub* Ch'ang-men). There was a place by the name of Ch'ang-men near Ch'ang-an, but nothing is said of any palace located there; *HHS*, Tr. 10: 5b, in quoting this passage, omits the word for "Palace." This word seems to have been an interpolation made by someone who knew about the Palace and did not know the place-name.

使者分敕城中諸獄囚徒皆校兵授兵孫飲其血與誓曰有不為新室

城下聞天水隗氏兵方到皆爭欲先入城貪立大功囷掠之利莽遣

安城當須更始帝大兵到即引軍至華陰治攻具而長安兵四會

千人假號稱漢將時李松鄧曄呂為京師小小倉尚未可下何況長

藍田王孟槐里汝臣盩厔王扶陽陵厳本杜陵厓門少之屬泉皆數

迎降大姓櫟陽申碭下邽王大皆率眾隨憲屬縣鄠春茂陵董喜

surrender. [People] of the powerful clans, Shen Tang of Yüeh-yang and Wang Ta of Hsia-kuei, both led their bands to follow [Wang] Hsien₄. From counties in [the capital commanderies], Chuang Ch'un from T'ai, Tung Hsi from Mou-ling, Wang Meng₄ᵦ from Lan-t'ien, Ju Ch'en from Huai-li, Wang Fu₂ᵦ from Chou-chih, Chuang Pen from Yang-ling, T'u-men Shao from Tu-ling, and the like, whose bands all [numbered] several thousand men, took titles and called themselves Generals of the Han [dynasty].

At this time, Li Sung and Teng Yeh considered that although the Capital Granary was a very small [place], if they had not yet been able to make it surrender, how much more [this would be the case with] the city of Ch'ang-an, so that it would be necessary for them to wait until the great army of the Keng-shih Emperor arrived [before attacking Ch'ang-an]. When they thereupon led their armies to Hua-yin to prepare implements for attacking [Ch'ang-an], troops from [places] neighboring Ch'ang-an however assembled from all quarters below the [Ch'ang-an] city walls. It was reported that the troops of the Wei clan from T'ien-shui [Commandery][26.3] would presently arrive, so they all rivaled [one another], wanting to be the first to enter the city, for they were covetous of the profit [they would gain by] achieving the great glory [of executing Wang Mang] and from kidnapping and plundering [in the palaces].

[Wang] Mang sent commissioners separately to amnesty the convicts in the various prisons within the city and gave them all arms. [The commissioners had] some swine killed, and had [the former convicts] drink the blood [of the swine, thereby] making an oath with them, saying, "If there is

The Kuan-chung People Welcome the Invaders.

25a

32a

Ch'ang-an Attacked

26b
A Convict Army Flees.

[26.3] Wei Ao and his followers, among whom were Pan Piao and Pan Ku; cf. HHS, Mem. 30 A: 1a. They had then taken An-ting Commandery, just over the border in the present Kansu, on the upper reaches of the Ching River; cf. HHS, Mem. 3: 4b.

anyone who is not for the House of Hsin, may the gods of the soils and the spirits remember it." The General of a New Beginning, Shih Shen, led them. They crossed the Wei [River] Bridge and all scattered and ran, [so that Shih] Shen returned empty-[handed].

The Hsin Tombs Opened and its Temples Destroyed

The bands of troops dug up the tomb-mounds of [Wang] Mang's wife, sons, father, and grandfather, and burnt their coffins and grave-vaults, together with his Nine [Ancestral] Temples, the *Ming-t'ang*, and the *Pi-yung*. The fire shone into the city.

Someone said to [Wang] Mang, "The soldiers at the city gates are people from the east, so that they cannot be trusted." [Wang] Mang [accordingly] changed them and mobilized men from the Picked Cavalry to be the guards [for the city gates], establishing one Colonel at each Gate with six hundred men.

Oct. 4
Ch'ang-an Entered

In the tenth month, on [the day] *mou-shen*, the first day of the month, the troops entered by way of the Hsüan-p'ing City Gate, which among the common people is called the Capital Gate. Chang₂ Han was inspecting the city gates, happened upon the troops, and was killed. Wang Yi₅, Wang Lin₂, Wang Hsün₂, Tai Yün, and others separately led troops to

32b

resist the attack outside the Northern Portal [of the Palace]. The Han troops were ambitious for enfeoffment [in reward for killing Wang] Mang and more than seven hundred of them fought strenuously. When it happened that the sun went down, [the people in] the government yamens, the lodges

25b

[for the commanderies and kingdoms], and the residences [adjoining the Palace] had all run away and fled.

Oct. 5
The Palace Set on Fire

On the second day [of the month, the day] *chi-yu*, some young people from within the city [of Ch'ang-an], Chu Ti, Chang Yü₂, and others, who had feared that they would be kidnapped or robbed, and had shouted vehemently in response to [the invaders],

者社鬼記之更始將軍史諶將度渭橋皆散走諶空還泉兵發掘莽妻

子父祖冢燒其棺椁及九廟明堂辟雍火照城中或謂莽曰城門辛東

方人不可信莽更發越騎士為衛門置六百人各一校尉十月戊申朔

兵從宣平城門入民間所謂都門也張邯行城門逢兵見殺王邑王林

王巡棻渾等分將兵距擊北闕下漢兵貪莽封力戰者七百餘人會日

莽官府邸第盡壞亡二日己酉城中少年朱弟張魚等恐見鹵掠趙謹

462

竝和燒作宣門㸃歌法聞謹曰反虜王莽何不出降

火及掖廷承明黃皇室主所居也莽避火宣室前殿

火輒隨之宮人婦女謼譁曰當奈何時莽紺袀服帶

重戴持虞帝匕首天文郎桉拭於前日時加其莽旋

set fire to the Artisans' Chamber Gate [an inner gate in the northwestern part of the Wei-yang Palace], and hacked open a side door of the [Hall] of Reverence for the Law, calling out,

"You rebellious caitiff, Wang Mang,
Why do you not come out and surrender?"[26.4]

The fire reached to the Ch'eng-ming [Hall] in the Lateral Courts, where the Princess of the Yellow Imperial House dwelt.   [Wang] Mang fled from the fire to the Hsüan Room, and the fire in the Front Hall immediately followed him.  The Palace Maids and women wailed, saying, "What must we do?"

At that time [Wang] Mang had on uniformly purple garments,[27.1] was girded with his imperial seals and apron and held the Lord of Yü, [Shun's], dagger with a spoon on the end of its hilt; an Astrological Gentleman held a diviner's board before him,[27.2] and for the day and hour he added [the appropriate] layout [on the board.  Wang] Mang had turned about

**27a**
**Magical**
**Defenses**

[26.4] There is a rime or assonance between the last words of these two lines: 莽, mang < mwâng < *mwâng, and 降, hsiang < yâng > *g'ông (Karlgren, *Gram. Serica*, #709a, 1015a).

[27.1] Yen Shih-ku explains, "*Kan* is a color that is a deep blue, showing a red [tinge] 紺深青而揚赤色也."  Dr. Duyvendak notes that purple is the color corresponding to the Pole Star, the imperial symbol.  *Mh* III, 340 gives the name "the Lilac Purple Palace (*tzu-kung* 紫宮)" to the four asterisms about the Pole Star.  The Supreme One, the divine ruler of the universe, has his regular habitation in the Pole Star (*Mh*, III, 339), so that the color of this area is appropriate to the human ruler of all under heaven.  *Kan* (deep purple) was a deeper purple than *tzu* (lilac purple).  By wearing the color of the Supreme One, Wang Mang was by sympathy attracting protection from this supreme power.

[27.2] The Official ed. has emended *an₁-shih₁* 桉拭 to *an₂-shih₂* 按栻.  Yen Shih-ku's comment reads, "A *shih₁* is what is used to divine the seasons and days," hence his text read *shih₂*.

*Chou-li* 26: 9a, *sub* the Grand Astrologer, (*T'ai-shih*) (Biot, II, 108 & n. 5), says, "When the great army [starts out, the Grand Astrologer] holds [the board for determining] Heaven's times, and [travels] in the same chariot as the Grand Master [of Music]."  Cheng Chung glosses, "When a great army starts out, then the Grand Astrologer has charge of holding the diviner's board, in order [to be able] to tell Heaven's times and to

his mat and sat according to [the position] of the handle to the [Heavenly] Bushel, saying, "Heaven begat the virtue that is in me. The Han troops—what can they do to me?"[27.3]

33a    For some time, [Wang] Mang had not eaten, which had lessened his energy, so that he had become exhausted. On the morning of the third day [of the

Oct. 6   month, the day] keng-hsü, when it was light, a group

Wang    of courtiers supported [Wang] Mang from the Front

Mang    Hall southwards down the Zanthoxylum Stairs, and

Flees to   westwards out of the White Tiger Gate. The Duke

The Tower  of Peace to [the House of] Hsin, Wang Yi₆, had

Bathed by  charge of the chariot and drove it outside the [Palace]

Water.    Gate. [Wang] Mang went in the chariot to the

27b    Tower Bathed [by Water], intending to rely upon the water of the pond [as a magical defence],[27.4] and planning to hold in his arms the mandates [given through] portents and majestic tou-[measures]. The

26a    ministers, Grandees, Palace Attendants, [Attendants of] the Yellow Gate, Gentlemen, and Royal Retinue, who were still more than a thousand persons, followed him.

Wang Yi₅ had been fighting day and night and was extremely fatigued; when his men had almost all been killed or wounded, they galloped into the Palace and, by a difficult and roundabout route, reached the

席隨斗柄而坐曰天生德於予漢兵其如予何莽時不食少
氣困矣三日庚戌晨旦明羣臣扶掖莽自前殿南下儌除西
出白虎門和新公王揖奉車待門外莽就車之漸臺欲阻池
水猶抱持符命威斗公卿大夫侍中黃門郎從官尚千餘人
隨之王邑晝夜戰罷極士死傷略盡馳入宮間關至漸臺見

determine whether they are lucky or unlucky." The bibliography in HS 30: 72a sub the school of the Five Powers, lists, "[Mr.] Hsien-men's Method [of Using] the Diviner's Board, in 20 rolls and [Mr.] Hsien-men's Divining Board, in 20 rolls." (For Hsien-men Tzu-kao, the immortal, cf. Mh II, 165, n. 1; III, 432, 436). The Ta-t'ang Liu-tien 14: 27b, sub the T'ai-p'u Ling, contains a description of the board used in T'ang times. It had the zodiacal constellations engraved on it. At the Wang Hsu Tomb and at the Painted Basket Tomb in Korea a set of Han divining boards were found; a photograph is found in Plate 6 to W. C. Rufus, "Korean Astronomy," in Trans. of Korea Br. Roy. As. Soc'y, vol. 26.

27.3 He made magical use of Confucius' saying in time of danger, "Heaven begat the virtue that is in me. Huan T'ui—what can he do to me?" Analects, VII, xxii.

27.4 Water, the element in the pond, puts out fire, the Han dynasty's element, represented by the attackers.

其子侍中睦解衣冠欲逃邑此之令還父子共守奔軍人入殿

中讙曰反虜王莽安在有美人出房曰在漸臺眾兵追之圍數

百重臺上亦弓弩與相射稍稍落去矢盡無日俊射短兵接王

邑父平憚王巡戰死莽入室下鋪時眾上臺王揖趙博苗

訢唐尊王盛中常侍王參等皆死臺上商人杜吳殺莽取其綬

Tower Bathed [By Water. When Wang Yi5] saw his son, the Palace Attendant, [Wang] Mu, taking off his robes and bonnet, with the intention of escaping, [Wang] Yi5 scolded him, ordering him to return, [so that the two], father and son, together defended [Wang] Mang.

When the men of the army entered the [Palace] Halls, they called out, "Where is the rebellious caitiff, Wang Mang?" and a Beauty came out of a room and said, "He is in the Tower Bathed [By Water]." The bands of soldiers pursued after him, and surrounded it several hundred deep. Those on the Tower also exchanged shots with them, using bows and crossbows, but gradually dropped out and left [off shooting]. When their arrows were exhausted, so that they had no way of returning shots, they met [the attackers] with their short weapons. Wang Yi5 and his son,[27.5] [Wang Mu], Tai Yün, and Wang Hsün2, died fighting, [whereupon Wang] Mang entered the room [on top of the Tower]. In the very late afternoon,[27.6] the bands of soldiers went up the tower. Wang Yi6, Chao Po, Miao Hsin, T'ang Tsunb, Wang Sheng, the Regular Palace Attendant Wang Ts'an, and others all died on top of the Tower. Tu Wu,[27.7] a man from [the prefecture of] Shang, killed [Wang] Mang and took his [seals][27.8] and cords. A Colonel

33b

Wang
Mang
Killed

[27.5] For 平, the Ching-yu ed., the Southern Academy ed., and the Official ed. read 子. Wang Yi5's father, Wang Shang, had died in 11 B.C.

[27.6] HS 26: 46b, in enumerating the periods of the day, lists the period hsia-pu 下鋪 as the period before sunset and after the period pu 鋪, which latter was about 3 to 5 p.m.

[27.7] The San-fu Chiu-shih (attributed to Wei Piao, d. A.D. 89; book lost) collected fragments, p. 15b, says, "A butcher, Tu Yü 虞, killed [Wang] Mang by his own hand." The Tung-kuan Han-chi (A.D. 58–225; book lost, fragments collected) 23: 4a also writes "Tu Yü." But HHS, Tr. 10: 5b, copying this sentence, says, "A man from Shang, Tu Wu 吳 killed [Wang] Mang." Chou Shou-ch'ang remarks that anciently wu and yü were interchanged. Shang was a place along the road through the Wu Pass to Ch'ang-an, so that this man probably came with the forces attacking the capital.

[27.8] The word "seals 璽" has probably dropped out before 綬. Previously (p. 27a), it is said that Wang Mang wore his seals; nowhere else is it said that anyone else secured the

from Tunghai [Commandery], Kung-pin Chiu, who had formerly been a [Gentleman] Dealing With the Rites, [a subordinate of] the Grand Messenger, saw [Tu] Wu and asked him where the owner of the seal-cords was. He replied, "In the room, in the north-east corner." [Kung-pin] Chiu recognized [Wang] Mang and cut off his head.[27.9] The men of the army cut [Wang] Mang's body to pieces. His members

**28a** and his flesh and bones were sliced and divided.[28.1] "Those who killed each other in the struggle [to secure parts of Wang Mang's body numbered] several tens of persons."[28.2] Kung-pin Chiu bore [Wang] Mang's head to Wang Hsien₄.

[Wang] Hsien₄ called himself a Han Generalissimo and the troops in the city, [numbering] several hun-

*26b* dred thousand [men], were all subordinate to him.
**Wang** He dwelt in the Eastern Palace, treated [the women
**Hsien's** in Wang] Mang's harem as his wives, rode in [Wang
**Fate** Mang's] carriages [and wore Wang Mang's] robes.
**Oct. 9** On the sixth day [of the month, the day] *kuei-ch'ou*, Li Sung and Teng Yeh entered Ch'ang-an. Generals Chao Meng and Shen-t'u Chien also arrived. Because Wang Hsien₄ had received the imperial seals and cords and had not immediately sent them [to the Keng-shih Emperor], had taken many

鄧曄入長安將軍趙萌中屠建亦至呂王憲得璽綬不輒上
數十萬皆屬馬舍東宮妻奔俊宮乘其車服六日癸丑李松
者數十人公賓就持莽首詣王憲憲自稱漢大將軍城中兵
北闕閒就識斬莽首軍人分裂莽身支節肌骨爭分牛相校
校尉東海公賓就故大行治禮見莽閒綬主所在曰室中西

imperial seals before they passed into the possession of Wang Hsien₄ (p. 28a). The seal-cords were threaded through the seals, so that it would be difficult to take the cords without also taking the seals.

[27.9] *Tung-kuan Han-chi* 23: 4a says, "Kung-pin Chiu secured his head and transmitted and took it to Yüan, [where the Keng-shih Emperor was], and was enfeoffed as the Marquis of Hua."

[28.1] Yen Shih-ku quotes the *San-fu Chiu-shih* (lost), as saying that *luan* 臠 is "to cut into a thousand pieces." Hsü Ling (507–583), in his "Letter to [the Northern Ch'i] Supervisor [of the Masters of Writing] Yang, [Tsun-yen]," in his works, *Hsü Hsiao-mu Chi* 4: 6a, says, "Wang Mang was mutilated by a thousand strokes." (Reference from Shen Ch'in-han.)

[28.2] This sentence is identical with the similar statement at the death of Hsiang Yü: cf. *SC* 7: 73 = *Mh* II, 320. It may have been a merely literary addition in Kung-pin Chiu's report of his deeds; cf. *HFHD*, III, 97.

新之嚴尤陳茂敗昆陽下走至沛郡譙自稱漢將召會吏民尤為稱說王
倉開莽死乃降更始義之皆封為侯太師王匡國將哀章降雒陽傳詣宛
九江連率貰萌皆守郡不降為漢兵所誅賞都大尹王欽及郭欽守京師
敦曰吾聞食人食者死其事拔劍自刺死及曹部監杜善陳定大尹沈意
切食其古莽楊州牧李聖守司命孔仁兵敗山東聖格死仁將其眾降已而
多挾宮女建天子鼓旗收斬之傳莽首詣更始縣宛市百姓共提擊之或

of the women in the palace, and had set up the drums
and flags of the Son of Heaven, he was arrested and
beheaded [for aspiring to the throne. Wang] Mang's    34a
head was transmitted to the Keng-shih Emperor and
was hung up in the market-place at Yüan. The
people all together picked up [things] and threw them
at it. Some cut out and ate his tongue.

     The troops of [Wang] Mang's Shepherd of Yang[28.3]    The Fate
Province, Li Sheng, and of the Director of Mandates    of Wang
[from the Five Majestic Principles], K'ung Jen, were    Mang's
defeated east of [the Kuan-chung] mountains. [Li]    Officials:
Sheng fought and was killed. [K'ung] Jen led his    Li Sheng
band and surrendered. Afterwards, he sighed and    K'ung Jen
said, "I have heard that he who eats another's food
must die in his service," so he drew his sword, stabbed
himself, and died. The Department Head and
Superintendant of a Division, Tu P'u, the Grand    Tu P'u
Governor of Ch'en-ting [Commandery], Shen Yi,    Shen Yi
and the Leader of a Combination at Chiu-chiang
[Commandery], Chia Meng, all moreover defended    **28b**
their commanderies, did not surrender, and were ex-    Chia Meng
ecuted by the Han troops. When the Grand Gov-
ernor of Shang-tu [Commandery], Wang Ch'in, and    Wang
Kuo Ch'in[b], who were defending the Capital Granary,    Ch'in
heard that [Wang] Mang was dead, they surrendered.    Kuo Ch'in
The Keng-shih [Emperor] [considered them] as
righteous, and enfeoffed them both as marquises.
The Grand Master, Wang K'uang[1a], and the State    Wang
General, Ai Chang, surrendered at Lo-yang. They    K'uang
were transported to Yüan, where they were beheaded.    Ai Chang

     After Chuang Yu and Ch'en Mou had been de-    Chuang Yu
feated below [the walls of] K'un-yang, they fled to    Ch'en Mou
Ch'iao in P'ei Commandery. They called them-
selves Han Generals and summoned and assembled
officials and common people. [Chuang] Yu gave
them an account, saying that Wang Mang had

---

[28.3] The Southern Academy ed. and Official ed. emend 楊 to the more correct 揚.
The Ching-yu ed. reads the former.

usurped the throne, that he would die at the time [allotted to him by] Heaven, and that the sage Han [dynasty] would revive again; [meanwhile Ch'en] Mou prostrated himself and wept. When they heard that the former Marquis of Chung-wu[b] [under] the Han [dynasty], Liu Sheng[5e], had collected a band in Ju-nan [Commandery] and was [going to be]entitled

**34b**
**27a**
by the imperial title, [Chuang] Yu and [Ch'en] Mou surrendered to him. He made [Chuang] Yu his Commander-in-chief and [Ch'en] Mou his Lieutenant Chancellor. [After] more than ten days, he was defeated [by the Keng-shih Emperor's Generalissimo, Liu Hsin[4a], and Chuang] Yu and [Ch'en] Mou

**Nov./**
**Dec.[28.4]**
both died.

The commanderies and counties all offered their cities [to the Keng-shih Emperor] and surrendered, so that the whole empire returned to the Han [dynasty].

**Ts'ui Fa**
Previously, Shen-t'u Chien had once served Ts'ui Fa [as a disciple, studying] the *Book of Odes*. When [Shen-t'u] Chien arrived, [Ts'ui] Fa surrendered to him, [but] later he again gave an [apologetic] account [of Wang Mang,[28.5] so Shen-t'u] Chien directed the Lieutenant Chancellor [of the Keng-shih Emperor], Liu Tz'u[4a], to behead [Ts'ui] Fa in order that he might accompany [his master, Wang Mang], in

**Shih Shen**
**Others**
death. Shih Shen, Wang Yen[2], Wang Lin[2], Wang Wu[2], and Chao Hung also surrendered but nevertheless were killed.

Previously those soldiers who had taken titles every one hoped to be enfeoffed as a marquis, [but] because Shen-t'u Chien had beheaded Wang Hsien[4] and also spread about [a report] that treacherous [persons from] the three capital commanderies had together

---

[28.4] Cf. *HHS*, Mem. 1: 3a.

[28.5] This apology was preserved; Emperor Kuang-wu had Yin Min 尹敏 rebut "a comparison written in behalf of Wang Mang by Ts'ui Fa"; *HHS*, Mem. 69 A: 10a. Cf. *HFHD*, III, 95–96.

輔黠共殺其主吏民惶恐屬縣屯聚建等不能下馳白更始二年

二月更始到長安下詔大赦非王莽子他皆除其罪故王氏宗族

得全三輔悉平更始都長安居樂宮府藏完具獨未央宮燒攻

莽三日死則案堵復故更始至歲餘政教不行明年夏赤眉樊崇

killed their lord, [Wang Mang], the officials and common people [of Ch'ang-an] became afraid and the counties subordinate [to Ch'ang-an] assembled [troops, hence Shen-t'u] Chien and the others were unable to make them surrender. He galloped and advised [the Keng-shih Emperor of the situation].

In [the period] Keng-shih, the second year, the second month, the Keng-shih [Emperor, Liu Hsüan₂ₐ Sheng-kung], reached Ch'ang-an. He issued an imperial edict [granting] a general amnesty, [stating that], except for the sons of Wang Mang, all others' crimes were expunged. Hence the [former imperial] Wang clan was able to be preserved and the three capital commanderies all became calm.

**II**
**A.D. 24**
**March**
**The Keng-shih Emperor Reaches Ch'ang-an**

The Keng-shih [Emperor] made Ch'ang-an his capital and lived in Ch'ang-lo Palace. The government repositories were all intact. Only the Wei-yang Palace had been burnt. After [Wang] Mang [had been attacked] for three days and he had died, [the people of the capital commanderies] had lived peacefully in their homes and [everything] was as previously.[29.1]

**29a**

After the Keng-shih [Emperor] had arrived for a year and more, his governmental instructions were no [longer] obeyed. In the next year, in the summer,[29.2] after the Red Eyebrows,[29.3] [led by] Fan Ch'ung and

**35a**
**III**
**A.D. 25**
**Summer**

[29.1] *Tung-kuan Han-chi* 23:2b states that after the Keng-shih Emperor reached Ch'ang-an, "the bells and drums, the women and eunuchs of the [imperial] apartments, the several thousand offices and yamens, and [the people of the various] wards were peacefully harmonious as formerly. The Keng-shih [Emperor] ascended [the throne] in the Front Hall [of the Wei-yang Palace]." Hence there was sufficient left of even the audience chamber in the Wei-yang Palace for the imperial throne to be set up in its former location.

[29.2] The Red Eyebrows entered Kuan-chung in Jan./Feb., A.D. 25, defeated the Keng-shih Emperor's generals in Feb./Mar. and Apr./May, set up Liu P'en-tzu as the Emperor in July/Aug., and entered Ch'ang-an in Oct./Nov. The Keng-shih Emperor fled and surrendered to them in Nov./Dec., upon the promise of a kingdom. He was probably murdered not long afterwards. Cf. Glossary, *sub* Fan Ch'ung & Liu Hsüan₂ₐ.

[29.3] A T'ang manuscript fragment of this chapter has been preserved, which consists of 2½ leaves, 38 columns of the passage at the end of this chapter. The words *shih*

The Red
Eyebrows
Capture
Ch'ang-an

others, a band of several hundred thousand men, had entered through the passes, [Fan Ch'ung and others] set up Liu P'en-tzu, giving him the imperial title, and attacked the Keng-shih [Emperor]. The Keng-shih [Emperor] surrendered to them.

　　　The Red Eyebrows thereupon burnt the palace-buildings, market-places, and wards in Ch'ang-an, and killed the Keng-shih [Emperor]. The common people starved and [even] ate others, so that the dead [numbered] several hundred thousand, Ch'ang-an became a waste, and inside the city walls there were no people going about.[29.4] The [imperial ancestral] temples, funerary parks, and tomb mounds were all dug up; only the Pa Tomb and the Tu Tomb were preserved intact.

*27b*

Aug. 5[29.5]
Emperor
Kuang-au
Enthroned

　　　In the sixth month, the Epochal Exemplar, [Emperor Kuang-wu], had ascended the throne, and thereafter the [imperial] ancestral temples and the mounds to the gods of the soils and grains were re-established [at Lo-yang], the empire was well governed and at peace.

The
Eulogy

　　　In eulogy we say: Wang Mang first arose [because he was one of] the maternal relatives [of Emperor

赞曰王莽始起外戚折節力行요名譽宗族稱孝師友
完六月世祖即位然後宗廟社稷復立天下乂安
萬長安為虛城中無人行宗廟園陵皆發掘唯霸陵杜陵
赤眉遂燒長安宮室市里害更始民飢餓相食死者數十
等衆數十萬人入關立劉盆子稱尊號攻更始更始降之

and *ming*, which were the personal name of the Grand Exemplar of the T'ang dynasty, Emperor Wen, (reigned 627–649), lack a stroke. This manuscript furthermore contains Yen Shih-ku's comments, hence it was written after 641, when Yen Shih-ku completed his work. The word Sung, the personal name for the Condescending Exemplar, (the Shun-tsung, reigned 805), is written correctly. In T'ang times, the names of the Eminent Founder and the Grand Exemplar and of the seven emperors immediately preceding the reigning emperor were tabooed, hence this manuscript was written some time in 641–804 or 860–907 A.D. A photographic reprint is published in vol. 4 of the *Ku-chi Ts'ung-ts'an*, under the editorship of Lo Cheng-yü. The other manuscripts in this volume are from the cave at Tun-huang, hence this one probably also came thence, although nothing is specially said to that effect. Its variant readings exhibit a tendency to improve the literary quality of the writing.

　　　In this manuscript, the word 眉 is regularly written 麋, which variant reading is now occasionally found in the *HHS*.

[29.4] The T'ang mss. interchanges the words 人行 to read 行人, a more literary reading.
[29.5] *HHS*, An. 1 A: 15b.

歸仁及其居位輔政成哀之際勤勞國家直道而行動見

稱迹豈所謂在家必聞在國必聞色取仁而行違者邪莽

阮不仁而有佞邪之材又乘四父歷世之權遭漢中微國

統三絕而太后壽考為之宗主玫得肆其姦慝呂成篡盜

之禍推迲言之亦天時非人力之致矣及其竊位南面處

Ch'eng].[29.6] He humbled himself and acted energetically, in order to seek for fame and reputation, so that his clan praised him as filial and his teachers and associates attributed benevolence to him.[29.7]

When he occupied [a high] position and acted as [chief] assistant in the government, [during] the time in [the reigns of Emperors] Ch'eng and Ai, he toiled **7 B.C.** diligently for the state and "pursued a straightforward course,"[29.8] [so that whenever he] acted, [his deeds] were reported in detail. Was he not [the sort of person] referred to [in the sayings, "Such a man] will certainly be heard of in his clan; he will certainly be heard of in his state," and "He assumes the appearance of benevolence, but his actions are contrary to it?"[29.9]

Since [Wang] Mang did not [possess] benevolence, **35b** but had a talent for flattery and evil and also took advantage of the power his four uncles, [Wang Feng, Wang Yin, Wang Shang₁b, and Wang Ken, had exercised for] successive generations,[29.10] and [because] it happened that the Han [dynasty] became weak in the midst [of its period] and the dynastic succession was thrice broken, so that in her old age the Empress **29b** Dowager [nee Wang] became the mistress of the [imperial] clan, hence [Wang Mang] was able to give free rein to his viciousness and thereby to bring to pass the calamity of his usurpation [of the throne]. If we speak of [the situation by] investigating it from this [aspect], it was[29.11] a time [set by] Heaven and not brought about by human effort.

When he had stolen the throne and faced south,

---

[29.6] In the T'ang mss., after the 戚, there are the words "支葉, an offshoot of."

[29.7] Cf. *HS* 99 A: 1b.

[29.8] A saying of Confucius, from *Analects* XV, xxiv, 2—high praise of Wang Mang indeed.

[29.9] Sayings of Confucius, from *Analects* XII, xx, 6, with minor changes.

[29.10] Instead of 歷世, the T'ang mss. reads 世業.

[29.11] After 亦, the T'ang mss. inserts the word 有.

so that he occupied [a position which] he should not
have seized, the influences[29.12] which would overthrow
[such a person] were more dangerous [in his case than
in the cases of] Chieh and Chou, yet [Wang] Mang
was tranquil and considered himself a second appearance of the Yellow [Lord] and Yü [Shun].   Then for
the first time he gave rein to his desires[29.13] and displayed his tyrannousness and deceitfulness, being
scornfully [hypocritical] towards Heaven[29.14] and
oppressive towards the common people, exhausting
28a   [the possibilities of] banefulness, and [attaining] the
limit of evil.   His poison diffused itself among all
Chinese and [his power of causing] disorder [even]
extended to the southern and northern barbarians,
but this did not yet satisfy his desires.

For this reason, [all] within the four seas[29.15] mur-
mured sadly and lost their joy in life.   Within and
outside [the country, people] were filled with resentment, [braves] far and near [the capital] all mobilized, his city-wall and moat was not defended, so
that his members were cut to pieces.   Thereupon he
caused the cities and towns of the empire to become
wastes, [while peoples'] grave mounds were [more-
over] dug into, so that he injured all living people, and
36a   his crimes reached [even] to rotten bones.

Of the rebellious ministers and evil sons and of the
unprincipled men who are recorded in books and
records, if we investigate the calamities [they pro-
duced] and the ruin [they wrought], there have not
been any as severe as [those produced by Wang]

---

[29.12] The T'ang mss. reads 勢 for 埶.

[29.13] In a note to *HHS*, Mem. 42: 2b[11], Li Hsien says, "*Tzu-hui* is an attitude of being
unwilling to heed the exhortations of others 恣睢自用之貌."

[29.14] An allusion to *Book of History*, I, iii, 11 (Legge, p. 24).   The reference is to the
Provider of Works of whom Yao says, "He appears to be respectful, [but he is actually]
scornful of Heaven."   The Han interpretation of this passage is found in *SC* 1: 29 =
MH I, 50.

[29.15] The T'ang mss. omits the words 四 and 之.

甚者也昔秦燔詩書曰立
私議莘誦六蓺呂文姦言
同歸殊塗俱用滅亡皆炕
龍絕氣非命之運紫色蠅

Mang. Anciently [the First Emperor of] the Ch'in [dynasty] burnt the *Books of Odes* and *of History* in order to establish his private proposals, while [Wang] Mang chanted the six canons in order to gloss over his wicked words. "They came to the same result but by different paths;"[29.16] both thereby [came to] destruction.[29.17] They were both "dragons [who had flown] too high"[29.18] and whose breath was cut off, which was not the destiny [originally bestowed upon them by Heaven's] decree. They were [like] a purple color[29.19] or a croaking sound,[29.20] or the left-

[29.16] A quotation of *Book of Changes*, App. III, ii, 31 (Legge, p. 389).

[29.17] After 亡, the T'ang mss. adds the word 此.

[29.18] An allusion to *Book of Changes*, App. II, Hex. 1, 6 (Legge, p. 267; Wilhelm, II, 5), "A dragon [that has flown] too high will have to repent it; a state of fullness cannot last long."

The Official ed. and the Southern Academy ed. write 亢 for the 炕, to accord with the reading in the *Book of Odes*, but the T'ang mss., the Ching-yu ed., and the Chi-ku-ko ed. confirm the reading in the latter reading.

[29.19] Ying Shao explains that purple is a mixed color. Professor Duyvendak notes the reference to *Analects* XVII, xviii, where Confucius states he dislikes purple and parallels it with obscene music. Professor Duyvendak explains that purple pretends to be red without being red.

[29.20] Ying Shao explains, "*Wa* 蠅 is an evil sound." In his *Yen-shih Chia-hsün*, ch. 17, sect. 16; B: 20a, Yen Chih-t'ui explains, "It probably means that it is not a blue color, [that of heaven], nor a yellow color, [that of earth], and that it is a sound which does not agree with the [twelve] musical tubes." Yen Shih-ku adds, "*Wa* is a disorderly sound in music, not [appropriate to] correct songs. Recent students say however that *wa* means merely the croaking of frogs,* [thus] mistaking its meaning. They also wish to change the *wa-sheng* of this eulogy to be 'the sound of 蠅 blue-flies (*ying*)', and quote the *Book of Odes* [I, VIII, i, 1; Legge, p. 150]:

'It was not the cock that was crowing—
It was the sound of blue flies,'

thus following their caprice still further." Professor Duyvendak explains that *wa* may denote "a croaking sound which is a parody of music."

At the sign *, after the word *wa*, the T'ang mss. adds the word 蛆, making the meaning clearer.

I have compared the variant readings of this T'ang manuscript with those of five other editions of the *HS*: the Ching-yu ed. of 1035, the Wang Wen-sheng ed. of 1546, the Chi-ku-ko ed. of 1642, a Te-fan-tsui-lo-hsien ed., prob. between 1457 and 1573, and Wang Hsien-ch'ien's ed. of 1900. Including items in the Chinese notes (which are not mentioned

over minutes [that are given] the place of an inter-

**30a** calation,[29.21] which are driven out by a sage-king.[30.1]

聲 閏 王 除
餘 位 之 云
分 聖 驅 爾

in my notes), there are nineteen differences between this T'ang manuscript and other editions. In each case, these other five editions agree against the T'ang manuscript. In many cases, it can be seen that the T'ang manuscript is endeavoring to make plainer or easier the original text (cf. my notes 29.4, 29.9, 29.11, and the preceding paragraph of this note); in other cases they are errors of transcription. Evidently this scribe was not careful in his work and his variants are textually unimportant.

[29.21] Fu Ch'ien explains, "It means that [Wang] Mang did not obtain the real [Heavenly] decree of a [true] king, as the left-over parts of the months in a year make an inter- calation."

[30.1] A phrase also found in *SC* 16: 3[8,9] = *Mh* III, 49. Su Lin explains that in this case the sage-king was Emperor Kuang-wu.

# APPENDIX I

## THE PASSAGES IN
## "THE TREATISE ON FOOD AND GOODS"
## DEALING WITH WANG MANG

The following two passages are the most important accounts of Wang Mang in the *HS* outside of his "Memoir" and are necessary in order to understand his period, hence they are translated here in full. They occur at the end of the first and second parts of this "Treatise."

There are a few additional passages dealing with this period: the section in the "Memoir on the Huns" (*HS* ch. 94) is translated in de Groot, *Die Hunnen der vorchristlichen Zeit*, ch. XX–XXII. The few scattered matters in the "Memoir on the Western Frontier Regions" (*HS* ch. 96) are to be found in his companion volume, *Chinesischen Urkunden zur Geschichte Asiens* (cf. his index *sub* Wang Mang). The passage (about a page) in the "Memoir on the Southwestern Barbarians" (*HS* ch. 95) is translated by A. Wylie in the *Journal* of the Royal Anthropological Institute, vol. 9 (1879/1880), p. 64, 65. There is also a brief section at the end of the "Treatise on the Suburban Sacrifices and State Offerings to the Spirits" (*HS* ch. 25, which is not translated; it deals with Wang Mang's alterations in the state sacrifices and his attempts to secure immortality). Other passages dealing with this period, found in the various biographies of the *HS* and *HHS*, are abstracted in the Glossary. With these accounts, the reader should be able to secure a well-rounded view of Wang Mang and his period.

After this translation had been prepared and sent to press, there appeared a translation of these two passages in *Food & Money in Ancient China, Han Shu 24*, by Nancy Lee Swann (Princeton University Press, 1950). The difficulty of altering a proof which was already in page form has however prevented me from referring to this translation.

## Chapter XXIV

## THE TREATISE ON FOOD AND GOODS

## PART A

**24A: 20b**    After Emperor P'ing died,[20.1] Wang Mang occupied
*19a 15b*    [the post of] Regent and thereupon usurped the
A.D. 6    throne. Wang Mang profited from the Han [dy-
Conditions    nasty's] estate, inheriting its peacefulness: the Huns
at the End    had pronounced themselves its tributaries and the
of the    many barbarians had submitted respectfully, so that
Former    wherever boats or carriages could go, all [people] were
Han    its male or female subjects,[20.2] and its yamens and
Dyansty    treasuries [exhibited] "the richness of its host of
officers,"[20.3] with the result that the empire was at
**21a**    rest. In one morning, [Wang] Mang possessed them
[all, but] his mind and intentions were not yet satis-
Wang    fied. He despised the institutions of the Han dy-
Mang    nasty, considering them to be lax.
Changes    Emperor Hsüan had first granted the [Hun] *Shan-*
Titles and    *yü* an imperial seal like that of the Son of Heaven,
Arouses    and [the Marquis of] Kou-t'ing, [Wu Po], a south-
Resent-    western barbarian, had been entitled a king. [Wang]
ment.    Mang however sent a commissioner to change the seal
A.D. 9[21.1]    of the *Shan-yü* [to be an ordinary official seal] and
degraded the King of Kou-t'ing to be a marquis.
*16a*    Not until then did these two quarters become resent-
A.D. 10/11    ful and trespass the borders. [Wang] Mang there-
Dec./    upon raised an army, mobilizing a multitude of three
Jan.[21.2]    hundred thousand [men], intending to go out [of the

[20.1] This statement is all that the Treatise says concerning the period when Wang Mang was ruling for Emperor P'ing.

[20.2] Cf. 99 A: n. 26.9.

[20.3] A quotation from *Analects* XIX, xxiii, 3.

[21.1] Cf. 99 B: 11b.

[21.2] Cf. 99 B: 14a ff.

減輕田租三十而稅一常有更賦罷癃咸出
不度時宜分裂州郡改職作官下令曰漢氏
北邊使者馳傳督趣海內擾矣又動欲暴古
徒丁男甲卒轉委輸兵器自負海江淮而至
欲同時十道並出一舉滅匈奴募發天下囚

country] simultaneously by ten routes and at one stroke to annihilate the Huns. He solicited and mobilized the empire's convicts, freemen, and armed soldiers, to transport supplies and bring military implements. From the seacoast, the Yangtze and the Huai Rivers, to the northern borders, commissioners, [riding in] galloping quadrigae, supervised and urged them, [so that all] within [the four] seas were disturbed.[21.3]

19b
Armies
Mobilized

Moreover, whenever [Wang Mang] acted, he desired to imitate ancient [practises], and did not consider what was appropriate to the times,[21.4] so he divided up the provinces and commanderies, altered the duties [of officials], and created [new] offices. He issued an ordinance,[21.5] which said,

"The Han dynasty reduced and lightened the land tax, taking [only] one-thirtieth, [but in addition] there were regularly [required] conscript service and capitation taxes, which [even] the sick and aged were all required to pay,[21.6] while powerful common people

A.D. 9[21.5]
Land and
Slaves
Not to be
Bought
or Sold

[21.3] A sentence also found in 99 B: 14b.

[21.4] A statement characteristic of the Legalists (Bodde, *China's First Unifier*, p. 214f); perhaps also of the Confucianists. Mencius says that Confucius was timely (V, II, i, 5).

[21.5] This ordinance is quoted in a more elaborate form in 99 B: 8a–9a, q.v.

[21.6] A T'ang manuscript of *HS* 24 A has been preserved in Japan in the Hōjōin of the Shimpuku Temple in Nagoya. Yang Shou-ching (1839–1915) had a tracing of it made in 1895; it was edited by Li Shu-ch'ang (1837–1897) and published as vol. 21 of the "Ku-yi Ts'ung-shu", under the title, *Ying T'ang-hsieh-pen HS Shih-huo Chih*. Unfortunately, this tracing is not always accurate. Dr. Takao Yamada has published a photolithographic facsimile, under the title, *Han-sho Shokka-shi* 漢書食貨志, under the auspices of the Koten Hozon-kai 古典保存會. This manuscript taboos the words *shih-min* 世民 (they usually lack a stroke; occasionally, as on folio leaf 7, reverse [b], column 7 of the facsimile, and 8a[1,5], the word 萌 is written for *min* [this latter form of taboo is not in Ch'en Yüan's list]). Shih-min was the personal name of Emperor Wen 文, the Grand Exemplar (the T'ai-tsung) of the T'ang dynasty. This manuscript also taboos the word *chih* 治, which was the personal name of Emperor Ta 大, the Eminent Exemplar (the Kao-tsung). The words *tan* 旦 (6a[4]) and *yü* 豫 (5a[3], 10a[3]), which were the personal names of the Penetrating Exemplar (the Jui-tsung) and the Dynastic Exemplar (the Tai-tsung), respectively, are however written

beset and encroached upon[21.7] [the poor, letting their     而裹民侵陵

correctly.  The word *yung* 用 (16a[9], 18b[8], 19a[2], 19b[2], 20a[7]), which formed part of the personal name of Li K'o-yung, the founder of the Later T'ang dynasty, is also written correctly.  At its inception, the T'ang rulers were quite lenient concerning taboos of imperial names.  But as Confucianism became more and more influential, the observance of these taboos became more and more stressed, until, in the period of the Five Dynasties, which followed upon the fall of the T'ang dynasty, imperial taboos were observed strictly. (Cf. Ch'en Yüan, *Shih-hui Chü-li*, p. 95b.)   In the T'ang period, there were tabooed the personal names of the seven immediately preceding generations of emperors, and also those of the dynastic founders, as well as that of the reigning emperor, i.e., those of the Eminent Founder (the Kao-tsu), the Grand Exemplar, the Eminent Exemplar, the seven emperors immediately preceding, and the reigning sovereign.  (Cf. *ibid.*, p. 49b.)   From the above noted phenomena, this manuscript was written in either of two periods: (1) between 650 (when the Eminent Exemplar began his reign) and the reign of the Penetrating Exemplar, i.e., 684 (when he was first enthroned) or 710 (when he began his independent reign), or else (2) after the seventh reign after that of the Dynastic Exemplar, down to the end of the T'ang period, i.e., in 847–904.

On the back of this scroll there has been transcribed the Buddhist Amida Sutra, with a colophon stating that it was written in the second year of the period Kaho 嘉保, a Japanese date corresponding to 1095.  The scroll is doubly boxed.  On the outer box is written the words, "橘逸勢眞跡 Handwriting of Tachibana no Hayanari."  The inner box also has this attribution inscribed on it; on the cover of this box is the signature of Kohitsu Ryôhan 古筆了伴 (1827–1853), who came of a family for generations acknowledged to be authorities on matters of ancient handwriting, so that this attribution is very likely from him.

Hayanari went to China in the closing years of the Enriki period (782–805) and after his return served in the court, being noted for his calligraphy.  At the end of the scroll is a vermillion seal, that of the Office of Civil Affairs, used on official documents from 770 to some date before 864.  It is then quite possible that this manuscript was written in the middle of the ix century by Hayanari, after his return from China.  In that case it represents an exemplar then preserved in Japan.  Hayanari was made Governor of Tajima Province in 840; the date of his death is unknown.  Dr. Yamada however seems to place little reliance upon the attribution of this scroll to Hayanari.  He and his colleagues believe that this scroll comes from the early Nara period (646–710).  (I thank Dr. Shio Sakanishi, formerly of the Library of Congress, for the above information.)

There is the further possibility that this manuscript is a copy by Hayanari or some other Japanese scribe of a Chinese exemplar then preserved in Japan.  Dr. Sakanishi states that no Japanese would have taken any liberties in copying an old Chinese manuscript, not even altering the writing to conform to Chinese taboos that had arisen after the exemplar had been written.  If so, this exemplar was written between 650 and 684 or 710 and the present manuscript was written between 650 and the first part of the ninth century, to possibly about 820, when that seal ceased to be used.

At this point, this T'ang manuscript omits the word 出 after the 咸.

[21.7] The T'ang manuscript reads 淩 for 陵, and omits the word 假, although space is

478

刑者衆後三年奔知民愁下詔諸食王田及私屬皆得賣買
族鄉黨犯令法至死制度又不定吏緣為姦天下警然陷
屬皆不得賣買其男口不滿八而田過一井者分餘田與九
為姦俱陷於辜刑用不錯今更名天下田曰王田奴婢曰私
分田劫假厥名三十貢什稅五也富者驕而為邪貧者窮而

own] fields [out on] shares, robbing them by the rentals [required for their land, so that while], in name, the [poor] were taxed [only one]-thirtieth, in reality, they were taxed or paid in rent five-tenths of their produce. The rich were proud[21.8] and did evil, and the poor became destitute and acted wickedly. Both [of them] fell into crime, so that the punishments [had to be] employed and could not be set aside.

"Now I am changing the names of the cultivated **21b** fields in the empire to be 'the King's fields,' and of male and female slaves to be 'private adherents.' All are not to be permitted to be bought or sold. Let it be that those [rich families with] eight males or less, who have more cultivated fields than those in one *ching* [900 *mou*], shall divide the cultivated fields that are in excess [of those in one *ching*] and give them to their nine [classes of] relatives or to [people in] their neighborhood." The punishment of those who violated this ordinance was as great as death.

The institutions and regulations were moreover not **20a** fixed, and the officials utilized [that fact] to do evil, so that the empire kept murmuring,[21.9] and those who fell into punishment were multitudes.

The third year[21.10] afterwards, [because Wang] A.D. 12
Mang knew that the common people hated [his *16b*
arrangements], he issued an imperial edict, [saying], The Order
"Those who enjoy the income from the King's fields Rescinded
together with [those who have] private adherents, are all to be permitted to sell or buy them, and are

left for it.

21.8 The Official ed. has emended 驕 to 質, but the T'ang mss. and other texts read the former word.

21.9 The T'ang mss. reads only one 謷, but in quoting Yen Shih-ku's note, it reads two.

21.10 The T'ang mss., the Ching-yu ed., and the Official ed. read 歲; the Chi-ku-ko ed. and Wang Hsien-ch'ien read 年.

This edict is also found in 99 B: 20a.

not to be restricted by the law." His punishments were however very severe, and in other[21.11] [respects] his government was contrary to reason and disorderly.

**The People Suffer**   The troops at the border, [numbering] more than two hundred thousand men, relied upon the imperial government for food and clothing; [since Wang Mang's] means were insufficient, he repeatedly [exacted] unreasonable poll-taxes and imposts, so that the common people became all the more poor and impoverished. They constantly suffered from withering droughts, and there were no abundant harvests, so that the prices of the grains soared and were high. In his last years, robbers and bandits arose in great numbers, and when he mobilized armies to attack them, the generals and officials acted with free license outside [the capital], so that at the northern borders and in the regions of Ch'ing and Hsü [Provinces],

**A.D. 21** people ate each other. At Lo-yang and east of it, grain was two thousand [cash per] picul,[21.12] [so

**A.D. 22** Wang] Mang sent [one of] the highest ministers and a general to open the various granaries in the eastern quarter, and to give and lend to those who were in extremity or indigent.[21.13] He also sent out by divisions grandees and internuncios to teach the common people to boil [parts of] trees and make a vegetable juice, [but] the vegetable juice could not be eaten,

**20b** [and the sending merely] made much trouble and

**22a** disturbance.[21.14] The vagrant common people who entered the passes [of Kuan-chung numbered] several hundred thousand persons, [so Wang Mang] established an Office for Maintenance and Relief,[22.1] in order to distribute [grain] to them, [but] the officials

---

[22.11] For 它 the T'ang mss. writes 他, a graphic variant not found in the *HS*.

[21.12] Taken from T'ien K'uang's memorial in 99 C: 16a.

[21.13] Repeated from the edict quoted in 99 C: 17a.

[21.14] Repeated in 99 C: 17b.

[22.1] Where this sentence is repeated in 99 C: 18a, 贍 is used for the 澹 here.

盜其稟飢死者什七八茲恥為政　所致迺下詔曰于遭陽九之阨百　六之會枯旱霜蝗饑饉荐臻蠻夷　猾夏寇賊姦軌百姓流離于甚悼　之害氣將究矣歲為此言曰至於亡

robbed them of their grain allowances, so that seven or eight-tenths of them died of hunger.[22.2]

[Wang] Mang was ashamed [to recognize that these events] had arrived because of his [mis]government, so he issued imperial edicts which said, "I have met with the distresses of the nine dry years and [the untoward] occurrences in the 106 [years], of withering droughts, frosts, locusts, famines, repeated arrivals of 'barbarians who have troubled the Chinese,' robbers and bandits [who follow] a wicked course, and people who become vagrants and fall into [crime]. I am greatly saddened by it. This injurious emanation will [soon] end." Year by year he produced this explanation, until he came to ruin.[22.3]

His Excuses

17a

[22.2] For the 飢 of the other texts, the T'ang mss. writes 餓.

I have compared this T'ang manuscript with the Ching-yu ed. of 1035, with what seems to be a copy of the 1131 Szechuan large character ed., also a Yüan reprint of a Sung Academy ed., the Te-fan-tsui-lo-hsien ed. (betw. 1457 & 1573), the Wang Wen-sheng ed. of 1546, the Chi-ku-ko ed. of 1642, and the Wang Hsien-ch'ien ed. of 1900. In the part translated here, there are ten differences between the T'ang manuscript and these other texts. Except for the difference noted in n. 21.10, in every case these other editions agree against the readings of the Japanese T'ang manuscript. Its variants are then textually unimportant. No significant variations occur and some are sheer blunders. Cf. also Pelliot, *BEFEO*, 2 (1902), 335.

[22.3] This passage does not seem to be a quotation from any single edict, but merely a summary; cf. 99 B: 21a, 28a; C: 8b, 17a for such utterances. "Barbarians who have troubled the Chinese" is a phrase from *Book of History* II, i, 20, Legge, p. 44.

## PART B

**24B: 21a**

19a *16a*
A.D. 7
June/
July[21.1]

When Wang Mang acted as Regent, he changed
the Han institutions. Because in the Chou [dy-
nasty] its cash were larger and smaller coins[21.1] which
acted as standards for each other,[21.2] [Wang Mang]

母相
權於
周
錢
有
子
變
漢
制
已
王
莽
居
攝

[21.1] Cf. *HS* 99 A: 30a for the complementary account.

[21.2] Cf. *HS* 24 B: 2b, 3a. The reference is to *Kuo-yü* (iv or iii cent. B.C.) 3: 13b–15b, sect. 5, (de Harlez, *Jour. Asiat.*, ser. 9, vol. 3 [Jan.–Feb. 1894], pp. 58–61) which says, "In the twenty-first year of King Ching [524 B.C.], when [the King] was about to have large cash cast, [seemingly for the purpose of securing more revenue], Duke Mu of Shan said, 'It should not be done. Anciently, when Heaven's visitations descended, thereupon [the ruler] evaluated [the state's] merchandise and currency, and standardized the weight [of the currency] in order to assist the common people. When the common people suffered [because the currency was too] light, then he made heavier currency in order to make [the lighter ones] circulate, whereupon the larger ones (*mu*) acted as a standard (*ch'üan*) for the smaller ones (*tzu*) and [the smaller ones] circulated, so that the common people secured [the benefits of] both [denominations of coins]. However, when [business conditions] would not support the heavier [coins], then [the ruler] made many lighter [coins] and circulated them, and also did not suppress the heavier ones, whereupon the smaller [coins] (*tzu*) acted as a standard (*ch'üan*) for the larger ones (*mu*) and [the larger ones] circulated, so that [both] the smaller and larger [coins] were beneficial. If now you, King, abolish the lighter [coins] and make heavier ones, and the common people lose their property, will they be able not to default [on their taxes]?' . . . But the King did not listen and eventually cast larger cash."

*Chi-chung Chou-shu* (possibly forged from ancient materials after the Han period), 2: 7b, 8a, also refers to this incident: "When the currency for the land tax was too light, [King Wen] made larger [coins] in order to make the smaller ones circulate and altered the price of merchandise, in order to adjust it for travelers, so that [merchandise] might have no obstacles [in trade]."

Ying Shao explains this economic policy as follows (in a note to *HS* 24 B: 2b, 3a): "The mother (*mu*) is the heavier one. It is a moiety larger, hence it is the mother (*mu*). The son (*tzu*) is the lighter. It is lighter and lesser by half, hence it is the son (*tzu*). When the common people suffered by the lightness of the currency and the expensiveness of goods, [the ruler] made heavy currency in order to equalize the [prices] and temporarily circulated these [coins] in order to do away with the light [coins]. Hence it is said, 'The mothers (*mu*, heavier ones) act as standards for the sons (*tzu*, lighter ones),' which is like saying that the heavier ones are used as the weights by which to weigh the lighter ones. The common people all secured them. Whether they were farmers or merchants, had or had no [property], they all secured benefits from them."

Meng K'ang adds, "The heavier ones were the mothers (*mu*) and the lighter ones

是　重　十　其　長
更　十　又　環　二
造　二　造　如　寸
大　銖　契　大　文
錢　文　刀　錢　曰
徑　曰　錯　身　契
寸　大　刀　形　刀
二　錢　契　如　五
分　五　刀　刀　百

thereupon changed [the currency] and [additionally] coined large cash, with a diameter of an inch and two *fen*, a weight of 12 *shu*, and a legend which reads, "Large cash (*ta-ch'ien*) [worth] fifty [cash]."[21.3] He also coined graving-knife (*ch'i-tao*) [coins] and [gold] inlaid knife (*ts'o-tao*) [coins]. The circular [heads] of the graving-knife [coins] are like the large cash; their bodies are shaped like knives and are two inches long. Their legend reads, "a graving-knife [coin], worth five hundred [cash]."[21.4] The inlaid knife

**Four Denominations of Money**

were the sons (*tzu*). It is like the selling of an article for eighty cash: the mother (*mu* [original cost]) was fifty [cash] and the son (*tzu*, [profit]), thirty [cash], comes from it."

This same precedent was used to justify paper money in Yüan times; cf. *HJAS* 2: 317 (the phrase mentioned there, *tzu-mu hsiang-ch'üan erh hsing*, is from the Kuo-yü.)

[21.3] Cf. James H. Stewart Lockhart, *The Stewart Lockhart Collection of Chinese Copper Coins*, "Royal Asiatic Society, North China Branch," Extra Volume no. 1 (1915), no. 144; H. Glathe, *The Origin and Development of Chinese Money*, p. 30, nos. 151–161, 163–167. Mr. H. F. Bowker of Oakland, Cal., an officer of the U. S. Navy, has loaned me a 50-cash coin of this issue which weighs 6.19 g. and is 27 mm. in diameter, as compared with the 7.68 g. and 27 mm. of the text.

[21.4] Cf. E. Chavannes, *Documents chinois*, no. 709; Glathe, *op. cit.*, p. 29, no. 103. The graving-knife coins in Lockhart, *ibid.*, nos. 152, 153, are both probably fakes: no. 152 because of the defective writing of the words for "five hundred" and no. 153 because of its size and the more modern form of the word *ch'i*. In this matter I am glad to have the concurrence of the numismatist, Mr. H. F. Bowker. *Chin-shih-so*, Chin, 4: 29a, b, contains diagrams of the graving-knife and inlaid-knife coins.

Mr. Bowker has very kindly loaned me an excellently-preserved specimen of a graving-knife coin, obtained from Gakuyo Katsuyama 勝山岳陽 of Tokyo, a highly esteemed Japanese archeologist, who guaranteed its authenticity. It corresponds exactly with the description in the *HS* text and with Chavannes' illustration. The cutting edge of the knife-blade has been sharpened by filing from both sides (with almost all of the bevel on the obverse side), so that the coin would actually cut. It weighs 15.80 g. or a little less than 25 *shu* (16.0 g.), which latter figure may have been its original weight. The circular head of the coin is 28 mm. in diameter (exactly corresponding to the text's "1 inch 2 *fen*" for the diameter of large cash; cf. *HFHD* I, 279 for equivalents), with a hole 13 mm. square; the blade is 46 mm. long (exactly 2 of Wang Mang's inches, as the text states).

Mr. Bowker has also loaned me what is plainly the circular head of a graving-knife coin, from which the blade has been broken off and the break smoothed, thus making a round cash out of the coin. It weighs 9.48 gm.; about two-thirds of the graving-knife coin's metal was in its head. Since the edges of cash were smooth and not milled, such a mutilation would be unnoticed until the inscription was read, which is "*ch'i-tao* (graving-knife)." Mr. Bowker has also loaned me three other coins which are similar round heads

483

[coins] are inlaid with actual gold. Their legend reads, "One knife [coin], worth five thousand [cash]."[21.5] Together with the five-*shu* cash, alto-

**21b** *16b*

錯刀曰　黃金錯　其文曰　一刀直　五千與

of inlaid knife-coins. Cf. Glathe, *ibid.*, p. 30, no. 162.

Chang Yen (iii cent.) plainly knew only these broken-off knife-coin heads, for he glosses this passage as follows: "In my opinion, in shape and substance, the graving-knife [coins] and inlaid knife-[coins] which are extant today are like [Wang Mang's] large cash, but the raised edges to their circumferences and holes are thick—different from those of these large cash. In shape [these knife-coins] are like the rings on swords. The shape of the body of the graving-knife [coins] is round, not two inches long. The legend to the left [of the hole] reads, '*ch'i* (graving),' and to the right reads, '*tao* (knife),' and they do not have the words, '*wu-po* (five hundred [cash]).' "

Yen Shih-ku (581–645) states that Chang Yen is mistaken and that the Wang Mang knife-coins of his day tallied with the description in the text. Chang Yen seems merely not to have known unmutilated knife-coins. (Cf. also the end of n. 21.5).

[21.5] Cf. Glathe, *op. cit.*, 29, no. 104. Mr. Bowker has also kindly loaned me a well-preserved Wang Mang inlaid knife-coin, also obtained from and guaranteed by the same archeologist. It corresponds with the description in the text (except for the substitution of *p'ing* for *chih*, which is discussed later). This coin weighs 23.74 g. (a little less than 38 *shu* [24.32 g.]), so that these coins probably originally weighed about 40 *shu*. The cutting edge of the blade has been filed sharp, with an even bevel on both sides. Its dimensions are exactly the same as those of the graving-knife coins, except that it is thicker and heavier. On the field of the circular part of the coin, above and below the hole, are the words, "*yi-tao* (one knife-[coin])," in seal characters, engraved into the body of the coin and inlaid with gold, level to the field of the coin. This gold inlay is mentioned in the *HS* text, without specifying what is inlaid. The blade of the coin bears the words, "*p'ing wu-ch'ien* (standardized at five thousand [cash])" in raised bronze characters, like the legends on other Han coins. The reverse of the coin is bare of any legend.

In the account of the legend on these coins, for "worth," the text reads the word *chih* 直. But this coin has *p'ing* 平. I suspect that the *chih* in the *HS* text is an error, from attraction to the word *chih* in the legend on the one-cash coins in Wang Mang's coinage of A.D. 9. *P'ing*, which meant "standardized," denoting the establishing by the government of a fixed value for an article, is much more appropriate for these coins, which were really fiat money. Liu Feng-shih (1041–1113), the Sung Ch'i ed. (xi or xii cent.), and Ch'ien Chan (1744–1806) moreover all quote the legend on these coins with the word *p'ing*. The latter of these writers noted that the words *yi-tao* are engraved and inlaid with gold, while the rest of the legend is raised.

Lockhart's inlaid knife-coins, *ibid.* nos. 146–152, seem all either to have been fakes or counterfeits or to have been copied incorrectly from Chinese numismatic books. He nowhere mentions the gold-inlaid characters, which are the most striking feature of these coins and are testified to as early as by Chang Yen in the third century. Mr. Bowker remarks that Lockhart "obviously did not have these coins or he would have mentioned the gold characters." The word *p'ing* in Lockhart's drawings is not correctly formed

五錢四並
銖凡品行

gether four denominations [of money] were to circulate at the same time.

(except perhaps in no. 147); the vertical line should project below the bottom horizontal line. Mr. Bowker writes me, "I have never seen a specimen like no. 148, and am sure it is a fake. The same applies to no. 147, on account of the incused line around the blade on both sides, not to mention the smallness of the characters." No. 149 comes closest to Mr. Bowker's specimen, but the proportions are somewhat incorrect.

Chang Yen knew only the circular heads of these inlaid knife-coins, from which the blades had been broken off. His gloss (trans. in n. 21.4) continues, "The inlaid knife-[coins] are moreover engraved with characters, which are filled with actual gold. Their legend, above [the hole], reads, 'yi (one),' and, below [the hole], reads, 'tao (knife-[coin]).' " This description agrees with Mr. Bowker's specimens. The heaviest of these heads weighs 15.97 g., so that about two-thirds of the metal was in the head. The amount of gold inlaid in the two engraved characters is negligible, so that it was not worth gouging out.

When Wang Mang ascended the throne and dispossessed the Han dynasty, these knife-coins became *nefastus*, unpropitious, since they denoted the Han surname, Liu (cf. p. 245f). After Wang Mang demonetized them, their possession probably became a mark of loyalty to the Han dynasty. Wealthy nobles, who had obediently exchanged their gold for these knife-coins, found them now not only worthless, but even dangerous to possess. Probably many nobles did not dare to melt down their knife-coins, for someone in their household would be sure to inform the ever-watchful government of the deed, and counterfeiting was a serious crime. Hence the blades were broken off these coins, making them into round cash. As such they would have been worth their weight in bronze or (perhaps more likely) they may have circulated on a par with the fifty-cash coins—the owners lost 99% of their money by turning a 5000-cash coin into a 50-cash coin, but that doubtless seemed better than losing the whole value of these coins and being punished for possessing them!

In the *Ch'üan-pi* 泉幣, issue 1, July, 1940 (pub. at Shanghai), Mr. Ts'ai Chi-hsiang 蔡季襄 publishes a photograph of a 10,000-cash coin, shaped like a circle with a square attached to it, with the legend, "Worth ten thousand [cash from] the chests of gold in the state's treasure 國寶金匱直萬." Mr. Ts'ai decides that it is a Wang Mang coin from the issue of A.D. 11.

I cannot agree with him. If it was from Wang Mang's age at all (the use of the word *chih*, instead of *p'ing*, raises doubts), it must have been intended for the issue of A.D. 7. At that time, Wang Mang "nationalized" gold, paying for it probably at the rate of 10,000 cash per catty (the value he set in A.D. 11), so that a 10,000-cash coin was really needed in making this exchange. The round shape denotes heaven and the square shape denotes earth. Mr. Ts'ai argues that the word *kuei* 匱 (chest) in its legend was the name for 10,000 catties of gold in Wang Mang's time (cf. *HS* 99 C: 25a), just as *Kuan-tzu* (ch. 5, "Shen-ma," sect. "Shih, nung, kung, shang"; Szu-pu Ts'ung-k'an ed. 1: 12b) states, "A hundred *yi* 鎰 of actual gold [make] one *ch'ieh* 篋 (box)," and *Nan-shih*, 53: 25b "Memoir of the King of Wu-ling, Hsiao Yüan-cheng," states, "One catty of actual gold makes one *ping* 餅 (cake) and a hundred *ping* make a *ch'ou* 籌 (secondary unit)." (Gold was cast

485

A.D. 9[21.6]

A.D. 10[21.6]
19b
Six Kinds
of
Valuable
Currency:

Cash

When Wang Mang became actual [Emperor], he considered that in the writing for the word Liu [there are the words] metal and knife, so he abolished the inlaid knife and the graving-knife [coins], together with the five-*shu* cash. [Later] he changed and made [six] kinds [of money]: gold, silver, tortoise-[shells], cowries, cash, and spade-money, [giving them] the name, "Valuable currency (*pao-huo*)."[21.7] The diminutive cash (*hsiao-ch'ien*) are six *fen* in diameter, one *shu* in weight, and their legend is, "Diminutive cash worth one [cash]."[21.8]    The next

恭即真呂為書劉字有金
刀迴罷錯刀契刀及五銖
錢而更作金銀龜貝錢布
之品名曰寶貨小錢徑六
分重一銖文曰小錢直一

into cake-shaped ingots; Mr. Ts'ai publishes photographs of such ingots from Chou and Former Han times.)

This 10,000-cash coin is not mentioned in any Chinese history.  It was needed in A.D. 7, but if such coins had been issued, they would have been used plentifully in purchasing the nobles' gold and would not be so rare and unmentioned.  But in the issue of A.D. 7, the coins of a higher denomination than one cash were all multiples of five: 50, 500, and 5000 cash.  (Five, along with the other odd numbers, is the number of Heaven, not Earth; cf. *Book of Changes*, App. III, i, 49; Legge, p. 365.)  Emperor P'ing was sickly; the knife-coins, with their symbolism of metal and knife [*HS* 24 B: 21b] denoted the Liu house; similarly the use of the number five, denoting Heaven [the Emperor was the Son of Heaven] was probably also magic to strengthen the Emperor.)  It would have been unlikely that a 10,000-cash coin (denoting both Heaven and Earth) would have been added to this (purely Heavenly) series.  In the issue of A.D. 11, the denominations increase by tens to 50, then by hundreds to 1000; it would have been unlikely that a 10,000-cash coin would have been added to such a series, leaving so great a gap between it and the next lower coin.  The largest denomination in the issue of A.D. 14 was 25-cash, so that this 10,000-cash coin could not have belonged to that series.  In my opinion, if this coin is really from Wang Mang's mint (concerning which I have no evidence), it can only have been a mint sample for the issue of A.D. 7, which coin was rejected because it spoiled the symmetry and magical effect of that issue.  (Cf. also the *Tung-yang Huo-pi Tsa-chih* 東洋貨幣雜誌, no. 218.)

[21.6] As a matter of fact, this coinage was not all begun at the same time.  The previous coinage was abolished, except for the twelve-*shu* large fifty-cash coins, in the spring of A.D. 9, when there were also first coined the one-*shu* diminutive cash coins, so that these two denominations circulated together (99 B: 7b).  Then in A.D. 10 (99 B: 15a), Wang Mang added the other 26 denominations of this coinage.  When compiling this "Treatise," Pan Ku evidently forgot that this coinage was not all enacted at the same time.

[21.7] Wang Mang took this name from that said to have been given by King Ching of the Chou dynasty to his large cash; cf. *HS* 24 B: 3a.

[21.8] Cf. Lockhart, *ibid.*, no. 145; Terrien de Lacouperie, *Catalogue of Chinese Coins in the British Museum*, p. 367, nos. 341–343; *Chin-shih-so*, Chin, 4: 28b.

486

次七分三銖曰么錢一十次八分五銖曰幼錢二十次九分
七銖曰中錢三十次一寸九銖曰壯錢四十因前大錢五十
是為銀貨六品直各如其文黃金重一斤直錢萬朱提銀重
八兩為一流直一千五百八它銀一流直千是為銀貨二
品元龜岷丹長尺二寸直二千一百六十萬大貝十朋公龜

are seven *fen* [in diameter] and three *shu* [in weight, with the legend], "Young cash (*yao-ch'ien*) [worth] ten [cash]."[21.9] The next are eight *fen* [in diameter **22a** and weigh] five *shu*, [with the legend], "Small cash (*yu-ch'ien*) [worth] twenty [cash]."[22.1] The next are nine *fen* [in diameter and weigh] seven *shu*, [with the legend], "Medium cash (*chung-ch'ien*) [worth] thirty [cash]."[22.2] The next are one inch [in diameter and weigh] nine *shu*, [with the legend], "Adult cash (*chuang-ch'ien*) [worth] forty [cash]."[22.3] [The use of] the previous large cash [worth] fifty [cash] was [also] continued.[22.4] These were the six denominations of cash currency, each of which are valued according to its legend.

Actual gold weighing one catty was [declared to be] **Gold** worth ten thousand cash.

Shu-shih silver weighing eight taels made [one **Silver** unit], (a *liu*), and was [declared to be] worth 1580 [cash].[22.5] One *liu* of other silver was [declared to be] worth one thousand cash. These were the two denominations of silver currency.

Sovereign's tortoise-[shells], the edges of whose **Tortoise-** carapaces reached a foot and two inches were [de- **shells** clared to be] worth 2160 [cash] and were [made the equivalent of] ten pairs of large cowries.[22.6]

[21.9] Cf. de Lacouperie, *ibid.*, p. 368, nos. 1711, 1712.

[22.1] Cf. *Ku-chin Ch'ien-lüeh*, by Ni Mo (1750–1825), 16: 6b; Glathe, *op. cit.*, p. 30, no. 171.

[22.2] Cf. de Lacouperie, *ibid.*, p. 369, nos. 1713, 1714; Glathe, *op. cit.*, no. 170.

[22.3] Cf. de Lacouperie, *ibid.*, nos. 344, 1715, 1716; Glathe, *op. cit.*, no. 169.

[22.4] Cf. de Lacouperie, *ibid.*, p. 370; Lockhart, nos. 136–143.

[22.5] Shu-shih was a prefecture in Chien-wei Commandery, which mined fine silver. For location, cf. Glossary, *sub voce*.

[22.6] Meng K'ang glosses, "*Jang* 冉 [means] the border of tortoise shells. . . . They measured the edge of the two sides of their backs as a foot and two inches." Li Tz'u-ming, in his *HS Cha-chi* 2: 6a, adds that *jang* should be 𪚢, which is defined in the *Shuo-wen* 13 B: 2b as, "The edge of a tortoise carapace. . . . [The edge of] great tortoise shells used for] the Son of Heaven is a foot and two inches; for the nobles, it is a foot; for grandees, it is eight inches; and for gentlemen, it is six inches." Meng K'ang seems to have had this latter word in mind. The *Shuo-wen* is quoting the ancient text of the *Lost Book*

Duke's tortoise-[shells, the edges of which reached]
nine inches [or more],[22.7] were [declared to be] worth

17a   five hundred [cash] and were [made the equivalent of]
ten pairs of big cowries.   Marquises' tortoise-[shells,

20a   the edges of which reached] seven inches or more were
[declared to be] worth three hundred [cash] and were
[made the equivalent of] ten pairs of small cowries.
Viscount's tortoise-[shells, the edges of which
reached] five inches or more were [declared to be]
worth a hundred [cash] and were [made the equivalent of] ten pairs of little cowries.  The [foregoing]
were the four denominations of tortoise-[shell]
currency.

Cowries   Of large cowries (*ta-pei*), four inches eight *fen* or
more [in length], two made one pair (*p'eng*), and were

22b   [declared to be] worth 216 [cash].   Of adult cowries
(*chuang-pei*), three inches six *fen* [in length] or more,
two made one pair, and were [declared to be] worth
fifty [cash].  Of little cowries (*yao-pei*), two inches
four *fen* [in length] or more, two made one pair and
were [declared to be] worth thirty [cash].  Of diminutive cowries (*hsiao-pei*), an inch two *fen* [in
length] or more, two made one pair and were [de-
clared to be] worth ten [cash].  Those which were
not fully an inch two *fen* and so were outside of these
regulations were not permitted to make pairs and
were [declared to be] generally worth three [cash]

九寸直五百為壯貝十朋　龜五寸直五百為壯貝十朋侯龜七寸巳上直三百為幺貝十朋子　五寸巳上直百為小貝十朋是為龜寶四品大貝四寸八分巳　上二枚為一朋直二寸六分巳上二枚為一朋　直五十幺貝二寸四分巳上二枚為一朋直三十小貝寸二分巳　上二枚為一朋直十不盈寸二分漏度不得為朋率枚直錢三是

of Rites (now lost), which is quoted by name in *Ch'u-hsüeh-chi* 30: 30a.

*Li-chi* XVII, ii, 26 (Legge, II, 114; Couvreur, II, 82) says, "[The standard] bordered
with blue and black was that [on which were represented] the Son of Heaven's precious
tortoise-[shells]."   The "precious" tortoise-shells were those used for divination.   *Kung-
yang Commentary*, 26: 3b, Dk. Ting. VIII, says "The treasures of Chin were . . . tortoise-
[shells] with blue borders," and Ho Hsiu glosses, "Tortoises [which live to] a thousand
years have blue beards."   (References from Shen Ch'in-han.)

[22.7] Wang Nien-sun asserts that after 寸 there were originally the words 以上, to agree
with the statements concerning the size of the next two sizes of tortoise-shells; K'ung
Ying-ta, in a note to *Li-chi*, ch. VIII, i, 6, in his *Li-chi Chu-su* 23 : 4a, and the *Ch'u-hsüeh-chi*
30: 32b quote this passage with these words; the *T'ung-tien*, ch. 8: 11a, (Com. Pr. ed.
p. 47) quotes it without them.

寸四分重一兩而直千錢矣是為布貨十品凡寶貨五物六名

長一分相重一銖文各為其布名直各加一百上至大布長一

布小布長寸五分重十五銖文曰小布一百自小布呂上各相

為貝貨五品大布次布弟布壯布中布差布厚布幼布幺布小

apiece.   The [foregoing] were the five denominations of cowry currency.

"Large spade-money (*ta-pu*)," the "next-[largest] spade-money (*tz'u-pu*)," the "third [largest] spade-money (*ti-pu*)," "adult spade-money (*chuang-pu*)," "medium spade-money (*chung-pu*)," "smaller [than medium] spade-money (*ch'a-pu*)," "[still] smaller [than medium] spade-money (*hsü-pu*),"[22.8] "young spade-money (*yu-pu*)," "little spade-money (*yao-pu*)," and "diminutive spade-money (*hsiao-pu*)" [were also coined]. The diminutive spade-money was one inch five *fen* long, weighed fifteen *shu*, and its legend was "Diminutive spade-money [worth] a hundred [cash]."[22.9] From the diminutive spade-money on upwards, each [denomination] was one *fen* longer and one *shu* heavier, and the legend of each [gave] the name of [that denomination of] spade-money, and each [denomination] was worth a hundred [cash] more [than the preceding denomination], up to the large spade-money, which was two[22.10] inches four *fen* long, weighed one tael, and was worth a thousand cash.[22.11] The [foregoing] were the ten denominations of spade-money currency. Altogether the "valuable currency" was made of five substances with six names, and [included] twenty-

**Spade-Money**

20b

23a

[22.8] Ts'ai Yün (d. ca. 1820), in his *Pi-t'an* 3: 8b, 9a, asserts that the text's *hou* 厚 should be *hsü* 序. He points out that the six denominations of cash were named "diminutive," "little," "young," "medium," "adult," and "large." There were ten denominations of spade-money, hence between "large" and "adult" there were added 次 and 第, both of which words mean "next"; and between "medium" and "young" there were added 差 and *hsü*, both of which also mean "next." *Hou*, "thick," does not fit the meaning at all; in the seal character, *hou* and *hsü* are very similar. A specimen of this "Still smaller than medium spade-money," loaned me by Mr. Bowker, bears plainly the seal-character form of the word *hsü*, which is practically identical with that found for *hsü* in the *Shuo-wen*, and is not the word *hou*.

[22.9] Cf. de Lacouperie, *ibid.*, p. 303, no. 1580.

[22.10] The Ching-yu ed. and the Official ed. read the obviously correct 二 for Wang Hsien-ch'ien's 一.

[22.11] For these spade-coins, cf. de Lacouperie, *ibid.*, pp. 302–306; *Ku-chin Ch'ien-lüeh* 16:

eight denominations.

In casting and making cash and spade-money, all [denominations] used copper and mixed it with lead

二 品 錢 用 呂
十 鑄 布 銅 連
八 作 皆 殽 錫

7b–9a and *Chin-shih So*, Chin, 4 : 30b–32a illustrate a complete set. The Yokohama Numismatic Society's 橫濱古泉會揚摸集, no. 9 (1912) and Glathe, *op. cit.*, pp. 28, 29, nos. 90–99 print a photograph of these ten spade-coins.

The legend on these 1000-cash pieces is "大布黃千 large spade-money valued at a thousand [cash]," for which legend there is ancient testimony. Ni Mo, in his *Ku-chin Ch'ien-lüeh* 16 : 9b, points out that the word *huang* 黃 in this legend is a cursive form of *heng*₁ 橫, and that *heng*₁ is used for *heng*₂ 衡, with which it was anciently interchanged. *Heng*₂, like *p'ing* 平, meant "to weigh," hence "to standardize at a given value." Karl-gren, *Grammata Serica* 707a & m, lists *huang* and *heng*₁ as having had the same archaic and ancient pronunciations. The fact that Wang Mang asserted he ruled by virtue of the element earth, whose color is yellow, *huang*, aided in forming this cursive form of *heng*₁.

Mr. Bowker has loaned me a complete set of these spade-coins, secured by him from Gakuyo Katsuyama. Herewith a comparison of these coins with the statements in the *HS*:

| Denomination (in cash) | Legal weight according to the *HS* (in grams) | Actual weight (in g.) | Legal length according to the *HS* (in mm.) | Actual length (in mm.) |
|---|---|---|---|---|
| 100 | 9.60 | 7.0 | 35 | 35 |
| 200 | 10.24 | 7.86 | 37 | 38 |
| 300 | 10.88 | 9.44 | 39 | 40 |
| 400 | 11.52 | 8.09 | 42 | 42 |
| 500 | 12.16 | 9.38 | 44 | 44 |
| 600 | 12.80 | 14.15 | 46 | 50 |
| 700 | 13.44 | 12.02 | 48.5 | 51 |
| 800 | 14.08 | 15.31 | 50.8 | 52.5 |
| 900 | 14.72 | 13.37 | 53.1 | 54 |
| 1000 | 15.25 | 8.42 | 55.4 | 53 |

It is to be noted that the first five and the 900-cash coin correspond very well with the sizes indicated in the *HS*, although their age has caused them to lose weight. The other four are, in my judgment, very likely ancient counterfeits or later fakes. Since the Han weights and measures were gradually *increased* to their present size, a later faker would make coins in accordance with the weights and measures of his own epoch, so that they would be larger and heavier than the Han standards required. Such seems to be the case with Mr. Bowker's 600-, 700-, and 800-cash coins. The 1000-cash coin may be an ancient light-weight counterfeit.

The outstanding feature of Wang Mang's bronze coinages is that as the nominal value of the coins increased, the amount of metal per cash decreased, so that the larger coins were the more depreciated.

文質周郭放漢五銖
錢云其金銀與它物
雜色不純好龜不盈
五寸貝不盈六分皆
不得為資貨元龜為

ore and tin.[23.1]  In their obverse and reverse and in  *17b* their raised rim all around, they imitated the Han [dynasty's] five-*shu* cash.  In this [currency], the gold and silver were mixed with other substances, and the alloy was not pure and good.  Tortoise-[shells] not fully five inches [in size], and cowries not fully six *fen* [in length] were all not permitted to be considered as valuable currency.  Large tortoise-

TABLE OF THE BRONZE COINAGES OF WANG MANG

| Nominal Value | Coinage of A.D. 7 | | Coinage of A.D. 9-10 | | Coinage of A.D. 14 | |
|---|---|---|---|---|---|---|
| | Total Weight | Shu per cash | Total Weight | No. of shu per cash | Total Weight | No. of shu per cash |
| 1 cash | 5 *shu* | 5 *shu* | 1 *shu* | 1 *shu* | 5 *shu* | 5 *shu* |
| 10 " | (same as Han dy- | | 3 " | 0.3 " | | |
| 20 " | nasty's cash; un- | | 5 " | 0.25 " | | |
| 25 " | changed since 118 | | | | 25 " | 1 " |
| 30 " | B.C.) | | 7 " | 0.23 " | | |
| 40 " | | | 9 " | 0.225 " | | |
| 50 " | 12 *shu* | 0.24 *shu* | 12 " | 0.24 " | | |
| 100 " | | | 15 " | 0.15 " | | |
| 200 " | | | 16 " | 0.080 " | | |
| 300 " | | | 17 " | 0.057 " | | |
| 400 " | | | 18 " | 0.045 " | | |
| 500 " | 25 *shu*? | 0.05 *shu*? | 19 " | 0.038 " | | |
| 600 " | | | 20 " | 0.036 " | | |
| 700 " | | | 21 " | 0.030 " | | |
| 800 " | | | 22 " | 0.027 " | | |
| 900 " | | | 23 " | 0.0244 " | | |
| 1000 " | | | 24 " | 0.0240 " | | |
| 5000 " | 40 *shu*? | 0.008 *shu*? | | | | |

On the origin of spade-coins, cf. Richard Schlösser, "Der Ursprung der Chinesischen *Pu*-münzen," *Artibus Asiae*, 1928, no. 1, pp. 12–34.  This article contains photographs of more ancient spade-coins (of which Wang Mang's coins were imitations), also of a complete set of Wang Mang's coins.  Cf. also his, "Die Münzereformversuche des Wang Mang," *Sinica* V (1930), 25–37.

[23.1] Meng K'ang glosses, "*Lien*₁ 連 is another name for tin," but Li Ch'i declares, "The name for lead and tin ore is *lien*₁."  Yen Shih-ku asserts that both are mistaken, because the *Shuo-wen* 14 A: 1b says, "*Lien*₂ 鏈 is [the same] sort [of thing as] copper." Shen Ch'in-han however replies that Li Ch'i is correct; the *Shuo-wen* is merely speaking in general terms; the *Kuang-ya* and the *Yü-p'ien* both state that *lien*₂ is lead ore.  F. C. Chang asserts that zinc was called *lien*; *Journal of Science* 8, 233–243; 9, 1116–1127 (in Chinese).  Certain Sung cash are found, upon analysis, to be copper with a considerable proportion of lead, a small proportion of tin, and a minute amount of zinc, the latter arising from the impurity of the ore used.

[shells were named] Ts'ai [shells],[23.2] and were not what the four [orders of] common people[23.3] were allowed to store up. Those who had them took them to the Grand Augur and received their value.

**Penalties for Using Other Coins**

The people were confused and troubled [by this coinage, so that Wang Mang's] currency did not circulate. The common people privately used five-*shu* cash in the markets and in purchases. [Wang] Mang was troubled by it and so issued an imperial edict that those who presumed to oppose the *ching* [system of] cultivated fields or hoard five-*shu* cash were misleading the multitude and 'should be thrown out to the four frontiers [and be made] to resist the

**21a** elves and goblins."[23.4] Thereupon farmers and merchants lost their business, food and goods were both rendered useless, and the common people wept and cried in the market-places and highways. Those who were sentenced for selling or buying fields, residences, slaves or slave-women, or for casting cash, and [thus] fell into crime, from the ministers and grandees down to ordinary people, could not be estimated or counted.

**23b All but Two Denominations Rescinded**

[Wang] Mang knew that the common people hated [his arrangements], so he only had the two denominations of diminutive cash worth one [cash] and the large cash worth fifty [cash] circulate together; the tortoise-[shells], cowries, spade-money, and the like were temporarily abandoned.

[Wang] Mang by nature was irascible and irritable, and could not [bring himself to a state of] non-activity. Every time there was something that he

---

[23.2] Ju Shen quotes *Analects* V, xvii, in which a tortoise is called a *t'sai*, and states that the state of Ts'ai produced large tortoises. Hence large tortoises were named Ts'ai.

[23.3] *Ku-liang Commentary* 13: 1b, Dk. Ch'eng, I, enumerates the four orders of common people as gentlemen, merchants, farmers, and artisans. *HS* 24 A: 2a however enumerates them as gentlemen, farmers, artisans, and merchants. The Han dynasty, following the Ch'in practise, degraded merchants.

[23.4] Cf. 99 B: 8b, 9a and n. 9.1.

蔡非四民所得居有者入大卜受直百姓憤亂其貨不行民私呂五

鑄錢抵罪者自公卿大夫至庶人不可稱數奸知民愁迺但行小錢

御魑魅於是農商失業食貨俱廢民涕泣於市道坐賣買田宅奴婢

鉢錢市買恭患之下詔敢非井田挾五鉢錢者為惑眾投諸四裔呂

直一與大錢五十二品並行龜貝布屬且寢茶性躁擾不能無為每

有五均傳記各有幹焉今開賒貸張
也莽乃下詔曰夫周禮有賒貸樂語
得即易所謂理財正辭禁民為非者
劉歆言周有泉府之官收不讐與欲
有所興造必欲依古得經文國師公

initiated or invented, he always wanted it to be in accordance with ancient [practises and tried to] secure the words of [some] classic [as a model]. The State Master and Highest Minister, Liu Hsin[1a], said that the Chou [dynasty] had a government Office for Money,[23.6] which collected what was not sold and gave to those who needed to obtain [such things], which was precisely what the *Book of Changes* means by "the right administration of wealth, correct instructions [to the people], and prohibitions to the common people against wrong-[doing."[23.7] Wang] Mang accordingly issued an imperial edict, saying, "Verily, the *Chou Offices* contains [regulations for] selling on credit and lending on interest,[23.8] the *Yo-yü* contains [an account of] the five equalizations,[23.9] and all the books and records speak of controls. Now that I open [offices for] selling on credit and lending on interest, set up the five equalizations, and estab-

*The Five Equalizations A.D. 10[23.5]*

*18a*

21b

[6]

23.5 Cf. 99 B: 12b. The numbers in square brackets in the margin and text, here and on pp. 24b, 25a, b are the same as those in the enumeration of the six monopolies in 99 B: 12b. There was no fixed order, so I use that list as a reference point.

23.6 *Chou-li* 15: 3b f (Biot, I, 326–328) lists as one of the Chou offices an Office for Money, which "collected what goods are not sold in the market-place, goods [whose sale] is slow, but which are used by the common people. [The Yamen] writes their selling-price on a post, in order to be ready for those in need who would buy them."

23.7 A quotation from *Book of Changes*, App. III, ii, 10 (Legge, 381).

23.8 *Chou-li*, 15: 4a (Biot, I, 327), *sub* the Office for Money (*Ch'üan-fu*), says, "Whoever buys on credit, for [purposes of] sacrificing, shall not exceed ten days [without paying interest], and for mourning ceremonies, shall not exceed three months [without paying interest]. Whenever common people wish to borrow on interest, [the head of the Office for Money] shall discuss it with his heads of departments and then only shall pay out [the loan; the people shall pay] interest in accordance with [the taxes paid] as their service to their state," [i.e., if the tax was a tithe, the interest would be a tithe per year].

23.9 Cheng Chan (fl. ca. 208) glosses, "The *Yo-yü* are sayings on the origin of music, which King Hsien of Ho-chien, [Liu Tê, d. 130 B.C.], transmitted [to Emperor Wu]. It speaks of the matter of the five equalizations." This book has been lost; the only quotations from it that have been preserved are three brief paragraphs in the *Po-hu-t'ung* (relating to other matters) and the following one:

Fu Tsan glosses, "Its words are, "When the Son of Heaven takes land from his nobles and uses it to establish the five equalizations, then in the market-places there are no two [different] prices [for the same thing, so that] the four [orders of] common people are constantly equalized [in their power]. If the strong are not permitted to oppress the weak and the rich are not permitted to use force upon the poor, then the government shows

lish the various monopolies (controls), it is in order that the crowd of people may be made equal and those who take concurrently [the advantages of other classes] may be repressed."[23.10]

Thereupon at Ch'ang-an and at five [commandery] capitals there were established Offices for the Five Equalizations. The name of the Prefects of the Eastern and Western Markets at Ch'ang-an, together with the Chiefs of the Markets at Lo-yang,

**24a**  Han-tan, Lin-tzu, Yüan, and Ch'eng-tu, were all changed to be the Masters in Charge of the Five Equalizations at the Markets.[24.1]   At the Eastern Market, in the title [of this official, the word] Capital [was used]; at the Western Market, in his title [the word] Court [was used]; at Lo-yang, in his title, [the word] Central [was used]; at the remaining four capitals one of [the words] Eastern, Western, Southern, and Northern, [respectively, was used] in his title.   At each [place] there were established five Assistants for Exchange, and one Assistant for the

**18b**  Office for Money.   Artisans and merchants who

---

additional kindness to the unimportant common people."

Shen Ch'in-han declares that this statement is based on the *Chi-chung Chou-shu*, 4: 7a, ch. 39, (possibly this latter book, which seems to be a later forgery, took them from the *Yo-yü*) which says, "When in the market-places there were the five equalizations, then morning and evening [prices] were the same.   [This office] accompanied the departing, invited those who are coming, assisted the distressed, and rescued the impoverished."

[23.10] Cf. *HFHD*, II, 68, n. 17.2.

[24.1] Wang Nien-sun points out that the word *ch'eng* 稱 after the 市 is an interpolation by attraction for the subsequent use of this word.   This title is quoted without the word *ch'eng* in *HS* 91: 11b (Master in Charge of the Capital Market) and in sundry quotations of this passage: *Wen-hsüan* 21: 23a, in a note to Pao Chao's "*Yung-shih Shih*"; *ibid.*, 36: 22a, in a note to the "*Yung-ming, XI Nien, Ts'ê Hsui-ts'ai Wen*"; *ibid.*, 53: 20b in a note to the "*Yün-ming Lun*"; T'ung-tien 11: 22a (Com. Pr. ed. p. 65); and *Tzu-chih T'ung-chien* 37: 8b.   *Wen-hsüan* 1: 8b, in a note to the "*Hsi-tu Fu*", however quotes this passage with the word *ch'eng*.

商能采金銀銅連錫登龜取貝者皆自占司市錢府順時氣而取

之又呂周官稅民凡田不耕為不殖出三夫之稅城郭中宅不毛者出三夫布一匹其不能出布

築者充作縣官衣食之諸取眾物鳥獸魚鼈百蟲於山林水澤及畜

牧者嬪婦桑織紝紡績補縫工匠醫巫卜祝及它方技商販賈

had been able to collect gold, silver, copper, lead ore, tin, to whom tortoises had presented themselves,[24.2] or who had gathered cowries, all themselves testified [their value to the Assistant for] the Office for Money of [the Master] in Charge of the Market, and he took them in accordance with the emanations of the seasons.

[Wang Mang] also [ordered], "In accordance with the [system of] taxing the common people in the *Chou Offices*,[24.3] all fields that are not plowed are 'unproductive [fields,' hence] shall pay taxes for three heads of households; residences inside the inner or outer city walls that are not planted [with fruit-trees] or cultivated [for garden produce] are 'denuded of vegetation,' and shall pay the hemp-cloth [tax] for three heads of households; common people who wander about and have no occupation must pay [the tax of] one roll of hemp-cloth for a head of a household. Those who are not able to pay the hemp-cloth [tax] shall work at incidental occupations for the imperial government and shall be clothed and fed by it.

"Those who collect articles of any kind, birds, beasts, fish, turtles, or the various insects from the mountains, forests, streams, or marshes, together with those who rear or care for domestic animals, women who collect mulberry leaves, rear silkworms, weave, spin, or sew, laborers, artisans, physicians, shamans, diviners, invokers, together with [people who have] other recipes or skills, peddlers, traders, merchants who sit down and spread out [their wares]

*The Offices for Money*

*22a Unused Land and Idle People Taxed*

*An Income Tax on Hunters, Fishermen, Sericulturists, Artisans, Professional Men and Merchants*

[24.2] I.e., those who had found tortoises. Ju Shun explains, "Tortoises have supernatural power 靈, hence it says that they present themselves 登."

[24.3] *Chou-li* 13:9a (Biot, I, 279 f) says, "All residences which are denuded [of vegetation] have the hempen-cloth [tax] for occupied land; all fields which were not plowed, pay grain for a house [occupied by three families]; all common people who do not have an occupation, pay the contribution of service for a head of a household." This passage enumerates the three types of taxes mentioned in *Mencius* VII, II, xxvii, 1 (Legge, p. 491).

**24b**

or who arrange them at stopping-places, or who visit houses, shall all and each themselves, at the places where they are, testify to the imperial government what they do, exclude their principal, calculate their [net] profit, divide off from it one-tenth, and use this one-[tenth] as their tribute. Those who presume not to testify themselves, or who themselves in testifying do not accord with the facts shall have all that they have collected or taken confiscated and paid [to the government] and shall work for the imperial government for one year.

22b *19a*
Equaliza-
tion of
Prices At
the Five
Market
Centers

"The [Masters] in Charge of Markets shall regularly, in the second month of [each of] the four seasons, determine the true [prices] of the articles that they take care of and make high, middle, and low prices [for the respective grades of these goods]. Each [Master] shall himself use [these prices] at his own market to equalize [prices there] and shall not restrict himself [by the prices] at other places. When the mass of common people have sold and bought the five [kinds of] grains or articles of hempen-cloth, silk cloth, silk thread, or silk wadding, which are used everywhere among the common people, whenever any has not been sold, and the office for equalization has examined and inspected the reality of that [fact, the office] shall take those [articles] at their cost price, so as not to cause [the people] to lose a cash. When [any of] the myriad things rise [in price and become] expensive, so that they surpass by one cash [the prices at which they have been] equalized, then [the accumulated stock] shall be sold to the common people in accordance with the price at which they have been equalized. If the price goes down and becomes cheap, below [the price at which it is to be] equalized, the common people shall be permitted to sell [goods] amongst each other at the market-place, in order to prevent any from storing [goods] up [for the purpose of keeping them until they become] expensive.[24.4]

萬物卬貴過平一錢則以平賈賣與民其賈氏賤減平者聽民自相與市以防貴庚
布帛絲縣之物周於民用而不讐者均官有以考撅厥賈用其本賈取之毋令折錢
四時中月賈定所掌為物上中下之賈各自用為其市平毋拘亡所衆民賣貫五穀
以其一為貢敢不自占自占不以貢者盡沒入所采取而作縣官一歲諸司市常以
人坐肆列里區謁舍皆各自占所為於其在所之縣官除其本計其利十一分之而

者民欲祭祀喪紀而無用者錢府旦所入工商之貢但賒之祭

祀無過旬日喪紀毋過三月民或之絕貸呂治產業者均授

之除其貴計所得受息毋過歲什一義和魯匡言名山大澤鹽

鐵錢布帛五均賒貸幹在縣官唯酒酤獨未幹酒者天之美祿

帝王所呂頤養天下享祀祈福扶衰養疾百禮之會非酒不行

"If any of the common people wish to sacrifice or perform funeral and mourning ceremonies, and have not the means, the Office for Money shall give to them on credit, without requiring interest, whatever laborers or merchants have paid in as tribute,[24.5] [in the case of] sacrifices, for not more than ten days, [and in the case of] mourning ceremonies, for not more than three months. If any of the common people are lacking and have no [means] or wish to borrow on interest in order to establish a productive occupation, [the money] shall be impartially given to them, and, after their expenses have been deducted, they shall calculate what [profit] they have made, and shall pay interest [to the amount of] not more than one-tenth [of his income] per year."[24.6]

**Government Loans to the People**

The Hsi-and-Ho, Lu K'uang, said, "The controls of [5] the famous mountains and great marshes, [2] salt and [3] iron, [4] cash and spade-money currency, [6] the five equalizations, selling on credit and lending on interest, are in [the hands of] the imperial government. Only [1] the selling of fermented drinks alone is not yet monopolized. Fermented drink is the most beautiful happiness from Heaven, whereby the lords and kings have nourished the country. Meetings for offering sacrifices, for praying for blessings, for succoring the decrepit, for caring for the sick, and all the rites, cannot be carried on without fermented drink.

23a

**25a Liquor Monopolized**

19b

[24.4] The procedure seems to have been that the Master fixed his prices for equalization as the fair prices for his market, and bought goods that were unsold in the market-place at their cost to the producer or at the current price, providing that this price was below his price for equalization. Then he sold those goods at the price for equalization whenever the market-price surpassed his price by one cash.

[24.5] I.e., as income-tax (cf. p. 24a).

[24.6] *HS* 99 B: 12b states however that interest was 3% per month. The usual rate of interest was 20% per year (91: 6a); so that the government was charging more than the current rate. This passage adds that borrowers were not to pay more than 10% of their net income as interest to the government.

"Hence the *Book of Odes* says,

'If I have no fermented drink, I buy it, do I,'[25.1] but the *Analects* says, '[Confucius] would not drink purchased fermented drink.'[25.2] These two are not contradictory.

"Verily, the ode refers to [a time when] peaceful reigns succeeded [each other, when] the fermented drink purchased at a [government] office was harmonious, agreeable, and suited to people, so that it could be offered [to others]. [In the time of] the *Analects*, Confucius [lived] in [the period when] the Chou [dynasty] was decaying and in disorder, so that the sale of fermented drink was in [the hands of] the common people, [and hence] was of poor quality, bad, and not free from adulteration. For this reason [Confucius] suspected it and would not drink it.

"If now the empire's fermented drink is cut off, then there will be no means of performing the rites or of cherishing others. If permission is given [to anyone to make it] and no limit is set [to its manufacture], then it will consume wealth and injure the common people. [Hence] I beg that you will imitate ancient [practises] and order the [government] offices to make fermented drink, taking 2500 piculs as one standard [unit] and accordingly open one shop[25.3] to **25b** 23b sell [this quantity]. If the selling of fifty fermentations is taken as one standard [unit]; one fermentation requires two *hu* of coarse grain and one *hu* of yeast, [from which] is obtained six *hu* six *tou* of finished fermented drink. If for each [fermentation] one counts up together the price of the three *hu* of grain and yeast, according to [the price at] the

---

[25.1] *Book of Odes* (no. 165), II, ɪ, v, 3 (Legge, 255).

[25.2] *Analects* X, viii, 5.

[25.3] Ju Shun explains, "When a liquor-seller opens a shop and waits for guests, he puts up a wine-jar. Hence a wine-jar (*lu* 鑪) is used as the name for the shop." Yen Shih-ku denies this plain interpretation, but Liu Feng-shih points out that Ju Shun must be correct.

*HS* 91: 7a states, "A large capital which communicates with [surrounding] towns sells a thousand fermentations in one year."

故詩曰無酒酤我而論語曰酤酒不食二者非相反也夫詩據承平之世酒

蘗米二斛麴一斛得成酒六斛六斗各以其市月朔米麴三斛并計其賈而

古今官作酒以二千五百石為一均率開一盧以賣豐五十釀用

臣疑而弗食今絶天下之酒則無以行禮相養放而亡限則貴財傷民矯法

酤在官和旨便人可以相御也論語孔子當周衰亂酒酤在民薄惡不誠是

故詩曰無酒酤我而論語曰酤酒不食二者非相反也夫詩據承平之世酒

嘉會之好醴曰農之本名山大澤饒衍之臧五均賒貸百姓所取平卬已給澹

空簿府臧不賣百姓俞病荐知民苦之復下詔曰夫鹽食肴之將酒百藥之長

貴洛陽薛子仲張長叔臨菑姓偉等乘傳求利交錯天下因與郡縣通姦多張

三及醴藏灰炭給工器薪樵之費義和置命士督五均六斡郡有數人皆用富

參分之呂其一為酒一斛之平除米麴本賈計其利而什分之呂其七入官其

market-place on the first day of the month, divide it 20a by three, and take one part as the average for one *hu* of [material for] fermented drink, if one deducts the original price of the grain and yeast and counts up the profit, then seven parts in ten will be paid to the government. The three [other parts], together with the lees, vinegar, ashes, and charcoal may be given to the workmen for the expense of the utensils and firewood."

The Hsi-and-Ho, [Lu K'uang], established [officials, ranking as] Mandated Officers, to supervise the five equalizations and the six monopolies. [In each] commandery there were several [such] men. Everywhere he employed rich merchants, [such as] Nieh Tzu-chung and Chang Ch'ang-shu from Lo-yang, Hsin Wei from Lin-tzu, and others. [Traveling] in riding quadrigae, they sought for profit and made numerous contacts [all over] the empire, and, availing [themselves of their opportunities], they communicated their wickedness to the commanderies and prefectures, and made many false accountings. The yamens and storehouses were not filled, and the people suffered all the more.

The Monopolies Cause Trouble

[Wang] Mang knew that the common people suffered from these [measures, so he] again issued an imperial edict, which said, "Verily, [2] salt is the greatest of foods; [1] fermented drink is the chief of all medicines and the best feature of auspicious assemblies; [3] iron is the fundamental [thing] in [the cultivation of] fields[25.4] and in agriculture; [5] the famous mountains and the great marshes are storehouses of abundance; [6] the five equalizations and and [the system of] selling on credit and lending on interest [are means by which] the people may receive the equalization of high [prices], in order to give as-

24a
An Edict Justifying Them

26a

[25.4] Ch'ien Ta-chao says that 日 should be 田; the Official ed. has made this emendation, and I have followed it.

sistance [to the people against profiteers]; [4] cash[26.1] and spade-money, and the casting of copper make wealth circulate and furnish [what is needed] for the common people's use.  These six [matters] are not [things that] the enrolled households of equal common people[26.2] are able to make in their homes, so that, if [the prices of these goods] are high in the market-place, although [these things] may be several times as expensive [as usual, the people] inevitably have no alternative but to purchase them, [hence] eminent common people and wealthy merchants can thereupon coerce the poor and weak.  The ancient sages knew that it would be so, hence they made controls (monopolies) of these [matters]."

*20b*

**Penalties for Violation**

For each control (monopoly) he established rules and precepts to interdict and prohibit [violations of the monopoly]; the penalties for violation extended to capital [punishment].[26.3]  Wicked officials and cunning common people both at the same time encroached upon the mass of people, so that every [person] was disquieted with life.

**A.D. 14 Two Denominations of Money**

The fifth year after, in [the period] T'ien-feng, the first year,[26.4] [Wang Mang] again sent down [a message], increasing and decreasing considerably the price and value of gold, silver, tortoise-[shell], and cowry currency, and abolishing the large and small cash.  Instead he made "currency spade-money (*huo-*

---

[26.1] Ch'ien Ta-chao remarks that the Fukien ed. (1549) has emended 鐵 to 錢, which seems correct, since iron was previously mentioned.

[26.2] In a note to *HS* 24 B: 17a, Ju Shun glosses, "*Ch'i* 齊 is 'of the same rank 等也.' When there are no honorable or inferior [grades] they are called the equal common-people (*ch'i-min* 民), just as at present we say *p'ing* 平 *-min*."   Chin Shao however declares, "They are Chinese instructed and regulated (*ch'i-cheng* 整) common people."   Chavannes (*Mh* III, 588 = *SC* 30: 35), who did not have Ju Shun's gloss available, follows Chin Shao, but Yen Shih-ku approves of Ju Shun's interpretation.

[26.3] This sentence is a doublet (except for verbal differences) of one in 99 C: 1b; that sentence seems however to refer to a second issuance of these rules.

[26.4] *HS* 99 C: 10a mentions this enactment under the date A.D. 20, because it was not to take full effect until that time.   Cf. 99 C: 10a & n. 10.4.

長二寸五分廣一寸首長八分有奇廣八
分其圓好徑二分半足枚長八分閒廣二
分其文右曰貨左曰布重二十五銖直貨
泉二十五貨泉徑一寸重五銖文右曰貨
左曰泉枚直一與貨布二品並行又曰大

pu)," two inches five *fen* in length and one inch in width, with their heads eight *fen* and a fraction long and eight *fen* wide, their circular holes two *fen* and a half in diameter, their feet eight *fen* long, their opening [between the feet] two *fen* wide, their legend, on the right reading, "Currency (*huo*)" and on the left reading, "Spade-money (*pu*)."[26.5] Their weight was twenty-five *shu*, and they were worth twenty-five of the currency cash. The currency cash (*huo-ch'üan*) were one inch in diameter, and weighed five *shu*. Their legend on the right reads "Currency (*huo*)" and on the left reads "Cash (*ch'üan*)."[26.6] One [such] was worth one [cash]; it and the currency spade-money [formed] two denominations, which circulated concurrently.

24b

Moreover, because the large cash had circulated

[26.5] Cf. Lockhart, *ibid.*, nos. 155, 156; de Lacouperie, *ibid.*, p. 306, nos. 112–115; Glathe, *op. cit.*, p. 29, no. 101; *Chin-shih-so*, Chin, 4:32a. Prof. P. M. L. Linebarger of Duke University has loaned me a well-preserved *ho-pu* coin of this issue, weighing 15.53 g. (legal weight, according to the *HS*, 16.0 g.); length, 57.7 mm. (legal, 58 mm.); width, 23.5 mm. (legal, 23.1 mm.); length of feet 19 mm. (legal, 18.5 mm.); width of opening, 4.8 mm. (legal, 4.6 mm.).

[26.6] Cf. Lockhart, *ibid.*, nos. 162-182; de Lacouperie, *ibid.*, p. 384, nos. 365–400; Glathe, *op. cit.*, p. 30, nos. 173–75; *Chin-shih-so*, Chin, 4:29a.

*HHS*, An. 1 B:23b says, "When Wang Mang had usurped the throne, he feared evil [because] the Liu clan had used the word *ch'ien* 錢 [as the word for 'cash'] and [the word for Liu 劉] contains [the words for] metal (*chin* 金) and knife (*tao* 刀), hence [Wang Mang] changed [the coinage and the word for 'cash'] and made it 'currency cash (*huo-ch'üan* 貨泉).' [But] someone considered that the words *huo-ch'üan* were 'The immortal of the White River (*Po-shui chen-jen*)'." Ying Shao, in his *Han-kuan-yi* (lost; quoted in *T'ai-p'ing Yü-lan* 835:6b, 7a) also remarks this circumstance, and adds, "This was an auspicious presage of the restoration under the Epochal Founder, [Emperor Kuang-wu]."

The word *ch'üan* 泉 is composed of the words *po* 白 and *shui* 水, and *huo* 貨 is composed of *jen* 人 and *chen* 眞, which make-up is particularly evident in the seal form on these coins, in which the *jen* extends all along the left side of the character. The White River was a stream which arises 50 *li* northeast of the present Tsao-yang, Hupeh (*Shina Rekidai Chimei Yoran*, p. 531); Emperor Kuang-wu came from the city of Ts'ai-yang, which was located southwest of the present Tsao-yang (*HHS*, An. 1 A:1a); hence it was not surprising that these coins issued by Wang Mang were later understood as a prophecy of Emperor Kuang-wu.

for a long time, [Wang Mang] abolished them, fearing that the common people would keep them and not stop [using them].[26.7]  So he ordered that the common people should only temporarily circulate the

**26b**  large cash, and that one [such large cash] should be worth one of the new currency cash, that their con-

A.D. 20  current circulation should be ended in the sixth year, and that [people] should not [then] be any more allowed to possess the large cash.[26.8]

Penalties  Each time that the money was changed, the com-
Make the  mon people were thereby ruined financially and fell
People  into serious punishment.  Because so many were
Suffer  those who violated the laws and [whoever] privately cast cash had to die and [whoever] criticized or put obstacles [in the circulation of] the valuable currency should be thrown out to the four borders, with the result that [their sentences] could not be entirely carried out, [Wang] Mang therefore changed and lightened these laws: those who privately cast or made cash or spade-money were confiscated with their wives and children and became government slaves or slave-women.  Officials and the group of five [families, of which the culprit was a member], who knew of [the crime] and did not bring it forward or denounce it, [were tried] with [the culprit as having committed] a like crime.  As to those who criticized or put obstacles [in the circulation of] the

*21a*  valuable currency: common people were to be punished [by being made] to work for one year and

為官奴婢吏及比伍知而不舉告與同罪非沮寶貨民罰
者多不可勝行迺更輕其法私鑄作泉布者與妻子沒入
破業而大陷刑莽呂私鑄錢死及非沮寶貨投四裔犯法
俱枚直一並行盡六年毋得復挾大錢矣每壹易錢民用
錢行久罷之恐民挾不止迺令民且獨行大錢與新貨泉

---

[26.7] The "large cash" weighed 12 *shu* and were nominally worth 50 cash (B: 21a), i.e., 0.24 *shu* per cash; the spade-money of 14 A.D. weighed 1 *shu* per cash and the round cash weighed 5 *shu* per cash; Wang Mang was trying to drive out light coins, something that rulers have always found difficult or impossible, because of the facts summed up in Gresham's law.

[26.8] Since the "large cash" had been worth 50 cash, and the new cash were worth 1 cash, such a valuation meant losing 49/50 of their nominal value.  Yet the large cash weighed more than twice as much as the new cash, so that private melting down and counterfeit casting became inevitable.

盡復曰與民民搖手觸禁不得耕桑餘役煩劇而枯旱蝗蟲
三十而取一又令公卿呂下至郡縣黃綬皆保養軍馬吏
寇甚莽大募天下囚徒人奴名曰豬突豨勇壹切稅吏民訾
鎮傳送長安鍾官愁苦死者什六七作貨布後六年句奴侵
作一歲吏免官犯者俞眾及五人相坐皆沒入郡國樞車鐵

officials were to be dismissed from their offices. When
violations became the more numerous and [the people
in the group of] five [families who were held responsi-
ble] were sentenced together with them and all were
confiscated to [the government penal service], the
commanderies and kingdoms, with accompanying
[guards], sent them in carts with cages, with iron
locks [about their necks], to the Office for Coinage
at Ch'ang-an. Six or seven out of [every] ten [of
these people] died from the hardships and suffering.

25a
Counter-
feiters
Enslaved
to the
Mint

The sixth year after the currency spade-money had
been issued,[26.9] the Huns made great incursions and
robberies, [hence Wang] Mang made a great solicitation of the empire's prisoners, convicts, and people's
slaves, naming them, "Boar braves who are porcupines rushing out." He temporarily taxed the
officials and common people, taking one-thirtieth of
their property. He also ordered that the ministers
and those of lower [rank, down] to the officials in the
commanderies and counties who wore yellow seal-
cords,[26.10] should all guarantee the rearing of horses
for the army, and the officials all in turn gave [these
horses to] the common people [to care for them].
Whenever the common people moved their hands,
they ran upon a prohibition. They could not plow
or cultivate silkworms, for the corvée service was
troublesome and distressing, and withering droughts
and [plagues of] insects and locusts[26.11] followed
each other.

A.D. 19
A Great
Levy and
Taxation

[26.9] Cf. 99 C: 4b.

[26.10] Cf. 99 C: n. 4.10.

[26.11] Wang Nien-sun points out that *huang-ch'ung* 蝗蟲 was originally *ch'ung-huang*.
He quotes the parallel expressions *ch'ung-ming* 螟 in *Li-chi* IV, IV, ii, 18 (Legge, I, 306;
Couvreur, I, 345); 草茅 in *Yi-li* 7: 8a (Steele, I, 50); 鳥烏 in *Tso-chuan*, Dk. Hsiang,
XVIII, autumn (Legge, 476[11]); 禽犢 in the *Hsün-tzu;* the present expression *ch'ung*-蟻;
*ch'ung-huang* in *HS* 27 Ca: 2b[10]; the present *huang-ch'ung*, which he says was originally
*ch'ung-huang* (cf. *Ching-yi Shu-wen*) in *Li-chi* IV, iii, 21 (Couvreur, I, 358); and *ch'ung-
huang* in *Shuo-wen* 13 A: 8b, *sub* 蠚. The *HS* uses *huang* just as the *Tso-chuan* uses

27a
Private
Illicit
Taxation

Moreover, because [Wang Mang's] establishment [of rites] and composition [of music] had not been settled, from the dukes and marquises on the one hand to the minor officials on the other, they all could not secure their salaries, so they made private taxations and collections, and goods and bribes flowed up from them.   Criminal trials and litigations were not settled, officials employed tyranny and violence in order to establish their power, and utilized [Wang] Mang's prohibitions to encroach upon and oppress the unimportant common people.

Banditry
25b

When the wealthy were not able to protect themselves and the poor had no way of keeping themselves alive, they arose and became thieves and robbers. Since they relied upon the fastnesses of the mountains and marshes [for refuge], the officials were not able to capture them, hence covered and hid the [fact], and the infection spread daily.   Thereupon in the regions of Ch'ing, Hsü, Ching, and Ch'u [Provinces, people] often by the ten-thousands battled and

*21b*

died, were taken captive at the borders by the various barbarians, fell into criminal punishment, or suffered from famine and epidemics, so that people ate each

Depopulation

other.   Before [Wang] Mang had been executed, the population of the empire had been reduced by half.[27.1]

邊四夷所係虜陷罪飢疫人相食及莽未誅而天下戶口減半
震藪之浸淫日廣於是青徐荊楚之地往往萬數戰鬬死亡綠
者不得自保貧者無以自存起為盜賊依阻山澤吏不能禽而
斂貨賂上流獄訟不決吏用奇暴立威旁緣莽禁侵刻小民富而
相固又用制作未定上自公侯下至小吏皆不得奉祿而私賦

*ch'ung* (as indicating an insect plague), so that it does not make sense to add a *ch'ung* after the *huang*, for the phrase *ch'ung-huang* means that the plague consisted of other insects in addition to the *huang*.   HS 27 Bb: 20a, b lists plagues of *ming* and *huang* from 130 to 89 B.C., hence in HS 75: 4a[4] Hsia-hou Sheng summed them up by saying that *ch'ung-huang* arose, i.e., both locusts and other insects appeared; the present reading of HS 75: 4a, *huang-ch'ung*, which means only locusts, is thus inexact.   People did not understand the meaning of *ch'ung-huang*, so changed it to *huang-ch'ung*.   Hence the phrase *huang-ch'ung* was originally *ch'ung-huang* in SC 106: 12[1] = HS 35: 7b[5], HS 75: 4a[4], HS 90: 17a[10] (which is quoted in a note to HHS, Mem. 67: 10a[11] without the *ch'ung*).

[27.1] H. Bielenstein, BMFEA, no. 19, pp. 125–163, in an illuminating paper, "The Census of China during the Period 2–742 A.D.," (esp. pp. 135–145), shows that, between 2 B.C. (when the population was 56.7 million) and A.D. 140, there was a decrease of 8 or 9 million, i.e., about 15%.   The population of northwestern and northeastern China had decreased nearly 18 million, whereas that of south China, especially the present Hunan, Kiangsi, Kwangtung, and Szechuan, had increased by roughly 9 million.   When we make allowance for the natural population increase in the subsequent century, Pan Ku's statement, that by A.D. 25 the population fell to half its former figure, is roughly corroborated, but for north China only.   He seems to have been unaware that millions had emigrated into central and southern China, so that the total loss in population was not as great as he believed.

In the fourth year after the "Boar braves who are    A.D. 23
porcupines rushing out" had been mobilized, the
Han troops executed [Wang] Mang. The second
year afterwards, the Epochal Founder, [Emperor    A.D. 25
Kuang-wu], received [Heaven's] mandate, washed
away these vexatious [ordinances] and tyrannous
[punishments], restored the five-*shu* cash, and gave a
new beginning to the empire.[27.2]

[27.2] *HHS* Tr. 13: 10b says, "In A.D. 30, boys in *Shu* circulated a saying,
'A yellow bull with a white belly,
The five-*shu* [cash] must be restored.'
At this time Kung-sun Shu had usurped the [imperial] title in Shu. At that time, people
said secretly that Wang Mang had taken yellow [for his color; Kung-sun] Shu wanted to
succeed him, hence he took white [for his color]. The five-*shu* cash were the currency of
the Han dynasty, [so that this saying] made plain that the Han dynasty must be restored.
[Kung-sun] Shu was thereupon executed and destroyed." Thus even a reference to a
particular coinage had political implications. (Reference from Chou Shou-ch'ang.)

# APPENDIX II

## WANG MANG'S ECONOMIC REFORMS

The economic changes made by Wang Mang constitute one of the very interesting experiments man has made with his social environment. In studying these reforms, we must recognize that they sprang from the Confucianism of that age. While Wang Mang was himself interested in changing government institutions—he liked nothing so much as to show his superiority by bringing about an improvement—yet the crucial test of any proposed change was whether it was classical, i.e., whether it had been practised or approved by some of the sages, as their deeds and sayings were recorded in the Classics and interpreted by the scholarly traditions of the time, handed down in the various schools. Wang Mang had moreover added certain books to the official Confucian canon: the *Tso-chuan*, the *Chou Offices*, the ancient text (since lost) of the *Book of History*, the lost chapters of that *Book*, etc. (99 A: 19a). The *Chou Offices*, for example, seems to have been prepared, in part at least, by idealistic Confucian antiquarians, who, consciously or unconsciously, wrote into the past their own conceptions of an ideal government. In these new canonical books there were naturally many traditions concerning economic matters. Wang Mang had acquired his popularity among the intelligentsia, which had brought him to the throne, by his complete conformity to Confucian ideals; when he ruled in person, he was then obligated to put into practise these Confucian ideals. Wang Mang was, first and foremost, a complete Confucian; the credit for his remarkable reforms must be given rather to the Confucian literati than to him.

Wang Mang was also a scheming courtier who wormed his way into power by clever intrigue. He came of a clan that had enriched itself, beyond all other clans, through imperial grants and through profiting from the perquisites of power. While Wang Mang himself held his acquisitive propensities severely in check, in order to appear liberal (99 A: 1b), yet at heart he was grasping and stingy (99 C: 1b). Hence he saw to it that his reforms benefited the throne. In his rule, he showed himself callous to the true interests of his people, with the result that their economic condition deteriorated, until, as a result of misgovernment, oppression, famine, banditry, and civil war, the population was reduced by half (24 B: 27a).

Such a result was however quite contrary to Confucian idealism, which was sympathetic with the people. To Confucians, it was axiomatic that all reforms which accord with the Classics will benefit the state and the people. Consequently, when any of Wang Mang's reforms brought discontent and economic disorganization, the conclusion was drawn that it was not really classical. Wang Mang did not follow classical precedents slavishly; he improved on them. The tradition was that King Wen had coined two denominations of money (24 B: n. 21.2), so Wang Mang instituted twenty-eight denominations (24 B: 23a), only later reducing them to two. Wang Mang found the word "controls (kuan)" in the Classics (24 B: 23b), whereupon he used this word as a justification for his monopolies; later, when these monopolies were seen to have oppressed the people, the term "controls" was interpreted otherwise and monopolies were held to be unclassical. As a result of Wang Mang's failure, Confucianism was not discarded by many intelligentsia, it was merely reinterpreted; the Later Han dynasty was at first more Confucian than the Former Han. But sceptical thinkers (even some members of Wang Mang's own clan, such as Wang Chi₇ [a distant cousin, cf. *HHS*, Mem. 9: 1a]) began now to be repelled by Confucianism and were attracted to Taoism, so that at this time there began the re-emergence of this doctrine after a century of almost total eclipse. Wang Mang's own grasping nature was an important reason for the failure of his reforms, in spite of their Confucian nature.

We shall consider his economic changes in the following order: (1) his monetary reforms, (2) his policy regarding land and slavery, (3) his monopolies and taxes, and (4) his attempt to speculate in staples and to loan money.

His monetary reforms came soon after he became Acting Emperor (A.D. 6). A tradition had been preserved that in Chou times, in order to compensate for fluctuations of prices, there had been two denominations of bronze coins, not merely one, as in Han times. (*HS* 24 B: 2b, 3a, 21a & n. 21.2). This tradition made varied coinage a Confucian practise, since a fundamental Confucian principle was the imitation of the ancient sages. Wang Mang accordingly coined four denominations of bronze coins, with the values of 1, 50, 500, and 5000 cash. The first two denominations were round cash; the latter two were in the form of knives. The fifty-cash coins had only $\frac{1}{20}$ as much metal per cash as the one-cash coins, and the others were proportionately lighter (about $\frac{1}{100}$ and $\frac{1}{625}$ as much metal per cash as the one-cash coins), so that there was much profit for the government in this coinage. In its early years, the Han dynasty had experimented with depreciating the coinage, but there had arisen opposition to that practise, and, for the last century and a quarter, there had been no change in the weight of coins, so that the evil effects of this depreciation were probably not anticipated. One result was a great increase in counterfeiting.

In addition, Wang Mang "nationalized" all gold, that is, he permitted only vassal kings to possess actual gold, other nobles and people being required to bring their gold to the Emperor's wardrobe, where they were to be given its value in bronze cash. Pan Ku states that they were not given its full value. Very probably they were paid in light-weight knife-coins of high denominations. Thus Wang Mang made much profit out of manipulating coinage and gold.

When in A.D. 9, Wang Mang became titular emperor and established his own dynasty, he had to do away with the knife-coins, because the Chinese word for knife, 刀, forms part of the word Liu 劉, the surname of the Han dynasty. Since a change in currency was thus necessary, he first did away with the knife-coins, only two denominations remaining (A.D. 9), and later (A.D. 10), added other denominations to make twenty-eight in all. Sixteen of these were of bronze. The others, in gold, silver, tortoise-shells, and cowries, were not coined, so that this legislation amounted to fixing a price for these four articles.

An important motive in this bronze coinage was undoubtedly to make a profit for the government. We are informed concerning the weight and value of each denomination (24 B: 21a–23a). The light-weight fifty-cash pieces were retained, but the heavy one-cash pieces were replaced by new cash weighing only one-fifth as much as the former one-cash pieces. The higher denominations were in the shape of trousers-cash or spade-money. The weights of these bronze coins were so arranged that the one-cash pieces contained proportionately the largest amount of metal, each higher denomination containing proportionately less metal, until the highest denomination, that of a thousand cash, contained only 2.4% as much metal per cash as the one-cash pieces (cf. 24 B: n. 22.11). This coinage was thus an issue of metal fiat money. People who had previously used the heavy one-cash pieces would hardly want to give them up in exchange for the new light coins. In order to make the coins of large denominations circulate, Wang Mang ordered that all persons who passed the likin stations at the passes, fords, and elsewhere must show large spade-coins of high denominations along with their passports; officials who used the government posts or who entered the palaces, must also show spade-money in order to be admitted (99 B: 15a). Since cash were cast, instead of being struck, counterfeiting was easy and many people were driven to it in order to preserve their wealth. To stop counterfeiting, Wang Mang made the possession of copper and charcoal an offense (99 B:

7b). This law proved too drastic and was moreover ineffective; it was consequently abolished in A.D. 13 (99 B: 22a). When the people refused to use the new coins, Wang Mang issued an edict that all those possessing the older heavy cash would be executed or exiled. Pan Ku says that as a consequence farmers could not sell their produce nor merchants their goods, and the common people wept in the market-places and highways, while uncounted people and officials, even of the highest ranks, were sentenced for crime (24 B: 23a).

When we note that the mere possession of the heavy coins was made a crime, and that an informer was given half of the illicit wealth seized as a result of his information, we can well believe Pan Ku's statement. In order to maintain a semblance of authority over the coinage, Wang Mang had to abandon all but two denominations of these new coins, and retain only the light one-cash pieces and the fifty-cash pieces (24 B: 23b).

Some years later (A.D. 14), Wang Mang again changed the coinage. The light-weight one-cash pieces had probably so disarranged prices that there had been a loud clamor for the restoration of the previous heavy cash. The people had been paying taxes in the light cash, and the officials had probably found that taxes and their salaries (which were payable half in coin) did not yield as much value as previously. The former coinage was therefore abolished and the previous heavy one-cash pieces, weighing five times as much as the light one-cash pieces, were restored. But the light one-cash coins were not exchanged for the new heavy cash; they were merely dropped. The one-cash pieces in circulation were thus demonetized. An edict was issued which declared that the previous fifty-cash coins (weighing two and one-half times as much as the new large one-cash coins) were to be worth as much as one of the new one-cash pieces (24 B: 26b), i.e., the government would take a former fifty-cash coin in place of a new one-cash coin.

The people were given six years in which to make this change; after that time, possession of the former fifty-cash pieces was to be forbidden. The result may easily be imagined. A person who had any large amount of money in fifty-cash pieces and who used it in accordance with the law, lost $\frac{49}{50}$ of his money. What he had in one-cash pieces became worth only so much metal. Few people could afford to make the exchange. By melting down cash, on the other hand, a person may have lost comparatively little, for cash were then probably worth approximately their weight in metal. All that was needed was new cash to use as models, clay for moulds, and a charcoal stove to melt the coins. It is not surprising that counterfeiting became ubiquitous. To stop it, people were grouped in lots of five families, who were responsible for each other; if one family was caught counterfeiting, all five families were punished. So many people, however, violated the law that the punishments could not be carried out. Wang Mang had to lighten the punishment for counterfeiting to enslavement of the counterfeiter to the government, together with his wife and children and those in his group of five families. These unfortunates were transported to the mint at the capital to work out their sentences. Pan Ku states that six or seven out of every ten died from the hardships and suffering (24 B: 26b).

There were also coined new twenty-five-cash pieces (in the shape of trousers-cash or spade-money), which contained one-fifth as much metal per cash as the new one-cash pieces. Thus the former principle was continued, of profiting by coining light-weight pieces of high denominations. Light-weight coins of high value would be a boon to anyone who must transport money, if their value could be maintained. But there is no evidence that the government did anything to maintain their value. The fact that the coins of high denominations in the second coinage were dropped and that the coins of high value in the third coinage were only twenty-five-cash pieces, instead of fifty-cash pieces as in the first coinage, would seem to indicate that the value of these coins was not maintained and that they depreciated in usage.

We must resort to inference in order to determine the precise economic effects upon Chinese society of Wang Mang's three changes in coinage and his nationalization of gold. The latter decree probably succeeded in mulcting the wealthy, especially the Han dynasty's nobility, who were the only persons likely to have possessed much gold. They needed gold for their yearly contribution to the throne (*HFHD* II, 126–128). Since Wang Mang allowed the highest nobles (the vassal kings) to retain their gold, he did not, even in A.D. 6, take gold completely out of circulation; the enactment of A.D. 10, which made gold one of the articles of currency, rescinded the prohibition against possessing gold.

At that time, gold was not coined, but circulated in the shape of square cakes an inch (0.9 in., Eng. meas.) on a side and weighing a catty (then 7.84 oz. troy, 244 g.; *HFHD*, I, 280). Such a catty of gold was worth ten thousand cash; imperial grants of gold were usually transmitted in terms of their equivalent in bronze cash. Ten catties of gold was the value of the property belonging to a median family (*HS* 4: 21a). By exchanging depreciated inlaid bronze knife-coins for actual gold, Wang Mang deprived all but his highest nobles of much of their wealth. His use of such knife-money in making grants saved him about 99.8% of the metal he would otherwise have disbursed. For the first three years after their gold had been taken away, the nobles probably did not feel the loss—they merely paid their annual required contribution in the form of gilded knife-money. When, however, in A.D. 9, these knife-coins were demonetized and suddenly became worth only their value in metal, the nobles found themselves mulcted and had to get rid of these knife-coins to show their loyalty to the new dynasty. Thus, by a clever trick, Wang Mang deprived the Han dynasty's nobility of much their wealth, before he dismissed them and set up his own nobility.

Wang Mang seems to have hoarded most of the gold he obtained. He was miserly, and failed to use his treasure, even in emergencies (cf. his payment to soldiers, 99 C: 25b). Pan Ku reports that when Wang Mang was finally killed, he still had much treasure. Ten thousand catties of gold made a chest and there were sixty chests of gold in the imperial apartments, as well as several chests in other offices of the palace, besides cash, silk, pearls, jade and valuables (99 C: 25a, b). This nationalization of gold seems merely to have withdrawn much of the empire's gold from circulation and to have concentrated it in the imperial palace. The nobles had been given depreciated bronze coins, nominally of the same value, but probably exchangeable in trade for far less, and these coins were soon demonetized, after which time gold was again allowed to circulate.

Sixty chests of gold, if all the chests were full, would be 146,400,000 grams or 4,706,867 oz. troy. There were also "several chests" in each of three other offices, so that the total amount, if correctly reported, must have been about 5,000,000 oz. of gold. Where did this huge amount of treasure come from? If the report is correct, it was a greater quantity than the entire visible stock of gold in Europe of the middle ages, which is estimated as not over 3,750,000 oz.[1]

The reliability of this report concerning the gold is probably quite high. Pan Ku was too careful a historian to insert such a statement into his account if he had no documentary source for it. He had no motive in exaggerating Wang Mang's wealth. This statement probably came from the report to the Keng-shih Emperor made in A.D. 23 by the captors of Ch'ang-an. They may indeed have exaggerated their report of Wang Mang's wealth. "Sixty" is a round number and so may not be exact. But the captors would not have exaggerated very much, for they would be held accountable if any large amount of treasure was missing. The Wei-yang Palace, in which were located the inner apartments containing this large treasure, was burnt in the attack upon Wang Mang, but Pan Ku says specifically that the government treasuries were nevertheless maintained intact (99 C: 29a). Proof that Wang Mang had possessed a

---

[1] Joseph Kitchin, *Encyclopedia of Social Sciences*, art. "Gold."

large amount of gold is also afforded by his betrothal present to the family of his second wife, nee Shih, which was 30,000 catties of actual gold or 235,343 oz. (7,320,000 g.; 99 C: 20a).[2] Thus Wang Mang must at one time have had about five million ounces of gold. China had never produced any large quantity of gold;[3] whence could he have obtained all this treasure?

[2] *SC* 30: 11 (= *Mh* III, 553 = *HS* 24 B: 8a) also states that in 123 B.C. (possibly in this *and* the preceding years since 135 B.C., when Emperor Wu began his war against the Huns) Emperor Wu gave out more than 200,000 catties of actual gold in rewards to his victorious troops—an amount over 1,568,000 oz. or 48,800,000 g. There may have been a set monetary grant for each head or prisoner taken (cf. 6: n. 7.8) or Emperor Wu may have been over-liberal in his grants. They seem to have exhausted the imperial treasury, for at this time a new military aristocracy was established, ranks in which were to be used in the future to reward victorious troops. In 135 B.C., Emperor Wu then possessed at least 1,600,000 oz. or 50,000,000 g. of gold, while in 23 A.D. Wang Mang had three times as much. It is attractive to speculate that in a century and a half the gold stock of China may have tripled. (It should however be noted that Emperor Wu did not attempt to monopolize his country's gold in the way Wang Mang did.)

[3] While gold is very widely distributed in China, it has nowhere been mined in very large amounts, and ancient references to gold production in China are quite uncommon. There seems to be only one in the *HS*—28 Aiii: 42b states that ten-odd *li* west of Wu-yang District 武陽鄉 in P'o-yang 鄱陽 County of Yü-chang Commandery there was a gold placer 黃金采 (this phrase is interpreted "where gold is taken"). Wu-yang was fifty *li* east of the present P'o-yang. (This placer is also mentioned in *Shui-ching-chu* 39: 17b.) But *HS* 28 Bii: 67a reports, "Yü-chang [Commandery] produces actual gold, but very little. The things that can be gotten with it are inadequate in exchange for the expense [of getting it]."

Probably other Chinese deposits were likewise poor. *Shui-ching-chu* 27: 12b mentions gold in the mountains along the Han River below the Hou-ching Rapids 猴徑灘 below Ch'eng-ku 城固, and also on the southern bank of the Yangtze, below its junction with the Hsiang River (*ibid.* 35: 4a), but neither of these places seems to have produced much gold. Curiously enough, Kiangsi is not at present credited with any gold production. Evidently its deposits were anciently exhausted. (Cf. *New Atlas & Commercial Gazetteer of China*; *Chinese Year Book*, 1938–1939, pp. 488–490.) According to a news release from the China Information Committee, dated Aug. 7, 1939, although efforts had been made to stimulate gold production by modern methods, for many years previous to 1938–9, gold production in China and outlying territories had averaged only 130,000 ounces yearly. (Communicated by Prof. T. T. Reed of Columbia University School of Mines.) With ancient primitive methods of mining, even if all the modern lodes were known in ancient times (which is not at all likely), the amount of production would have been very much less. If there had been any large production of gold in ancient China, we would undoubtedly have been informed of it. Ancient Chinese production cannot explain Wang Mang's hoard of gold.

Outside of the above few references, gold production is mentioned in the *HS* only in two regions outside the Chinese area: in Chi-pin (Kabul or northern India) and in Wu-yi-shan-li (Seistan; *HS* 96 A: 24a, 29a = de Groot, *Die Westlande*, pp. 87, 91; for identifi-

It undoubtedly came to China in return for Chinese exports, the chief of which was silk. Gold has indeed a tendency to form hoards. Siberia was then the largest and nearest source of gold. Much of the gold possessed by ancient oriental empires seems to have come from this region. Parthia, Bactria, Sogdiana, and India produced little or no gold, although Bactria was famed in ancient times for its gold.[4] An abundance of golden articles has however been found in Scythian graves in South Russia and Siberia. In the fifth century, the Massagetae, who were northern neighbors of Bactria, had so much gold that they used it to make bits and trappings for their horses.[5] Probably most of this gold came from placer mining along the headwaters of Siberian rivers; even at the beginning of the present century, the main Siberian sources were the washings along the Lena and Amur. Possibly the Obi and Yenisei systems also furnished gold; new gold fields are said to have recently been discovered near the head waters of both rivers. Probably gold was obtained over a very large area; Siberia is today asserted to have larger amounts of gold

cation, cf. Tarn, *Greeks in Bactria*, pp. 340 ff, 347). But Tarn (*ibid.* p. 103–4) indicates that these regions produced no gold; their gold was an importation from Siberia. The *HS* says nothing, either in its "Treatise on the Principles of Geographical Arrangements" (ch. 28) or elsewhere, about any gold washings in Yünnan or elsewhere, such as those mentioned by Marco Polo (II, ch. 47–48). *HHS*, Tr. 23 A: 24a however notes gold produced in the southern borders of Po-nan 博南 County in Yung-ch'ang Commandery, which is the present Yung-ch'ang 永昌, Yünnan. This gold seems however to have first become known between the time Pan Ku wrote in 58–84 A.D. and the age in which Szu-ma Piao (ca. 240–306) compiled the *HHS* Treatises. According to the *Hua-yang Kuo Chih* (by Ch'ang Ch'ü, fl. dur. 302–347), 4: 5b, chap. "Nan-chung *Chih*," this gold seems to have been produced abundantly only after the conquest of this region in A.D. 225. Hence the gold of Yünnan did not contribute to Wang Mang's hoard. While it is always dangerous to argue from negatives, yet the *HS* is careful in mentioning outstanding products and seems to be interested in deposits of gold. We are hence probably safe in concluding that nowhere in the Chinese world of Han times were there produced any large amounts of gold, so that Wang Mang's store must have been largely imported from outside China.

[4] W. W. Tarn, *The Greeks in Bactria and India*, p. 107 f, points out that the Greeks had to teach the Indians about gold and silver mining and that the Greek invaders got no gold in India (*ibid.* 108; 106, n. 6). In Darius' inscription, no gold came from Sogdiana. Yet in legend, Bactria had been a golden land (e.g., the golden Treasure of the Oxus in v and iv cent. B.C.); from Bactria the Persian empire had drawn its gold; but Bactria itself produced no gold. After Euthydemus (d. ca. 189 B.C.), no Greek king of Bactria coined any gold, although gold coinage was prized. Even in India, no Greek or Saca king coined any gold (*ibid.* pp. 104 f). Bactrian and Indian gold was an importation chiefly from Siberia or the Mediterranean world.

[5] *Herodotus* I, 215.

than any other country.[6]   There may also have been gold mines in the Urals and Altai, but mining was so laborious in comparison with washing that most of the gold probably came from the rivers.   Anciently this supply must have seemed inexhaustible.

The Chinese probably obtained a goodly share of this Siberian gold by trade with their northern neighbors.   Although these peoples did not wear silk, yet their leaders would want it as an article of luxury; other Chinese articles of luxury were likewise exported to these peoples.   The Chinese traded actively with the Huns and other northern neighbors (except when they were at war with them) along the whole northern border, and (at least during the first century B.C.) Chinese envoys traveled regularly through much of southern Siberia, along with whom went merchants, who took advantage of the envoy's escort and probably paid his expenses.

Gold was also mined in Europe and possibly in Asia Minor.   There were important gold mines in Transylvania, where the Romans obtained much gold.[7]   Once silk became available, the Romans eagerly sought for it, just as they imported large quantities of Indian spices and other goods. In Wang Mang's time, the silk trade with Greek Asia and India via the Tarim basin had been actively carried on for some centuries.   We know little of it before the time of Emperor Wu, but the fact that Chang Ch'ien reported conditions in Bactria shows that before the Chinese conquered the Tarim basin, trade was going on between the Greek orient and China. After that conquest, with the establishment of peace, trade doubtless increased several-fold.   In 67 B.C., a Protector-General was established for the Western Frontier Regions and in 48 B.C. the army of the Mou-and-Chi Colonel was established there to maintain order.

At the same time, silk was becoming more and more popular in Rome. Julius Caesar (d. 44 B.C.) is reported to have possessed silken curtains, but the introduction of silk to Rome in quantities began only in the reign of Augustus (27 B.C.–A.D. 14) and may be traced to Marcus Antonius, who communicated with the Bactrians.   Tiberius (A.D. 14–37) censured the wearing of silk by both sexes and forbad its wearing by men. Gaius (37–41) revived the wearing of silk, at least by the emperor.   But clothing made wholly of silk was rare until Elagabalus (218–222) set the example, this material normally being woven into linen or woolen fabrics after importation.   At the same time that they were using silk, the

[6] Most of this information is taken from Tarn, *Greeks in Bactria*, pp. 105 f.

[7] E. H. Minns, *Scythians and Greeks*, p. 7.

Romans were importing much larger quantities of goods from India; Pliny says that at the lowest computation, India, Seres, and Arabia drained from the Roman empire a hundred million sesterces (over five million dollars-worth) annually, more than half of which went to India.[8] Thus wealthy Romans began to use a certain amount of silk in the last century of the Former Han period; in the time of Wang Mang, sumptuary legislation was enacted against it, and in Later Han times its use became common among the wealthy.

Before silk became sought after in Rome, its use had probably become likewise popular in the kingdoms of central and western Asia and in India. As early as the time of Emperor Wu, traders were taking silk to India by sea (*HS* 28 Bii: 68b); this sea-borne trade seems however to have represented a drain of gold rather than an accession of it. There was also some trade to India via Yünnan and Burma. But these two routes can hardly have carried any large quantities of trade; the geographical obstacles were too great. The chief route of export was by way of the Tarim basin, which led into Sogdiana and Bactria, and thence to India or to the Mediterranean world.

It is doubtful whether there was much return trade to China in goods by this route. The road was so long and difficult that only goods which combined high value with small bulk would be profitable to carry. In Europe, silk was worth its weight in gold. Some jewels (including pearls from India) and a few Hellenistic works of art seem to have been all that the Chinese imported. But their appeal was limited, so that large quantities would hardly be carried to China. Hence the return trade was largely in gold, which alone, together with silk, fulfilled the conditions for profitable trade. Thus China may have drained the Hellenistic Euthydemids of gold in the first century B.C., just as in the time of Wang Mang the Roman use of silk threatened the Roman stock of gold. It is an interesting fact that, although gold was mined in Europe, in late antiquity, accumulated stocks of gold seem to have disappeared from that region. Much of this gold found its way to India, but some must have come to China. Large hoards of gold coins dating from Hellenistic and Roman times have been found in India, but finds of such coins are extremely rare in Chinese territory. Trade between the Roman empire and India went direct; that between the Roman empire and the Chinese seems only to have been carried by middlemen, until Later Han times. The Chinese were furthermore accustomed to using gold in the form of bullion squares, so that they melted down Greek and Roman coins. In China there was a customary ratio between gold and cash (10,000 cash to 1 catty of gold, 130 to 1). Wang Mang's stock of gold probably came

[8] E. H. Warmington, *The Commerce Between the Roman Empire and India*, p. 175, 41, 42, 274.

chiefly from Siberia, somewhat from Hellenistic Asia and India, and some from Europe.

At the beginning of the Former Han period, gold seems to have been used in China freely in exchange; imperial grants were frequently in "actual gold." By the latter part of that period, actual gold seems to have been used much less frequently. Probably the opening of the copper mines in the lower Yangtze region and elsewhere had made bronze cash so plentiful that even large sums were transferred in the form of cash. In A.D. 3, Wang Mang was given 40,000,000 cash and 23,000,000 cash as betrothal presents for his daughter (99 A: 10a). With large quantities of cash available, it would have been natural that gold should have accumulated in the treasuries of the wealthy, who were chiefly the nobles. When Wang Mang demonetized gold, these nobles would have been especially careful to deliver up their stores of gold, in order to avoid the punishment (dismissal and confiscation) for retaining any of it. Thus Wang Mang probably secured much of the gold in China, which country had been draining gold from Asia and Europe.

The changes in the bronze coinage probably affected Han China much less than a similar depreciation would have done in modern times. China had already changed from a barter economy to a limited money economy. The land tax was still payable in kind, but money was exacted for the numerous other taxes. The salaries of officials were quoted in so many piculs of grain, and were paid, half in grain and half in money (*HHS*, Tr. 28: 14b, 15a). Poll-taxes, levied upon all adults and all children over their seventh year, were in cash. Artisans and professional men paid an income tax in money, (established by Wang Mang; 24 B: 24a, b). The Han satrapies each sent an annual accounting to the imperial government, and probably at the same time remitted a certain proportion of the taxes they had gathered. Nearer commanderies remitted at least a portion in the form of grain. We hear of corvée service for the transportation of grain and of a special canal to Ch'ang-an dug for its conveyance. Distant commanderies probably remitted cash or valuables. An effort seems to have been made to transport to the capital no more grain than was necessary to feed the people in that region. The capital region had been irrigated, and had been one of the most productive areas in the empire. Hence taxes could largely be remitted in money, which had been used to purchase grain in the capital area. Each city had its market-place (or bazaar); the capital had two. There was thus a large sum of money in circulation for purposes of taxation and trade.

The farmers probably used very little money. They stored their grain and used it themselves or sold small amounts in order to purchase articles in the markets.  The farmers who possessed money were probably only those who had accumulated surplus wealth.  The poorer people affected by Wang Mang's changes in coinage were chiefly those who were in debt. Interest rates were quite high.  We have no way of knowing how many farmers were involved in debt, for we hear nothing of farm debts.  Since merchants were prohibited from owning cultivated fields, they would hardly lend money on farm land, for they could not foreclose such a mortgage.

A real, though limited money economy was only a few centuries old in the China of Wang Mang's time, so that a mortgage system may have not yet developed.  The only moneyed people besides merchants were nobles and officials.  Some decades previously, the Grandee Secretary, Kung Yü, (d. 43 B.C.) had memorialized the throne that the court officials should not be allowed to buy or sell or to make money off the people, but this memorial had not been acted upon (*HS* 72: 14a).  Hence some wealthy officials did actually engage in business, but that procedure was frowned upon and was not considered proper.  There had been a long-standing prejudice and prohibition against merchants entering government positions.

The higher nobles undoubtedly considered it beneath their dignity to engage in business.  Some of the wealthier ones however maintained "guests," i.e., persons of ability who came voluntarily to their house, became part of their household, receiving support from them, and in return executed various commissions for them.  We hear of guests who gave clever advice, of others who wrote books for their host, of still others who avenged their host's feud, and even of guests who robbed for their host, bringing their booty into his house and being protected by him. Some nobles had guests who engaged in business for their hosts.  But here again the aristrocratic prejudice against merchants probably prevented this carrying on of business by proxy from becoming a very common practise.

We hear of one wealthy merchant who sent his slaves out to conduct businesses (91: 10a), and of a wealthy family that lent money, but these loans were to other merchants or artisans (91: 9b).  When Wang Mang established an office for making loans, his enactment implies that debts were incurred chiefly for the performing of religious sacrifices (especially burials) and for buying farm land or setting up businesses (24 B: 24b). In an emergency, a certain wealthy man made loans to those newly enfeoffed nobles who needed supplies for a military expedition against rebels (154 B.C.; he exacted a tenfold repayment; 91: 11b).

But nowhere do we hear of any extensive loans to farmers, except those made by the government in time of drought or calamity. The government would sometimes settle landless people on vacant or newly opened land, giving them seed, food, and oxen for plowing. They were expected to repay these debts, but this provision was frequently waived by an imperial act of grace. The only large farm debts may have been of this variety; but on such debts, the government, if it wished, doubtless found means whereby a change in coinage would not diminish its revenues. Wealthy land-owners probably exacted their rents in terms of grain, rather than money, as is still the case in rural China. Hence farmers (except the wealthy ones) were probably little affected by the depreciation of money.

Merchants and other wealthy persons (who were probably bureaucrats or their descendants) were the ones who felt the deprecations of the coinage, for they possessed most of the money not in the hands of the government. The policy of the Han dynasty was to discourage trade and foster agriculture in every possible manner. Trade was penalized drastically. Merchants were considered parasites and were compelled to pay larger taxes than farmers. They and their descendants were not ordinarily allowed to hold official positions.

How far the depreciations of the coinage actually deprived merchants of their wealth is difficult to determine. The extremely rich, settled merchants, who had large establishments, probably found it possible to melt down their cash promptly and recoin it into the new forms. They may even had made money by the change, just as did the government. Wealthy officials probably kept most of their property in the form of goods or jewels. Those who suffered were the smaller merchants and pedlars, who did not have facilities for counterfeiting, and whose small shops could easily be watched. The worst suffering was among the unfortunates who were caught counterfeiting; they were punished with their innocent neighbors who had failed to report the crime. The chief effect of the changes in coinage was probably the transfer of wealth from the smaller merchants to some rich merchants and especially to the government.

Wang Mang had incurred great expenses, and his income was inadequate for the government expenses. It was thus only natural that he should have depreciated the coinage in order to secure money. Government loans had not yet been thought of. The circumstances occasioning the monetary changes and the nature of the changes in the coinages were such that Wang Mang could hardly have had any genuine revolutionary policy in mind—his purpose was probably to make money for the government by a change in coinage which superficially had classical sanctions.

In his land policy, Wang Mang encountered similar difficulties. Population had increased considerably during the peaceful years of the Han dynasty. North China (then the only thickly populated part of the country) is a region of periodic droughts and floods; many poor farmers, unable to keep reserves enough to tide them over a drought, had been forced to sell their hand in bad years, in order to get food. It had been the policy of the Han government to maintain great granaries for famine relief, to make loans to the poor, and to settle landless refugees upon vacant lands. Nevertheless large holdings of land and tenancy had increased and had long been a problem, because tenants could scarcely accumulate the reserves necessary to tide them over a famine. A famine year inevitably produced great hordes of vagrants, who died on the roads and thronged into regions where there was food. Since the government levied poll-taxes upon adults and children over seven years of age, in addition to the land-tax, this vagrancy meant not only human suffering, but also a great loss of income to the government.

In the year that he took the throne (A.D. 9), Wang Mang reformed the tenure of land by establishing the *ching* 井 system (99 B: 8a, b; 24 A: 21a, b).[9] The Confucian tradition was that this system had been universal in Chou times in all flat regions, and that other types of terrain had been parcelled out proportionately (*HS* 24 A: 3a). According to this system, an area one *li* or about 1350 feet square (Eng. meas.) was divided into nine equal squares. One of the outer squares, containing 100 *mou* or about $4\frac{1}{2}$ acres, was given to each of eight families to cultivate for its own use. (For the size of the *li* and *mou*, cf. 99 A: n. 9.7.) Each family also cultivated one-ninth of the central square ($\frac{1}{2}$ acre), the produce of which was to be paid to the government in lieu of taxes. The remaining ninth of the central square was reserved for houses and buildings. Thus the farmer paid as taxes only one-tenth of his produce, and paid it in kind, not in money. Land was moreover distributed according to the needs of the people, so that one household, containing five persons and one male worker, cultivated one unit. A youth received land in his twentieth year and returned it to the government in his sixtieth year. (Cf. Pan Ku's account, in *HS* 24 A: 2a ff.)[10]

[9] Cf. also K. A. Wittfogel, "Foundations and Stages of Chinese Economic History," *Zeit. f. Sozialforschung*, 4 (1935), p. 44 f.

[10] In estimating the areas of land concerned, I have used the Han figure for the *li*; the length of the Chou *li* and size of the Chou *ching* are uncertain. Since however the underlying unit was the *pu* 步 or double-pace (300 *pu* made a *li*), which is a natural and

This *ching* system looks excellent on paper; but its practical difficulties make doubtful its use without changes over any large area. Land cannot always be divided into exact squares; streams, hills, and roads interfere with such a division. Five acres could not support a family except on the best soil; Pan Ku, in describing this system (24 A: 2b), states that two or three times as much land of the poorer varieties was necessary for a family. A tax amounting to only a tithe of the produce would provide very little for the officials in poor years, when they needed a larger income than in good years. This sum was furthermore too small for the requirements of a developed government, which maintained an expensive and luxurious court, an elaborate bureaucracy with post-roads and post-stations, a standing army, government schools, a government university, etc., etc. Hence there had been added to the tax on land other taxes, such as a regular conscript system, which required three days a month service at the distant frontiers (regularly commuted to a money payment for substitutes, who became a standing army). In addition, there were heavy poll-taxes of various sorts. Tung Chung-shu said, in a memorial to Emperor Wu (24 A: 16b), that farm tenants paid out five-tenths of their income to their landlords. In Han times, money had come to be the usual medium of exchange, so that the payment of all taxes in kind was a special boon granted by the throne to the farmers only on special occasions, when grain was extraordinarily low in price. Thus the *ching* system seems to have been a dream of idealistic scholars; it had probably been tried only in a restricted area and in much simpler times, and, if applied literally, was quite impractical in a society like that of Han China. (In recent centuries, it has been considered by orthodox Confucian authorities as a practise suitable only for Spring and Autumn times. That conclusion is however probably a consequence from the experience of Wang Mang and others with this scheme.) The *ching* system had however the great merit of doing away with tenancy and large land-holdings, from both of which China suffered.

This system had great authority, for it had been urged by Mencius (III, A, iii, 13–20; Legge, 243–5) and was said to have been the system employed by the Confucian sages. Tung Chung-shu, the great Confucian authority, had urged it upon Emperor Wu (24 A: 17a), and Shih$_1$ Tan,

not an arbitrary unit, the difference in these two larger measures between Chou and Han times may not have been large. The Chou foot was one or two inches (Eng. meas.) shorter than the Han foot, but the Chou *pu* contained eight Chou feet while the Han *pu* contained only 6 Han feet (cf. 99 A: n. 9.7), so that the two *pu* seem to have been about the same length.

another Confucian, had urged it upon Emperor Ai in 7 B.C. (24 A: 20a), probably because they felt that the land needed redistribution and taxes were too onerous. Wang Mang, who had secured the throne because he followed Confucian practises whole-heartedly, naturally ordered its enactment.

In order to prevent any increase in tenancy, he at the same time nationalized all land. He named all cultivated fields, "the King's fields, *wang-t'ien* 王田," and ordered that they could not be bought or sold. Thus farmers were deprived of the opportunity to alienate their land, even in extremities. The amount of land that one family could hold was also limited. A family containing nine adult males or less was allowed to possess a maximum of 900 *mou* (102 acres or 41.5 ha.) of arable land; any family with less than that number of adult males and more than that amount of land must distribute its excess land to relatives or neighbors. Thus land ceased to have any market-value and wealthy land-owners were compelled to get rid of all but a small part of their land. Wang Mang must have realized the extremely drastic nature of this reform and the resentment it would arouse, for he added that anyone who dared even to criticize the *ching* system would be exiled beyond the frontiers or suffer execution.

At the same time, slavery, which had also been disapproved by Confucians, was to be abolished. Tung Chung-shu had urged its abolition more than a century previously (24 A: 17a). As a consequence of Shih₁ Tan's proposals in 7 B.C., it had actually been ordered that vassal kings might own only 200 slaves, marquises and princesses only 100 slaves, and others only 30 slaves, but this law had been dropped and had never been enforced (11: 3a). Wang Mang now produced a text from the Confucian canon, which was interpreted to assert that slavery was lawful only for the government, i.e., there should be no slaves except those in penal servitude to the government. Private slaves were renamed "private adherents 私屬" and were not to be bought or sold.

The limitation of land holdings was a specifically Confucian measure. Tung Chung-shu had advocated the limitation of the amount of land that could be held by an individual (24 A: 17a). Shih₁ Tan had repeated that statement (24 A: 20b). When Emperor Ai had agreed, his officials suggested that kings and marquises should be allowed unrestricted amounts of private land within their kingdoms or marquisates; outside these areas they should be restricted to 3000 *mou* (342 acres or 136 ha.). It was also proposed that the number of slaves be restricted. The Emperor's maternal relatives had however found this restriction inconvenient, and prevented it from being put into effect (11: 3a; 24 A:20b). The *ching* system and the limitation of land had the backing of Confucian tradition and sentiment.

A customary practise, like the free ownership of land, cannot be changed overnight. Land had been bought and sold freely in China for several centuries. After Wang Mang's edict was published, it was but natural that the wealthy should seek to convert their excess land and slaves into money. Pan Ku reports that countless people, nobles, ministers, and commoners, were sentenced for purchasing or selling land or slaves (99 B: 9a). It is not surprising that two years later the prohibition against buying or selling land or slaves was rescinded (24 A: 21b).

In A.D. 17, a tax of 3600 cash per slave was levied upon all slave-owners, including nobles (99 C: 1b). The intent of this tax was not to eliminate slavery, but merely to obtain money. Since rich households depended upon slaves for domestic service, this law bore chiefly upon the wealthy nobles and high officials.

In the abolition of slavery and the restriction of land holdings, Wang Mang was undoubtedly making a needed reform. It is possible that the more thoroughgoing nature of this enactment, as compared with previous proposals of the kind, indicates a genuine altruism on his part and a desire to help the poor. The severity with which violations of his enactment were punished may have also been merely a general characteristic of his government. He very likely conceived of himself as altruistic. The drastic nature of his enactments may however have been merely his conception of the lengths to which a new and thoroughly Confucian dynasty should go in carrying out supposedly ancient practises and an expression of his sense of power. This latter supposal is moreover more in harmony with the rest of his deeds. Certainly he seems to have shown no pity for those who suffered from his reforms.

Since these reforms were all rescinded within two years, someone was evidently able to bring so much pressure upon him that he had to revoke this reform of land tenure and slavery. We are not told who it was, so shall be compelled to resort again to inference.

No large part of the population in China has ever been enslaved except by a general conquest. Slaves have rarely, if ever, been used for agricultural work. Skilled artisans, who are able to make money by plying their trades, tend to become freemen; free labor is more efficient than slave labor and clever slaves purchase their freedom. Chinese slavery was limited chiefly to domestic service and rough labor. The government was undoubtedly the largest slave-owner; criminals were frequently condemned to forced labor for a period of years or for life and were put to work in the government offices. (C. M. Wilbur, *Slavery in China During the Former Han Dynasty,* pp. 241–44.) The menial labor at the various bureaux was performed by these slaves. Thousands of such enslaved criminals were employed in the government iron and salt monopolies. A capital sentence could sometimes be commuted, at the culprit's request, to castration, whereupon he became a eunuch in the imperial palace—a eunuch government slave. Many, perhaps most of the palace eunuchs must have originated in this manner. We hear of thousands of slaves in the imperial palace and occasionally even of a highly educated slave-girl, such as Emperor Ch'eng's inamorata, Ts'ao Kung (*HFHD*, II, 369). Government slaves were freed when their terms were completed. Government slaves were sometimes bestowed upon imperial relatives or favorites; occasionally at least, they were sold (Wilbur, *op. cit.*, p. 446). There may have been hereditary slaves, but there is some evidence that children of slaves were automatically free, at least by the fourth generation, unless (as must have very commonly been the case) they were, as children, sold or given into slavery by their parents, in order that they might be reared. The Huns captured large numbers of Chinese in their raids upon the borders; these people were often sold, many, in all probability, to Chinese. The slave-market was however chiefly maintained from children sold by their poor parents or from children or adults kidnapped by powerful people (perhaps given actually unjust, but technically legal sentences of enslavement). Criminals who were enslaved by the government would rarely be of high caliber and would be suitable chiefly for rough labor; for entertainers and other trained domestic slaves, the nobles and wealthy had to depend chiefly upon the slave market.[11]

Outside the government service, the largest number of slaves were in the noble houses. The nobles maintained slaves as entertainers as well as domestic servants. Rich merchants also had such slaves; sometimes slaves were used for manufacturing. The prohibition of the sale or purchase of slaves would have limited severely the supply of high quality domestic slaves and it would have made the government the only remaining source of slaves. At the time, it produced little immediate change, except among merchants who had bought slaves for resale. We may well conclude that it was Wang Mang's nobles, probably his close relatives, who persuaded him to rescind this measure, for these nobles would have

---

[11] Concerning slaves in agricultural colonies in A.D. 275, cf. *HJAS* 9, 161. This agricultural slavery was probably little different from other agricultural colonies, except that in this case the colonists were criminals made to farm.

found it impossible to replenish the high quality slaves in their households. Since the revocation came so soon, the measure had a negligible effect upon slavery.

Just how Wang Mang put the *ching* system into effect is not told. He could not cut the land up into regular squares; probably he did not change the boundaries of fields, but merely limited to 900 *mou* the amount of land one family might possess. The Han land-tax was one-fifteenth, so that the introduction of the *ching* system probably meant an increase in the land tax to one-tenth. The other taxes, such as the poll-tax on adults, (*suan*), the poll-money (levied on children), the military taxes (*fu*), likin duties (collected at the Wu Pass and probably at the other passes), were probably continued. Then the actual effect of the *ching* system was very likely limited to prohibiting the sale of cultivated land, limiting land holdings, and an increase in the land tax.

The ban on selling cultivated land was probably a benefit to the poor farmers. It prevented them from losing their land in time of drought. Hence they were compelled to fall back upon the government for relief and to become vagrants when that relief was not available. We are not told about any mortgages upon farm land. This prohibition of the sale of farm land merely fixed the existing farm population upon the farms they then occupied. It was rescinded within two years and so had little actual effect.

The limitation of the amount of cultivated land that could be owned by a single small family was plainly an attempt to diminish tenancy and distribute the land more widely among the people. It only affected large land-owners. These large land-owners were chiefly the bureaucrats and nobility (these two classes were largely identical, since the Han nobilities had been mostly discontinued and Wang Mang's nobles were his relatives and officials); merchants were not allowed to own farm land. The reason that the nobles would wish to own large private farm estates requires explanation.

The Han dynasty's full marquises (which Wang Mang replaced by four degrees of nobility: marquises, earls, viscounts, and barons) all had their noble estates located outside of Kuan-chung (the capital region, roughly the present central Shensi), some at considerable distances from the capital—in the present southern Honan, Hunan, Shantung, or Hopei. The nobles had little control over their fiefs; these estates were managed by chancellors, who were appointed by the central government; in practise, nobles received merely the income from these estates in the form of 200 cash per household or its equivalent in grain, out of which they had to pay their annual contributions to the imperial court (91: 6a). But the

524

transport of grain or even of bronze cash from a distance to the capital presented difficulties because of banditry, and sometimes cost more than the value of the grain itself. It may have been impossible to make regular deliveries to the capital from the noble estates, because of the distance. Most of the nobles, moreover, lived at the imperial capital, Ch'ang-an, the center of culture, civilization, and political power. Hence it became the practise for such nobles to purchase private land in Kuan-chung, the income of which they used for their expenses. Such neighboring lands could be watched, and rents brought to the capital with ease. The largest private land-owners were the same rich nobles who had large numbers of slaves. Wang Mang's uncles are described as having, at the time of Wang Mang's childhood, "several tens of concubines in their harems, slaves by the thousands or hundreds, musicians, singers, actors, dogs, horses, large residences with earthen mountains inside, cave gates, high verandas and pavillions, double passage-ways," etc. (98: 7b). To keep up such extravagent establishments, large estates were essential.

Wang Mang did not interfere with the feudal estates of his nobles, he merely required them to distribute their excess *private* fields among their relatives or neighbors. It would not have been difficult for some nobles to find members of their clans to take these excess cultivated fields, manage them, and remit part or most of the proceeds to the original owner. There was, however, the danger that these new owners would cease paying rents to the original owner. Those nobles who could not or would not use such subterfuges and who did not have adequate official salaries would be compelled to retire from the court to their feudal estates. That meant, however, leaving civilization to live in the "sticks," the abandonment of one's social life and of the source of political perquisites. Exclusion from the capital was a penalty considered more severe than dismissal from office; it was visited upon officials who had become obnoxious to the court. Wang Mang had suffered three years of such exile and knew its bitterness; his intimates and the members of his clan probably reminded him of the suffering he was preparing for them and of the ease with which certain nobles were circumventing his enactment. So much pressure was brought upon him (in all probability, practically the whole court, except the conscientious Confucians, were unanimous in this matter) that he had to rescind his enactment. In the end, this reform of land tenure amounted to nothing.

We can only speculate concerning Wang Mang's motive in attempting to alter land tenure. He might have been moved by compassion for the miserable condition of the peasant farmers, but in my opinion, any such attitude on his part is doubtful. He did not commonly indulge in compassion; his great increases in taxation would seem to preclude any real concern for the poor. His concern was rather to carry out Confucian policies. The *ching* system was one of the outstanding Confucian economic policies; if he had not attempted to put into practise a policy recommended by Mencius, Tung Chung-shu, and other outstanding Confucians, he would have appeared lukewarm, so that one important source of his unusual popularity would have been gravely undermined. Statecraft and ambition, not compassion, were his driving ambitions.

* * *

The third group of economic measures enacted by Wang Mang were the six monopolies (established A.D. 10; 99 B: 12b; C: 1b) and increased taxes. Government monopolies were by no means new in China. More than half a millennium earlier, in the first half of the seventh century B.C., Duke Huan of Ch'i is said to have made himself powerful through a government monopoly in the manufacture of salt and iron. (Maspero rejects this tradition; Karlgren defends it.) The Ch'in dynasty, which first unified China under a single government, continued these two monopolies (24 A: 16b). Emperor Wen (180–157 B.C.) had allowed the common people to evaporate salt, smelt iron, and coin money (*Discourse on Salt and Iron*, Gale, p. 28), but Emperor Wu had withdrawn these privileges. Tung Chung-shu had protested against these monopolies without avail (24 A: 17a). In the famous discussion of 81 B.C. (reported in the *Discourses on Salt and Iron*), when the economic policies of the government were reviewed, the Confucian literati likewise protested against these monopolies (*HS* 7: 5a). In 44 B.C., Emperor Yüan, who was attempting to be a good Confucian, abolished these monopolies, but the loss of revenue compelled him to reestablish them three years later (41 B.C.; *HS* 9: 6b, 9a). Confucianism in general opposed government monopolies, so that these measures can hardly be said to have been Confucian. Wang Mang, however, found references in Confucian literature to something called controls or *kuan*, 筦 or 榦, so he changed the name of these monopolies to "controls," and continued them as Confucian enactments. He needed money too much to dispense with them.

A third monopoly was that in fermented liquors. Originally established by Emperor Wu in 98 B.C., it had been abolished in 81 B.C., because of popular criticism. The people were then permitted to brew liquors upon payment of a tax. A high official of Wang Mang produced texts from which one could infer that a government monopoly of liquor was an ancient institution approved by Confucius; he pointed out to Wang Mang that a 70% profit could be made in brewing and selling liquor (24 B: 25a, b). Wang Mang therefore included it as one of his "controls," and established it as another government business.

A fourth monopoly was that of coinage, which probably included the mining and smelting of copper. In this enterprise, Wang Mang was continuing a long-standing Chinese practise. In 175 B.C., Emperor Wen had indeed allowed free coinage (4: 12b), but the consequent depreciation of the currency had caused his son, Emperor Ching, to rescind this privilege in 144 B.C. and to establish a death sentence for counter-feiting (5: 7b).

The fifth monopoly was concerned with the products of the mountains and marshes; these included forestry, fishing, hunting, and the taking of other wild products, such as wild honey, etc. Such occupations had been the resource of the poor in ordinary times and of all in time of famine. (The mining of copper and or iron were probably included in the monopo-lies of coinage [which was of bronze] and of iron, respectively.) For these monopolies too, Wang Mang could cite classical texts. The *Chou Offices* mentions a Forester of the Mountains 山虞, whose duty it was to enforce the prohibitions concerning these regions, keeping people out of the forests at improper times. He had a subordinate who collected the revenue from the forests. Thus it is implied that there had been a tax upon those who cut trees. This book also lists a Forester of the Marshes 澤虞, who had the local people go into the marshes and waters at the proper times to take the articles of those places, delivering the proper amount to the imperial treasury (as a tax) and keeping the rest for them-selves (*Chou-li* 16: 6b–8b; Biot, I, 370–375). *Li-ki* III, iii, 11 (Legge, I, 227; Couvreur, I, 293) says, "Anciently, [people] went into the forests at the foot of the mountains and the waters of the marshes at the [proper] seasons without being prohibited," in which statement the qualification "at the proper seasons" implies that there were prohibitions against cutting trees at certain seasons of the year (*Chou-li* 16: 7a [Biot, I, 372] specifies spring and autumn), and so implies a government supervision of these regions with an impost upon those working there, to support that supervision. Elsewhere, the *Li-chi* (IV, i, iii, 12; iv, ii, 21; Legge, I, 265, 301; Couvreur, I, 350, 396) mentions a Forester of the Wastes 野虞 and a Forester of the Waters 水虞, whose duties were to prevent the cutting of trees at certain times and to collect the revenues from rivers, springs, ponds, and meres. Thus there was ample classical prece-dent for a taxation of forests and marshes. Wang Mang merely broad-ened these precedents into a government monopoly and made it cover all forests and marsh products.

The Ch'in dynasty had actually made the rivers, marshes, mountains, and forests a government monopoly (24 A: 16b). In Han times, the revenue from the mountains, streams, parks, ponds, market-places, and shops had been reserved for those overlords who were enfeoffed as their private estates with the regions containing these places, such as kings, marquises, baronets, and princesses. From regions not given in fief, this revenue was reserved for the imperial private purse, in charge of the Privy Treasurer, and was not put into the imperial public treasury, in charge of the Grand Minister of Agriculture (*HS* 24 A: 9b = *Mh* III, 541 f). The Privy Treasurer could hardly supervise these regions throughout the empire, hence it is probable that, except for certain areas near the capital, especially Kuan-chung, which he could conveniently supervise, the mountains and waters in most of China had been actually free to the people. Hunting had been prohibited in the imperial parks, which were hunted and fished by government agents; it may not have been restricted elsewhere, especially outside Kuan-chung. Wang Mang seems then to have extended systematically throughout the whole country the Ch'in and Han practise of taxing mountains and waters, and to have made all the occupations related to forests and marshes government monopolies, permitted only to those who paid certain fees. (Possibly only certain of such occupations had previously been taxed.) In A.D. 22, in a time of famine, the mountains and marshes were freely opened to the people (99 C: 17b), possibly because they could not be kept from utilizing these resources.

Detailed laws were made for each of these monopolies; the penalties for violation were as severe as death (99 C: 1b), in which latter respect too, Wang Mang was following classical precedent—*Chou-li* 16: 7b mentions execution 誅 in this connection (Biot, I, 374 softens this word to "châti-ments"). These monopolies were opposed. When the Communicator (the state treasurer), Feng Ch'ang, remonstrated against them, Wang Mang became extremely incensed and summarily dismissed him from office (99 C: 2a). There had been successive years of drought, and there was much banditry. In A.D. 18, a new governor, Fei Hsing, was ap- pointed for a province in the Yangtze valley. When asked what would be his plans upon reaching his province, he replied that these people made much of fishing; the monopolies and taxes on the mountains and marshes had taken away peoples' profits, so that they were starving; he would summon back to farm land those who had taken to banditry and would exempt them from taxes, loan them seed and food, and thus bring peace to the region. Wang Mang was incensed at the covert criticism of his monopolies and dismissed Fei Hsing (99 C: 2b, 3a).

The economic effect of these five monopolies was chiefly to raise and stabilize the price of certain necessities. This objection had been made to monopolies by the Confucians in the famous debate of 81 B.C. They said that the price of salt had become so high that people had to forego it, and that the iron implements made by the government manufactories were inferior and unsuitable. Similar objections were made to the liquor monopoly. The effect of these three monopolies, together with coinage, was, indeed, to put into the hands of the government the most profitable manufacturing enterprises of the time. Only the monopoly in liquors was new in the time of Wang Mang. Its effect was to take away the livelihood of those merchants who had engaged in brewing and liquor dealing, except for those who now became government agents. It probably also raised the price of liquor to the common people. There was no thought of restricting its use. The abuse of alcoholic liquors has rarely become an important problem in China.

The effect of the fifth monopoly, that on the mountains and marshes, was to deprive of their livelihood the country's poor, who had engaged in hunting and fishing, or to compel them to pay for the privilege of continuing their occupations. These monopolies constituted an additional tax upon the poor.

As a whole, these monopolies were thus means of obtaining additional revenue for the government. I can find no other purpose in them. They were a burden upon the poor and common people, since they were a tax upon necessities. They could be counted on to bring in revenue, and were in no sense revolutionary.

This policy of mulcting the people for the benefit of the government also showed itself in Wang Mang's new taxes. A special tax upon merchants and artisans had previously been attempted by Emperor Wu (119 B.C.), compelling them to testify to the total amount of their property and to pay a tax of $9\frac{1}{2}\%$ and $4\frac{3}{4}\%$ respectively, upon their capital (*HFHD*, II, 65, n. 15.13; 24 B: 13a, b). This tax had, however, soon been abolished (24 B: 20a).

In A.D. 9, Wang Mang imposed an income tax upon all hunters, fishermen, sericulturalists, artisans, and professional men. They were each to testify to their income for the year, and pay a tithe of it as a tax. Those who refused to testify to their income or who testified falsely were to be sentenced to a year at penal servitude (24 B: 24b). At the same time, it was ordered that all uncultivated fields, whether inside or outside the city, should pay three times the usual land tax. This latter provision was taken from the classical *Chou-li* (13: 9a; Biot, I, 279f; *HS* 24 B: 24a & n. 24.3). Wang Mang moreover attempted to systematize the previous practise, begun by Emperor Hsüan (8: 6b & n. 6.4), that official salaries were reduced in time of flood or drought. He enacted that salaries were to be reduced proportionately each year, according to the state of the harvest in each part of the empire (99 B: 29a, b). This system proved cumbersome, for officials hence did not know what their salary was to be until the year was almost over. They therefore made various collections and exactions (24 B: 27a). When they were suspected of having accumulated much property, in A.D. 18, Wang Mang ordered that all but the lowest officials should be required to deliver up four-fifths of their wealth, for the use of the army at the borders. Pan Ku states that inquisitors galloped all over the empire, persuading slaves and subordinates to inform on their masters or superiors (99 C: 3a). We can imagine the limitless opportunities for blackmail and bribery, the repaying of old scores by inquisitors and informers. In the same year, when a serious attempt was made to put down the bandits and rebels, a levy was made, consisting of $\frac{1}{30}$ of all property. This levy was immediately repeated, because property had not been assessed at its full value (99 C: 4b, 5b). All officials were also required to make additional contributions out of their salaries, for the rearing of horses (99 C: 4b). It is not surprising that when serious rebellion finally arose against Wang Mang, the bureaucracy did little to stop it.

Wang Mang's fiscal policy seems to have been one of exploiting all the sources of revenue he could find, regardless of the effect his measures had upon the empire. While some of them mulcted the rich, other measures burdened the poor. It is but natural that the enthusiasm for him, which was so abundantly evident before he took the throne, should have evaporated rapidly once he attained unchecked rule. He incurred large and unusual expenses, which were aggravated by the corruption of his officials. His fiscal measures show a remarkable lack of tact and a phenomenal disregard of their effect upon the empire.

\* \* \*

The most interesting of Wang Mang's economic experiments was the sixth control, which he called the "Five Equalizations," by which fluctuations of prices in staple goods were to be prevented and loans were to be made by the government. These measures, too, had had their predecessors.

Four centuries earlier, Li K'uei, a student of Confucius' personal disciple, Tzu-hsia, became Chancellor to Marquis Wen of Wei_h (reigned 424–387 B.C.) and attempted to equalize the price of grain. In good years, the state of Wei_h purchased grain in large or small amounts according to the state of the crop, while in poor years, it sold grain, thus attempting to prevent fluctuations in its price (*HS* 24 A: 7b–8b). Unfortunately, we are given no information concerning the success of this policy of speculating in grain, except that it is said to have made "the state of Wei$_h$ wealthy and powerful."

This policy was again tried in 54 B.C., when Keng Shou-ch'ang, the Palace Assistant Grand Minister of Agriculture under Emperor Hsüan, built Constantly Equalizing Granaries in the border commanderies. These granaries purchased grain when its price was low and sold it when the price was high (24 A: 19b). Granaries were not built at the imperial capital, probably because irrigation had eliminated bad seasons in that region. These Constantly Equalizing Granaries seem to have become sources of expense rather than of benefit to the people; they were abolished by Emperor Yüan in 44 B.C., ten years after being built, in a fit of imperial economy, when other expensive government projects were also abolished, such as the imperial ateliers for silk and metal manufacture and the government monopolies of salt and iron (9: 6a, b; 24 A: 20a).

When moreover, in 115 B.C., Emperor Wu needed money, Sang Hung-yang, an official who had come from a mercantile family, suggested speculation in goods. Prices differed widely in different parts of the empire; Sang Hung-yang had the government purchase goods where they were cheap and transport them to places where they were dear, thus making a profit (24 B: 19b). Since the government had built roads and set up a system of posts, and since criminals sentenced to penal servitude could be used to supply the necessary labor, the government had an advantage over private traders and could make great profits in this manner. The system also prevented undue fluctuations in prices; when prices rose in one region, goods were brought in from other places. We are not told that this system was abolished. It was complained of in 81 B.C., but not abolished; probably the increasing freedom of intercourse led to an approximate equalization of prices in different regions, so that this method of equalization became unprofitable and gradually ceased to function. At least we hear nothing of it after the reign of Emperor Chao. Wang Mang directed the Masters in Charge of the Five Equalizations to neglect prices at other markets (24 B: 24b), so that in his time the government had plainly ceased to transport goods.

Liu Hsin$_{1a}$, who brought the *Chou Offices* to people's attention and induced Wang Mang to make it an officially recognized classic, pointed out to Wang Mang that the Chou dynasty, according to this classic, had a government Office for Money (24 B: 23b). This book recounts that in the Chou period there was an office for the collection of goods unsold in the market-place of the capital and for their storage until people wished to buy them. There was also an office which lent money without interest for a period of three months to people who needed it for ancestral sacrifices

531

or mourning ceremonies, after which time, they paid 10% interest per year (*Chou-li* 15: 3b f; Biot, I, 326–328; *HS* 24 B: n. 23.6, 23.8). The *Yo-yü* (now lost), which was a commentary on the *Classic of Music*, told of an institution called the Five Equalizations, by which prices were stabilized, probably for the five fundamental commodities (*HS* 24 B: 23b & n. 23.9). It is impossible to tell whether these measures had ever been actually put into practise; they were very likely the inventions of Confucians who were idealizing the past.

When Wang Mang came to the throne in A.D. 9, he accordingly established offices for lending and for the Five Equalizations. At the imperial capital and at five other large cities in the empire, Lo-yang, Han-tan, Lin-tzu, Yüan, and Ch'eng-tu, there were set up Masters in Charge of the Five Equalizations at the Markets, each with five Assistants for Exchange and one Assistant for the Office for Money. Storehouses were built at these places. In the middle of each quarter, the Master at each market was to determine a price for equalization for each of three grades of goods (high, middle, and low). These prices were to apply to the five kinds of grains (hemp and similar seeds, glutinous millet, panicled millet, wheat, and beans), linen cloth and silk cloth, thread, and wadding. When any of these goods remained unsold in the market (as they were brought in by farmers), the office for equalization was to buy them at cost or at the market price (provided that price was lower than the price for equalization), so that the people would lose nothing by being compelled to receive a lower price in the market. When the price rose above the price for equalization by one cash, the office for equalization was to sell its goods at the price for equalization. Fluctuations of prices in the market were thus to be prevented, merchants were not to be allowed to corner goods or fleece the country people, and the farmers were to be assured of a market for their goods.

People who needed money for sacrifices or for mourning ceremonies were to have what they needed lent them, from the payments of the income-tax, without interest for ten days or three months, respectively. Others who needed money for working capital were to be given loans, paying interest at 3% per month.

It was an interesting and idealistic experiment. Hu Shih says that Wang Mang's exposition of his monopolies and of the Five Equalizations was "the earliest conscious statement of the theory of state socialism in the history of the social and political thought of mankind" (*JNChRAS*, 59 [1928]: 229). How far that statement is true may be gaged from the information here given. The credit for this experiment should not however be given to Wang Mang, but to the Confucian author of the passage

in the *Chou Offices* dealing with these matters, and in some degree to Hsin₁ₐ.

Rich merchants were selected to operate these offices. Few other would be capable of controlling, without great loss, offices essentiall intended for speculating in goods and lending money. Pan Ku says tha these merchants communicated their wickedness to various places in th empire and made many false accountings; that the offices and storehouses for goods were not filled (24 B: 25b). If they had been well stocked with goods, their very presence would have kept prices down, without actually purchasing any more goods, until a scarcity arose. Since however these storehouses were not filled, and since they utterly failed to prevent the rise of prices in time of famine (99 C: 16a), this attempt to control prices probably achieved very little, except for providing certain sinecure positions in the bureaucracy.

It is not difficult to discover the reason that this attempt to speculate in goods had only slight economic effects. If the price for equalization was set too high, the storehouses would be filled with goods unsalable at the current price. Hence the Masters, to protect their offices from losing money, probably set their prices for equalization low, with the result that they refused to take goods from the common people, because the current price was too high. Then farmers would not bring their goods to the storehouses except under stress of necessity. We are told that the storehouses remained empty.

When a scarcity was impending, the grain remaining in these storehouses was probably sold rapidly, before famine actually arrived, for goods had to be sold at the price for equalization plus one cash. In times of abundant harvest, because the prices for equalization were set every quarter, these prices decreased before the harvest was reaped, since grain was expected to become plentiful. Thus the farmers were not helped, unless there was a sudden and unexpected fall in prices, such as that caused by a glut on the market. Such gluts were perhaps the only economic situations in which farmers were regularly benefited. The Masters knew that Wang Mang needed money, and they undoubtedly looked upon the storehouses as means of making profits, just as with the other monopolies. They did not accordingly dare to risk a loss. The Masters were former merchants, who hence took the same attitude to the farmers that the merchants did. It is therefore only natural that the farmers should not have been greatly benefited.

The loans made to needy persons were to be taken out of the payments for income-taxes made by professional men. We are not told how much money was loaned. The rate of interest, 3% per month, was however

much higher than the usual commercial rate, which was 20% per year (91: 6a), so that few loans were probably made, except for short terms, for which periods the commercial rate was probably also high. There was furthermore a provision that the borrower was not to pay more than 10% of his net income as interest, so that the Masters probably refused to make large loans. These storehouses and lending agencies benefited few except their managers.

Their purpose was undoubtedly good—that of preventing exploitation of the farmers by the merchants. In view of the fact that the Chinese state had been carrying on at least two businesses (the manufacture and sale of salt and iron) for several centuries, Wang Mang's measures can hardly be called state socialism or revolutionary. The Five Equalizations was merely another measure to benefit the people, advocated by the Confucians with the same motive as the *ching* system and other economic plans.

This motive on the part of the Confucians who first invented these proposals does not however mean that Wang Mang had any strong urge to benefit the people. His chief purpose was undoubtedly to follow Confucian tradition—the practise by which he first secured his popularity and as a result of which he was able to ascend the throne. He was morally obligated to put Confucian policies into practise. Had he really been deeply concerned for the people, he would have removed the monopolies on salt and iron, which pressed most severely upon them. But he showed no inclination to do so; on the contrary, he dismissed any official who manifested an inclination even to relax these monopolies.

*   *   *

Wang Mang was in no sense a revolutionist. He was merely a clever intriguer, who found a new way of gaining popular approval and who clung to it tenaciously. He achieved the throne by playing upon the Confucian attitude of the educated class and becoming a whole-hearted Confucian. Confucianism is an idealistic philosophy that sought to benefit the whole people, and the Confucian literati were in close touch with the common people of their own clans, so that they largely reflected the attitude of the common people to the government. When Wang Mang actually came to the throne, he proceeded to enact various Confucian proposals, but his decrees were not based upon a clear knowledge of the people or of their needs.

He had passed his life as a member of the governing clan, which gained wealth and position merely because it was related to the reigning Emperor. He made his way to leadership by intrigue and secured popularity by espousing the popular Confucian religion of the educated class.

When chance made him the dictator of the government and regent for an infant, people found no difficulty in interpreting Confucian teachings so that they were thought to require his enthronement.  He then had to put into practise the economic policies embodied in the Confucian tradition, including the particular Confucian books he had newly accepted as authoritative.

His economic policies proceeded from the Confucian tradition, not from any need of the people.  His forced colonization of Kokonor (99 A: 24b) and his increased taxation demonstrate his utter callousness to the real needs of the people.  His changes in the coinage were a means of mulcting the merchants and moneyed class.  His nationalization of land, the establishment of the *ching* system, the restrictions on large holdings of land and on slaves proved onerous even to his own relatives and followers.  These measures were therefore quickly rescinded, even though they were in accord with Confucian tradition and would have proved helpful to the common people.

The first four monopolies were plainly means of seizing for the government the most profitable private enterprises, a procedure that had long been a government policy.  It was especially oppressive under Wang Mang, because he added to the number of enterprises taken over by the government and to the severity of the punishments for offending against these monopolies.  They put added burdens upon the poorer people, virtually taxing necessities.  The fifth monopoly was clearly directed against the poorer people and was in effect a direct tax on certain occupations.  The Five Equalizations, an attempt to stabilize prices and make loans to those who needed them, was inexpertly planned and failed to achieve anything of note.  Thus Wang Mang's economic policies were either futile or oppressive in their operation.  He seems to have oppressed all the economic classes in the empire.

When, in the winter of A.D. 22, the whole empire was in rebellion and Wang Mang at last realized the extremity of the situation, it was decided to rescind all the imperial edicts and ordinances that had been made since he had ascended the throne, especially the economic reforms we have been discussing.  Messengers were prepared to be sent out (99 C: 19b).  Such an act would have meant a drastic loss of face.  The imperial forces, however, achieved a preliminary minor success, and the messengers were not actually dispatched.  Such a drastic proposal is evidence that Wang Mang was at last driven to recognize the unpopularity of his economic reforms.  Thereafter events happened too rapidly.  The rebels continued to gain, and by October of the next year, the capital had been captured and Wang Mang killed by the people of the capital itself.  Thus his phenomenal popularity changed within fifteen years into the most bitter hatred. His economic measures must bear much of the blame for that reversal of public opinion.[12] (Reproduced by permission, with omissions and additions, from an article with the same title in the *T'oung Pao*, vol. 35, [1940], Livr. 4, pp. 219–265.)

[12] An account of Wang Mang's policies is also to be found in Hans O. Stange, *Leben, Persönlichkeit und Werk Wang Mang's*, Inaugural-Dissertation zur Friedrich-Wilhelms-Universitäts zur Berlin, 1934, which is not always quite carefully done. Cf. also Dr. Stange's *Die Monographie über Wang Mang, kritisch bearbeitet, übersetzt, und erklärt*, Leipzig, 1939.

O. Franke, *Geschichte des Chinesischen Reiches*, I, 375, likens Wang Mang to Richard the Third in Shakespeare; his economic reforms are described on pp. 379–383.

O. Franke, "Staatssozialistische Versuche im alten und mittelalterlichen China," *SPAW* (1931), Phil.-hist. Kl., 218–242, touches upon Wang Mang in passing.

An excellent summary of economic matters during the Han period is to be found in W. Eberhard, "Zur Landwirtschaft der Han-Zeit," *MSOS*, 35 (1932): 74–105; K. A. Wittfogel, "Foundations and Stages of Chinese Economic History," *Zeit. f. Sozialforchung*, vol. 4 (1935), pp. 26–60.

# APPENDIX III

## THE *KANG-MAO* AMULETS

The mention of the *kang-mao* amulets in 99 B: 7a has induced the commentators to give us an account of these curious objects, which show the prevalence of superstition in that age.

Fu Ch'ien (ca. 125–195) glosses, "The *kang-mao* [amulets] are made in the first month, on a *mao* day, and are worn at the waist. They are three inches[1] long, one inch wide, and foursquare [in cross-section]. Sometimes jade[2] is used, sometimes metal is used, and sometimes peach-[wood] is used. A thong is attached to them to wear them at the waist. Now jade[2] ones still exist. The inscription on one of them, on its side, reads, 'The first month *kang-mao* [amulet].'" 剛卯以正月卯日作，佩之，長三尺，[1] 廣一寸，四方，或用五，[2] 或用金，或用桃，著革帶佩之。今有五[2] 在者，銘其一，面，曰，正月剛卯 Yen Shih-ku (581–645) adds, "Today frequently in the soil there are obtained jade *kang-mao* [amulets]. According to my opinion, as regards their size and their inscriptions, the explanation of Fu [Ch'ien] is correct."

Chin Shao (fl. ca. 275) however glosses, "The *kang-mao* [amulets] are one inch long, five *fen* broad, and four-square [in cross-section]. In the center, there is a hole made lengthwise, in order that it may be threaded[3] to the bottom with variegated silk, like the threads of the fringe on the top of a hat. Two lines of writing are engraved on their faces. The inscription says, 'When the first month *kang-mao* [amulet] is in the center [of the girdle ornaments], it is a supernatural baton[4] [which influences] the four quarters. Red, blue, white, and yellow, these four colors are my defences. The Lord [Shun] ordered Chu-yung[5] to teach K'uei and Lung[6] [to infuse power into it, so that] of the many epidemics and serious (*kang*)

---

[1] Wang Hsien-ch'ien's text reads 尺; the Ching-yu and the Official ed. read 寸.

[2] Wang's text reads 五; the Ching-yu and the Official ed. read 玉.

[3] The text reads 茸; the Official ed. has emended it to 葺. The Ching-yu ed. reads 笇.

[4] 殳 should probably be read as *hai* 殺. But it is better to read without emending or changing. Shen Ch'in-han, in his *HS Su-cheng* 36: 9b, quotes the *Han-shih Wai-chuan* 10: 8b (ed. "Ku-ching-chieh Hui-han") and thinks that *ling* 靈-*shu* denotes the *tao* 桃-*shu*, the peach-wood baton, which was a popular apotropaic implement.

[5] Chu-yung was the Red Lord; he presides over the first month.

[6] K'uei and Lung were ministers of Shun.

diseases, none will presume to touch me.' On the other [of the pair], the inscription says, 'On the worst of unlucky days, [the day] *mao*, the Lord [Shun] ordered K'uei to transform [this object, saying], "In accordance with your firmness and subtlety, do you transform this thing into a supernatural baton.[4] It should be completely upright, completely straight, completely angular, and completely square, so that of the many epidemics and severe (*kang*) diseases, none will presume to touch me." ' " 剛卯長一寸，廣五分，四方，當中央從穿作孔，以采絲茸[3] 其底，如冠纓頭 緌，刻其上面，作兩行書，文曰，正月剛卯旣央，靈殳[4] 四方。赤青白黃， 四色是當。帝令祝融，以敎夔龍，庶疫剛癉，莫我敢當。其一銘曰，疾日嚴 卯，帝令夔化，順爾固伏，化茲靈殳[4] ，旣正旣眞，旣觚旣方，庶疫剛癉， 莫我敢當.

*HHS*, Tr. 30: 13a, b (by Szu-ma Piao, ca. 240–306) says, "The girdle ornaments are a pair of seals[7] one inch two *fen* long and six *fen* square. The emperor, vassal kings, dukes, and full marquises use white jade for them. [Officials ranking at] fully 2000 piculs and lower, down to [those ranking at] 400 piculs, all use black rhinoceros [horn. Those ranking at] 200 piculs [and lower, down] to disciples of private schools, all use ivory. They are attached above by silk. The Emperor uses a cord threaded with white pearls and red wool threads. Vassal kings and those of lower [rank] use a band with red silk threads. The cords and bands are each according to the material of the seal. The engraved writing reads, 'When the first month *kang-mao* [amulets] is in the center,[8] it is a supernatural baton,[4] [which influences] the four quarters. Red, blue, white, and yellow, these four colors are my defense. The Lord [Shun] ordered Chu-yung to teach K'uei and Lung [to transform this object into an amulet, so that] of the many epidemics and severe diseases, none will presume to touch me.' [The inscription on the other one of the pair reads], 'On the worst of unlucky days, [the day] *mao*, the Lord [Shun] ordered K'uei to transform [this object, saying], "Do you care for subtle things all around. Transform this [thing] into a supernatural baton.[4] It should be completely upright, completely straight, completely angular, and completely square, so that of the many epidemics and severe (*kang*) diseases, none will presume to touch me." ' In all there are 66 words." 佩，雙印長寸

---

[7] These amulets were probably called seals because they were worn at the waist just as seals were.

[8] The text reads 決; I have read 央, as in the *HS* note.

二分，方六分。乘輿，諸侯王，公，列侯，曰白玉。中二千石曰下至四百石，皆曰黑犀，二白石曰至私學弟子，皆曰象牙。上合絲。乘輿曰縢貫白珠赤罽蕤。諸侯王曰下，曰綈赤絲蕤。縢縏各如其印質。刻書文曰，正月剛卯既決[8]，靈殳[4]四方，赤青白黃，四色是當。帝令祝融，曰敎夔龍，庶疫剛癉，莫我敢當。疫日嚴卯，帝令夔化，愼爾周伏，化茲靈殳[4]，既正既直，既觚既方，庶疫剛癉，莫我敢當。凡六十六字。

*Shuo-wen* 3 B: 6b defines *hai* 殺 as follows: "The *hai-szu* 攺 is a large *kang-mao* [amulet]. It is used to expel influences and demons." (From Shen Ch'in-han.)

*Chi-chiu-p'ien* 41b, a word-list written by Shih Yu during 48–33 B.C., contains the following line: "The *Shih-ch'i* [lit., "the shooter of infant-like demons"] and the *Pi-hsieh* [lit., "the expeller of perversities"] eliminate the many banefulnesses 射魑辟邪除羣凶," and Yen Shih-ku explains, "*Shih-ch'i* and *Pi-hsieh* are both the names of supernatural animals. The *ch'i* is a demon [in the shape of] a small infant. *Shih-ch'i* means that it is able to hit and drive away infant-like demons. *Pi-hsieh* means that it is able to expel and ward off monstrosities and perversities. [These terms] refer to [articles made of] precious jade and the like. The forms of [these] two animals were used to hang on [peoples'] girdles to drive away baneful calamities and to protect their persons.

"It is also said that *shih-ch'i* refers to the large *kang-mao* [amulets]. Gold, jade, and peach-wood were carved to make them. Another name for them is *hai-szu*. On top of them there was an inscription and on their sides a hole was pierced, which was threaded with many-colored silk. They were used to attach to the forearm and were also a means of expelling influences and animal-shaped demons." (Yen Shih-ku's error about the location of the inscription and hole on these amulets indicates that he had never seen them; he is merely summing up the literary tradition about them.)

Hui Tung (1697–1758) confirms Fu Ch'ien's implication that the day *mao* was evil, by quoting *Tso-chuan*, Dk. Chao, IX (Legge, p. 626), "If the day is *tzu* or *mao*, it is called an evil day." Motze, ch. 31 (Mei, p. 170) however mentions the day *ting-mao* as a propitious day for sacrifices. The difference was that there were both *kang* (severe)-*mao* and *jou* (gentle)-*mao* days, and the day *ting-mao* belonged to the latter group.

T'ao Tsung-yi (fl. 1360), in his *Cho-keng-lu* 24: 5a–7b, discusses these *kang-mao* amulets and states that they were called 大堅, great firmness." Hence the word *kang* may refer to the hardness of the material used for them, this hardness implying their strong power to ward off disease. The *Kang* found in the inscription on them says that they ward off *kang* (severe) diseases.

*Kang* also has a third meaning. *Li-chi* 3: 8b (Legge, I, 94; Couvreur, I, 60) says, "For external matters, a *kang* (odd) day should be used, and for internal affairs a *jou* 柔 (even) day should be used." K'ung Ying-ta explains, "*Kang* [refers to] the odd (*chi* 奇) days. In ten days there are five odd and five even (*ou* 偶). The five odd [days] *chia, ping, mou, keng,* and *jen* are *kang* (strong). External affairs [need] strong (*kang*) purposes, hence *kang* days are used. . . . The five even [days], *yi, ting, chi, hsin,* and *kuei* are *jou* (gentle)." *Kang* and *jou* are also used in the *Book of Changes* to refer to the undivided and divided lines of the hexagrams. Thus the term *kang-mao* has a number of meanings upon which diviners undoubtedly rang the changes. *Kang* refers to the strength of the amulet, the hardness of its material, the severity of the disasters it warded off, as well as the odd days in the decenary cycle of stems and certain lines of the hexagrams.

In Han times, the word *mao* had a special significance. The character *liu* 劉, which was the surname of the imperial clan, is made up of the three characters *mao, chin* (metal), and knife (*tao*), as Wang Mang notes (cf. 99 B: 7a & n. 7.2). Hence *mao* denoted the Han imperial house. The continuance of this interpretation is to be found in the biography of Liu Fang 昉, who in A.D. 586 was executed for conspiracy against the newly enthroned Emperor Wu, the founder of the Sui dynasty. Liu Fang is declared to have said, "My surname is *mao*, metal, and knife, and my given name is 'one, ten-thousand, and days 一万日,' so that the Liu clan will infallibly rule as kings and be the sons of Heaven [emperors] for ten thousand days." (*Pei-shih* 74: 3b; *Sui-shu* 38: 4a). It is then not surprising that Wang Mang and the Wei dynasty did away with these *kang-mao* amulets and that the Han emperors wore them.

Wu Ta-cheng (1844–1902), in his *Ku-yü T'u K'ao*, pp. 130 & 132, presents drawings with a discussion of four jade *kang-mao* amulets from Han times. He remarks that their construction and inscriptions are very similar and that many of the words are written in a cursive manner or with borrowed characters. The inscription on them all is as follows: "[When] the *yu*-month *kang-mao* [amulet] is in the center [an unreadable word, possibly "it influences"] the four quarters. Red, blue, white, yellow, these four colors are my defense. The Lord commanded to hold and complete it. Of the many epidemics and severe sicknesses, (three characters unreadable) *mao*, none will presume to touch me." 酉月剛卯，央□四方，赤青白黃，四色是當，帝令執成，□□□卯，庶疫剛癉，莫我敢當. Wu Ta-cheng asserts he has seen no *kang-mao* amulets of the dimensions Fu Ch'ien speaks of, and states that his amulets are of the size described by Chin Shao. Possibly Fu Ch'ien's amulets were what the *Shuo-wen* calls "large *kang-mao* [amulets]."

These *kang-mao* amulets were part of the regular Han court costume during the Wang Mang and Later Han periods at least, and were worn in the center of the girdle ornaments. They were worn by all grades of officials, even students in private schools. Their function was frankly that of being amulets intended to ward off disease demons. Even the emperor and his highest officials wore them, which circumstance illustrates vividly the prevalence of superstition among the most educated persons of the age.

We do not know when they first became popular. Wei Hung (fl. ca. 25), in his *Han-chiu-yi* A: 1b, declares, "In the Ch'in and earlier [periods], the common people all wore seal-cords on their girdles, with seals, an inch square, made of gold, jade, silver, bronze, rhinoceros[-horn], or ivory, each one wearing what he liked." While the passage concerns itself with actual seals, yet these amulets were also called seals, so that they may date back to Chou times. They seem to have gone out of fashion some time after the Later Han and before the T'ang period, for Yen Shih-ku had not seen them and they are not mentioned in the Sung books on rites, such as Nieh Ch'ung-yi's *San-li-t'u* (presented 962) and Ch'en Hsiang-tao's (1053–1093) *Li-shu*.

Yen Shih-ku states that there were *kang-mao* amulets made of peach-wood. The peach is indigenous to China, so that it was naturally used for apotropaic purposes. The *Tso-chuan* (Dk. Hsiang, yr. XXIX; Legge, pp. 544[2], 547b) recounts that when, in 544 B.C., Duke Hsiang of Lu was required to go in person to present shrouds to the deceased King K'ang of Ch'u, he first had shamans asperse the corpse with peach-wood and broom-straw in order to drive away the dead king's ghost and other evil spirits, so that no harm should come to the Duke. This book also (Dk. Chao, yr. IV; Legge, pp. 592[3], 596a) states that when stored ice was brought out of the ice-house, a bow of peach-wood and thorn arrows were used to drive away evil influences. It likewise (Dk. Chao, XII; Legge, 637[18], 641a) reports that when the first ancestor of the Ch'u line, Hsiung-yi, who was supposed to have lived at the time of King Ch'eng of the Chou dynasty, waited upon that King, he bore a peach-wood bow and thorn arrows. Tu Yü (222–284) states that these implements were for apotropaic purposes (*Tso-chuan Cheng-yi* 45: 19a). *Chou-li* 32: 8b (Biot, II, 248) states: "[The royal companion of the right in the war-chariot (*jung-yu*)] assists [at the making of a solemn oath by holding] the ox's ear, [which is cut off to secure blood for making the oath, and he assists by using] peach-wood and broom-straw [to asperse this blood and drive away any harmful influences]." Since peach-wood thus came to have the meaning of driving away harm, sword-makers were entitled "the Peach-wood Clan (*t'ao-shih*)" in the *K'ao-kung-chi*, which was appended to the *Chou-li* (Biot, II, 491, 496).

In *Han-shih Wai-chuan* 10: 11b (by Han Ying, fl. 179–141 B.C.), Duke Huan of Ch'i (685–643 B.C.) is represented as having met, while on a trip, an old man on foot, carrying a peach-wood baton (*t'ao-shu*). When the Duke asked him about it, he replied, "This is named a double [strength] peach-wood [implement]. The way peach-wood acts is called 'to destroy.' ... The warning to plebeians [against destructive conduct] lies in peach-wood batons." The story continues, "By the first month of the next year, the plebeians [at the Duke's court] all wore [these peach-wood batons]." Shen Ch'in-han, in his *HS Su-cheng* 36: 9b, 10a (my attention was called to this passage by P. van der Loon), quotes this passage and concludes, "In my opinion, this was the origin of wearing *kang-mao* [amulets]." It appears to me, however, to have been more probably a rationalization, written in Han times, for a practise common then.

Wang Su's (195–256) *Sang-fu Yao-chi* (this book is lost and the passage is quoted from *T'ai-p'ing Yü-lan* 967: 3b by the *Han-Wei Yi-shu Ts'ao*, 2b) said, "When Duke Ai of Lu (494–468 B.C.) was sacrificing preparatory to the funeral of his father, ... Confucius asked [Duke Ai], 'Would it not be better to use triply [extracted] peach-wood water?' [The Duke] replied, 'No. [The use of] peach-wood [water] arose when Duke Ling of Wei₈ [534–493 B.C.] had a daughter who was married to [the prince of] Ch'u. Her nurse was accompanying her to her husband's household, when she was a newly [wedded] wife, and on the way she heard that her husband had died. The nurse wanted to have the new wife return [home. But] the new wife replied, "A woman has the three obediences. Now I belong to this man. He has died and I must complete the mourning." Thereupon she had a plain chariot yoked with white horses and proceded to her husband's house. She made some triply [extracted] peach-wood water and used it to wash the hair of the deceased. She went out of the eastern gate at the northern corner [of the eastern wall of the city] and completed the ceremony with three bows, in order to make the deceased not hate her. My father has nothing to hate. What would be the use of triply [extracted] peach-wood water?' " Here is given a classical sanction for apotropaic implements and ceremonies put into the mouth of the greatest of sages. It is also a mere rationalization of a later practise.

Evidence that *kang-mao* amulets were placed upon doors (as are the present door-gods) in Han times is furnished by *HHS*, Tr. 5: 4b–5a:

"In the central month of summer [the fifth month], all things are then flourishing and the sun comes to its summer maximum [northward journey]. The *yin* emanations [thereupon] begin to work, so that it is to be feared that things will not [continue to] grow. The [proper] rites for this [situation] are to employ scarlet cordage plants joining strong smelling vegetables, to exorcise injurious insects, rodents (?), black magic (*ku*), and noises (?), and to use peach-wood seals, six inches long and three inches square, vari-colored, on which are written characters according to the regular procedure, and display them on gates and doors.

"The [various] dynasties used as ornaments [articles] they esteemed according to [the elementary powers by which they ruled]. The clan of the Hsia sovereigns [had as their elementary power] metal. Their roads were made of the stalks of rushes, meaning that essences should mingle [and the people be fruitful]. The Yin people had water as their [elementary] virtue. They used snail shells, stressing cautiousness, that their closing up [against evil emanations] should be like that by snails. The Chou people had wood as their [elementary] virtue. They used peach-wood for apotropaic purposes, meaning that emanations should be blocked [from operating] upon them. In Han [times] all were used. Hence on the fifth day of the fifth month, scarlet cordage plants and vari-colored seal-[shaped blocks of peach-wood] were used as ornaments for gates and doors in order to present obstacles and block evil emanations."

Huang Shan (fl. 1915) quotes the *Shih-wu Chi-yüan* (by Kao Ch'eng, fl. 1078–1085, book later greatly added to) as recording, "In the Han [period, people] used scarlet cordage plants joining vari-colored *kang-mao* [amulets] as decorations for their gates and doors." According to the passage from *HHS*, Tr. 30 translated above, the *kang-mao* amulets worn at people's waists were also called "seals," so that these large "seals" on doors were likewise *kang-mao* amulets.

Liu Chao (fl. dur. 502–520) glosses *HHS*, Tr. 5: 5a as follows: "The peach-wood seals were originally a Han institution and a means of reinforcing [the power of] the *mao*-metal-[knife clan, i.e., the Han dynasty]. The Wei [dynasty] did away with them." Perhaps Liu Chao's statement is as far as we can go concerning the origin of these amulets.

# APPENDIX IV

## ECLIPSES DURING THE RULE OF WANG MANG

i. In Chü-shê I, x (the tenth month), on the day *ping-ch'en*, the first day of the month, an eclipse of the sun is recorded (99 A: 29b; *Han-chi* 30: 7b). Hoang equates this date with Nov. 10, A.D. 6, but there was no eclipse on that date.

In the 12 years between the previous eclipse of A.D. 2 and the next correctly recorded eclipse in 14 A.D., there were 28 solar eclipses, of which three were visible in China.[1] These three were all calculated by Neugebauer's tables, and the following results were reached: The eclipse of Apr. 8, 4 A.D. was invisible in Ch'ang-an, but at the present Peking it reached a magnitude of 0.15 at 4:06 p.m., local time. The eclipse of Sept. 11, A.D. 6 reached a magnitude of 0.95 at Ch'ang-an at 3:59 p.m., local time. Hoang and Chen Yuan (*Comparative Daily Calender*) both equate this date with Chü-shê I, vii, last day, *ping-ch'en*. Then 十 is an error for 七 and 朔 is an error for 晦 or, since these calenders might have been a day in error, the eclipse might well have happened on the first day of the eighth month, so that 十 is an error for 八. The eclipse of June 30, 10, was invisible at Ch'ang-an and Peking, but at So-fang, the present Ning-hsia, it reached a magnitude of 0.46 at sunset.

In view of the nearness in time and the magnitude of the eclipse, the eclipse of 6 A.D. is undoubtedly the one referred to in the text; it requires merely a slight emendation in the text, an error that may have been in Pan Ku's source.

ii. On T'ien-feng I, iii, *jen-shen*, the last day, a second eclipse is recorded. (*HS* 99 B: 23a; *Han-chi* 30: 13b.) Hoang and Yuan both equate this date with Apr. 18, 14 A.D., for which Oppolzer calculates his solar eclipse no. 2917. It was merely partial; calculation according to Neugebauer's tables shows that at Ch'ang-an it reached a magnitude of 0.30 at 6:19 a.m. local time.

---

[1] Besides those charted by Oppolzer, the following partial eclipses were located near the south pole: nos. 2889, 2890, 2899, 2900, 2909, and 2916. The following were calculated by Oppolzer's elements and shown plainly invisible in China: nos. 2891, 2898, 2901, 2908. The following umbral eclipses were also calculated by Oppolzer's elements and found invisible: nos. 2895, 2896, 2903, 2904, 2910, 2911, 2915.

iii. On T'ien-feng III, vii, *mou-tzu*, the last day, a third eclipse of the sun is recorded (*HS* 99 B: 29b; *Han-chi* 30: 14b). Hoang and Yuan both equate this date with Aug. 21, 16 A.D., for which Oppolzer calculates his solar eclipse no. 2923. He charts the path of totality as passing through the present Canton and the Philippines.

In the two years since the preceding recorded eclipse, 5 solar eclipses occurred, of which one was visible in China.[2] This one occurred on Sept. 2, 15 A.D. Calculation shows that it was invisible in Ch'ang-an, but at the present Peiping it reached a magnitude of 0.07 at 9:10 a.m., local time.

In the 9 years from the time of this recorded eclipse to the first eclipse recorded by the *HHS* in the reign of Emperor Kuang-wu, which occurred on Feb. 6, 26 A.D., there were 24 solar eclipses, of which only one was visible in China.[3] This one occurred on Dec. 15, 19 A.D. Calculation by Neugebauer's elements shows that it was invisible in Ch'ang-an and north China, but at the present Canton it reached a magnitude of 0.03 at 7:47 a.m., local time, so that it was hardly visible in China.

[2] Two were merely partial; ✳2919 was located near the south pole; the other, ✳2918 was calculated by Oppolzer's elements and found invisible as far south as China.

[3] Eleven were merely partial; nos. 2926, 2929, 2935, 2936, 2945, 2946 were located near the south pole. Of the others, nos. 2927, 2928, 2930, 2932, 2934, 2937, 2939, 2944, 2947 were so far outside of China that a rough calculation by Oppolzer's elements was sufficient to determine them to be invisible in China. The remaining one, not charted, no. 2937, on Nov. 23, 21, was calculated by Neugebauer's tables and found to have been too far north to have been visible in China.

The eclipse of Feb. 16, 25 was listed in the *Ku-chin Chu* (about 300 A.D.), according to a note to *HHS*, Tr. 18: 1a. (It is not in the present text of that book.) Oppolzer calculated his eclipse no. 2944 for that date, and both Hoang, *Catalogue des eclipses*, and Chu Wen-chin, *Li-tai Jih-shih K'ao*, list this eclipse among Chinese eclipses. Calculation by Neugebauer's tables shows that on the morning of Feb. 17 it was visible in Alaska. western United States and Canada, and the eastern Pacific Ocean. But it was invisible in China. It was merely partial. This eclipse could not have been observed, and must have been calculated by Chinese astronomers. The listing of this eclipse by Hoang and Chu shows how dangerous it is to assume an eclipse to have been observed, without calculating its circumstances, especially when it was merely partial.

Of the umbral eclipses, those on June 10, 20 and Nov. 23, 21 seemed promising; they were also calculated by Neugebauer's tables, and both found invisible in China. The first one was located too far south, and the other too far north.

# APPENDIX V

## SOLAR ECLIPSES DURING THE FORMER HAN PERIOD

The results derived from an examination of the eclipses reported in the *HS* are here summarized. During this period of 230 years (including the reign of Wang Mang) there occurred 559 solar eclipses, of which 98 or 17.5% were visible in some part of China. Fifteen of these were very small eclipses or were invisible in the capital, so that we should not expect Chinese astronomers to have noticed them. Of the remaining 83 solar eclipses, 55 or almost two-thirds seem to have been recorded by Chinese astronomers. In order to examine this unusually good record, I present here a list of the solar eclipses visible in China from 206 B.C. to A.D. 23, with my conclusions.[1]

As sources for these eclipses recordings, there is (1) the *SC*, which contains very few of these recordings, so that its value is almost negligible. (2) The "Annals" and ch. 99 of the *HS* constitute a second source, giving only the dates of these eclipses. (3) *HS* ch. 27, "The Treatise on the Five Powers," near the end, contains a list of solar eclipses, which partly duplicates the information contained in the "Annals" and partly amplifies it by noting a few additional solar eclipses, giving the heavenly location of many eclipses, sometimes other information, and often presenting their astrological interpretation. This list ends with the reign of Emperor P'ing, so that the eclipses during A.D. 6 to 23 are only mentioned in ch. 99 of the *HS*. (4) The *Han-chi* seems to be an entirely secondary

---

[1] The visibility of these eclipses has been computed by the method discussed in *HFHD* I: app. III. Both P. Hoang, *Catalogue des éclipses de soleil et de lune relatées dans les documents chinois et collationées avec le Canon de Th. Ritter v. Oppolzer*, "Variétés sinologiques," no. 56, and Chu Wen-hsin, *Li-tai Jih-shih K'ao* are not altogether reliable, since they do not discuss these eclipses in detail and sometimes list an eclipse that was invisible in China as the one referred to by the Chinese historian.

In dating these eclipses, capital roman letters refer to the year of a reign or year-period, small roman letters to the (lunar) month, and arabic numbers to the day of the month. European dates are given by the Julian system, as in Oppolzer, but years are B.C., not astronomical years. (Hoang uses the Gregorian calendar for dates B.C., but the Julian for the first millennium A.D.) In references, arabic figures followed by a colon denote chapters of the *HS*, app. denotes appendices of those chapters, and small roman numbers particular eclipses in those appendices.

source, and has copied its dates from the *HS* Annals. Since however it was written in the second century A.D., it constitutes an early check upon the text of the *HS*, and very occasionally furnishes additional information. The information found in these four sources is discussed in the appendixes of the various chapters concerning eclipses, and need not be repeated here.

## SOLAR ECLIPSES VISIBLE IN CHINA, 206 B.C. to A.D. 23

206 B.C., July 6.  Not noticed.

205, Jan. 1.  Not noticed.

205, Dec. 20.  Recorded correctly (*HFHD*, I, 165, i).

201, Oct. 8.  Possibly recorded (*ibid.*, ii); if so, as for all eclipses not noted as "recorded correctly," the Chinese date must be emended.

198, Aug. 7.  Recorded correctly (*HFHD*, I, 166, iii).

197, July 26.  Not noticed.

195, June 6.  Not noticed.

194, May 26.  Not noticed.

192, Sept. 29.  Probably recorded (*HFHD*, I, 188, i).

188, July 17.  Recorded as total (*HFHD*, II, 189, ii).

A false solar eclipse is listed for July 26, 186 (*HFHD*, I, 211–12, i).

184, May 6.  Hardly visible and seemingly not noticed (*ibid.*).

181, Mar. 4.  Recorded correctly, total at the capital (*HFHD*, I, 212, ii).

178, Jan. 2.  Recorded correctly (*HFHD*, I, 284, i).  A small partial eclipse, only reaching a magnitude of 0.20 (totality = 1.00) at the capital.

The *SC* notes a solar eclipse for Jan. 17, 178, which was actually the date of a lunar eclipse (*ibid.*, ii).

178, Dec. 22.  Recorded correctly (*ibid.*, iii).

176, June, 6.  Probably recorded (*HFHD*, I, 285, iv).

174, Oct. 10.  Not noticed.

173, May 4.  Not noticed.

169, July 17.  Not noticed.

167, May 28.  Not noticed

166, May 17.  Not noticed.

164, Mar. 26.  Hardly visible, magnitude 0.02 (*ibid.*).

162, Mar. 5.  Hardly visible.  Invisible in the north (*ibid.*).

161, Aug. 16.  Possibly recorded (*HFHD*, I, 286, v).

155, Oct. 10.  Possibly recorded (*ibid.*, vi).

154, Apr. 4.  Recorded (*HFHD*, I, 335, i).  The three sources here all disagree on the day of the eclipse.

An eclipse listed for 153 may have been dittography for the eclipse of 145 (*ibid.*, ii).

547

152, Aug. 8.   Hardly visible (*ibid*.).   Invisible at the capital; magnitude of 0.08 at Peiping.

151, Feb. 2.   Hardly visible (*ibid*.); magnitude of 0.03 at the capital.

150, Jan. 22.   Recorded correctly (*ibid*., 336, iii).

149, June 7.   Very probably recorded (*ibid*., iv).
An eclipse listed for Oct. 22, 148 is almost certainly dittography for the eclipse of 147 (*ibid*., 337, v).

147, Nov. 10.   Recorded correctly (*ibid*., vi); almost total (0.77).

145, Mar. 26.   Possibly recorded (*ibid*., 338, vii); if so, reported from the tip of eastern Shantung.

144, Sept. 8.   Recorded correctly (*ibid*., viii).

143, Aug. 28.   Recorded correctly (*ibid*., 339, ix).
The *SC* states that in the month Nov. 16–Dec. 14, 142, "the sun and moon were both eclipsed and red for five days."   The *HS* does not mention this eclipse, which may have been a dust storm (*ibid*. x).

141, July 8.   Possibly recorded (*HFHD*, II, 136, i).

138, Nov. 1.   Recorded correctly (*ibid*., ii).

136, Apr. 15.   Probably recorded (*ibid*., iii).

135, Apr. 5.   Probably recorded (*ibid*., 137, iv).

134, Aug. 19.   Recorded correctly (*ibid*., 138, v).

127, Apr. 6.   Recorded correctly (*ibid*., vi).

124, Feb. 3.   Hardly visible and that only in southern Mongolia (*ibid*. 139, vii).

123, Jan. 23.   Very probably recorded (*ibid*.).

122, July 9.   Recorded correctly (*ibid*., viii).

115, Aug. 19.   Reached a magnitude of 0.28 at 11:21 a.m. at the capital, so that it was not conspicuous.   But smaller eclipses were recorded (*ibid*., 140).

112, June 18.   Recorded correctly (*ibid*., ix).

108, Apr. 6.   Possibly recorded; reached a magnitude of 0.32 at the capital (*ibid*., x).

107, Sept. 19.   Invisible at the capital; reached a magnitude of 0.34 at Peiping at sunrise, where it was conspicuous.   Not mentioned (*ibid*.)

104, July 19.   Not mentioned; reached a magnitude of 0.62 at the capital (*ibid*.).

103, Dec. 3.   Not mentioned; reached a magnitude of 0.12 at the capital (*ibid*.).

101, May 17.   Not mentioned; reached a magnitude of 0.45 at the capital (*ibid*.).

96, Feb. 23.   Recorded correctly, if Hoang's calendar is corrected by altering the intercalary month according to a recently excavated contemporary calendar (*ibid.*, 141, xi).

93, Dec. 12.  Recorded correctly (*ibid.*, xii).

90, Oct. 11.  Not conspicuous; reached a magnitude of 0.17 at sunrise at the capital (*ibid.*, 142, xiii).

89, Sept. 29.  Recorded correctly (*ibid.*).

84, Dec. 3.  Recorded correctly (*HFHD*, II, 178, i).

82, May 18.  Not mentioned (*ibid.*, 179).

81, May 6.  Not mentioned; invisible at the capital, but reached a magnitude of 0.47 shortly after sunrise at Peiping (*ibid.*).

80, Sept. 20.  Recorded correctly; almost total at the capital and total in the provinces, from which its totality was reported (*ibid.*, 178, ii).

75, Jan. 3.  Visible only in south China (*HFHD*, II, 275, i).

73, May 8.  Not mentioned (*ibid.*)

69, Feb. 25.  Not mentioned (*ibid.*).

68, Feb. 13.  Recorded correctly, although at the capital it only reached a magnitude of 0.10 at 4:20 p.m. (*ibid.*).

68, Aug. 9.  Not mentioned (*ibid.*, 276).

61, Sept. 20.  Not mentioned (*ibid.*).

58, July 20.  Not mentioned (*ibid.*).

57, July 9.  Not mentioned (*ibid.*).

56, Jan. 3.  Recorded correctly, although it was invisible at the capital and at Peiping it only reached a magnitude of 0.18 at sunrise (*ibid.*, 275, ii).

54, May 9.  Recorded correctly (*ibid.*, 276, iii).

53, Oct. 21.  Not mentioned (*HFHD*, II, 354, i).

50, Aug. 21.  Not mentioned (*ibid.*).

49, Aug. 9.  Not mentioned (*ibid.*).

47, June 19.  Not mentioned (*ibid.*).

42, Mar. 28.  Recorded correctly (*ibid.*).

40, July 31.  Recorded correctly (*ibid.*, ii).

39, July 20.  Hardly visible; only reached a magnitude of 0.07 at the capital (*ibid.*, 355, iii).

38, Jan. 14.  Hardly visible; only reached a magnitude of 0.02 at sunset at the capital (*ibid.*).

36, Nov. 12.  Not mentioned.  Reached a magnitude of 0.29 at sunrise at the capital (*ibid.*).

35, Nov. 1.  Recorded, with an error of a year in the date.  The record indicates that it was a sunset eclipse of large magnitude; this is the only eclipse of the sort within many years (*ibid.*).

29, Jan. 5.  Recorded correctly (*HFHD*, II, 419, i).

28, June 19.  Recorded correctly; total near the capital; the Annals say it was total, but the Treatise says it was almost total (*ibid.*, ii).

26, Oct. 23.  Recorded correctly (*ibid.*, iii).

25, Apr. 18.  Recorded correctly (*ibid.*, 420, iv).

24, Apr. 7.  Recorded correctly (*ibid.*, v).

16, Nov. 1.  Recorded correctly (*ibid.*, vi).  The Treatise says it was seen only in the capital.  At that place it only reached a magnitude of 0.08 at 4:29 p.m.; its small magnitude prevented it being noticed elsewhere.  It could only have been seen by using a mirror, smoked glass, or other special means.  The court astronomers must have been watching carefully for eclipses.

15, Mar. 29.  Recorded correctly (*ibid.*, 421, vii).  The Treatise states that clouds prevented this eclipse being seen in the capital, but it was seen elsewhere, proving that reports of eclipses were sent in to the central government.

14, Mar. 18.  Recorded correctly (*ibid.*, viii).

13, Aug. 31.  Recorded correctly (*ibid.*, ix).

12, Jan. 26.  Recorded correctly (*ibid.*, 422, x).  It only reached a magnitude of 0.07 at the capital and lasted only 67 minutes.

2, Feb. 5.  Recorded correctly (*HFHD*, III, ch. 11: app. II, i).  Almost total at the capital.

1 B.C., June 20.  Recorded with an error in the day (ch. 11: app. II, ii).  It only reached a magnitude of 0.06 at sunset at the capital.

A.D. 1, June 10.  Recorded correctly (12: app., i).

2, Nov. 23.  Recorded correctly (12: app., ii).  It is stated to have been total, but its totality was visible in northern Shensi and Honan, so that this fact was reported from outside the capital.

4, Apr. 8.  Hardly visible; invisible at the capital, and at Peiping reached only a magnitude of 0.15 (99: app. IV, i).

6, Sept. 11.  Recorded with a slight textual error in the date.  It reached a magnitude of 0.95 at the capital (*ibid.*, 544, i).

10, June 30.  Hardly visible.  Only visible in present Ninghsia (99: app. IV, i).

14, Apr. 18.  Recorded correctly (*ibid.*, ii).

15, Sept. 2.  Hardly visible; invisible at the capital; at Peiping it only reached a magnitude of 0.07 (*ibid.*, 545, iii).

16, Aug. 21.  Recorded correctly (*ibid.*).

19, Dec. 15.  Hardly visible.  Visible only in south China; at Canton it only reached a magnitude of 0.03 (*ibid.*).

From a study of the above material, there emerge several interesting conclusions:

1. The records of eclipses in Former Han times are predominatingly

reliable. More than two-thirds of the recorded eclipses, some 38 in all, are recorded correctly in the present text. Considering the length of time since the *HS* was written in the first century A.D., and the many opportunities for mistakes, both by astronomers and annalists before the *HS* was compiled and the opportunities for errors in transmitting the *HS* text, this is an excellent record. Fourteen other eclipses can be fitted into the actual dates, usually by only slight changes in the text. Only at most three recordings are hopelessly erroneous; two of these are due to errors in the transmission of the data. When we consider how very easy it is to write mistakenly the number of a month or the cyclical day, the essential correctness of the *HS* is a marked evidence of the care that was exercised in compiling it and in preserving and copying faithfully its text.

It does not seem to have been the case in Han times, as was sometimes later the case, that the dates given in the history were those on which the emperor was informed of an event, rather than the dates on which events occurred. The eclipse of 15 B.C. is said to have been reported from outside the capital and to have been invisible in the capital, so that some days must have elapsed between its occurrence and its being reported to the throne. But it is dated correctly.

2. In the case of some eclipses that are not listed correctly, it is plain that the errors of dating occurred before the *HS* was compiled. In other cases the evidence is not so clear, but it looks as if the same thing happened. The description of the eclipse of 35 B.C. as being large and ending at sunset is such that the actual eclipse can be unmistakeably identified by calculation. In the chronological account of events in the Annals, this eclipse is put more than a year later than it actually happened; between the actual date and the date at which the Annals put it, several events are recorded. Hence it is plain that when Pan Ku composed the "Annals," this eclipse was already misdated. In the eclipses of 192 and 141, it also seems very likely that the error of dating occurred before Pan Ku prepared his *HS*. He or his sources probably had somewhat illegible astronomical records of eclipses, which were easily misread. As a whole, there seem indeed to have been made more errors of dating before the *HS* was written than have occurred in the transmission of the text since that time.

In other cases, minor changes have plainly been made since the *HS* was composed. With the eclipse of 192, there seems to have been later conflation between the account in the "Annals" and that in the "Treatise." A later correction of a date has possibly been made in connection with the eclipse of A.D. 1. For the eclipse of 154, three different cyclical dates are given by our three sources.

# SOLAR ECLIPSES DURING THE FORMER HAN PERIOD

Dittography in Pan Ku's *sources* seems to have been responsible for the eclipse listed for 153, and almost certainly for that listed for 148. The reign of Emperor Ching (157–141 B.C.) was the worst period in accuracy of eclipse recordings. During this period there are five eclipses incorrectly dated, two dittographies, and only four correctly recorded eclipses. The "Annals" for this period are also the least satisfactory of all the "Annals" in the *HS*. The original sources for this reign seem to have been defective.

3. Ch'ang-an, the imperial capital, was not the only place from which eclipses were observed. The remarks in the *HS* in connection with the eclipse of 15 B.C. establish by direct testimony the fact that eclipses were reported from outside the capital. The eclipses of 136, 135, 80, and 56 must also have been reported from outside the capital. It is hence dangerous to take the capital as the sole point of observation, as Hoang and others have done. Nothing less than the whole of China should be taken as the possible locus of observation. For Han times, there is however some evidence that eclipses were not reported to the capital from central and southern China; the eclipse of 2 B.C. was total in the present southern Szechuan, southern Hunan, and Foochow, but no statement of its totality got into the *HS*.

4. During long periods of years, all eclipses plainly visible in China (and some quite small ones) are reported, while during other periods, groups of eclipses are missed. The following table indicates the number of eclipses not mentioned in the *HS* and the number of years after the last unreported and plainly visible eclipse during which all plainly visible eclipses were reported:

| Number of missed eclipses | 2 | 1 | 3 | 5 | 1 | 3 | 1 | 1 | 2 | 4 | 4 | 1 |
|---|---|---|---|---|---|---|---|---|---|---|---|---|
| Years in which all plainly visible eclipses were recorded | 1 | 1 | 18 | 51 | 9 | 8 | 6 | 7 | 1 | 2 | 9 | 61 |

It is especially remarkable that there were two periods of over half a century during which all plainly visible eclipses were recorded—from 166 to 115 B.C. and from 35 B.C. to the first eclipse correctly recorded in Later Han times (A.D. 26). What could have been the reason for such periods of complete success followed by periods of failure? For example, the five plainly visible eclipses between 174 and 166 B.C. were all missed, then all plainly visible eclipses during 51 years down to 115 B.C. were recorded.

Bad weather could hardly be the reason; eclipses were reported from outside the capital, so that local bad weather would hardly prevent an eclipse visible to the naked eye from being recorded. There is however a small correlation between the number of eclipses missed and the time of the year:

| | MONTHS | | | | | | | | | | | |
|---|---|---|---|---|---|---|---|---|---|---|---|---|
| | Jan. | Feb. | Mar. | Apr. | May | June | July | Aug. | Sept. | Oct. | Nov. | Dec. |
| Number of eclipses missed in the month | 1 | 1 | 0 | 0 | 7 | 2 | 5 | 3 | 1 | 3 | 1 | 1 |
| Number of eclipses recorded in the month | 6 | 3 | 3 | 8 | 3 | 6 | 4 | 6 | 5 | 3 | 5 | 4 |
| Aver. number of overcast days in month at Ch'ang-an[2] | 9 | 8 | 9 | 12 | 9 | 9 | 7 | 10 | 9 | 10 | 10 | 10 |

The missed eclipses seem to be concentrated during the summer months, especially May and July, more than half coming during four consecutive months. Yet the correlation between the number of eclipses missed in each month and the number recorded is only −0.34, with a probable error of ±0.17. There is thus only a very moderate degree of association between the number missed and the number recorded, and the number of instances is too low to make the correlation reliable. The correlation between the number of eclipses missed and the average number of overcast days is −0.39 ± 0.17, a negligible amount. It however looks very much as if the interest taken in the observation of solar eclipses by the responsible observers determined whether eclipses were or were not observed. To be conspicuous (so that an eclipse could not be missed by ordinary people) an eclipse must reach a magnitude of 0.75 when the sun is high or a magnitude of 0.33 when the sun is near the horizon. Many of the eclipses recorded in the HS are much smaller than these magnitudes, so that they could not have been perceived unless astronomers were expecting them and used special means to observe them. Hence the attitude of the responsible observers or astronomers probably had much to do with the observation or non-observation of solar eclipses.

5. The Chinese used special means to observe eclipses and watched for them during the two or three days at the end and beginning of the Chinese months when solar eclipses were to be expected. Unless an

[2] The data for overcast days are for the years 1924–1936 and have been very kindly reported to me by Fr. E. Gherzi, S.J., Director of the Siccawei Observatory.

eclipse is conspicuous, it is easily missed; under other circumstances, the diminution of light is too small to be perceived. Unless the sun is near the horizon or is covered by light clouds, it cannot moreover be watched with naked eyes. The necessary diminution of light can be obtained by looking through smoked mica or at the reflection of the sun in water or in a mirror. (Smoked glass may have been available at the time, mica was actually used as a screen, cf. 99 B: 16b.) Some of the recorded eclipses were so small that such special means were certainly used by Chinese astronomers. The eclipse of 178 only reached a magnitude of 0.20; that of 68 only a magnitude of 0.10; that of 16, only 0.08; that of 12, only a magnitude of 0.07 lasting only 67 minutes; that of 1 B.C., only a magnitude of 0.06. That such small eclipses were recorded demonstrates that eclipses were expected and watched for, using special means. There was an office at the capital entitled the Office for Watching the Heavens (cf. Glossary, *sub voce*), the members of which probably scrutinized the sun for eclipses. Probably this practise of watching for eclipses was however confined to the capital; the eclipse of 16 B.C. was not reported from outside the capital, although at the present Peiping it reached a magnitude of almost twice that at the capital. Thus astronomical activity reached high levels at the capital and was largely confined there.

6. As is to be expected, the method of calculation given by Neugebauer shows itself remarkably accurate when its results are compared with Chinese records. In the eclipse of 181, Chinese records show that at Ch'ang-an the eclipse was total; calculation by Neugebauer's tables reaches that result, but Oppolzer and Ginzel both reach a different result. For the eclipse of 89, Chinese records give its time, late afternoon, which also checks, to a reasonable degree of accuracy, with the results of calculation by Neugebauer's tables. In this case, the eclipse seems merely not to have been noticed until some time after it began.

By Neugebauer's tables, the time of an eclipse may be determined to within fifteen minutes and the magnitude to within 0.03.[3] The eclipse of 136 may have actually been observed at the capital, although, according to Neugebauer's method of calculation, the capital was just outside the area of visibility.

7. The differences between the statements about eclipses in the "Annals" and in the "Treatise on the Five Powers" (*HS* ch. 27) indicate that the latter probably represents the list of eclipses kept by the astrologers at the capital, while the "Annals" also employ reports from outside

[3] A. Pogo, "Additions and Corrections to Oppolzer's *Canon der Mondfinsternisse*," the *Astronomical Journal*, 1938, no. 1083.

the capital. In three cases, in the eclipses of 188, 80, and 28, the "Annals" state that the eclipse was total, while the "Treatise" says it was almost total. In each case, calculation demonstrates that at Ch'ang-an it was almost total, while at some other places in China it was total. Thus we can identify the "Treatise" with the reports of the astronomers at the capital.

Yet the astrologers at the capital sometimes utilized reports from elsewhere. The "Treatise" specifically mentions the observation of an eclipse in other parts of China, in connection with the eclipse of 15. It lists the eclipse of 135, which was not visible at the capital, as well as that of 136, which was close to the borderline of visibility there. The "Treatise" also records the eclipse of A.D. 2 as total, whereas calculation shows that at Ch'ang-an it was not quite total.

8. It is possible that the eclipse listed for 186 was a deliberate fabrication for the purpose of warning the ruler, the Empress of Emperor Kao, that Heaven disapproved of her acts. This listing seems hardly explicable by any other means. The eclipse discussed under the date 155 is also either a fabrication or else an actual eclipse dated a few years ahead. The eclipse of 201 is likewise doubtful. That only these three eclipses, all near the beginning of this period, should be doubtful, is a high testimony to the accuracy of Chinese recordings at this time. According to Chinese law, it was a serious and capital crime to report falsely a prodigy (such as an eclipse of the sun, cf. *HS* 100 A: 5b, to be translated in the Preliminary Volume of this series).

9. There is no evidence that the Chinese by calculation reached the dates of any eclipses recorded in the period. In the most promising cases, those of 201, 184, 155, and 145 B.C., I tried to calculate these eclipses by the methods that might have been used, and in each case reached negative results.

For the mistakenly dated eclipse of 201, I counted forwards from the date given for this eclipse to the end of the Former Han period by the Han eclipse period of $3986\frac{2}{3}$ days, by the Han *chang* of 6939 61/81 days, and by the saros of 6585.3 days, without coming upon any solar eclipses. Since it might have been possible for Chinese astronomers to know that there is a lunar period lasting one month, during which two solar eclipses and one lunar eclipse or two lunar eclipses and one solar eclipse may occur (although no evidence of this knowledge is found in Han records), I also took periods of one lunation from the dates found by this counting, but came upon no solar eclipse visible in China. This eclipse could thus hardly have been a calculation and its date must merely have been an error of some sort.

In the case of the eclipses listed in 186 and 145, I performed a similar calculation, with similar negative results. For the actual eclipse of 145 (not the mistaken date given in the "Annals," which does not correspond to any actual eclipse), I counted forwards and backwards for the whole Former Han period by the Chinese eclipse period of $3986\frac{2}{3}$ days. At each date thus found, an eclipse had occurred, but most of these eclipses were invisible in China. The second eclipse period after was the date of the eclipse of 123, the sixth was that of the eclipse of 80, the eleventh, that of 25, and the twelfth, that of 14 B.C. In addition, the eclipses of 167, 58, 47 B.C. and A.D. 19 occurred in this series, but these four eclipses are not recorded in the *HS*. The four recorded eclipses do not occur in any regular sequence, so that the probabilities are decidedly against this eclipse having been calculated by the Chinese eclipse period. I made a similar calculation, using the Han *chang* of 6939 61/81 days, but no recorded eclipse was found, only the missed eclipse of 164 and two invisible eclipses. Calculation by the saros of 6585.3 days, used by Greek astronomers, brought the eclipses of 181, 145, 127, and 1 B.C., the missed eclipse of 73, together with invisible eclipses. The saros does not however seem to have been known to the ancient Chinese. Thus even calculation of a difficultly visible eclipse from the actual date of that eclipse does not bring any results that would seem to encourage the computation of eclipses or to make probable the hypothesis that they were computed by the ancient Chinese.

It is however interesting that the first eclipse listed for Later Han times, dated on Feb. 16, A.D. 25, was almost certainly calculated. It is not found in the list of eclipses in the relevant "Treatise" of the *History of the Later Han Dynasty*, which was compiled by Szu-ma Piao, who lived ca. 240–306. This eclipse is listed in the *Ku-chin Chu*, written about A.D. 300. Calculation shows that this partial eclipse was invisible in Asia, and was confined to Alaska, western North America, and the eastern Pacific Ocean (cf. p. 509, n. 3). This date cannot thus have been the result of any Chinese observation; since the Chinese listing agrees with the date of the actual but invisible eclipse, it must have been calculated. Both Hoang and Chu Wen-hsin however include it in their lists of Chinese eclipses. This eclipse shows how dangerous it is to accept an eclipse listing without scrutiny.

Perhaps the most peculiar eclipse is that of 145 B.C., which was visible only at sunrise at the tip of the Shantung peninsula. I have pointed out that for it calculation was quite unlikely; since it was visible to the naked eye, it was probably observed and reported to the capital.

10. The court astronomers seem to have kept lists of lunar eclipses as

well as of solar eclipses, although no such lists have come down to us. One such lunar eclipse got into the *SC* (that of 178), probably because Szu-ma Ch'ien or his source misread the word for "lunar" as "solar" in his source. Eclipses of the moon were not believed to portend anything important, so were not recorded in the histories.

11. Where the dates in the Chinese text do not correspond to any actual eclipse, slight emendations nearly always enable us to show what was the original date. The eclipse of 35 B.C. shows that such emendations actually reach the original dating. In this case, the eclipse is described in such a way that there is no doubt which eclipse is denoted by the recording. To reach the correct date, it is necessary to change a 5 in the year to a 4, a 6 in the month to a 9, and a *jen-shen* 壬申 in the date to a *ting-ch'ou* 丁丑, all of which are mistakes easily made in copying records. These mistakes occurred before Pan Ku compiled his History.

In other cases, slighter or greater changes are necessary. They have been noted in the appendices dealing with those eclipses. Altogether the dates of thirteen eclipses were rectified with a considerable degree of probability; those of 192, 176, 161, 149, 145, 141, 136, 135, 123, 108, 35, 1 B.C., and A.D. 6. The eclipses of 201, 151, and 155 also present difficulties.

12. The calendars of correspondences between Chinese and European dates are essentially correct. Hoang, who prepared the best of the calendars dealing with this period, based his tables largely on previous Chinese studies and partly on the correctly recorded eclipses, as is quite proper. He also published a table of Chinese eclipses, indicating the correspondence between astronomically calculated and Chinese dates, which he took as the basis for his calendar. In those eclipses for which I have been able to identify the original of a now incorrect date, and in which the correct date was unknown to Hoang, it is possible to test Hoang's calendar. In every case it is shown to be reliable (within close limits) for the Han period.

The most interesting case is the eclipse of 96, in which a change in the intercalary month from one year to the next (which is required by a contemporary calendar for this year discovered by Stein in the desert; cf. Chavannes, *Documents chinois*, p. 71) furnishes, unknown to Hoang, a date from his calendar correct within one day to that obtained from astronomical calculation. Thus modern science justifies Chinese calendrical calculations.

There are however slight discrepancies. These never amount to more than three days (except for the intercalary month mentioned above), so that the essential accuracy of Hoang's table is maintained. More recent calendars are no better; concerning the eclipse A.D. 6, which is misdated in the text by two months, and is said to have occurred on the first day of the month, both Hoang and Chen Yuan's *Comparative Daily Calendar* (*Chung-hsi-hui Jih-li*) equate the actual date with the last day of the month, so that both these calendars seem to be a day in error here. Because of inaccuracies in Han calculations, it is quite possible that months which our present calendars calculate as having 29 days actually had 30 days, so that modern calendrical computations may in some years be a few days in error. Such seems actually to have been the case. Hoang's calendar requires minor reworking.

13. In 37 cases, the position of the sun at the time of a solar eclipse is given. By the use of Neugebauer's *Sterntafeln*, the positions of the stars mentioned in the Chinese sources have been calculated for the date of these eclipses. The comparison of these records with the calculated position of the sun does not furnish any convincing proof that these positions were the result of any observation. In partial eclipses, the stars could not have been observed; almost all of these eclipses were observed as partial. For the total eclipse of 181, when the stars could have been observed, the position is 14° in error. For erroneously dated eclipses, the position, if given, is grossly in error, and corresponds more to the (erroneous) date than to the actual position of the sun at the time of the actual eclipse. For the five eclipses whose dates are corrected and in which positions are given, the errors in the dates are 3 yrs. 9 mo., 3 yrs. 4 mo., 1 yr. 7 mo., 10 mo., and 1 yr. 8 mo., while the errors in the position are 103°, 130°, 66°, and 105° respectively. Towards the end of the Former Han period, these positions are no longer given exactly in degrees, only the constellation being given. It looks as though someone had calculated the position of the sun from the date in the calendar at some time towards the end of the Former Han period, possibly about 27 B.C. (Liu Hsiang?), at which time the dates of many eclipses were already in error.

Yet more of the positions are fairly correct. Of the 37 eclipses for which positions are given, 24 are correct to 8° or less in R.A.; seven more are in error only 10 to 14°. (Since Chinese astronomical observations were always made with reference to the equator, not the ecliptic, celestial positions are reduced to right ascension for purposes of comparison.) The other six are grossly in error, from 42° to 105°. These are the eclipses of 201, 192, 176, 161, 141, and 80. The first five of these are incorrectly dated in the *HS*. For the others whose dates are correct, there possibly has been some corruption in the original names of the Chinese constellations.

These positions cannot have much significence and may be neglected. Their use in Han times was astrological; the various parts of the sky were taken to correspond to various localities on earth, hence an eclipse in a certain part of the sky indicated something in the corresponding locality on earth. It is possible that the heavenly location of the eclipse was falsified in order to make the eclipse interpret some earthly event. In however only six cases in the whole period are we given an interpretation of the eclipse in terms of its heavenly location. Much more common was an interpretation in terms of its month or day. Of the eclipses whose location is grossly erroneous, only those of 201 and 141 were interpreted in terms of their location. Hence it is not likely that many of the erroneous heavenly locations were deliberate falsifications.

In conclusion: The outstanding impression left by the Chinese recordings of eclipses in the Former Han period is their high degree of fidelity to fact. The Chinese were not to any great extent interested in fabricating eclipses as portents and it was dangerous to do so. They had not yet begun to predict eclipses. They watched for eclipses, at times with great pertinacity, and succeeded in observing eclipses that were quite small and required the use of special means to be seen. It is but natural that the original records should have suffered errors of transmission; as a whole they are surprisingly correct. This fact constitutes an unimpeachable testimony to the fidelity of the *HS* to fact. (Reproduced by permission and with alterations from *Osiris*, vol. 5 [1938], pp. 499–522.)

# ADDENDA ET CORRIGENDA TO VOLUMES ONE & TWO

(Roman numerals denote volumes; arabic numbers, pages; superscript numerals, lines.)

I 56, *add to note 3*: Yen Shih-ku explains, " 'Insignia' denoted the tallies that could be matched together, which constituted documents [of credit]. 'Credentials' were made with feathers. At the top and bottom they were double. They took [their names] from their form. 'Bamboo credentials' got their name in this manner. Those who bore commands held them in order that they might be trusted."

I 66[29], *for* Yuan *read* Yüan    (From L. C. Goodrich).

I 79[6], *for* blowing away *read* unroofing

I 88[13], *for* T'ung *read* Ch'ê

I 91[11], *for* punishing a merciless *read* exterminate a

I 98[27], *delete* -an

I 123[33], *for* Li-Chi *read* Li-chi    (From L. C. G.)

I 142[30], *for* Decree *read* Mandate

I 155[15], *for* autumn *read* winter    (From A. C. Moule).

I 157[35], *for* 180 *read* 178

I 165[33], *for* proceeding *read* preceding

I 192[20], *before* decrees *insert* written

I 192[21], *before* edicts *insert* written

I 207[22], delete sentence in square brackets.

I 208[14], *for* his *read* the imperial

I 216[23], *for* testimentary *read* testamentary    (From L. C. G.)

I 219[11], *for* extravagently *read* extravagantly    (From L. C. G.)

I 225[22], *delete* King

I 225[34,35,38], *delete* Emperor

I 237[22,23], *for* the Prefect, or an official *read* or a foreman clerk

I 238[21], *for* Palace Military Commander *read* Commandant of the Capital

I 238[25], *for* Guards *read* Guard

I 243[32], *for* In *read* An original note to

I 243[33], *before* Lu Shih *add* on

I 243[34], *delete* in his own comment on his

I 243[34,35], *for* is quoted as saying *read* says

I 244[4,5], *for* speaking evil and criticizing *read* slandering [the government]

I 247[1], *for* ch'üen *read* ch'üan    (From L. C. G.)

I 250[20], *for* towers screening *read* crenelated screening wall[3] at the towers outside

I 250[42], *for* [palace] portal with the towers *read* tower outside the [palace] portal with the crenelated screening walls

I 251[10], *for* towers of the eastern gate *read* crenelated screening wall at the eastern tower

I 251[11], *for* screen towers are small *read* fou-szu are irregular

I 251[25], *add at end*: Probably in Han times the *fou-szu* was merely a crenelated screening wall connecting the two detached look-out towers before the palace gate, whereas by T'ang times there had been added to the wall various turrets and the term *fou-szu* had come to be applied to both turrets and screening wall.

I 266[22], *for* decree *read* edict

I 270[28], *for* ch'ü *read* chü    (From L. C. G.)

# ADDENDA

I 275[5], *for* despized *read* despised    (From L. C. G.)

I 284[20], *for* emenation *read* emendation    (From L. C. G.)

II 24[35], *for* fifty-odd, *read* the fifty-odd scholars whom he had summoned to advise him,

II 27[20], *for* Marquises. *read* marquises.

II 35[32], *for* Ou *read* Ch'ü

II 37[35], *for* 9a *read* 6b

II 48[16], *before* imperial *add* written

II 57[3], *for* an office for rewarding military merits *read* a distinguished service order for military merit

II 91[35], *for* Hsin *read* Hsien    (From L. C. G.)

II 93[34], *for* Exempler *read* Exemplar    (From L. C. G.)

II 95[23], *for* Ching *read* Ch'ing    (From L. C. G.)

II 96[30], *for* suevotaurilia *read* suovetaurilia

II 100[40], *for* ch'ou *read* ch'u

II 101[25], at end of line, *add* have to

II 101[30], *after* five *add* [domestic]

II 101[31], *after* Room *add* or Impluvium.

II 101[32], *for* vi *read* iv

II 102[29], 284[27], 335[25], *for* P'an *read* P'o

II 114[6], *for* blew away *read* unroofed

II 156[1], *shift* Winter *into the margin.*

II 166[23], *after* all *add* [pardoned and]

II 167[17] margin, *for* 79 *read* 78

II 167[21], *after* animals' *add* [in HS 96 B: 38b]

II 168[27], *for* fortelling *read* foretelling    (From L. C. G.)

II 176[31,32], *for* for Military Officers *read* [kept by] the Commandant [of Justice]

II 201[26], *for* order *read* edict

II 213[28], *for* their attendants *read* imperial retinue

II 227[14], *for* the first ordinance *read* in the first [section] of the ordinances

II 230[16], *for* classics *read* canons

II 245[20], *for* Hung *read* Heng    (From L. C. G.)

II 245[30], *for* they [really had [ *read* there were some who occupied [this position with

II 245[31,32], *for* allowed [to receive] the full [amount called for by their] rank *read* secured the rank of fully [two thousand piculs].

II 246[37], *for* Ho- *read* Hu-    (From L. C. G.)

II 267[10], *for* order *read* ordered    (From L. C. G.)

II 269[23], *for* 季 *read* 秀

II 269[27], *after* 121 *add* or later    (From L. C. G.)

II 295[38], *for* punished *read* mutilated

II 299[32], *for* Lin *read* Liu    (From L. C. G.)

II 307[11], *after* made *add* fall

II 307[13], *delete* fall

II 312[38], *for* to this chapter *read* , pp. 295, 297,

II 315[31], *for* irrevokable *read* irrevocable    (From L. C. G.)

II 316[4], *before* Retinue *add* the Imperial

II 317[31], *after* over *add* ,

II 328, Chinese text, column 5, character 2, should be 潁

561

II 329[14], *for* Tung-tu *read* the

II 329[15], *after* Gate *add* Towards the Eastern Capital

II 335[25], *for* P'an] *read* [P'an]   (From L. C. G.)

II 335[26], *for* [In *read* In   (From L. C. G.)

II 339[11], *for* and write *read* the *and after* characters *add* of [Shih] Chou's Fascicles

II 339[23], *for* these *read* the following

II 344[12], *for* works of a certain P'an Yü, an eclectic philosopher who *read* book P'an-yü, an eclectic philosophy which

II 349[5], *for* -two *read* -three

II 353[26], *for* JOAS *read* JAOS

II 365[32], *for* Chen *read* Cheng

II 377, Chinese text, column 5, last character should be deleted.

II 378, Chinese text, column 5, character 19 should be 郊

II 381[41], *for* armpits *read* arms

II 385[2], *for* cruel and injurious persons *read* injurious villains

II 385[3], *after* sent *add* far

II 385[29], *after* the *add* melted

II 386[29], *for* potent *read* portent

II 389[27], *add* In defence of the common interpretation, "black heads," there is however the fact that in 221 B.C. the First Emperor "changed the name of the common people to be 'black heads'."   (SC 6: 28 = *Mh* II, 133).   That designation seems to have been merely an extension of the First Emperor's exaltation of the power water, whose corresponding color is black.   Calling the people "black heads" was asserting that by nature they were subjects of the Ch'in dynasty.

II 396[8], *after* offices *add* ,

II 409[14], *for* regulations *read* regulatory decrees.

II 409[23], *for* decreed *read* commanded

II 425[20], *for* 4.4 *read* −4.4,

II 425[33], *for* the *read* True

II 425[42], *for* Ying *read* Chao

For the sake of *uniformity of usage* with the other volumes in this series, the following changes should be made:

*For* Auxiliary *read* Attendant *at* II 118[23].

*For* Chief of Police *read* Commandant *at* I 75[9].

*For* Chief of Palace Police in the Capital *read* Bearer of the Gilded Mace *at* II 163[34], 400[31,32].

*Delete* Custodian *at* I 230[33], II 118[24,25], 151[20].

*For* friendship *read* alliance by marriage *at* I 262[24,37], 264[21], 310[9], 313[13], II 243[23], 250[13].

*For* Governor of the Capital *read* Capital Adjunct *at* II 208[23].

*For* Inspector of Fields *read* Bailiff *at* I 237[22], II 185[17].

*For* Junior Chief of the Multitude *read* Chief of the Multitude on the Left *at* II 229[37].

*For* Junior Chieftain of Conscripts *read* Chieftain of Conscripts on the Left *at* II 209[4], 229[35].

*For* Kuan-nei Marquis *read* Marquis of the Imperial Domain *at* I 200[20], 240[33], 305[41], II 127[31], 128[16,19], 162[14,15], 208[6,24], 220[5], 246[1], 253[25], 285[17], 308[29], 309[27], 310[26,30], 336[11],

# ADDENDA

$377^{11}$, $405^{15}$.

*For* prefecture *read* county *passim.*

*For* of the Protecting *read* and Commissioner Over the *at* II, $39^{12,13}$, $256^{15}$.

*For* Officials *read* Clerks *at* I, $175^{2,11}$; II, $229^{14}$.

*For* Ordinary Chieftain of Conscripts *read* Chieftain of Conscripts in the Center *at* II, $229^{12,32,35}$.

*For* Palace Military Commander *read* Commandant of the Capital *at* I, $135^{19}$, $206^{26,27}$, $207^{13,26}$, $223^{5}$, $238^{21}$, $247^{4,5}$, $256^{4}$, $271^{5}$, $320^{4}$; II, $81^{14,15}$, $82^{27}$.

*For* Prefect *read* Clerk *at* I, $256^{19}$, $271^{13}$; II, $163^{8}$.

*For* prescribed equipage *read* legal carriage of state *at* I, $236^{5,6}$.

*For* Pretors of the Waters *read* Szu-hu *at* I, $207^{14}$.

*For* Public *read* Government *at* I, $105^{4,17}$, $120^{5}$.

*For* Senior Chief of the Multitude *read* Chief of the Multitude on the Right *at* I, $326^{22}$; II, $58^{12}$, $221^{6}$, $229^{36}$, $308^{30}$.

*For* Senior Chieftain of Conscripts *read* Chieftain of Conscripts on the Right *at* II, $403^{25,39}$.

*For* Superior Accomplished *read* Distinguished Accomplishment *at* I, $176^{7}$.

*Delete* tsu *at* I, $239^{5,10}$.

# ADDENDA